Understanding the
LINUX
KERNEL

Related titles from O'Reilly

Understanding the
LINUX
KERNEL

SECOND EDITION

Daniel P. Bovet and Marco Cesati

O'REILLY®

Beijing · Cambridge · Farnham · Köln · Paris · Sebastopol · Taipei · Tokyo

Understanding the Linux Kernel, Second Edition
by Daniel P. Bovet and Marco Cesati

Published by O'Reilly & Associates, Inc., 1005 Gravenstein Highway North, Sebastopol, CA 95472.

O'Reilly & Associates books may be purchased for educational, business, or sales promotional use. Online editions are also available for most titles (*safari.oreilly.com*). For more information, contact our corporate/institutional sales department: (800) 998-9938 or *corporate@oreilly.com*.

Editor:	Andy Oram
Production Editor:	Mary Brady
Cover Designer:	Edie Freedman
Interior Designer:	David Futato

Printing History:

December 2002:   First Edition.

ISBN: 0-596-00213-0
[M]

Table of Contents

Preface ix

1. **Introduction** **1**
   Linux Versus Other Unix-Like Kernels   2
   Hardware Dependency   6
   Linux Versions   7
   Basic Operating System Concepts   8
   An Overview of the Unix Filesystem   12
   An Overview of Unix Kernels   18

2. **Memory Addressing** **34**
   Memory Addresses   34
   Segmentation in Hardware   35
   Segmentation in Linux   40
   Paging in Hardware   44
   Paging in Linux   54

3. **Processes** **72**
   Processes, Lightweight Processes, and Threads   72
   Process Descriptor   74
   Process Switch   89
   Creating Processes   99
   Destroying Processes   106

4. **Interrupts and Exceptions** **109**
   The Role of Interrupt Signals   110
   Interrupts and Exceptions   111
   Nested Execution of Exception and Interrupt Handlers   121
   Initializing the Interrupt Descriptor Table   122

Exception Handling 125
Interrupt Handling 128
Softirqs, Tasklets, and Bottom Halves 145
Returning from Interrupts and Exceptions 156

5. Kernel Synchronization **161**
Kernel Control Paths 161
When Synchronization Is Not Necessary 162
Synchronization Primitives 163
Synchronizing Accesses to Kernel Data Structures 184
Examples of Race Condition Prevention 189

6. Timing Measurements **193**
Hardware Clocks 194
The Linux Timekeeping Architecture 197
CPU's Time Sharing 202
Updating the Time and Date 203
Updating System Statistics 204
Software Timers 206
System Calls Related to Timing Measurements 213

7. Memory Management **217**
Page Frame Management 217
Memory Area Management 239
Noncontiguous Memory Area Management 256

8. Process Address Space **263**
The Process's Address Space 264
The Memory Descriptor 265
Memory Regions 268
Page Fault Exception Handler 285
Creating and Deleting a Process Address Space 298
Managing the Heap 300

9. System Calls **303**
POSIX APIs and System Calls 303
System Call Handler and Service Routines 304
Kernel Wrapper Routines 316

10. Signals **318**
    The Role of Signals   318
    Generating a Signal   327
    Delivering a Signal   332
    System Calls Related to Signal Handling   343

11. Process Scheduling **348**
    Scheduling Policy   348
    The Scheduling Algorithm   352
    System Calls Related to Scheduling   367

12. The Virtual Filesystem **372**
    The Role of the Virtual Filesystem (VFS)   372
    VFS Data Structures   378
    Filesystem Types   394
    Filesystem Mounting   397
    Pathname Lookup   407
    Implementations of VFS System Calls   416
    File Locking   420

13. Managing I/O Devices **427**
    I/O Architecture   427
    Device Files   437
    Device Drivers   441
    Block Device Drivers   449
    Character Device Drivers   471

14. Disk Caches **474**
    The Page Cache   476
    The Buffer Cache   481

15. Accessing Files **497**
    Reading and Writing a File   497
    Memory Mapping   513
    Direct I/O Transfers   523

16. Swapping: Methods for Freeing Memory **528**
    What Is Swapping?   529
    Swap Area   531
    The Swap Cache   545

Transferring Swap Pages   548
Swapping Out Pages   551
Swapping in Pages   556
Reclaiming Page Frame   559

17. The Ext2 and Ext3 Filesystems **574**
General Characteristics of Ext2   574
Ext2 Disk Data Structures   577
Ext2 Memory Data Structures   584
Creating the Ext2 Filesystem   588
Ext2 Methods   590
Managing Ext2 Disk Space   592
The Ext3 Filesystem   600

18. Networking **608**
Main Networking Data Structures   609
System Calls Related to Networking   618
Sending Packets to the Network Card   627
Receiving Packets from the Network Card   629

19. Process Communication **632**
Pipes   633
FIFOs   642
System V IPC   644

20. Program Execution **661**
Executable Files   662
Executable Formats   674
Execution Domains   676
The exec Functions   678

A. System Startup **685**

B. Modules **692**

C. Source Code Structure **702**

Bibliography **707**

Source Code Index **711**

Index **749**

Preface

In the spring semester of 1997, we taught a course on operating systems based on Linux 2.0. The idea was to encourage students to read the source code. To achieve this, we assigned term projects consisting of making changes to the kernel and performing tests on the modified version. We also wrote course notes for our students about a few critical features of Linux such as task switching and task scheduling.

Out of this work—and with a lot of support from our O'Reilly editor Andy Oram—came the first edition of *Understanding the Linux Kernel* and the end of 2000, which covered Linux 2.2 with a few anticipations on Linux 2.4. The success encountered by this book encouraged us to continue along this line, and in the fall of 2001 we started planning a second edition covering Linux 2.4. However, Linux 2.4 is quite different from Linux 2.2. Just to mention a few examples, the virtual memory system is entirely new, support for multiprocessor systems is much better, and whole new classes of hardware devices have been added. As a result, we had to rewrite from scratch two-thirds of the book, increasing its size by roughly 25 percent.

As in our first experience, we read thousands of lines of code, trying to make sense of them. After all this work, we can say that it was worth the effort. We learned a lot of things you don't find in books, and we hope we have succeeded in conveying some of this information in the following pages.

The Audience for This Book

All people curious about how Linux works and why it is so efficient will find answers here. After reading the book, you will find your way through the many thousands of lines of code, distinguishing between crucial data structures and secondary ones—in short, becoming a true Linux hacker.

Our work might be considered a guided tour of the Linux kernel: most of the significant data structures and many algorithms and programming tricks used in the kernel are discussed. In many cases, the relevant fragments of code are discussed line by line. Of course, you should have the Linux source code on hand and should be willing to spend some effort deciphering some of the functions that are not, for sake of brevity, fully described.

On another level, the book provides valuable insight to people who want to know more about the critical design issues in a modern operating system. It is not specifically addressed to system administrators or programmers; it is mostly for people who want to understand how things really work inside the machine! As with any good guide, we try to go beyond superficial features. We offer a background, such as the history of major features and the reasons why they were used.

Organization of the Material

When we began to write this book, we were faced with a critical decision: should we refer to a specific hardware platform or skip the hardware-dependent details and concentrate on the pure hardware-independent parts of the kernel?

Others books on Linux kernel internals have chosen the latter approach; we decided to adopt the former one for the following reasons:

- Efficient kernels take advantage of most available hardware features, such as addressing techniques, caches, processor exceptions, special instructions, processor control registers, and so on. If we want to convince you that the kernel indeed does quite a good job in performing a specific task, we must first tell what kind of support comes from the hardware.

- Even if a large portion of a Unix kernel source code is processor-independent and coded in C language, a small and critical part is coded in assembly language. A thorough knowledge of the kernel therefore requires the study of a few assembly language fragments that interact with the hardware.

When covering hardware features, our strategy is quite simple: just sketch the features that are totally hardware-driven while detailing those that need some software support. In fact, we are interested in kernel design rather than in computer architecture.

Our next step in choosing our path consisted of selecting the computer system to describe. Although Linux is now running on several kinds of personal computers and workstations, we decided to concentrate on the very popular and cheap IBM-compatible personal computers—and thus on the 80×86 microprocessors and on some support chips included in these personal computers. The term *80×86 microprocessor* will be used in the forthcoming chapters to denote the Intel 80386, 80486, Pentium, Pentium Pro, Pentium II, Pentium III, and Pentium 4 microprocessors or compatible models. In a few cases, explicit references will be made to specific models.

One more choice we had to make was the order to follow in studying Linux components. We tried a bottom-up approach: start with topics that are hardware-dependent and end with those that are totally hardware-independent. In fact, we'll make many references to the 80×86 microprocessors in the first part of the book, while the rest of it is relatively hardware-independent. One significant exception is made in Chapter 13. In practice, following a bottom-up approach is not as simple as it looks, since the areas of memory management, process management, and filesystems are intertwined; a few forward references—that is, references to topics yet to be explained—are unavoidable.

Each chapter starts with a theoretical overview of the topics covered. The material is then presented according to the bottom-up approach. We start with the data structures needed to support the functionalities described in the chapter. Then we usually move from the lowest level of functions to higher levels, often ending by showing how system calls issued by user applications are supported.

Level of Description

Linux source code for all supported architectures is contained in more than 8,000 C and assembly language files stored in about 530 subdirectories; it consists of roughly 4 million lines of code, which occupy over 144 megabytes of disk space. Of course, this book can cover only a very small portion of that code. Just to figure out how big the Linux source is, consider that the whole source code of the book you are reading occupies less than 3 megabytes of disk space. Therefore, we would need more than 40 books like this to list all code, without even commenting on it!

So we had to make some choices about the parts to describe. This is a rough assessment of our decisions:

- We describe process and memory management fairly thoroughly.
- We cover the Virtual Filesystem and the Ext2 and Ext3 filesystems, although many functions are just mentioned without detailing the code; we do not discuss other filesystems supported by Linux.
- We describe device drivers, which account for a good part of the kernel, as far as the kernel interface is concerned, but do not attempt analysis of each specific driver, including the terminal drivers.
- We cover the inner layers of networking in a rather sketchy way, since this area deserves a whole new book by itself.

The book describes the official 2.4.18 version of the Linux kernel, which can be downloaded from the web site, *http://www.kernel.org*.

Be aware that most distributions of GNU/Linux modify the official kernel to implement new features or to improve its efficiency. In a few cases, the source code provided by your favorite distribution might differ significantly from the one described in this book.

In many cases, the original code has been rewritten in an easier-to-read but less efficient way. This occurs at time-critical points at which sections of programs are often written in a mixture of hand-optimized C and Assembly code. Once again, our aim is to provide some help in studying the original Linux code.

While discussing kernel code, we often end up describing the underpinnings of many familiar features that Unix programmers have heard of and about which they may be curious (shared and mapped memory, signals, pipes, symbolic links, etc.).

Overview of the Book

To make life easier, Chapter 1, *Introduction*, presents a general picture of what is inside a Unix kernel and how Linux competes against other well-known Unix systems.

The heart of any Unix kernel is memory management. Chapter 2, *Memory Addressing*, explains how 80×86 processors include special circuits to address data in memory and how Linux exploits them.

Processes are a fundamental abstraction offered by Linux and are introduced in Chapter 3, *Processes*. Here we also explain how each process runs either in an unprivileged User Mode or in a privileged Kernel Mode. Transitions between User Mode and Kernel Mode happen only through well-established hardware mechanisms called *interrupts* and *exceptions*. These are introduced in Chapter 4, *Interrupts and Exceptions*.

In many occasions, the kernel has to deal with bursts of interrupts coming from different devices. Synchronization mechanisms are needed so that all these requests can be serviced in an interleaved way by the kernel: they are discussed in Chapter 5, *Kernel Synchronization*, for both uniprocessor and multiprocessor systems.

One type of interrupt is crucial for allowing Linux to take care of elapsed time; further details can be found in Chapter 6, *Timing Measurements*.

Next we focus again on memory: Chapter 7, *Memory Management*, describes the sophisticated techniques required to handle the most precious resource in the system (besides the processors, of course), available memory. This resource must be granted both to the Linux kernel and to the user applications. Chapter 8, *Process Address Space*, shows how the kernel copes with the requests for memory issued by greedy application programs.

Chapter 9, *System Calls*, explains how a process running in User Mode makes requests to the kernel, while Chapter 10, *Signals*, describes how a process may send synchronization signals to other processes. Chapter 11, *Process Scheduling*, explains how Linux executes, in turn, every active process in the system so that all of them can progress toward their completions. Now we are ready to move on to another essential topic, how Linux implements the filesystem. A series of chapters cover this topic. Chapter 12, *The Virtual Filesystem*, introduces a general layer that supports many different filesystems. Some Linux files are special because they provide trap-doors to reach hardware devices; Chapter 13, *Managing I/O Devices*, offers insights on these special files and on the corresponding hardware device drivers.

Another issue to consider is disk access time; Chapter 14, *Disk Caches*, shows how a clever use of RAM reduces disk accesses, therefore improving system performance significantly. Building on the material covered in these last chapters, we can now explain in Chapter 15, *Accessing Files*, how user applications access normal files. Chapter 16, *Swapping: Methods for Freeing Memory*, completes our discussion of Linux memory management and explains the techniques used by Linux to ensure that enough memory is always available. The last chapter dealing with files is Chapter 17, *The Ext2 and Ext3 Filesystems*, which illustrates the most frequently used Linux filesystem, namely Ext2 and its recent evolution, Ext3.

Chapter 18, *Networking*, deals with the lower layers of networking.

The last two chapters end our detailed tour of the Linux kernel: Chapter 19, *Process Communication*, introduces communication mechanisms other than signals available to User Mode processes; Chapter 20, *Program Execution*, explains how user applications are started.

Last, but not least, are the appendixes: Appendix A, *System Startup*, sketches out how Linux is booted, while Appendix B, *Modules*, describes how to dynamically reconfigure the running kernel, adding and removing functionalities as needed. Appendix C, *Source Code Structure*, is just a list of the directories that contain the Linux source code. The Source Code Index includes all the Linux symbols referenced in the book; here you will find the name of the Linux file defining each symbol and the book's page number where it is explained. We think you'll find it quite handy.

Background Information

No prerequisites are required, except some skill in C programming language and perhaps some knowledge of Assembly language.

Conventions in This Book

The following is a list of typographical conventions used in this book:

Constant Width
> Is used to show the contents of code files or the output from commands, and to indicate source code keywords that appear in code.

Italic
> Is used for file and directory names, program and command names, command-line options, URLs, and for emphasizing new terms.

How to Contact Us

Please address comments and questions concerning this book to the publisher:

O'Reilly & Associates, Inc.
1005 Gravenstein Highway North
Sebastopol, CA 95472
(800) 998-9938 (in the United States or Canada)
(707) 829-0515 (international or local)
(707) 829-0104 (fax)

We have a web page for this book, where we list errata, examples, or any additional information. You can access this page at:

> *http://www.oreilly.com/catalog/linuxkernel2/*

To comment or ask technical questions about this book, send email to:

> *bookquestions@oreilly.com*

For more information about our books, conferences, Resource Centers, and the O'Reilly Network, see our web site at:

> *http://www.oreilly.com*

Acknowledgments

This book would not have been written without the precious help of the many students of the University of Rome school of engineering "Tor Vergata" who took our course and tried to decipher lecture notes about the Linux kernel. Their strenuous efforts to grasp the meaning of the source code led us to improve our presentation and correct many mistakes.

Andy Oram, our wonderful editor at O'Reilly & Associates, deserves a lot of credit. He was the first at O'Reilly to believe in this project, and he spent a lot of time and energy deciphering our preliminary drafts. He also suggested many ways to make the book more readable, and he wrote several excellent introductory paragraphs.

Many thanks also to the O'Reilly staff, especially Rob Romano, the technical illustrator, and Lenny Muellner, for tools support.

We had some prestigious reviewers who read our text quite carefully. The first edition was checked by (in alphabetical order by first name) Alan Cox, Michael Kerrisk, Paul Kinzelman, Raph Levien, and Rik van Riel.

Erez Zadok, Jerry Cooperstein, John Goerzen, Michael Kerrisk, Paul Kinzelman, Rik van Riel, and Walt Smith reviewed this second edition. Their comments, together with those of many readers from all over the world, helped us to remove several errors and inaccuracies and have made this book stronger.

—Daniel P. Bovet
Marco Cesati
September 2002

CHAPTER 1
Introduction

Linux is a member of the large family of Unix-like operating systems. A relative new-comer experiencing sudden spectacular popularity starting in the late 1990s, Linux joins such well-known commercial Unix operating systems as System V Release 4 (SVR4), developed by AT&T (now owned by the SCO Group); the 4.4 BSD release from the University of California at Berkeley (4.4BSD); Digital Unix from Digital Equipment Corporation (now Hewlett-Packard); AIX from IBM; HP-UX from Hewlett-Packard; Solaris from Sun Microsystems; and Mac OS X from Apple Computer, Inc.

Linux was initially developed by Linus Torvalds in 1991 as an operating system for IBM-compatible personal computers based on the Intel 80386 microprocessor. Linus remains deeply involved with improving Linux, keeping it up to date with various hardware developments and coordinating the activity of hundreds of Linux developers around the world. Over the years, developers have worked to make Linux available on other architectures, including Hewlett-Packard's Alpha, Itanium (the recent Intel's 64-bit processor), MIPS, SPARC, Motorola MC680x0, PowerPC, and IBM's zSeries.

One of the more appealing benefits to Linux is that it isn't a commercial operating system: its source code under the GNU Public License* is open and available to anyone to study (as we will in this book); if you download the code (the official site is *http://www.kernel.org*) or check the sources on a Linux CD, you will be able to explore, from top to bottom, one of the most successful, modern operating systems. This book, in fact, assumes you have the source code on hand and can apply what we say to your own explorations.

---

* The GNU project is coordinated by the Free Software Foundation, Inc. (*http://www.gnu.org*); its aim is to implement a whole operating system freely usable by everyone. The availability of a GNU C compiler has been essential for the success of the Linux project.

Technically speaking, Linux is a true Unix kernel, although it is not a full Unix operating system because it does not include all the Unix applications, such as filesystem utilities, windowing systems and graphical desktops, system administrator commands, text editors, compilers, and so on. However, since most of these programs are freely available under the GNU General Public License, they can be installed onto one of the filesystems supported by Linux.

Since the Linux kernel requires so much additional software to provide a useful environment, many Linux users prefer to rely on commercial distributions, available on CD-ROM, to get the code included in a standard Unix system. Alternatively, the code may be obtained from several different FTP sites. The Linux source code is usually installed in the */usr/src/linux* directory. In the rest of this book, all file pathnames will refer implicitly to that directory.

Linux Versus Other Unix-Like Kernels

The various Unix-like systems on the market, some of which have a long history and show signs of archaic practices, differ in many important respects. All commercial variants were derived from either SVR4 or 4.4BSD, and all tend to agree on some common standards like IEEE's Portable Operating Systems based on Unix (POSIX) and X/Open's Common Applications Environment (CAE).

The current standards specify only an application programming interface (API)— that is, a well-defined environment in which user programs should run. Therefore, the standards do not impose any restriction on internal design choices of a compliant kernel.*

To define a common user interface, Unix-like kernels often share fundamental design ideas and features. In this respect, Linux is comparable with the other Unix-like operating systems. Reading this book and studying the Linux kernel, therefore, may help you understand the other Unix variants too.

The 2.4 version of the Linux kernel aims to be compliant with the IEEE POSIX standard. This, of course, means that most existing Unix programs can be compiled and executed on a Linux system with very little effort or even without the need for patches to the source code. Moreover, Linux includes all the features of a modern Unix operating system, such as virtual memory, a virtual filesystem, lightweight processes, reliable signals, SVR4 interprocess communications, support for Symmetric Multiprocessor (SMP) systems, and so on.

By itself, the Linux kernel is not very innovative. When Linus Torvalds wrote the first kernel, he referred to some classical books on Unix internals, like Maurice Bach's *The Design of the Unix Operating System* (Prentice Hall, 1986). Actually,

---

* As a matter of fact, several non-Unix operating systems, such as Windows NT, are POSIX-compliant.

Linux still has some bias toward the Unix baseline described in Bach's book (i.e., SVR4). However, Linux doesn't stick to any particular variant. Instead, it tries to adopt the best features and design choices of several different Unix kernels.

The following list describes how Linux competes against some well-known commercial Unix kernels:

Monolithic kernel

It is a large, complex do-it-yourself program, composed of several logically different components. In this, it is quite conventional; most commercial Unix variants are monolithic. (A notable exception is Carnegie-Mellon's Mach 3.0, which follows a microkernel approach.)

Compiled and statically linked traditional Unix kernels

Most modern kernels can dynamically load and unload some portions of the kernel code (typically, device drivers), which are usually called modules. Linux's support for modules is very good, since it is able to automatically load and unload modules on demand. Among the main commercial Unix variants, only the SVR4.2 and Solaris kernels have a similar feature.

Kernel threading

Some modern Unix kernels, such as Solaris 2.x and SVR4.2/MP, are organized as a set of kernel threads. A kernel thread is an execution context that can be independently scheduled; it may be associated with a user program, or it may run only some kernel functions. Context switches between kernel threads are usually much less expensive than context switches between ordinary processes, since the former usually operate on a common address space. Linux uses kernel threads in a very limited way to execute a few kernel functions periodically; since Linux kernel threads cannot execute user programs, they do not represent the basic execution context abstraction. (That's the topic of the next item.)

Multithreaded application support

Most modern operating systems have some kind of support for multithreaded applications—that is, user programs that are well designed in terms of many relatively independent execution flows that share a large portion of the application data structures. A multithreaded user application could be composed of many *lightweight processes* (LWP), which are processes that can operate on a common address space, common physical memory pages, common opened files, and so on. Linux defines its own version of lightweight processes, which is different from the types used on other systems such as SVR4 and Solaris. While all the commercial Unix variants of LWP are based on kernel threads, Linux regards lightweight processes as the basic execution context and handles them via the nonstandard clone( ) system call.

Nonpreemptive kernel

Linux 2.4 cannot arbitrarily interleave execution flows while they are in privileged mode.* Several sections of kernel code assume they can run and modify data structures without fear of being interrupted and having another thread alter those data structures. Usually, fully preemptive kernels are associated with special real-time operating systems. Currently, among conventional, general-purpose Unix systems, only Solaris 2.x and Mach 3.0 are fully preemptive kernels. SVR4.2/MP introduces some *fixed preemption points* as a method to get limited preemption capability.

Multiprocessor support

Several Unix kernel variants take advantage of multiprocessor systems. Linux 2.4 supports symmetric multiprocessing (SMP): the system can use multiple processors and each processor can handle any task—there is no discrimination among them. Although a few parts of the kernel code are still serialized by means of a single "big kernel lock," it is fair to say that Linux 2.4 makes a near optimal use of SMP.

Filesystem

Linux's standard filesystems come in many flavors, You can use the plain old Ext2 filesystem if you don't have specific needs. You might switch to Ext3 if you want to avoid lengthy filesystem checks after a system crash. If you'll have to deal with many small files, the ReiserFS filesystem is likely to be the best choice. Besides Ext3 and ReiserFS, several other journaling filesystems can be used in Linux, even if they are not included in the vanilla Linux tree; they include IBM AIX's Journaling File System (JFS) and Silicon Graphics Irix's XFS filesystem. Thanks to a powerful object-oriented Virtual File System technology (inspired by Solaris and SVR4), porting a foreign filesystem to Linux is a relatively easy task.

STREAMS

Linux has no analog to the STREAMS I/O subsystem introduced in SVR4, although it is included now in most Unix kernels and has become the preferred interface for writing device drivers, terminal drivers, and network protocols.

This somewhat modest assessment does not depict, however, the whole truth. Several features make Linux a wonderfully unique operating system. Commercial Unix kernels often introduce new features to gain a larger slice of the market, but these features are not necessarily useful, stable, or productive. As a matter of fact, modern Unix kernels tend to be quite bloated. By contrast, Linux doesn't suffer from the restrictions and the conditioning imposed by the market, hence it can freely evolve according to the ideas of its designers (mainly Linus Torvalds). Specifically, Linux offers the following advantages over its commercial competitors:

---

* This restriction has been removed in the Linux 2.5 development version.

Linux is free. You can install a complete Unix system at no expense other than the hardware (of course).

Linux is fully customizable in all its components. Thanks to the General Public License (GPL), you are allowed to freely read and modify the source code of the kernel and of all system programs.*

Linux runs on low-end, cheap hardware platforms. You can even build a network server using an old Intel 80386 system with 4 MB of RAM.

Linux is powerful. Linux systems are very fast, since they fully exploit the features of the hardware components. The main Linux goal is efficiency, and indeed many design choices of commercial variants, like the STREAMS I/O subsystem, have been rejected by Linus because of their implied performance penalty.

Linux has a high standard for source code quality. Linux systems are usually very stable; they have a very low failure rate and system maintenance time.

The Linux kernel can be very small and compact. It is possible to fit both a kernel image and full root filesystem, including all fundamental system programs, on just one 1.4 MB floppy disk. As far as we know, none of the commercial Unix variants is able to boot from a single floppy disk.

Linux is highly compatible with many common operating systems. It lets you directly mount filesystems for all versions of MS-DOS and MS Windows, SVR4, OS/2, Mac OS, Solaris, SunOS, NeXTSTEP, many BSD variants, and so on. Linux is also able to operate with many network layers, such as Ethernet (as well as Fast Ethernet and Gigabit Ethernet), Fiber Distributed Data Interface (FDDI), High Performance Parallel Interface (HIPPI), IBM's Token Ring, AT&T Wave-LAN, and DEC RoamAbout DS. By using suitable libraries, Linux systems are even able to directly run programs written for other operating systems. For example, Linux is able to execute applications written for MS-DOS, MS Windows, SVR3 and R4, 4.4BSD, SCO Unix, XENIX, and others on the 80×86 platform.

Linux is well supported. Believe it or not, it may be a lot easier to get patches and updates for Linux than for any other proprietary operating system. The answer to a problem often comes back within a few hours after sending a message to some newsgroup or mailing list. Moreover, drivers for Linux are usually available a few weeks after new hardware products have been introduced on the market. By contrast, hardware manufacturers release device drivers for only a few commercial operating systems—usually Microsoft's. Therefore, all commercial Unix variants run on a restricted subset of hardware components.

With an estimated installed base of several tens of millions, people who are used to certain features that are standard under other operating systems are starting to

---

* Several commercial companies have started to support their products under Linux. However, most of them aren't distributed under an open source license, so you might not be allowed to read or modify their source code.

expect the same from Linux. In that regard, the demand on Linux developers is also increasing. Luckily, though, Linux has evolved under the close direction of Linus to accommodate the needs of the masses.

Hardware Dependency

Linux tries to maintain a neat distinction between hardware-dependent and hardware-independent source code. To that end, both the *arch* and the *include* directories include nine subdirectories that correspond to the nine hardware platforms supported. The standard names of the platforms are:

alpha
> Hewlett-Packard's Alpha workstations

arm
> ARM processor-based computers and embedded devices

cris
> "Code Reduced Instruction Set" CPUs used by Axis in its thin-servers, such as web cameras or development boards

i386
> IBM-compatible personal computers based on 80×86 microprocessors

ia64
> Workstations based on Intel 64-bit Itanium microprocessor

m68k
> Personal computers based on Motorola $MC680 \times 0$ microprocessors

mips
> Workstations based on MIPS microprocessors

mips64
> Workstations based on 64-bit MIPS microprocessors

parisc
> Workstations based on Hewlett Packard HP 9000 PA-RISC microprocessors

ppc
> Workstations based on Motorola-IBM PowerPC microprocessors

s390
> 32-bit IBM ESA/390 and zSeries mainframes

s390x
> IBM 64-bit zSeries servers

sh
> SuperH embedded computers developed jointly by Hitachi and STMicroelectronics

sparc
> Workstations based on Sun Microsystems SPARC microprocessors

sparc64
> Workstations based on Sun Microsystems 64-bit Ultra SPARC microprocessors

Linux Versions

Linux distinguishes stable kernels from development kernels through a simple numbering scheme. Each version is characterized by three numbers, separated by periods. The first two numbers are used to identify the version; the third number identifies the release.

As shown in Figure 1-1, if the second number is even, it denotes a stable kernel; otherwise, it denotes a development kernel. At the time of this writing, the current stable version of the Linux kernel is 2.4.18, and the current development version is 2.5.22. The 2.4 kernel—which is the basis for this book—was first released in January 2001 and differs considerably from the 2.2 kernel, particularly with respect to memory management. Work on the 2.5 development version started in November 2001.

Figure 1-1. Numbering Linux versions

New releases of a stable version come out mostly to fix bugs reported by users. The main algorithms and data structures used to implement the kernel are left unchanged.*

Development versions, on the other hand, may differ quite significantly from one another; kernel developers are free to experiment with different solutions that occasionally lead to drastic kernel changes. Users who rely on development versions for running applications may experience unpleasant surprises when upgrading their kernel to a newer release. This book concentrates on the most recent stable kernel that we had available because, among all the new features being tried in experimental kernels, there's no way of telling which will ultimately be accepted and what they'll look like in their final form.

---

* The practice does not always follow the theory. For instance, the virtual memory system has been significantly changed, starting with the 2.4.10 release.

Basic Operating System Concepts

Each computer system includes a basic set of programs called the *operating system*. The most important program in the set is called the *kernel*. It is loaded into RAM when the system boots and contains many critical procedures that are needed for the system to operate. The other programs are less crucial utilities; they can provide a wide variety of interactive experiences for the user—as well as doing all the jobs the user bought the computer for—but the essential shape and capabilities of the system are determined by the kernel. The kernel provides key facilities to everything else on the system and determines many of the characteristics of higher software. Hence, we often use the term "operating system" as a synonym for "kernel."

The operating system must fulfill two main objectives:

- Interact with the hardware components, servicing all low-level programmable elements included in the hardware platform.
- Provide an execution environment to the applications that run on the computer system (the so-called user programs).

Some operating systems allow all user programs to directly play with the hardware components (a typical example is MS-DOS). In contrast, a Unix-like operating system hides all low-level details concerning the physical organization of the computer from applications run by the user. When a program wants to use a hardware resource, it must issue a request to the operating system. The kernel evaluates the request and, if it chooses to grant the resource, interacts with the relative hardware components on behalf of the user program.

To enforce this mechanism, modern operating systems rely on the availability of specific hardware features that forbid user programs to directly interact with low-level hardware components or to access arbitrary memory locations. In particular, the hardware introduces at least two different execution modes for the CPU: a nonprivileged mode for user programs and a privileged mode for the kernel. Unix calls these *User Mode* and *Kernel Mode*, respectively.

In the rest of this chapter, we introduce the basic concepts that have motivated the design of Unix over the past two decades, as well as Linux and other operating systems. While the concepts are probably familiar to you as a Linux user, these sections try to delve into them a bit more deeply than usual to explain the requirements they place on an operating system kernel. These broad considerations refer to virtually all Unix-like systems. The other chapters of this book will hopefully help you understand the Linux kernel internals.

Multiuser Systems

A *multiuser system* is a computer that is able to concurrently and independently execute several applications belonging to two or more users. *Concurrently* means that applications can be active at the same time and contend for the various resources such as CPU, memory, hard disks, and so on. *Independently* means that each application can perform its task with no concern for what the applications of the other users are doing. Switching from one application to another, of course, slows down each of them and affects the response time seen by the users. Many of the complexities of modern operating system kernels, which we will examine in this book, are present to minimize the delays enforced on each program and to provide the user with responses that are as fast as possible.

Multiuser operating systems must include several features:

- An authentication mechanism for verifying the user's identity
- A protection mechanism against buggy user programs that could block other applications running in the system
- A protection mechanism against malicious user programs that could interfere with or spy on the activity of other users
- An accounting mechanism that limits the amount of resource units assigned to each user

To ensure safe protection mechanisms, operating systems must use the hardware protection associated with the CPU privileged mode. Otherwise, a user program would be able to directly access the system circuitry and overcome the imposed bounds. Unix is a multiuser system that enforces the hardware protection of system resources.

Users and Groups

In a multiuser system, each user has a private space on the machine; typically, he owns some quota of the disk space to store files, receives private mail messages, and so on. The operating system must ensure that the private portion of a user space is visible only to its owner. In particular, it must ensure that no user can exploit a system application for the purpose of violating the private space of another user.

All users are identified by a unique number called the *User ID*, or *UID*. Usually only a restricted number of persons are allowed to make use of a computer system. When one of these users starts a working session, the operating system asks for a *login name* and a *password*. If the user does not input a valid pair, the system denies access. Since the password is assumed to be secret, the user's privacy is ensured.

To selectively share material with other users, each user is a member of one or more *groups*, which are identified by a unique number called a *Group ID*, or *GID*. Each file is associated with exactly one group. For example, access can be set so the user owning the file has read and write privileges, the group has read-only privileges, and other users on the system are denied access to the file.

Any Unix-like operating system has a special user called *root*, *superuser*, or *supervisor*. The system administrator must log in as root to handle user accounts, perform maintenance tasks such as system backups and program upgrades, and so on. The root user can do almost everything, since the operating system does not apply the usual protection mechanisms to her. In particular, the root user can access every file on the system and can interfere with the activity of every running user program.

Processes

All operating systems use one fundamental abstraction: the *process*. A process can be defined either as "an instance of a program in execution" or as the "execution context" of a running program. In traditional operating systems, a process executes a single sequence of instructions in an *address space*; the address space is the set of memory addresses that the process is allowed to reference. Modern operating systems allow processes with multiple execution flows—that is, multiple sequences of instructions executed in the same address space.

Multiuser systems must enforce an execution environment in which several processes can be active concurrently and contend for system resources, mainly the CPU. Systems that allow concurrent active processes are said to be *multiprogramming* or *multiprocessing*.* It is important to distinguish programs from processes; several processes can execute the same program concurrently, while the same process can execute several programs sequentially.

On uniprocessor systems, just one process can hold the CPU, and hence just one execution flow can progress at a time. In general, the number of CPUs is always restricted, and therefore only a few processes can progress at once. An operating system component called the *scheduler* chooses the process that can progress. Some operating systems allow only *nonpreemptive* processes, which means that the scheduler is invoked only when a process voluntarily relinquishes the CPU. But processes of a multiuser system must be *preemptive*; the operating system tracks how long each process holds the CPU and periodically activates the scheduler.

Unix is a multiprocessing operating system with preemptive processes. Even when no user is logged in and no application is running, several system processes monitor the peripheral devices. In particular, several processes listen at the system terminals waiting for user logins. When a user inputs a login name, the listening process runs a program that validates the user password. If the user identity is acknowledged, the process creates another process that runs a shell into which commands are entered. When a graphical display is activated, one process runs the window manager, and each window on the display is usually run by a separate process. When a user creates a graphics shell, one process runs the graphics windows and a second process runs the shell into which the user can enter the commands. For each user command, the shell process creates another process that executes the corresponding program.

Unix-like operating systems adopt a *process/kernel model*. Each process has the illusion that it's the only process on the machine and it has exclusive access to the operating system services. Whenever a process makes a system call (i.e., a request to the

---

* Some multiprocessing operating systems are not multiuser; an example is Microsoft's Windows 98.

kernel), the hardware changes the privilege mode from User Mode to Kernel Mode, and the process starts the execution of a kernel procedure with a strictly limited purpose. In this way, the operating system acts within the execution context of the process in order to satisfy its request. Whenever the request is fully satisfied, the kernel procedure forces the hardware to return to User Mode and the process continues its execution from the instruction following the system call.

Kernel Architecture

As stated before, most Unix kernels are monolithic: each kernel layer is integrated into the whole kernel program and runs in Kernel Mode on behalf of the current process. In contrast, *microkernel* operating systems demand a very small set of functions from the kernel, generally including a few synchronization primitives, a simple scheduler, and an interprocess communication mechanism. Several system processes that run on top of the microkernel implement other operating system–layer functions, like memory allocators, device drivers, and system call handlers.

Although academic research on operating systems is oriented toward microkernels, such operating systems are generally slower than monolithic ones, since the explicit message passing between the different layers of the operating system has a cost. However, microkernel operating systems might have some theoretical advantages over monolithic ones. Microkernels force the system programmers to adopt a modularized approach, since each operating system layer is a relatively independent program that must interact with the other layers through well-defined and clean software interfaces. Moreover, an existing microkernel operating system can be easily ported to other architectures fairly easily, since all hardware-dependent components are generally encapsulated in the microkernel code. Finally, microkernel operating systems tend to make better use of random access memory (RAM) than monolithic ones, since system processes that aren't implementing needed functionalities might be swapped out or destroyed.

To achieve many of the theoretical advantages of microkernels without introducing performance penalties, the Linux kernel offers *modules*. A module is an object file whose code can be linked to (and unlinked from) the kernel at runtime. The object code usually consists of a set of functions that implements a filesystem, a device driver, or other features at the kernel's upper layer. The module, unlike the external layers of microkernel operating systems, does not run as a specific process. Instead, it is executed in Kernel Mode on behalf of the current process, like any other statically linked kernel function.

The main advantages of using modules include:

A modularized approach
> Since any module can be linked and unlinked at runtime, system programmers must introduce well-defined software interfaces to access the data structures handled by modules. This makes it easy to develop new modules.

Platform independence
> Even if it may rely on some specific hardware features, a module doesn't depend on a fixed hardware platform. For example, a disk driver module that relies on the SCSI standard works as well on an IBM-compatible PC as it does on Hewlett-Packard's Alpha.

Frugal main memory usage
> A module can be linked to the running kernel when its functionality is required and unlinked when it is no longer useful. This mechanism also can be made transparent to the user, since linking and unlinking can be performed automatically by the kernel.

No performance penalty
> Once linked in, the object code of a module is equivalent to the object code of the statically linked kernel. Therefore, no explicit message passing is required when the functions of the module are invoked.*

An Overview of the Unix Filesystem

The Unix operating system design is centered on its filesystem, which has several interesting characteristics. We'll review the most significant ones, since they will be mentioned quite often in forthcoming chapters.

Files

A Unix file is an information container structured as a sequence of bytes; the kernel does not interpret the contents of a file. Many programming libraries implement higher-level abstractions, such as records structured into fields and record addressing based on keys. However, the programs in these libraries must rely on system calls offered by the kernel. From the user's point of view, files are organized in a tree-structured namespace, as shown in Figure 1-2.

All the nodes of the tree, except the leaves, denote directory names. A directory node contains information about the files and directories just beneath it. A file or directory name consists of a sequence of arbitrary ASCII characters,† with the exception of / and of the null character \0. Most filesystems place a limit on the length of a filename, typically no more than 255 characters. The directory corresponding to the root of the tree is called the *root directory*. By convention, its name is a slash (/). Names must be different within the same directory, but the same name may be used in different directories.

---

* A small performance penalty occurs when the module is linked and unlinked. However, this penalty can be compared to the penalty caused by the creation and deletion of system processes in microkernel operating systems.

† Some operating systems allow filenames to be expressed in many different alphabets, based on 16-bit extended coding of graphical characters such as Unicode.

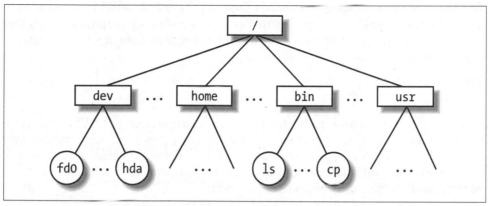

Figure 1-2. An example of a directory tree

Unix associates a *current working directory* with each process (see the section "The Process/Kernel Model" later in this chapter); it belongs to the process execution context, and it identifies the directory currently used by the process. To identify a specific file, the process uses a *pathname*, which consists of slashes alternating with a sequence of directory names that lead to the file. If the first item in the pathname is a slash, the pathname is said to be *absolute*, since its starting point is the root directory. Otherwise, if the first item is a directory name or filename, the pathname is said to be *relative*, since its starting point is the process's current directory.

While specifying filenames, the notations "." and ".." are also used. They denote the current working directory and its parent directory, respectively. If the current working directory is the root directory, "." and ".." coincide.

Hard and Soft Links

A filename included in a directory is called a *file hard link*, or more simply, a *link*. The same file may have several links included in the same directory or in different ones, so it may have several filenames.

The Unix command:

```
$ ln f1 f2
```

is used to create a new hard link that has the pathname f2 for a file identified by the pathname f1.

Hard links have two limitations:

- Users are not allowed to create hard links for directories. This might transform the directory tree into a graph with cycles, thus making it impossible to locate a file according to its name.
- Links can be created only among files included in the same filesystem. This is a serious limitation, since modern Unix systems may include several filesystems located on different disks and/or partitions, and users may be unaware of the physical divisions between them.

To overcome these limitations, *soft links* (also called *symbolic links*) have been introduced. Symbolic links are short files that contain an arbitrary pathname of another file. The pathname may refer to any file located in any filesystem; it may even refer to a nonexistent file.

The Unix command:

```
$ ln -s f1 f2
```

creates a new soft link with pathname f2 that refers to pathname f1. When this command is executed, the filesystem extracts the directory part of f2 and creates a new entry in that directory of type symbolic link, with the name indicated by f2. This new file contains the name indicated by pathname f1. This way, each reference to f2 can be translated automatically into a reference to f1.

File Types

Unix files may have one of the following types:

- Regular file
- Directory
- Symbolic link
- Block-oriented device file
- Character-oriented device file
- Pipe and named pipe (also called FIFO)
- Socket

The first three file types are constituents of any Unix filesystem. Their implementation is described in detail in Chapter 17.

Device files are related to I/O devices and device drivers integrated into the kernel. For example, when a program accesses a device file, it acts directly on the I/O device associated with that file (see Chapter 13).

Pipes and sockets are special files used for interprocess communication (see the section "Synchronization and Critical Regions" later in this chapter; also see Chapter 18 and Chapter 19)

File Descriptor and Inode

Unix makes a clear distinction between the contents of a file and the information about a file. With the exception of device and special files, each file consists of a sequence of characters. The file does not include any control information, such as its length or an End-Of-File (EOF) delimiter.

All information needed by the filesystem to handle a file is included in a data structure called an *inode*. Each file has its own inode, which the filesystem uses to identify the file.

While filesystems and the kernel functions handling them can vary widely from one Unix system to another, they must always provide at least the following attributes, which are specified in the POSIX standard:

- File type (see the previous section)
- Number of hard links associated with the file
- File length in bytes
- Device ID (i.e., an identifier of the device containing the file)
- Inode number that identifies the file within the filesystem
- User ID of the file owner
- Group ID of the file
- Several timestamps that specify the inode status change time, the last access time, and the last modify time
- Access rights and file mode (see the next section)

Access Rights and File Mode

The potential users of a file fall into three classes:

- The user who is the owner of the file
- The users who belong to the same group as the file, not including the owner
- All remaining users (others)

There are three types of access rights—*Read*, *Write*, and *Execute*—for each of these three classes. Thus, the set of access rights associated with a file consists of nine different binary flags. Three additional flags, called *suid* (*Set User ID*), *sgid* (*Set Group ID*), and *sticky*, define the file mode. These flags have the following meanings when applied to executable files:

suid

> A process executing a file normally keeps the User ID (UID) of the process owner. However, if the executable file has the suid flag set, the process gets the UID of the file owner.

sgid

> A process executing a file keeps the Group ID (GID) of the process group. However, if the executable file has the sgid flag set, the process gets the ID of the file group.

sticky

> An executable file with the sticky flag set corresponds to a request to the kernel to keep the program in memory after its execution terminates.[*]

---

[*] This flag has become obsolete; other approaches based on sharing of code pages are now used (see Chapter 8).

When a file is created by a process, its owner ID is the UID of the process. Its owner group ID can be either the GID of the creator process or the GID of the parent directory, depending on the value of the sgid flag of the parent directory.

File-Handling System Calls

When a user accesses the contents of either a regular file or a directory, he actually accesses some data stored in a hardware block device. In this sense, a filesystem is a user-level view of the physical organization of a hard disk partition. Since a process in User Mode cannot directly interact with the low-level hardware components, each actual file operation must be performed in Kernel Mode. Therefore, the Unix operating system defines several system calls related to file handling.

All Unix kernels devote great attention to the efficient handling of hardware block devices to achieve good overall system performance. In the chapters that follow, we will describe topics related to file handling in Linux and specifically how the kernel reacts to file-related system calls. To understand those descriptions, you will need to know how the main file-handling system calls are used; these are described in the next section.

Opening a file

Processes can access only "opened" files. To open a file, the process invokes the system call:

```
fd = open(path, flag, mode)
```

The three parameters have the following meanings:

path
Denotes the pathname (relative or absolute) of the file to be opened.

flag
Specifies how the file must be opened (e.g., read, write, read/write, append). It can also specify whether a nonexisting file should be created.

mode
Specifies the access rights of a newly created file.

This system call creates an "open file" object and returns an identifier called a *file descriptor*. An open file object contains:

- Some file-handling data structures, such as a pointer to the kernel buffer memory area where file data will be copied, an offset field that denotes the current position in the file from which the next operation will take place (the so-called *file pointer*), and so on.

- Some pointers to kernel functions that the process can invoke. The set of permitted functions depends on the value of the flag parameter.

We discuss open file objects in detail in Chapter 12. Let's limit ourselves here to describing some general properties specified by the POSIX semantics.

- A file descriptor represents an interaction between a process and an opened file, while an open file object contains data related to that interaction. The same open file object may be identified by several file descriptors in the same process.

- Several processes may concurrently open the same file. In this case, the filesystem assigns a separate file descriptor to each file, along with a separate open file object. When this occurs, the Unix filesystem does not provide any kind of synchronization among the I/O operations issued by the processes on the same file. However, several system calls such as flock( ) are available to allow processes to synchronize themselves on the entire file or on portions of it (see Chapter 12).

To create a new file, the process may also invoke the creat( ) system call, which is handled by the kernel exactly like open( ).

Accessing an opened file

Regular Unix files can be addressed either sequentially or randomly, while device files and named pipes are usually accessed sequentially (see Chapter 13). In both kinds of access, the kernel stores the file pointer in the open file object—that is, the current position at which the next read or write operation will take place.

Sequential access is implicitly assumed: the read( ) and write( ) system calls always refer to the position of the current file pointer. To modify the value, a program must explicitly invoke the lseek( ) system call. When a file is opened, the kernel sets the file pointer to the position of the first byte in the file (offset 0).

The lseek( ) system call requires the following parameters:

```
newoffset = lseek(fd, offset, whence);
```

which have the following meanings:

fd
    Indicates the file descriptor of the opened file

offset
    Specifies a signed integer value that will be used for computing the new position of the file pointer

whence
    Specifies whether the new position should be computed by adding the offset value to the number 0 (offset from the beginning of the file), the current file pointer, or the position of the last byte (offset from the end of the file)

The read( ) system call requires the following parameters:

```
nread = read(fd, buf, count);
```

which have the following meaning:

fd
    Indicates the file descriptor of the opened file

buf
> Specifies the address of the buffer in the process's address space to which the data will be transferred

count
> Denotes the number of bytes to read

When handling such a system call, the kernel attempts to read count bytes from the file having the file descriptor fd, starting from the current value of the opened file's offset field. In some cases—end-of-file, empty pipe, and so on—the kernel does not succeed in reading all count bytes. The returned nread value specifies the number of bytes effectively read. The file pointer is also updated by adding nread to its previous value. The write( ) parameters are similar.

Closing a file

When a process does not need to access the contents of a file anymore, it can invoke the system call:

```
res = close(fd);
```

which releases the open file object corresponding to the file descriptor fd. When a process terminates, the kernel closes all its remaining opened files.

Renaming and deleting a file

To rename or delete a file, a process does not need to open it. Indeed, such operations do not act on the contents of the affected file, but rather on the contents of one or more directories. For example, the system call:

```
res = rename(oldpath, newpath);
```

changes the name of a file link, while the system call:

```
res = unlink(pathname);
```

decrements the file link count and removes the corresponding directory entry. The file is deleted only when the link count assumes the value 0.

An Overview of Unix Kernels

Unix kernels provide an execution environment in which applications may run. Therefore, the kernel must implement a set of services and corresponding interfaces. Applications use those interfaces and do not usually interact directly with hardware resources.

The Process/Kernel Model

As already mentioned, a CPU can run in either User Mode or Kernel Mode. Actually, some CPUs can have more than two execution states. For instance, the 80×86 microprocessors have four different execution states. But all standard Unix kernels use only Kernel Mode and User Mode.

When a program is executed in User Mode, it cannot directly access the kernel data structures or the kernel programs. When an application executes in Kernel Mode, however, these restrictions no longer apply. Each CPU model provides special instructions to switch from User Mode to Kernel Mode and vice versa. A program usually executes in User Mode and switches to Kernel Mode only when requesting a service provided by the kernel. When the kernel has satisfied the program's request, it puts the program back in User Mode.

Processes are dynamic entities that usually have a limited life span within the system. The task of creating, eliminating, and synchronizing the existing processes is delegated to a group of routines in the kernel.

The kernel itself is not a process but a process manager. The process/kernel model assumes that processes that require a kernel service use specific programming constructs called *system calls*. Each system call sets up the group of parameters that identifies the process request and then executes the hardware-dependent CPU instruction to switch from User Mode to Kernel Mode.

Besides user processes, Unix systems include a few privileged processes called *kernel threads* with the following characteristics:

- They run in Kernel Mode in the kernel address space.
- They do not interact with users, and thus do not require terminal devices.
- They are usually created during system startup and remain alive until the system is shut down

On a uniprocessor system, only one process is running at a time and it may run either in User or in Kernel Mode. If it runs in Kernel Mode, the processor is executing some kernel routine. Figure 1-3 illustrates examples of transitions between User and Kernel Mode. Process 1 in User Mode issues a system call, after which the process switches to Kernel Mode and the system call is serviced. Process 1 then resumes execution in User Mode until a timer interrupt occurs and the scheduler is activated in Kernel Mode. A process switch takes place and Process 2 starts its execution in User Mode until a hardware device raises an interrupt. As a consequence of the interrupt, Process 2 switches to Kernel Mode and services the interrupt.

Unix kernels do much more than handle system calls; in fact, kernel routines can be activated in several ways:

- A process invokes a system call.
- The CPU executing the process signals an *exception*, which is an unusual condition such as an invalid instruction. The kernel handles the exception on behalf of the process that caused it.

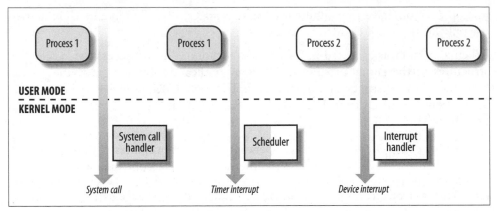

Figure 1-3. Transitions between User and Kernel Mode

- A peripheral device issues an *interrupt signal* to the CPU to notify it of an event such as a request for attention, a status change, or the completion of an I/O operation. Each interrupt signal is dealt by a kernel program called an *interrupt handler*. Since peripheral devices operate asynchronously with respect to the CPU, interrupts occur at unpredictable times.

- A kernel thread is executed. Since it runs in Kernel Mode, the corresponding program must be considered part of the kernel.

Process Implementation

To let the kernel manage processes, each process is represented by a *process descriptor* that includes information about the current state of the process.

When the kernel stops the execution of a process, it saves the current contents of several processor registers in the process descriptor. These include:

- The program counter (PC) and stack pointer (SP) registers
- The general purpose registers
- The floating point registers
- The processor control registers (Processor Status Word) containing information about the CPU state
- The memory management registers used to keep track of the RAM accessed by the process

When the kernel decides to resume executing a process, it uses the proper process descriptor fields to load the CPU registers. Since the stored value of the program counter points to the instruction following the last instruction executed, the process resumes execution at the point where it was stopped.

When a process is not executing on the CPU, it is waiting for some event. Unix kernels distinguish many wait states, which are usually implemented by queues of process descriptors; each (possibly empty) queue corresponds to the set of processes waiting for a specific event.

Reentrant Kernels

All Unix kernels are *reentrant*. This means that several processes may be executing in Kernel Mode at the same time. Of course, on uniprocessor systems, only one process can progress, but many can be blocked in Kernel Mode when waiting for the CPU or the completion of some I/O operation. For instance, after issuing a read to a disk on behalf of some process, the kernel lets the disk controller handle it, and resumes executing other processes. An interrupt notifies the kernel when the device has satisfied the read, so the former process can resume the execution.

One way to provide reentrancy is to write functions so that they modify only local variables and do not alter global data structures. Such functions are called *reentrant functions*. But a reentrant kernel is not limited just to such reentrant functions (although that is how some real-time kernels are implemented). Instead, the kernel can include nonreentrant functions and use locking mechanisms to ensure that only one process can execute a nonreentrant function at a time. Every process in Kernel Mode acts on its own set of memory locations and cannot interfere with the others.

If a hardware interrupt occurs, a reentrant kernel is able to suspend the current running process even if that process is in Kernel Mode. This capability is very important, since it improves the throughput of the device controllers that issue interrupts. Once a device has issued an interrupt, it waits until the CPU acknowledges it. If the kernel is able to answer quickly, the device controller will be able to perform other tasks while the CPU handles the interrupt.

Now let's look at kernel reentrancy and its impact on the organization of the kernel. A *kernel control path* denotes the sequence of instructions executed by the kernel to handle a system call, an exception, or an interrupt.

In the simplest case, the CPU executes a kernel control path sequentially from the first instruction to the last. When one of the following events occurs, however, the CPU interleaves the kernel control paths:

- A process executing in User Mode invokes a system call, and the corresponding kernel control path verifies that the request cannot be satisfied immediately; it then invokes the scheduler to select a new process to run. As a result, a process switch occurs. The first kernel control path is left unfinished and the CPU resumes the execution of some other kernel control path. In this case, the two control paths are executed on behalf of two different processes.

- The CPU detects an exception—for example, access to a page not present in RAM—while running a kernel control path. The first control path is suspended, and the CPU starts the execution of a suitable procedure. In our example, this type of procedure can allocate a new page for the process and read its contents from disk. When the procedure terminates, the first control path can be resumed. In this case, the two control paths are executed on behalf of the same process.

- A hardware interrupt occurs while the CPU is running a kernel control path with the interrupts enabled. The first kernel control path is left unfinished and the CPU starts processing another kernel control path to handle the interrupt. The first kernel control path resumes when the interrupt handler terminates. In this case, the two kernel control paths run in the execution context of the same process, and the total elapsed system time is accounted to it. However, the interrupt handler doesn't necessarily operate on behalf of the process.

Figure 1-4 illustrates a few examples of noninterleaved and interleaved kernel control paths. Three different CPU states are considered:

- Running a process in User Mode (User)
- Running an exception or a system call handler (Excp)
- Running an interrupt handler (Intr)

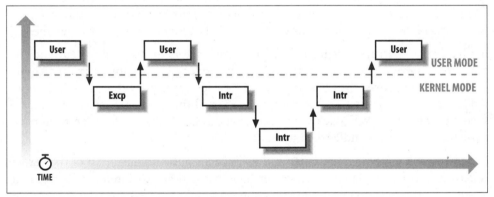

Figure 1-4. Interleaving of kernel control paths

Process Address Space

Each process runs in its private address space. A process running in User Mode refers to private stack, data, and code areas. When running in Kernel Mode, the process addresses the kernel data and code area and uses another stack.

Since the kernel is reentrant, several kernel control paths—each related to a different process—may be executed in turn. In this case, each kernel control path refers to its own private kernel stack.

While it appears to each process that it has access to a private address space, there are times when part of the address space is shared among processes. In some cases, this sharing is explicitly requested by processes; in others, it is done automatically by the kernel to reduce memory usage.

If the same program, say an editor, is needed simultaneously by several users, the program is loaded into memory only once, and its instructions can be shared by all of the users who need it. Its data, of course, must not be shared because each user will have separate data. This kind of shared address space is done automatically by the kernel to save memory.

Processes can also share parts of their address space as a kind of interprocess communication, using the "shared memory" technique introduced in System V and supported by Linux.

Finally, Linux supports the mmap( ) system call, which allows part of a file or the memory residing on a device to be mapped into a part of a process address space. Memory mapping can provide an alternative to normal reads and writes for transferring data. If the same file is shared by several processes, its memory mapping is included in the address space of each of the processes that share it.

Synchronization and Critical Regions

Implementing a reentrant kernel requires the use of synchronization. If a kernel control path is suspended while acting on a kernel data structure, no other kernel control path should be allowed to act on the same data structure unless it has been reset to a consistent state. Otherwise, the interaction of the two control paths could corrupt the stored information.

For example, suppose a global variable V contains the number of available items of some system resource. The first kernel control path, A, reads the variable and determines that there is just one available item. At this point, another kernel control path, B, is activated and reads the same variable, which still contains the value 1. Thus, B decrements V and starts using the resource item. Then A resumes the execution; because it has already read the value of V, it assumes that it can decrement V and take the resource item, which B already uses. As a final result, V contains −1, and two kernel control paths use the same resource item with potentially disastrous effects.

When the outcome of some computation depends on how two or more processes are scheduled, the code is incorrect. We say that there is a *race condition*.

In general, safe access to a global variable is ensured by using *atomic operations*. In the previous example, data corruption is not possible if the two control paths read and decrement V with a single, noninterruptible operation. However, kernels contain many data structures that cannot be accessed with a single operation. For example, it usually isn't possible to remove an element from a linked list with a single operation because the kernel needs to access at least two pointers at once. Any section of code that should be finished by each process that begins it before another process can enter it is called a *critical region*.[*]

---

[*] Synchronization problems have been fully described in other works; we refer the interested reader to books on the Unix operating systems (see the bibliography).

These problems occur not only among kernel control paths, but also among processes sharing common data. Several synchronization techniques have been adopted. The following section concentrates on how to synchronize kernel control paths.

Nonpreemptive kernels

In search of a drastically simple solution to synchronization problems, most traditional Unix kernels are nonpreemptive: when a process executes in Kernel Mode, it cannot be arbitrarily suspended and substituted with another process. Therefore, on a uniprocessor system, all kernel data structures that are not updated by interrupts or exception handlers are safe for the kernel to access.

Of course, a process in Kernel Mode can voluntarily relinquish the CPU, but in this case, it must ensure that all data structures are left in a consistent state. Moreover, when it resumes its execution, it must recheck the value of any previously accessed data structures that could be changed.

Nonpreemptability is ineffective in multiprocessor systems, since two kernel control paths running on different CPUs can concurrently access the same data structure.

Interrupt disabling

Another synchronization mechanism for uniprocessor systems consists of disabling all hardware interrupts before entering a critical region and reenabling them right after leaving it. This mechanism, while simple, is far from optimal. If the critical region is large, interrupts can remain disabled for a relatively long time, potentially causing all hardware activities to freeze.

Moreover, on a multiprocessor system, this mechanism doesn't work at all. There is no way to ensure that no other CPU can access the same data structures that are updated in the protected critical region.

Semaphores

A widely used mechanism, effective in both uniprocessor and multiprocessor systems, relies on the use of *semaphores*. A semaphore is simply a counter associated with a data structure; it is checked by all kernel threads before they try to access the data structure. Each semaphore may be viewed as an object composed of:

- An integer variable
- A list of waiting processes
- Two atomic methods: down( ) and up( )

The down( ) method decrements the value of the semaphore. If the new value is less than 0, the method adds the running process to the semaphore list and then blocks (i.e., invokes the scheduler). The up( ) method increments the value of the semaphore and, if its new value is greater than or equal to 0, reactivates one or more processes in the semaphore list.

Each data structure to be protected has its own semaphore, which is initialized to 1. When a kernel control path wishes to access the data structure, it executes the down( ) method on the proper semaphore. If the value of the new semaphore isn't negative, access to the data structure is granted. Otherwise, the process that is executing the kernel control path is added to the semaphore list and blocked. When another process executes the up( ) method on that semaphore, one of the processes in the semaphore list is allowed to proceed.

Spin locks

In multiprocessor systems, semaphores are not always the best solution to the synchronization problems. Some kernel data structures should be protected from being concurrently accessed by kernel control paths that run on different CPUs. In this case, if the time required to update the data structure is short, a semaphore could be very inefficient. To check a semaphore, the kernel must insert a process in the semaphore list and then suspend it. Since both operations are relatively expensive, in the time it takes to complete them, the other kernel control path could have already released the semaphore.

In these cases, multiprocessor operating systems use *spin locks*. A spin lock is very similar to a semaphore, but it has no process list; when a process finds the lock closed by another process, it "spins" around repeatedly, executing a tight instruction loop until the lock becomes open.

Of course, spin locks are useless in a uniprocessor environment. When a kernel control path tries to access a locked data structure, it starts an endless loop. Therefore, the kernel control path that is updating the protected data structure would not have a chance to continue the execution and release the spin lock. The final result would be that the system hangs.

Avoiding deadlocks

Processes or kernel control paths that synchronize with other control paths may easily enter a *deadlocked* state. The simplest case of deadlock occurs when process *p1* gains access to data structure *a* and process *p2* gains access to *b*, but *p1* then waits for *b* and *p2* waits for *a*. Other more complex cyclic waits among groups of processes may also occur. Of course, a deadlock condition causes a complete freeze of the affected processes or kernel control paths.

As far as kernel design is concerned, deadlocks become an issue when the number of kernel semaphores used is high. In this case, it may be quite difficult to ensure that no deadlock state will ever be reached for all possible ways to interleave kernel control paths. Several operating systems, including Linux, avoid this problem by introducing a very limited number of semaphores and requesting semaphores in an ascending order.

Signals and Interprocess Communication

Unix *signals* provide a mechanism for notifying processes of system events. Each event has its own signal number, which is usually referred to by a symbolic constant such as SIGTERM. There are two kinds of system events:

Asynchronous notifications
> For instance, a user can send the interrupt signal SIGINT to a foreground process by pressing the interrupt keycode (usually CTRL-C) at the terminal.

Synchronous errors or exceptions
> For instance, the kernel sends the signal SIGSEGV to a process when it accesses a memory location at an illegal address.

The POSIX standard defines about 20 different signals, two of which are user-definable and may be used as a primitive mechanism for communication and synchronization among processes in User Mode. In general, a process may react to a signal delivery in two possible ways:

- Ignore the signal.
- Asynchronously execute a specified procedure (the signal handler).

If the process does not specify one of these alternatives, the kernel performs a *default action* that depends on the signal number. The five possible default actions are:

- Terminate the process.
- Write the execution context and the contents of the address space in a file (*core dump*) and terminate the process.
- Ignore the signal.
- Suspend the process.
- Resume the process's execution, if it was stopped.

Kernel signal handling is rather elaborate since the POSIX semantics allows processes to temporarily block signals. Moreover, the SIGKILL and SIGSTOP signals cannot be directly handled by the process or ignored.

AT&T's Unix System V introduced other kinds of interprocess communication among processes in User Mode, which have been adopted by many Unix kernels: *semaphores*, *message queues*, and *shared memory*. They are collectively known as *System V IPC*.

The kernel implements these constructs as *IPC resources*. A process acquires a resource by invoking a shmget( ), semget( ), or msgget( ) system call. Just like files, IPC resources are persistent: they must be explicitly deallocated by the creator process, by the current owner, or by a superuser process.

Semaphores are similar to those described in the section "Synchronization and Critical Regions," earlier in this chapter, except that they are reserved for processes in User Mode. Message queues allow processes to exchange messages by using the msgsnd( ) and msgget( ) system calls, which insert a message into a specific message queue and extract a message from it, respectively.

Shared memory provides the fastest way for processes to exchange and share data. A process starts by issuing a shmget( ) system call to create a new shared memory having a required size. After obtaining the IPC resource identifier, the process invokes the shmat( ) system call, which returns the starting address of the new region within the process address space. When the process wishes to detach the shared memory from its address space, it invokes the shmdt( ) system call. The implementation of shared memory depends on how the kernel implements process address spaces.

Process Management

Unix makes a neat distinction between the process and the program it is executing. To that end, the fork( ) and _exit( ) system calls are used respectively to create a new process and to terminate it, while an exec( )-like system call is invoked to load a new program. After such a system call is executed, the process resumes execution with a brand new address space containing the loaded program.

The process that invokes a fork( ) is the *parent*, while the new process is its *child*. Parents and children can find one another because the data structure describing each process includes a pointer to its immediate parent and pointers to all its immediate children.

A naive implementation of the fork( ) would require both the parent's data and the parent's code to be duplicated and assign the copies to the child. This would be quite time consuming. Current kernels that can rely on hardware paging units follow the Copy-On-Write approach, which defers page duplication until the last moment (i.e., until the parent or the child is required to write into a page). We shall describe how Linux implements this technique in the section "Copy On Write" in Chapter 8.

The _exit( ) system call terminates a process. The kernel handles this system call by releasing the resources owned by the process and sending the parent process a SIGCHLD signal, which is ignored by default.

Zombie processes

How can a parent process inquire about termination of its children? The wait( ) system call allows a process to wait until one of its children terminates; it returns the process ID (PID) of the terminated child.

When executing this system call, the kernel checks whether a child has already terminated. A special *zombie* process state is introduced to represent terminated processes: a process remains in that state until its parent process executes a wait( ) system call on it. The system call handler extracts data about resource usage from the process descriptor fields; the process descriptor may be released once the data is collected. If no child process has already terminated when the wait( ) system call is executed, the kernel usually puts the process in a wait state until a child terminates.

Many kernels also implement a `waitpid( )` system call, which allows a process to wait for a specific child process. Other variants of `wait( )` system calls are also quite common.

It's good practice for the kernel to keep around information on a child process until the parent issues its `wait( )` call, but suppose the parent process terminates without issuing that call? The information takes up valuable memory slots that could be used to serve living processes. For example, many shells allow the user to start a command in the background and then log out. The process that is running the command shell terminates, but its children continue their execution.

The solution lies in a special system process called *init*, which is created during system initialization. When a process terminates, the kernel changes the appropriate process descriptor pointers of all the existing children of the terminated process to make them become children of *init*. This process monitors the execution of all its children and routinely issues `wait( )` system calls, whose side effect is to get rid of all zombies.

Process groups and login sessions

Modern Unix operating systems introduce the notion of *process groups* to represent a "job" abstraction. For example, in order to execute the command line:

```
$ ls | sort | more
```

a shell that supports process groups, such as `bash`, creates a new group for the three processes corresponding to `ls`, `sort`, and `more`. In this way, the shell acts on the three processes as if they were a single entity (the job, to be precise). Each process descriptor includes a *process group ID* field. Each group of processes may have a *group leader*, which is the process whose PID coincides with the process group ID. A newly created process is initially inserted into the process group of its parent.

Modern Unix kernels also introduce *login sessions*. Informally, a login session contains all processes that are descendants of the process that has started a working session on a specific terminal—usually, the first command shell process created for the user. All processes in a process group must be in the same login session. A login session may have several process groups active simultaneously; one of these process groups is always in the foreground, which means that it has access to the terminal. The other active process groups are in the background. When a background process tries to access the terminal, it receives a `SIGTTIN` or `SIGTTOUT` signal. In many command shells, the internal commands `bg` and `fg` can be used to put a process group in either the background or the foreground.

Memory Management

Memory management is by far the most complex activity in a Unix kernel. More than a third of this book is dedicated just to describing how Linux does it. This section illustrates some of the main issues related to memory management.

Virtual memory

All recent Unix systems provide a useful abstraction called *virtual memory*. Virtual memory acts as a logical layer between the application memory requests and the hardware Memory Management Unit (MMU). Virtual memory has many purposes and advantages:

- Several processes can be executed concurrently.
- It is possible to run applications whose memory needs are larger than the available physical memory.
- Processes can execute a program whose code is only partially loaded in memory.
- Each process is allowed to access a subset of the available physical memory.
- Processes can share a single memory image of a library or program.
- Programs can be relocatable—that is, they can be placed anywhere in physical memory.
- Programmers can write machine-independent code, since they do not need to be concerned about physical memory organization.

The main ingredient of a virtual memory subsystem is the notion of *virtual address space*. The set of memory references that a process can use is different from physical memory addresses. When a process uses a virtual address,* the kernel and the MMU cooperate to locate the actual physical location of the requested memory item.

Today's CPUs include hardware circuits that automatically translate the virtual addresses into physical ones. To that end, the available RAM is partitioned into *page frames* 4 or 8 KB in length, and a set of Page Tables is introduced to specify how virtual addresses correspond to physical addresses. These circuits make memory allocation simpler, since a request for a block of contiguous virtual addresses can be satisfied by allocating a group of page frames having noncontiguous physical addresses.

Random access memory usage

All Unix operating systems clearly distinguish between two portions of the random access memory (RAM). A few megabytes are dedicated to storing the kernel image (i.e., the kernel code and the kernel static data structures). The remaining portion of RAM is usually handled by the virtual memory system and is used in three possible ways:

- To satisfy kernel requests for buffers, descriptors, and other dynamic kernel data structures
- To satisfy process requests for generic memory areas and for memory mapping of files
- To get better performance from disks and other buffered devices by means of caches

---

* These addresses have different nomenclatures, depending on the computer architecture. As we'll see in Chapter 2, Intel manuals refer to them as "logical addresses."

Each request type is valuable. On the other hand, since the available RAM is limited, some balancing among request types must be done, particularly when little available memory is left. Moreover, when some critical threshold of available memory is reached and a page-frame-reclaiming algorithm is invoked to free additional memory, which are the page frames most suitable for reclaiming? As we shall see in Chapter 16, there is no simple answer to this question and very little support from theory. The only available solution lies in developing carefully tuned empirical algorithms.

One major problem that must be solved by the virtual memory system is *memory fragmentation*. Ideally, a memory request should fail only when the number of free page frames is too small. However, the kernel is often forced to use physically contiguous memory areas, hence the memory request could fail even if there is enough memory available but it is not available as one contiguous chunk.

Kernel Memory Allocator

The *Kernel Memory Allocator* (*KMA*) is a subsystem that tries to satisfy the requests for memory areas from all parts of the system. Some of these requests come from other kernel subsystems needing memory for kernel use, and some requests come via system calls from user programs to increase their processes' address spaces. A good KMA should have the following features:

- It must be fast. Actually, this is the most crucial attribute, since it is invoked by all kernel subsystems (including the interrupt handlers).
- It should minimize the amount of wasted memory.
- It should try to reduce the memory fragmentation problem.
- It should be able to cooperate with the other memory management subsystems to borrow and release page frames from them.

Several proposed KMAs, which are based on a variety of different algorithmic techniques, include:

- Resource map allocator
- Power-of-two free lists
- McKusick-Karels allocator
- Buddy system
- Mach's Zone allocator
- Dynix allocator
- Solaris's Slab allocator

As we shall see in Chapter 7, Linux's KMA uses a Slab allocator on top of a buddy system.

Process virtual address space handling

The address space of a process contains all the virtual memory addresses that the process is allowed to reference. The kernel usually stores a process virtual address space as a list of *memory area descriptors*. For example, when a process starts the execution of some program via an exec( )-like system call, the kernel assigns to the process a virtual address space that comprises memory areas for:

- The executable code of the program
- The initialized data of the program
- The uninitialized data of the program
- The initial program stack (i.e., the User Mode stack)
- The executable code and data of needed shared libraries
- The heap (the memory dynamically requested by the program)

All recent Unix operating systems adopt a memory allocation strategy called *demand paging*. With demand paging, a process can start program execution with none of its pages in physical memory. As it accesses a nonpresent page, the MMU generates an exception; the exception handler finds the affected memory region, allocates a free page, and initializes it with the appropriate data. In a similar fashion, when the process dynamically requires memory by using malloc( ) or the brk( ) system call (which is invoked internally by malloc( )), the kernel just updates the size of the heap memory region of the process. A page frame is assigned to the process only when it generates an exception by trying to refer its virtual memory addresses.

Virtual address spaces also allow other efficient strategies, such as the Copy-On-Write strategy mentioned earlier. For example, when a new process is created, the kernel just assigns the parent's page frames to the child address space, but marks them read-only. An exception is raised as soon the parent or the child tries to modify the contents of a page. The exception handler assigns a new page frame to the affected process and initializes it with the contents of the original page.

Swapping and caching

To extend the size of the virtual address space usable by the processes, the Unix operating system uses *swap areas* on disk. The virtual memory system regards the contents of a page frame as the basic unit for swapping. Whenever a process refers to a swapped-out page, the MMU raises an exception. The exception handler then allocates a new page frame and initializes the page frame with its old contents saved on disk.

On the other hand, physical memory is also used as cache for hard disks and other block devices. This is because hard drives are very slow: a disk access requires several milliseconds, which is a very long time compared with the RAM access time. Therefore, disks are often the bottleneck in system performance. As a general rule, one of the policies already implemented in the earliest Unix system is to defer writing to disk as long as possible by loading into RAM a set of disk buffers that correspond to blocks read from disk. The sync( ) system call forces disk synchronization by writing all of the "dirty" buffers (i.e., all the buffers whose contents differ from that of the corresponding disk blocks) into disk. To avoid data loss, all operating systems take care to periodically write dirty buffers back to disk.

Device Drivers

The kernel interacts with I/O devices by means of *device drivers*. Device drivers are included in the kernel and consist of data structures and functions that control one or more devices, such as hard disks, keyboards, mouses, monitors, network interfaces, and devices connected to a SCSI bus. Each driver interacts with the remaining part of the kernel (even with other drivers) through a specific interface. This approach has the following advantages:

- Device-specific code can be encapsulated in a specific module.
- Vendors can add new devices without knowing the kernel source code; only the interface specifications must be known.
- The kernel deals with all devices in a uniform way and accesses them through the same interface.
- It is possible to write a device driver as a module that can be dynamically loaded in the kernel without requiring the system to be rebooted. It is also possible to dynamically unload a module that is no longer needed, therefore minimizing the size of the kernel image stored in RAM.

Figure 1-5 illustrates how device drivers interface with the rest of the kernel and with the processes.

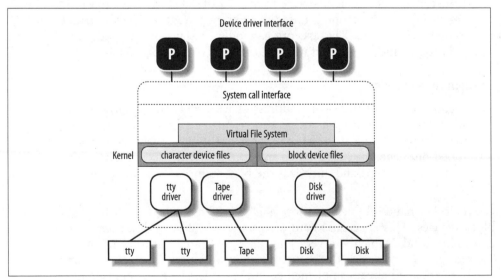

Figure 1-5. Device driver interface

Some user programs (P) wish to operate on hardware devices. They make requests to the kernel using the usual file-related system calls and the device files normally found in the */dev* directory. Actually, the device files are the user-visible portion of the device driver interface. Each device file refers to a specific device driver, which is invoked by the kernel to perform the requested operation on the hardware component.

At the time Unix was introduced, graphical terminals were uncommon and expensive, so only alphanumeric terminals were handled directly by Unix kernels. When graphical terminals became widespread, ad hoc applications such as the X Window System were introduced that ran as standard processes and accessed the I/O ports of the graphics interface and the RAM video area directly. Some recent Unix kernels, such as Linux 2.4, provide an abstraction for the frame buffer of the graphic card and allow application software to access them without needing to know anything about the I/O ports of the graphics interface (see the section "Levels of Kernel Support" in Chapter 13.)

CHAPTER 2
Memory Addressing

This chapter deals with addressing techniques. Luckily, an operating system is not forced to keep track of physical memory all by itself; today's microprocessors include several hardware circuits to make memory management both more efficient and more robust in case of programming errors.

As in the rest of this book, we offer details in this chapter on how 80×86 microprocessors address memory chips and how Linux uses the available addressing circuits. You will find, we hope, that when you learn the implementation details on Linux's most popular platform you will better understand both the general theory of paging and how to research the implementation on other platforms.

This is the first of three chapters related to memory management; Chapter 7 discusses how the kernel allocates main memory to itself, while Chapter 8 considers how linear addresses are assigned to processes.

Memory Addresses

Programmers casually refer to a *memory address* as the way to access the contents of a memory cell. But when dealing with 80×86 microprocessors, we have to distinguish three kinds of addresses:

Logical address
> Included in the machine language instructions to specify the address of an operand or of an instruction. This type of address embodies the well-known 80×x86 segmented architecture that forces MS-DOS and Windows programmers to divide their programs into segments. Each logical address consists of a *segment* and an *offset* (or *displacement*) that denotes the distance from the start of the segment to the actual address.

Linear address (also known as virtual address)
> A single 32-bit unsigned integer that can be used to address up to 4 GB—that is, up to 4,294,967,296 memory cells. Linear addresses are usually represented in hexadecimal notation; their values range from 0x00000000 to 0xffffffff.

Physical address
> Used to address memory cells in memory chips. They correspond to the electrical signals sent along the address pins of the microprocessor to the memory bus. Physical addresses are represented as 32-bit unsigned integers.

The CPU control unit transforms a logical address into a linear address by means of a hardware circuit called a *segmentation unit*; subsequently, a second hardware circuit called a *paging unit* transforms the linear address into a physical address (see Figure 2-1).

Figure 2-1. Logical address translation

In multiprocessor systems, all CPUs share the same memory; this means that RAM chips may be accessed concurrently by independent CPUs. Since read or write operations on a RAM chip must be performed serially, a hardware circuit called a *memory arbiter* is inserted between the bus and every RAM chip. Its role is to grant access to a CPU if the chip is free and to delay it if the chip is busy servicing a request by another processor. Even uniprocessor systems use memory arbiters, since they include a specialized processor called DMA that operates concurrently with the CPU (see the section "Direct Memory Access (DMA)" in Chapter 13). In the case of multiprocessor systems, the structure of the arbiter is more complex since it has more input ports. The dual Pentium, for instance, maintains a two-port arbiter at each chip entrance and requires that the two CPUs exchange synchronization messages before attempting to use the common bus. From the programming point of view, the arbiter is hidden since it is managed by hardware circuits.

Segmentation in Hardware

Starting with the 80386 model, Intel microprocessors perform address translation in two different ways called *real mode* and *protected mode*. These are described in the next sections. Real mode exists mostly to maintain processor compatibility with older models and to allow the operating system to bootstrap (see Appendix A for a short description of real mode).

Segmentation Registers

A logical address consists of two parts: a segment identifier and an offset that specifies the relative address within the segment. The segment identifier is a 16-bit field called the *Segment Selector*, while the offset is a 32-bit field.

To make it easy to retrieve segment selectors quickly, the processor provides *segmentation registers* whose only purpose is to hold Segment Selectors; these registers are called cs, ss, ds, es, fs, and gs. Although there are only six of them, a program can reuse the same segmentation register for different purposes by saving its content in memory and then restoring it later.

Three of the six segmentation registers have specific purposes:

cs   The code segment register, which points to a segment containing program instructions

ss   The stack segment register, which points to a segment containing the current program stack

ds   The data segment register, which points to a segment containing static and external data

The remaining three segmentation registers are general purpose and may refer to arbitrary data segments.

The cs register has another important function: it includes a 2-bit field that specifies the Current Privilege Level (CPL) of the CPU. The value 0 denotes the highest privilege level, while the value 3 denotes the lowest one. Linux uses only levels 0 and 3, which are respectively called Kernel Mode and User Mode.

Segment Descriptors

Each segment is represented by an 8-byte *Segment Descriptor* (see Figure 2-2) that describes the segment characteristics. Segment Descriptors are stored either in the *Global Descriptor Table* (*GDT*) or in the *Local Descriptor Table* (*LDT*).

Usually only one GDT is defined, while each process is permitted to have its own LDT if it needs to create additional segments besides those stored in the GDT. The address of the GDT in main memory is contained in the gdtr processor register and the address of the currently used LDT is contained in the ldtr processor register.

Each Segment Descriptor consists of the following fields:

- A 32-bit Base field that contains the linear address of the first byte of the segment.
- A G granularity flag. If it is cleared (equal to 0), the segment size is expressed in bytes; otherwise, it is expressed in multiples of 4096 bytes.
- A 20-bit Limit field that denotes the segment length in bytes (segments that have a Limit field equal to zero are considered null). When G is set to 0, the size of a non-null segment may vary between 1 byte and 1 MB; otherwise, it may vary between 4 KB and 4 GB.
- An S system flag. If it is cleared, the segment is a system segment that stores kernel data structures; otherwise, it is a normal code or data segment.
- A 4-bit Type field that characterizes the segment type and its access rights. The following list shows Segment Descriptor types that are widely used.

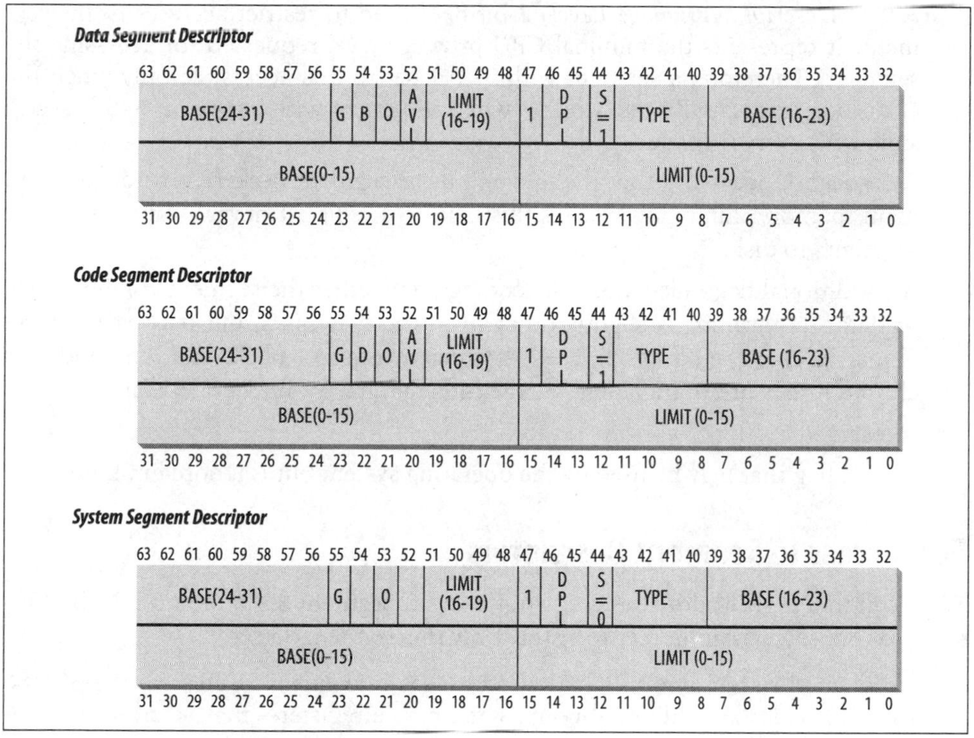

Data Segment Descriptor

63 62 61 60 59 58 57 56 55 54 53 52	51 50 49 48	47	46 45	44	43 42 41 40	39 38 37 36 35 34 33 32
BASE(24-31)	G B 0 AVL	LIMIT (16-19)	1	DP	S=1	TYPE	BASE (16-23)

31 30 29 28 27 26 25 24 23 22 21 20 19 18 17 16	15 14 13 12 11 10 9 8 7 6 5 4 3 2 1 0
BASE(0-15)	LIMIT (0-15)

Code Segment Descriptor

63 62 61 60 59 58 57 56 55 54 53 52	51 50 49 48	47	46 45	44	43 42 41 40	39 38 37 36 35 34 33 32
BASE(24-31)	G D 0 AVL	LIMIT (16-19)	1	DP	S=1	TYPE	BASE (16-23)

31 30 29 28 27 26 25 24 23 22 21 20 19 18 17 16	15 14 13 12 11 10 9 8 7 6 5 4 3 2 1 0
BASE(0-15)	LIMIT (0-15)

System Segment Descriptor

63 62 61 60 59 58 57 56 55 54 53 52	51 50 49 48	47	46 45	44	43 42 41 40	39 38 37 36 35 34 33 32
BASE(24-31)	G 0	LIMIT (16-19)	1	DP	S=0	TYPE	BASE (16-23)

31 30 29 28 27 26 25 24 23 22 21 20 19 18 17 16	15 14 13 12 11 10 9 8 7 6 5 4 3 2 1 0
BASE(0-15)	LIMIT (0-15)

Figure 2-2. Segment Descriptor format

Code Segment Descriptor

Indicates that the Segment Descriptor refers to a code segment; it may be included either in the GDT or in the LDT. The descriptor has the S flag set.

Data Segment Descriptor

Indicates that the Segment Descriptor refers to a data segment; it may be included either in the GDT or in the LDT. The descriptor has the S flag set. Stack segments are implemented by means of generic data segments.

Task State Segment Descriptor (TSSD)

Indicates that the Segment Descriptor refers to a Task State Segment (TSS)—that is, a segment used to save the contents of the processor registers (see the section "Task State Segment" in Chapter 3); it can appear only in the GDT. The corresponding Type field has the value 11 or 9, depending on whether the corresponding process is currently executing on a CPU. The S flag of such descriptors is set to 0.

Local Descriptor Table Descriptor (LDTD)

Indicates that the Segment Descriptor refers to a segment containing an LDT; it can appear only in the GDT. The corresponding Type field has the value 2. The S flag of such descriptors is set to 0. The next section shows how 80×86 processors are able to decide whether a segment descriptor is stored in the GDT or in the LDT of the process.

- A DPL (*Descriptor Privilege Level*) 2-bit field used to restrict accesses to the segment. It represents the minimal CPU privilege level requested for accessing the segment. Therefore, a segment with its DPL set to 0 is accessible only when the CPL is 0—that is, in Kernel Mode—while a segment with its DPL set to 3 is accessible with every CPL value.

- A Segment-Present flag that is equal to 0 if the segment is currently not stored in main memory. Linux always sets this field to 1, since it never swaps out whole segments to disk.

- An additional flag called D or B depending on whether the segment contains code or data. Its meaning is slightly different in the two cases, but it is basically set (equal to 1) if the addresses used as segment offsets are 32 bits long and it is cleared if they are 16 bits long (see the Intel manual for further details).

- A reserved bit (bit 53) always set to 0.

- An AVL flag that may be used by the operating system but is ignored in Linux.

Fast Access to Segment Descriptors

We recall that logical addresses consist of a 16-bit Segment Selector and a 32-bit Offset, and that segmentation registers store only the Segment Selector.

To speed up the translation of logical addresses into linear addresses, the 80×86 processor provides an additional nonprogrammable register—that is, a register that cannot be set by a programmer—for each of the six programmable segmentation registers. Each nonprogrammable register contains the 8-byte Segment Descriptor (described in the previous section) specified by the Segment Selector contained in the corresponding segmentation register. Every time a Segment Selector is loaded in a segmentation register, the corresponding Segment Descriptor is loaded from memory into the matching nonprogrammable CPU register. From then on, translations of logical addresses referring to that segment can be performed without accessing the GDT or LDT stored in main memory; the processor can just refer directly to the CPU register containing the Segment Descriptor. Accesses to the GDT or LDT are necessary only when the contents of the segmentation register change (see Figure 2-3). Each Segment Selector includes the following fields:

- A 13-bit index (described further in the text following this list) that identifies the corresponding Segment Descriptor entry contained in the GDT or in the LDT

- A TI (*Table Indicator*) flag that specifies whether the Segment Descriptor is included in the GDT (TI = 0) or in the LDT (TI = 1)

- An RPL (*Requestor Privilege Level*) 2-bit field, which is precisely the Current Privilege Level of the CPU when the corresponding Segment Selector is loaded into the cs register[*]

---

[*] The RPL field may also be used to selectively weaken the processor privilege level when accessing data segments; see Intel documentation for details.

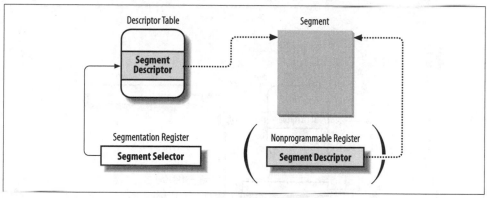

Figure 2-3. Segment Selector and Segment Descriptor

Since a Segment Descriptor is 8 bytes long, its relative address inside the GDT or the LDT is obtained by multiplying the 13-bit index field of the Segment Selector by 8. For instance, if the GDT is at 0x00020000 (the value stored in the gdtr register) and the index specified by the Segment Selector is 2, the address of the corresponding Segment Descriptor is 0x00020000 + (2 × 8), or 0x00020010.

The first entry of the GDT is always set to 0. This ensures that logical addresses with a null Segment Selector will be considered invalid, thus causing a processor exception. The maximum number of Segment Descriptors that can be stored in the GDT is 8,191 (i.e., , $2^{13}-1$).

Segmentation Unit

Figure 2-4 shows in detail how a logical address is translated into a corresponding linear address. The segmentation unit performs the following operations:

- Examines the TI field of the Segment Selector to determine which Descriptor Table stores the Segment Descriptor. This field indicates that the Descriptor is either in the GDT (in which case the segmentation unit gets the base linear address of the GDT from the gdtr register) or in the active LDT (in which case the segmentation unit gets the base linear address of that LDT from the ldtr register).

- Computes the address of the Segment Descriptor from the index field of the Segment Selector. The index field is multiplied by 8 (the size of a Segment Descriptor), and the result is added to the content of the gdtr or ldtr register.

- Adds the offset of the logical address to the Base field of the Segment Descriptor, thus obtaining the linear address.

Notice that, thanks to the nonprogrammable registers associated with the segmentation registers, the first two operations need to be performed only when a segmentation register has been changed.

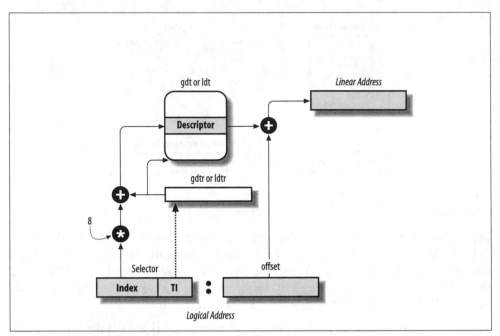

Figure 2-4. Translating a logical address

Segmentation in Linux

Segmentation has been included in 80×86 microprocessors to encourage programmers to split their applications into logically related entities, such as subroutines or global and local data areas. However, Linux uses segmentation in a very limited way. In fact, segmentation and paging are somewhat redundant since both can be used to separate the physical address spaces of processes: segmentation can assign a different linear address space to each process, while paging can map the same linear address space into different physical address spaces. Linux prefers paging to segmentation for the following reasons:

- Memory management is simpler when all processes use the same segment register values—that is, when they share the same set of linear addresses.

- One of the design objectives of Linux is portability to a wide range of architectures; RISC architectures in particular have limited support for segmentation.

The 2.4 version of Linux uses segmentation only when required by the 80×86 architecture. In particular, all processes use the same logical addresses, so the total number of segments to be defined is quite limited, and it is possible to store all Segment Descriptors in the Global Descriptor Table (GDT). This table is implemented by the array gdt_table referred to by the gdt variable. If you look in the Source Code Index, you can see that these symbols are defined in the file *arch/i386/kernel/head.S*. Every macro, function, and other symbol in this book is listed in the Source Code Index, so you can quickly find it in the source code.

Local Descriptor Tables are not used by the kernel, although a system call called modify_ldt( ) exists that allows processes to create their own LDTs. This turns out to be useful to applications (such as Wine) that execute segment-oriented Microsoft Windows applications.

Here are the segments used by Linux:

- A kernel code segment. The fields of the corresponding Segment Descriptor in the GDT have the following values:
  - Base = 0x00000000
  - Limit = 0xfffff
  - G (granularity flag) = 1, for segment size expressed in pages
  - S (system flag) = 1, for normal code or data segment
  - Type = 0xa, for code segment that can be read and executed
  - DPL (Descriptor Privilege Level) = 0, for Kernel Mode
  - D/B (32-bit address flag) = 1, for 32-bit offset addresses

  Thus, the linear addresses associated with that segment start at 0 and reach the addressing limit of $2^{32} -1$. The S and Type fields specify that the segment is a code segment that can be read and executed. Its DPL value is 0, so it can be accessed only in Kernel Mode. The corresponding Segment Selector is defined by the _ _KERNEL_CS macro. To address the segment, the kernel just loads the value yielded by the macro into the cs register.

- A kernel data segment. The fields of the corresponding Segment Descriptor in the GDT have the following values:
  - Base = 0x00000000
  - Limit = 0xfffff
  - G (granularity flag) = 1, for segment size expressed in pages
  - S (system flag) = 1, for normal code or data segment
  - Type = 2, for data segment that can be read and written
  - DPL (Descriptor Privilege Level) = 0, for Kernel Mode
  - D/B (32-bit address flag) = 1, for 32-bit offset addresses

  This segment is identical to the previous one (in fact, they overlap in the linear address space), except for the value of the Type field, which specifies that it is a data segment that can be read and written. The corresponding Segment Selector is defined by the _ _KERNEL_DS macro.

- A user code segment shared by all processes in User Mode. The fields of the corresponding Segment Descriptor in the GDT have the following values:
  - Base = 0x00000000
  - Limit = 0xfffff

— G (granularity flag) = 1, for segment size expressed in pages

— S (system flag) = 1, for normal code or data segment

— Type = 0xa, for code segment that can be read and executed

— DPL (Descriptor Privilege Level) = 3, for User Mode

— D/B (32-bit address flag) = 1, for 32-bit offset addresses

The S and DPL fields specify that the segment is not a system segment and its privilege level is equal to 3; it can thus be accessed both in Kernel Mode and in User Mode. The corresponding Segment Selector is defined by the __USER_CS macro.

- A user data segment shared by all processes in User Mode. The fields of the corresponding Segment Descriptor in the GDT have the following values:

— Base = 0x00000000

— Limit = 0xfffff

— G (granularity flag) = 1, for segment size expressed in pages

— S (system flag) = 1, for normal code or data segment

— Type = 2, for data segment that can be read and written

— DPL (Descriptor Privilege Level) = 3, for User Mode

— D/B (32-bit address flag) = 1, for 32-bit offset addresses

This segment overlaps the previous one: they are identical, except for the value of Type. The corresponding Segment Selector is defined by the __USER_DS macro.

- A Task State Segment (TSS) for each processor. The linear address space corresponding to each TSS is a small subset of the linear address space corresponding to the kernel data segment. All the Task State Segments are sequentially stored in the init_tss array; in particular, the Base field of the TSS descriptor for the nth CPU points to the nth component of the init_tss array. The G (granularity) flag is cleared, while the Limit field is set to 0xeb, since the TSS segment is 236 bytes long. The Type field is set to 9 or 11 (available 32-bit TSS), and the DPL is set to 0, since processes in User Mode are not allowed to access TSS segments. You will find details on how Linux uses TSSs in the section "Task State Segment" in Chapter 3.

- A default Local Descriptor Table (LDT) that is usually shared by all processes. This segment is stored in the default_ldt variable. The default LDT includes a single entry consisting of a null Segment Descriptor. Each processor has its own LDT Segment Descriptor, which usually points to the common default LDT segment; its Base field is set to the address of default_ldt and its Limit field is set to 7. When a process requiring a nonempty LDT is running, the LDT descriptor in the GDT corresponding to the executing CPU is replaced by the descriptor associated with the LDT that was built by the process. You will find more details of this mechanism in Chapter 3.

- Four segments related to the Advanced Power Management (APM) support. APM consists of a set of BIOS routines devoted to the management of the power states of the system. If the kernel supports APM, four entries in the GDT store the descriptors of two data segments and two code segments containing APM-related kernel functions.

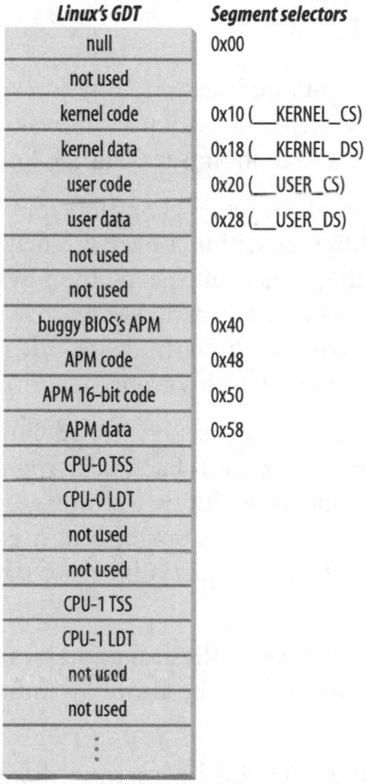

Linux's GDT	Segment selectors
null	0x00
not used	
kernel code	0x10 (__KERNEL_CS)
kernel data	0x18 (__KERNEL_DS)
user code	0x20 (__USER_CS)
user data	0x28 (__USER_DS)
not used	
not used	
buggy BIOS's APM	0x40
APM code	0x48
APM 16-bit code	0x50
APM data	0x58
CPU-0 TSS	
CPU-0 LDT	
not used	
not used	
CPU-1 TSS	
CPU-1 LDT	
not used	
not used	
⋮	

Figure 2-5. The Global Descriptor Table

In conclusion, as shown in Figure 2-5, the GDT includes a set of common descriptors plus a pair of segment descriptors for each existing CPU—one for the TSS segment and one for the LDT segment. For efficiency, some entries in the GDT table are left unused, so that segment descriptors usually accessed together are kept in the same 32-byte line of the hardware cache (see the section "Hardware Cache" later in this chapter).

As stated earlier, the Current Privilege Level of the CPU indicates whether the processor is in User or Kernel Mode and is specified by the RPL field of the Segment Selector stored in the cs register. Whenever the CPL is changed, some segmentation registers must be correspondingly updated. For instance, when the CPL is equal to 3 (User Mode), the ds register must contain the Segment Selector of the user data segment, but when the CPL is equal to 0, the ds register must contain the Segment Selector of the kernel data segment.

A similar situation occurs for the ss register. It must refer to a User Mode stack inside the user data segment when the CPL is 3, and it must refer to a Kernel Mode stack inside the kernel data segment when the CPL is 0. When switching from User Mode to Kernel Mode, Linux always makes sure that the ss register contains the Segment Selector of the kernel data segment.

Paging in Hardware

The paging unit translates linear addresses into physical ones. It checks the requested access type against the access rights of the linear address. If the memory access is not valid, it generates a Page Fault exception (see Chapter 4 and Chapter 7).

For the sake of efficiency, linear addresses are grouped in fixed-length intervals called *pages*; contiguous linear addresses within a page are mapped into contiguous physical addresses. In this way, the kernel can specify the physical address and the access rights of a page instead of those of all the linear addresses included in it. Following the usual convention, we shall use the term "page" to refer both to a set of linear addresses and to the data contained in this group of addresses.

The paging unit thinks of all RAM as partitioned into fixed-length *page frames* (sometimes referred to as *physical pages*). Each page frame contains a page—that is, the length of a page frame coincides with that of a page. A page frame is a constituent of main memory, and hence it is a storage area. It is important to distinguish a page from a page frame; the former is just a block of data, which may be stored in any page frame or on disk.

The data structures that map linear to physical addresses are called *Page Tables*; they are stored in main memory and must be properly initialized by the kernel before enabling the paging unit.

In 80×86 processors, paging is enabled by setting the PG flag of a control register named cr0. When PG = 0, linear addresses are interpreted as physical addresses.

Regular Paging

Starting with the 80386, the paging unit of Intel processors handles 4 KB pages.

The 32 bits of a linear address are divided into three fields:

Directory
    The most significant 10 bits

Table
    The intermediate 10 bits

Offset
    The least significant 12 bits

The translation of linear addresses is accomplished in two steps, each based on a type of translation table. The first translation table is called the *Page Directory* and the second is called the *Page Table*.

The aim of this two-level scheme is to reduce the amount of RAM required for per-process Page Tables. If a simple one-level Page Table was used, then it would require up to 2^{20} entries (i.e., at 4 bytes per entry, 4 MB of RAM) to represent the Page Table for each process (if the process used a full 4 GB linear address space), even though a process does not use all addresses in that range. The two-level scheme reduces the memory by requiring Page Tables only for those virtual memory regions actually used by a process.

Each active process must have a Page Directory assigned to it. However, there is no need to allocate RAM for all Page Tables of a process at once; it is more efficient to allocate RAM for a Page Table only when the process effectively needs it.

The physical address of the Page Directory in use is stored in a control register named cr3. The Directory field within the linear address determines the entry in the Page Directory that points to the proper Page Table. The address's Table field, in turn, determines the entry in the Page Table that contains the physical address of the page frame containing the page. The Offset field determines the relative position within the page frame (see Figure 2-6). Since it is 12 bits long, each page consists of 4,096 bytes of data.

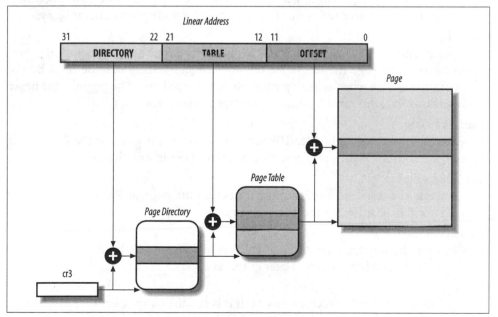

Figure 2-6. Paging by 80x86 processors

Both the Directory and the Table fields are 10 bits long, so Page Directories and Page Tables can include up to 1,024 entries. It follows that a Page Directory can address up to $1024 \times 1024 \times 4096 = 2^{32}$ memory cells, as you'd expect in 32-bit addresses.

The entries of Page Directories and Page Tables have the same structure. Each entry includes the following fields:

Present *flag*
> If it is set, the referred-to page (or Page Table) is contained in main memory; if the flag is 0, the page is not contained in main memory and the remaining entry bits may be used by the operating system for its own purposes. If the entry of a Page Table or Page Directory needed to perform an address translation has the Present flag cleared, the paging unit stores the linear address in a control register named cr2 and generates the exception 14: the Page Fault exception. (We shall see in Chapter 16 how Linux usea this field.)

Field containing the 20 most significant bits of a page frame physical address
> Since each page frame has a 4-KB capacity, its physical address must be a multiple of 4,096 so the 12 least significant bits of the physical address are always equal to 0. If the field refers to a Page Directory, the page frame contains a Page Table; if it refers to a Page Table, the page frame contains a page of data.

Accessed *flag*
> Sets each time the paging unit addresses the corresponding page frame. This flag may be used by the operating system when selecting pages to be swapped out. The paging unit never resets this flag; this must be done by the operating system.

Dirty *flag*
> Applies only to the Page Table entries. It is set each time a write operation is performed on the page frame. As for the Accessed flag, Dirty may be used by the operating system when selecting pages to be swapped out. The paging unit never resets this flag; this must be done by the operating system.

Read/Write *flag*
> Contains the access right (Read/Write or Read) of the page or of the Page Table (see the section "Hardware Protection Scheme" later in this chapter).

User/Supervisor *flag*
> Contains the privilege level required to access the page or Page Table (see the later section "Hardware Protection Scheme").

PCD *and* PWT *flags*
> Controls the way the page or Page Table is handled by the hardware cache (see the section "Hardware Cache" later in this chapter).

Page Size *flag*
> Applies only to Page Directory entries. If it is set, the entry refers to a 2 MB– or 4 MB–long page frame (see the following sections).

Global *flag*

Applies only to Page Table entries. This flag was introduced in the Pentium Pro to prevent frequently used pages from being flushed from the TLB cache (see the section "Translation Lookaside Buffers (TLB)" later in this chapter). It works only if the Page Global Enable (PGE) flag of register cr4 is set.

Extended Paging

Starting with the Pentium model, 80×86 microprocessors introduce *extended paging*, which allows page frames to be 4 MB instead of 4 KB in size (see Figure 2-7).

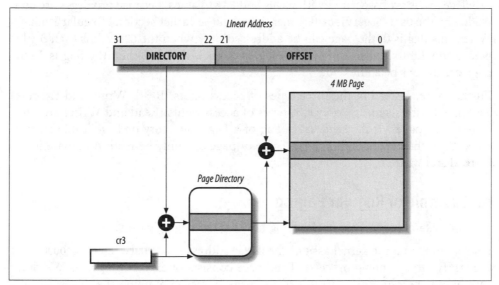

Figure 2-7. Extended paging

As mentioned in the previous section, extended paging is enabled by setting the Page Size flag of a Page Directory entry. In this case, the paging unit divides the 32 bits of a linear address into two fields:

Directory
The most significant 10 bits

Offset
The remaining 22 bits

Page Directory entries for extended paging are the same as for normal paging, except that:

- The Page Size flag must be set.
- Only the 10 most significant bits of the 20-bit physical address field are significant. This is because each physical address is aligned on a 4-MB boundary, so the 22 least significant bits of the address are 0.

Extended paging coexists with regular paging; it is enabled by setting the PSE flag of the cr4 processor register. Extended paging is used to translate large contiguous linear address ranges into corresponding physical ones; in these cases, the kernel can do without intermediate Page Tables and thus save memory and preserve TLB entries (see the section "Translation Lookaside Buffers (TLB)").

Hardware Protection Scheme

The paging unit uses a different protection scheme from the segmentation unit. While 80×86 processors allow four possible privilege levels to a segment, only two privilege levels are associated with pages and Page Tables, because privileges are controlled by the User/Supervisor flag mentioned in the earlier section "Regular Paging." When this flag is 0, the page can be addressed only when the CPL is less than 3 (this means, for Linux, when the processor is in Kernel Mode). When the flag is 1, the page can always be addressed.

Furthermore, instead of the three types of access rights (Read, Write, and Execute) associated with segments, only two types of access rights (Read and Write) are associated with pages. If the Read/Write flag of a Page Directory or Page Table entry is equal to 0, the corresponding Page Table or page can only be read; otherwise it can be read and written.

An Example of Regular Paging

A simple example will help in clarifying how regular paging works.

Let's assume that the kernel assigns the linear address space between 0x20000000 and 0x2003ffff to a running process.* This space consists of exactly 64 pages. We don't care about the physical addresses of the page frames containing the pages; in fact, some of them might not even be in main memory. We are interested only in the remaining fields of the Page Table entries.

Let's start with the 10 most significant bits of the linear addresses assigned to the process, which are interpreted as the Directory field by the paging unit. The addresses start with a 2 followed by zeros, so the 10 bits all have the same value, namely 0x080 or 128 decimal. Thus the Directory field in all the addresses refers to the 129th entry of the process Page Directory. The corresponding entry must contain the physical address of the Page Table assigned to the process (see Figure 2-8). If no other linear addresses are assigned to the process, all the remaining 1,023 entries of the Page Directory are filled with zeros.

---

* As we shall see in the following chapters, the 3 GB linear address space is an upper limit, but a User Mode process is allowed to reference only a subset of it.

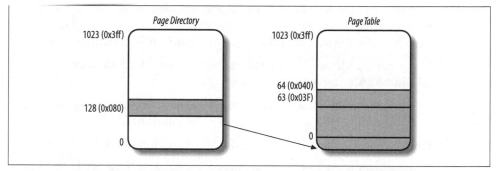

Figure 2-8. An example of paging

The values assumed by the intermediate 10 bits, (that is, the values of the Table field) range from 0 to 0x03f, or from 0 to 63 decimal. Thus, only the first 64 entries of the Page Table are significant. The remaining 960 entries are filled with zeros.

Suppose that the process needs to read the byte at linear address 0x20021406. This address is handled by the paging unit as follows:

1. The Directory field 0x80 is used to select entry 0x80 of the Page Directory, which points to the Page Table associated with the process's pages.
2. The Table field 0x21 is used to select entry 0x21 of the Page Table, which points to the page frame containing the desired page.
3. Finally, the Offset field 0x406 is used to select the byte at offset 0x406 in the desired page frame.

If the Present flag of the 0x21 entry of the Page Table is cleared, the page is not present in main memory; in this case, the paging unit issues a Page Fault exception while translating the linear address. The same exception is issued whenever the process attempts to access linear addresses outside of the interval delimited by 0x20000000 and 0x2003ffff since the Page Table entries not assigned to the process are filled with zeros; in particular, their Present flags are all cleared.

Three-Level Paging

Two-level paging is used by 32-bit microprocessors. But in recent years, several microprocessors (such as Hewlett-Packard's Alpha, Intel's Itanium, and Sun's Ultra-SPARC) have adopted a 64-bit architecture. In this case, two-level paging is no longer suitable and it is necessary to move up to three-level paging. Let's use a thought experiment to explain why.

Start by assuming as large a page size as is reasonable (since you have to account for pages being transferred routinely to and from disk). Let's choose 16 KB for the page size. Since 1 KB covers a range of 2^{10} addresses, 16 KB covers 2^{14} addresses, so the Offset field is 14 bits. This leaves 50 bits of the linear address to be distributed between the Table and the Directory fields. If we now decide to reserve 25 bits for each of these two fields, this means that both the Page Directory and the Page Tables of each process includes 2^{25} entries—that is, more than 32 million entries.

Even if RAM is getting cheaper and cheaper, we cannot afford to waste so much memory space just for storing the Page Tables.

The solution chosen for the Hewlett-Packard's Alpha microprocessor—one of the first 64-bit CPUs that appeared on the market—is the following:

- Page frames are 8 KB long, so the Offset field is 13 bits long.
- Only the least significant 43 bits of an address are used. (The most significant 21 bits are always set to 0.)
- Three levels of Page Tables are introduced so that the remaining 30 bits of the address can be split into three 10-bit fields (see Figure 2-11 later in this chapter). Thus, the Page Tables include $2^{10} = 1024$ entries as in the two-level paging schema examined previously.

As we shall see in the section "Paging in Linux" later in this chapter, Linux's designers decided to implement a paging model inspired by the Alpha architecture.

The Physical Address Extension (PAE) Paging Mechanism

The amount of RAM supported by a processor is limited by the number of address pins connected to the address bus. Older Intel processors from the 80386 to the Pentium used 32-bit physical addresses. In theory, up to 4 GB of RAM could be installed on such systems; in practice, due to the linear address space requirements of User Mode processes, the kernel cannot directly address more than 1 GB of RAM, as we shall see in the later section "Paging in Linux."

However, some demanding applications running on large servers require more than 1 GB of RAM, and in recent years this created a pressure on Intel to expand the amount of RAM supported on the 32-bit 80386 architecture.

Intel has satisfied these requests by increasing the number of address pins on its processors from 32 to 36. Starting with the Pentium Pro, all Intel processors are now able to address up to $2^{36} = 64$ GB of RAM. However, the increased range of physical addresses can be exploited only by introducing a new paging mechanism that translates 32-bit linear addresses into 36-bit physical ones.

With the Pentium Pro processor, Intel introduced a mechanism called *Physical Address Extension (PAE)*. Another mechanism, Page Size Extension (PSE-36), was introduced in the Pentium III processor, but Linux does not use it and we won't discuss it further in this book.

PAE is activated by setting the Physical Address Extension (PAE) flag in the cr4 control register. The Page Size Extension (PSE) flag in the cr4 control register enables large page sizes (2 MB when PAE is enabled).

Intel has changed the paging mechanism in order to support PAE.

- The 64 GB of RAM are split into 2^{24} distinct page frames, and the physical address field of Page Table entries has been expanded from 20 to 24 bits. Since a PAE Page Table entry must include the 12 flag bits (described in the earlier section "Regular Paging") and the 24 physical address bits, for a grand total of 36, the Page Table entry size has been doubled from 32 bits to 64 bits. As a result, a 4 KB PAE Page Table includes 512 entries instead of 1,024.

- A new level of Page Table called the Page Directory Pointer Table (PDPT) consisting of four 64-bit entries has been introduced.

- The cr3 control register contains a 27-bit Page Directory Pointer Table base address field. Since PDPTs are stored in the first 4 GB of RAM and aligned to a multiple of 32 bytes (2^5), 27 bits are sufficient to represent the base address of such tables.

- When mapping linear addresses to 4 KB pages (PS flag cleared in Page Directory entry), the 32 bits of a linear address are interpreted in the following way:

cr3
> Points to a PDPT

bits 31–30
> Point to one of 4 possible entries in PDPT

bits 29–21
> Point to one of 512 possible entries in Page Directory

bits 20–12
> Point to one of 512 possible entries in Page Table

bits 11–0
> Offset of 4 KB page

- When mapping linear addresses to 2 MB pages (PS flag set in Page Directory entry), the 32 bits of a linear address are interpreted in the following way:

cr3
> Points to a PDPT

bits 31–30
> Point to one of 4 possible entries in PDPT

bits 29–21
> Point to one of 512 possible entries in Page Directory

bits 20–0
> Offset of 2 MB page

To summarize, once cr3 is set, it is possible to address up to 4 GB of RAM. If we want to address more RAM, we'll have to put a new value in cr3 or change the content of the PDPT. However, the main problem with PAE is that linear addresses are still 32-bits long. This forces programmers to reuse the same linear addresses to map different areas of RAM. We'll sketch how Linux initializes Page Tables when PAE is enabled in the later section, "Final kernel Page Table when RAM size is more than 4096 MB."

Hardware Cache

Today's microprocessors have clock rates of several gigahertz, while dynamic RAM (DRAM) chips have access times in the range of hundreds of clock cycles. This means that the CPU may be held back considerably while executing instructions that require fetching operands from RAM and/or storing results into RAM.

Hardware cache memories were introduced to reduce the speed mismatch between CPU and RAM. They are based on the well-known *locality principle*, which holds both for programs and data structures. This states that because of the cyclic structure of programs and the packing of related data into linear arrays, addresses close to the ones most recently used have a high probability of being used in the near future. It therefore makes sense to introduce a smaller and faster memory that contains the most recently used code and data. For this purpose, a new unit called the *line* was introduced into the 80×86 architecture. It consists of a few dozen contiguous bytes that are transferred in burst mode between the slow DRAM and the fast on-chip static RAM (SRAM) used to implement caches.

The cache is subdivided into subsets of lines. At one extreme, the cache can be *direct mapped*, in which case a line in main memory is always stored at the exact same location in the cache. At the other extreme, the cache is *fully associative*, meaning that any line in memory can be stored at any location in the cache. But most caches are to some degree *N-way set associative*, where any line of main memory can be stored in any one of N lines of the cache. For instance, a line of memory can be stored in two different lines of a two-way set associative cache.

As shown in Figure 2-9, the cache unit is inserted between the paging unit and the main memory. It includes both a *hardware cache memory* and a *cache controller*. The cache memory stores the actual lines of memory. The cache controller stores an array of entries, one entry for each line of the cache memory. Each entry includes a *tag* and a few flags that describe the status of the cache line. The tag consists of some bits that allow the cache controller to recognize the memory location currently mapped by the line. The bits of the memory physical address are usually split into three groups: the most significant ones correspond to the tag, the middle ones to the cache controller subset index, and the least significant ones to the offset within the line.

When accessing a RAM memory cell, the CPU extracts the subset index from the physical address and compares the tags of all lines in the subset with the high-order bits of the physical address. If a line with the same tag as the high-order bits of the address is found, the CPU has a *cache hit*; otherwise, it has a *cache miss*.

When a cache hit occurs, the cache controller behaves differently, depending on the access type. For a read operation, the controller selects the data from the cache line and transfers it into a CPU register; the RAM is not accessed and the CPU saves time,

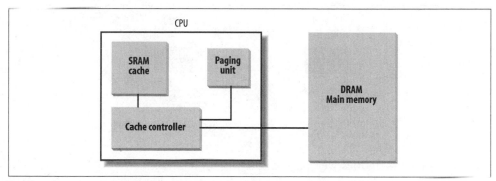

Figure 2-9. Processor hardware cache

which is why the cache system was invented. For a write operation, the controller may implement one of two basic strategies called *write-through* and *write-back*. In a write-through, the controller always writes into both RAM and the cache line, effectively switching off the cache for write operations. In a write-back, which offers more immediate efficiency, only the cache line is updated and the contents of the RAM are left unchanged. After a write-back, of course, the RAM must eventually be updated. The cache controller writes the cache line back into RAM only when the CPU executes an instruction requiring a flush of cache entries or when a FLUSH hardware signal occurs (usually after a cache miss).

When a cache miss occurs, the cache line is written to memory, if necessary, and the correct line is fetched from RAM into the cache entry.

Multiprocessor systems have a separate hardware cache for every processor, and therefore need additional hardware circuitry to synchronize the cache contents. As shown in Figure 2-10, each CPU has its own local hardware cache. But now updating becomes more time consuming: whenever a CPU modifies its hardware cache, it must check whether the same data is contained in the other hardware cache; if so, it must notify the other CPU to update it with the proper value. This activity is often called *cache snooping*. Luckily, all this is done at the hardware level and is of no concern to the kernel.

Cache technology is rapidly evolving. For example, the first Pentium models included a single on-chip cache called the *L1-cache*. More recent models also include another larger, slower on-chip cache called the *L2-cache*. The consistency between the two cache levels is implemented at the hardware level. Linux ignores these hardware details and assumes there is a single cache.

The CD flag of the cr0 processor register is used to enable or disable the cache circuitry. The NW flag, in the same register, specifies whether the write-through or the write-back strategy is used for the caches.

Another interesting feature of the Pentium cache is that it lets an operating system associate a different cache management policy with each page frame. For this purpose, each Page Directory and each Page Table entry includes two flags: PCD (Page

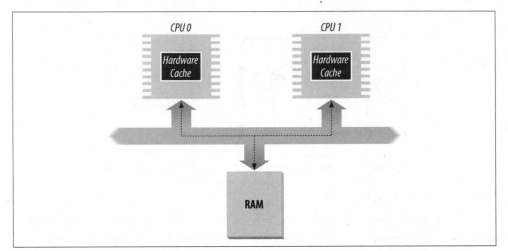

Figure 2-10. The caches in a dual processor.

Cache Disable), which specifies whether the cache must be enabled or disabled while accessing data included in the page frame; and PWT (Page Write-Through), which specifies whether the write-back or the write-through strategy must be applied while writing data into the page frame. Linux clears the PCD and PWT flags of all Page Directory and Page Table entries; as a result, caching is enabled for all page frames and the write-back strategy is always adopted for writing.

Translation Lookaside Buffers (TLB)

Besides general-purpose hardware caches, 80×86 processors include other caches called *Translation Lookaside Buffers (TLB)* to speed up linear address translation. When a linear address is used for the first time, the corresponding physical address is computed through slow accesses to the Page Tables in RAM. The physical address is then stored in a TLB entry so that further references to the same linear address can be quickly translated.

In a multiprocessor system, each CPU has its own TLB, called the *local TLB* of the CPU. Contrary to the L1 cache, the corresponding entries of the TLB need not be synchronized because processes running on the existing CPUs may associate the same linear address with different physical ones.

When the cr3 control register of a CPU is modified, the hardware automatically invalidates all entries of the local TLB.

Paging in Linux

As we explained earlier in the section "Three-Level Paging," Linux adopted a three-level paging model so paging is feasible on 64-bit architectures. Figure 2-11 shows the model, which defines three types of paging tables.

- Page Global Directory
- Page Middle Directory
- Page Table

The Page Global Directory includes the addresses of several Page Middle Directories, which in turn include the addresses of several Page Tables. Each Page Table entry points to a page frame. The linear address is thus split into four parts. Figure 2-11 does not show the bit numbers because the size of each part depends on the computer architecture.

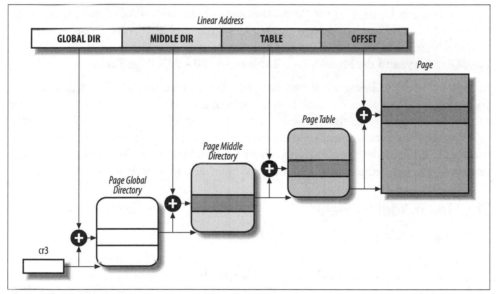

Figure 2-11. The Linux paging model

Linux's handling of processes relies heavily on paging. In fact, the automatic translation of linear addresses into physical ones makes the following design objectives feasible:

- Assign a different physical address space to each process, ensuring an efficient protection against addressing errors.

- Distinguish pages (groups of data) from page frames (physical addresses in main memory). This allows the same page to be stored in a page frame, then saved to disk and later reloaded in a different page frame. This is the basic ingredient of the virtual memory mechanism (see Chapter 16).

As we shall see in Chapter 8, each process has its own Page Global Directory and its own set of Page Tables. When a process switch occurs (see the section "Process Switch" in Chapter 3), Linux saves the cr3 control register in the descriptor of the process previously in execution and then loads cr3 with the value stored in the descriptor of the process to be executed next. Thus, when the new process resumes its execution on the CPU, the paging unit refers to the correct set of Page Tables.

What happens when this three-level paging model is applied to the Pentium, which uses only two types of Page Tables? Linux essentially eliminates the Page Middle Directory field by saying that it contains zero bits. However, the position of the Page Middle Directory in the sequence of pointers is kept so that the same code can work on 32-bit and 64-bit architectures. The kernel keeps a position for the Page Middle Directory by setting the number of entries in it to 1 and mapping this single entry into the proper entry of the Page Global Directory.

However, when Linux uses the Physical Address Extension (PAE) mechanism of the Pentium Pro and later processors, the Linux's Page Global Directory corresponds to the 80×86's Page Directory Pointer Table, the Page Middle Directory to the 80×86's Page Directory, and the Linux's Page Table to the 80×86's Page Table.

Mapping logical to linear addresses now becomes a mechanical task, although it is still somewhat complex. The next few sections of this chapter are a rather tedious list of functions and macros that retrieve information the kernel needs to find addresses and manage the tables; most of the functions are one or two lines long. You may want to just skim these sections now, but it is useful to know the role of these functions and macros because you'll see them often in discussions throughout this book.

The Linear Address Fields

The following macros simplify Page Table handling:

PAGE_SHIFT
> Specifies the length in bits of the Offset field; when applied to 80×86 processors, it yields the value 12. Since all the addresses in a page must fit in the Offset field, the size of a page on 80×86 systems is 2^{12} or the familiar 4,096 bytes; the PAGE_SHIFT of 12 can thus be considered the logarithm base 2 of the total page size. This macro is used by PAGE_SIZE to return the size of the page. Finally, the PAGE_MASK macro yields the value 0xfffff000 and is used to mask all the bits of the Offset field.

PMD_SHIFT
> The total length in bits of the Middle Directory and Table fields of a linear address; in other words, the logarithm of the size of the area a Page Middle Directory entry can map. The PMD_SIZE macro computes the size of the area mapped by a single entry of the Page Middle Directory—that is, of a Page Table. The PMD_MASK macro is used to mask all the bits of the Offset and Table fields.
>
> When PAE is disabled, PMD_SHIFT yields the value 22 (12 from Offset plus 10 from Table), PMD_SIZE yields 2^{22} or 4 MB, and PMD_MASK yields 0xffc00000. Conversely, when PAE is enabled, PMD_SHIFT yields the value 21 (12 from Offset plus 9 from Table), PMD_SIZE yields 2^{21} or 2 MB, and PMD_MASK yields 0xffe00000.

PGDIR_SHIFT

Determines the logarithm of the size of the area a Page Global Directory entry can map. The PGDIR_SIZE macro computes the size of the area mapped by a single entry of the Page Global Directory. The PGDIR_MASK macro is used to mask all the bits of the Offset, Table, and Middle Dir fields.

When PAE is disabled, PGDIR_SHIFT yields the value 22 (the same value yielded by PMD_SHIFT), PGDIR_SIZE yields 2^{22} or 4 MB, and PGDIR_MASK yields 0xffc00000. Conversely, when PAE is enabled, PGDIR_SHIFT yields the value 30 (12 from Offset plus 9 from Table plus 9 from Middle Dir), PGDIR_SIZE yields 2^{30} or 1 GB, and PGDIR_MASK yields 0xc0000000.

PTRS_PER_PTE, PTRS_PER_PMD, *and* PTRS_PER_PGD

Compute the number of entries in the Page Table, Page Middle Directory, and Page Global Directory. They yield the values 1,024, 1, and 1,024, respectively, when PAE is disabled, and the values 4, 512, and 512, respectively, when PAE is enabled

Page Table Handling

pte_t, pmd_t, and pgd_t describe the format of, respectively, a Page Table, a Page Middle Directory, and a Page Global Directory entry. They are 32-bit data types, except for pte_t, which is a 64-bit data type when PAE is enabled and a 32-bit data type otherwise. pgprot_t is another 32-bit data type that represents the protection flags associated with a single entry.

Four type-conversion macros—__pte( ), __pmd( ), __pgd( ), and __pgprot( )—cast a unsigned integer into the required type. Four other type-conversion macros—pte_val( ), pmd_val( ), pgd_val( ), and pgprot_val( )—perform the reverse casting from one of the four previously mentioned specialized types into a unsigned integer.

The kernel also provides several macros and functions to read or modify Page Table entries:

- The pte_none( ), pmd_none( ), and pgd_none( ) macros yield the value 1 if the corresponding entry has the value 0; otherwise, they yield the value 0.

- The pte_present( ), pmd_present( ), and pgd_present( ) macros yield the value 1 if the Present flag of the corresponding entry is equal to 1—that is, if the corresponding page or Page Table is loaded in main memory.

- The pte_clear( ), pmd_clear( ), and pgd_clear( ) macros clear an entry of the corresponding Page Table, thus forbidding a process to use the linear addresses mapped by the Page Table entry.

The macros pmd_bad( ) and pgd_bad( ) are used by functions to check Page Global Directory and Page Middle Directory entries passed as input parameters. Each macro yields the value 1 if the entry points to a bad Page Table—that is, if at least one of the following conditions applies:

- The page is not in main memory (Present flag cleared).
- The page allows only Read access (Read/Write flag cleared).
- Either Accessed or Dirty is cleared (Linux always forces these flags to be set for every existing Page Table).

No pte_bad( ) macro is defined because it is legal for a Page Table entry to refer to a page that is not present in main memory, not writable, or not accessible at all. Instead, several functions are offered to query the current value of any of the flags included in a Page Table entry:

pte_read( )
Returns the value of the User/Supervisor flag (indicating whether the page is accessible in User Mode).

pte_write( )
Returns 1 if the Read/Write flag is set (indicating whether the page is writable).

pte_exec( )
Returns the value of the User/Supervisor flag (indicating whether the page is accessible in User Mode). Notice that pages on the 80×86 processor cannot be protected against code execution.

pte_dirty( )
Returns the value of the Dirty flag (indicating whether the page has been modified).

pte_young( )
Returns the value of the Accessed flag (indicating whether the page has been accessed).

Another group of functions sets the value of the flags in a Page Table entry:

pte_wrprotect( )
Clears the Read/Write flag

pte_rdprotect *and* pte_exprotect( )
Clear the User/Supervisor flag

pte_mkwrite( )
Sets the Read/Write flag

pte_mkread( ) *and* pte_mkexec( )
Set the User/Supervisor flag

pte_mkdirty( ) *and* pte_mkclean( )
Set the Dirty flag to 1 and to 0, respectively, marking the page as modified or unmodified

pte_mkyoung( ) *and* pte_mkold( )
> Set the Accessed flag to 1 and to 0, respectively, marking the page as accessed (young) or nonaccessed (old)

pte_modify(p,v)
> Sets all access rights in a Page Table entry p to a specified value v

set_pte, set_pmd, *and* set_pgd
> Writes a specified value into a Page Table, Page Middle Directory, and Page Global Directory entry, respectively

The ptep_set_wrprotect() and ptep_mkdirty() functions are similar to pte_wrprotect() and pte_mkdirty(), respectively, except that they act on pointers to a Page Table entry. The ptep_test_and_clear_dirty() and ptep_test_and_clear_young() functions also act on pointers and are similar to pte_mkclean() and pte_mkold(), respectively, except that they return the old value of the flag.

Now come the macros that combine a page address and a group of protection flags into a page entry or perform the reverse operation of extracting the page address from a Page Table entry:

mk_pte
> Accepts a linear address and a group of access rights as arguments and creates a Page Table entry.

mk_pte_phys
> Creates a Page Table entry by combining the physical address and the access rights of the page.

pte_page( )
> Returns the address of the descriptor of the page frame referenced by a Page Table entry (see the section "Page Descriptors" in Chapter 7).

pmd_page( )
> Returns the linear address of a Page Table from its Page Middle Directory entry.

pgd_offset(p,a)
> Receives as parameters a memory descriptor p (see Chapter 8) and a linear address a. The macro yields the address of the entry in a Page Global Directory that corresponds to the address a; the Page Global Directory is found through a pointer within the memory descriptor p. The pgd_offset_k( ) macro is similar, except that it refers to the master kernel Page Tables (see the later section "Kernel Page Tables").

pmd_offset(p,a)
> Receives as a parameter a Page Global Directory entry p and a linear address a; it yields the address of the entry corresponding to the address a in the Page Middle Directory referenced by p.

pte_offset(p,a)

    Similar to pmd_offset, but p is a Page Middle Directory entry and the macro yields the address of the entry corresponding to a in the Page Table referenced by p.

The last group of functions of this long list were introduced to simplify the creation and deletion of Page Table entries.

When two-level paging is used (and PAE is disabled), creating or deleting a Page Middle Directory entry is trivial. As we explained earlier in this section, the Page Middle Directory contains a single entry that points to the subordinate Page Table. Thus, the Page Middle Directory entry *is* the entry within the Page Global Directory too. When dealing with Page Tables, however, creating an entry may be more complex because the Page Table that is supposed to contain it might not exist. In such cases, it is necessary to allocate a new page frame, fill it with zeros, and add the entry.

If PAE is enabled, the kernel uses three-level paging. When the kernel creates a new Page Global Directory, it also allocates the four corresponding Page Middle Directories; these are freed only when the parent Page Global Directory is released.

As we shall see in the section "Page Frame Management" in Chapter 7, the allocations and deallocations of page frames are expensive operations. Therefore, when the kernel destroys a Page Table, it makes sense to add the corresponding page frame to a suitable memory cache. Linux 2.4.18 already includes some functions and data structures, such as pte_quicklist or pgd_quicklist, to implement such cache; however, the code is not mature and the cache is not used yet.

Now comes the last round of functions and macros. As usual, we'll stick to the 80×86 architecture.

pgd_alloc(m)

    Allocates a new Page Global Directory by invoking the get_pgd_slow( ) function. If PAE is enabled, the latter function also allocates the four children Page Middle Directories. The argument m (the address of a memory descriptor) is ignored on the 80×86 architecture.

pmd_alloc(m,p,a)

    Defined so three-level paging systems can allocate a new Page Middle Directory for the linear address a. If PAE is not enabled, the function simply returns the input parameter p—that is, the address of the entry in the Page Global Directory. If PAE is enabled, the function returns the address of the Page Middle Directory that was allocated when the Page Global Directory was created. The argument m is ignored.

pte_alloc(m,p,a)

    Receives as parameters the address of a Page Middle Directory entry p and a linear address a, and returns the address of the Page Table entry corresponding to a. If the Page Middle Directory entry is null, the function must allocate a new

Page Table. The page frame is allocated by invoking pte_alloc_one( ). If a new Page Table is allocated, the entry corresponding to a is initialized and the User/ Supervisor flag is set. The argument m is ignored.

pte_free( ) *and* pgd_free( )

Release a Page Table. The pmd_free( ) function does nothing, since Page Middle Directories are allocated and deallocated together with their parent Page Global Directory.

free_one_pmd( )

Invokes pte_free( ) to release a Page Table and sets the corresponding entry in the Page Middle Directory to NULL.

free_one_pgd( )

Releases all Page Tables of a Page Middle Directory by using free_one_pmd( ) repeatedly. Then it releases the Page Middle Directory by invoking pmd_free( ).

clear_page_tables( )

Clears the contents of the Page Tables of a process by iteratively invoking free_one_pgd( ).

Reserved Page Frames

The kernel's code and data structures are stored in a group of reserved page frames. A page contained in one of these page frames can never be dynamically assigned or swapped to disk.

As a general rule, the Linux kernel is installed in RAM starting from the physical address 0x00100000—i.e., from the second megabyte. The total number of page frames required depends on how the kernel is configured. A typical configuration yields a kernel that can be loaded in less than 2 MBs of RAM.

Why isn't the kernel loaded starting with the first available megabyte of RAM? Well, the PC architecture has several peculiarities that must be taken into account. For example:

- Page frame 0 is used by BIOS to store the system hardware configuration detected during the *Power-On Self-Test* (*POST*); the BIOS of many laptops, moreover, write data on this page frame even after the system is initialized.

- Physical addresses ranging from 0x000a0000 to 0x000fffff are usually reserved to BIOS routines and to map the internal memory of ISA graphics cards. This area is the well-known hole from 640 KB to 1 MB in all IBM-compatible PCs: the physical addresses exist but they are reserved, and the corresponding page frames cannot be used by the operating system.

- Additional page frames within the first megabyte may be reserved by specific computer models. For example, the IBM ThinkPad maps the 0xa0 page frame into the 0x9f one.

In the early stage of the boot sequence (see Appendix A), the kernel queries the BIOS and learns the size of the physical memory. In recent computers, the kernel also invokes a BIOS procedure to build a list of physical address ranges and their corresponding memory types.

Later, the kernel executes the setup_memory_region( ) function, which fills a table of physical memory regions, shown in Table 2-1. Of course, the kernel builds this table on the basis of the BIOS list, if this is available; otherwise the kernel builds the table following the conservative default setup. All page frames with numbers from 0x9f (LOWMEMSIZE( )) to 0x100 (HIGH_MEMORY) are marked as reserved.

Table 2-1. Example of BIOS-provided physical addresses map

Start	End	Type
0x00000000	0x0009ffff	Usable
0x000f0000	0x000fffff	Reserved
0x00100000	0x07fefffff	Usable
0x07ff0000	0x07ff2fff	ACPI data
0x07ff3000	0x07ffffff	ACPI NVS
0xffff0000	0xffffffff	Reserved

A typical configuration for a computer having 128 MB of RAM is shown in Table 2-1. The physical address range from 0x07ff0000 to 0x07ff2fff stores information about the hardware devices of the system written by the BIOS in the POST phase; during the initialization phase, the kernel copies such information in a suitable kernel data structure, and then considers these page frames usable. Conversely, the physical address range of 0x07ff3000 to 0x07ffffff is mapped on ROM chips of the hardware devices. The physical address range starting from 0xffff0000 is marked as reserved since it is mapped by the hardware to the BIOS's ROM chip (see Appendix A). Notice that the BIOS may not provide information for some physical address ranges (in the table, the range is 0x000a0000 to 0x000effff). To be on the safe side, Linux assumes that such ranges are not usable.

To avoid loading the kernel into groups of noncontiguous page frames, Linux prefers to skip the first megabyte of RAM. Clearly, page frames not reserved by the PC architecture will be used by Linux to store dynamically assigned pages.

Figure 2-12 shows how the first 2 MB of RAM are filled by Linux. We have assumed that the kernel requires less than one megabyte of RAM (this is a bit optimistic).

The symbol _text, which corresponds to physical address 0x00100000, denotes the address of the first byte of kernel code. The end of the kernel code is similarly identified by the symbol _etext. Kernel data is divided into two groups: *initialized* and *uninitialized*. The initialized data starts right after _etext and ends at _edata. The uninitialized data follows and ends up at _end.

0   1   0x9f   0x100   0x1ff

                                                                                           _text   _etext   _edata   _end

■ Unavailable page frames
□ Available page frames
▨ Kernel code
▨ Initialized kernel data
■ Uninitialized kernel data

Figure 2-12. The first 512 page frames (2 MB) in Linux 2.4

The symbols appearing in the figure are not defined in Linux source code; they are produced while compiling the kernel.*

Process Page Tables

The linear address space of a process is divided into two parts:

- Linear addresses from 0x00000000 to 0xbfffffff can be addressed when the process is in either User or Kernel Mode.
- Linear addresses from 0xc0000000 to 0xffffffff can be addressed only when the process is in Kernel Mode.

When a process runs in User Mode, it issues linear addresses smaller than 0xc0000000; when it runs in Kernel Mode, it is executing kernel code and the linear addresses issued are greater than or equal to 0xc0000000. In some cases, however, the kernel must access the User Mode linear address space to retrieve or store data.

The PAGE_OFFSET macro yields the value 0xc0000000; this is the offset in the linear address space of a process where the kernel lives. In this book, we often refer directly to the number 0xc0000000 instead.

The content of the first entries of the Page Global Directory that map linear addresses lower than 0xc0000000 (the first 768 entries with PAE disabled) depends on the specific process. Conversely, the remaining entries should be the same for all processes and equal to the corresponding entries of the kernel master Page Global Directory (see the following section).

---

* You can find the linear address of these symbols in the file *System.map*, which is created right after the kernel is compiled.

Kernel Page Tables

The kernel maintains a set of Page Tables for its own use, rooted at a so-called *master kernel Page Global Directory*. After system initialization, this set of Page Tables are never directly used by any process or kernel thread; rather, the highest entries of the master kernel Page Global Directory are the reference model for the corresponding entries of the Page Global Directories of every regular process in the system.

We explain how the kernel ensures that changes to the master kernel Page Global Directory are propagated to the Page Global Directories that are actually used by the processes in the system in the section "Handling Noncontiguous Memory Area Accesses" in Chapter 8.

We now describe how the kernel initializes its own Page Tables. This is a two-phase activity. In fact, right after the kernel image is loaded into memory, the CPU is still running in real mode; thus, paging is not enabled.

In the first phase, the kernel creates a limited 8 MB address space, which is enough for it to install itself in RAM.

In the second phase, the kernel takes advantage of all of the existing RAM and sets up the paging tables properly. The next sections examine how this plan is executed.

Provisional kernel Page Tables

A provisional Page Global Directory is initialized statically during kernel compilation, while the provisional Page Tables are initialized by the startup_32( ) assembly language function defined in *arch/i386/kernel/head.S*. We won't bother mentioning the Page Middle Directories anymore since they are equated to Page Global Directory entries. PAE support is not enabled at this stage.

The Page Global Directory is contained in the swapper_pg_dir variable, while the two Page Tables that span the first 8 MB of RAM are contained in the pg0 and pg1 variables.

The objective of this first phase of paging is to allow these 8 MB to be easily addressed both in real mode and protected mode. Therefore, the kernel must create a mapping from both the linear addresses 0x00000000 through 0x007fffff and the linear addresses 0xc0000000 through 0xc007fffff into the physical addresses 0x00000000 through 0x007fffff. In other words, the kernel during its first phase of initialization can address the first 8 MB of RAM by either linear addresses identical to the physical ones or 8 MB worth of linear addresses, starting from 0xc0000000.

The kernel creates the desired mapping by filling all the swapper_pg_dir entries with zeroes, except for entries 0, 1, 0×300 (decimal 768), and 0×301 (decimal 769); the latter two entries span all linear addresses between 0xc0000000 and 0xc007fffff. The 0, 1, 0×300, and 0×301 entries are initialized as follows:

- The address field of entries 0 and 0×300 is set to the physical address of pg0, while the address field of entries 1 and 0×301 is set to the physical address of pg1.

- The Present, Read/Write, and User/Supervisor flags are set in all four entries.
- The Accessed, Dirty, PCD, PWD, and Page Size flags are cleared in all four entries.

The startup_32() assembly language function also enables the paging unit. This is achieved by loading the physical address of swapper_pg_dir into the cr3 control register and by setting the PG flag of the cr0 control register, as shown in the following equivalent code fragment:

```
movl $swapper_pg_dir-0xc0000000,%eax
movl %eax,%cr3          /* set the page table pointer.. */
movl %cr0,%eax
orl $0x80000000,%eax
movl %eax,%cr0          /* ..and set paging (PG) bit */
```

Final kernel Page Table when RAM size is less than 896 MB

The final mapping provided by the kernel Page Tables must transform linear addresses starting from 0xc0000000 into physical addresses starting from 0.

The _pa macro is used to convert a linear address starting from PAGE_OFFSET to the corresponding physical address, while the _va macro does the reverse.

The *kernel master Page Global Directory* is still stored in swapper_pg_dir. It is initialized by the paging_init() function, which does the following:

1. Invokes pagetable_init() to set up the Page Table entries properly
2. Writes the physical address of swapper_pg_dir in the cr3 control register
3. Invokes flush_tlb_all() to invalidate all TLB entries

The actions performed by pagetable_init() depend on both the amount of RAM present and on the CPU model. Let's start with the simplest case. Our computer has less than 896 MB* of RAM, 32-bit physical addresses are sufficient to address all the available RAM, and there is no need to activate the PAE mechanism. (See the earlier section "The Physical Address Extension (PAE) Paging Mechanism.")

The swapper_pg_dir Page Global Directory is reinitialized by a cycle equivalent to the following:

```
pgd = swapper_pg_dir + 768;
address = 0xc0000000;
while (address < end) {
    pe = _PAGE_PRESENT + _PAGE_RW + _PAGE_ACCESSED +
         _PAGE_DIRTY + _PAGE_PSE + _PAGE_GLOBAL + __pa(address);
    set_pgd(pgd, __pgd(pe));
    ++pgd;
    address += 0x400000;
}
```

---

* The highest 128 MB of linear addresses are left available for several kinds of mappings (see sections "Fix-Mapped Linear Addresses" later in this chapter and "Noncontiguous Memory Area Management" in Chapter 7). The kernel address space left for mapping the RAM is thus 1 GB – 128 MB = 896 MB.

The end variable stores the linear address in the fourth gigabyte corresponding to the end of usable physical memory. We assume that the CPU is a recent 80×86 microprocessor supporting 4 MB pages and "global" TLB entries. Notice that the User/Supervisor flags in all Page Global Directory entries referencing linear addresses above 0xc0000000 are cleared, thus denying processes in User Mode access to the kernel address space.

The identity mapping of the first 8 MB of physical memory built by the startup_32() function is required to complete the initialization phase of the kernel. When this mapping is no longer necessary, the kernel clears the corresponding Page Table entries by invoking the zap_low_mappings() function.

Actually, this description does not state the whole truth. As we shall see in the later section "Fix-Mapped Linear Addresses," the kernel also adjusts the entries of Page Tables corresponding to the "fix-mapped linear addresses."

Final kernel Page Table when RAM size is between 896 MB and 4096 MB

In this case, the RAM cannot be mapped entirely into the kernel linear address space. The best Linux can do during the initialization phase is to map a RAM window having size of 896 MB into the kernel linear address space. If a program needs to address other parts of the existing RAM, some other linear address interval must be mapped to the required RAM. This implies changing the value of some Page Table entries. We'll defer discussing how this kind of dynamic remapping is done in Chapter 7.

To initialize the Page Global Directory, the kernel uses the same code as in previous case.

Final kernel Page Table when RAM size is more than 4096 MB

Let's now consider kernel Page Table initialization for computers with more than 4 GB; more precisely, we deal with cases in which the following happens:

- The CPU model supports Physical Address Extension (PAE).
- The amount of RAM is larger than 4 GB.
- The kernel is compiled with PAE support.

Although PAE handles 36-bit physical addresses, linear addresses are still 32-bit addresses. As in the previous case, Linux maps a 896-MB RAM window into the kernel linear address space; the remaining RAM is left unmapped and handled by dynamic remapping, as described in Chapter 7. The main difference with the previous case is that a three-level paging model is used, so the Page Global Directory is initialized as follows:

```
for (i = 0; i < 3; i++)
    set_pgd(swapper_pg_dir + i, __pgd(1 + __pa(empty_zero_page)));
pgd = swapper_pg_dir + 3;
address = 0xc0000000;
```

```
set_pgd(pgd, __pgd(__pa(pmd) + 0x1));
while (address < 0xe8000000) {
    pe = _PAGE_PRESENT + _PAGE_RW + _PAGE_ACCESSED +
         _PAGE_DIRTY + _PAGE_PSE + _PAGE_GLOBAL + __pa(address);
    set_pmd(pmd, __pmd(pe));
    pmd++;
    address += 0x200000;
}
pgd_base[0] = pgd_base[3];
```

The kernel initializes the first three entries in the Page Global Directory corresponding to the user linear address space with the address of an empty page (empty_zero_page). The fourth entry is initialized with the address of a Page Middle Directory (pmd). The first 448 entries in the Page Middle Directory (there are 512 entries, but the last 64 are reserved for noncontiguous memory allocation) are filled with the physical address of the first 896 MB of RAM.

Notice that all CPU models that support PAE also support large 2 MB pages and global pages. As in the previous case, whenever possible, Linux uses large pages to reduce the number of Page Tables.

Fix-Mapped Linear Addresses

We saw that the initial part of the fourth gigabyte of kernel linear addresses maps the physical memory of the system. However, at least 128 MB of linear addresses are always left available because the kernel uses them to implement noncontiguous memory allocation and fix-mapped linear addresses.

Noncontiguous memory allocation is just a special way to dynamically allocate and release pages of memory, and is described in the section "Noncontiguous Memory Area Management" in Chapter 7. In this section, we focus on fix-mapped linear addresses.

Basically, a *fix-mapped linear address* is a constant linear address like 0xffffffdf0 whose corresponding physical address can be set up in an arbitrary way. Thus, each fix-mapped linear address maps one page frame of the physical memory.

Fix-mapped linear addresses are conceptually similar to the linear addresses that map the first 896 MB of RAM. However, a fix-mapped linear address can map any physical address, while the mapping established by the linear addresses in the initial portion of the fourth gigabyte is linear (linear address X maps physical address X-PAGE_OFFSET).

With respect to variable pointers, fix-mapped linear addresses are more efficient. In fact, dereferencing a variable pointers requires that one memory access more than dereferencing an immediate constant address. Moreover, checking the value of a variable pointer before dereferencing it is a good programming practice; conversely, the check is never required for a constant linear address.

Each fix-mapped linear address is represented by an integer index defined in the enum fixed_addresses data structure:

```
enum fixed_addresses {
    FIX_APIC_BASE,
    FIX_IO_APIC_BASE_0,
    [...]
    __end_of_fixed_addresses
};
```

Fix-mapped linear addresses are placed at the end of the fourth gigabyte of linear addresses. The fix_to_virt() function computes the constant linear address starting from the index:

```
inline unsigned long fix_to_virt(const unsigned int idx)
{
    if (idx >= __end_of_fixed_addresses)
        __this_fixmap_does_not_exist();
    return (0xffffe000UL - (idx << PAGE_SHIFT));
}
```

Let's assume that some kernel function invokes fix_to_virt(FIX_IOAPIC_BASE_0). Since the function is declared as "inline," the C compiler does not invoke fix_to_virt(), but just inserts its code in the calling function. Moreover, the check on the index value is never performed at runtime. In fact, FIX_IOAPIC_BASE_0 is a constant, so the compiler can cut away the if statement because its condition is false at compile time. Conversely, if the condition is true or the argument of fix_to_virt() is not a constant, the compiler issues an error during the linking phase because the symbol __this_fixmap_does_not_exist is not defined elsewhere. Eventually, the compiler computes 0xffffe000-(1<<PAGE_SHIFT) and replaces the fix_to_virt() function call with the constant linear address 0xffffd000.

To associate a physical address with a fix-mapped linear address, the kernel uses the set_fixmap(idx,phys) and set_fixmap_nocache(idx,phys) functions. Both of them initialize the Page Table entry corresponding to the fix_to_virt(idx) linear address with the physical address phys; however, the second function also sets the PCD flag of the Page Table entry, thus disabling the hardware cache when accessing the data in the page frame (see the section "Hardware Cache" earlier in this chapter).

Handling the Hardware Cache and the TLB

Hardware caches and Translation Lookaside Buffers play a crucial role in boosting the performances of modern computer architectures. Several techniques are used by kernel developers to reduce the number of cache and TLB misses.

Handling the hardware cache

As mentioned earlier in this chapter, hardware cache are addressed by cache lines. The L1_CACHE_BYTES macro yields the size of a cache line in bytes. On Intel models earlier than the Pentium 4, the macro yields the value 32; on a Pentium 4, it yields the value 128.

To optimize the cache hit rate, the kernel considers the architecture in making the following decisions.

- The most frequently used fields of a data structure are placed at the low offset within the data structure so they can be cached in the same line.
- When allocating a large set of data structures, the kernel tries to store each of them in memory so that all cache lines are used uniformly.
- When performing a process switch, the kernel has a small preference for processes that use the same set of Page Tables as the previously running process (see the section "The schedule() Function" in Chapter 11).

Handling the TLB

As a general rule, any process switch implies changing the set of active Page Tables. Local TLB entries relative to the old Page Tables must be flushed; this is done automatically when the kernel writes the address of the new Page Global Directory into the cr3 control register. In some cases, however, the kernel succeeds in avoiding TLB flushes, which are listed here:

- When performing a process switch between two regular processes that use the same set of Page Tables (see the section "The schedule() Function" in Chapter 11).
- When performing a process switch between a regular process and a kernel thread. In fact, we'll see in the section "Memory Descriptor of Kernel Threads" in Chapter 8, that kernel threads do not have their own set of Page Tables; rather, they use the set of Page Tables owned by the regular process that was scheduled last for execution on the CPU.

Beside process switches, there are other cases in which the kernel needs to flush some entries in a TLB. For instance, when the kernel assigns a page frame to a User Mode process and stores its physical address into a Page Table entry, it must flush any local TLB entry that refers to the corresponding linear address. On multiprocessor systems, the kernel must also flush the same TLB entry on the CPUs that are using the same set of Page Tables, if any.

To invalidate TLB entries, the kernel uses the following functions and macros:

__flush_tlb_one
    Invalidates the local TLB entry of the page, including the specified address.

flush_tlb_page
    Invalidates all TLB entries of the page, including the specified address on all CPUs. To do this, the kernel sends an Interprocessor Interrupt to the other CPUs (see the section "Interprocessor Interrupt Handling" in Chapter 4).

`local_flush_tlb` *and* `__flush_tlb`

> Flushes the local TLB entries relative to all pages of the current process. To do this, the current value of the `cr3` register is rewritten back into it. On Pentium Pro and later processors, only TLB entries of nonglobal pages (pages whose Global flag is clear) are invalidated.

`flush_tlb`

> Flushes the TLB entries relative to the nonglobal pages of all current processes. Essentially, all CPUs receive an Interprocessor Interrupt that forces them to execute `__flush_tlb`.

`flush_tlb_mm`

> Flushes the TLB entries relative to all nonglobal pages in a specified set of Page Tables (see the section "The Memory Descriptor" in Chapter 8). As we shall see in the next chapter, on multiprocessor systems, two or more CPUs might be executing processes that share the same set of Page Tables. On the 80×86 architecture, this function forces every CPU to invalidate all local TLB entries relative to nonglobal pages of the specified set of Page Tables.

`flush_tlb_range`

> Invalidates all TLB entries of the nonglobal pages in a specified address range of a given set of Page Tables. On the 80×86 architecture, this macro is equivalent to `flush_tlb_mm`.

`__flush_tlb_all`

> Flushes all local TLB entries (regardless of the Global flag settings of the Page Table entries in Pentium Pro and later processors). To do this, the kernel temporarily clears the PGE flag in `cr4` and then writes into the `cr3` register.

`flush_tlb_all`

> Flushes all TLB entries in all CPUs (regardless of the Global flag settings of the Page Table entries in Pentium Pro and later processors). Essentially, all CPUs receive an Interprocessor Interrupt that forces them to execute `__flush_tlb_all`.

To avoid useless TLB flushing in multiprocessor systems, the kernel uses a technique called *lazy TLB mode*. The basic idea is if several CPUs are using the same Page Tables and a TLB entry must be flushed on all of them, then TLB flushing may, in some cases, be delayed on CPUs running kernel threads.

In fact, each kernel thread does not have its own set of Page Tables; rather, it makes use of the set of Page Tables belonging to a regular process. However, there is no need to invalidate a TLB entry that refers to a User Mode linear address because no kernel thread accesses the User Mode address space.[*]

---

[*] By the way, the `flush_tlb_all` macro does not use the lazy TLB mode mechanism; it is usually invoked whenever the kernel modifies a Page Table entry relative to the Kernel Mode address space.

When some CPU starts running a kernel thread, the kernel sets it into lazy TLB mode. When requests are issued to clear some TLB entries, each CPU in lazy TLB mode does not flush the corresponding entries; however, the CPU remembers that its current process is running on a set of Page Tables whose TLB entries for the User Mode addresses are invalid. As soon as the CPU in lazy TLB mode switches to a regular process with a different set of Page Tables, the hardware automatically flushes the TLB entries, and the kernel sets the CPU back in nonlazy TLB mode. However, if a CPU in lazy TLB mode switches to a regular process that owns the same set of Page Tables used by the previously running kernel thread, then any deferred TLB invalidation must be effectively applied by the kernel; this "lazy" invalidation is effectively achieved by flushing all nonglobal TLB entries of the CPU.

Some extra data structures are needed to implement the lazy TLB mode. The cpu_tlbstate variable is a static array of NR_CPUS structures (one for every CPU in the system) consisting of an active_mm field pointing to the memory descriptor of the current process (see Chapter 8) and a state flag that can assume only two values: TLBSTATE_OK (non-lazy TLB mode) or TLBSTATE_LAZY (lazy TLB mode). Furthermore, each memory descriptor includes a cpu_vm_mask field that stores the indices of the CPUs that should receive Interprocessor Interrupts related to TLB flushing; this field is meaningful only when the memory descriptor belongs to a process currently in execution.

When a CPU starts executing a kernel thread, the kernel sets the state field of its cpu_tlbstate element to TLBSTATE_LAZY; moreover, the cpu_vm_mask field of the active memory descriptor stores the indices of all CPUs in the system, including the one that is entering in lazy TLB mode. When another CPU wants to invalidate the TLB entries of all CPUs relative to a given set of Page Tables, it delivers an Interprocessor Interrupt to all CPUs whose indices are included in the cpu_vm_mask field of the corresponding memory descriptor.

When a CPU receives an Interprocessor Interrupt related to TLB flushing and verifies that it affects the set of Page Tables of its current process, it checks whether the state field of its cpu_tlbstate element is equal to TLBSTATE_LAZY; in this case, the kernel refuses to invalidate the TLB entries and removes the CPU index from the cpu_vm_mask field of the memory descriptor. This has two consequences:

- Until the CPU remains in lazy TLB mode, it will not receive other Interprocessor Interrupts related to TLB flushing.
- If the CPU switches to another process that is using the same set of Page Tables as the kernel thread that is being replaced, the kernel invokes local_flush_tlb to invalidate all nonglobal TLB entries of the CPU.

CHAPTER 3
Processes

The concept of a *process* is fundamental to any multiprogramming operating system. A process is usually defined as an instance of a program in execution; thus, if 16 users are running *vi* at once, there are 16 separate processes (although they can share the same executable code). Processes are often called *tasks* or *threads* in the Linux source code.

In this chapter, we discuss static properties of processes and then describe how process switching is performed by the kernel. The last two sections describe how processes can be created and destroyed. We also describe how Linux supports multithreaded applications—as mentioned in Chapter 1, it relies on so-called lightweight processes (LWP).

Processes, Lightweight Processes, and Threads

The term "process" is often used with several different meanings. In this book, we stick to the usual OS textbook definition: a *process* is an instance of a program in execution. You might think of it as the collection of data structures that fully describes how far the execution of the program has progressed.

Processes are like human beings: they are generated, they have a more or less significant life, they optionally generate one or more child processes, and eventually they die. A small difference is that sex is not really common among processes—each process has just one parent.

From the kernel's point of view, the purpose of a process is to act as an entity to which system resources (CPU time, memory, etc.) are allocated.

When a process is created, it is almost identical to its parent. It receives a (logical) copy of the parent's address space and executes the same code as the parent, beginning at the next instruction following the process creation system call. Although the parent and child may share the pages containing the program code (text), they have separate copies of the data (stack and heap), so that changes by the child to a memory location are invisible to the parent (and vice versa).

While earlier Unix kernels employed this simple model, modern Unix systems do not. They support *multithreaded applications*—user programs having many relatively independent execution flows sharing a large portion of the application data structures. In such systems, a process is composed of several *user threads* (or simply *threads*), each of which represents an execution flow of the process. Nowadays, most multithreaded applications are written using standard sets of library functions called *pthread (POSIX thread) libraries*.

Older versions of the Linux kernel offered no support for multithreaded applications. From the kernel point of view, a multithreaded application was just a normal process. The multiple execution flows of a multithreaded application were created, handled, and scheduled entirely in User Mode, usually by means of a POSIX-compliant *pthread* library.

However, such an implementation of multithreaded applications is not very satisfactory. For instance, suppose a chess program uses two threads: one of them controls the graphical chessboard, waiting for the moves of the human player and showing the moves of the computer, while the other thread ponders the next move of the game. While the first thread waits for the human move, the second thread should run continuously, thus exploiting the thinking time of the human player. However, if the chess program is just a single process, the first thread cannot simply issue a blocking system call waiting for a user action; otherwise, the second thread is blocked as well. Instead, the first thread must employ sophisticated nonblocking techniques to ensure that the process remains runnable.

Linux uses *lightweight processes* to offer better support for multithreaded applications. Basically, two lightweight processes may share some resources, like the address space, the open files, and so on. Whenever one of them modifies a shared resource, the other immediately sees the change. Of course, the two processes must synchronize themselves when accessing the shared resource.

If lightweight processes are available, a straightforward way to implement multithreaded applications is to associate a lightweight process with each thread. In this way, the threads can access the same set of application data structures by simply sharing the same memory address space, the same set of open files, and so on; at the same time, each thread can be scheduled independently by the kernel so that one may sleep while another remains runnable. Two examples of POSIX-compliant *pthread* libraries that use Linux's lightweight processes are *LinuxThreads* and the recently released IBM's *Next Generation Posix Threading Package (NGPT)*.

Process Descriptor

To manage processes, the kernel must have a clear picture of what each process is doing. It must know, for instance, the process's priority, whether it is running on a CPU or blocked on an event, what address space has been assigned to it, which files it is allowed to address, and so on. This is the role of the *process descriptor*—a task_ struct type structure whose fields contain all the information related to a single process. As the repository of so much information, the process descriptor is rather complex. In addition to a large number of fields containing process attributes, the process descriptor contains several pointers to other data structures that, in turn, contain pointers to other structures. Figure 3-1 describes the Linux process descriptor schematically.

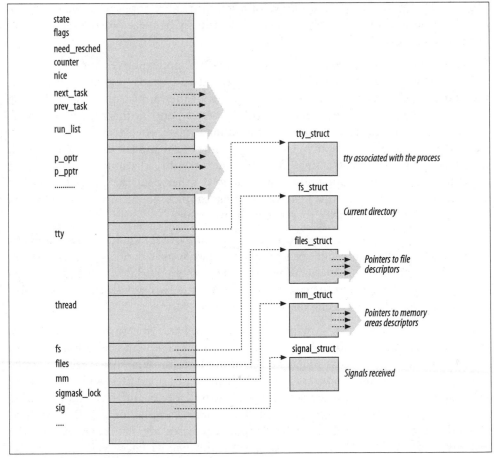

Figure 3-1. The Linux process descriptor

The five data structures on the right side of the figure refer to specific resources owned by the process. These resources are covered in future chapters. This chapter focuses on two types of fields that refer to the process state and to process parent/child relationships.

Process State

As its name implies, the state field of the process descriptor describes what is currently happening to the process. It consists of an array of flags, each of which describes a possible process state. In the current Linux version, these states are mutually exclusive, and hence exactly one flag of state is set; the remaining flags are cleared. The following are the possible process states:

TASK_RUNNING
> The process is either executing on a CPU or waiting to be executed.

TASK_INTERRUPTIBLE
> The process is suspended (sleeping) until some condition becomes true. Raising a hardware interrupt, releasing a system resource the process is waiting for, or delivering a signal are examples of conditions that might wake up the process (put its state back to TASK_RUNNING).

TASK_UNINTERRUPTIBLE
> Like the previous state, except that delivering a signal to the sleeping process leaves its state unchanged. This process state is seldom used. It is valuable, however, under certain specific conditions in which a process must wait until a given event occurs without being interrupted. For instance, this state may be used when a process opens a device file and the corresponding device driver starts probing for a corresponding hardware device. The device driver must not be interrupted until the probing is complete, or the hardware device could be left in an unpredictable state.

TASK_STOPPED
> Process execution has been stopped; the process enters this state after receiving a SIGSTOP, SIGTSTP, SIGTTIN, or SIGTTOU signal. When a process is being monitored by another (such as when a debugger executes a ptrace( ) system call to monitor a test program), each signal may put the process in the TASK_STOPPED state.

TASK_ZOMBIE
> Process execution is terminated, but the parent process has not yet issued a wait( )-like system call—wait( ), wait3( ), wait4( ), or waitpid( )—to return information about the dead process. Before the wait( )-like call is issued, the kernel cannot discard the data contained in the dead process descriptor because the parent might need it. (See the section "Process Removal" near the end of this chapter.)

The value of the state field is usually set with a simple assignment. For instance:

```
procdesc_ptr->state = TASK_RUNNING;
```

The kernel also uses the set_task_state and set_current_state macros: they set the state of a specified process and of the process currently executed, respectively. Moreover, these macros ensure that the assignment operation is not mixed with other instructions by the compiler or the CPU control unit. Mixing the instruction order may sometimes lead to catastrophic results (see Chapter 5).

Identifying a Process

As a general rule, each execution context that can be independently scheduled must have its own process descriptor; therefore, even lightweight processes, which share a large portion of their kernel data structures, have their own task_struct structures.

The strict one-to-one correspondence between the process and process descriptor makes the 32-bit process descriptor address[*] a useful means for the kernel to identify processes. These addresses are referred to as *process descriptor pointers*. Most of the references to processes that the kernel makes are through process descriptor pointers.

On the other hand, Unix-like operating systems allow users to identify processes by means of a number called the *Process ID* (or *PID*), which is stored in the pid field of the process descriptor. PIDs are numbered sequentially: the PID of a newly created process is normally the PID of the previously created process incremented by one. However, for compatibility with traditional Unix systems developed for 16-bit hardware platforms, the maximum PID number allowed on Linux is 32,767. When the kernel creates the 32,768th process in the system, it must start recycling the lower, unused PIDs.

Linux associates a different PID with each process or lightweight process in the system. (As we shall see later in this chapter, there is a tiny exception on multiprocessor systems.) This approach allows the maximum flexibility, since every execution context in the system can be uniquely identified.

On the other hand, Unix programmers expect threads in the same group to have a common PID. For instance, it should be possible to a send a signal specifying a PID that affects all threads in the group. In fact, the POSIX 1003.1c standard states that all threads of a multithreaded application must have the same PID.

To comply with this standard, Linux 2.4 introduces the notion of *thread group*. A thread group is essentially a collection of lightweight processes that correspond to the threads of a multithreaded application. All descriptors of the lightweight processes in the same thread group are collected in a doubly linked list implemented through the thread_group field of the task_struct structure. The identifier shared by

---

[*] Technically, these 32 bits are only the offset component of a logical address. However, since Linux uses a single kernel data segment, we can consider the offset to be equivalent to a whole logical address. Furthermore, since the base addresses of the code and data segments are set to 0, we can treat the offset as a linear address.

the threads is the PID of the first lightweight process in the group; it is stored in the tgid field of the process descriptors. The getpid() system call returns current->tgid instead of current->pid, so all the threads of a multithreaded application share the same identifier. The tgid field has the same value as the pid field, both for normal processes and for lightweight processes not included in a thread group. Therefore, the getpid() system call works as usual for them.

Later, we'll show you how it is possible to derive a true process descriptor pointer efficiently from its respective PID. Efficiency is important because many system calls such as kill() use the PID to denote the affected process.

Processor descriptors handling

Processes are dynamic entities whose lifetimes range from a few milliseconds to months. Thus, the kernel must be able to handle many processes at the same time, and process descriptors are stored in dynamic memory rather than in the memory area permanently assigned to the kernel. Linux stores two different data structures for each process in a single 8 KB memory area: the process descriptor and the Kernel Mode process stack.

In the section "Segmentation in Linux" in Chapter 2, we learned that a process in Kernel Mode accesses a stack contained in the kernel data segment, which is different from the stack used by the process in User Mode. Since kernel control paths make little use of the stack, only a few thousand bytes of kernel stack are required. Therefore, 8 KB is ample space for the stack and the process descriptor.

Figure 3-2 shows how the two data structures are stored in the 2-page (8 KB) memory area. The process descriptor resides at the beginning of the memory area and the stack grows downward from the end.

The esp register is the CPU stack pointer, which is used to address the stack's top location. On Intel systems, the stack starts at the end and grows toward the beginning of the memory area. Right after switching from User Mode to Kernel Mode, the kernel stack of a process is always empty, and therefore the esp register points to the byte immediately following the memory area.

The value of the esp is decremented as soon as data is written into the stack. Since the process descriptor is less than 1,000 bytes long, the kernel stack can expand up to 7,200 bytes.

The C language allows the process descriptor and the kernel stack of a process to be conveniently represented by means of the following union construct:

```
union task_union {
    struct task_struct task;
    unsigned long stack[2048];
};
```

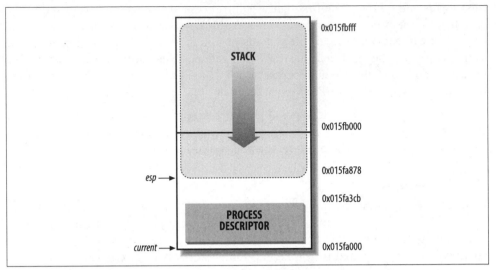

Figure 3-2. *Storing the process descriptor and the process kernel stack*

The process descriptor shown in Figure 3-2 is stored starting at address 0x015fa000, and the stack is stored starting at address 0x015fc000. The value of the esp register points to the current top of the stack at 0x015fa878.

The kernel uses the alloc_task_struct and free_task_struct macros to allocate and release the 8 KB memory area storing a process descriptor and a kernel stack.

The current macro

The close association between the process descriptor and the Kernel Mode stack just described offers a key benefit in terms of efficiency: the kernel can easily obtain the process descriptor pointer of the process currently running on a CPU from the value of the esp register. In fact, since the memory area is 8 KB (2^{13} bytes) long, all the kernel has to do is mask out the 13 least significant bits of esp to obtain the base address of the process descriptor. This is done by the current macro, which produces assembly language instructions like the following:

```
movl $0xffffe000, %ecx
andl %esp, %ecx
movl %ecx, p
```

After executing these three instructions, p contains the process descriptor pointer of the process running on the CPU that executes the instruction.*

---

* One drawback to the shared-storage approach is that, for efficiency reasons, the kernel stores the 8-KB memory area in two consecutive page frames with the first page frame aligned to a multiple of 2^{13}. This may turn out to be a problem when little dynamic memory is available.

The current macro often appears in kernel code as a prefix to fields of the process descriptor. For example, current->pid returns the process ID of the process currently running on the CPU.

Another advantage of storing the process descriptor with the stack emerges on multiprocessor systems: the correct current process for each hardware processor can be derived just by checking the stack, as shown previously. Linux 2.0 did not store the kernel stack and the process descriptor together. Instead, it was forced to introduce a global static variable called current to identify the process descriptor of the running process. On multiprocessor systems, it was necessary to define current as an array—one element for each available CPU.

The process list

To allow an efficient search through processes of a given type (for instance, all processes in a runnable state), the kernel creates several lists of processes. Each list consists of pointers to process descriptors. A list pointer (that is, the field that each process uses to point to the next process) is embedded right in the process descriptor's data structure. When you look at the C-language declaration of the task_struct structure, the descriptors may seem to turn in on themselves in a complicated recursive manner. However, the concept is no more complicated than any list, which is a data structure containing a pointer to the next instance of itself.

A circular doubly linked list (see Figure 3-3) links all existing process descriptors; we will call it the *process list*. The prev_task and next_task fields of each process descriptor are used to implement the list. The head of the list is the init_task descriptor referenced by the first element of the task array; it is the ancestor of all processes, and is called *process 0* or *swapper* (see the section "Kernel Threads" later in this chapter). The prev_task field of init_task points to the process descriptor inserted last in the list.

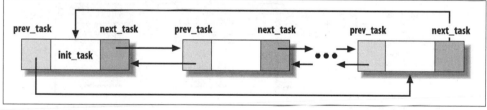

Figure 3-3. The process list

The SET_LINKS and REMOVE_LINKS macros are used to insert and to remove a process descriptor in the process list, respectively. These macros also take care of the parenthood relationship of the process (see the section "Parenthood Relationships Among Processes" later in this chapter).

Another useful macro, called for_each_task, scans the whole process list. It is defined as:

```
#define for_each_task(p) \
    for (p = &init_task ; (p = p->next_task) != &init_task ; )
```

The macro is the loop control statement after which the kernel programmer supplies the loop. Notice how the init_task process descriptor just plays the role of list header. The macro starts by moving past init_task to the next task and continues until it reaches init_task again (thanks to the circularity of the list).

Doubly linked lists

The process list is a special doubly linked list. However, as you may have noticed, the Linux kernel uses hundreds of doubly linked lists that store the various kernel data structures.

For each list, a set of primitive operations must be implemented: initializing the list, inserting and deleting an element, scanning the list, and so on. It would be both a waste of programmers' efforts and a waste of memory to replicate the primitive operations for each different list.

Therefore, the Linux kernel defines the list_head data structure, whose fields next and prev represent the forward and back pointers of a generic doubly linked list element, respectively. It is important to note, however, that the pointers in a list_head field store the addresses of other list_head fields rather than the addresses of the whole data structures in which the list_head structure is included (see Figure 3-4).

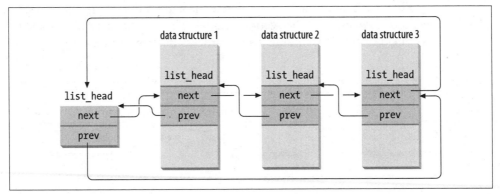

Figure 3-4. A doubly linked list built with list_head data structures

A new list is created by using the LIST_HEAD(list_name) macro. It declares a new variable named list_name of type list_head, which is the conventional first element of the new list (much as init_task is the conventional first element of the process list).

Several functions and macros implement the primitives, including those shown in the following list.

```
list_add(n,p)
```
Inserts an element pointed by n right after the specified element pointed by p (to insert n at the beginning of the list, set p to the address of the conventional first element)

```
list_add_tail(n,h)
```
Inserts an element pointed by n at the end of the list specified by the address h of its conventional first element

```
list_del(p)
```
Deletes an element pointed by p (there is no need to specify the conventional first element of the list)

```
list_empty(p)
```
Checks if the list specified by the address of its conventional first element is empty

```
list_entry(p,t,f)
```
Returns the address of the data structure of type t in which the list_head field that has the name f and the address p is included

```
list_for_each(p,h)
```
Scans the elements of the list specified by the address h of the conventional first element (similar to for_each_task for the process list)

The list of TASK_RUNNING processes

When looking for a new process to run on the CPU, the kernel has to consider only the runnable processes (that is, the processes in the TASK_RUNNING state). Since it is rather inefficient to scan the whole process list, a doubly linked circular list of TASK_RUNNING processes called *runqueue* has been introduced. This list is implemented through the run_list field of type list_head in the process descriptor. As in the previous case, the init_task process descriptor plays the role of list header. The nr_running variable stores the total number of runnable processes.

The add_to_runqueue( ) function inserts a process descriptor at the beginning of the list, while del_from_runqueue( ) removes a process descriptor from the list. For scheduling purposes, two functions, move_first_runqueue( ) and move_last_runqueue( ), are provided to move a process descriptor to the beginning or the end of the runqueue, respectively. The task_on_runqueue( ) function checks whether a given process is inserted into the runqueue.

Finally, the wake_up_process( ) function is used to make a process runnable. It sets the process state to TASK_RUNNING and invokes add_to_runqueue( ) to insert the process in the runqueue list. It also forces the invocation of the scheduler when the process has a dynamic priority larger than that of the current process or, in SMP systems, that of a process currently executing on some other CPU (see Chapter 11).

The pidhash table and chained lists

In several circumstances, the kernel must be able to derive the process descriptor pointer corresponding to a PID. This occurs, for instance, in servicing the kill( ) system call. When process P1 wishes to send a signal to another process, P2, it invokes the kill( ) system call specifying the PID of P2 as the parameter. The kernel derives the process descriptor pointer from the PID and then extracts the pointer to the data structure that records the pending signals from P2's process descriptor.

Scanning the process list sequentially and checking the pid fields of the process descriptors is feasible but rather inefficient. To speed up the search, a pidhash hash table consisting of PIDHASH_SZ elements has been introduced (PIDHASH_SZ is usually set to 1,024). The table entries contain process descriptor pointers. The PID is transformed into a table index using the pid_hashfn macro:

```
#define pid_hashfn(x) ((((x) >> 8) ^ (x)) & (PIDHASH_SZ - 1))
```

As every basic computer science course explains, a hash function does not always ensure a one-to-one correspondence between PIDs and table indexes. Two different PIDs that hash into the same table index are said to be *colliding*.

Linux uses *chaining* to handle colliding PIDs; each table entry is a doubly linked list of colliding process descriptors. These lists are implemented by means of the pidhash_next and pidhash_pprev fields in the process descriptor. Figure 3-5 illustrates a pidhash table with two lists. The processes having PIDs 199 and 26,799 hash into the 200th element of the table, while the process having PID 26,800 hashes into the 217th element of the table.

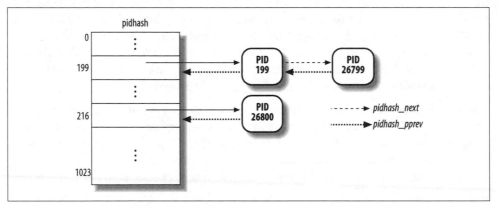

Figure 3-5. The pidhash table and chained lists

Hashing with chaining is preferable to a linear transformation from PIDs to table indexes because at any given instance, the number of processes in the system is usually far below 32,767 (the maximum allowed PID). It is a waste of storage to define a table consisting of 32,768 entries, if, at any given instance, most such entries are unused.

The hash_pid( ) and unhash_pid( ) functions are invoked to insert and remove a process in the pidhash table, respectively. The find_task_by_pid( ) function searches the hash table and returns the process descriptor pointer of the process with a given PID (or a null pointer if it does not find the process).

Parenthood Relationships Among Processes

Processes created by a program have a parent/child relationship. When a process creates multiple children, these children have sibling relationships. Several fields must be introduced in a process descriptor to represent these relationships. Processes 0 and 1 are created by the kernel; as we shall see later in the chapter, process 1 (*init*) is the ancestor of all other processes. The descriptor of a process P includes the following fields:

p_opptr (*original parent*)
> Points to the process descriptor of the process that created P or to the descriptor of process 1 (*init*) if the parent process no longer exists. Therefore, when a shell user starts a background process and exits the shell, the background process becomes the child of *init*.

p_pptr (*parent*)
> Points to the current parent of P (this is the process that must be signaled when the child process terminates); its value usually coincides with that of p_opptr. It may occasionally differ, such as when another process issues a ptrace( ) system call requesting that it be allowed to monitor P (see the section "Execution Tracing" in Chapter 20).

p_cptr (*child*)
> Points to the process descriptor of the youngest child of P—that is, of the process created most recently by it.

p_ysptr (*younger sibling*)
> Points to the process descriptor of the process that has been created immediately after P by P's current parent.

p_osptr (*older sibling*)
> Points to the process descriptor of the process that has been created immediately before P by P's current parent.

Figure 3-6 illustrates the parent and sibling relationships of a group of processes. Process P0 successively created P1, P2, and P3. Process P3, in turn, created process P4. Starting with p_cptr and using the p_osptr pointers to siblings, P0 is able to retrieve all its children.

How Processes Are Organized

The runqueue list groups all processes in a TASK_RUNNING state. When it comes to grouping processes in other states, the various states call for different types of treatment, with Linux opting for one of the choices shown in the following list.

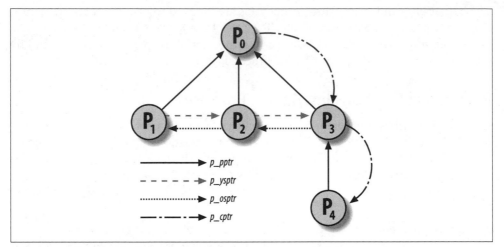

Figure 3-6. Parenthood relationships among five processes

- Processes in a TASK_STOPPED or in a TASK_ZOMBIE state are not linked in specific lists. There is no need to group processes in either of these two states, since stopped and zombie processes are accessed only via PID or via linked lists of the child processes for a particular parent.

- Processes in a TASK_INTERRUPTIBLE or TASK_UNINTERRUPTIBLE state are subdivided into many classes, each of which corresponds to a specific event. In this case, the process state does not provide enough information to retrieve the process quickly, so it is necessary to introduce additional lists of processes. These are called *wait queues*.

Wait queues

Wait queues have several uses in the kernel, particularly for interrupt handling, process synchronization, and timing. Because these topics are discussed in later chapters, we'll just say here that a process must often wait for some event to occur, such as for a disk operation to terminate, a system resource to be released, or a fixed interval of time to elapse. Wait queues implement conditional waits on events: a process wishing to wait for a specific event places itself in the proper wait queue and relinquishes control. Therefore, a wait queue represents a set of sleeping processes, which are woekn up by the kernel when some condition becomes true.

Wait queues are implemented as doubly linked lists whose elements include pointers to process descriptors. Each wait queue is identified by a *wait queue head*, a data structure of type wait_queue_head_t:

```
struct __wait_queue_head {
    spinlock_t lock;
    struct list_head task_list;
};
typedef struct __wait_queue_head wait_queue_head_t;
```

Since wait queues are modified by interrupt handlers as well by major kernel functions, the doubly linked lists must be protected from concurrent accesses, which could induce unpredictable results (see Chapter 5). Synchronization is achieved by the lock spin lock in the wait queue head.

Elements of a wait queue list are of type wait_queue_t:

```
struct __wait_queue {
    unsigned int flags;
    struct task_struct * task;
    struct list_head task_list;
};
typedef struct __wait_queue wait_queue_t;
```

Each element in the wait queue list represents a sleeping process, which is waiting for some event to occur; its descriptor address is stored in the task field. However, it is not always convenient to wake up *all* sleeping processes in a wait queue.

For instance, if two or more processes are waiting for exclusive access to some resource to be released, it makes sense to wake up just one process in the wait queue. This process takes the resource, while the other processes continue to sleep. (This avoids a problem known as the "thundering herd," with which multiple processes are awoken only to race for a resource that can be accessed by one of them, and the result is that remaining processes must once more be put back to sleep.)

Thus, there are two kinds of sleeping processes: *exclusive processes* (denoted by the value 1 in the flags field of the corresponding wait queue element) are selectively woken up by the kernel, while *nonexclusive processes* (denoted by the value 0 in flags) are always woken up by the kernel when the event occurs. A process waiting for a resource that can be granted to just one process at a time is a typical exclusive process. Processes waiting for an event like the termination of a disk operation are nonexclusive.

Handling wait queues

The add_wait_queue() function inserts a nonexclusive process in the first position of a wait queue list. The add_wait_queue_exclusive() function inserts an exclusive process in the last position of a wait queue list. The remove_wait_queue() function removes a process from a wait queue list. The waitqueue_active() function checks whether a given wait queue list is empty.

A new wait queue may be defined by using the DECLARE_WAIT_QUEUE_HEAD(name) macro, which statically declares and initializes a new wait queue head variable called name. The init_waitqueue_head() function may be used to initialize a wait queue head variable that was allocated dynamically.

A process wishing to wait for a specific condition can invoke any of the functions shown in the following list.

- The sleep_on() function operates on the current process:

```
void sleep_on(wait_queue_head_t *q)
{
    unsigned long flags;
    wait_queue_t wait;
    wait.flags = 0;
    wait.task = current;
    current->state = TASK_UNINTERRUPTIBLE;
    add_wait_queue(q, &wait);
    schedule();
    remove_wait_queue(q, &wait);
}
```

  The function sets the state of the current process to TASK_UNINTERRUPTIBLE and inserts it into the specified wait queue. Then it invokes the scheduler, which resumes the execution of another process. When the sleeping process is woken, the scheduler resumes execution of the sleep_on() function, which removes the process from the wait queue.

- The interruptible_sleep_on() is identical to sleep_on(), except that it sets the state of the current process to TASK_INTERRUPTIBLE instead of setting it to TASK_UNINTERRUPTIBLE so that the process can also be woken up by receiving a signal.

- The sleep_on_timeout() and interruptible_sleep_on_timeout() functions are similar to the previous ones, but they also allow the caller to define a time interval after which the process will be woken up by the kernel. To do this, they invoke the schedule_timeout() function instead of schedule() (see the section "An Application of Dynamic Timers" in Chapter 6).

- The wait_event and wait_event_interruptible macros, introduced in Linux 2.4, put the calling process to sleep on a wait queue until a given condition is verified. For instance, the wait_event_interruptible(wq,condition) macro essentially yields the following fragment (we have omitted the code related to signal handling and return values on purpose):

```
if (!(condition)) {
    wait_queue_t __wait;
    init_waitqueue_entry(&__wait, current);
    add_wait_queue(&wq, &__wait);
    for (;;) {
        set_current_state(TASK_INTERRUPTIBLE);
        if (condition)
            break;
        schedule();
    }
    current->state = TASK_RUNNING;
    remove_wait_queue(&wq, &__wait);
}
```

  These macros should be used instead of the older sleep_on() and interruptible_sleep_on(), because the latter functions cannot test a condition and atomically put the process to sleep when the condition is not verified and are thus a well-known source of race conditions.

Notice that any process put to sleep by one of the above functions or macros is non-exclusive. Whenever the kernel wants to insert an exclusive process into a wait queue, it invokes add_wait_queue_exclusive() directly.

Processes inserted in a wait queue enter the TASK_RUNNING state by means of one of the following macros: wake_up, wake_up_nr, wake_up_all, wake_up_sync, wake_up_sync_nr, wake_up_interruptible, wake_up_interruptible_nr, wake_up_interruptible_all, wake_up_interruptible_sync, and wake_up_interruptible_sync_nr. We can understand what each of these ten macros does from its name:

- All macros take into consideration sleeping processes in TASK_INTERRUPTIBLE state; if the macro name does not include the string "interruptible," sleeping processes in TASK_UNINTERRUPTIBLE state are also considered.

- All macros wake all nonexclusive processes having the required state (see the previous bullet item).

- The macros whose name include the string "nr" wake a given number of exclusive processes having the required state; this number is a parameter of the macro. The macros whose name include the string "all" wake all exclusive processes having the required state. Finally, the macros whose names don't include "nr" or "all" wake exactly one exclusive process that has the required state.

- The macros whose names don't include the string "sync" check whether the priority of the woken processes is higher than that of the processes currently running in the systems and invoke schedule() if necessary. These checks are not made by the macros whose names include the string "sync."

For instance, the wake_up macro is equivalent to the following code fragment:

```
void wake_up(wait_queue_head_t *q)
{
    struct list_head *tmp;
    wait_queue_t *curr;

    list_for_each(tmp, &q->task_list) {
        curr = list_entry(tmp, wait_queue_t, task_list);
        wake_up_process(curr->task);
        if (curr->flags)
            break;
    }
}
```

The list_for_each macro scans all items in the doubly linked list of q. For each item, the list_entry macro computes the address of the correspondent wait_queue_t variable. The task field of this variable stores the pointer to the process descriptor, which is then passed to the wake_up_process() function. If the woken process is exclusive, the loop terminates. Since all nonexclusive processes are always at the beginning of the doubly linked list and all exclusive processes are at the end, the function always waken the nonexclusive processes and then wakes one exclusive process, if any exists.* Notice that awoken processes are not removed from the wait queue. A process could be awoken while the wait condition is still false; in this case, the process may suspend itself again in the same wait queue.

Process Resource Limits

Each process has an associated set of *resource limits*, which specify the amount of system resources it can use. These limits keep a user from overwhelming the system (its CPU, disk space, and so on). Linux recognizes the following resource limits:

RLIMIT_AS
>   The maximum size of process address space, in bytes. The kernel checks this value when the process uses malloc( ) or a related function to enlarge its address space (see the section "The Process's Address Space" in Chapter 8).

RLIMIT_CORE
>   The maximum core dump file size, in bytes. The kernel checks this value when a process is aborted, before creating a core file in the current directory of the process (see the section "Actions Performed upon Delivering a Signal" in Chapter 10). If the limit is 0, the kernel won't create the file.

RLIMIT_CPU
>   The maximum CPU time for the process, in seconds. If the process exceeds the limit, the kernel sends it a SIGXCPU signal, and then, if the process doesn't terminate, a SIGKILL signal (see Chapter 10).

RLIMIT_DATA
>   The maximum heap size, in bytes. The kernel checks this value before expanding the heap of the process (see the section "Managing the Heap" in Chapter 8).

RLIMIT_FSIZE
>   The maximum file size allowed, in bytes. If the process tries to enlarge a file to a size greater than this value, the kernel sends it a SIGXFSZ signal.

RLIMIT_LOCKS
>   The maximum number of file locks. The kernel checks this value when the process enforces a lock on a file (see the section "File Locking" in Chapter 12).

RLIMIT_MEMLOCK
>   The maximum size of nonswappable memory, in bytes. The kernel checks this value when the process tries to lock a page frame in memory using the mlock( ) or mlockall( ) system calls (see the section "Allocating a Linear Address Interval" in Chapter 8).

RLIMIT_NOFILE
>   The maximum number of open file descriptors. The kernel checks this value when opening a new file or duplicating a file descriptor (see Chapter 12).

---

* By the way, it is rather uncommon that a wait queue includes both exclusive and nonexclusive processes.

RLIMIT_NPROC

> The maximum number of processes that the user can own (see the section "The clone( ), fork( ), and vfork( ) System Calls" later in this chapter).

RLIMIT_RSS

> The maximum number of page frames owned by the process. The kernel checks this value when the process uses malloc( ) or a related function to enlarge its address space (see the section "The Process's Address Space" in Chapter 8).

RLIMIT_STACK

> The maximum stack size, in bytes. The kernel checks this value before expanding the User Mode stack of the process (see the section "Page Fault Exception Handler" in Chapter 8).

The resource limits are stored in the rlim field of the process descriptor. The field is an array of elements of type struct rlimit, one for each resource limit:

```
struct rlimit {
    unsigned long rlim_cur;
    unsigned long rlim_max;
};
```

The rlim_cur field is the current resource limit for the resource. For example, current->rlim[RLIMIT_CPU].rlim_cur represents the current limit on the CPU time of the running process.

The rlim_max field is the maximum allowed value for the resource limit. By using the getrlimit( ) and setrlimit( ) system calls, a user can always increase the rlim_cur limit of some resource up to rlim_max. However, only the superuser (or, more precisely, a user who has the CAP_SYS_RESOURCE capability) can increase the rlim_max field or set the rlim_cur field to a value greater than the corresponding rlim_max field.

Most resource limits contain the value RLIM_INFINITY (0xffffffff), which means that no user limit is imposed on the corresponding resource (of course, real limits exist due to kernel design restrictions, available RAM, available space on disk, etc.). However, the system administrator may choose to impose stronger limits on some resources. Whenever a user logs into the system, the kernel creates a process owned by the superuser, which can invoke setrlimit( ) to decrease the rlim_max and rlim_cur fields for a resource. The same process later executes a login shell and becomes owned by the user. Each new process created by the user inherits the content of the rlim array from its parent, and therefore the user cannot override the limits enforced by the system.

Process Switch

To control the execution of processes, the kernel must be able to suspend the execution of the process running on the CPU and resume the execution of some other process previously suspended. This activity goes variously by the names *process switch*, *task switch*, or *context switch*. The next sections describe the elements of process switching in Linux.

Hardware Context

While each process can have its own address space, all processes have to share the CPU registers. So before resuming the execution of a process, the kernel must ensure that each such register is loaded with the value it had when the process was suspended.

The set of data that must be loaded into the registers before the process resumes its execution on the CPU is called the *hardware context*. The hardware context is a subset of the process execution context, which includes all information needed for the process execution. In Linux, a part of the hardware context of a process is stored in the process descriptor, while the remaining part is saved in the Kernel Mode stack.

In the description that follows, we will assume the prev local variable refers to the process descriptor of the process being switched out and next refers to the one being switched in to replace it. We can thus define a *process switch* as the activity consisting of saving the hardware context of prev and replacing it with the hardware context of next. Since process switches occur quite often, it is important to minimize the time spent in saving and loading hardware contexts.

Old versions of Linux took advantage of the hardware support offered by the Intel architecture and performed a process switch through a far jmp instruction* to the selector of the Task State Segment Descriptor of the next process. While executing the instruction, the CPU performs a *hardware context switch* by automatically saving the old hardware context and loading a new one. But Linux 2.4 uses software to perform a process switch for the following reasons:

- Step-by-step switching performed through a sequence of mov instructions allows better control over the validity of the data being loaded. In particular, it is possible to check the values of segmentation registers. This type of checking is not possible when using a single far jmp instruction.

- The amount of time required by the old approach and the new approach is about the same. However, it is not possible to optimize a hardware context switch, while there might be room for improving the current switching code.

Process switching occurs only in Kernel Mode. The contents of all registers used by a process in User Mode have already been saved before performing process switching (see Chapter 4). This includes the contents of the ss and esp pair that specifies the User Mode stack pointer address.

Task State Segment

The 80×86 architecture includes a specific segment type called the *Task State Segment* (TSS), to store hardware contexts. Although Linux doesn't use hardware

---

* far jmp instructions modify both the cs and eip registers, while simple jmp instructions modify only eip.

context switches, it is nonetheless forced to set up a TSS for each distinct CPU in the system. This is done for two main reasons:

- When an 80×86 CPU switches from User Mode to Kernel Mode, it fetches the address of the Kernel Mode stack from the TSS (see Chapter 4).
- When a User Mode process attempts to access an I/O port by means of an in or out instruction, the CPU may need to access an I/O Permission Bitmap stored in the TSS to verify whether the process is allowed to address the port.

  More precisely, when a process executes an in or out I/O instruction in User Mode, the control unit performs the following operations:

  1. It checks the 2-bit IOPL field in the eflags register. If it is set to 3, the control unit executes the I/O instructions. Otherwise, it performs the next check.
  2. It accesses the tr register to determine the current TSS, and thus the proper I/O Permission Bitmap.
  3. It checks the bit of the I/O Permission Bitmap corresponding to the I/O port specified in the I/O instruction. If it is cleared, the instruction is executed; otherwise, the control unit raises a "General protection error" exception.

The tss_struct structure describes the format of the TSS. As already mentioned in Chapter 2, the init_tss array stores one TSS for each different CPU on the system. At each process switch, the kernel updates some fields of the TSS so that the corresponding CPU's control unit may safely retrieve the information it needs.

Each TSS has its own 8-byte *Task State Segment Descriptor* (TSSD). This Descriptor includes a 32-bit Base field that points to the TSS starting address and a 20-bit Limit field. The S flag of a TSSD is cleared to denote the fact that the corresponding TSS is a *System Segment*.

The Type field is set to either 9 or 11 to denote that the segment is actually a TSS. In the Intel's original design, each process in the system should refer to its own TSS; the second least significant bit of the Type field is called the *Busy bit*; it is set to 1 if the process is being executed by a CPU, and to 0 otherwise. In Linux design, there is just one TSS for each CPU, so the Busy bit is always set to 1.

The TSSDs created by Linux are stored in the Global Descriptor Table (GDT), whose base address is stored in the gdtr register of each CPU. The tr register of each CPU contains the TSSD Selector of the corresponding TSS. The register also includes two hidden, nonprogrammable fields: the Base and Limit fields of the TSSD. In this way, the processor can address the TSS directly without having to retrieve the TSS address from the GDT.

The thread field

At every process switch, the hardware context of the process being replaced must be saved somewhere. It cannot be saved on the TSS, as in the original Intel design, because we cannot make assumptions about when the process being replaced will resume execution and what CPU will execute it again.

Thus, each process descriptor includes a field called thread of type thread_struct, in which the kernel saves the hardware context whenever the process is being switched out.

As we shall see later, this data structure includes fields for most of the CPU registers, such as the general-purpose registers, the floating point registers, and so on.

Performing the Process Switch

A process switch may occur at just one well-defined point: the schedule() function (discussed at length in Chapter 11). Here, we are only concerned with how the kernel performs a process switch.

Essentially, every process switch consists of two steps:

1. Switching the Page Global Directory to install a new address space; we'll describe this step in Chapter 8.
2. Switching the Kernel Mode stack and the hardware context, which provides all the information needed by the kernel to execute the new process, including the CPU registers.

Again, we assume that prev points to the descriptor of the process being replaced, and next to the descriptor of the process being activated. As we shall see in Chapter 11, prev and next are local variables of the schedule() function.

The second step of the process switch is performed by the switch_to macro. It is one of the most hardware-dependent routines of the kernel, and it·takes some effort to understand what it does.

First of all, the macro has three parameters called prev, next, and last. The actual invocation of the macro in schedule() is:

```
switch_to(prev, next, prev);
```

You might easily guess the role of prev and next—they are just placeholders for the local variables prev and next—but what about the third parameter last? Well, the point is that in any process switch, three processes are involved, not just two.

Suppose the kernel decides to switch off process A and to activate process B. In the schedule() function, prev points to A's descriptor and next points to B's descriptor. As soon as the switch_to macro deactivates A, the execution flow of A freezes.

Later, when the kernel wants to reactivate A, it must switch off another process C (in general, this is different from B) by executing another switch_to macro with prev pointing to C and next pointing to A. When A resumes its execution flow, it finds its old Kernel Mode stack, so the prev local variable points to A's descriptor and next points to B's descriptor. The kernel, which is now executing on behalf of process A, has lost any reference to C.

The last parameter of the switch_to macro reinserts the address of C's descriptor into the prev local variable. The mechanism exploits the state of registers during function calls. The first prev parameter corresponds to a CPU register, which is loaded with the content of the prev local variable when the macro starts. When the macro ends, it writes the content of the same register in the last parameter—namely, in the prev local variable. However, the CPU register doesn't change across the process switch, so prev receives the address of C's descriptor (as we shall see in Chapter 11, the scheduler checks whether C should be readily executed on another CPU).

Here is a description of what the switch_to macro does on an 80×86 microprocessor:

1. Saves the values of prev and next in the eax and edx registers, respectively:

   ```
   movl prev,%eax
   movl next,%edx
   ```

   The eax and edx registers correspond to the prev and next parameters of the macro.

2. Saves another copy of prev in the ebx register; ebx corresponds to the last parameter of the macro:

   ```
   movl %eax,%ebx
   ```

3. Saves the contents of the esi, edi, and ebp registers in the prev Kernel Mode stack. They must be saved because the compiler assumes that they will stay unchanged until the end of switch_to:

   ```
   pushl %esi
   pushl %edi
   pushl %ebp
   ```

4. Saves the content of esp in prev->thread.esp so that the field points to the top of the prev Kernel Mode stack:

   ```
   movl %esp, 616(%eax)
   ```

   The 616(%eax) operand identifies the memory cell whose address is the contents of eax plus 616.

5. Loads next->thread.esp in esp. From now on, the kernel operates on the Kernel Mode stack of next, so this instruction performs the actual process switch from prev to next. Since the address of a process descriptor is closely related to that of the Kernel Mode stack (as explained in the section "Identifying a Process" earlier in this chapter), changing the kernel stack means changing the current process:

   ```
   movl 616(%edx), %esp
   ```

6. Saves the address labeled 1 (shown later in this section) in prev->thread.eip. When the process being replaced resumes its execution, the process executes the instruction labeled as 1:

   ```
   movl $1f, 612(%eax)
   ```

7. On the Kernel Mode stack of next, the macro pushes the next->thread.eip value, which, in most cases, is the address labeled 1:

```
pushl 612(%edx)
```

8. Jumps to the __switch_to( ) C function:

```
jmp __switch_to
```

This function acts on the prev and next parameters that denote the former process and the new process. This function call is different from the average function call, though, because __switch_to( ) takes the prev and next parameters from the eax and edx (where we saw they were stored), not from the stack like most functions. To force the function to go to the registers for its parameters, the kernel uses the __attribute__ and regparm keywords, which are nonstandard extensions of the C language implemented by the gcc compiler. The __switch_to( ) function is declared in the *include/asm-i386/system.h* header file as follows:

```
__switch_to(struct task_struct *prev,
            struct task_struct *next)
    __attribute__(regparm(3))
```

The __switch_to( ) function completes the process switch started by the switch_to( ) macro. It includes extended inline assembly language code that makes for rather complex reading because the code refers to registers by means of special symbols:

a. Executes the code yielded by the unlazy_fpu( ) macro (see the section "Saving the FPU, MMX, and XMM Registers" later in this chapter) to optionally save the contents of the FPU, MMX, and XMM registers. As we shall see, there is no need to load the corresponding registers of next while performing the context switch:

```
unlazy_fpu(prev);
```

b. Loads next->esp0 in the esp0 field of the TSS relative to the current CPU so that any future privilege level change from User Mode to Kernel Mode automatically forces this address into the esp register:

```
init_tss[smp_processor_id()].esp0 = next->thread.esp0;
```

The smp_processor_id( ) macro yields the index of the executing CPU.

c. Stores the contents of the fs and gs segmentation registers in prev->thread.fs and prev->thread.gs, respectively; the corresponding assembly language instructions are:

```
movl %fs,620(%esi)
movl %gs,624(%esi)
```

The esi register points to the prev->thread structure.

d. Loads the fs and gs segment registers with the values contained in next->thread.fs and next->thread.gs, respectively. This step logically complements the actions performed in the previous step. The corresponding assembly language instructions are:

```
movl 12(%ebx),%fs
movl 17(%ebx),%gs
```

The ebx register points to the next->thread structure. The code is actually more intricate, as an exception might be raised by the CPU when it detects an invalid segment register value. The code takes this possibility into account by adopting a "fix-up" approach (see the section "Dynamic Address Checking: The Fixup Code" in Chapter 9).

e. Loads six debug registers* with the contents of the next->thread.debugreg array. This is done only if next was using the debug registers when it was suspended (that is, field next->thread.debugreg[7] is not 0). As we shall see in Chapter 20, these registers are modified only by writing in the TSS, so there is no need to save the corresponding registers of prev:

```
if (next->thread.debugreg[7]){
    loaddebug(&next->thread, 0);
    loaddebug(&next->thread, 1);
    loaddebug(&next->thread, 2);
    loaddebug(&next->thread, 3);
    /* no 4 and 5 */
    loaddebug(&next->thread, 6);
    loaddebug(&next->thread, 7);
}
```

f. Updates the I/O bitmap in the TSS, if necessary. This must be done when either next or prev have their own customized I/O Permission Bitmap:

```
if (next->thread.ioperm) {
    memcpy(init_tss[smp_processor_id()].io_bitmap, next->thread.io_bitmap,
        128));
    init_tss[smp_processor_id()].bitmap = 104;
} else if (prev->thread.ioperm)
    init_tss[smp_processor_id()].bitmap = 0x8000;
```

The customized I/O Permission Bitmap of a process is stored in a buffer pointed to by the thread.io_bitmap field of the process descriptor. If next has a customized bitmap, it is copied into the io_bitmap field of the TSS. Otherwise, if next doesn't have it, the kernel checks whether prev defined such a bitmap. In this case, the bitmap must be invalidated.

g. Terminates. Like any other function, __switch_to( ) ends by means of a ret assembly language instruction, which loads the eip program counter with the return address stored into the stack. However, the __switch_to( ) function has been invoked simply by jumping into it. Therefore the ret assembly language instruction finds on the stack the address of the instruction shown in the following item and labeled 1, which was pushed by the switch_ to macro. If next was never suspended before because it is being executed for the first time, the function finds the starting address of the ret_from_ fork( ) function (see the section "The clone(), fork(), and vfork() System Calls" later in this chapter).

---

* The 80×86 debug registers allow a process to be monitored by the hardware. Up to four breakpoint areas may be defined. Whenever a monitored process issues a linear address included in one of the breakpoint areas, an exception occurs.

9. Includes a few instructions that restore the contents of the esi, edi, and ebp registers. The first of these three instructions is labeled 1:

```
1:
    popl %ebp
    popl %edi
    popl %esi
```

Notice how these pop instructions refer to the kernel stack of the prev process. They will be executed when the scheduler selects prev as the new process to be executed on the CPU, thus invoking switch_to with prev as the second parameter. Therefore, the esp register points to the prev's Kernel Mode stack.

10. Copies the content of the ebx register (corresponding to the last parameter of the switch_to macro) into the prev local variable:

```
movl %ebx,prev
```

As discussed earlier, the ebx register points to the descriptor of the process that has just been replaced.

Saving the FPU, MMX, and XMM Registers

Starting with the Intel 80486, the arithmetic floating-point unit (FPU) has been integrated into the CPU. The name *mathematical coprocessor* continues to be used in memory of the days when floating-point computations were executed by an expensive special-purpose chip. To maintain compatibility with older models, however, floating-point arithmetic functions are performed with *ESCAPE instructions*, which are instructions with a prefix byte ranging between 0xd8 and 0xdf. These instructions act on the set of floating point registers included in the CPU. Clearly, if a process is using ESCAPE instructions, the contents of the floating point registers belong to its hardware context.

In later Pentium models, Intel introduced a new set of assembly language instructions into its microprocessors. They are called *MMX instructions* and are supposed to speed up the execution of multimedia applications. MMX instructions act on the floating point registers of the FPU. The obvious disadvantage of this architectural choice is that programmers cannot mix floating-point instructions and MMX instructions. The advantage is that operating system designers can ignore the new instruction set, since the same facility of the task-switching code for saving the state of the floating-point unit can also be relied upon to save the MMX state.

MMX instructions speed up multimedia applications because they introduce a single-instruction multiple-data (SIMD) pipeline inside the processor. The Pentium III model extends such SIMD capability: it introduces the *SSE extensions* (Streaming SIMD Extensions), which adds facilities for handling floating-point values contained in eight 128-bit registers (the XMM registers). Such registers do not overlap with the FPU and MMX registers, so SSE and FPU/MMX instructions may be freely mixed. The Pentium 4 model introduces yet another feature: the SSE2 extensions, which is basically an extension of SSE supporting higher-precision floating-point values. SSE2 uses the same set of XMM registers as SSE.

The 80×86 microprocessors do not automatically save the FPU, MMX, and XMM registers in the TSS. However, they include some hardware support that enables kernels to save these registers only when needed. The hardware support consists of a TS (Task-Switching) flag in the cr0 register, which obeys the following rules:

- Every time a hardware context switch is performed, the TS flag is set.
- Every time an ESCAPE, MMX, SSE, or SSE2 instruction is executed when the TS flag is set, the control unit raises a "Device not available" exception (see Chapter 4).

The TS flag allows the kernel to save and restore the FPU, MMX, and XMM registers only when really needed. To illustrate how it works, suppose that a process A is using the mathematical coprocessor. When a context switch occurs, the kernel sets the TS flag and saves the floating point registers into the TSS of process A. If the new process B does not use the mathematical coprocessor, the kernel won't need to restore the contents of the floating point registers. But as soon as B tries to execute an ESCAPE or MMX instruction, the CPU raises a "Device not available" exception, and the corresponding handler loads the floating point registers with the values saved in the TSS of process B.

Let's now describe the data structures introduced to handle selective loading of the FPU, MMX, and XMM registers. They are stored in the thread.i387 subfield of the process descriptor, whose format is described by the i387_union union:

```
union i387_union {
    struct i387_fsave_struct    fsave;
    struct i387_fxsave_struct   fxsave;
    struct i387_soft_struct     soft;
};
```

As you see, the field may store just one of three different types of data structures. The i387_soft_struct type is used by CPU models without a mathematical coprocessor; the Linux kernel still supports these old chips by emulating the coprocessor via software. We don't discuss this legacy case further, however. The i387_fsave_struct type is used by CPU models with a mathematical coprocessor and, optionally, a MMX unit. Finally, the i387_fxsave_struct type is used by CPU models featuring SSE and SSE2 extensions.

The process descriptor includes two additional flags:

- The PF_USEDFPU flag, which is included in the flags field. It specifies whether the process used the FPU, MMX, or XMM registers in the current execution run.
- The used_math field. This flag specifies whether the contents of the thread.i387 subfield are significant. The flag is cleared (not significant) in two cases, shown in the following list.

— When the process starts executing a new program by invoking an execve( ) system call (see Chapter 20). Since control will never return to the former program, the data currently stored in thread.i387 is never used again.

— When a process that was executing a program in User Mode starts executing a signal handler procedure (see Chapter 10). Since signal handlers are asynchronous with respect to the program execution flow, the floating point registers could be meaningless to the signal handler. However, the kernel saves the floating point registers in thread.i387 before starting the handler and restores them after the handler terminates. Therefore, a signal handler is allowed to use the mathematical coprocessor, but it cannot carry on a floating-point computation started during the normal program execution flow.

As stated earlier, the __switch_to( ) function executes the unlazy_fpu macro, passing the process descriptor of the process being replaced as an argument. The macro checks the value of the PF_USEDFPU flags of prev. If the flag is set, prev has used a FPU, MMX, SSE, or SSE2 instructions in this run of execution; therefore, the kernel must save the relative hardware context:

```
if (prev->flags & PF_USEDFPU)
    save_init_fpu(prev);
```

The save_init_fpu( ) function, in turn, executes the following operations:

1. Dumps the contents of the FPU registers in the process descriptor of prev and then re-initializes the FPU. If the CPU uses SSE/SSE2 extensions, it also dumps the contents of the XMM registers and re-initialize the SSE/SSE2 unit. A couple of powerful assembly language instructions take care of everything, either:

   ```
   asm volatile( "fxsave %0 ; fnclex"
       : "=m" (tsk->thread.i387.fxsave) );
   ```

   if the CPU uses SSE/SSE2 extensions, or otherwise:

   ```
   asm volatile( "fnsave %0 ; fwait"
       : "=m" (tsk->thread.i387.fsave) );
   ```

2. Resets the PF_USEDFPU flag of prev:

   ```
   prev->flags &= ~PF_USEDFPU;
   ```

3. Sets the TS flag of cr0 by means of the stts( ) macro, which in practice yields the following assembly language instructions:

   ```
   movl %cr0, %eax
   orl $8,%eax
   movl %eax, %cr0
   ```

The contents of the floating point registers are not restored right after a process resumes execution. However, the TS flag of cr0 has been set by unlazy_fpu( ). Thus, the first time the process tries to execute an ESCAPE, MMX, or SSE/SSE2 instruction, the control unit raises a "Device not available" exception, and the kernel (more precisely, the exception handler involved by the exception) runs the math_state_ restore( ) function:

```
void math_state_restore()
{
    asm("clts"); /* clear the TS flag of cr0 */
    if (current->used_math) {
        restore_fpu(current);
    } else {
        /* initialize the FPU unit */
        asm("fninit");
        /* and also the SSE/SSE2 unit, if present */
        if ( cpu_has_xmm )
            load_mxcsr(0x1f80);
        current->used_math = 1;
    }
    current->flags |= PF_USEDFPU;
}
```

Since the process is executing an FPU, MMX, or SSE/SSE2 instruction, this function sets the PF_USEDFPU flag. Moreover, the function clears the TS flags of cr0 so that further FPU, MMX, or SSE/SSE2 instructions executed by the process won't trigger the "Device is not available" exception. If the data stored in the thread.i387 field is valid, the restore_fpu( ) function loads the registers with the proper values. To do this, either the fxrstor or the frstor assembly language instructions are used, depending on whether the CPU supports SSE/SSE2 extensions. Otherwise, if the data stored in the thread.i387 field is not valid, the FPU/MMX unit is re-initialized and all its registers are cleared. To re-initialize the SSE/SSE2 unit, it is sufficient to load a value in a XMM register.

Creating Processes

Unix operating systems rely heavily on process creation to satisfy user requests. For example, the shell creates a new process that executes another copy of the shell whenever the user enters a command.

Traditional Unix systems treat all processes in the same way: resources owned by the parent process are duplicated in the child process. This approach makes process creation very slow and inefficient, since it requires copying the entire address space of the parent process. The child process rarely needs to read or modify all the resources inherited from the parent; in many cases, it issues an immediate execve( ) and wipes out the address space that was so carefully copied.

Modern Unix kernels solve this problem by introducing three different mechanisms:

- The Copy On Write technique allows both the parent and the child to read the same physical pages. Whenever either one tries to write on a physical page, the kernel copies its contents into a new physical page that is assigned to the writing process. The implementation of this technique in Linux is fully explained in Chapter 8.

- Lightweight processes allow both the parent and the child to share many per-process kernel data structures, such as the paging tables (and therefore the entire User Mode address space), the open file tables, and the signal dispositions.

- The vfork( ) system call creates a process that shares the memory address space of its parent. To prevent the parent from overwriting data needed by the child, the parent's execution is blocked until the child exits or executes a new program. We'll learn more about the vfork( ) system call in the following section.

The clone( ), fork( ), and vfork( ) System Calls

Lightweight processes are created in Linux by using a function named clone( ), which uses four parameters:

fn

> Specifies a function to be executed by the new process; when the function returns, the child terminates. The function returns an integer, which represents the exit code for the child process.

arg

> Points to data passed to the fn( ) function.

flags

> Miscellaneous information. The low byte specifies the signal number to be sent to the parent process when the child terminates; the SIGCHLD signal is generally selected. The remaining three bytes encode a group of clone flags, which specify the resources to be shared between the parent and the child process as follows:

CLONE_VM

> Shares the memory descriptor and all Page Tables (see Chapter 8).

CLONE_FS

> Shares the table that identifies the root directory and the current working directory, as well as the value of the bitmask used to mask the initial file permissions of a new file (the so-called file *umask*).

CLONE_FILES

> Shares the table that identifies the open files (see Chapter 12).

CLONE_PARENT

> Sets the parent of the child (p_pptr and p_opptr fields in the process descriptor) to the parent of the calling process.

CLONE_PID

> Shares the PID.*

---

* As we shall see later, the CLONE_PID flag can be used only by a process having a PID of 0; in a uniprocessor system, no two lightweight processes have the same PID.

CLONE_PTRACE

> If a ptrace( ) system call is causing the parent process to be traced, the child will also be traced.

CLONE_SIGHAND

> Shares the table that identifies the signal handlers (see Chapter 10).

CLONE_THREAD

> Inserts the child into the same thread group of the parent, and the child's tgid field is set accordingly. If this flag is true, it implicitly enforces CLONE_PARENT.

CLONE_SIGNAL

> Equivalent to setting both CLONE_SIGHAND and CLONE_THREAD, so that it is possible to send a signal to all threads of a multithreaded application.

CLONE_VFORK

> Used for the vfork( ) system call (see later in this section).

child_stack

> Specifies the User Mode stack pointer to be assigned to the esp register of the child process. If it is equal to 0, the kernel assigns the current parent stack pointer to the child. Therefore, the parent and child temporarily share the same User Mode stack. But thanks to the Copy On Write mechanism, they usually get separate copies of the User Mode stack as soon as one tries to change the stack. However, this parameter must have a non-null value if the child process shares the same address space as the parent.

clone( ) is actually a wrapper function defined in the C library (see the section "POSIX APIs and System Calls" in Chapter 9), which in turn uses a clone( ) system call hidden to the programmer. This system call receives only the flags and child_stack parameters; the new process always starts its execution from the instruction following the system call invocation. When the system call returns to the clone( ) function, it determines whether it is in the parent or the child and forces the child to execute the fn( ) function.

The traditional fork( ) system call is implemented by Linux as a clone( ) system call whose flags parameter specifies both a SIGCHLD signal and all the clone flags cleared, and whose child_stack parameter is 0.

The vfork( ) system call, described in the previous section, is implemented by Linux as a clone( ) system call whose first parameter specifies both a SIGCHLD signal and the flags CLONE_VM and CLONE_VFORK, and whose second parameter is equal to 0.

When either a clone( ), fork( ), or vfork( ) system call is issued, the kernel invokes the do_fork( ) function, which executes the following steps:

1. If the CLONE_PID flag is specified, the do_fork( ) function checks whether the PID of the parent process is not 0; if so, it returns an error code. Only the *swapper* process is allowed to set CLONE_PID; this is required when initializing a multiprocessor system.

2. The `alloc_task_struct( )` function is invoked to get a new 8 KB union `task_union` memory area to store the process descriptor and the Kernel Mode stack of the new process.

3. The function follows the `current` pointer to obtain the parent process descriptor and copies it into the new process descriptor in the memory area just allocated.

4. A few checks occur to make sure the user has the resources necessary to start a new process. First, the function checks whether `current->rlim[RLIMIT_NPROC]`. `rlim_cur` is smaller than or equal to the current number of processes owned by the user. If so, an error code is returned, unless the process has root privileges. The function gets the current number of processes owned by the user from a per-user data structure named `user_struct`. This data structure can be found through a pointer in the `user` field of the process descriptor.

5. The function checks that the number of processes is smaller than the value of the `max_threads` variable. The initial value of this variable depends on the amount of RAM in the system. The general rule is that the space taken by all process descriptors and Kernel Mode stacks cannot exceed 1/8 of the physical memory. However, the system administrator may change this value by writing in the */proc/sys/kernel/threads-max* file.

6. If the parent process uses any kernel modules, the function increments the corresponding reference counters. As we shall see in Appendix B, each kernel module has its own reference counter, which ensures that the module will not be unloaded while it is being used.

7. The function then updates some of the flags included in the `flags` field that have been copied from the parent process:

    a. It clears the `PF_SUPERPRIV` flag, which indicates whether the process has used any of its superuser privileges.

    b. It clears the `PF_USEDFPU` flag.

    c. It sets the `PF_FORKNOEXEC` flag, which indicates that the child process has not yet issued an execve( ) system call.

8. Now the function has taken almost everything that it can use from the parent process; the rest of its activities focus on setting up new resources in the child and letting the kernel know that this new process has been born. First, the function invokes the get_pid( ) function to obtain a new PID, which will be assigned to the child process (unless the `CLONE_PID` flag is set).

9. The function then updates all the process descriptor fields that cannot be inherited from the parent process, such as the fields that specify the process parenthood relationships.

10. Unless specified differently by the `flags` parameter, it invokes copy_files( ), copy_fs( ), copy_sighand( ), and copy_mm( ) to create new data structures and copy into them the values of the corresponding parent process data structures.

11. The do_fork() function invokes copy_thread() to initialize the Kernel Mode stack of the child process with the values contained in the CPU registers when the clone() call was issued (these values have been saved in the Kernel Mode stack of the parent, as described in Chapter 9). However, the function forces the value 0 into the field corresponding to the eax register. The thread.esp field in the descriptor of the child process is initialized with the base address of the child's Kernel Mode stack, and the address of an assembly language function (ret_from_fork()) is stored in the thread.eip field. The copy_thread() function also invokes unlazy_fpu() on the parent and duplicates the contents of the thread.i387 field.

12. If either CLONE_THREAD or CLONE_PARENT is set, the function copies the value of the p_opptr and p_pptr fields of the parent into the corresponding fields of the child. The parent of the child thus appears as the parent of the current process. Otherwise, the function stores the process descriptor address of current into the p_opptr and p_pptr fields of the child.

13. If the CLONE_PTRACE flag is not set, the function sets the ptrace field in the child process descriptor to 0. This field stores a few flags used when a process is being traced by another process. Even if the current process is being traced, the child will not.

14. Conversely, if the CLONE_PTRACE flag is set, the function checks whether the parent process is being traced because in this case, the child should be traced too. Therefore, if PT_PTRACED is set in current->ptrace, the function copies the current->p_pptr field into the corresponding field of the child.

15. The do_fork() function checks the value of CLONE_THREAD. If the flag is set, the function inserts the child in the thread group of the parent and copies in the tgid field the value of the parent's tgid; otherwise, the function sets the tgid field to the value of the pid field.

16. The function uses the SET_LINKS macro to insert the new process descriptor in the process list.

17. The function invokes hash_pid() to insert the new process descriptor in the pidhash hash table.

18. The function increments the values of nr_threads and current->user->processes.

19. If the child is being traced, the function sends a SIGSTOP signal to it so that the debugger has a chance to look at it before it starts the execution.

20. It invokes wake_up_process() to set the state field of the child process descriptor to TASK_RUNNING and to insert the child in the runqueue list.

21. If the CLONE_VFORK flag is specified, the function inserts the parent process in a wait queue and suspends it until the child releases its memory address space (that is, until the child either terminates or executes a new program).

22. The do_fork() function returns the PID of the child, which is eventually read by the parent process in User Mode.

Now we have a complete child process in the runnable state. But it isn't actually running. It is up to the scheduler to decide when to give the CPU to this child. At some future process switch, the schedule bestows this favor on the child process by loading a few CPU registers with the values of the thread field of the child's process descriptor. In particular, esp is loaded with thread.esp (that is, with the address of child's Kernel Mode stack), and eip is loaded with the address of ret_from_fork( ). This assembly language function, in turn, invokes the ret_from_sys_call( ) function (see Chapter 9), which reloads all other registers with the values stored in the stack and forces the CPU back to User Mode. The new process then starts its execution right at the end of the fork( ), vfork( ), or clone( ) system call. The value returned by the system call is contained in eax: the value is 0 for the child and equal to the PID for the child's parent.

The child process executes the same code as the parent, except that the fork returns a 0. The developer of the application can exploit this fact, in a manner familiar to Unix programmers, by inserting a conditional statement in the program based on the PID value that forces the child to behave differently from the parent process.

Kernel Threads

Traditional Unix systems delegate some critical tasks to intermittently running processes, including flushing disk caches, swapping out unused page frames, servicing network connections, and so on. Indeed, it is not efficient to perform these tasks in strict linear fashion; both their functions and the end user processes get better responses if they are scheduled in the background. Since some of the system processes run only in Kernel Mode, modern operating systems delegate their functions to *kernel threads*, which are not encumbered with the unnecessary User Mode context. In Linux, kernel threads differ from regular processes in the following ways:

- Each kernel thread executes a single specific kernel C function, while regular processes execute kernel functions only through system calls.

- Kernel threads run only in Kernel Mode, while regular processes run alternatively in Kernel Mode and in User Mode.

- Since kernel threads run only in Kernel Mode, they use only linear addresses greater than PAGE_OFFSET. Regular processes, on the other hand, use all four gigabytes of linear addresses, in either User Mode or Kernel Mode.

Creating a kernel thread

The kernel_thread( ) function creates a new kernel thread and can be executed only by another kernel thread. The function contains mostly inline assembly language code, but it is roughly equivalent to the following:

```
int kernel_thread(int (*fn)(void *), void * arg, unsigned long flags)
{
    int p;
```

```
    p - clonc( 0, flags | CLONE_VM );
    if ( p )        /* parent */
        return p;
    else {          /* child */
        fn(arg);
        exit( );
    }
}
```

Process 0

The ancestor of all processes, called *process 0* or, for historical reasons, the *swapper process*, is a kernel thread created from scratch during the initialization phase of Linux by the start_kernel( ) function (see Appendix A). This ancestor process uses the following data structures:

- A process descriptor and a Kernel Mode stack stored in the init_task_union variable. The init_task and init_stack macros yield the addresses of the process descriptor and the stack, respectively.
- The following tables, which the process descriptor points to:
  — init_mm
  — init_fs
  — init_files
  — init_signals

  The tables are initialized, respectively, by the following macros:
  — INIT_MM
  — INIT_FS
  — INIT_FILES
  — INIT_SIGNALS
- The master kernel Page Global Directory stored in swapper_pg_dir (see the section "Kernel Page Tables" in Chapter 2).

The start_kernel( ) function initializes all the data structures needed by the kernel, enables interrupts, and creates another kernel thread, named *process 1* (more commonly referred to as the *init process*):

```
kernel_thread(init, NULL, CLONE_FS | CLONE_FILES | CLONE_SIGNAL);
```

The newly created kernel thread has PID 1 and shares all per-process kernel data structures with process 0. Moreover, when selected from the scheduler, the *init* process starts executing the init( ) function.

After having created the *init* process, process 0 executes the cpu_idle( ) function, which essentially consists of repeatedly executing the hlt assembly language instruction with the interrupts enabled (see Chapter 4). Process 0 is selected by the scheduler only when there are no other processes in the TASK_RUNNING state.

Process 1

The kernel thread created by process 0 executes the init( ) function, which in turn completes the initialization of the kernel. Then init( ) invokes the execve( ) system call to load the executable program *init*. As a result, the *init* kernel thread becomes a regular process having its own per-process kernel data structure (see Chapter 20). The *init* process stays alive until the system is shut down, since it creates and monitors the activity of all processes that implement the outer layers of the operating system.

Other kernel threads

Linux uses many other kernel threads. Some of them are created in the initialization phase and run until shutdown; others are created "on demand," when the kernel must execute a task that is better performed in its own execution context.

The most important kernel threads (beside process 0 and process 1) are:

keventd
> Executes the tasks in the qt_context task queue (see the section "Bottom Halves" in Chapter 4).

kapm
> Handles the events related to the Advanced Power Management (APM).

kswapd
> Performs memory reclaiming, as described in the section "The kswapd Kernel Thread" in Chapter 16.

kflushd (also bdflush)
> Flushes "dirty" buffers to disk to reclaim memory, as described in the section "Writing Dirty Buffers to Disk" in Chapter 14.

kupdated
> Flushes old "dirty" buffers to disk to reduce risks of filesystem inconsistencies, as described in the section "Writing Dirty Buffers to Disk" in Chapter 14.

ksoftirqd
> Runs the tasklets (see section "Softirqs, Tasklets, and Bottom Halves" in Chapter 4); there is one kernel thread for each CPU in the system.

Destroying Processes

Most processes "die" in the sense that they terminate the execution of the code they were supposed to run. When this occurs, the kernel must be notified so that it can release the resources owned by the process; this includes memory, open files, and any other odds and ends that we will encounter in this book, such as semaphores.

The usual way for a process to terminate is to invoke the exit( ) library function, which releases the resources allocated by the C library, executes each function registered by the programmer, and ends up invoking the _exit( ) system call. The exit( )

function may be inserted by the programmer explicitly. Additionally, the C compiler always inserts an exit( ) function call right after the last statement of the main( ) function.

Alternatively, the kernel may force a process to die. This typically occurs when the process has received a signal that it cannot handle or ignore (see Chapter 10) or when an unrecoverable CPU exception has been raised in Kernel Mode while the kernel was running on behalf of the process (see Chapter 4).

Process Termination

All process terminations are handled by the do_exit( ) function, which removes most references to the terminating process from kernel data structures. The do_exit( ) function executes the following actions:

1. Sets the PF_EXITING flag in the flag field of the process descriptor to indicate that the process is being eliminated.

2. Removes, if necessary, the process descriptor from an IPC semaphore queue via the sem_exit( ) function (see Chapter 19) or from a dynamic timer queue via the del_timer_sync( ) function (see Chapter 6).

3. Examines the process's data structures related to paging, filesystem, open file descriptors, and signal handling, respectively, with the __exit_mm( ), __exit_files( ), __exit_fs( ), and exit_sighand( ) functions. These functions also remove each of these data structures if no other process are sharing them.

4. Decrements the resource counters of the modules used by the process.

5. Sets the exit_code field of the process descriptor to the process termination code. This value is either the _exit( ) system call parameter (normal termination), or an error code supplied by the kernel (abnormal termination).

6. Invokes the exit_notify( ) function to update the parenthood relationships of both the parent process and the child processes. All child processes created by the terminating process become children of another process in the same thread group, if any, or of the *init* process. Moreover, exit_notify( ) sets the state field of the process descriptor to TASK_ZOMBIE. We shall see what happens to zombie processes in the following section.

7. Invokes the schedule( ) function (see Chapter 11) to select a new process to run. Since a process in a TASK_ZOMBIE state is ignored by the scheduler, the process stops executing right after the switch_to macro in schedule( ) is invoked.

Process Removal

The Unix operating system allows a process to query the kernel to obtain the PID of its parent process or the execution state of any of its children. A process may, for instance, create a child process to perform a specific task and then invoke a wait( )-like system call to check whether the child has terminated. If the child has terminated, its termination code will tell the parent process if the task has been carried out successfully.

To comply with these design choices, Unix kernels are not allowed to discard data included in a process descriptor field right after the process terminates. They are allowed to do so only after the parent process has issued a wait( )-like system call that refers to the terminated process. This is why the TASK_ZOMBIE state has been introduced: although the process is technically dead, its descriptor must be saved until the parent process is notified.

What happens if parent processes terminate before their children? In such a case, the system could be flooded with zombie processes that might end up using all the available task entries. As mentioned earlier, this problem is solved by forcing all orphan processes to become children of the *init* process. In this way, the *init* process will destroy the zombies while checking for the termination of one of its legitimate children through a wait( )-like system call.

The release_task( ) function releases the process descriptor of a zombie process by executing the following steps:

1. Decrements by 1 the number of processes created up to now by the user owner of the terminated process. This value is stored in the user_struct structure mentioned earlier in the chapter.

2. Invokes the free_uid( ) function to decrement by 1 the resource counter of the user_struct structure.

3. Invokes unhash_process( ), which in turn:
   a. Decrements by 1 the nr_threads variable
   b. Invokes unhash_pid( ) to remove the process descriptor from the pidhash hash table
   c. Uses the REMOVE_LINKS macro to unlink the process descriptor from the process list
   d. Removes the process from its thread group, if any

4. Invokes the free_task_struct( ) function to release the 8-KB memory area used to contain the process descriptor and the Kernel Mode stack.

CHAPTER 4

Interrupts and Exceptions

An *interrupt* is usually defined as an event that alters the sequence of instructions executed by a processor. Such events correspond to electrical signals generated by hardware circuits both inside and outside the CPU chip.

Interrupts are often divided into *synchronous* and *asynchronous* interrupts:

- *Synchronous* interrupts are produced by the CPU control unit while executing instructions and are called synchronous because the control unit issues them only after terminating the execution of an instruction.

- *Asynchronous* interrupts are generated by other hardware devices at arbitrary times with respect to the CPU clock signals.

Intel microprocessor manuals designate synchronous and asynchronous interrupts as *exceptions* and *interrupts*, respectively. We'll adopt this classification, although we'll occasionally use the term "interrupt signal" to designate both types together (synchronous as well as asynchronous).

Interrupts are issued by interval timers and I/O devices; for instance, the arrival of a keystroke from a user sets off an interrupt. Exceptions, on the other hand, are caused either by programming errors or by anomalous conditions that must be handled by the kernel. In the first case, the kernel handles the exception by delivering to the current process one of the signals familiar to every Unix programmer. In the second case, the kernel performs all the steps needed to recover from the anomalous condition, such as a Page Fault or a request (via an int instruction) for a kernel service.

We start by describing in the next section the motivation for introducing such signals. We then show how the well-known IRQs (Interrupt ReQuests) issued by I/O devices give rise to interrupts, and we detail how 80×86 processors handle interrupts and exceptions at the hardware level. Then we illustrate, in the section "Initializing the Interrupt Descriptor Table," how Linux initializes all the data structures required by the Intel interrupt architecture. The remaining three sections describe how Linux handles interrupt signals at the software level.

One word of caution before moving on: in this chapter, we cover only "classic" interrupts common to all PCs; we do not cover the nonstandard interrupts of some architectures. For instance, laptops generate types of interrupts not discussed here.

The Role of Interrupt Signals

As the name suggests, interrupt signals provide a way to divert the processor to code outside the normal flow of control. When an interrupt signal arrives, the CPU must stop what it's currently doing and switch to a new activity; it does this by saving the current value of the program counter (i.e., the content of the eip and cs registers) in the Kernel Mode stack and by placing an address related to the interrupt type into the program counter.

There are some things in this chapter that will remind you of the context switch described in the previous chapter, carried out when a kernel substitutes one process for another. But there is a key difference between interrupt handling and process switching: the code executed by an interrupt or by an exception handler is not a process. Rather, it is a kernel control path that runs on behalf of the same process that was running when the interrupt occurred (see the later section "Nested Execution of Exception and Interrupt Handlers"). As a kernel control path, the interrupt handler is lighter than a process (it has less context and requires less time to set up or tear down).

Interrupt handling is one of the most sensitive tasks performed by the kernel, since it must satisfy the following constraints:

- Interrupts can come at any time, when the kernel may want to finish something else it was trying to do. The kernel's goal is therefore to get the interrupt out of the way as soon as possible and defer as much processing as it can. For instance, suppose a block of data has arrived on a network line. When the hardware interrupts the kernel, it could simply mark the presence of data, give the processor back to whatever was running before, and do the rest of the processing later (such as moving the data into a buffer where its recipient process can find it and then restarting the process). The activities that the kernel needs to perform in response to an interrupt are thus divided into two parts: a *top half* that the kernel executes right away and a *bottom half* that is left for later. The kernel keeps a queue pointing to all the functions that represent bottom halves waiting to be executed and pulls them off the queue to execute them at particular points in processing.

- Since interrupts can come at any time, the kernel might be handling one of them while another one (of a different type) occurs. This should be allowed as much as possible since it keeps the I/O devices busy (see the later section "Nested Execution of Exception and Interrupt Handlers"). As a result, the interrupt handlers must be coded so that the corresponding kernel control paths can be executed in a nested manner. When the last kernel control path terminates, the kernel must be able to resume execution of the interrupted process or switch to another process if the interrupt signal has caused a rescheduling activity.

- Although the kernel may accept a new interrupt signal while handling a previous one, some critical regions exist inside the kernel code where interrupts must be disabled. Such critical regions must be limited as much as possible since, according to the previous requirement, the kernel, and particularly the interrupt handlers, should run most of the time with the interrupts enabled.

Interrupts and Exceptions

The Intel documentation classifies interrupts and exceptions as follows:

- Interrupts:

    Maskable interrupts

    All Interrupt Requests (IRQs) issued by I/O devices give rise to maskable interrupts. A maskable interrupt can be in two states: masked or unmasked; a masked interrupt is ignored by the control unit as long as it remains masked.

    Nonmaskable interrupts

    Only a few critical events (such as hardware failures) give rise to nonmaskable interrupts. Nonmaskable interrupts are always recognized by the CPU.

- Exceptions:

    Processor-detected exceptions

    Generated when the CPU detects an anomalous condition while executing an instruction. These are further divided into three groups, depending on the value of the eip register that is saved on the Kernel Mode stack when the CPU control unit raises the exception.

    Faults

    Can generally be corrected; once corrected, the program is allowed to restart with no loss of continuity. The saved value of eip is the address of the instruction that caused the fault, and hence that instruction can be resumed when the exception handler terminates. As we shall see in the section "Page Fault Exception Handler" in Chapter 8, resuming the same instruction is necessary whenever the handler is able to correct the anomalous condition that caused the exception.

    Traps

    Reported immediately following the execution of the trapping instruction; after the kernel returns control to the program, it is allowed to continue its execution with no loss of continuity. The saved value of eip is the address of the instruction that should be executed after the one that caused the trap. A trap is triggered only when there is no need to reexecute the instruction that terminated. The main use of traps is for debugging purposes. The role of the interrupt signal in this case is to notify the debugger that a specific instruction has been executed (for instance, a breakpoint has been reached within a program). Once the user has examined the data provided by the debugger, she may ask that execution of the debugged program resume, starting from the next instruction.

Aborts

A serious error occurred; the control unit is in trouble, and it may be unable to store in the eip register the precise location of the instruction causing the exception. Aborts are used to report severe errors, such as hardware failures and invalid or inconsistent values in system tables. The interrupt signal sent by the control unit is an emergency signal used to switch control to the corresponding abort exception handler. This handler has no choice but to force the affected process to terminate.

Programmed exceptions

Occur at the request of the programmer. They are triggered by int or int3 instructions; the into (check for overflow) and bound (check on address bound) instructions also give rise to a programmed exception when the condition they are checking is not true. Programmed exceptions are handled by the control unit as traps; they are often called *software interrupts*. Such exceptions have two common uses: to implement system calls and to notify a debugger of a specific event (see Chapter 9).

Each interrupt or exception is identified by a number ranging from 0 to 255; Intel calls this 8-bit unsigned number a *vector*. The vectors of nonmaskable interrupts and exceptions are fixed, while those of maskable interrupts can be altered by programming the Interrupt Controller (see the next section).

IRQs and Interrupts

Each hardware device controller capable of issuing interrupt requests has an output line designated as an Interrupt ReQuest (*IRQ*). All existing IRQ lines are connected to the input pins of a hardware circuit called the *Interrupt Controller*, which performs the following actions:

1. Monitors the IRQ lines, checking for raised signals.
2. If a raised signal occurs on an IRQ line:
   a. Converts the raised signal received into a corresponding vector.
   b. Stores the vector in an Interrupt Controller I/O port, thus allowing the CPU to read it via the data bus.
   c. Sends a raised signal to the processor INTR pin—that is, issues an interrupt.
   d. Waits until the CPU acknowledges the interrupt signal by writing into one of the Programmable Interrupt Controllers (PIC) I/O ports; when this occurs, clears the INTR line.
3. Goes back to Step 1.

The IRQ lines are sequentially numbered starting from 0; therefore, the first IRQ line is usually denoted as IRQ0. Intel's default vector associated with IRQn is $n+32$. As mentioned before, the mapping between IRQs and vectors can be modified by issuing suitable I/O instructions to the Interrupt Controller ports.

Each IRQ line can be selectively disabled. Thus, the PIC can be programmed to disable IRQs. That is, the PIC can be told to stop issuing interrupts that refer to a given IRQ line, or to enable them. Disabled interrupts are not lost; the PIC sends them to the CPU as soon as they are enabled again. This feature is used by most interrupt handlers since it allows them to process IRQs of the same type serially.

Selective enabling/disabling of IRQs is not the same as global masking/unmasking of maskable interrupts. When the IF flag of the eflags register is clear, each maskable interrupt issued by the PIC is temporarily ignored by the CPU. The cli and sti assembly language instructions, respectively, clear and set that flag. Masking and unmasking interrupts on a multiprocessor system is trickier since each CPU has its own eflags register. We'll deal with this topic in Chapter 5.

Traditional PICs are implemented by connecting "in cascade" two 8259A-style external chips. Each chip can handle up to eight different IRQ input lines. Since the INT output line of the slave PIC is connected to the IRQ2 pin of the master PIC, the number of available IRQ lines is limited to 15.

The Advanced Programmable Interrupt Controller (APIC)

The previous description refers to PICs designed for uniprocessor systems. If the system includes a single CPU, the output line of the master PIC can be connected in a straightforward way to the INTR pin the CPU. However, if the system includes two or more CPUs, this approach is no longer valid and more sophisticated PICs are needed.

Being able to deliver interrupts to each CPU in the system is crucial for fully exploiting the parallelism of the SMP architecture. For that reason, Intel has introduced a new component designated as the *I/O Advanced Programmable Interrupt Controller (I/O APIC)*, which replaces the old 8259A Programmable Interrupt Controller. Moreover, all current Intel CPUs include a *local APIC*. Each Local APIC has 32-bit registers, an internal clock, a local timer device, and two additional IRQ lines LINT0 and LINT1 reserved for local interrupts. All local APICs are connected to an external I/O APIC, giving raise to a multi-APIC system.

Figure 4-1 illustrates in a schematic way the structure of a multi-APIC system. An *APIC bus* connects the "frontend" I/O APIC to the local APICs. The IRQ lines coming from the devices are connected to the I/O APIC, which therefore acts as a router with respect to the local APICs. In the motherboards of the Pentium III and earlier processors, the APIC bus was a serial three-line bus; starting with the Pentium 4, the APIC bus is implemented by means of the system bus. However, since the APIC bus and its messages are invisible to software, we won't give further details.

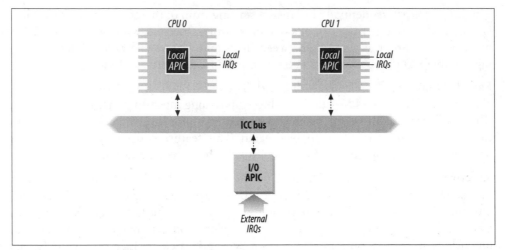

Figure 4-1. Multi-APIC system

The I/O APIC consists of a set of 24 IRQ lines, a 24-entry *Interrupt Redirection Table*, programmable registers, and a message unit for sending and receiving APIC messages over the APIC bus. Unlike IRQ pins of the 8259A, interrupt priority is not related to pin number: each entry in the Redirection Table can be individually programmed to indicate the interrupt vector and priority, the destination processor, and how the processor is selected. The information in the Redirection Table is used to translate each external IRQ signal into a message to one or more local APIC units via the APIC bus.

Interrupt requests coming from external hardware devices can be distributed among the available CPUs in two ways:

Static distribution

> The IRQ signal is delivered to the local APICs listed in the corresponding Redirection Table entry. The interrupt is delivered to one specific CPU, to a subset of CPUs, or to all CPUs at once (broadcast mode).

Dynamic distribution

> The IRQ signal is delivered to the local APIC of the processor that is executing the process with the lowest priority.

> Any local APIC has a programmable *task priority register* (TPR), which is used to compute the priority of the currently running process. Intel expects this register to be modified in an operating system kernel by each process switch.

> If two or more CPUs share the lowest priority, the load is distributed between them using a technique called *arbitration*. Each CPU is assigned an arbitration priority ranging from 0 to 15 in the arbitration priority register of the local APIC. Every local APIC has a unique value

> Every time an interrupt is delivered to a CPU, its corresponding arbitration priority is automatically set to 0, while the arbitration priorities of every other CPU

is incremented. When the arbitration priority register becomes greater than 15, it is set to the previous arbitration priority of the winning CPU incremented by 1. Therefore, interrupts are distributed in a round-robin fashion among CPUs with the same task priority.*

Besides distributing interrupts among processors, the multi-APIC system allows CPUs to generate *interprocessor interrupts*. When a CPU wishes to send an interrupt to another CPU, it stores the interrupt vector and the identifier of the target's local APIC in the Interrupt Command Register (ICR) of its own local APIC. A message is then sent via the APIC bus to the target's local APIC, which therefore issues a corresponding interrupt to its own CPU.

Interprocessor interrupts (in short, IPIs) are part of the SMP architecture and are actively used by Linux to exchange messages among CPUs (see the section "Interrupt service routines" later in this chapter).

Most of the current uniprocessor systems include an I/O APIC chip, which may be configured in two distinct ways:

- As a standard 8259A-style external PIC connected to the CPU. The local APIC is disabled and the two LINT0 and LINT1 local IRQ lines are configured, respectively, as the INTR and NMI pins.

- As a standard external I/O APIC. The local APIC is enabled and all external interrupts are received through the I/O APIC.

Exceptions

The 80×86 microprocessors issue roughly 20 different exceptions.† The kernel must provide a dedicated exception handler for each exception type. For some exceptions, the CPU control unit also generates a *hardware error code* and pushes it in the Kernel Mode stack before starting the exception handler.

The following list gives the vector, the name, the type, and a brief description of the exceptions found in 80×86 processors. Additional information may be found in the Intel technical documentation.

0 - *"Divide error"* (fault)
Raised when a program issues an integer division by 0.

1 - *"Debug"* (trap or fault)
Raised when the T flag of eflags is set (quite useful to implement step-by-step execution of a debugged program) or when the address of an instruction or

---

* The Pentium 4 local APIC doesn't have an arbitration priority register; the arbitration mechanism is hidden in the bus arbitration circuitry. The Intel manuals state that if the operating system kernel does not regularly update the task priority registers, performances may be suboptimal because interrupts might always be serviced by the same CPU.

† The exact number depends on the processor model.

operand falls within the range of an active debug register (see the section "Hard-ware Context" in Chapter 3).

2 - Not used

Reserved for nonmaskable interrupts (those that use the NMI pin).

3 - "Breakpoint" (trap)

Caused by an int3 (breakpoint) instruction (usually inserted by a debugger).

4 - "Overflow" (trap)

An into (check for overflow) instruction has been executed when the OF (over-flow) flag of eflags is set.

5 - "Bounds check" (fault)

A bound (check on address bound) instruction is executed with the operand out-side of the valid address bounds.

6 - "Invalid opcode" (fault)

The CPU execution unit has detected an invalid opcode (the part of the machine instruction that determines the operation performed).

7 - "Device not available" (fault)

An ESCAPE, MMX, or XMM instruction has been executed with the TS flag of cr0 set (see the section "Saving the FPU, MMX, and XMM Registers" in Chapter 3).

8 - "Double fault" (abort)

Normally, when the CPU detects an exception while trying to call the handler for a prior exception, the two exceptions can be handled serially. In a few cases, however, the processor cannot handle them serially, so it raises this exception.

9 - "Coprocessor segment overrun" (abort)

Problems with the external mathematical coprocessor (applies only to old 80386 microprocessors).

10 - "Invalid TSS" (fault)

The CPU has attempted a context switch to a process having an invalid Task State Segment.

11 - "Segment not present" (fault)

A reference was made to a segment not present in memory (one in which the Segment-Present flag of the Segment Descriptor was cleared).

12 - "Stack segment" (fault)

The instruction attempted to exceed the stack segment limit, or the segment identified by ss is not present in memory.

13 - "General protection" (fault)

One of the protection rules in the protected mode of the 80×86 has been violated.

14 - "Page Fault" (fault)

The addressed page is not present in memory, the corresponding Page Table entry is null, or a violation of the paging protection mechanism has occurred.

15 - Reserved by Intel

16 - "Floating-point error" (fault)

The floating-point unit integrated into the CPU chip has signaled an error condition, such as numeric overflow or division by 0.*

17 - "Alignment check" (fault)

The address of an operand is not correctly aligned (for instance, the address of a long integer is not a multiple of 4).

18 - "Machine check" (abort)

A machine-check mechanism has detected a CPU or bus error.

19 - "SIMD floating point" (fault)

The SSE or SSE2 unit integrated in the CPU chip has signaled an error condition on a floating-point operation.

The values from 20 to 31 are reserved by Intel for future development. As illustrated in Table 4-1, each exception is handled by a specific exception handler (see the section "Exception Handling" later in this chapter), which usually sends a Unix signal to the process that caused the exception.

Table 4-1. Signals sent by the exception handlers

#	Exception	Exception handler	Signal
0	Divide error	divide_error( )	SIGFPE
1	Debug	debug( )	SIGTRAP
2	NMI	nmi( )	None
3	Breakpoint	int3( )	SIGTRAP
4	Overflow	overflow( )	SIGSEGV
5	Bounds check	bounds( )	SIGSEGV
6	Invalid opcode	invalid_op( )	SIGILL
7	Device not available	device_not_available( )	SIGSEGV
8	Double fault	double_fault( )	SIGSEGV
9	Coprocessor segment overrun	coprocessor_segment_overrun( )	SIGFPE
10	Invalid TSS	invalid_tss( )	SIGSEGV
11	Segment not present	segment_not_present( )	SIGBUS
12	Stack exception	stack_segment( )	SIGBUS
13	General protection	general_protection( )	SIGSEGV

---

* The 80×86 microprocessors also generate this exception when performing a signed division whose result cannot be stored as a signed integer (for instance, a division between −2147483648 and −1).

Table 4-1. Signals sent by the exception handlers (continued)

#	Exception	Exception handler	Signal
14	Page Fault	page_fault( )	SIGSEGV
15	Intel reserved	None	None
16	Floating-point error	coprocessor_error( )	SIGFPE
17	Alignment check	alignment_check( )	SIGBUS
18	Machine check	machine_check( )	None
19	SIMD floating point	simd_coprocessor_error( )	SIGFPE

Interrupt Descriptor Table

A system table called *Interrupt Descriptor Table* (IDT) associates each interrupt or exception vector with the address of the corresponding interrupt or exception handler. The IDT must be properly initialized before the kernel enables interrupts.

The IDT format is similar to that of the GDT and the LDTs examined in Chapter 2. Each entry corresponds to an interrupt or an exception vector and consists of an 8-byte descriptor. Thus, a maximum of 256×8=2048 bytes are required to store the IDT.

The idtr CPU register allows the IDT to be located anywhere in memory: it specifies both the IDT base physical address and its limit (maximum length). It must be initialized before enabling interrupts by using the lidt assembly language instruction.

The IDT may include three types of descriptors; Figure 4-2 illustrates the meaning of the 64 bits included in each of them. In particular, the value of the Type field encoded in the bits 40–43 identifies the descriptor type.

The descriptors are:

Task gate
> Includes the TSS selector of the process that must replace the current one when an interrupt signal occurs. Linux does not use task gates.

Interrupt gate
> Includes the Segment Selector and the offset inside the segment of an interrupt or exception handler. While transferring control to the proper segment, the processor clears the IF flag, thus disabling further maskable interrupts.

Trap gate
> Similar to an interrupt gate, except that while transferring control to the proper segment, the processor does not modify the IF flag.

As we shall see in the later section "Interrupt, Trap, and System Gates," Linux uses interrupt gates to handle interrupts and trap gates to handle exceptions.

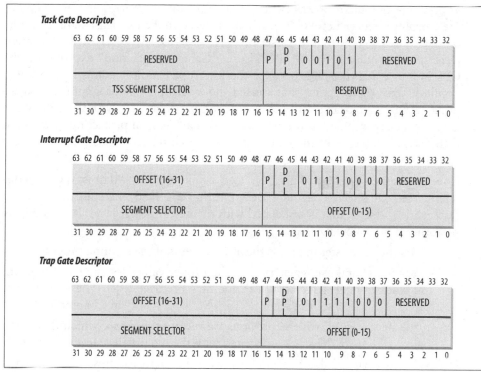

Figure 4-2. Gate descriptors' format

Hardware Handling of Interrupts and Exceptions

We now describe how the CPU control unit handles interrupts and exceptions. We assume that the kernel has been initialized and thus the CPU is operating in Protected Mode.

After executing an instruction, the cs and eip pair of registers contain the logical address of the next instruction to be executed. Before dealing with that instruction, the control unit checks whether an interrupt or an exception occurred while the control unit executed the previous instruction. If one occurred, the control unit does the following:

1. Determines the vector i ($0 \leq i \leq 255$) associated with the interrupt or the exception.

2. Reads the ith entry of the IDT referred by the idtr register (we assume in the following description that the entry contains an interrupt or a trap gate).

3. Gets the base address of the GDT from the gdtr register and looks in the GDT to read the Segment Descriptor identified by the selector in the IDT entry. This descriptor specifies the base address of the segment that includes the interrupt or exception handler.

4. Makes sure the interrupt was issued by an authorized source. First, it compares the Current Privilege Level (CPL), which is stored in the two least significant bits of the cs register, with the Descriptor Privilege Level (DPL) of the Segment Descriptor included in the GDT. Raises a "General protection" exception if the CPL is lower than the DPL because the interrupt handler cannot have a lower privilege than the program that caused the interrupt. For programmed exceptions, it makes a further security check. It compares the CPL with the DPL of the gate descriptor included in the IDT and raises a "General protection" exception if the DPL is lower than the CPL. This last check makes it possible to prevent access by user applications to specific trap or interrupt gates.

5. Checks whether a change of privilege level is taking place—that is, if CPL is different from the selected Segment Descriptor's DPL. If so, the control unit must start using the stack that is associated with the new privilege level. It does this by performing the following steps:

    a. Reads the tr register to access the TSS segment of the running process.

    b. Loads the ss and esp registers with the proper values for the stack segment and stack pointer associated with the new privilege level. These values are found in the TSS (see the section "Task State Segment" in Chapter 3).

    c. In the new stack, saves the previous values of ss and esp, which define the logical address of the stack associated with the old privilege level.

6. If a fault has occurred, loads cs and eip with the logical address of the instruction that caused the exception so that it can be executed again.

7. Saves the contents of eflags, cs, and eip in the stack.

8. If the exception carries a hardware error code, saves it on the stack.

9. Loads cs and eip, respectively, with the Segment Selector and the Offset fields of the Gate Descriptor stored in the ith entry of the IDT. These values define the logical address of the first instruction of the interrupt or exception handler.

The last step performed by the control unit is equivalent to a jump to the interrupt or exception handler. In other words, the instruction processed by the control unit after dealing with the interrupt signal is the first instruction of the selected handler.

After the interrupt or exception is processed, the corresponding handler must relinquish control to the interrupted process by issuing the iret instruction, which forces the control unit to:

1. Load the cs, eip, and eflags registers with the values saved on the stack. If a hardware error code has been pushed in the stack on top of the eip contents, it must be popped before executing iret.

2. Check whether the CPL of the handler is equal to the value contained in the two least significant bits of cs (this means the interrupted process was running at the same privilege level as the handler). If so, iret concludes execution; otherwise, go to the next step.

3. Load the ss and esp registers from the stack and return to the stack associated with the old privilege level.

4. Examine the contents of the ds, es, fs, and gs segment registers; if any of them contains a selector that refers to a Segment Descriptor whose DPL value is lower than CPL, clear the corresponding segment register. The control unit does this to forbid User Mode programs that run with a CPL equal to 3 from using segment registers previously used by kernel routines (with a DPL equal to 0). If these registers were not cleared, malicious User Mode programs could exploit them in order to access the kernel address space.

Nested Execution of Exception and Interrupt Handlers

When handling an interrupt or an exception, the kernel begins a new *kernel control path*, or separate sequence of instructions. When a process issues a system call request, for instance, the first instructions of the corresponding kernel control path are those that save the content of the registers in the Kernel Mode stack, while the last instructions are those that restore the content of the registers and put the CPU back into User Mode.

Linux design does not allow process switching while the CPU is executing a kernel control path associated with an interrupt. However, such kernel control paths may be arbitrarily nested; an interrupt handler may be interrupted by another interrupt handler, thus giving raise to a nested execution of kernel threads. We emphasize that the current process doesn't change while the kernel is handling a nested set of kernel control paths.

Assuming that the kernel is bug free, most exceptions can occur only while the CPU is in User Mode. Indeed, they are either caused by programming errors or triggered by debuggers. However, the Page Fault exception may occur in Kernel Mode. This happens when the process attempts to address a page that belongs to its address space but is not currently in RAM. While handling such an exception, the kernel may suspend the current process and replace it with another one until the requested page is available. The kernel control path that handles the Page fault exception resumes execution as soon as the process gets the processor again.

Since the Page Fault exception handler never gives rise to further exceptions, at most two kernel control paths associated with exceptions (the first one caused by a system call invocation, the second one caused by a Page Fault) may be stacked, one on top of the other.

In contrast to exceptions, interrupts issued by I/O devices do not refer to data structures specific to the current process, although the kernel control paths that handle them run on behalf of that process. As a matter of fact, it is impossible to predict which process will be running when a given interrupt occurs.

An interrupt handler may preempt both other interrupt handlers and exception handlers. Conversely, an exception handler never preempts an interrupt handler. The only exception that can be triggered in Kernel Mode is Page Fault, which we just described. But interrupt handlers never perform operations that can induce Page Faults, and thus, potentially, process switch.

Linux interleaves kernel control paths for two major reasons:

- To improve the throughput of programmable interrupt controllers and device controllers. Assume that a device controller issues a signal on an IRQ line: the PIC transforms it into an external interrupt, and then both the PIC and the device controller remain blocked until the PIC receives an acknowledgment from the CPU. Thanks to kernel control path interleaving, the kernel is able to send the acknowledgment even when it is handling a previous interrupt.

- To implement an interrupt model without priority levels. Since each interrupt handler may be deferred by another one, there is no need to establish predefined priorities among hardware devices. This simplifies the kernel code and improves its portability.

On multiprocessor systems, several kernel control paths may execute concurrently. Moreover, a kernel control path associated with an exception may start executing on a CPU and, due to a process switch, migrate on another CPU.

Initializing the Interrupt Descriptor Table

Now that you understand what the Intel processor does with interrupts and exceptions at the hardware level, we can move on to describe how the Interrupt Descriptor Table is initialized.

Remember that before the kernel enables the interrupts, it must load the initial address of the IDT table into the idtr register and initialize all the entries of that table. This activity is done while initializing the system (see Appendix A).

The int instruction allows a User Mode process to issue an interrupt signal that has an arbitrary vector ranging from 0 to 255. Therefore, initialization of the IDT must be done carefully, to block illegal interrupts and exceptions simulated by User Mode processes via int instructions. This can be achieved by setting the DPL field of the Interrupt or Trap Gate Descriptor to 0. If the process attempts to issue one of these interrupt signals, the control unit checks the CPL value against the DPL field and issues a "General protection" exception.

In a few cases, however, a User Mode process must be able to issue a programmed exception. To allow this, it is sufficient to set the DPL field of the corresponding Interrupt or Trap Gate Descriptors to 3—that is, as high as possible.

Let's now see how Linux implements this strategy.

Interrupt, Trap, and System Gates

As mentioned in the earlier section "Interrupt Descriptor Table," Intel provides three types of interrupt descriptors: Task, Interrupt, and Trap Gate Descriptors. Task Gate Descriptors are irrelevant to Linux, but its Interrupt Descriptor Table contains several Interrupt and Trap Gate Descriptors. Linux classifies them as follows, using a slightly different breakdown and terminology from Intel:

Interrupt gate
> An Intel interrupt gate that cannot be accessed by a User Mode process (the gate's DPL field is equal to 0). All Linux interrupt handlers are activated by means of interrupt gates, and all are restricted to Kernel Mode.

System gate
> An Intel trap gate that can be accessed by a User Mode process (the gate's DPL field is equal to 3). The four Linux exception handlers associated with the vectors 3, 4, 5, and 128 are activated by means of system gates, so the four assembly language instructions int3, into, bound, and int $0x80 can be issued in User Mode.

Trap gate
> An Intel trap gate that cannot be accessed by a User Mode process (the gate's DPL field is equal to 0). Most Linux exception handlers are activated by means of trap gates.

The following architecture-dependent functions are used to insert gates in the IDT:

set_intr_gate(n,addr)
> Inserts an interrupt gate in the nth IDT entry. The Segment Selector inside the gate is set to the kernel code's Segment Selector. The Offset field is set to addr, which is the address of the interrupt handler. The DPL field is set to 0.

set_system_gate(n,addr)
> Inserts a trap gate in the nth IDT entry. The Segment Selector inside the gate is set to the kernel code's Segment Selector. The Offset field is set to addr, which is the address of the exception handler. The DPL field is set to 3.

set_trap_gate(n,addr)
> Similar to the previous function, except the DPL field is set to 0.

Preliminary Initialization of the IDT

The IDT is initialized and used by the BIOS routines when the computer still operates in Real Mode. Once Linux takes over, however, the IDT is moved to another area of RAM and initialized a second time, since Linux does not use any BIOS routines (see Appendix A).

The idt variable points to the IDT, while the IDT itself is stored in the idt_table table, which includes 256 entries.* The 6-byte idt_descr variable stores both the size of the IDT and its address and is used only when the kernel initializes the idtr register with the lidt assembly language instruction.

During kernel initialization, the setup_idt( ) assembly language function starts by filling all 256 entries of idt_table with the same interrupt gate, which refers to the ignore_int( ) interrupt handler:

```
setup_idt:
    lea ignore_int, %edx
    movl $(__KERNEL_CS << 16), %eax
    movw %dx, %ax        /* selector = 0x0010 = cs */
    movw $0x8e00, %dx    /* interrupt gate, dpl=0, present */
    lea idt_table, %edi
    mov $256, %ecx
rp_sidt:
    movl %eax, (%edi)
    movl %edx, 4(%edi)
    addl $8, %edi
    dec %ecx
    jne rp_sidt
    ret
```

The ignore_int( ) interrupt handler, which is in assembly language, may be viewed as a null handler that executes the following actions:

1. Saves the content of some registers in the stack
2. Invokes the printk( ) function to print an "Unknown interrupt" system message
3. Restores the register contents from the stack
4. Executes an iret instruction to restart the interrupted program

The ignore_int( ) handler should never be executed. The occurrence of "Unknown interrupt" messages on the console or in the log files denotes either a hardware problem (an I/O device is issuing unforeseen interrupts) or a kernel problem (an interrupt or exception is not being handled properly).

Following this preliminary initialization, the kernel makes a second pass in the IDT to replace some of the null handlers with meaningful trap and interrupt handlers. Once this is done, the IDT includes a specialized interrupt, trap, or system gate for each different exception issued by the control unit and for each IRQ recognized by the interrupt controller.

The next two sections illustrate in detail how this is done for exceptions and interrupts.

---

* Some Pentium models have the notorious "f00f" bug, which allows a User Mode program to freeze the system. When executing on such CPUs, Linux uses a workaround based on storing the IDT in a write-protected page frame. The workaround for the bug is offered as an option when the user compiles the kernel.

Exception Handling

Most exceptions issued by the CPU are interpreted by Linux as error conditions. When one of them occurs, the kernel sends a signal to the process that caused the exception to notify it of an anomalous condition. If, for instance, a process performs a division by zero, the CPU raises a "Divide error" exception and the corresponding exception handler sends a SIGFPE signal to the current process, which then takes the necessary steps to recover or (if no signal handler is set for that signal) abort.

There are a couple of cases, however, where Linux exploits CPU exceptions to manage hardware resources more efficiently. A first case is already described in section "Saving the FPU, MMX, and XMM Registers" in Chapter 3. The "Device not available" exception is used together with the TS flag of the cr0 register to force the kernel to load the floating point registers of the CPU with new values. A second case refers to the Page Fault exception, which is used to defer allocating new page frames to the process until the last possible moment. The corresponding handler is complex because the exception may, or may not, denote an error condition (see the section "Page Fault Exception Handler" in Chapter 8).

Exception handlers have a standard structure consisting of three parts:

1. Save the contents of most registers in the Kernel Mode stack (this part is coded in assembly language).
2. Handle the exception by means of a high-level C function.
3. Exit from the handler by means of the ret_from_exception( ) function.

To take advantage of exceptions, the IDT must be properly initialized with an exception handler function for each recognized exception. It is the job of the trap_init( ) function to insert the final values—the functions that handle the exceptions—into all IDT entries that refer to nonmaskable interrupts and exceptions. This is accomplished through the set_trap_gate, set_intr_gate, and set_system_gate macros:

```
set_trap_gate(0,&divide_error);
set_trap_gate(1,&debug);
set_intr_gate(2,&nmi);
set_system_gate(3,&int3);
set_system_gate(4,&overflow);
set_system_gate(5,&bounds);
set_trap_gate(6,&invalid_op);
set_trap_gate(7,&device_not_available);
set_trap_gate(8,&double_fault);
set_trap_gate(9,&coprocessor_segment_overrun);
set_trap_gate(10,&invalid_TSS);
set_trap_gate(11,&segment_not_present);
set_trap_gate(12,&stack_segment);
set_trap_gate(13,&general_protection);
set_intr_gate(14,&page_fault);
set_trap_gate(16,&coprocessor_error);
set_trap_gate(17,&alignment_check);
```

```
set_trap_gate(18,&machine_check);
set_trap_gate(19,&simd_coprocessor_error);
set_system_gate(128,&system_call);
```

Now we will look at what a typical exception handler does once it is invoked.

Saving the Registers for the Exception Handler

Let's use handler_name to denote the name of a generic exception handler. (The actual names of all the exception handlers appear on the list of macros in the previous section.) Each exception handler starts with the following assembly language instructions:

```
handler_name:
    pushl $0 /* only for some exceptions */
    pushl $do_handler_name
    jmp error_code
```

If the control unit is not supposed to automatically insert a hardware error code on the stack when the exception occurs, the corresponding assembly language fragment includes a pushl $0 instruction to pad the stack with a null value. Then the address of the high-level C function is pushed on the stack; its name consists of the exception handler name prefixed by do_.

The assembly language fragment labeled as error_code is the same for all exception handlers except the one for the "Device not available" exception (see the section "Saving the FPU, MMX, and XMM Registers" in Chapter 3). The code performs the following steps:

1. Saves the registers that might be used by the high-level C function on the stack.

2. Issues a cld instruction to clear the direction flag DF of eflags, thus making sure that autoincrements on the edi and esi registers will be used with string instructions.[*]

3. Copies the hardware error code saved in the stack at location esp+36 in eax. Stores the value –1 in the same stack location. As we shall see in the section "Reexecution of System Calls" in Chapter 10, this value is used to separate 0x80 exceptions from other exceptions.

4. Loads edi with the address of the high-level do_handler_name( ) C function saved in the stack at location esp+32; writes the contents of es in that stack location.

5. Loads the kernel data Segment Selector into the ds and es registers, then sets the ebx register to the address of the current process descriptor (see the section "Identifying a Process" in Chapter 3).

---

[*] A single assembly language "string instruction," such as rep;movsb, is able to act on a whole block of data (string).

6. Stores the parameters to be passed to the high-level C function on the stack, namely, the exception hardware error code and the address of the stack location where the contents of User Mode registers is saved.

7. Invokes the high-level C function whose address is now stored in edi.

After the last step is executed, the invoked function finds the following on the top locations of the stack:

- The return address of the instruction to be executed after the C function terminates (see the next section)
- The stack address of the saved User Mode registers
- The hardware error code

Entering and Leaving the Exception Handler

As already explained, the names of the C functions that implement exception handlers always consist of the prefix do_ followed by the handler name. Most of these functions store the hardware error code and the exception vector in the process descriptor of current, and then send a suitable signal to that process. This is done as follows:

```
current->tss.error_code = error_code;
current->tss.trap_no = vector;
force_sig(sig_number, current);
```

The current process takes care of the signal right after the termination of exception handler. The signal will be handled either in User Mode by the process's own signal handler (if it exists) or in Kernel Mode. In the latter case, the kernel usually kills the process (see Chapter 10). The signals sent by the exception handlers are already in Table 4-1.

The exception handler always checks whether the exception occurred in User Mode or in Kernel Mode and, in the latter case, whether it was due to an invalid argument of a system call. We'll describe in the section "Dynamic Address Checking: The Fixup Code" in Chapter 9 how the kernel defends itself against invalid arguments of system calls. Any other exception raised in Kernel Mode is due to a kernel bug. In this case, the exception handler knows the kernel is misbehaving and, in order to avoid data corruption on the hard disks, the handler invokes the die( ) function, which prints the contents of all CPU registers on the console (this dump is called *kernel oops*) and terminates the current process by calling do_exit( ) (see Chapter 20).

When the C function that implements the exception handling terminates, control is transferred to the following assembly language fragment:

```
addl $8, %esp
jmp ret_from_exception
```

The code pops the stack address of the saved User Mode registers and the hardware error code from the stack, and then performs a jmp instruction to the ret_from_exception( ) function. This function is described in the later section "Returning from Interrupts and Exceptions."

Interrupt Handling

As we explained earlier, most exceptions are handled simply by sending a Unix signal to the process that caused the exception. The action to be taken is thus deferred until the process receives the signal; as a result, the kernel is able to process the exception quickly.

This approach does not hold for interrupts because they frequently arrive long after the process to which they are related (for instance, a process that requested a data transfer) has been suspended and a completely unrelated process is running. So it would make no sense to send a Unix signal to the current process.

Interrupt handling depends on the type of interrupt. For our purposes, we'll distinguish three main classes of interrupts:

I/O interrupts
> Some I/O devices require attention; the corresponding interrupt handler must query the device to determine the proper course of action. We cover this type of interrupt in the later section "I/O Interrupt Handling."

Timer interrupts
> Some timer, either a local APIC timer or an external timer, has issued an interrupt; this kind of interrupt tells the kernel that a fixed-time interval has elapsed. These interrupts are handled mostly as I/O interrupts; we discuss the peculiar characteristics of timer interrupts in Chapter 6.

Interprocessor interrupts
> A CPU issued an interrupt to another CPU of a multiprocessor system. We cover such interrupts in the later section "Interprocessor Interrupt Handling."

I/O Interrupt Handling

In general, an I/O interrupt handler must be flexible enough to service several devices at the same time. In the PCI bus architecture, for instance, several devices may share the same IRQ line. This means that the interrupt vector alone does not tell the whole story. In the example shown in Table 4-3, the same vector 43 is assigned to the USB port and to the sound card. However, some hardware devices found in older PC architectures (like ISA) do not reliably operate if their IRQ line is shared with other devices.

Interrupt handler flexibility is achieved in two distinct ways, as discussed in the following list.

IRQ sharing

The interrupt handler executes several *interrupt service routines* (*ISRs*). Each ISR is a function related to a single device sharing the IRQ line. Since it is not possible to know in advance which particular device issued the IRQ, each ISR is executed to verify whether its device needs attention; if so, the ISR performs all the operations that need to be executed when the device raises an interrupt.

IRQ dynamic allocation

An IRQ line is associated with a device at the last possible moment; for instance, the IRQ line of the floppy device is allocated only when a user accesses the floppy disk device. In this way, the same IRQ vector may be used by several hardware devices even if they cannot share the IRQ line, although not at the same time.

Not all actions to be performed when an interrupt occurs have the same urgency. In fact, the interrupt handler itself is not a suitable place for all kind of actions. Long noncritical operations should be deferred, since while an interrupt handler is running, the signals on the corresponding IRQ line are temporarily ignored. Most important, the process on behalf of which an interrupt handler is executed must always stay in the TASK_RUNNING state, or a system freeze can occur. Therefore, interrupt handlers cannot perform any blocking procedure such as an I/O disk operation. Linux divides the actions to be performed following an interrupt into three classes:

Critical

Actions such as acknowledging an interrupt to the PIC, reprogramming the PIC or the device controller, or updating data structures accessed by both the device and the processor. These can be executed quickly and are critical because they must be performed as soon as possible. Critical actions are executed within the interrupt handler immediately, with maskable interrupts disabled.

Noncritical

Actions such as updating data structures that are accessed only by the processor (for instance, reading the scan code after a keyboard key has been pushed). These actions can also finish quickly, so they are executed by the interrupt handler immediately, with the interrupts enabled.

Noncritical deferrable

Actions such as copying a buffer's contents into the address space of some process (for instance, sending the keyboard line buffer to the terminal handler process). These may be delayed for a long time interval without affecting the kernel operations; the interested process will just keep waiting for the data. Noncritical deferrable actions are performed by means of separate functions that are discussed in the later section "Softirqs, Tasklets, and Bottom Halves."

Regardless of the kind of circuit that caused the interrupt, all I/O interrupt handlers perform the same four basic actions:

1. Save the IRQ value and the registers contents in the Kernel Mode stack.
2. Send an acknowledgment to the PIC that is servicing the IRQ line, thus allowing it to issue further interrupts.

---

3. Execute the interrupt service routines (ISRs) associated with all the devices that share the IRQ.

4. Terminate by jumping to the ret_from_intr( ) address.

Several descriptors are needed to represent both the state of the IRQ lines and the functions to be executed when an interrupt occurs. Figure 4-3 represents in a schematic way the hardware circuits and the software functions used to handle an interrupt. These functions are discussed in the following sections.

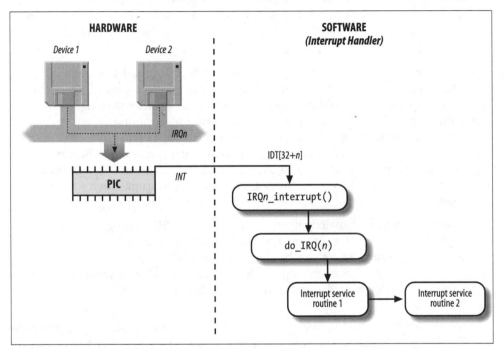

Figure 4-3. I/O interrupt handling

Interrupt vectors

As illustrated in Table 4-2, physical IRQs may be assigned any vector in the range 32–238. However, Linux uses vector 128 to implement system calls.

The IBM-compatible PC architecture requires that some devices be statically connected to specific IRQ lines. In particular:

- The interval timer device must be connected to the IRQ0 line (see Chapter 6).
- The slave 8259A PIC must be connected to the IRQ2 line (although more advanced PICs are now being used, Linux still supports 8259A-style PICs).
- The external mathematical coprocessor must be connected to the IRQ13 line (although recent 80×86 processors no longer use such a device, Linux continues to support the hardy 80386 model).

- In general, an I/O device can be connected to a limited number of IRQ lines. (As a matter of fact, when playing with an old PC where IRQ sharing is not possible, you might not succeed in installing a new card because of IRQ conflicts with other already present hardware devices.)

Table 4-2. Interrupt vectors in Linux

Vector range	Use
0–19 (0x0-0x13)	Nonmaskable interrupts and exceptions
20–31 (0x14–0x1f)	Intel-reserved
32–127 (0x20–0x7f)	External interrupts (IRQs)
128 (0x80)	Programmed exception for system calls (see Chapter 9)
129–238 (0x81–0xee)	External interrupts (IRQs)
239 (0xef)	Local APIC timer interrupt (see Chapter 6)
240–250 (0xf0–0xfa)	Reserved by Linux for future use
251–255 (0xfb–0xff)	Interprocessor interrupts (see the section "Interprocessor Interrupt Handling" later in this chapter)

There are three ways to select a line for an IRQ-configurable device:

- By setting some hardware jumpers (only on very old device cards).
- By a utility program shipped with the device and executed when installing it. Such a program may either ask the user to select an available IRQ number or probe the system to determine an available number by itself.
- By a hardware protocol executed at system startup. Peripheral devices declare which interrupt lines they are ready to use; the final values are then negotiated to reduce conflicts as much as possible. Once this is done, each interrupt handler can read the assigned IRQ by using a function that accesses some I/O ports of the device. For instance, drivers for devices that comply with the Peripheral Component Interconnect (PCI) standard use a group of functions such as pci_read_config_byte( ) to access the device configuration space.

Table 4-3 shows a fairly arbitrary arrangement of devices and IRQs, such as those that might be found on one particular PC.

Table 4-3. An example of IRQ assignment to I/O devices

IRQ	INT	Hardware Device
0	32	Timer
1	33	Keyboard
2	34	PIC cascading
3	35	Second serial port
4	36	First serial port
6	38	Floppy disk
8	40	System clock

Table 4-3. An example of IRQ assignment to I/O devices (continued)

IRQ	INT	Hardware Device
10	42	Network interface
11	43	USB port, sound card
12	44	PS/2 mouse
13	45	Mathematical coprocessor
14	46	EIDE disk controller's first chain
15	47	EIDE disk controller's second chain

The kernel must discover the correspondence between the IRQ number and the I/O device before enabling interrupts. Otherwise, how could the kernel handle a signal from, for example, a SCSI disk without knowing which vector corresponds to the device? The correspondence is established while initializing each device driver (see Chapter 13).

IRQ data structures

As always, when discussing complicated operations involving state transitions, it helps to understand first where key data is stored. Thus, this section explains the data structures that support interrupt handling and how they are laid out in various descriptors. Figure 4-4 illustrates schematically the relationships between the main descriptors that represent the state of the IRQ lines. (The figure does not illustrate the data structures needed to handle softirqs, tasklets, and bottom halves; they are discussed later in this chapter.)

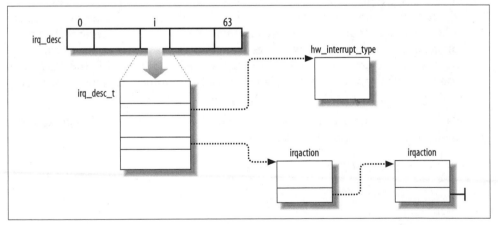

Figure 4-4. IRQ descriptors

An `irq_desc` array groups together `NR_IRQS` (usually 224) `irq_desc_t` descriptors, which include the following fields:

status
    A set of flags describing the IRQ line status (see Table 4-4).

Table 4-4. Flags describing the IRQ line status

Flag name	Description
IRQ_INPROGRESS	A handler for the IRQ is being executed.
IRQ_DISABLED	The IRQ line has been deliberately disabled by a device driver.
IRQ_PENDING	An IRQ has occurred on the line; its occurrence has been acknowledged to the PIC, but it has not yet been serviced by the kernel.
IRQ_REPLAY	The IRQ line has been disabled but the previous IRQ occurrence has not yet been acknowledged to the PIC.
IRQ_AUTODETECT	The kernel uses the IRQ line while performing a hardware device probe.
IRQ_WAITING	The kernel uses the IRQ line while performing a hardware device probe; moreover, the corresponding interrupt has not been raised.
IRQ_LEVEL	Not used on the 80 × 86 architecture.
IRQ_MASKED	Not used.
IRQ_PER_CPU	Not used on the 80 × 86 architecture.

handler

Points to the hw_interrupt_type descriptor that identifies the PIC circuit servicing the IRQ line.

action

Identifies the interrupt service routines to be invoked when the IRQ occurs. The field points to the first element of the list of irqaction descriptors associated with the IRQ. The irqaction descriptor is described later in the chapter.

depth

Shows 0 if the IRQ line is enabled and a positive value if it has been disabled at least once. Every time the disable_irq( ) or disable_irq_nosync( ) function is invoked, the field is incremented; if depth was equal to 0, the function disables the IRQ line and sets its IRQ_DISABLED flag.* Conversely, each invocation of the enable_irq( ) function decrements the field; if depth becomes 0, the function enables the IRQ line and clears its IRQ_DISABLED flag.

lock

A spin lock used to serialize the accesses to the IRQ descriptor (see Chapter 5).

During system initialization, the init_IRQ( ) function sets the status field of each IRQ main descriptor to IRQ_DISABLED. Moreover, init_IRQ() updates the IDT by replacing the provisional interrupt gates with new ones. This is accomplished through the following statements:

```
for (i = 0; i < NR_IRQS; i++)
    if (i+32 != 128)
        set_intr_gate(i+32,interrupt[i]);
```

---

* Contrary to disable_irq_nosync( ), disable_irq(n) waits until all interrupt handlers for IRQ*n* that are running on other CPUs have completed before returning.

This code looks in the interrupt array to find the interrupt handler addresses that it uses to set up the interrupt gates. The interrupt handler for IRQ*n* is named IRQ*n*_interrupt( ) (see the later section "Saving the registers for the interrupt handler").

Some of the interrupt gates will never be used; others will be used only in multiprocessor systems; finally, some of them are always used. Thus, some of the interrupt gates are set to their final values, while others aren't. More precisely:

- The gates of the first 16 IRQs (vectors 32–47) are set to their final values.
- In multiprocessor systems, the gates of the interprocessor interrupts and the gate of the local APIC timer interrupt are also set properly (see the section "Interrupt service routines" later in this chapter).
- Vector 128 is left untouched, since it is used for the system call's programmed exception.
- All remaining gates are reserved for interrupts issued from devices connected to a PCI bus. In this case, the handler field of the irq_desc element is initialized to the no_irq_type null handler.

In addition to the 8259A chip that was mentioned near the beginning of this chapter, Linux supports several other PIC circuits such as the SMP IO-APIC, PIIX4's internal 8259 PIC, and SGI's Visual Workstation Cobalt (IO-)APIC. To handle all such devices in a uniform way, Linux uses a "PIC object," consisting of the PIC name and seven PIC standard methods. The advantage of this object-oriented approach is that drivers need not to be aware of the kind of PIC installed in the system. Each driver-visible interrupt source is transparently wired to the appropriate controller. The data structure that defines a PIC object is called hw_interrupt_type (also called hw_irq_controller).

For the sake of concreteness, let's assume that our computer is a uniprocessor with two 8259A PICs, which provide 16 standard IRQs. In this case, the handler field in each of the 16 irq_desc_t descriptors points to the i8259A_irq_type variable, which describes the 8259A PIC. This variable is initialized as follows:

```
struct hw_interrupt_type i8259A_irq_type = {
    "XT-PIC",
    startup_8259A_irq,
    shutdown_8259A_irq,
    enable_8259A_irq,
    disable_8259A_irq,
    mask_and_ack_8259A,
    end_8259A_irq,
    NULL
};
```

The first field in this structure, "XT-PIC", is the PIC name. Next come the pointers to six different functions used to program the PIC. The first two functions start up and shut down an IRQ line of the chip, respectively. But in the case of the 8259A chip, these functions coincide with the third and fourth functions, which enable and disable the line. The mask_and_ack_8259A( ) function acknowledges the IRQ received by sending the proper bytes to the 8259A I/O ports. The end_8259A_irq() function is invoked when the interrupt handler for the IRQ line terminates. The last set_affinity method is set to NULL: it is used in multiprocessor systems to declare the "affinity" of CPUs for specified IRQs—that is, which CPUs are enabled to handle specific IRQs.

As described earlier, multiple devices can share a single IRQ. Therefore, the kernel maintains irqaction descriptors, each of which refers to a specific hardware device and a specific interrupt. The descriptor includes the following fields:

handler

> Points to the interrupt service routine for an I/O device. This is the key field that allows many devices to share the same IRQ.

flags

> Describes the relationships between the IRQ line and the I/O device (see Table 4-5).

Table 4-5. Flags of the irqaction descriptor

Flag name	Description
SA_INTERRUPT	The handler must execute with interrupts disabled.
SA_SHIRQ	The device permits its IRQ line to be shared with other devices.
SA_SAMPLE_RANDOM	The device may be considered a source of events that occurs randomly; it can thus be used by the kernel random number generator. (Users can access this feature by taking random numbers from the */dev/random* and */dev/urandom* device files.)

name

> The name of the I/O device (shown when listing the serviced IRQs by reading the */proc/interrupts* file).

dev_id

> A private field for the I/O device. Typically, it identifies the I/O device itself (for instance, it could be equal to its major and minor numbers; see the section "Device Files" in Chapter 13), or it points to a device driver's data.

next

> Points to the next element of a list of irqaction descriptors. The elements in the list refer to hardware devices that share the same IRQ.

Finally, the irq_stat array includes NR_CPUS entries, one for each CPU in the system. Each entry is of type irq_cpustat_t, and includes a few counters and flags used by the kernel to keep track of what any CPU is currently doing. The most important fields are usually accessed through some macros having as a parameter the CPU logical number (that is, the index of the array).

In particular, the local_irq_count(n) macro selects the __local_irq_count field of the nth entry of the array. The field is a counter of how many interrupt handlers are stacked in the CPU—that is, how many interrupt handlers have been started and are not yet terminated.

IRQ distribution in multiprocessor systems

Linux sticks to the Symmetric Multiprocessing model (SMP); this means, essentially, that the kernel should not have any bias toward one CPU with respect to the others. As a consequence, the kernel tries to distribute the IRQ signals coming from the hardware devices in a round-robin fashion among all the CPUs. Therefore, all the CPUs spend approximately the same fraction of their execution time servicing I/O interrupts.

In the earlier section "The Advanced Programmable Interrupt Controller (APIC)," we said that the multi-APIC system has sophisticated mechanisms to dynamically distribute the IRQ signals among the CPUs. Therefore, the Linux kernel has to do very little to enforce the round-robin distribution scheme.

During system bootstrap, the booting CPU executes the setup_IO_APIC_irqs() function to initialize the I/O APIC chip. The 24 entries of the Interrupt Redirection Table of the chip are filled so that all IRQ signals from the I/O hardware devices can be routed to each CPU in the system according to the "lowest priority" scheme. During system bootstrap, moreover, all CPUs execute the setup_local_APIC() function, which takes care of initializing the local APICs. In particular, the task priority register (TPR) of each chip is initialized to a fixed value, meaning that the CPU is willing to handle any kind of IRQ signal, regardless of its priority. The Linux kernel never modifies this value after its initialization.

Since all task priority registers contain the same value, all CPUs always have the same priority. To break tie, the multi-APIC system uses the values in the arbitration priority registers of local APICs, as explained earlier. Since such values are automatically changed after every interrupt, the IRQ signals are fairly distributed among all CPUs.[*]

In short, when a hardware device raises an IRQ signal, the multi-APIC system selects one of the CPUs and delivers the signal to the corresponding local APIC, which in turn interrupts its CPU. All other CPUs are not notified of the event. All this is magically done by the hardware, so it is of no concern for the kernel after multi-APIC system initialization.

Saving the registers for the interrupt handler

When a CPU receives an interrupt, it starts executing the code at the address found in the corresponding gate of the IDT (see the earlier section "Hardware Handling of Interrupts and Exceptions").

---

[*] There is an exception, though. Linux usually sets up the local APICs in such a way to honor the *focus processor*. When an IRQ signal is raised, the focus processor for that IRQ is the CPU to which a previous occurrence of the same IRQ has been already sent; moreover, either the interrupt is still pending (waiting to be handled) or the CPU is still servicing the corresponding interrupt handler. When focus mode is enabled, an interrupt is always sent to its focus processor, if it exists. However, Intel has dropped support for focus processors in the Pentium 4 model.

As with other context switches, the need to save registers leaves the kernel developer with a somewhat messy coding job because the registers have to be saved and restored using assembly language code. However, within those operations, the processor is expected to call and return from a C function. In this section, we describe the assembly language task of handling registers; in the next, we show some of the acrobatics required in the C function that is subsequently invoked.

Saving registers is the first task of the interrupt handler. As already mentioned, the interrupt handler for IRQn is named IRQn_interrupt, and its address is included in the interrupt gate stored in the proper IDT entry.

In uniprocessor systems, the same BUILD_IRQ macro is duplicated 16 times, once for each IRQ number, in order to yield 16 different interrupt handler entry points. In multiprocessor systems, the macro is duplicated 14 × 16 times for a grand total of 224 interrupt handler entry points. Each macro occurrence expands to the following assembly language fragment:

```
IRQn_interrupt:
    pushl $n-256
    jmp common_interrupt
```

The result is to save on the stack the IRQ number associated with the interrupt minus 256.* The same code for all interrupt handlers can then be executed while referring to this number. The common code can be found in the BUILD_COMMON_IRQ macro, which expands to the following assembly language fragment:

```
common_interrupt:
    SAVE_ALL
    call do_IRQ
    jmp $ret_from_intr
```

The SAVE_ALL macro, in turn, expands to the following fragment:

```
cld
push %es
push %ds
pushl %eax
pushl %ebp
pushl %edi
pushl %esi
pushl %edx
pushl %ecx
pushl %ebx
movl $__KERNEL_DS,%edx
movl %edx,%ds
movl %edx,%es
```

SAVE_ALL saves all the CPU registers that may be used by the interrupt handler on the stack, except for eflags, cs, eip, ss, and esp, which are already saved automatically by

---

* Subtracting 256 from an IRQ number yields a negative number. Positive numbers are reserved to identify system calls (see Chapter 9).

the control unit (see the earlier section "Hardware Handling of Interrupts and Exceptions"). The macro then loads the selector of the kernel data segment into ds and es.

After saving the registers, BUILD_COMMON_IRQ invokes the do_IRQ() function. Then, when the ret instruction of do_IRQ() is executed (when that function terminates) control is transferred to ret_from_intr() (see the later section "Returning from Interrupts and Exceptions").

The do_IRQ( ) function

The do_IRQ() function is invoked to execute all interrupt service routines associated with an interrupt. When it starts, the kernel stack contains, from the top down:

- The do_IRQ()'s return address (the starting address of ret_from_intr())
- The group of register values pushed on by SAVE_ALL
- The encoding of the IRQ number
- The registers saved automatically by the control unit when it recognized the interrupt

Since the C compiler places all the parameters on top of the stack, the do_IRQ() function is declared as follows:

```
unsigned int do_IRQ(struct pt_regs regs)
```

where the pt_regs structure consists of 15 fields:

- The first nine fields are the register values pushed by SAVE_ALL.
- The tenth field, referenced through a field called orig_eax, encodes the IRQ number.
- The remaining fields correspond to the register values pushed on automatically by the control unit.*

The do_IRQ() function is equivalent to the following code fragment. Don't be scared by this function—we are going to explain the code line by line.

```
int irq = regs.orig_eax & 0xff;
spin_lock(&(irq_desc[irq].lock));
irq_desc[irq].handler->ack(irq);
irq_desc[irq].status &= ~(IRQ_REPLAY | IRQ_WAITING);
irq_desc[irq].status |= IRQ_PENDING;
if (!(irq_desc[irq].status & (IRQ_DISABLED | IRQ_INPROGRESS)) && irq_desc[irq].
action) {
    irq_desc[irq].status |= IRQ_INPROGRESS;
    do {
        irq_desc[irq].status &= ~IRQ_PENDING;
        spin_unlock(&(irq_desc[irq].lock));
```

---

* The ret_from_intr() return address is missing from the pt_regs structure because the C compiler expects a return address on top of the stack. It takes this into account when generating the instructions to address parameters.

```
        handle_IRQ_event(irq, &regs, irq_desc[irq].action);
        spin_lock(&(irq_desc[irq].lock));
    } while (irq_desc[irq].status & IRQ_PENDING);
    irq_desc[irq].status &= ~IRQ_INPROGRESS;
}
irq_desc[irq].handler->end(irq);
spin_unlock(&(irq_desc[irq].lock));
if (softirq_pending(smp_processor_id()))
    do_softirq();
```

First of all, the do_IRQ( ) function gets the IRQ vector passed as a parameter on the stack and puts it in the irq local variable. This value is used as an index to access the proper element of the irq_desc array (the IRQ main descriptor).

Before accessing the main IRQ descriptor, the kernel acquires the corresponding spin lock. We'll see in Chapter 5 that the spin lock protects against concurrent accesses by different CPUs (in a uniprocessor system, the spin_lock() function does nothing). This spin lock is necessary in a multiprocessor system because other interrupts of the same kind may be raised, and other CPUs might take care of the new interrupt occurrences. Without the spin lock, the main IRQ descriptor would be accessed concurrently by several CPUs. As we'll see, this situation must be absolutely avoided.

After acquiring the spin lock, the function invokes the ack method of the main IRQ descriptor. In a uniprocessor system, the corresponding mask_and_ack_8259A() function acknowledges the interrupt on the PIC and also disables the IRQ line. Masking the IRQ line ensures that the CPU does not accept further occurrences of this type of interrupt until the handler terminates. Remember that the do_IRQ() function runs with local interrupts disabled; in fact, the CPU control unit automatically clears the IF flag of the eflags register because the interrupt handler is invoked through an IDT's interrupt gate. However, we'll see shortly that the kernel might re-enable local interrupts before executing the interrupt service routines of this interrupt.

In a multiprocessor system, however, things are much more complicated. Depending on the type of interrupt, acknowledging the interrupt could either be done by the ack method or delayed until the interrupt handler terminates (that is, acknowledgement could be done by the end method). In either case, we can take for granted that the local APIC doesn't accept further interrupts of this type until the handler terminates, although further occurrences of this type of interrupt may be accepted by other CPUs (main IRQ descriptor's spin lock comes to the rescue!).

The do_IRQ( ) function then initializes a few flags of the main IRQ descriptor. It sets the IRQ_PENDING flag because the interrupt has been acknowledged (well, sort of), but not yet really serviced; it also clears the IRQ_WAITING and IRQ_REPLAY flags (but we don't have to care about them now).

Now do_IRQ( ) checks whether it must really handle the interrupt. There are three cases in which nothing has to be done. These are discussed in the following list.

IRQ_DISABLED *is set*

A CPU might execute the do_IRQ() function even if the corresponding IRQ line is disabled; you'll find an explanation for this nonintuitive case in the later section "Reviving a lost interrupt." Moreover, buggy motherboards may generate spurious interrupts even when the IRQ line is disabled in the PIC.

IRQ_INPROGRESS *is set*

In a multiprocessor system, another CPU might be handling a previous occurrence of the same interrupt. Why not defer the handling of *this* occurrence to *that* CPU? This is exactly what is done by Linux. This leads to a simpler kernel architecture because device drivers' interrupt service routines need not to be reentrant (their execution is serialized). Moreover, the freed CPU can quickly return to what it was doing, without dirtying its hardware cache; this is beneficial to system performances. The IRQ_INPROGRESS flag is set whenever a CPU is committed to execute the interrupt service routines of the interrupt; therefore, the do_IRQ() function checks it before starting the real work.

irc_desc[irq].action *is* NULL

This case occurs when there is no interrupt service routines associated with the interrupt. Normally, this happens only when the kernel is probing a hardware device.

Let's suppose that none of the three cases holds, so the interrupt has to be serviced. do_IRQ() sets the IRQ_INPROGRESS flag and starts a loop. In each iteration, the function clears the IRQ_PENDING flag, releases the interrupt spin lock, and executes the interrupt services routines by invoking handle_IRQ_event()(described in the later section "Interrupt service routines"). When the latter function terminates, do_IRQ() acquires the spin lock again and checks the value of the IRQ_PENDING flag. If it is clear, no further occurrence of the interrupt has been delivered to another CPU, so the loop ends. Conversely, if IRQ_PENDING is set, another CPU has executed the do_IRQ() function for this type of interrupt while this CPU was executing handle_IRQ_event(). Therefore, do_IRQ() performs another iteration of the loop, servicing the new occurrence of the interrupt.*

Our do_IRQ() function is now going to terminate, either because it has already executed the interrupt service routines or because it had nothing to do. The function invokes the end method of the main IRQ descriptor. On uniprocessor systems, the corresponding end_8259A_irq() function re-enables the IRQ line (unless the interrupt occurrence was spurious). On multiprocessor systems, the end method acknowledges the interrupt (if not already done by the ack method).

Finally, do_IRQ() releases the spin lock: the hard work is finished! Before returning, however, the function checks whether deferrable kernel functions are waiting to be

---

* Because IRQ_PENDING is a flag and not a counter, only the second occurrence of the interrupt can be recognized. Further occurrences in each iteration of the do_IRQ()'s loop are simply lost.

executed (see the section "Softirqs, Tasklets, and Bottom Halves" later in this chapter). In the affirmative case, it invokes the do_softirq() function. When do_IRQ() terminates, the control is transferred to the ret_from_intr() function.

Reviving a lost interrupt

The do_IRQ() function is small and simple, yet it works properly in most cases. Indeed, the IRQ_PENDING, IRQ_INPROGRESS, and IRQ_DISABLED flags ensure that interrupts are correctly handled even when the hardware is misbehaving. However, things may not work so smoothly in a multiprocessor system.

Suppose that a CPU has an IRQ line enabled. A hardware device raises the IRQ line, and the multi-APIC system selects our CPU for handling the interrupt. Before the CPU acknowledges the interrupt, the IRQ line is masked out by another CPU; as a consequence, the IRQ_DISABLED flag is set. Right afterwards, our CPU starts handling the pending interrupt; therefore, the do_IRQ() function acknowledges the interrupt and then returns without executing the interrupt service routines because it finds the IRQ_DISABLED flag set. Therefore, the interrupt occurred before IRQ line disabling, yet it got lost.

To cope with this scenario, when the enable_irq() function re-enables the IRQ line, it forces the hardware to generate a new occurrence of the lost interrupt:

```
spin_lock_irqsave(&(irq_desc[irq].lock), flags);
if (--irq_desc[irq].depth == 0) {
    irq_desc[irq].status &= ~IRQ_DISABLED;
    if (irq_desc[irq].status & (IRQ_PENDING | IRQ_REPLAY)) == IRQ_PENDING) {
        irq_desc[irq].status |= IRQ_REPLAY;
        send_IPI_self(irq|32);
    }
    irq_desc[irq].handler->enable(irq);
}
spin_lock_irqrestore(&(irq_desc[irq].lock), flags);
```

The function detects that an interrupt was lost by checking the value of the IRQ_PENDING flag. The flag is always cleared when leaving the interrupt handler; therefore, if the IRQ line is disabled and the flag is set, then an interrupt occurrence has been acknowledged but not yet serviced. In this case it is necessary to issue a new interrupt. This is obtained by forcing the local APIC to generate a self-interrupt (see the later section "Interprocessor Interrupt Handling"). The role of the IRQ_REPLAY flag is to ensure that exactly one self-interrupt is generated. Remember that the do_IRQ() function clears that flag when it starts handling the interrupt.

Interrupt service routines

As mentioned previously, an interrupt service routine implements a device-specific operation. When an interrupt handler must execute the ISRs, it invokes the handle_IRQ_event() function. This function essentially performs the steps shown in the following list.

1. Invokes the `irq_enter( )` function to increment the `__local_irq_count` field of the `irq_stat` entry of the executing CPU (to learn how many interrupt handlers are stacked in the CPU, see the earlier section "IRQ data structures"). As we shall see in Chapter 5, this function also checks that interrupts are not globally disabled.

2. Enables the local interrupts with the `sti` assembly language instruction if the `SA_INTERRUPT` flag is clear.

3. Executes each interrupt service routine of the interrupt through the following code:

```
do {
    action->handler(irq, action->dev_id, regs);
    action = action->next;
} while (action);
```

   At the start of the loop, `action` points to the start of a list of `irqaction` data structures that indicate the actions to be taken upon receiving the interrupt (see Figure 4-4 earlier in this chapter).

4. Disables the local interrupts with the `cli` assembly language instruction.

5. Invokes `irq_exit( )` to decrement the `__local_irq_count` field of the `irq_stat` entry of the executing CPU.

All interrupt service routines act on the same parameters:

irq
    The IRQ number

dev_id
    The device identifier

regs
    A pointer to the Kernel Mode stack area containing the registers saved right after the interrupt occurred

The first parameter allows a single ISR to handle several IRQ lines, the second one allows a single ISR to take care of several devices of the same type, and the last one allows the ISR to access the execution context of the interrupted kernel control path. In practice, most ISRs do not use these parameters.

The `SA_INTERRUPT` flag of the main IRQ descriptor determines whether interrupts must be enabled or disabled when the `do_IRQ( )` function invokes an ISR. An ISR that has been invoked with the interrupts in one state is allowed to put them in the opposite state. In a uniprocessor system, this can be achieved by means of the `cli` (disable interrupts) and `sti` (enable interrupts) assembly language instructions. Globally enabling or disabling interrupts in a multiprocessor system is a much more complicated task; we'll deal with it in Chapter 5.

The structure of an ISR depends on the characteristics of the device handled. We'll give a few examples of ISRs in Chapter 6, Chapter 13, and Chapter 18.

Dynamic allocation of IRQ lines

As noticed in section "Interrupt vectors," a few vectors are reserved for specific devices, while the remaining ones are dynamically handled. There is, therefore, a way in which the same IRQ line can be used by several hardware devices even if they do not allow IRQ sharing. The trick is to serialize the activation of the hardware devices so that just one owns the IRQ line at a time.

Before activating a device that is going to use an IRQ line, the corresponding driver invokes request_irq(). This function creates a new irqaction descriptor and initializes it with the parameter values; it then invokes the setup_irq() function to insert the descriptor in the proper IRQ list. The device driver aborts the operation if setup_irq() returns an error code, which means that the IRQ line is already in use by another device that does not allow interrupt sharing. When the device operation is concluded, the driver invokes the free_irq() function to remove the descriptor from the IRQ list and release the memory area.

Let's see how this scheme works on a simple example. Assume a program wants to address the */dev/fd0* device file, which corresponds to the first floppy disk on the system.[*] The program can do this either by directly accessing */dev/fd0* or by mounting a filesystem on it. Floppy disk controllers are usually assigned IRQ6; given this, the floppy driver issues the following request:

```
request_irq(6, floppy_interrupt,
        SA_INTERRUPT|SA_SAMPLE_RANDOM, "floppy", NULL);
```

As can be observed, the floppy_interrupt() interrupt service routine must execute with the interrupts disabled (SA_INTERRUPT set) and no sharing of the IRQ (SA_SHIRQ flag cleared). The SA_SAMPLE_RANDOM flag set means that accesses to the floppy disk are a good source of random events to be used for the kernel random number generator. When the operation on the floppy disk is concluded (either the I/O operation on */dev/fd0* terminates or the filesystem is unmounted), the driver releases IRQ6:

```
free_irq(6, NULL);
```

To insert an irqaction descriptor in the proper list, the kernel invokes the setup_irq() function, passing to it the parameters irq_nr, the IRQ number, and new (the address of a previously allocated irqaction descriptor). This function:

1. Checks whether another device is already using the irq_nr IRQ and, if so, whether the SA_SHIRQ flags in the irqaction descriptors of both devices specify that the IRQ line can be shared. Returns an error code if the IRQ line cannot be used.

2. Adds *new (the new irqaction descriptor pointed to by new) at the end of the list to which irq_desc[irq_nr]->action points.

---

[*] Floppy disks are "old" devices that do not usually allow IRQ sharing.

3. If no other device is sharing the same IRQ, clears the `IRQ_DISABLED`, `IRQ_AUTODETECT`, and `IRQ_INPROGRESS` flags in the `flags` field of `*new` and invokes the startup method of the `irq_desc[irq_nr]->handler` PIC object to make sure that IRQ signals are enabled.

Here is an example of how `setup_irq()` is used, drawn from system initialization. The kernel initializes the `irq0` descriptor of the interval timer device by executing the following instructions in the `time_init()` function (see Chapter 6):

```
struct irqaction irq0 =
    {timer_interrupt, SA_INTERRUPT, 0, "timer", NULL,};
setup_irq(0, &irq0);
```

First, the `irq0` variable of type `irqaction` is initialized: the `handler` field is set to the address of the `timer_interrupt()` function, the `flags` field is set to `SA_INTERRUPT`, the `name` field is set to `"timer"`, and the last field is set to `NULL` to show that no `dev_id` value is used. Next, the kernel invokes `setup_irq()` to insert `irq0` in the list of `irqaction` descriptors associated with IRQ0.

Interprocessor Interrupt Handling

On multiprocessor systems, Linux defines the following five kinds of interprocessor interrupts (see also Table 4-2):

CALL_FUNCTION_VECTOR *(vector 0xfb)*
> Sent to all CPUs but the sender, forcing those CPUs to run a function passed by the sender. The corresponding interrupt handler is named `call_function_interrupt()`. The function passed as a parameter may, for instance, force all other CPUs to stop, or may force them to set the contents of the Memory Type Range Registers (MTRRs).[*] Usually this interrupt is sent to all CPUs except the CPU executing the calling function by means of the `smp_call_function()` facility function.

RESCHEDULE_VECTOR *(vector 0xfc)*
> When a CPU receives this type of interrupt, the corresponding handler—named `reschedule_interrupt()`—limits itself to acknowledge the interrupt. All the rescheduling is done automatically when returning from the interrupt (see the section "Returning from Interrupts and Exceptions" later in this chapter).

INVALIDATE_TLB_VECTOR *(vector 0xfd)*
> Sent to all CPUs but the sender, forcing them to invalidate their Translation Lookaside Buffers. The corresponding handler, named `invalidate_interrupt()`, flushes some TLB entries of the processor as described in the section "Handling the Hardware Cache and the TLB" in Chapter 2.

---

[*] Starting with the Pentium Pro model, Intel microprocessors include these additional registers to easily customize cache operations. For instance, Linux may use these registers to disable the hardware cache for the addresses mapping the frame buffer of a PCI/AGP graphic card while maintaining the "write combining" mode of operation: the paging unit combines write transfers into larger chunks before copying them into the frame buffer.

ERROR_APIC_VECTOR *(vector* 0xfe)
> This interrupt should never occur.

SPURIOUS_APIC_VECTOR *(vector* 0xff)
> This interrupt should never occur.

Thanks to the following group of functions, issuing interprocessor interrupts (IPIs) becomes an easy task:

send_IPI_all( )
> Sends an IPI to all CPUs (including the sender)

send_IPI_allbutself( )
> Sends an IPI to all CPUs except the sender

send_IPI_self( )
> Sends an IPI to the sender CPU

send_IPI_mask( )
> Sends an IPI to a group of CPUs specified by a bit mask

The assembly language code of the interprocessor interrupt handlers is generated by the BUILD_SMP_INTERRUPT macro; the code is almost identical to the code generated by the BUILD_IRQ macro (see the earlier section "Saving the registers for the interrupt handler").

Each interprocessor interrupt has a different high-level handler, which has the same name as the low-level handler preceded by smp_. For instance, the high-level handler of the RESCHEDULE_VECTOR interprocessor interrupt that is invoked by the low-level reschedule_interrupt( ) handler is named smp_reschedule_interrupt( ). Each high-level handler acknowledges the interprocessor interrupt on the local APIC and then performs the specific action triggered by the interrupt.

Softirqs, Tasklets, and Bottom Halves

We mentioned earlier in the section "Interrupt Handling" that several tasks among those executed by the kernel are not critical: they can be deferred for a long period of time, if necessary. Remember that the interrupt service routines of an interrupt handler are serialized, and often there should be no occurrence of an interrupt until the corresponding interrupt handler has terminated. Conversely, the deferrable tasks can execute with all interrupts enabled. Taking them out of the interrupt handler helps keep kernel response time small. This is a very important property for many time-critical applications that expect their interrupt requests to be serviced in a few milliseconds.

Linux 2.4 answers such a challenge by using three kinds of deferrable and interruptible kernel functions (in short, *deferrable functions*[*]): *softirqs*, *tasklets*, and *bottom halves*. Although these three kinds of deferrable functions work in different ways, they are strictly correlated. Tasklets are implemented on top of softirqs, and bottom halves are implemented by means of tasklets. As a matter of fact, the term "softirq," which appears in the kernel source code, often denotes all kinds of deferrable functions.

As a general rule, no softirq can be interrupted to run another softirq on the same CPU; the same rule holds for tasklets and bottom halves built on top of softirqs. On a multiprocessor system, however, several deferrable functions can run concurrently on different CPUs. The degree of concurrency depends on the type of deferrable function, as shown in Table 4-6.

Table 4-6. Differences between softirqs, tasklets, and bottom halves

Deferrable function	Dynamic allocation	Concurrency
Softirq	No	Softirqs of the same type can run concurrently on several CPUs.
Tasklet	Yes	Tasklets of different types can run concurrently on several CPUs, but tasklets of the same type cannot.
Bottom half	No	Bottom halves cannot run concurrently on several CPUs.

Softirqs and bottom halves are statically allocated (i.e., defined at compile time), while tasklets can also be allocated and initialized at runtime (for instance, when loading a kernel module).

Many softirqs can always be executed concurrently on several CPUs, even if they are of the same type. Generally speaking, softirqs are re-entrant functions and must explicitly protect their data structures with spin locks.

Tasklets differ from softirqs because a tasklet is always serialized with respect to itself; in other words, a tasklet cannot be executed by two CPUs at the same time. However, different tasklets can be executed concurrently on several CPUs. Serializing the tasklet simplifies the life of device driver developers, since the tasklet function needs not to be re-entrant.

Finally, bottom halves are globally serialized. When one bottom half is in execution on some CPU, the other CPUs cannot execute any bottom half, even if it is of different type. This is a quite strong limitation, since it degrades the performances of the Linux kernel on multiprocessor systems. As a matter of fact, bottom halves continue to be supported by the kernel for compatibility reasons only, and device driver developers are expected to update their old drivers and replace bottom halves with

---

[*] These are also called *software interrupts*, but we denote them as "deferrable functions" to avoid confusion with programmed exceptions, which are referred to as "software interrupts" in Intel manuals.

tasklets. Therefore, it is likely that bottom halves will disappear in a future version of Linux.

In any case, deferrable functions must be executed serially. Any deferrable function cannot be interleaved with other deferrable functions on the same CPU.

Generally speaking, four kinds of operations can be performed on deferrable functions:

Initialization

Defines a new deferrable function; this operation is usually done when the kernel initializes itself.

Activation

Marks a deferrable function as "pending"—to be run in the next round of executions of the deferrable functions. Activation can be done at any time (even while handling interrupts).

Masking

Selectively disables a deferrable function in such a way that it will not be executed by the kernel even if activated. We'll see in the section "Disabling Deferrable Functions" in Chapter 5 that disabling deferrable functions is sometimes essential.

Execution

Executes a pending deferrable function together with all other pending deferrable functions of the same type; execution is performed at well-specified times, explained later in the section "Softirqs."

Activation and execution are somehow bound together: a deferrable function that has been activated by a given CPU must be executed on the same CPU. There is no self-evident reason suggesting that this rule is beneficial for system performances. Binding the deferrable function to the activating CPU could in theory make better use of the CPU hardware cache. After all, it is conceivable that the activating kernel thread accesses some data structures that will also be used by the deferrable function. However, the relevant lines could easily be no longer in the cache when the deferrable function is run because its execution can be delayed a long time. Moreover, binding a function to a CPU is always a potentially "dangerous" operation, since a CPU might end up very busy while the others are mostly idle.

Softirqs

Linux 2.4 uses a limited number of softirqs. For most purposes, tasklets are good enough and are much easier to write because they do not need to be re-entrant.

As a matter of fact, only the four kinds of softirqs listed in Table 4-7 are currently defined.

Table 4-7. Softirqs used in Linux 2.4

Softirq	Index (priority)	Description
HI_SOFTIRQ	0	Handles high-priority tasklets and bottom halves
NET_TX_SOFTIRQ	1	Transmits packets to network cards
NET_RX_SOFTIRQ	2	Receives packets from network cards
TASKLET_SOFTIRQ	3	Handles tasklets

The index of a sofirq determines its priority: a lower index means higher priority because softirq functions will be executed starting from index 0.

The main data structure used to represent softirqs is the softirq_vec array, which includes 32 elements of type softirq_action. The priority of a softirq is the index of the corresponding softirq_action element inside the array. As shown in Table 4-7, only the first four entries of the array are effectively used. The softirq_action data structure consists of two fields: a pointer to the softirq function and a pointer to a generic data structure that may be needed by the softirq function.

The irq_stat array, already introduced in the section "IRQ data structures," includes several fields used by the kernel to implements softirqs (and also tasklets and bottom halves, which depend on softirqs). Each element of the array, corresponding to a given CPU, includes:

- A __softirq_pending field that points to a softirq_action structure (the pending softirq). This field may easily be accessed through the softirq_pending macro.

- A __local_bh_count field that disables the execution of the softirqs (as well as tasklets and bottom halves). This field may easily be accessed through the local_bh_count macro. If it is set to zero, the softirqs are enabled; alternatively, if the field stores a positive integer, the softirqs are disabled. The local_bh_disable macro increments the field, while the local_bh_enable macro decrements it. If the kernel invokes local_bh_disable twice, it must also call local_bh_enable twice to re-enable softirqs.[*]

- A __ksoftirqd_task field that stores the process descriptor address of a *ksoftirqd_CPUn* kernel thread, which is devoted to the execution of deferrable functions. (There is one such thread per CPU, and the *n* in *ksoftiqd_CPUn* represents the CPU index, as described later in the section "The softirq kernel threads.") This field can be accessed through the ksoftirqd_task macro.

The open_softirq() function takes care of softirq initialization. It uses three parameters: the softirq index, a pointer to the softirq function to be executed, and a second pointer to a data structure that may be required by the softirq function. open_softirq() limits itself to initialize the proper entry of the softirq_vec array.

---

[*] Better names for these two macros could be local_softirq_disable and local_softirq_enable. The actual names are vestiges of old kernel versions.

Softirqs are activated by invoking by the __cpu_raise_softirq macro, which receives as parameters the CPU number cpu and the softirq index nr, and sets the nrth bit of softirq_pending(cpu). The cpu_raise_softirq() function is similar to the __cpu_raise_softirq macro, except that it might also wake up the *ksoftirqd_CPUn* kernel thread.

Checks for pending softirqs are performed in a few points of the kernel code. Currently, this is done in the following cases (be warned that number and position of the softirq check points change both with the kernel version and with the supported hardware architecture):

- When the local_bh_enable macro re-enables the softirqs
- When the do_IRQ() function finishes handling an I/O interrupt
- When the smp_apic_timer_interrupt() function finishes handling a local timer interrupt (see the section "Timekeeping Architecture in Multiprocessor Systems" in Chapter 6)
- When one of the special *ksoftirqd_CPUn* kernel threads is awoken
- When a packet is received on a network interface card (see Chapter 18)

In each check point, the kernel reads softirq_pending(cpu); if this field is not null, the kernel invokes do_softirq() to execute the softirq functions. It performs the following actions:

1. Gets the logical number cpu of the CPU that executes the function.
2. Returns if local_irq_count(cpu) is not set to zero. In this case, do_softirq() is invoked while terminating a nested interrupt handler, and we know that deferrable functions must run outside of interrupt service routines.
3. Returns if local_bh_count(cpu) is not set to zero. In this case, all deferrable functions are disabled.
4. Saves the state of the IF flag and clears it to disable local interrupts.
5. Checks the softirq_pending(cpu) field of irq_stat. If no softirqs are pending, restores the value of the IF flag saved in the previous step, and then returns.
6. Invokes local_bh_disable(cpu) to increment the local_bh_count(cpu) field of irq_stat. In this way, deferrable functions are effectively serialized on the CPU because any further invocation of do_softirq() returns without executing the softirq functions (see check at Step 3).
7. Executes the following loop:

```
pending = softirq_pending(cpu);
softirq_pending(cpu) = 0;
mask = 0;
do {
    mask &= ~pending;
    asm("sti");
    for (i=0; pending; pending >>= 1, i++)
```

```
            if (pending & 1)
                softirq_vec[i].action(softirq_vec+i);
        asm("cli");
        pending = softirq_pending(cpu);
    } while (pending & mask);
```

As you may see, the function stores the pending softirqs in the pending local variable, and then resets the softirq_pending(cpu) field to zero. In each iteration of the loop, the function:

    a. Updates the mask local variable; it stores the indices of the softirqs that are already executed in this invocation of the do_softirq() function.

    b. Enables local interrupts.

    c. Executes the softirq functions of all pending softirqs (inner loop).

    d. Disables local interrupts.

    e. Reloads the pending local variable with the contents of the softirq_pending(cpu) field. An interrupt handler, or even a softirq function, could have invoked cpu_raise_softirq() while softirq functions were executing.

    f. Performs another iteration of the loop if a softirq that has not been handled in this invocation of do_softirq() is activated.

8. Decrements the local_bh_count(cpu) field, thus re-enabling the softirqs.

9. Checks the value of the pending local variable. If it is not zero, a softirq that was handled in this invocation of do_softirq() is activated again. To trigger another execution of the do_softirq() function, the function wakes up the *ksoftirqd_CPUn* kernel thread.

10. Restores the status of IF flag (local interrupts enabled or disabled) saved in Step 4 and returns.

The softirq kernel threads

In recent kernel versions, each CPU has its own *ksoftirqd_CPUn* kernel thread (where *n* is the logical number of the CPU). Each *ksoftirqd_CPUn* kernel thread runs the ksoftirqd() function, which essentially executes the following loop:

```
for(;;) {
    set_current_state(TASK_INTERRUPTIBLE);
    schedule();
    /* now in TASK_RUNNING state */
    while (softirq_pending(cpu)) {
        do_softirq();
        if (current->need_resched)
            schedule();
    }
}
```

When awoken, the kernel thread checks the softirq_pending(*n*) field and invokes, if necessary, do_softirq().

The *ksoftirqd_CPUn* kernel threads represent a solution for a critical trade-off problem.

Softirq functions may re-activate themselves; actually, both the networking softirqs and the tasklet softirqs do this. Moreover, external events, like packet flooding on a network card, may activate softirqs at very high frequency.

The potential for a continuous high-volume flow of softirqs creates a problem that is solved by introducing kernel threads. Without them, developers are essentially faced with two alternative strategies.

The first strategy consists of ignoring new softirqs that occur while do_softirq() is running. In other words, the do_softirq() function determines what softirqs are pending when the function is started, and then executes their functions. Next, it terminates without rechecking the pending softirqs. This solution is not good enough. Suppose that a softirq function is re-activated during the execution of do_softirq(). In the worst case, the softirq is not executed again until the next timer interrupt, even if the machine is idle. As a result, softirq latency time is unacceptable for networking developers.

The second strategy consists of continuously rechecking for pending softirqs. The do_softirq() function keeps checking the pending softirqs and terminates only when none of them is pending. While this solution might satisfy networking developers, it can certainly upset normal users of the system: if a high-frequency flow of packets is received by a network card or a softirq function keeps activating itself, the do_softirq() function never returns and the User Mode programs are virtually stopped.

The *ksoftirqd_CPUn* kernel threads try to solve this difficult trade-off problem. The do_softirq() function determines what softirqs are pending and executes their functions. If an already executed softirq is activated again, the function wakes up the kernel thread and terminates (Step 9 in of do_softirq()). The kernel thread has low priority, so user programs have a chance to run; but if the machine is idle, the pending softirqs are executed quickly.

Tasklets

Tasklets are the preferred way to implement deferrable functions in I/O drivers. As already explained, tasklets are built on top of two softirqs named HI_SOFTIRQ and TASKLET_SOFTIRQ. Several tasklets may be associated with the same softirq, each tasklet carrying its own function. There is no real difference between the two softirqs, except that do_softirq() executes HI_SOFTIRQ's tasklets before TASKLET_SOFTIRQ's tasklets.

Tasklets and high-priority tasklets are stored in the tasklet_vec and tasklet_hi_vec arrays, respectively. Both of them include NR_CPUS elements of type tasklet_head, and each element consists of a pointer to a list of *tasklet descriptors*. The tasklet descriptor is a data structure of type tasklet_struct, whose fields are shown in Table 4-8.

Table 4-8. The fields of the tasklet descriptor

Field name	Description
next	Pointer to next descriptor in the list
state	Status of the tasklet
count	Lock counter
func	Pointer to the tasklet function
data	An unsigned long integer that may be used by the tasklet function

The state field of the tasklet descriptor includes two flags:

TASKLET_STATE_SCHED

> When set, this indicates that the tasklet is pending (has been scheduled for execution); it also means that the tasklet descriptor is inserted in one of the lists of the tasklet_vec and tasklet_hi_vec arrays.

TASKLET_STATE_RUN

> When set, this indicates that the tasklet is being executed; on a uniprocessor system this flag is not used because there is no need to check whether a specific tasklet is running.

Let's suppose you're writing a device driver and you want to use a tasklet: what has to be done? First of all, you should allocate a new tasklet_struct data structure and initialize it by invoking tasklet_init(); this function receives as parameters the address of the tasklet descriptor, the address of your tasklet function, and its optional integer argument.

Your tasklet may be selectively disabled by invoking either tasklet_disable_nosync() or tasklet_disable(). Both functions increment the count field of the tasklet descriptor, but the latter function does not return until an already running instance of the tasklet function has terminated. To re-enable your tasklet, use tasklet_enable().

To activate the tasklet, you should invoke either the tasklet_schedule() function or the tasklet_hi_schedule() function, according to the priority that you require for your tasklet. The two functions are very similar; each of them performs the following actions:

1. Checks the TASKLET_STATE_SCHED flag; if it is set, returns (the tasklet has already been scheduled)
2. Gets the logical number of the CPU that is executing the function
3. Saves the state of the IF flag and clears it to disable local interrupts
4. Adds the tasklet descriptor at the beginning of the list pointed to by tasklet_vec[cpu] or tasklet_hi_vec[cpu]
5. Invokes cpu_raise_softirq() to activate either the TASKLET_SOFTIRQ softirq or the HI_SOFTIRQ softirq
6. Restores the value of the IF flag saved in Step 3 (local interrupts enabled or disabled)

Finally, let's see how your tasklet is executed. We know from the previous section that, once activated, softirq functions are executed by the do_softirq() function. The softirq function associated with the HI_SOFTIRQ softirq is named tasklet_hi_action(), while the function associated with TASKLET_SOFTIRQ is named tasklet_action(). Once again, the two functions are very similar; each of them:

1. Gets the logical number of the CPU that is executing the function.
2. Disables local interrupts, saving the previous state of the IF flag.
3. Stores the address of the list pointed to by tasklet_vec[cpu] or tasklet_hi_vec[cpu] in the list local variable.
4. Puts a NULL address in tasklet_vec[cpu] or tasklet_hi_vec[cpu]; thus, the list of scheduled tasklet descriptors is emptied.
5. Enables local interrupts.
6. For each tasklet descriptor in the list pointed to by list:

    a. In multiprocessor systems, checks the TASKLET_STATE_RUN flag of the tasklet. If it is set, a tasklet of the same type is already running on another CPU, so the function reinserts the task descriptor in the list pointed to by tasklet_vec[cpu] or tasklet_hi_vec[cpu] and activates the TASKLET_SOFTIRQ or HI_SOFTIRQ softirq again. In this way, execution of the tasklet is deferred until other tasklets of the same type are running on other CPUs.

    b. If the TASKLET_STATE_RUN flag is not set, the tasklet is not running on other CPUs. In multiprocessor systems, the function sets the flag so that the tasklet function cannot be executed on other CPUs.

    c. Checks whether the tasklet is disabled by looking at the count field of the tasklet descriptor. If it is disabled, it reinserts the task descriptor in the list pointed to by tasklet_vec[cpu] or tasklet_hi_vec[cpu]; then the function activates the TASKLET_SOFTIRQ or HI_SOFTIRQ softirq again.

    d. If the tasklet is enabled, clears the TASKLET_STATE_SCHED flag and executes the tasklet function.

Notice that, unless the tasklet function re-activates itself, every tasklet activation triggers at most one execution of the tasklet function.

Bottom Halves

A bottom half is essentially a high-priority tasklet that cannot be executed concurrently with any other bottom half, even if it is of a different type and on another CPU. The global_bh_lock spin lock is used to ensure that at most one bottom half is running.

Linux uses an array called the bh_base table to group all bottom halves together. It is an array of pointers to bottom halves and can include up to 32 entries, one for each type of bottom half. In practice, Linux uses about half of them; the types are listed in

Table 4-9. As you can see from the table, some of the bottom halves are associated with hardware devices that are not necessarily installed in the system or that are specific to platforms besides the IBM PC compatible. But TIMER_BH, TQUEUE_BH, SERIAL_BH, and IMMEDIATE_BH still see widespread use. We describe the TQUEUE_BH and IMMEDIATE_BH bottom half later in this chapter and the TIMER_BH bottom half in Chapter 6.

Table 4-9. The Linux bottom halves

Bottom half	Peripheral device
TIMER_BH	Timer
TQUEUE_BH	Periodic task queue
DIGI_BH	DigiBoard PC/Xe
SERIAL_BH	Serial port
RISCOM8_BH	RISCom/8
SPECIALIX_BH	Specialix I08+
AURORA_BH	Aurora multiport card (SPARC)
ESP_BH	Hayes ESP serial card
SCSI_BH	SCSI interface
IMMEDIATE_BH	Immediate task queue
CYCLADES_BH	Cyclades Cyclom-Y serial multiport
CM206_BH	CD-ROM Philips/LMS cm206 disk
MACSERIAL_BH	Power Macintosh's serial port
ISICOM_BH	MultiTech's ISI cards

The bh_task_vec array stores 32 tasklet descriptors, one for each bottom half. During kernel initialization, these tasklet descriptors are initialized in the following way:

```
for (i=0; i<32; ++i)
    tasklet_init(bh_task_vec+i, bh_action, i);
```

As usual, before a bottom half is invoked for the first time, it must be initialized. This is done by invoking init_bh(n, routine), which inserts the routine address as the nth entry of bh_base. Conversely, remove_bh(n) removes the nth bottom half from the table.

Bottom-half activation is done by invoking mark_bh( ). Since bottom halves are high-priority tasklets, mark_bh(n) just reduces to tasklet_hi_schedule(bh_task_vec+n).

The bh_action( ) function is the tasklet function common to all bottom halves. It receives as a parameter the index of the bottom half and performs the following steps:

1. Gets the logical number of the CPU executing the tasklet function.
2. Checks whether the global_bh_lock spin lock has already been acquired. In this case, another CPU is running a bottom half. The function invokes mark_bh( ) to re-activate the bottom half and returns.

3. Otherwise, the function acquires the global_bh_lock spin lock so that no other bottom half can be executed in the system.

4. Checks that the local_irq_count field is set to zero (bottom halves are supposed to be run outside interrupt service routines), and that global interrupts are enabled (see Chapter 5). If one of these cases doesn't hold, the function releases the global_bh_lock spin lock and terminates.

5. Invokes the bottom half function stored in the proper entry of the bh_base array.

6. Releases the global_bh_lock spin lock and returns.

Extending a bottom half

The motivation for introducing deferrable functions is to allow a limited number of functions related to interrupt handling to be executed in a deferred manner. This approach has been stretched in two directions:

- To allow not only a function that services an interrupt, but also a generic kernel function to be executed as a bottom half

- To allow several kernel functions, instead of a single one, to be associated with a bottom half

Groups of functions are represented by *task queues*, which are lists of tq_struct structures whose fields are shown in Table 4-10.

Table 4-10. The fields of the tq_struct structure

Field name	Description
list	Links for doubly linked list
sync	Used to prevent multiple activations
routine	Function to call
data	Argument for the function

As we shall see in Chapter 13, I/O device drivers use task queues to require the execution of several related functions when a specific interrupt occurs.

The DECLARE_TASK_QUEUE macro allocates a new task queue, while queue_task( ) inserts a new function in a task queue. The run_task_queue( ) function executes all the functions included in a given task queue.

It's worth mentioning three particular task queues:

- The tq_immediate task queue, run by the IMMEDIATE_BH bottom half, includes kernel functions to be executed together with the standard bottom halves. The kernel invokes mark_bh( ) to activate the IMMEDIATE_BH bottom half whenever a function is added to the tq_immediate task queue. It is executed as soon as do_softirq( ) is invoked.

- The `tq_timer` task queue is run by the `TQUEUE_BH` bottom half, which is activated at every timer interrupt. As we'll see in Chapter 6, that means it runs about every 10 ms.

- The `tq_context` task queue is not associated with a bottom half, but it is run by the *keventd* kernel thread. The `schedule_task()` function adds a function to the task queue; its execution is deferred until the scheduler selects the *keventd* kernel thread as the next process to run.

The main advantage of `tq_context`, with respect to the other task queues based on deferrable functions, is that its functions can freely perform blocking operations. On the other hand, softirqs (and therefore tasklets and bottom halves) are similar to interrupt handlers in that kernel developers cannot make any assumption on the process that will execute the deferrable functions. From a practical point of view, this means that softirqs cannot perform blocking operations like accessing a file, acquiring a semaphore, or sleeping in a wait queue.

The price to pay is that, once scheduled for execution in `tq_context`, a function might be delayed for quite a long time interval.

Returning from Interrupts and Exceptions

We will finish the chapter by examining the termination phase of interrupt and exception handlers. Although the main objective is clear—namely, to resume execution of some program—several issues must be considered before doing it:

Number of kernel control paths being concurrently executed
 If there is just one, the CPU must switch back to User Mode.

Pending process switch requests
 If there is any request, the kernel must perform process scheduling; otherwise, control is returned to the current process.

Pending signals
 If a signal is sent to the current process, it must be handled.

The kernel assembly language code that accomplishes all these things is not, technically speaking, a function, since control is never returned to the functions that invoke it. It is a piece of code with four different entry points called `ret_from_intr`, `ret_from_exception`, `ret_from_sys_call`, and `ret_from_fork`. We will refer to it as four different functions since this makes the description simpler, and we shall refer quite often to the following three entry points as functions:

`ret_from_exception( )`
 Terminates all exceptions except the 0x80 ones

`ret_from_intr( )`
 Terminates interrupt handlers

ret_from_sys_call()

Terminates system calls (i.e., kernel control paths engendered by 0x80 programmed exceptions)

ret_from_fork()

Terminates the fork( ), vfork( ), or clone( ) system calls (child only).

The general flow diagram with the corresponding four entry points is illustrated in Figure 4-5. The ret_from_exception() and ret_from_intr() entry points look the same in the picture, but they aren't. In the former case, the kernel knows the descriptor of the process that caused the exception; in the latter case, no process descriptor is associated with the interrupt. Besides the labels corresponding to the entry points, a few others have been added to allow you to relate the assembly language code more easily to the flow diagram. Let's now examine in detail how the termination occurs in each case.

The ret_from_exception( ) Function

The ret_from_exception( ) function is essentially equivalent to the following assembly language code:

```
ret_from_exception:
    movl 0x30(%esp),%eax
    movb 0x2C(%esp),%al
    testl $(0x000200003),%eax
    jne ret_from_sys_call
restore_all:
    popl %ebx
    popl %ecx
    popl %edx
    popl %esi
    popl %edi
    popl %ebp
    popl %eax
    popl %ds
    popl %es
    addl $4,%esp
    iret
```

The values of the cs and eflags registers, which were pushed on the stack when the exception occurred, are used by the function to determine whether the interrupted program was running in User Mode or if the VM flag of eflags was set.* In either case, a jump is made to the ret_from_sys_call() function. Otherwise, the interrupted kernel control path is to be restarted. The function loads the registers with the values saved by the SAVE_ALL macro when the exception started, and the function yields control to the interrupted program by executing the iret instruction.

---

* This flag allows programs to be executed in Virtual-8086 Mode; see the Pentium manuals for more details.

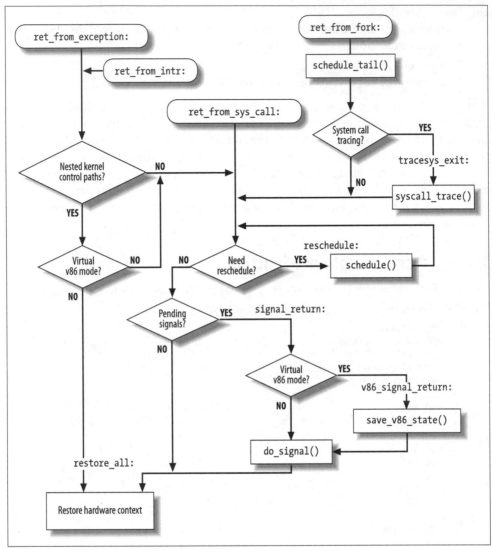

Figure 4-5. Returning from interrupts and exceptions

The ret_from_intr( ) Function

The ret_from_intr( ) function is essentially equivalent to ret_from_exception( ):

```
ret_from_intr:
    movl $0xffffe000,%ebx
    andl %esp,%ebx
    jmp ret_from_exception
```

Before invoking ret_from_exception( ), ret_from_intr( ) loads in the ebx register the address of the current's process descriptor (see the section "Identifying a Process" in

Chapter 3). This is necessary because the ret_from_sys_call() function, which can be invoked by ret_from_exception(), expects to find that address in ebx. On the other hand, when ret_from_exception() starts, the ebx register has already been loaded with current's address by the exception handler (see the section "Saving the Registers for the Exception Handler" earlier in this chapter).

The ret_from_sys_call( ) Function

The ret_from_sys_call() function is equivalent to the following assembly language code:

```
ret_from_sys_call:
    cli
    cmpl $0,20(%ebx)
    jne reschedule
    cmpl $0,8(%ebx)
    jne signal_return
    jmp restore_all
```

As we said previously, the ebx register points to the current process descriptor; within that descriptor, the need_resched field is at offset 20, which is checked by the first cmpl instruction. Therefore, if the need_resched field is 1, the schedule() function is invoked to perform a process switch:

```
reschedule:
    call schedule
    jmp ret_from_sys_call
```

The offset of the sigpending field inside the process descriptor is 8. If it is null, current resumes execution in User Mode by restoring the hardware context of the process saved on the stack. Otherwise, the function jumps to signal_return to process the pending signals of current:

```
signal_return:
    sti
    testl $(0x00020000),0x30(%esp)
    movl %esp,%eax
    jne v86_signal_return
    xorl %edx,%edx
    call do_signal
    jmp restore_all
v86_signal_return:
    call save_v86_state
    movl %eax,%esp
    xorl %edx,%edx
    call do_signal
    jmp restore_all
```

If the interrupted process was in VM86 mode, the save_v86_state() function is invoked. The do_signal() function (see Chapter 10) is then invoked to handle the pending signals. Finally, current can resume execution in User Mode.

The ret_from_fork( ) Function

The ret_from_fork( ) function is executed by the child process right after its creation through a fork( ), vfork( ), or clone( ) system call (see the section "The clone(), fork(), and vfork() System Calls" in Chapter 3). It is essentially equivalent to the following assembly language code:

```
ret_from_fork:
    pushl %ebx
    call schedule_tail
    addl $4,%esp
    movl $0xffffe000,%ebx
    andl %esp,%ebx
    testb $0x02,24(%ebx)
    jne tracesys_exit
    jmp ret_from_sys_call
tracesys_exit:
    call syscall_trace
    jmp ret_from_sys_call
```

Initially, the ebx register stores the address of the parent's process descriptor; this value is passed to the schedule_tail() function as a parameter (see Chapter 11). When that function returns, ebx is reloaded with the current's process descriptor address. Then the ret_from_fork() function checks the value of the ptrace field of the current (at offset 24 of the process descriptor). If the field is not null, the fork( ), vfork( ), or clone( ) system call is traced, so the syscall_trace( ) function is invoked to notify the debugging process. We give more details on system call tracing in Chapter 9.

CHAPTER 5

Kernel Synchronization

You could think of the kernel as a server that answers requests; these requests can come either from a process running on a CPU or an external device issuing an interrupt request. We make this analogy to underscore that parts of the kernel are not run serially, but in an interleaved way. Thus, they can give rise to race conditions, which must be controlled through proper synchronization techniques. A general introduction to these topics can be found in the section "An Overview of Unix Kernels" in Chapter 1.

We start this chapter by reviewing when, and to what extent, kernel requests are executed in an interleaved fashion. We then introduce the basic synchronization primitives implemented by the kernel and describe how they are applied in the most common cases. Finally we illustrate a few practical examples.

Kernel Control Paths

In the section "Nested Execution of Exception and Interrupt Handlers" in Chapter 4, a kernel control path was defined as a sequence of instructions executed by the kernel to handle interrupts of different kinds.

Each kernel request is handled by a different kernel control path, which usually executes several different kernel functions. For example, when a User Mode process issues a system call request, the system_call( ) function (see Chapter 9) begins this particular kernel control path and the ret_from_sys_call( ) function ends it (see the section "Returning from Interrupts and Exceptions" in Chapter 4).

As we said, kernel requests may be issued in several possible ways:

- A process executing in User Mode causes an exception—for instance, by executing an int 0x80 assembly language instruction.

- An external device sends a signal to a Programmable Interrupt Controller by using an IRQ line, and the corresponding interrupt is enabled.

- A process executing in Kernel Mode causes a Page Fault exception (see the section "Page Fault Exception Handler" in Chapter 8).

- A process running in a multiprocessor system and executing in Kernel Mode raises an interprocessor interrupt (see the section "Interprocessor Interrupt Handling" in Chapter 4).

Kernel control paths play a role similar to that of processes, except they are much more rudimentary. First, a descriptor is not attached to them; second, they are not scheduled through a single function, but rather by inserting sequences of instructions that stop or resume the paths into the kernel code.

In the simplest cases, the CPU executes a kernel control path sequentially from the first instruction to the last. However, the CPU interleaves kernel control paths when one of the following events happens:

- A process switch occurs. As we shall see in Chapter 11, a process switch can occur only when the schedule( ) function is invoked.

- An interrupt occurs while the CPU is running a kernel control path with interrupts enabled. In this case, the first kernel control path is left unfinished and the CPU starts processing another kernel control path to handle the interrupt.

- A deferrable function is executed. As we explained in the section "Softirqs" in Chapter 4, deferrable functions can be triggered by several events, such as interrupt occurrences or invocations of the local_bh_enable( ) function.

It is important to interleave kernel control paths to implement multiprocessing. In addition, as already noted in the section, "Nested Execution of Exception and Interrupt Handlers" in Chapter 4, interleaving improves the throughput of programmable interrupt controllers and device controllers.

While interleaving kernel control paths, special care must be applied to data structures that contain several related member variables—for instance, a buffer and an integer indicating its length. All statements affecting such a data structure must be put into a single critical section; otherwise, the data structure is in danger of being corrupted.

When Synchronization Is Not Necessary

As already pointed out, the Linux kernel is not preemptive—that is, a running process cannot be preempted (replaced by a higher-priority process) while it remains in Kernel Mode. In particular, the following assertions always hold in Linux:

- No process running in Kernel Mode may be replaced by another process, except when the former voluntarily relinquishes control of the CPU.[*]

---

[*] Of course, all process switches are performed in Kernel Mode. However, a process switch may occur only when the current process is going to return in User Mode.

- Interrupt, exception, or softirq handling can interrupt a process running in Kernel Mode; however, when the handler terminates, the kernel control path of the process is resumed.

- A kernel control path performing interrupt handling cannot be interrupted by a kernel control path executing a deferrable function or a system call service routine.

Thanks to these assertions, on uniprocessor systems kernel control paths dealing with nonblocking system calls are atomic with respect to other control paths started by system calls. This simplifies the implementation of many kernel functions: any kernel data structures that are not updated by interrupt, exception, or softirq handlers can be safely accessed. However, if a process in Kernel Mode voluntarily relinquishes the CPU, it must ensure that all data structures are left in a consistent state. Moreover, when it resumes its execution, it must recheck the value of all previously accessed data structures that could be changed. The change could be caused by a different kernel control path, possibly running the same code on behalf of a separate process.

As you would expect, things are much more complicated in multiprocessor systems. Many CPUs may execute kernel code at the same time, so kernel developers cannot assume that a data structure can be safely accessed just because it is never touched by an interrupt, exception, or softirq handler.

The rest of this chapter describes what to do when synchronization *is* necessary—i.e., how to prevent data corruption due to unsafe accesses to shared data structures.

Synchronization Primitives

Chapter 1 introduced the concepts of race condition and critical region for processes. The same definitions apply to kernel control paths. In this chapter, a race condition can occur when the outcome of a computation depends on how two or more interleaved kernel control paths are nested. A *critical region* is any section of code that must be completely executed by any kernel control path that enters it before another kernel control path can enter it.

We now examine how kernel control paths can be interleaved while avoiding race conditions among shared data. Table 5-1 lists the synchronization techniques used by the Linux kernel. The "Applies to" column indicates whether the synchronization technique applies to all CPUs in the system or to a single CPU. For instance, local interrupts disabling applies to just one CPU (other CPUs in the system are not affected); conversely, an atomic operation affects all CPUs in the system (atomic operations on several CPUs cannot interleave while accessing the same data structure).

Table 5-1. Various types of synchronization techniques used by the kernel

Technique	Description	Scope
Atomic operation	Atomic read-modify-write instruction to a counter	All CPUs
Memory barrier	Avoid instruction re-ordering	Local CPU
Spin lock	Lock with busy wait	All CPUs
Semaphore	Lock with blocking wait (sleep)	All CPUs
Local interrupt disabling	Forbid interrupt handling on a single CPU	Local CPU
Local softirq disabling	Forbid deferrable function handling on a single CPU	Local CPU
Global interrupt disabling	Forbid interrupt and softirq handling on all CPUs	All CPUs

Let's now briefly discuss each synchronization technique. In the later section "Synchronizing Accesses to Kernel Data Structures," we show how these synchronization techniques can be combined to effectively protect kernel data structures.

Atomic Operations

Several assembly language instructions are of type "read-modify-write"—that is, they access a memory location twice, the first time to read the old value and the second time to write a new value.

Suppose that two kernel control paths running on two CPUs try to "read-modify-write" the same memory location at the same time by executing nonatomic operations. At first, both CPUs try to read the same location, but the *memory arbiter* (a hardware circuit that serializes accesses to the RAM chips) steps in to grant access to one of them and delay the other. However, when the first read operation has completed, the delayed CPU reads exactly the same (old) value from the memory location. Both CPUs then try to write the same (new) value on the memory location; again, the bus memory access is serialized by the memory arbiter, and eventually both write operations succeed. However, the global result is incorrect because both CPUs write the same (new) value. Thus, the two interleaving "read-modify-write" operations act as a single one.

The easiest way to prevent race conditions due to "read-modify-write" instructions is by ensuring that such operations are atomic at the chip level. Any such operation must be executed in a single instruction without being interrupted in the middle and avoiding accesses to the same memory location by other CPUs. These very small *atomic operations* can be found at the base of other, more flexible mechanisms to create critical sections.

Let's review 80×86 instructions according to that classification.

- Assembly language instructions that make zero or one aligned memory access are atomic.[*]

- Read-modify-write assembly language instructions (such as inc or dec) that read data from memory, update it, and write the updated value back to memory are atomic if no other processor has taken the memory bus after the read and before the write. Memory bus stealing never happens in a uniprocessor system.

- Read-modify-write assembly language instructions whose opcode is prefixed by the lock byte (0xf0) are atomic even on a multiprocessor system. When the control unit detects the prefix, it "locks" the memory bus until the instruction is finished. Therefore, other processors cannot access the memory location while the locked instruction is being executed.

- Assembly language instructions (whose opcode is prefixed by a rep byte (0xf2, 0xf3), which forces the control unit to repeat the same instruction several times) are not atomic. The control unit checks for pending interrupts before executing a new iteration.

When you write C code, you cannot guarantee that the compiler will use a single, atomic instruction for an operation like a=a+1 or even for a++. Thus, the Linux kernel provides a special atomic_t type (a 24-bit atomically accessible counter) and some special functions (see Table 5-2) that act on atomic_t variables and are implemented as single, atomic assembly language instructions. On multiprocessor systems, each such instruction is prefixed by a lock byte.

Table 5-2. Atomic operations in Linux

Function	Description
atomic_read(v)	Return *v
atomic_set(v,i)	Set *v to i
atomic_add(i,v)	Add i to *v
atomic_sub(i,v)	Subtract i from *v
atomic_sub_and_test(i, v)	Subtract i from *v and return 1 if the result is zero; 0 otherwise
atomic_inc(v)	Add 1 to *v
atomic_dec(v)	Subtract 1 from *v
atomic_dec_and_test(v)	Subtract 1 from *v and return 1 if the result is zero; 0 otherwise
atomic_inc_and_test(v)	Add 1 to *v and return 1 if the result is zero; 0 otherwise
atomic_add_negative(i, v)	Add i to *v and return 1 if the result is negative; 0 otherwise

[*] A data item is aligned in memory when its address is a multiple of its size in bytes. For instance, the address of an aligned short integer must be a multiple of two, while the address of an aligned integer must be a multiple of four. Generally speaking, a unaligned memory access is not atomic.

Another class of atomic functions operate on bit masks (see Table 5-3). In this case, a bit mask is a generic integer variable.

Table 5-3. Atomic bit handling functions in Linux

Function	Description
test_bit(nr, addr)	Return the value of the nr^{th} bit of *addr
set_bit(nr, addr)	Set the nr^{th} bit of *addr
clear_bit(nr, addr)	Clear the nr^{th} bit of *addr
change_bit(nr, addr)	Invert the nr^{th} bit of *addr
test_and_set_bit(nr, addr)	Set the nr^{th} bit of *addr and return its old value
test_and_clear_bit(nr, addr)	Clear the nr^{th} bit of *addr and return its old value
test_and_change_bit(nr, addr)	Invert the nr^{th} bit of *addr and return its old value
atomic_clear_mask(mask, addr)	Clear all bits of addr specified by mask
atomic_set_mask(mask, addr)	Set all bits of addr specified by mask

Memory Barriers

When using optimizing compilers, you should never take for granted that instructions will be performed in the exact order in which they appear in the source code. For example, a compiler might reorder the assembly language instructions in such a way to optimize how registers are used. Moreover, modern CPUs usually execute several instructions in parallel, and might reorder memory accesses. These kinds of reordering can greatly speed up the program.

When dealing with synchronization, however, instructions reordering must be avoided. As a matter of fact, all synchronization primitives act as memory barriers. Things would quickly become hairy if an instruction placed after a synchronization primitive is executed before the synchronization primitive itself.

A *memory barrier* primitive ensures that the operations placed before the primitive are finished before starting the operations placed after the primitive. Thus, a memory barrier is like a firewall that cannot be passed by any assembly language instruction.

In the 80×86 processors, the following kinds of assembly language instructions are said to be "serializing" because they act as memory barriers:

- All instructions that operate on I/O ports
- All instructions prefixed by the lock byte (see the section "Atomic Operations")
- All instructions that write into control registers, system registers, or debug registers (for instance, cli and sti, which change the status of the IF flag in the eflags register)
- A few special assembly language instructions; among them, the iret instruction that terminates an interrupt or exception handler

Linux uses six memory barrier primitives, which are shown in Table 5-4. "Read memory barriers" act only on instructions that read from memory, while "write memory barriers" act only on instructions that write to memory. Memory barriers can be useful both in multiprocessor systems and in uniprocessor systems. The smp_ xxx() primitives are used whenever the memory barrier should prevent race conditions that might occur only in multiprocessor systems; in uniprocessor systems, they do nothing. The other memory barriers are used to prevent race conditions occurring both in uniprocessor and multiprocessor systems.

Table 5-4. Memory barriers in Linux

Macro	Description
mb()	Memory barrier for MP and UP
rmb()	Read memory barrier for MP and UP
wmb()	Write memory barrier for MP and UP
smp_mb()	Memory barrier for MP only
smp_rmb()	Read memory barrier for MP only
smp_wmb()	Write memory barrier for MP only

The implementations of the memory barrier primitives depend on the architecture of the system. For instance, on the Intel platform, the rmb() macro expands into asm volatile("lock;addl $0,0(%%esp)":::"memory"). The asm instruction tells the compiler to insert some assembly language instructions. The volatile keyword forbids the compiler to reshuffle the asm instruction with the other instructions of the program. The memory keyword forces the compiler to assume that all memory locations in RAM have been changed by the assembly language instruction; therefore, the compiler cannot optimize the code by using the values of memory locations stored in CPU registers before the asm instruction. Finally, the lock;addl $0,0(%%esp) assembly language instruction adds zero to the memory location on top of the stack; the instruction is useless by itself, but the lock prefix makes the instruction a memory barrier for the CPU. The wmb() macro on Intel is actually simpler because it expands into asm volatile("":::"memory"). This is because Intel processors never reorder write memory accesses, so there is no need to insert a serializing assembly language instruction in the code. The macro, however, forbids the compiler to reshuffle the instructions.

Notice that in multiprocessor systems, all atomic operations described in the earlier section "Atomic Operations" act as memory barriers because they use the lock byte.

Spin Locks

A widely used synchronization technique is *locking*. When a kernel control path must access a shared data structure or enter a critical region, it needs to acquire a "lock" for it. A resource protected by a locking mechanism is quite similar to a resource confined in a room whose door is locked when someone is inside. If a kernel control path wishes to access the resource, it tries to "open the door" by acquiring the lock. It succeeds only if the resource is free. Then, as long as it wants to use the resource, the door remains locked. When the kernel control path releases the lock, the door is unlocked and another kernel control path may enter the room.

Figure 5-1 illustrates the use of locks. Five kernel control paths (P0, P1, P2, P3, and P4) are trying to access two critical regions (C1 and C2). Kernel control path P0 is inside C1, while P2 and P4 are waiting to enter it. At the same time, P1 is inside C2, while P3 is waiting to enter it. Notice that P0 and P1 could run concurrently. The lock for critical region C3 is open since no kernel control path needs to enter it.

Figure 5-1. Protecting critical regions with several locks

Spin locks are a special kind of lock designed to work in a multiprocessor environment. If the kernel control path finds the spin lock "open," it acquires the lock and continues its execution. Conversely, if the kernel control path finds the lock "closed" by a kernel control path running on another CPU, it "spins" around, repeatedly executing a tight instruction loop, until the lock is released.

Of course, spin locks are useless in a uniprocessor environment, since the waiting kernel control path would keep running, so the kernel control path that is holding the lock would not have any chance to release it.

The instruction loop of spin locks represents a "busy wait." The waiting kernel control path keeps running on the CPU, even if it has nothing to do besides waste time. Nevertheless, spin locks are usually very convenient, since many kernel resources are locked for a fraction of a millisecond only; therefore, it would be far more time-consuming to release the CPU and reacquirie it later.

In Linux, each spin lock is represented by a spinlock_t structure consisting of a single lock field; the value 1 corresponds to the unlocked state, while any negative value and zero denote the locked state.

Five functions shown in Table 5-5 are used to initialize, test, and set spin locks. On uniprocessor systems, none of these functions do anything, except for spin_trylock(), which always returns 1. All these functions are based on atomic operations; this ensures that the spin lock will be properly updated by a process running on a CPU even if other processes running on different CPUs attempt to modify the spin lock at the same time.*

Table 5-5. Spin lock functions

Function	Description
spin_lock_init()	Set the spin lock to 1 (unlocked)
spin_lock()	Cycle until spin lock becomes 1 (unlocked), then set it to 0 (locked)
spin_unlock()	Set the spin lock to 1 (unlocked)
spin_unlock_wait()	Wait until the spin lock becomes 1 (unlocked)
spin_is_locked()	Return 0 if the spin lock is set to 1 (unlocked); 0 otherwise
spin_trylock()	Set the spin lock to 0 (locked), and return 1 if the lock is obtained; 0 otherwise

Let's discuss in detail the spin_lock macro, which is used to acquire a spin lock. It takes the address slp of the spin lock as its parameter and yields essentially the following assembly language code:†

```
1: lock; decb slp
   jns  3f
2: cmpb $0,slp
   pause
   jle 2b
   jmp 1b
3:
```

The decb assembly language instruction decrements the spin lock value; the instruction is atomic because it is prefixed by the lock byte. A test is then performed on the sign flag. If it is clear, it means that the spin lock was set to 1 (unlocked), so normal execution continues at label 3 (the f suffix denotes the fact that the label is a "forward" one; it appears in a later line of the program). Otherwise, the tight loop at label 2 (the b suffix denotes a "backward" label) is executed until the spin lock assumes a positive value. Then execution restarts from label 1, since it is unsafe to proceed without checking whether another processor has grabbed the lock. The pause assembly language instruction, which was introduced in the Pentium 4 model, is designed to optimize the execution of spin lock loops. By introducing a small

---

* Spin locks, ironically enough, are global and therefore must themselves be protected against concurrent accesses.

† The actual implementation of spin_lock is slightly more complicated. The code at label 2, which is executed only if the spin lock is busy, is included in an auxiliary section so that in the most frequent case (free spin lock) the hardware cache is not filled with code that won't be executed. In our discussion, we omit these optimization details.

delay, it speeds up the execution of code following the lock and reduces power consumption. The pause instruction is backward compatible with earlier models of Intel processors because it corresponds to the instructions rep;nop, which essentially do nothing.

The spin_unlock macro releases a previously acquired spin lock; it essentially yields the following code:

```
lock; movb $1, slp
```

Again, the lock byte ensures that the loading instruction is atomic.

Read/Write Spin Locks

Read/write spin locks have been introduced to increase the amount of concurrency inside the kernel. They allow several kernel control paths to simultaneously read the same data structure, as long as no kernel control path modifies it. If a kernel control path wishes to write to the structure, it must acquire the write version of the read/ write lock, which grants exclusive access to the resource. Of course, allowing concurrent reads on data structures improves system performance.

Figure 5-2 illustrates two critical regions (C1 and C2) protected by read/write locks. Kernel control paths R0 and R1 are reading the data structures in C1 at the same time, while W0 is waiting to acquire the lock for writing. Kernel control path W1 is writing the data structures in C2, while both R2 and W2 are waiting to acquire the lock for reading and writing, respectively.

Figure 5-2. Read/write spin locks

Each read/write spin lock is a rwlock_t structure; its lock field is a 32-bit field that encodes two distinct pieces of information:

- A 24-bit counter denoting the number of kernel control paths currently reading the protected data structure. The two's complement value of this counter is stored in bits 0–23 of the field.
- An unlock flag that is set when no kernel control path is reading or writing, and clear otherwise. This unlock flag is stored in bit 24 of the field.

Notice that the lock field stores the number 0x01000000 if the spin lock is idle (unlock flag set and no readers), the number 0x00000000 if it has been acquired for writing (unlock flag clear and no readers), and any number in the sequence 0x00ffffff, 0x00fffffe, and so on, if it has been acquired for reading by one, two, and more processes (unlock flag clear and the two's complement on 24 bits of the number of readers).

The rwlock_init macro initializes the lock field of a read/write spin lock to 0x01000000 (unlocked).

Getting and releasing a lock for reading

The read_lock macro, applied to the address rwlp of a read/write spin lock, essentially yields the following code:

```
        movl $rwlp,%eax
        lock; subl $1,(%eax)
        jns 1f
        call __read_lock_failed
    1:
```

where __read_lock_failed( ) is the following assembly language function:

```
    __read_lock_failed:
        lock; incl (%eax)
    1:  cmpl $1,(%eax)
        js 1b
        lock; decl (%eax)
        js __read_lock_failed
        ret
```

The read_lock macro atomically decreases the spin lock value by 1, thus incrementing the number of readers. The spin lock is acquired if the decrement operation yields a nonnegative value; otherwise, the __read_lock_failed( ) function is invoked. The function atomically increments the lock field to undo the decrement operation performed by the read_lock macro, and then loops until the field becomes positive (greater than or equal to 1). Next, __read_lock_failed( ) tries to get the spin lock again (another kernel control path could acquire the spin lock for writing right after the cmpl instruction).

Releasing the read lock is quite simple because the read_unlock macro must simply increment the counter in the lock field to decrease the number of readers; thus, the macro yields the following assembly language instruction:

```
    lock; incl rwlp
```

Getting and releasing a lock for writing

The write_lock function applied to the address rwlp of a read/write spin lock yields the following instructions:

```
        movl $rwlp,%eax
        lock; subl $0x01000000,(%eax)
```

```
        jz 1f
        call __write_lock_failed
    1:
```

where __write_lock_failed( ) is the following assembly language function:

```
    __write_lock_failed:
        lock; addl $0x01000000,(%eax)
    1:  cmpl $0x01000000,(%eax)
        jne 1b
        lock; subl $0x01000000,(%eax)
        jnz __write_lock_failed
        ret
```

The write_lock macro atomically subtracts 0x01000000 from the spin lock value, thus clearing the unlock flag. The spin lock is acquired if the subtraction operation yields zero (no readers); otherwise, the __write_lock_failed( ) function is invoked. This function atomically adds 0x01000000 to the lock field to undo the subtraction operation performed by the write_lock macro, and then loops until the spin lock becomes idle (lock field equal to 0x01000000). Next, __write_lock_failed( ) tries to get the spin lock again (another kernel control path could acquire the spin lock right after the cmpl instruction).

Once again, releasing the write lock is much simpler because the write_unlock macro must simply set the unlock flag in the lock field. Thus, the macro yields the following assembly language instruction:

```
        lock; addl $0x01000000,rwlp
```

The Big Reader Lock

Read/write spin locks are useful for data structures that are accessed by many readers and a few writers. They are more convenient than normal spin locks because they allow several readers to concurrently access the protected data structure. However, any time a CPU acquires a read/write spin lock, the counter in rwlock_t must be updated. A further access to the rwlock_t data structure performed by another CPU incurs in a significant performance penalty because the hardware caches of the two processors must be synchronized. Even worse, the new CPU changes the rwlock_t data structure, so the cache of the former CPU becomes invalid and there is another performance penalty when the former CPU releases the lock. In short, reader CPUs are playing ping-pong with the cache line containing the read/write spin lock data structure.

A special type of read/write spin locks, named *big reader read/write spin locks*, was designed to address this problem. The idea is to split the "reader" portion of the lock across all CPUs, so that each per-CPU data structure lies in its own line of the hardware caches. Readers do not need to stomp one another, so no reader CPU "snoops" the reader lock of another CPU. Conversely, the "writer" portion of the lock is common to all CPUs because only one CPU can acquire the lock for writing.

The __brlock_array array stores the "reader" portions of the big reader read/write spin locks; for every such lock, and for every CPU in the system, the array includes a lock flag, which is set to 1 when the lock is closed for reading by the corresponding CPU. Conversely, the __br_write_locks array stores the "writer" portions of the big reader spin locks—that is, a normal spin lock that is set when the big reader spin lock has been acquired for writing.

The br_read_lock() function acquires the spin lock for reading. It just sets the lock flag in __brlock_array corresponding to the executing CPU and the big reader spin lock to 1, and then waits until the spin lock in __br_write_locks is open. Conversely, the br_read_unlock() function simply clears the lock flag in _brlock_array.

The br_write_lock() function acquires the spin lock for writing. It invokes spin_lock to get the spin lock in __br_write_locks corresponding to the big reader spin lock, and then checks that all lock flags in __brlock_array corresponding to the big reader lock are cleared; if not, it releases the spin lock in __br_write_locks and starts again. The br_write_unlock() function simply invokes spin_unlock to release the spin lock in __br_write_locks.

As you may notice, acquiring an open big reader spin lock for reading is really fast, but acquiring it for writing is very slow because the CPU must acquire a spin lock and check several lock flags. Thus, big reader spin locks are rarely used. On the Intel architecture, there is just one big reader spin lock, used in the networking code.

Semaphores

We have already introduced semaphores in the section "Synchronization and Critical Regions" in Chapter 1. Essentially, they implement a locking primitive that allows waiters to sleep until the desired resource becomes free.

Actually, Linux offers two kinds of semaphores:

- Kernel semaphores, which are used by kernel control paths
- System V IPC semaphores, which are used by User Mode processes

In this section, we focus on kernel semaphores, while IPC semaphores are described in Chapter 19.

A kernel semaphore is similar to a spin lock, in that it doesn't allow a kernel control path to proceed unless the lock is open. However, whenever a kernel control path tries to acquire a busy resource protected by a kernel semaphore, the corresponding process is suspended. It becomes runnable again when the resource is released. Therefore, kernel semaphores can be acquired only by functions that are allowed to sleep; interrupt handlers and deferrable functions cannot use them.

A kernel semaphore is an object of type struct semaphore, containing the fields shown in the following list.

count
> Stores an atomic_t value. If it is greater than 0, the resource is free—that is, it is currently available. If count is equal to 0, the semaphore is busy but no other process is waiting for the protected resource. Finally, if count is negative, the resource is unavailable and at least one process is waiting for it.

wait
> Stores the address of a wait queue list that includes all sleeping processes that are currently waiting for the resource. Of course, if count is greater than or equal to 0, the wait queue is empty.

sleepers
> Stores a flag that indicates whether some processes are sleeping on the semaphore. We'll see this field in operation soon.

The init_MUTEX and init_MUTEX_LOCKED macros may be used to initialize a semaphore for exclusive access: they set the count field to 1 (free resource with exclusive access) and 0 (busy resource with exclusive access currently granted to the process that initializes the semaphore). Note that a semaphore could also be initialized with an arbitrary positive value n for count. In this case, at most n processes are allowed to concurrently access the resource.

Getting and releasing semaphores

Let's start by discussing how to release a semaphore, which is much simpler than getting one. When a process wishes to release a kernel semaphore lock, it invokes the up( ) assembly language function. This function is essentially equivalent to the following code:

```
        movl $sem,%ecx
        lock; incl (%ecx)
        jg 1f
        pushl %eax
        pushl %edx
        pushl %ecx
        call __up
        popl %ecx
        popl %edx
        popl %eax
    1:
```

where __up( ) is the following C function:

```
    void __up(struct semaphore *sem)
    {
        wake_up(&sem->wait);
    }
```

The up( ) function increments the count field of the *sem semaphore (at offset 0 of the semaphore structure), and then it checks whether its value is greater than 0. The increment of count and the setting of the flag tested by the following jump instruction must be atomically executed; otherwise, another kernel control path could concurrently access the field value, with disastrous results. If count is greater than 0, there was no process sleeping in the wait queue, so nothing has to be done. Otherwise, the __up() function is invoked so that one sleeping process is woken up.

Conversely, when a process wishes to acquire a kernel semaphore lock, it invokes the down() function. The implementation of down() is quite involved, but it is essentially equivalent to the following:

```
down:
    movl $sem,%ecx
    lock; decl (%ecx);
    jns 1f
    pushl %eax
    pushl %edx
    pushl %ecx
    call __down
    popl %ecx
    popl %edx
    popl %eax
1:
```

where __down() is the following C function:

```
void __down(struct semaphore * sem)
{
    DECLARE_WAITQUEUE(wait, current);
    current->state = TASK_UNINTERRUPTIBLE;
    add_wait_queue_exclusive(&sem->wait, &wait);
    spin_lock_irq(&semaphore_lock);
    sem->sleepers++;
    for (;;) {
        if (!atomic_add_negative(sem->sleepers-1, &sem->count)) {
            sem->sleepers = 0;
            break;
        }
        sem->sleepers = 1;
        spin_unlock_irq(&semaphore_lock);
        schedule();
        current->state = TASK_UNINTERRUPTIBLE;
        spin_lock_irq(&semaphore_lock);
    }
    spin_unlock_irq(&semaphore_lock);
    remove_wait_queue(&sem->wait, &wait);
    current->state = TASK_RUNNING;
    wake_up(&sem->wait);
}
```

The down() function decrements the count field of the *sem semaphore (at offset 0 of the semaphore structure), and then checks whether its value is negative. Again, the decrement and the test must be atomically executed. If count is greater than or equal to 0, the current process acquires the resource and the execution continues normally. Otherwise, count is negative and the current process must be suspended. The contents of some registers are saved on the stack, and then __down() is invoked.

Essentially, the __down() function changes the state of the current process from TASK_RUNNING to TASK_UNINTERRUPTIBLE, and puts the process in the semaphore wait queue. Before accessing other fields of the semaphore structure, the function also gets the semaphore_lock spin lock and disables local interrupts. This ensures that no process running on another CPU is able to read or modify the fields of the semaphore while the current process is updating them.

The main task of the __down() function is to suspend the current process until the semaphore is released. However, the way in which this is done is quite involved. To easily understand the code, keep in mind that the sleepers field of the semaphore is usually set to 0 if no process is sleeping in the wait queue of the semaphore, and it is set to 1 otherwise. Let's try to explain the code by considering a few typical cases.

*MUTEX semaphore open (*count *equal to 1,* sleepers *equal to 0)*
> The down macro just sets the count field to 0 and jumps to the next instruction of the main program; therefore, the __down() function is not executed at all.

*MUTEX semaphore closed, no sleeping processes (*count *equal to 0,* sleepers *equal to 0)*
> The down macro decrements count and invokes the __down() function with the count field set to −1 and the sleepers field set to 0. In each iteration of the loop, the function checks whether the count field is negative. (Observe that the count field is not changed by atomic_add_negative() because sleepers is equal to 0 when the function is invoked.)
>
> - If the count field is negative, the function invokes schedule() to suspend the current process. The count field is still set to −1, and the sleepers field to 1. The process picks up its run subsequently inside this loop and issues the test again.
> - If the count field is not negative, the function sets sleepers to 0 and exits from the loop. It tries to wake up another process in the semaphore wait queue (but in our scenario, the queue is now empty), and terminates holding the semaphore. On exit, both the count field and the sleepers field are set to 0, as required when the semaphore is closed but no process is waiting for it.

*MUTEX semaphore closed, other sleeping processes (*count *equal to −1,* sleepers *equal to 1)*
> The down macro decrements count and invokes the __down() function with count set to −2 and sleepers set to 1. The function temporarily sets sleepers to 2, and then undoes the decrement performed by the down macro by adding the value sleepers−1 to count. At the same time, the function checks whether count is still negative (the semaphore could have been released by the holding process right before __down() entered the critical region).

- If the count field is negative, the function resets sleepers to 1 and invokes schedule( ) to suspend the current process. The count field is still set to -1, and the sleepers field to 1.

- If the count field is not negative, the function sets sleepers to 0, tries to wake up another process in the semaphore wait queue, and exits holding the semaphore. On exit, the count field is set to 0 and the sleepers field to 0. The values of both fields look wrong, because *there are* other sleeping processes. However, consider that another process in the wait queue has been woken up. This process does another iteration of the loop; the atomic_add_ negative( ) function subtracts 1 from count, restoring it to −1; moreover, before returning to sleep, the woken-up process resets sleepers to 1.

As you may easily verify, the code properly works in all cases. Consider that the wake_up( ) function in __down( ) wakes up at most one process because the sleeping processes in the wait queue are exclusive (see the section "How Processes Are Organized" in Chapter 3).

Only exception handlers, and particularly system call service routines, can use the down( ) function. Interrupt handlers or deferrable functions must not invoke down( ), since this function suspends the process when the semaphore is busy.* For this reason, Linux provides the down_trylock( ) function, which may be safely used by one of the previously mentioned asynchronous functions. It is identical to down( ) except when the resource is busy. In this case, the function returns immediately instead of putting the process to sleep.

A slightly different function called down_interruptible( ) is also defined. It is widely used by device drivers since it allows processes that receive a signal while being blocked on a semaphore to give up the "down" operation. If the sleeping process is woken up by a signal before getting the needed resource, the function increments the count field of the semaphore and returns the value -EINTR. On the other hand, if down_ interruptible( ) runs to normal completion and gets the resource, it returns 0. The device driver may thus abort the I/O operation when the return value is -EINTR.

Finally, since processes usually find semaphores in an open state, the semaphore functions are optimized for this case. In particular, the up( ) function does not enter in a critical region if the semaphore wait queue is empty; similarly, the down( ) function does not enter in a critical region if the semaphore is open. Much of the complexity of the semaphore implementation is precisely due to the effort of avoiding costly instructions in the main branch of the execution flow.

---

* Exception handlers can block on a semaphore. Linux takes special care to avoid the particular kind of race condition in which two nested kernel control paths compete for the same semaphore; if that happens, one of them waits forever because the other cannot run and free the semaphore.

Read/Write Semaphores

Read/write semaphores are a new feature of Linux 2.4. They are similar to the read/write spin locks described earlier in the section "Read/Write Spin Locks," except that waiting processes are suspended until the semaphore becomes open again.

Many kernel control paths may concurrently acquire a read/write semaphore for reading; however, any writer kernel control path must have exclusive access to the protected resource. Therefore, the semaphore can be acquired for writing only if no other kernel control path is holding it for either read or write access. Read/write semaphores improve the amount of concurrency inside the kernel and improve overall system performance.

The kernel handles all processes waiting for a read/write semaphore in strict FIFO order. Each reader or writer that finds the semaphore closed is inserted in the last position of a semaphore's wait queue list. When the semaphore is released, the processes in the first positions of the wait queue list is checked. The first process is always awoken. If it is a writer, the other processes in the wait queue continue to sleep. If it is a reader, any other reader following the first process is also woken up and gets the lock. However, readers that have been queued after a writer continue to sleep.

Each read/write semaphore is described by a rw_semaphore structure that includes the following fields:

count
> Stores two 16-bit counters. The counter in the most significant word encodes in two's complement form the sum of the number of nonwaiting writers (either 0 or 1) and the number of waiting kernel control paths. The counter in the less significant word encodes the total number of nonwaiting readers and writers.

wait_list
> Points to a list of waiting processes. Each element in this list is a rwsem_waiter structure, including a pointer to the descriptor of the sleeping process and a flag indicating whether the process wants the semaphore for reading or for writing.

wait_lock
> A spin lock used to protect the wait queue list and the rw_semaphore structure itself.

The init_rwsem() function initializes a rw_semaphore structure by setting the count field to 0, the wait_lock spin lock to unlocked, and wait_list to the empty list.

The down_read() and down_write() functions acquire the read/write semaphore for reading and writing, respectively. Similarly, the up_read() and up_write() functions release a read/write semaphore previously acquired for reading and for writing. The implementation of these four functions is long, but easy to follow because it resembles the implementation of normal semaphores; therefore, we avoid describing them.

Completions

Linux 2.4 also makes use of another synchronization primitive similar to semaphores: the *completions*. They have been introduced to solve a subtle race condition that occurs in multiprocessor systems when process A allocates a temporary semaphore variable, initializes it as closed MUTEX, passes its address to process B, and then invokes down() on it. Later on, process B running on a different CPU invokes up() on the same semaphore. However, the current implementation of up() and down() also allows them to execute concurrently on the same semaphore. Thus, process A can be woken up and destroy the temporary semaphore while process B is still executing the up() function. As a result, up() might attempt to access a data structure that no longer exists.

Of course, it is possible to change the implementation of down() and up() to forbid concurrent executions on the same semaphore. However, this change would require additional instructions, which is a bad thing to do for functions that are so heavily used.

The completion is a synchronization primitive that is specifically designed to solve this problem. The completion data structure includes a wait queue head and a flag:

```
struct completion {
    unsigned int done;
    wait_queue_head_t wait;
};
```

The function corresponding to up() is called complete(). It receives as an argument the address of a completion data structure, sets the done field to 1, and invokes wake_up() to wake up the exclusive process sleeping in the wait wait queue.

The function corresponding to down() is called wait_for_completion(). It receives as an argument the address of a completion data structure and checks the value of the done flag. If it is set to 1, wait_for_completion() terminates because complete() has already been executed on another CPU. Otherwise, the function adds current to the tail of the wait queue as an exclusive process and puts current to sleep in the TASK_UNINTERRUPTIBLE state. Once woken up, the function removes current from the wait queue, sets done to 0, and terminates.

The real difference between completions and semaphores is how the spin lock included in the wait queue is used. Both complete() and wait_for_completion() use this spin lock to ensure that they cannot execute concurrently, while up() and down() use it only to serialize accesses to the wait queue list.

Local Interrupt Disabling

Interrupt disabling is one of the key mechanisms used to ensure that a sequence of kernel statements is treated as a critical section. It allows a kernel control path to continue executing even when hardware devices issue IRQ signals, thus providing an effective way to protect data structures that are also accessed by interrupt handlers. By itself, however, local interrupt disabling does not protect against concurrent accesses to data structures by interrupt handlers running on other CPUs, so in multiprocessor systems, local interrupt disabling is often coupled with spin locks (see the later section "Synchronizing Accesses to Kernel Data Structures").

Interrupts can be disabled on a CPU with the cli assembly language instruction, which is yielded by the __cli() macro. Interrupts can be enabled on a CPU by means of the sti assembly language instruction, which is yielded by the __sti() macro. Recent kernel versions also define the local_irq_disable() and local_irq_enable() macros, which are equivalent respectively to __cli() and __sti(), but whose names are not architecture dependent and are also much easier to understand.

When the kernel enters a critical section, it clears the IF flag of the eflags register to disable interrupts. But at the end of the critical section, often the kernel can't simply set the flag again. Interrupts can execute in nested fashion, so the kernel does not necessarily know what the IF flag was before the current control path executed. In these cases, the control path must save the old setting of the flag and restore that setting at the end.

Saving and restoring the eflags content is achieved by means of the __save_flags and __restore_flags macros, respectively. Typically, these macros are used in the following way:

```
__save_flags(old);
__cli();
[...]
__restore_flags(old);
```

The __save_flags macro copies the content of the eflags register into the old local variable; the IF flag is then cleared by __cli(). At the end of the critical region, the macro __restore_flags restores the original content of eflags; therefore, interrupts are enabled only if they were enabled before this control path issued the __cli() macro. Recent kernel versions also define the local_irq_save() and local_irq_restore() macros, which are essentially equivalent to __save_flags() and __restore_flags(), but whose names are easier to understand.

Global Interrupt Disabling

Some critical kernel functions can execute on a CPU only if no interrupt handler or deferrable function is running on any other CPU. This synchronization requirement is satisfied by *global interrupt disabling*. A typical scenario consists of a driver that needs to reset the hardware device. Before fiddling with I/O ports, the driver performs global interrupt disabling, ensuring that no other driver will access the same ports.

As we shall see in this section, global interrupt disabling significantly lowers the system concurrency level; it is deprecated because it can be replaced by more efficient synchronization techniques.

Global interrupt disabling is performed by the cli() macro. On uniprocessor system, the macro just expands into __cli(), disabling local interrupts. On multiprocessor systems, the macro waits until all interrupt handlers and all deferrable functions in the other CPUs terminate, and then acquires the global_irq_lock spin lock. The key activities required for multiprocessor systems occur inside the __global_cli() function, which is called by cli():

```
__save_flags(flags);
if (!(flags & 0x00000200)) /* testing IF flag */ {
    __cli();
    if (!local_irq_count[smp_processor_id()])
        get_irqlock(smp_processor_id());
}
```

First of all, __global_cli() checks the value of the IF flag of the eflags register because it refuses to "promote" the disabling of a local interrupt to a global one. Deadlock conditions can easily occur if this constraint is removed and global interrupts are disabled inside a critical region protected by a spin lock. For instance, consider a spin lock that is also accessed by interrupt handlers. Before acquiring the spin lock, the kernel must disable local interrupts, otherwise an interrupt handler could freeze waiting until the interrupted program released the spin lock. Now, suppose that a kernel control path disables local interrupts, acquires the spin lock, and then invokes cli(). The latter macro waits until all interrupt handlers on the other CPUs terminate; however, an interrupt handler could be stuck waiting for the spin lock to be released. To avoid this kind of deadlock, __global_cli() refuses to run if local interrupts are already disabled before its invocation.

If cli() is invoked with local interrupts enabled, __global_cli() disables them. If cli() is invoked inside an interrupt service routine (i.e., local_irq_count macro returns a value different than 0), __global_cli() returns without performing any further action.* Otherwise, __global_irq() invokes the get_irqlock() function, which acquires the global_irq_lock spin lock and waits for the termination of all interrupt handlers running on the other CPUs. Moreover, if cli() is not invoked by a deferrable function, get_irqlock() waits for the termination of all bottom halves running on the other CPUs.

global_irq_lock differs from normal spin locks because invoking get_irqlock() does not freeze the CPU if it already owns the lock. In fact, the global_irq_holder variable contains the logical identifier of the CPU that is holding the lock; this value is checked by get_irqlock() before starting the tight loop of the spin lock.

---

* This case should never occur because protection against concurrent execution of interrupt handlers should be based on spin locks rather than on global interrupt disabling. In short, an interrupt service routine should never execute the cli() macro.

Once cli( ) returns, no other interrupt handler on other CPUs starts running until interrupts are re-enabled by invoking the sti( ) macro. On multiprocessor systems, sti( ) invokes the __global_sti( ) function:

```
cpu = smp_processor_id( );
if (!local_irq_count[cpu])
    release_irqlock(cpu);
__sti( );
```

The release_irqlock( ) function releases the global_irq_lock spin lock. Notice that similar to cli( ), the sti( ) macro invoked inside an interrupt service routine is equivalent to __sti( ) because it doesn't release the spin lock.

Linux also provides global versions of the __save_flags and __restore_flags macros, which are also called save_flags and restore_flags. They save and reload, respectively, information controlling the interrupt handling for the executing CPU. As illustrated in Figure 5-3, save_flags yields an integer value that depends on three conditions; restore_flags performs actions based on the value yielded by save_flags.

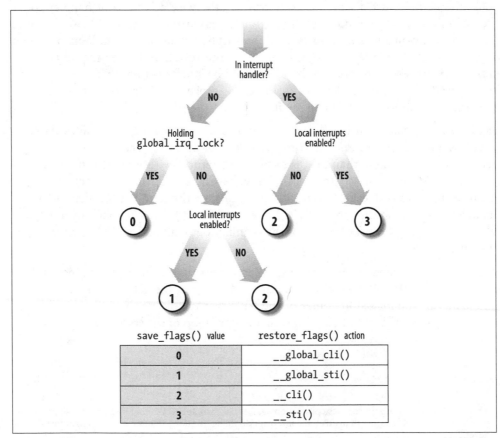

save_flags( ) value	restore_flags( ) action
0	__global_cli( )
1	__global_sti( )
2	__cli( )
3	__sti( )

Figure 5-3. Actions performed by save_flags() and restore_flags()

Finally, the synchronize_irq( ) function is called when a kernel control path wishes to synchronize itself with all interrupt handlers:

```
for (i = 0; i < smp_num_cpus; i++)
    if (local_irq_count(i)) {
        cli();
        sti();
        break;
    }
```

By invoking cli( ), the function acquires the global_irq_lock spin lock and then waits until all executing interrupt handlers terminate; once this is done, it reenables interrupts. The synchronize_irq( ) function is usually called by device drivers when they want to make sure that all activities carried on by interrupt handlers are over.

Disabling Deferrable Functions

In the section "Softirqs" in Chapter 4, we explained that deferrable functions can be executed at unpredictable times (essentially, on termination of hardware interrupt handlers). Therefore, data structures accessed by deferrable functions must be protected against race conditions.

A trivial way to forbid deferrable functions execution on a CPU is to disable interrupts on that CPU. Since no interrupt handler can be activated, softirq actions cannot be started asynchronously.

Globally disabling interrupts on all CPUs also disable deferrable functions on all CPUs. In fact, recall that the do_softirq() function refuses to execute the softirqs when the global_irq_lock spin lock is closed. When the cli() macro returns, the invoking kernel control path can assume that no deferrable function is in execution on any CPU, and that none are started until interrupts are globally re-enabled.

As we shall see in the next section, however, the kernel sometimes needs to disable deferrable functions without disabling interrupts. Local deferrable functions can be disabled on each CPU by setting the __local_bh_count field of the irq_stat structure associated with the CPU to a nonzero value. Recall that the do_softirq() function never executes the softirqs if it finds a nonzero value in this field. Moreover, tasklets and bottom halves are implemented on top of softirqs, so writing a nonzero value in the field disables the execution of all deferrable functions on a given CPU, not just softirqs.

The local_bh_disable macro increments the __local_bh_count field by 1, while the local_bh_enable macro decrements it. The kernel can thus use several nested invocations of local_bh_disable; deferrable functions will be enabled again only by the local_bh_enable macro matching the first local_bh_disable invocation.

Synchronizing Accesses to Kernel Data Structures

A shared data structure can be protected against race conditions by using some of the synchronization primitives shown in the previous section. Of course, system performances may vary considerably, depending on the kind of synchronization primitive selected. Usually, the following rule of thumb is adopted by kernel developers: *always keep the concurrency level as high as possible in the system.*

In turn, the concurrency level in the system depends on two main factors:

1. The number of I/O devices that operate concurrently
2. The number of CPUs that do productive work

To maximize I/O throughput, interrupts should be disabled for very short periods of time. As described in the section "IRQs and Interrupts" in Chapter 4, when interrupts are disabled, IRQs issued by I/O devices are temporarily ignored by the PIC and no new activity can start on such devices.

To use CPUs efficiently, synchronization primitives based on spin locks should be avoided whenever possible. When a CPU is executing a tight instruction loop waiting for the spin lock to open, it is wasting precious machine cycles.

Let's illustrate a couple of cases in which synchronization can be achieved while still maintaining a high concurrency level.

- A shared data structure consisting of a single integer value can be updated by declaring it as an atomic_t type and by using atomic operations. An atomic operation is faster than spin locks and interrupt disabling, and it slows down only kernel control paths that concurrently access the data structure.

- Inserting an element into a shared linked list is never atomic since it consists of at least two pointer assignments. Nevertheless, the kernel can sometimes perform this insertion operation without using locks or disabling interrupts. As an example of why this works, we'll consider the case where a system call service routine (see "System Call Handler and Service Routines" in Chapter 9") inserts new elements in a simply linked list, while an interrupt handler or deferrable function asynchronously looks up the list.

  In the C language, insertion is implemented by means of the following pointer assignments:

  ```
  new->next = list_element->next;
  list_element->next = new;
  ```

  In assembly language, insertion reduces to two consecutive atomic instructions. The first instruction sets up the next pointer of the new element, but it does not modify the list. Thus, if the interrupt handler sees the list between the execution of the first and second instructions, it sees the list without the new element. If the handler sees the list after the execution of the second instruction, it sees the list with the new element. The important point is that in either case, the list is consistent and in an uncorrupted state. However, this integrity is assured only if the interrupt handler does not modify the list. If it does, the next pointer that was just set within the new element might become invalid.

However, developers must ensure that the order of the two assignment operations cannot be subverted by the compiler or the CPU's control unit; otherwise, if the system call service routine is interrupted by the interrupt handler between the two assignments, the handler finds a corrupted list. Therefore, a write memory barrier primitive is required:

```
new->next = list_element->next;
wmb();
list_element->next = new;
```

Choosing Among Spin Locks, Semaphores, and Interrupt Disabling

Unfortunately, access patterns to most kernel data structures are a lot more complex than the simple examples just shown, and kernel developers are forced to use semaphores, spin locks, interrupts, and softirq disabling. Generally speaking, choosing the synchronization primitives depends on what kinds of kernel control paths access the data structure, as shown in Table 5-6.

Table 5-6. Protection required by data structures accessed by kernel control paths

Kernel control paths accessing the data structure	UP protection	MP further protection
Exceptions	Semaphore	None
Interrupts	Local interrupt disabling	Spin lock
Deferrable functions	None	None or spin lock (see Table 5-8)
Exceptions + Interrupts	Local interrupt disabling	Spin lock
Exceptions + Deferrable functions	Local softirq disabling	Spin lock
Interrupts + Deferrable functions	Local interrupt disabling	Spin lock
Exceptions + Interrupts + Deferrable functions	Local interrupt disabling	Spin lock

Notice that global interrupt disabling does not appear in the table. Delaying interrupts on all CPUs significantly lowers the system concurrency level, so global interrupt disabling is usually deprecated and should be replaced by other synchronization techniques. As a matter of fact, this synchronization technique is still available in Linux 2.4 to support old device drivers; it has been removed from the Linux 2.5 current development version.

Protecting a data structure accessed by exceptions

When a data structure is accessed only by exception handlers, race conditions are usually easy to understand and prevent. The most common exceptions that give rise to synchronization problems are the system call service routines (see the section "System Call Handler and Service Routines" in Chapter 9) in which the CPU operates in Kernel Mode to offer a service to a User Mode program. Thus, a data structure accessed only by an exception usually represents a resource that can be assigned to one or more processes.

Race conditions are avoided through semaphores because these primitives allow the process to sleep until the resource becomes available. Notice that semaphores work equally well both in uniprocessor and multiprocessor systems.

Protecting a data structure accessed by interrupts

Suppose that a data structure is accessed by only the "top half" of an interrupt handler. We learned in the section "Interrupt Handling" in Chapter 4 that each interrupt handler is serialized with respect to itself—that is, it cannot execute more than once concurrently. Thus, accessing the data structure does not require any synchronization primitive.

Things are different, however, if the data structure is accessed by several interrupt handlers. A handler may interrupt another handler, and different interrupt handlers may run concurrently in multiprocessor systems. Without synchronization, the shared data structure might easily become corrupted.

In uniprocessor systems, race conditions must be avoided by disabling interrupts in all critical regions of the interrupt handler. Nothing less will do because no other synchronization primitives accomplish the job. A semaphore can block the process, so it cannot be used in an interrupt handler. A spin lock, on the other hand, can freeze the system: if the handler accessing the data structure is interrupted, it cannot release the lock; therefore, the new interrupt handler keeps waiting on the tight loop of the spin lock.

Multiprocessor systems, as usual, are even more demanding. Race conditions cannot be avoided by simply disabling local interrupts. In fact, even if interrupts are disabled on a CPU, interrupt handlers can still be executed on the other CPUs. The most convenient method to prevent the race conditions is to disable local interrupts (so that other interrupt handlers running on the same CPU won't interfere) *and* to acquire a spin lock or a read/write spin lock that protects the data structure. Notice that these additional spin locks cannot freeze the system because even if an interrupt handler finds the lock closed, eventually the interrupt handler on the other CPU that owns the lock will release it.

The Linux kernel uses several macros that couple local interrupts enabling/disabling with spin lock handling. Table 5-7 describes all of them. In uniprocessor systems, these macros just enable or disable local interrupts because the spin lock handling macros does nothing.

Table 5-7. Interrupt-aware spin lock macros

Function	Description
spin_lock_irq(l)	local_irq_disable(); spin_lock(l)
spin_unlock_irq(l)	spin_unlock(l); local_irq_enable()
spin_lock_irqsave(l,f)	local_irq_save(f); spin_lock(l)
spin_unlock_irqrestore(l,f)	spin_unlock(l); local_irq_restore(f)
read_lock_irq(l)	local_irq_disable(); read_lock(l)
read_unlock_irq(l)	read_unlock(l); local_irq_enable()
write_lock_irq(l)	local_irq_disable(); write_lock(l)
write_unlock_irq(l)	write_unlock(l); local_irq_enable()
read_lock_irqsave(l,f)	local_irq_save(f); read_lock(l)
read_unlock_irqrestore(l,f)	read_unlock(l); local_irq_restore(f)
write_lock_irqsave(l,f)	local_irq_save(f); write_lock(l)
write_unlock_irqrestore(l,f)	write_unlock(l); local_irq_restore(f)

Protecting a data structure accessed by deferrable functions

What kind of protection is required for a data structure accessed only by deferrable functions? Well, it mostly depends on the kind of deferrable function. In the section "Softirqs, Tasklets, and Bottom Halves" in Chapter 4, we explained that softirqs, tasklets, and bottom halves essentially differ in their degree of concurrency.

First of all, no race condition may exist in uniprocessor systems. This is because execution of deferrable functions is always serialized on a CPU—that is, a deferrable function cannot be interrupted by another deferrable function. Therefore, no synchronization primitive is ever required.

Conversely, in multiprocessor systems, race conditions do exist because several deferrable functions may run concurrently. Table 5-8 lists all possible cases.

Table 5-8. Protection required by data structures accessed by deferrable functions in SMP

Deferrable functions accessing the data structure	Protection
Softirqs	Spin lock
One tasklet	None
Many tasklets	Spin lock
Bottom halves	None

A data structure accessed by a softirq must always be protected, usually by means of a spin lock, because the same softirq may run concurrently on two or more CPUs. Conversely, a data structure accessed by just one kind of tasklet need not be protected, because tasklets of the same kind cannot run concurrently. However, if the data structure is accessed by several kinds of tasklets, then it must be protected.

Finally, a data structure accessed only by bottom halves need not be protected because bottom halves never run concurrently.

Notice that it is also possible to prevent the race conditions by globally disabling the deferrable functions by means of the cli( ) macro. However, this should be avoided because the macro also disables the execution of interrupt handlers on all CPUs of the system.

Protecting a data structure accessed by exceptions and interrupts

Let's consider now a data structure that is accessed both by exceptions (for instance, system call service routines) and interrupt handlers.

On uniprocessor systems, race condition prevention is quite simple because interrupt handlers are not re-entrant and cannot be interrupted by exceptions. So long as the kernel accesses the data structure with local interrupts disabled, the kernel cannot be interrupted when accessing the data structure. However, if the data structure is accessed by just one kind of interrupt handler, the interrupt handler can freely access the data structure without disabling local interrupts.

On multiprocessor systems, we have to take care of concurrent executions of exceptions and interrupts on other CPUs. Local interrupt disabling must be coupled with a spin lock, which forces the concurrent kernel control paths to wait until the handler accessing the data structure finishes its work.

Sometimes it might be preferable to replace the spin lock with a semaphore. Since interrupt handlers cannot be suspended, they must acquire the semaphore using a tight loop and the down_trylock( ) function; for them, the semaphore acts essentially as a spin lock. System call service routines, on the other hand, may suspend the calling processes when the semaphore is busy. For most system calls, this is the expected behavior; it is preferable because it increases the degree of concurrency of the system.

Protecting a data structure accessed by exceptions and deferrable functions

A data structure accessed both by exception handlers and deferrable functions can be treated like a data structure accessed by exception and interrupt handlers. In fact, deferrable functions are essentially activated by interrupt occurrences, and no exception can be raised while a deferrable function is running. Coupling local interrupt disabling with a spin lock is therefore sufficient.

Actually, this is much more than sufficient: the exception handler can simply disable deferrable functions instead of local interrupts by using the local_bh_disable( ) macro (see the section "Softirqs" in Chapter 4). Disabling only the deferrable functions is preferable to disabling interrupts because interrupts continue to be serviced on the CPU. Execution of deferrable functions on each CPU is serialized, so no race condition exists.

As usual, in multiprocessor systems, spin locks are required to ensure that the data structure is accessed at any time by just one kernel control path.[*]

Protecting a data structure accessed by interrupts and deferrable functions

This case is similar to that of a data structure accessed by interrupt and exception handlers. An interrupt might be raised while a deferrable function is running, but no deferrable function can stop an interrupt handler. Therefore, race conditions must be avoided by disabling local interrupts. However, an interrupt handler can freely touch the data structure accessed by the deferrable function without disabling interrupts, provided that no other interrupt handler accesses that data structure.

Again, in multiprocessor systems, a spin lock is always required to forbid concurrent accesses to the data structure on several CPUs.

Protecting a data structure accessed by exceptions, interrupts, and deferrable functions

Similarly to previous cases, disabling local interrupts and acquiring a spin lock is almost always necessary to avoid race conditions. Notice that there is no need to explicitly disable deferrable functions because they are essentially activated when terminating the execution of interrupt handlers; disabling local interrupts is therefore sufficient.

Examples of Race Condition Prevention

Kernel developers are expected to identify and solve the synchronization problems raised interleaving by kernel control paths. However, avoiding race conditions is a hard task because it requires a clear understanding of how the various components of the kernel interact. To give a feeling of what's really inside the kernel code, let's mention a few typical usages of the synchronization primitives defined in this chapter.

Reference Counters

Reference counters are widely used inside the kernel to avoid race conditions due to the concurrent allocation and releasing of a resource. A *reference counter* is just an atomic_t counter associated with a specific resource like a memory page, a module, or a file. The counter is atomically incremented when a kernel control path starts using the resource, and it is decremented when a kernel control path finishes using the resource. When the reference counter becomes zero, the resource is not being used, and it can be released if necessary.

---

[*] The spin lock is required even when the data structure is accessed only by exception handlers and bottom halves (see the section "Softirqs, Tasklets, and Bottom Halves" in Chapter 4). The kernel ensures that two bottom halves never run concurrently, but this is not enough to prevent race conditions.

The Global Kernel Lock

In earlier Linux kernel versions, a *global kernel lock* (also known as *big kernel lock*, or *BKL*) was widely used. In Version 2.0, this lock was a relatively crude spin lock, ensuring that only one processor at a time could run in Kernel Mode. The 2.2 kernel was considerably more flexible and no longer relied on a single spin lock; rather, a large number of kernel data structures were protected by specialized spin locks. The global kernel lock, on other hand, was still present because splitting a big lock into several smaller locks is not trivial—both deadlocks and race conditions must be carefully avoided. Several unrelated parts of the kernel code were still serialized by the global kernel lock.

Linux kernel Version 2.4 reduces still further the role of the global kernel lock. In the current stable version, the global kernel lock is mostly used to serialize accesses to the Virtual File System and avoid race conditions when loading and unloading kernel modules. The main progress with respect to the earlier stable version is that the networking transfers and file accessing (like reading or writing into a regular file) are no longer serialized by the global kernel lock.

The global kernel lock is a spin lock named `kernel_flag`. Every process descriptor includes a `lock_depth` field, which allows the same process to acquire the global kernel lock several times. Therefore, two consecutive requests for it will not hang the processor (as for normal spin locks). If the process does not want the lock, the field has the value −1. If the process wants it, the field value plus 1 specifies how many times the lock has been requested. The `lock_depth` field is crucial for interrupt handlers, exception handlers, and bottom halves. Without it, any asynchronous function that tries to get the global kernel lock could generate a deadlock if the current process already owns the lock.

The `lock_kernel( )` and `unlock_kernel( )` functions are used to get and release the global kernel lock. The former function is equivalent to:

```
if (++current->lock_depth == 0)
    spin_lock(&kernel_flag);
```

while the latter is equivalent to:

```
if (--current->lock_depth < 0)
    spin_unlock(&kernel_flag);
```

Notice that the `if` statements of the `lock_kernel( )` and `unlock_kernel( )` functions need not be executed atomically because `lock_depth` is not a global variable—each CPU addresses a field of its own current process descriptor. Local interrupts inside the `if` statements do not induce race conditions either. Even if the new kernel control path invokes `lock_kernel( )`, it must release the global kernel lock before terminating.

Memory Descriptor Read/Write Semaphore

Each memory descriptor of type mm_struct includes its own semaphore in the mmap_ sem field (see the section "The Memory Descriptor" in Chapter 8). The semaphore protects the descriptor against race conditions that could arise because a memory descriptor can be shared among several lightweight processes.

For instance, let's suppose that the kernel must create or extend a memory region for some process; to do this, it invokes the do_mmap( ) function, which allocates a new vm_area_struct data structure. In doing so, the current process could be suspended if no free memory is available, and another process sharing the same memory descriptor could run. Without the semaphore, any operation of the second process that requires access to the memory descriptor (for instance, a Page Fault due to a Copy on Write) could lead to severe data corruption.

The semaphore is implemented as a read/write semaphore because some kernel functions, such as the Page Fault exception handler (see the section "Page Fault Exception Handler" in Chapter 8), need only to scan the memory descriptors.

Slab Cache List Semaphore

The list of slab cache descriptors (see the section "Cache Descriptor" in Chapter 7) is protected by the cache_chain_sem semaphore, which grants an exclusive right to access and modify the list.

A race condition is possible when kmem_cache_create( ) adds a new element in the list, while kmem_cache_shrink( ) and kmem_cache_reap( ) sequentially scan the list. However, these functions are never invoked while handling an interrupt, and they can never block while accessing the list. Since the kernel is nonpreemptive, these functions cannot overlap on a uniprocessor system. However, this semaphore plays an active role in multiprocessor systems.

Inode Semaphore

As we shall see in Chapter 12, Linux stores the information on a disk file in a memory object called an *inode*. The corresponding data structure includes its own semaphore in the i_sem field.

A huge number of race conditions can occur during filesystem handling. Indeed, each file on disk is a resource held in common for all users, since all processes may (potentially) access the file content, change its name or location, destroy or duplicate it, and so on. For example, let's suppose that a process lists the files contained in some directory. Each disk operation is potentially blocking, and therefore even in uniprocessor systems, other processes could access the same directory and modify its content while the first process is in the middle of the listing operation. Or, again, two different processes could modify the same directory at the same time. All these race conditions are avoided by protecting the directory file with the inode semaphore.

Whenever a program uses two or more semaphores, the potential for deadlock is present because two different paths could end up waiting for each other to release a semaphore. Generally speaking, Linux has few problems with deadlocks on semaphore requests, since each kernel control path usually needs to acquire just one semaphore at a time. However, in a couple of cases, the kernel must get two semaphore locks. Inode semaphores are prone to this scenario; for instance, this occurs in the service routines of the rmdir( ) and the rename( ) system calls (notice that in both cases two different inodes are involved in the operation, so both semaphores must be taken). To avoid such deadlocks, semaphore requests are performed in address order: the semaphore request whose semaphore data structure is located at the lowest address is issued first.

CHAPTER 6
Timing Measurements

Countless computerized activities are driven by timing measurements, often behind the user's back. For instance, if the screen is automatically switched off after you have stopped using the computer's console, it is due to a timer that allows the kernel to keep track of how much time has elapsed since you pushed a key or moved the mouse. If you receive a warning from the system asking you to remove a set of unused files, it is the outcome of a program that identifies all user files that have not been accessed for a long time. To do these things, programs must be able to retrieve a timestamp identifying its last access time from each file. Such a timestamp must be automatically written by the kernel. More significantly, timing drives process switches along with even more visible kernel activities like checking for time-outs.

We can distinguish two main kinds of timing measurement that must be performed by the Linux kernel:

- Keeping the current time and date so they can be returned to user programs through the time( ), ftime( ), and gettimeofday( ) system calls (see the section "The time(), ftime(), and gettimeofday() System Calls" later in this chapter) and used by the kernel itself as timestamps for files and network packets

- Maintaining timers—mechanisms that are able to notify the kernel (see the later section "Software Timers") or a user program (see the later section "The setitimer( ) and alarm( ) System Calls") that a certain interval of time has elapsed

Timing measurements are performed by several hardware circuits based on fixed-frequency oscillators and counters. This chapter consists of four different parts. The first two sections describe the hardware devices that underlie timing and give an overall picture of Linux timekeeping architecture. The following sections describe the main time-related duties of the kernel: implementing CPU time sharing, updating system time and resource usage statistics, and maintaining software timers. The last section discusses the system calls related to timing measurements and the corresponding service routines.

Hardware Clocks

On the 80×86 architecture, the kernel must explicitly interact with four kinds of clocks: the Real Time Clock, the Time Stamp Counter, the Programmable Interval Timer, and the timer of the local APICs in SMP systems. The first two hardware devices allow the kernel to keep track of the current time of day. The PIC device and the timers of the local APICs are programmed by the kernel so that they issue interrupts at a fixed, predefined frequency; such periodic interrupts are crucial for implementing the timers used by the kernel and the user programs.

Real Time Clock

All PCs include a clock called *Real Time Clock* (*RTC*), which is independent of the CPU and all other chips.

The RTC continues to tick even when the PC is switched off, since it is energized by a small battery or accumulator. The CMOS RAM and RTC are integrated in a single chip (the Motorola 146818 or an equivalent).

The RTC is capable of issuing periodic interrupts on IRQ8 at frequencies ranging between 2 Hz and 8,192 Hz. It can also be programmed to activate the IRQ8 line when the RTC reaches a specific value, thus working as an alarm clock.

Linux uses the RTC only to derive the time and date; however, it allows processes to program the RTC by acting on the */dev/rtc* device file (see Chapter 13). The kernel accesses the RTC through the 0x70 and 0x71 I/O ports. The system administrator can set up the clock by executing the *clock* Unix system program that acts directly on these two I/O ports.

Time Stamp Counter

All 80×86 microprocessors include a CLK input pin, which receives the clock signal of an external oscillator.

Starting with the Pentium, many recent 80×86 microprocessors include a 64-bit *Time Stamp Counter* (*TSC*) register that can be read by means of the rdtsc assembly language instruction. This register is a counter that is incremented at each clock signal—if, for instance, the clock ticks at 400 MHz, the Time Stamp Counter is incremented once every 2.5 nanoseconds.

Linux takes advantage of this register to get much more accurate time measurements than those delivered by the Programmable Interval Timer. To do this, Linux must determine the clock signal frequency while initializing the system. In fact, since this frequency is not declared when compiling the kernel, the same kernel image may run on CPUs whose clocks may tick at any frequency.

The task of figuring out the actual frequency of a CPU is accomplished during the system's boot. The `calibrate_tsc( )` function computes the frequency by counting the number of clock signals that occur in a relatively long time interval, namely 50.00077 milliseconds. This time constant is produced by properly setting up one of the channels of the Programmable Interval Timer (see the next section). The long execution time of `calibrate_tsc( )` does not create problems, since the function is invoked only during system initialization.*

Programmable Interval Timer

Besides the Real Time Clock and the Time Stamp Counter, IBM-compatible PCs include another type of time-measuring device called *Programmable Interval Timer* (*PIT*). The role of a PIT is similar to the alarm clock of a microwave oven: it makes the user aware that the cooking time interval has elapsed. Instead of ringing a bell, this device issues a special interrupt called *timer interrupt*, which notifies the kernel that one more time interval has elapsed.† Another difference from the alarm clock is that the PIT goes on issuing interrupts forever at some fixed frequency established by the kernel. Each IBM-compatible PC includes at least one PIT, which is usually implemented by a 8254 CMOS chip using the 0x40–0x43 I/O ports.

As we shall see in detail in the next paragraphs, Linux programs the PIT to issue timer interrupts on the IRQ0 at a (roughly) 100-Hz frequency—that is, once every 10 milliseconds. This time interval is called a *tick*, and its length in microseconds is stored in the `tick` variable. The ticks beat time for all activities in the system; in some sense, they are like the ticks sounded by a metronome while a musician is rehearsing.

Generally speaking, shorter ticks result in higher resolution timers, which help with smoother multimedia playback and faster response time when performing synchronous I/O multiplexing (`poll( )` and `select( )` system calls). This is a trade-off however: shorter ticks require the CPU to spend a larger fraction of its time in Kernel Mode—that is, a smaller fraction of time in User Mode. As a consequence, user programs run slower. Therefore, only very powerful machines can adopt very short ticks and afford the consequent overhead. Currently, most Hewlett-Packard's Alpha and Intel's IA-64 ports of the Linux kernel issue 1,024 timer interrupts per second, corresponding to a tick of roughly 1 millisecond. The Rawhide Alpha station adopts the highest tick frequency and issues 1,200 timer interrupts per second.

A few macros in the Linux code yield some constants that determine the frequency of timer interrupts. These are discussed in the following list.

---

* To avoid loosing significant digits in the integer divisions, `calibrate_tsc( )` returns the duration, in microseconds, of a clock tick multiplied by 2^{32}.

† The PIT is also used to drive an audio amplifier connected to the computer's internal speaker.

- HZ yields the number of timer interrupts per second—that is, their frequency. This value is set to 100 for IBM PCs and most other hardware platforms.

- CLOCK_TICK_RATE yields the value 1,193,180, which is the 8254 chip's internal oscillator frequency.

- LATCH yields the ratio between CLOCK_TICK_RATE and HZ. It is used to program the PIT.

The first PIT is initialized by init_IRQ( ) as follows:

```
outb_p(0x34,0x43);
outb_p(LATCH & 0xff , 0x40);
outb(LATCH >> 8 , 0x40);
```

The outb( ) C function is equivalent to the outb assembly language instruction: it copies the first operand into the I/O port specified as the second operand. The outb_ p( ) function is similar to outb( ), except that it introduces a pause by executing a no-op instruction. The first outb_p( ) invocation is a command to the PIT to issue interrupts at a new rate. The next two outb_p( ) and outb( ) invocations supply the new interrupt rate to the device. The 16-bit LATCH constant is sent to the 8-bit 0x40 I/O port of the device as two consecutive bytes. As a result, the PIT issues timer interrupts at a (roughly) 100-Hz frequency (that is, once every 10 ms).

CPU Local Timers

The local APIC present in recent Intel processors (see the section "Interrupts and Exceptions" in Chapter 4) provides yet another time-measuring device: the *CPU local timer*.

The CPU local timer is a device that can issue one-shot or periodic interrupts, which is similar to the Programmable Interval Timer just described. There are, however, a few differences:

- The APIC's timer counter is 32-bits long, while the PIT's timer counter is 16-bits long; therefore, the local timer can be programmed to issue interrupts at very low frequencies (the counter stores the number of ticks that must elapse before the interrupt is issued).

- The local APIC timer sends an interrupt only to its processor, while the PIT raises a global interrupt, which may be handled by any CPU in the system.

- The APIC's timer is based on the bus clock signal (or the APIC bus signal, in older machines). It can be programmed in such a way to decrement the timer counter every 1, 2, 4, 8, 16, 32, 64, or 128 bus clock signals. Conversely, the PIT has its own internal clock oscillator.

Now that we understand what the hardware timers are, we may discuss how the Linux kernel exploits them to conduct all activities of the system.

The Linux Timekeeping Architecture

Linux must carry on several time-related activities. For instance, the kernel periodically:

- Updates the time elapsed since system startup.
- Updates the time and date.
- Determines, for every CPU, how long the current process has been running, and preempts it if it has exceeded the time allocated to it. The allocation of time slots (also called *quanta*) is discussed in Chapter 11.
- Updates resource usage statistics.
- Checks whether the interval of time associated with each software timer (see the later section "Software Timers") has elapsed.

Linux's *timekeeping architecture* is the set of kernel data structures and functions related to the flow of time. Actually, Intel-based multiprocessor machines have a timekeeping architecture that is slightly different from the timekeeping architecture of uniprocessor machines:

- In a uniprocessor system, all time-keeping activities are triggered by interrupts raised by the Programmable Interval Timer.
- In a multiprocessor system, all general activities (like handling of software timers) are triggered by the interrupts raised by the PIT, while CPU-specific activities (like monitoring the execution time of the currently running process) are triggered by the interrupts raised by the local APIC timers.

Unfortunately, the distinction between the two cases is somewhat blurred. For instance, some early SMP systems based on Intel 80486 processors didn't have local APICs. Even nowadays, there are SMP motherboards so buggy that local timer interrupts are not usable at all. In these cases, the SMP kernel must resort to the UP timekeeping architecture. On the other hand, recent uniprocessor systems have a local APIC and an I/O APIC, so the kernel may use the SMP timekeeping architecture. Another significant case holds when a SMP-enabled kernel is running on a uniprocessor machine. However, to simplify our description, we won't discuss these hybrid cases and will stick to the two "pure" timekeeping architectures.

Linux's timekeeping architecture depends also on the availability of the Time Stamp Counter (TSC). The kernel uses two basic timekeeping functions: one to keep the current time up to date and another to count the number of microseconds that have elapsed within the current second. There are two different ways to get the last value. One method is more precise and is available if the CPU has a Time Stamp Counter; a less-precise method is used in the opposite case (see the later section "The time( ), ftime( ), and gettimeofday( ) System Calls").

Timekeeping Architecture in Uniprocessor Systems

In a uniprocessor system, all time-related activities are triggered by the interrupts raised by the Programmable Interval Timer on IRQ line 0. As usual, in Linux, some of these activities are executed as soon as possible after the interrupt is raised (in the "top half" of the interrupt handler), while the remaining activities are delayed (in the "bottom half" of the interrupt handler).

PIT's interrupt service routine

The time_init( ) function sets up the interrupt gate corresponding to IRQ0 during kernel setup. Once this is done, the handler field of IRQ0's irqaction descriptor contains the address of the timer_interrupt( ) function. This function starts running with the interrupts disabled, since the status field of IRQ0's main descriptor has the SA_INTERRUPT flag set. It performs the following steps:

1. If the CPU has a TSC register, it performs the following substeps:

   a. Executes an rdtsc assembly language instruction to store the 32 least-significant bits of the TSC register in the last_tsc_low variable.

   b. Reads the state of the 8254 chip device internal oscillator and computes the delay between the timer interrupt occurrence and the execution of the interrupt service routine.*

   c. Stores that delay (in microseconds) in the delay_at_last_interrupt variable; as we shall see in the section "The time(), ftime(), and gettimeofday() System Calls," this variable is used to provide the correct time to user processes.

2. It invokes do_timer_interrupt( ).

do_timer_interrupt( ), which may be considered the PIT's interrupt service routine common to all 80×86 models, essentially executes the following operations:

1. It invokes the do_timer( ) function, which is fully explained shortly.

2. If the timer interrupt occurred in Kernel Mode, it invokes the x86_do_profile( ) function (see the section "Profiling the Kernel Code" later in this chapter).

3. If an adjtimex( ) system call is issued, it invokes the set_rtc_mmss( ) function once every 660 seconds (every 11 minutes) to adjust the Real Time Clock. This feature helps systems on a network synchronize their clocks (see the later section "The adjtimex() System Call").

The do_timer( ) function, which runs with the interrupts disabled, must be executed as quickly as possible. For this reason, it simply updates one fundamental value—the

---

* The 8254 oscillator drives a counter that is continuously decremented. When the counter becomes 0, the chip raises an IRQ0. Thus, reading the counter indicates how much time has elapsed since the interrupt occurred.

time elapsed from system startup—and checks whether the running processes have exhausted its time quantum while delegating all remaining activities to the TIMER_BH bottom half.

The function is equivalent to:

```
void do_timer(struct pt_regs * regs)
{
    jiffies++;
    update_process_times(user_mode(regs)); /* UP only */
    mark_bh(TIMER_BH);
    if (TQ_ACTIVE(tq_timer))
        mark_bh(TQUEUE_BH);
}
```

The jiffies global variable stores the number of elapsed ticks since the system was started. It is set to 0 during kernel initialization and incremented by 1 when a timer interrupt occurs—that is, on every tick. Since jiffies is a 32-bit unsigned integer, it returns to 0 about 497 days after the system has been booted. However, the kernel is smart enough to handle the overflow without getting confused.

The update_process_times() function essentially checks how long the current process has been running; it is described in the section "CPU's Time Sharing" later in this chapter.

Finally do_timer() activates the TIMER_BH bottom half; if the tq_timer task queue is not empty (see the section "Softirqs, Tasklets, and Bottom Halves" in Chapter 4), the function also activates the TQUEUE_BH bottom half.

The TIMER_BH bottom half

Each invocation of the "top half" PIT's timer interrupt handler marks the TIMER_BH bottom half as active. As soon as the kernel leaves interrupt mode, the timer_bh() function, which is associated with TIMER_BH, starts:

```
void timer_bh(void)
{
    update_times();
    run_timer_list();
}
```

The update_times() function updates the system date and time and computes the current system load; these activities are discussed later in the sections "Updating the Time and Date" and "Updating System Statistics." The run_timer_list() function takes care of software timers handling; it is discussed in the later section "Software Timers."

Timekeeping Architecture in Multiprocessor Systems

In multiprocessor systems, timer interrupts raised by the Programmable Interval Timer still play an important role. Indeed, the corresponding interrupt handler takes care of activities not related to a specific CPU, such as the handling of software timers and keeping the system time up to date. As in the uniprocessor case, the most urgent activities are performed by the "top half" of the interrupt handler (see the section "PIT's interrupt service routine" earlier in this chapter), while the remaining activities are delayed until the execution of the TIMER_BH bottom half (see the earlier section "The TIMER_BH bottom half").

However, the SMP version of the PIT's interrupt service routine differs from the UP version in a few points:

- The timer_interrupt() function acquires the xtime_lock read/write spin lock for writing. Although local interrupts are disabled, the kernel must protect the xtime, last_tsc_low, and delay_at_last_interrupt global variables from concurrent read and write accesses performed by other CPUs (see the section "Updating the Time and Date" later in this chapter).

- The do_timer_interrupt() function does not invoke the x86_do_profile() function because this function performs actions related to a specific CPU.

- The do_timer() function does not invoke update_process_times() because this function also performs actions related to a specific CPU.

There are two timekeeping activities related to every specific CPU in the system:

- Monitoring how much time the current process has been running on the CPU

- Updating the resource usage statistics of the CPU

To simplify the overall timekeeping architecture, in Linux 2.4, every CPU takes care of these activities in the handler of the local timer interrupt raised by the APIC device embedded in the CPU. In this way, the number of accessed spin locks is minimized, since every CPU tends to access only its own "private" data structures.

Initialization of the timekeeping architecture

During kernel initialization, each APIC has to be told how often to generate a local time interrupt. The setup_APIC_clocks() function programs the local APICs of all CPUS to generate interrupts as follows:

```
void setup_APIC_clocks (void)
{
    __cli();
    calibration_result = calibrate_APIC_clock();
    setup_APIC_timer((void *)calibration_result);
    __sti();
    smp_call_function(setup_APIC_timer, (void *)calibration_result, 1, 1);
}
```

The calibrate_APIC_clock() function computes how many local timer interrupts are generated by the local APIC of the booting CPU during a tick (10 ms). This exact value is then used to program the local APICs in such a way to generate one local timer interrupt every tick. This is done by the setup_APIC_timer() function, which is invoked directly on the booting CPU, and through the CALL_FUNCTION_VECTOR Interprocessor Interrupts (IPI) on the other CPUs (see the section "Interprocessor Interrupt Handling" in Chapter 4).

All local APIC timers are synchronized because they are based on the common bus clock signal. This means that the value computed by calibrate_APIC_clock() for the booting CPU is good also for the other CPUs in the system. However, we don't really want to have all local timer interrupts generated at exactly the same time because this could induce a substantial performance penalty due to waits on spin locks. For the same reason, a local timer interrupt handler should not run on a CPU when a PIT's timer interrupt handler is being executed on another CPU.

Therefore, the setup_APIC_timer() function spreads the local timer interrupts inside the tick interval. Figure 6-1 shows an example. In a multiprocessor systems with four CPUs, the beginning of the tick is marked by the PIT's timer interrupt. Two milliseconds after the PIT's timer interrupt, the local APIC of CPU 0 raises its local timer interrupt; two milliseconds later, it is the turn of the local APIC of CPU 1, and so on. Two milliseconds after the local timer interrupt of CPU 3, the PIT raises another timer interrupt on IRQ 0 line and starts a new tick.

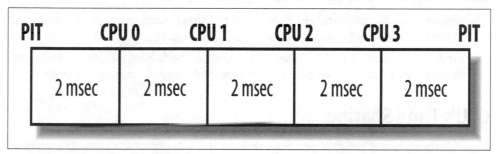

Figure 6-1. Spreading local timer interrupts inside a tick

setup_APIC_timer() programs the local APIC in such a way to raise timer interrupts that have vector LOCAL_TIMER_VECTOR (usually, 0xef); moreover, the init_IRQ() function associates LOCAL_TIMER_VECTOR to the low-level interrupt handler apic_timer_interrupt().

The local timer interrupt handler

The apic_timer_interrupt() assembly language function is equivalent to the following code:

```
apic_timer_interrupt:
    pushl $LOCAL_TIMER_VECTOR-256
    SAVE_ALL
    movl %esp,%eax
    pushl %eax
    call smp_apic_timer_interrupt
    addl $4,%esp
    jmp ret_from_intr
```

As you can see, the low-level handler is very similar to the other low-level interrupt handlers already described in Chapter 4. The high-level interrupt handler called `smp_apic_timer_interrupt()` executes the following steps:

1. Gets the CPU logical number (say n)
2. Increments the nth entry of the `apic_timer_irqs` array by 1 (see "Checking the NMI Watchdogs" later in this chapter)
3. Acknowledges the interrupt on the local APIC
4. Calls the `irq_enter()` function to increment the nth entry of the `local_irq_count` array and to honor the `global_irq_lock` spin lock (see Chapter 5)
5. Invokes the `smp_local_timer_interrupt()` function
6. Calls the `irq_exit()` function to decrement the nth entry of the `local_irq_count` array
7. Invokes `do_softirq()` if some softirqs are pending (see the section "Softirqs" in Chapter 4)

The `smp_local_timer_interrupt()` function executes the per-CPU timekeeping activities. Actually, it performs the following steps:

1. Invokes the `x86_do_profile()` function if the timer interrupt occurred in Kernel Mode (see the section "Profiling the Kernel Code" later in this chapter)
2. Invokes the `update_process_times()` function to check how long the current process has been running (see the section "Software Timers" later in this chapter)[*]

CPU's Time Sharing

Timer interrupts are essential for time-sharing the CPU among runnable processes (that is, those in the TASK_RUNNING state). As we shall see in Chapter 11, each process is usually allowed a *quantum* of time of limited duration: if the process is not terminated when its quantum expires, the `schedule()` function selects the new process to run.

The counter field of the process descriptor specifies how many ticks of CPU time are left to the process. The quantum is always a multiple of a tick—a multiple of about 10 ms. The value of counter is updated at every tick by `update_process_times()`, which is invoked by either the PIT's timer interrupt handler on uniprocessor systems or the local timer interrupt handler in multiprocessor systems. The code is equivalent to the following:

---

[*] The system administrator can change the sample frequency of the kernel code profiler. To do this, the kernel changes the frequency at which local timer interrupts are generated. However, the `smp_local_timer_interrupt()` function keeps invoking the `update_process_times()` function exactly once every tick. Unfortunately, changing the frequency of a local timer interrupt destroys the elegant spreading of the local timer interrupts inside a tick interval.

```
if (current->pid) {
    --current->counter;
    if (current->counter <= 0) {
        current->counter = 0;
        current->need_resched = 1;
    }
}
```

The snippet of code starts by making sure the kernel is not handling a process with PID 0—the *swapper* process associated with the executing CPU. It must not be time-shared because it is the process that runs on the CPU when no other TASK_RUNNING processes exist (see the section "Identifying a Process" in Chapter 3).

When counter becomes smaller than 0, the need_resched field of the process descriptor is set to 1. In this case, the schedule( ) function is invoked before resuming User Mode execution, and other TASK_RUNNING processes will have a chance to resume execution on the CPU.

Updating the Time and Date

User programs get the current time and date from the xtime variable of type struct timeval. The kernel also occasionally refers to it, for instance, when updating inode timestamps (see the section "File Descriptor and Inode" in Chapter 1). In particular, xtime.tv_sec stores the number of seconds that have elapsed since midnight of January 1, 1970 (UTC), while xtime.tv_usec stores the number of microseconds that have elapsed within the last second (its value ranges between 0 and 999999).

During kernel initialization, the time_init( ) function is invoked to set up the time and date. It reads them from the Real Time Clock by invoking the get_cmos_time( ) function, then it initializes xtime. Once this has been done, the kernel does not need the RTC anymore; it relies instead on the TIMER_BH bottom half, which is usually activated once every tick.

The update_times( ) function is equivalent to the following:

```
void update_times(void)
{
    unsigned long ticks;
    write_lock_irq(&xtime_lock);
    ticks = jiffies - wall_jiffies;
    if (ticks) {
        wall_jiffies += ticks;
        update_wall_time(ticks);
    }
    write_unlock_irq(&xtime_lock);
    calc_load(ticks);
}
```

On a uniprocessor system, the write_lock_irq( ) and write_unlock_irq( ) functions simply disable and enable the interrupts on the executing CPU; on multiprocessor systems, they also acquire and release the xtime_lock spin lock, which protects against concurrent accesses to the xtime variable.

The wall_jiffies variable stores the time of the last update of the xtime variable. Observe that the value of wall_jiffies can be smaller than jiffies-1, since the execution of the bottom half can be delayed; in other words, the kernel does not necessarily update the xtime variable at every tick. However, no tick is definitively lost, and in the long run, xtime stores the correct system time.

The update_wall_time( ) function invokes the update_wall_time_one_tick( ) function ticks consecutive times; each invocation adds 10,000 to the xtime.tv_usec field.* If xtime.tv_usec becomes greater than 999,999, the update_wall_time( ) function also updates the tv_sec field of xtime.

Updating System Statistics

The kernel, among the other time-related duties, must periodically collect several data used to:

- Checking the CPU resource limit of the running processes
- Computing the average system load
- Profiling the kernel code

Checking the Current Process CPU Resource Limit

The update_process_times( ) function (invoked by either the PIT's timer interrupt handler on uniprocessor systems or the local timer interrupt handler in multiprocessor systems) updates some kernel statistics stored in the kstat variable of type kernel_stat; it then invokes update_one_process( ) to update some fields storing statistics that can be exported to user programs through the times( ) system call. In particular, a distinction is made between CPU time spent in User Mode and in Kernel Mode. The function performs the following actions:

1. Updates the per_cpu_utime field of current's process descriptor, which stores the number of ticks during which the process has been running in User Mode.

2. Updates the per_cpu_stime field of current's process descriptor, which stores the number of ticks during which the process has been running in Kernel Mode.

3. Invokes do_process_times( ), which checks whether the total CPU time limit has been reached; if so, it sends SIGXCPU and SIGKILL signals to current. The section "Process Resource Limits" in Chapter 3 describes how the limit is controlled by the rlim[RLIMIT_CPU].rlim_cur field of each process descriptor.

---

* In fact, the function is much more complex since it might tune the value 10,000 slightly. This may be necessary if an adjtimex( ) system call has been issued (see the section "The adjtimex( ) System Call" later in this chapter).

Two additional fields called times.tms_cutime and times.tms_cstime are provided in the process descriptor to count the number of CPU ticks spent by the process children in User Mode and Kernel Mode, respectively. For reasons of efficiency, these fields are not updated by update_one_process( ), but rather when the parent process queries the state of one of its children (see the section "Destroying Processes" in Chapter 3).

Keeping Track of System Load

Any Unix kernel keeps track of how much CPU activity is being carried on by the system. These statistics are used by various administration utilities such as top. A user who enters the uptime command sees the statistics as the "load average" relative to the last minute, the last 5 minutes, and the last 15 minutes. On a uniprocessor system, a value of 0 means that there are no active processes (besides the *swapper* process 0) to run, while a value of 1 means that the CPU is 100 percent busy with a single process, and values greater than 1 mean that the CPU is shared among several active processes.[*]

The system load data is collected by the calc_load( ) function, which is invoked by update_times( ). This activity is therefore performed in the TIMER_BH bottom half. calc_load( ) counts the number of processes in the TASK_RUNNING or TASK_UNINTERRUPTIBLE state and uses this number to update the CPU usage statistics.

Profiling the Kernel Code

Linux includes a minimalist code profiler used by Linux developers to discover where the kernel spends its time in Kernel Mode. The profiler identifies the *hot spots* of the kernel—the most frequently executed fragments of kernel code. Identifying the kernel hot spots is very important because they may point out kernel functions that should be further optimized.

The profiler is based on a very simple Monte Carlo algorithm: at every timer interrupt occurrence, the kernel determines whether the interrupt occurred in Kernel Mode; if so, the kernel fetches the value of the eip register before the interruption from the stack and uses it to discover what the kernel was doing before the interrupt. In the long run, the samples accumulate on the hot spots.

The x86_do_profile( ) function collects the data for the code profiler. It is invoked either by the do_timer_interrupt( ) function in uniprocessor systems (by the PIT's timer interrupt handler) or by the smp_local_timer_interrupt( ) function in multiprocessor systems (by the local timer interrupt handler).

---

[*] Linux includes in the load average all processes that are in TASK_RUNNING and TASK_UNINTERRUPTIBLE states. However, in normal conditions, there are few TASK_UNINTERRUPTIBLE processes, so a high load usually means that the CPU is busy.

To enable the code profiler, the Linux kernel must be booted by passing as a parameter the string profile=N, where 2^N denotes the size of the code fragments to be profiled. The collected data can be read from the */proc/profile* file. The counters are reset by writing in the same file; in multiprocessor systems, writing into the file can also change the sample frequency (see the earlier section "Timekeeping Architecture in Multiprocessor Systems"). However, kernel developers do not usually access */proc/profile* directly; instead, they use the *readprofile* system command.

Checking the NMI Watchdogs

In multiprocessor systems, Linux offers yet another feature to kernel developers: a *watchdog system*, which might be quite useful to detect kernel bugs that cause a system freeze. To activate such watchdog, the kernel must be booted with the nmi_watchdog parameter.

The watchdog is based on a clever hardware feature of multiprocessor motherboards: they can broadcast the PIT's interrupt timer as NMI interrupts to all CPUs. Since NMI interrupts are not masked by the cli assembly language instruction, the watchdog can detect deadlocks even when interrupts are disabled.

As a consequence, once every tick, all CPUs, regardless of what they are doing, start executing the NMI interrupt handler; in turn, the handler invokes do_nmi( ). This function gets the logical number n of the CPU, and then checks the nth entry of the apic_timer_irqs array. If the CPU is working properly, the value must be different from the value read at the previous NMI interrupt. When the CPU is running properly, the nth entry of the apic_timer_irqs array is incremented by the local timer interrupt handler (see the earlier section "The local timer interrupt handler"); if the counter is not incremented, the local timer interrupt handler has not been executed in a whole tick. Not a good thing, you know.

When the NMI interrupt handler detects a CPU freeze, it rings all the bells: it logs scary messages in the system log files, dumps the contents of the CPU registers and of the kernel stack (kernel oops), and finally kills the current process. This gives kernel developers a chance to discover what's gone wrong.

Software Timers

A *timer* is a software facility that allows functions to be invoked at some future moment, after a given time interval has elapsed; a *time-out* denotes a moment at which the time interval associated with a timer has elapsed.

Timers are widely used both by the kernel and by processes. Most device drivers use timers to detect anomalous conditions—floppy disk drivers, for instance, use timers to switch off the device motor after the floppy has not been accessed for a while, and parallel printer drivers use them to detect erroneous printer conditions.

Timers are also used quite often by programmers to force the execution of specific functions at some future time (see the later section "The setitimer( ) and alarm( ) System Calls").

Implementing a timer is relatively easy. Each timer contains a field that indicates how far in the future the timer should expire. This field is initially calculated by adding the right number of ticks to the current value of jiffies. The field does not change. Every time the kernel checks a timer, it compares the expiration field to the value of jiffies at the current moment, and the timer expires when jiffies is greater or equal to the stored value. This comparison is made via the time_after, time_before, time_after_eq, and time_before_eq macros, which take care of possible overflows of jiffies.

Linux considers two types of timers called *dynamic timers* and *interval timers*. The first type is used by the kernel, while interval timers may be created by processes in User Mode.[*]

One word of caution about Linux timers: since checking for timer functions is always done by bottom halves that may be executed a long time after they have been activated, the kernel cannot ensure that timer functions will start right at their expiration times. It can only ensure that they are executed either at the proper time or after with a delay of up to a few hundreds of milliseconds. For this reason, timers are not appropriate for real-time applications in which expiration times must be strictly enforced.

Dynamic Timers

Dynamic timers may be dynamically created and destroyed. No limit is placed on the number of currently active dynamic timers.

A dynamic timer is stored in the following timer_list structure:

```
struct timer_list {
    struct list_head list;
    unsigned long expires;
    unsigned long data;
    void (*function)(unsigned long);
};
```

The function field contains the address of the function to be executed when the timer expires. The data field specifies a parameter to be passed to this timer function. Thanks to the data field, it is possible to define a single general-purpose function that handles the time-outs of several device drivers; the data field could store the device ID or other meaningful data that could be used by the function to differentiate the device.

---

[*] Earlier versions of Linux use a third type of kernel timers: the so-called *static timers*. Static timers are very rudimental because they cannot be dynamically allocated or destroyed, and at most there could be 32 of them. Static timers were replaced by dynamic timers, and new kernels (starting from Version 2.4) no longer support them.

The expires field specifies when the timer expires; the time is expressed as the number of ticks that have elapsed since the system started up. All timers that have an expires value smaller than or equal to the value of jiffies are considered to be expired or decayed.

The list field includes the links for a doubly linked circular list. There are 512 doubly linked circular lists to hold dynamic timers. Each timer is inserted into one of the lists based on the value of the expires field. The algorithm that uses this list is described later in this chapter.

To create and activate a dynamic timer, the kernel must:

1. Create a new timer_list object—for example, t. This can be done in several ways by:
   - Defining a static global variable in the code.
   - Defining a local variable inside a function; in this case, the object is stored on the Kernel Mode stack.
   - Including the object in a dynamically allocated descriptor.

2. Initialize the object by invoking the init_timer(&t) function. This simply sets the links in the list field to NULL.

3. Load the function field with the address of the function to be activated when the timer decays. If required, load the data field with a parameter value to be passed to the function.

4. If the dynamic timer is not already inserted in a list, assign a proper value to the expires field. Otherwise, update the expires field by invoking the mod_timer( ) function, which also takes care of moving the object into the proper list (discussed shortly).

5. If the dynamic timer is not already inserted in a list, insert the t element in the proper list by invoking the add_timer(&t) function.

Once the timer has decayed, the kernel automatically removes the t element from its list. Sometimes, however, a process should explicitly remove a timer from its list using the del_timer( ) or del_timer_sync( ) functions. Indeed, a sleeping process may be woken up before the time-out is over; in this case, the process may choose to destroy the timer. Invoking del_timer( ) or del_timer_sync( ) on a timer already removed from a list does no harm, so removing the timer within the timer function is considered a good practice.

Dynamic timers and race conditions

Being asynchronously activated, dynamic timers are prone to race conditions. For instance, consider a dynamic timer whose function acts on a discardable resource (e.g., a kernel module or a file data structure). Releasing the resource without stopping the timer may lead to data corruption if the timer function got activated when the resource no longer exists. Thus, a rule of thumb is to stop the timer *before* releasing the resource:

```
...
del_timer(&t);
X_Release_Resources();
...
```

In multiprocessor systems, however, this code is not safe because the timer function might already be running on another CPU when del_timer() is invoked. As a result, resources may be released while the timer function is still acting on them. To avoid this kind of race condition, the kernel offers the del_timer_sync() function. It removes the timer from the list, and then it checks whether the timer function is executed on another CPU; in such a case, del_timer_sync() waits until the timer function terminates.

Other types of race conditions exist, of course. For instance, the right way to modify the expires field of an already activated timer consists of using mod_timer(), rather than deleting the timer and recreating it thereafter. In the latter approach, two kernel control paths that want to modify the expires field of the same timer may mix each other up badly. The implementation of the timer functions is made SMP-safe by means of the timerlist_lock spin lock: every time the kernel must access the lists of dynamic timers, it disables the interrupts and acquires this spin lock.

Dynamic timers handling

Choosing the proper data structure to implement dynamic timers is not easy. Stringing together all timers in a single list would degrade system performances, since scanning a long list of timers at every tick is costly. On the other hand, maintaining a sorted list would not be much more efficient, since the insertion and deletion operations would also be costly.

The adopted solution is based on a clever data structure that partitions the expires values into blocks of ticks and allows dynamic timers to percolate efficiently from lists with larger expires values to lists with smaller ones.

The main data structure is an array called tvecs, whose elements point to five groups of lists identified by the tv1, tv2, tv3, tv4, and tv5 structures (see Figure 6-2).

The tv1 structure is of type struct timer_vec_root, which includes an index field and a vec array of 256 list_head elements—that is, lists of dynamic timers. It contains all dynamic timers that will decay within the next 255 ticks.

The index field specifies the currently scanned list; it is initialized to 0 and incremented by 1 (modulo 256) at every tick. The list referenced by index contains all dynamic timers that expired during the current tick; the next list contains all dynamic timers that will expire in the next tick; the (index+k)[th] list contains all dynamic timers that will expire in exactly k ticks. When index returns to 0, it signifies that all the timers in tv1 have been scanned. In this case, the list pointed to by tv2.vec[tv2.index] is used to replenish tv1.

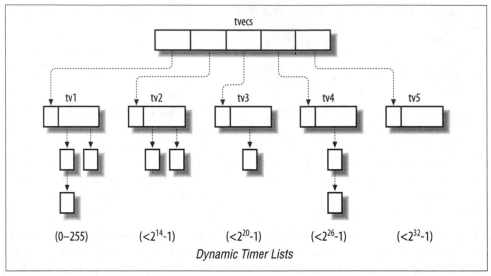

Figure 6-2. The groups of lists associated with dynamic timers

The tv2, tv3, and tv4 structures of type struct timer_vec contain all dynamic timers that will decay within the next $2^{14}-1$, $2^{20}-1$, and $2^{26}-1$ ticks, respectively.

The tv5 structure is identical to the previous ones, except that the last entry of the vec array includes dynamic timers with extremely large expires fields. It never needs to be replenished from another array.

The timer_vec structure is very similar to timer_vec_root: it contains an index field and a vec array of 64 pointers to dynamic timer lists. The index field specifies the currently scanned list; it is incremented by 1 (modulo 64) every 256^{i-1} ticks, where i, ranging between 2 and 5, is the tv$i$ group number. As in the case of tv1, when index returns to 0, the list pointed to by tv$j$.vec[tv$j$.index] is used to replenish tv$i$ (i ranges between 2 and 4, j is equal to $i+1$).

Thus, the first element of tv2 holds a list of all timers that expire in the 256 ticks following the tv1 timers; the timers in this list are sufficient to replenish the whole array tv1. The second element of tv2 holds all timers that expire in the following 256 ticks, and so on. Similarly, a single entry of tv3 is sufficient to replenish the whole array tv2.

Figure 6-2 shows how these data structures are connected.

The timer_bh() function associated with the TIMER_BH bottom half invokes the run_timer_list() auxiliary function to check for decayed dynamic timers. The function relies on a variable similar to jiffies that is called timer_jiffies. This new variable is needed because a few timer interrupts might occur before the activated TIMER_BH bottom half has a chance to run; this happens typically when several interrupts of different types are issued in a short interval of time.

The value of timer_jiffies represents the expiration time of the dynamic timer list yet to be checked: if it coincides with the value of jiffies, no backlog of bottom half functions has accumulated; if it is smaller than jiffies, then bottom half functions that refer to previous ticks must be dealt with. The variable is set to 0 at system startup and is incremented only by run_timer_list( ). Its value can never be greater than jiffies.

The run_timer_list( ) function is essentially equivalent the following C fragment:

```
struct list_head *head, *curr;
struct timer_list *timer;
void (*fn)(unsigned long);
unsigned long data;

spin_lock_irq(&timerlist_lock);
while ((long)(jiffies - timer_jiffies) >= 0) {
    if (!tv1.index) {
        int n = 1;
        do {
            cascade_timers(tvecs[n]);
        } while (tvecs[n]->index == 1 && ++n < 5));
    }
    head = &tv1.vec[tv1.index];
    for (curr = head->next; curr != head; curr = head->next) {
        timer = list_entry(curr, struct timer_list, list);
        fn = timer->function;
        data= timer->data;

        detach_timer(timer);
        timer->list.next = timer->list.prev = NULL;
        running_timer = timer;
        spin_unlock_irq(&timerlist_lock);
        fn(data);
        spin_lock_irq(&timerlist_lock);
        running_timer = NULL;
    }
    ++timer_jiffies;
    tv1.index = (tv1.index + 1) & 0xff;
}
spin_unlock_irq(&timerlist_lock);
```

The outermost while loop ends when timer_jiffies becomes greater than the value of jiffies. Since the values of jiffies and timer_jiffies usually coincide, the outermost while cycle is often executed only once. In general, the outermost loop is executed jiffies - timer_jiffies + 1 consecutive times. Moreover, if a timer interrupt occurs while run_timer_list( ) is being executed, dynamic timers that decay at this tick occurrence are also considered, since the jiffies variable is asynchronously incremented by the PIT's interrupt handler (see the earlier section "PIT's interrupt service routine").

During a single execution of the outermost while cycle, the dynamic timer functions included in the `tv1.vec[tv1.index]` list are executed. Before executing a dynamic timer function, the loop invokes the `detach_timer( )` function to remove the dynamic timer from the list. Once the list is emptied, the value of `tv1.index` is incremented (modulo 256) and the value of `timer_jiffies` is incremented.

When `tv1.index` becomes equal to 0, all the lists of `tv1` have been checked; in this case, it is necessary to refill the `tv1` structure. This is accomplished by the `cascade_timers( )` function, which transfers the dynamic timers included in `tv2.vec[tv2.index]` into `tv1.vec`, since they will necessarily decay within the next 256 ticks. If `tv2.index` is equal to 0, the `tv2` array of lists must be refilled with the elements of `tv3.vec[tv3.index]`.

Notice that `run_timer_list( )` disables interrupts and acquires the `timerlist_lock` spin lock just before entering the outermost loop; interrupts are enabled and the spin lock is released right before invoking each dynamic timer function, until its termination. This ensures that the dynamic timer data structures are not corrupted by interleaved kernel control paths.

To sum up, this rather complex algorithm ensures excellent performance. To see why, assume for the sake of simplicity that the `TIMER_BH` bottom half is executed right after the corresponding timer interrupt occurs. Then, in 255 timer interrupt occurrences out of 256 (in 99.6% of the cases), the `run_timer_list( )` function just runs the functions of the decayed timers, if any. To replenish `tv1.vec` periodically, it is sufficient 63 times out of 64 to partition the list pointed to by `tv2.vec[tv2.index]` into the 256 lists pointed to by `tv1.vec`. The `tv2.vec` array, in turn, must be replenished in 0.02 percent of the cases (that is, once every 163 seconds). Similarly, `tv3` is replenished every 2 hours and 54 minutes, and `tv4` is replenished every 7 days and 18 hours. `tv5` doesn't need to be replenished.

An Application of Dynamic Timers

To show how the outcome of all the previous activities are actually used in the kernel, we'll show an example of the creation and use of a *process time-out*.

Let's assume that the kernel decides to suspend the current process for two seconds. It does this by executing the following code:

```
timeou = 2 * HZ;
set_current_state(TASK_INTERRUPTIBLE); /* or TASK_UNINTERRUPTIBLE */
remaining = schedule_timeout(timeout);
```

The kernel implements process time-outs by using dynamic timers. They appear in the `schedule_timeout( )` function, which essentially executes the following statements:

```
struct timer_list timer;
expire = timeout + jiffies;
init_timer(&timer);
```

```
timer.expires = expire;
timer.data = (unsigned long) current;
timer.function = process_timeout;
add_timer(&timer);
schedule();      /* process suspended until timer expires */
del_timer_sync(&timer);
timeout = expire - jiffies;
return (timeout < 0 ? 0 : timeout);
```

When schedule( ) is invoked, another process is selected for execution; when the former process resumes its execution, the function removes the dynamic timer. In the last statement, the function either returns 0, if the time-out is expired, or it returns the number of ticks left to the time-out expiration if the process was awoken for some other reason.

When the time-out expires, the kernel executes the following function:

```
void process_timeout(unsigned long data)
{
    struct task_struct * p = (struct task_struct *) data;
    wake_up_process(p);
}
```

The run_timer_list( ) function invokes process_timeout( ), passing as its parameter the process descriptor pointer stored in the data field of the timer object. As a result, the suspended process is woken up.

System Calls Related to Timing Measurements

Several system calls allow User Mode processes to read and modify the time and date and to create timers. Let's briefly review these and discuss how the kernel handles them.

The time( ), ftime( ), and gettimeofday( ) System Calls

Processes in User Mode can get the current time and date by means of several system calls:

time( )

> Returns the number of elapsed seconds since midnight at the start of January 1, 1970 (UTC).

ftime( )

> Returns, in a data structure of type timeb, the number of elapsed seconds since midnight of January 1, 1970 (UTC) and the number of elapsed milliseconds in the last second.

gettimeofday( )

> Returns, in a data structure named timeval, the number of elapsed seconds since midnight of January 1, 1970 (UTC) (a second data structure named timezone is not currently used).

The former system calls are superseded by gettimeofday( ), but they are still included in Linux for backward compatibility. We don't discuss them further.

The gettimeofday( ) system call is implemented by the sys_gettimeofday( ) function. To compute the current date and time of the day, this function invokes do_gettimeofday( ), which executes the following actions:

1. Disables the interrupts and acquires the xtime_lock read/write spin lock for reading.

2. Gets the number of microseconds elapsed in the last second by using the function whose address is stored in do_gettimeoffset:

   ```
   usec = do_gettimeoffset();
   ```

   If the CPU has a Time Stamp Counter, the do_fast_gettimeoffset( ) function is executed. It reads the TSC register by using the rdtsc assembly language instruction; it then subtracts the value stored in last_tsc_low to obtain the number of CPU cycles elapsed since the last timer interrupt was handled. The function converts that number to microseconds and adds in the delay that elapsed before the activation of the timer interrupt handler (stored in the delay_at_last_interrupt variable mentioned earlier in the section "PIT's interrupt service routine").

   If the CPU does not have a TSC register, do_gettimeoffset points to the do_slow_gettimeoffset( ) function. It reads the state of the 8254 chip device internal oscillator and then computes the time length elapsed since the last timer interrupt. Using that value and the contents of jiffies, it can derive the number of microseconds elapsed in the last second.

3. Further increases the number of microseconds in order to take into account all timer interrupts whose bottom halves have not yet been executed:

   ```
   usec += (jiffies - wall_jiffies) * (1000000/HZ);
   ```

4. Copies the contents of xtime into the user-space buffer specified by the system call parameter tv, adding to the following fields:

   ```
   tv->tv_sec = xtime->tv_sec;
   tv->tv_usec = xtime->tv_usec + usec;
   ```

5. Releases the xtime_lock spin lock and reenables the interrupts.

6. Checks for an overflow in the microseconds field, adjusting both that field and the second field if necessary:

   ```
   while (tv->tv_usec >= 1000000) {
       tv->tv_usec -= 1000000;
       tv->tv_sec++;
   }
   ```

Processes in User Mode with root privilege may modify the current date and time by using either the obsolete stime( ) or the settimeofday( ) system call. The sys_settimeofday( ) function invokes do_settimeofday( ), which executes operations complementary to those of do_gettimeofday( ).

Notice that both system calls modify the value of xtime while leaving the RTC registers unchanged. Therefore, the new time is lost when the system shuts down, unless the user executes the *clock* program to change the RTC value.

The adjtimex( ) System Call

Although clock drift ensures that all systems eventually move away from the correct time, changing the time abruptly is both an administrative nuisance and risky behavior. Imagine, for instance, programmers trying to build a large program and depending on filetime stamps to make sure that out-of-date object files are recompiled. A large change in the system's time could confuse the make program and lead to an incorrect build. Keeping the clocks tuned is also important when implementing a distributed filesystem on a network of computers. In this case, it is wise to adjust the clocks of the interconnected PCs so that the timestamp values associated with the inodes of the accessed files are coherent. Thus, systems are often configured to run a time synchronization protocol such as Network Time Protocol (NTP) on a regular basis to change the time gradually at each tick. This utility depends on the adjtimex( ) system call in Linux.

This system call is present in several Unix variants, although it should not be used in programs intended to be portable. It receives as its parameter a pointer to a timex structure, updates kernel parameters from the values in the timex fields, and returns the same structure with current kernel values. Such kernel values are used by update_wall_time_one_tick( ) to slightly adjust the number of microseconds added to xtime.tv_usec at each tick.

The setitimer( ) and alarm( ) System Calls

Linux allows User Mode processes to activate special timers called *interval timers.*[*] The timers cause Unix signals (see Chapter 10) to be sent periodically to the process. It is also possible to activate an interval timer so that it sends just one signal after a specified delay. Each interval timer is therefore characterized by:

- The frequency at which the signals must be emitted, or a null value if just one signal has to be generated
- The time remaining until the next signal is to be generated

---

[*] These software constructs have nothing in common with the Programmable Interval Timer chips described earlier in this chapter.

The earlier warning about accuracy applies to these timers. They are guaranteed to execute after the requested time has elapsed, but it is impossible to predict exactly when they will be delivered.

Interval timers are activated by means of the POSIX setitimer( ) system call. The first parameter specifies which of the following policies should be adopted:

ITIMER_REAL

> The actual elapsed time; the process receives SIGALRM signals.

ITIMER_VIRTUAL

> The time spent by the process in User Mode; the process receives SIGVTALRM signals.

ITIMER_PROF

> The time spent by the process both in User and in Kernel Mode; the process receives SIGPROF signals.

To implement an interval timer for each of the preceding policies, the process descriptor includes three pairs of fields:

- it_real_incr and it_real_value
- it_virt_incr and it_virt_value
- it_prof_incr and it_prof_value

The first field of each pair stores the interval in ticks between two signals; the other field stores the current value of the timer.

The ITIMER_REAL interval timer is implemented by using dynamic timers because the kernel must send signals to the process even when it is not running on the CPU. Therefore, each process descriptor includes a dynamic timer object called real_timer. The setitimer( ) system call initializes the real_timer fields and then invokes add_timer( ) to insert the dynamic timer in the proper list. When the timer expires, the kernel executes the it_real_fn( ) timer function. In turn, the it_real_fn( ) function sends a SIGALRM signal to the process; if it_real_incr is not null, it sets the expires field again, reactivating the timer.

The ITIMER_VIRTUAL and ITIMER_PROF interval timers do not require dynamic timers, since they can be updated while the process is running. The do_it_virt( ) and do_it_prof( ) functions are invoked by update_one_process( ), which is called either by the PIT's timer interrupt handler (UP) or by the local timer interrupt handlers (SMP). Therefore, the two interval timers are updated once every tick, and if they are expired, the proper signal is sent to the current process.

The alarm( ) system call sends a SIGALRM signal to the calling process when a specified time interval has elapsed. It is very similar to setitimer( ) when invoked with the ITIMER_REAL parameter, since it uses the real_timer dynamic timer included in the process descriptor. Therefore, alarm( ) and setitimer( ) with parameter ITIMER_REAL cannot be used at the same time.

CHAPTER 7

Memory Management

We saw in Chapter 2 how Linux takes advantage of 80×86's segmentation and paging circuits to translate logical addresses into physical ones. We also mentioned that some portion of RAM is permanently assigned to the kernel and used to store both the kernel code and the static kernel data structures.

The remaining part of the RAM is called *dynamic memory*. It is a valuable resource, needed not only by the processes but also by the kernel itself. In fact, the performance of the entire system depends on how efficiently dynamic memory is managed. Therefore, all current multitasking operating systems try to optimize the use of dynamic memory, assigning it only when it is needed and freeing it as soon as possible.

This chapter, which consists of three main sections, describes how the kernel allocates dynamic memory for its own use. The sections "Page Frame Management" and "Memory Area Management" illustrate two different techniques for handling physically contiguous memory areas, while the section "Noncontiguous Memory Area Management" illustrates a third technique that handles noncontiguous memory areas.

Page Frame Management

We saw in the section "Paging in Hardware" in Chapter 2 how the Intel Pentium processor can use two different page frame sizes: 4 KB and 4 MB (or 2 MB if PAE is enabled—see the section "The Physical Address Extension (PAE) Paging Mechanism" in Chapter 2). Linux adopts the smaller 4 KB page frame size as the standard memory allocation unit. This makes things simpler for two reasons:

- The Page Fault exceptions issued by the paging circuitry are easily interpreted. Either the page requested exists but the process is not allowed to address it, or the page does not exist. In the second case, the memory allocator must find a free 4 KB page frame and assign it to the process.

- The 4 KB size is a multiple of most disk block sizes, so transfers of data between main memory and disks are more efficient. Yet this smaller size is much more manageable than the 4 MB size.

Page Descriptors

The kernel must keep track of the current status of each page frame. For instance, it must be able to distinguish the page frames that are used to contain pages that belong to processes from those that contain kernel code or kernel data structures. Similarly, it must be able to determine whether a page frame in dynamic memory is free. A page frame in dynamic memory is free if it does not contain any useful data. It is not free when the page frame contains data of a User Mode process, data of a software cache, dynamically allocated kernel data structures, buffered data of a device driver, code of a kernel module, and so on.

State information of a page frame is kept in a page descriptor of type struct page, whose fields are shown in Table 7-1. All page descriptors are stored in the mem_map array. Since each descriptor is less than 64 bytes long, mem_map requires about four page frames for each megabyte of RAM.

Table 7-1. The fields of the page descriptor

Type	Name	Description
struct list_head	list	Contains pointers to next and previous items in a doubly linked list of page descriptors
struct address_space *	mapping	Used when the page is inserted into the page cache (see the section "The Page Cache" in Chapter 14)
unsigned long	index	Either the position of the data stored in the page within the page's disk image (see Chapter 14) or a swapped-out page identifier (see Chapter 16)
struct page *	next_hash	Contains pointer to next item in a doubly linked circular list of the page cache hash table
atomic_t	count	Page's reference counter
unsigned long	flags	Array of flags (see Table 7-2)
struct list_head	lru	Contains pointers to the least recently used doubly linked list of pages
wait_queue_head_t	wait	Page's wait queue
struct page **	pprev_hash	Contains pointer to previous item in a doubly linked circular list of the page cache hash table
struct buffer_head *	buffers	Used when the page stores buffers (see the section "Page I/O operations" in Chapter 13)
void *	virtual	Linear address of the page frame in the fourth gigabyte (see the section "Requesting and Releasing Page Frames" later in this chapter)
struct zone_struct *	zone	The zone to which the page frame belongs (see the section "Memory Zones")

You don't have to fully understand the role of all fields in the page descriptor right now. In the following chapters, we often come back to the fields of the page descriptor. Moreover, several fields have different meaning, according to whether the page frame is free and what kernel component is using the page frame.

Let's describe in greater detail two of the fields:

count

A usage reference counter for the page. If it is set to 0, the corresponding page frame is free and can be assigned to any process or to the kernel itself. If it is set to a value greater than 0, the page frame is assigned to one or more processes or is used to store some kernel data structures.

flags

Includes up to 32 flags (see Table 7-2) that describe the status of the page frame. For each PG_*xyz* flag, the kernel defines some macros that manipulate its value. Usually, the PageXyz macro returns the value of the flag, while the SetPageXyz and ClearPageXyz macro set and clear the corresponding bit, respectively.

Table 7-2. Flags describing the status of a page frame

Flag name	Meaning
PG_locked	The page is involved in a disk I/O operation.
PG_error	An I/O error occurred while transferring the page.
PG_referenced	The page has been recently accessed for a disk I/O operation.
PG_uptodate	The flag is set after completing a read operation, unless a disk I/O error happened.
PG_dirty	The page has been modified (see the section "The try_to_swap_out( ) Function" in Chapter 16).
PG_lru	The page is in the active or inactive page list (see the section "The Least Recently Used (LRU) Lists" in Chapter 16).
PG_active	The page is in the active page list (see the section "The Least Recently Used (LRU) Lists" in Chapter 16).
PG_slab	The page frame is included in a slab (see the section "Memory Area Management" later in this chapter).
PG_skip	Not used.
PG_highmem	The page frame belongs to the ZONE_HIGHMEM zone (see the section "Memory Zones").
PG_checked	The flag used by the Ext2 filesystem (see Chapter 17).
PG_arch_1	Not used on the 80×86 architecture.
PG_reserved	The page frame is reserved to kernel code or is unusable.
PG_launder	The page is involved in an I/O operation triggered by shrink_cache( ) (see the section "The shrink_cache( ) Function" in Chapter 16).

Memory Zones

In an ideal computer architecture, a page frame is a memory storage unit that can be used for anything: storing kernel and user data, buffering disk data, and so on. Any kind of page of data can be stored in any page frame, without limitations.

However, real computer architectures have hardware constraints that may limit the way page frames can be used. In particular, the Linux kernel must deal with two hardware constraints of the 80×86 architecture:

- The Direct Memory Access (DMA) processors for ISA buses have a strong limitation: they are able to address only the first 16 MB of RAM.
- In modern 32-bit computers with lots of RAM, the CPU cannot directly access all physical memory because the linear address space is too small.

To cope with these two limitations, Linux partitions the physical memory in three *zones*:

ZONE_DMA
> Contains pages of memory below 16 MB

ZONE_NORMAL
> Contains pages of memory at and above 16 MB and below 896 MB

ZONE_HIGHMEM
> Contains pages of memory at and above 896 MB

The ZONE_DMA zone includes memory pages that can be used by old ISA-based devices by means of the DMA. (The section "Direct Memory Access (DMA)" in Chapter 13 gives further details on DMA.)

The ZONE_DMA and ZONE_NORMAL zones include the "normal" pages of memory that can be directly accessed by the kernel through the linear mapping in the fourth gigabyte of the linear address space (see the section "Kernel Page Tables" in Chapter 2). Conversely, the ZONE_HIGHMEM zone includes pages of memory that cannot be directly accessed by the kernel through the linear mapping in the fourth gigabyte of linear address space (see the section "Kernel Mappings of High-Memory Page Frames" later in this chapter). The ZONE_HIGHMEM zone is not used on 64-bit architectures.

Each memory zone has its own descriptor of type struct zone_struct (or equivalently, zone_t). Its fields are shown in Table 7-3.

Table 7-3. The fields of the zone descriptor

Type	Name	Description
char *	name	Contains a pointer to the conventional name of the zone: "DMA," "Normal," or "HighMem"
unsigned long	size	Number of pages in the zone
spinlock_t	lock	Spin lock protecting the descriptor
unsigned long	free_pages	Number of free pages in the zone
unsigned long	pages_min	Minimum number of pages of the zone that should remain free (see the section "Reclaiming Page Frame" in Chapter 16)
unsigned long	pages_low	Lower threshold value for the zone's page balancing algorithm (see the section "Reclaiming Page Frame" in Chapter 16)

Table 7-3. The fields of the zone descriptor (continued)

Type	Name	Description
unsigned long	pages_high	Upper threshold value for the zone's page balancing algorithm (see the section "Reclaiming Page Frame" in Chapter 16)
int	need_balance	Flag indicating that the zone's page balancing algorithm should be activated (see the section "Reclaiming Page Frame" in Chapter 16)
free_area_t []	free_area	Used by the buddy system page allocator (see the later section "The Buddy System Algorithm")
struct pglist_data *	zone_pgdat	Pointer to the descriptor of the node to which this zone belongs
struct page *	zone_mem_map	Array of page descriptors of the zone (see the later section "The Buddy System Algorithm")
unsigned long	zone_start_paddr	First physical address of the zone
unsigned long	zone_start_mapnr	First page descriptor index of the zone

The zone field in the page descriptor points to the descriptor of the zone to which the corresponding page frame belongs.

The zone_names array stores the canonical names of the three zones: "DMA," "Normal," and "HighMem."

When the kernel invokes a memory allocation function, it must specify the zones that contain the requested page frames. The kernel usually specifies which zones it's willing to use. For instance, if a page frame must be directly mapped in the fourth gigabyte of linear addresses but it is not going to be used for ISA DMA transfers, then the kernel requests a page frame either in ZONE_NORMAL or in ZONE_DMA. Of course, the page frame should be obtained from ZONE_DMA only if ZONE_NORMAL does not have free page frames. To specify the preferred zones in a memory allocation request, the kernel uses the struct zonelist_struct data structure (or equivalently zonelist_t), which is an array of zone descriptor pointers.

Non-Uniform Memory Access (NUMA)

We are used to thinking of the computer's memory as an homogeneous, shared resource. Disregarding the role of the hardware caches, we expect the time required for a CPU to access a memory location is essentially the same, regardless of the location's physical address and the CPU. Unfortunately, this assumption is not true in some architectures. For instance, it is not true for some multiprocessor Alpha or MIPS computers.

Linux 2.4 supports the *Non-Uniform Memory Access* (NUMA) model, in which the access times for different memory locations from a given CPU may vary. The physical memory of the system is partitioned in several *nodes*. The time needed by any given CPU to access pages within a single node is the same. However, this time might not be the same for two different CPUs. For every CPU, the kernel tries to minimize the number of accesses to costly nodes by carefully selecting where the kernel data structures that are most often referenced by the CPU are stored.

The physical memory inside each node can be split in several zones, as we saw in the previous section. Each node has a descriptor of type pg_data_t, whose fields are shown in Table 7-4. All node descriptors are stored in a simply linked list, whose first element is pointed to by the pgdat_list variable.

Table 7-4. The fields of the node descriptor

Type	Name	Description
zone_t []	node_zones	Array of zone descriptors of the node
zonelist_t []	node_zonelists	Array of zonelist_t data structures used by the page allocator (see the later section "Requesting and Releasing Page Frames")
int	nr_zones	Number of zones in the node
struct page *	node_mem_map	Array of page descriptors of the node
unsigned long *	valid_addr_bitmap	Bitmap of usable physical addresses for the node
struct bootmem_data *	bdata	Used in the kernel initialization phase
unsigned long	node_start_paddr	First physical address of the node
unsigned long	node_start_mapnr	First page descriptor index of the node
unsigned long	node_size	Size of the node (in pages)
int	node_id	Identifier of the node
pg_data_t *	node_next	Next item in the node list

As usual, we are mostly concerned with the 80×86 architecture. IBM-compatible PCs use the Uniform Access Memory model (UMA), thus the NUMA support is not really required. However, even if NUMA support is not compiled in the kernel, Linux makes use of a single node that includes all system physical memory; the corresponding descriptor is stored in the contig_page_data variable.

On the 80×86 architecture, grouping the physical memory in a single node might appear useless; however, this approach makes the memory handling code more portable, because the kernel may assume that the physical memory is partitioned in one or more nodes in all architectures.*

Initialization of the Memory Handling Data Structures

Dynamic memory and the values used to refer to it are illustrated in Figure 7-1. The zones of memory are now drawn to scale; ZONE_NORMAL is usually larger than ZONE_

---

* We have another example of this kind of design choice: Linux uses three levels of Page Tables even when the hardware architecture defines just two levels (see the section "Paging in Linux" in Chapter 2).

DMA, and, if present, ZONE_HIGHMEM is usually larger than ZONE_NORMAL. Notice that ZONE_HIGHMEM starts from physical address 0x38000000, which corresponds to 896 MB.

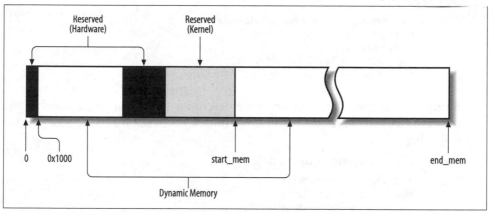

Figure 7-1. Memory layout

We already described how the paging_init() function initializes the kernel Page Tables according to the amount of RAM in the system in the section "Kernel Page Tables" in Chapter 2. Beside Page Tables, the paging_init() function also initializes other memory handling data structures. It invokes kmap_init(), which essentially sets up the kmap_pte variable to create "windows" of linear addresses that allow the kernel to address the ZONE_HIGHMEM zone (see the section "Temporary kernel mappings" later in this chapter). Then, paging_init() invokes the free_area_init() function, passing an array storing the sizes of the three memory zones to it.

The free_area_init() function sets up both the zone descriptors and the page descriptors. The function receives the zones_size array (size of each memory zone) as its parameter, and executes the following operations:*

1. Computes the total number of page frames in RAM by adding the value in zones_size, and stores the result in the totalpages local variable.

2. Initializes the active_list and inactive_list lists of page descriptors (see Chapter 16).

3. Allocates space for the mem_map array of page descriptors. The space needed is the product of totalpages by the page descriptor size.

4. Initializes some fields of the node descriptor contig_page_data:

```
contig_page_data.node_size = totalpages;
contig_page_data.node_start_paddr = 0x00000000;
contig_page_data.node_start_mapnr = 0;
```

---

* In NUMA architectures, these operations must be performed separately on every node. However, we are focusing on the 80×86 architecture, which has just one node.

5. Initializes some fields of all page descriptors. All page frames are marked as reserved, but later, the PG_reserved flag of the page frames in dynamic memory will be cleared:

```
for (p = mem_map; p < mem_map + totalpages; p++) {
    p->count = 0;
    SetPageReserved(p);
    init_waitqueue_head(&p->wait);
    p->list.next = p->list.prev = p;
}
```

6. Stores the address of the memory zone descriptor in the zone local variable and for each element of the zone_names array (index j between 0 and 2), performs the following steps:

   a. Initializes some fields of the descriptor:

   ```
   zone->name = zone_names[j];
   zone->size = zones_size[j];
   zone->lock = SPIN_LOCK_UNLOCKED;
   zone->zone_pgdat = & contig_page_data;
   zone->free_pages = 0;
   zone->need_balance = 0;
   ```

   b. If the zone is empty (that is, it does not include any page frame), the function goes back to the beginning of Step 6 and continues with the next zone.

   c. Otherwise, the zone includes at least one page frame and the function initializes the pages_min, pages_low, and pages_high fields of the zone descriptor (see Chapter 16).

   d. Sets up the zone_mem_map field of the zone descriptor to the address of the first page descriptor in the zone.

   e. Sets up the zone_start_mapnr field of the zone descriptor to the index of the first page descriptor in the zone.

   f. Sets up the zone_start_paddr field of the zone descriptor to the physical address of the first page frame in the zone.

   g. Stores the address of the zone descriptor in the zone field of the page descriptor for each page frame of the zone.

   h. If the zone is either ZONE_DMA or ZONE_NORMAL, stores the linear address in the fourth gigabyte that maps the page frame into the virtual field of every page descriptor of the zone.

   i. Initializes the free_area_t structures in the free_area array of the zone descriptor (see the section "The Buddy System Algorithm" later in this chapter).

7. Initializes the node_zonelists array of the contig_page_data node descriptor. The array includes 16 elements; each element corresponds to a different type of memory request and specifies the zones (in order of preference) from where the page frames could be retrieved. See the section "Requesting and Releasing Page Frames" later in this chapter for further details.

When the paging_init( ) function terminates, dynamic memory is not yet usable because the PG_reserved flag of all pages is set. Memory initialization is further carried on by the mem_init( ) function, which is invoked subsequently to paging_init( ).

Essentially, the mem_init( ) function initializes the value of num_physpages, the total number of page frames present in the system. It then scans all page frames associated with the dynamic memory; for each of them, the function sets the count field of the corresponding descriptor to 1, resets the PG_reserved flag, sets the PG_highmem flag if the page belongs to ZONE_HIGHMEM, and calls the free_page( ) function on it. Besides releasing the page frame (see the section "The Buddy System Algorithm" later in this chapter), free_page( ) also increments the value of the free_pages field of the memory zone descriptor that owns the page frame. The free_pages fields of all zone descriptors are used by the nr_free_pages( ) function to compute the total number of free page frames in the dynamic memory.

The mem_init( ) function also counts the number of page frames that are not associated with dynamic memory. Several symbols produced while compiling the kernel (some are described in the section "Reserved Page Frames" in Chapter 2) enable the function to count the number of page frames reserved for the hardware, kernel code, and kernel data, and the number of page frames used during kernel initialization that can be successively released.

Requesting and Releasing Page Frames

After having seen how the kernel allocates and initializes the data structures for page frame handling, we now look at how page frames are allocated and released.

Page frames can be requested by using six slightly different functions and macros. Unless otherwise stated, they return the linear address of the first allocated page, or return NULL if the allocation failed.

alloc_pages(gfp_mask, order)
> Function used to request 2^{order} contiguous page frames. It returns the address of the descriptor of the first allocated page frame or returns NULL if the allocation failed.

alloc_page(gfp_mask)
> Macro used to get a single page frame; it expands to:
>> alloc_pages(gfp_mask, 0)
>
> It returns the address of the descriptor of the allocated page frame or returns NULL if the allocation failed.

__get_free_pages(gfp_mask, order)
> Function that is similar to alloc_pages( ), but it returns the linear address of the first allocated page.

__get_free_page(gfp_mask)
> Macro used to get a single page frame; it expands to:
>> __get_free_pages(gfp_mask, 0)

get_zeroed_page(gfp_mask), *or equivalently* get_free_page(gfp_mask)
    Function that invokes:

        alloc_pages(gfp_mask, 0)

    and then fills the page frame obtained with zeros.

__get_dma_pages(gfp_mask, order)
    Macro used to get page frames suitable for DMA; it expands to:

        __get_free_pages(gfp_mask | __GFP_DMA, order)

The parameter gfp_mask specifies how to look for free page frames. It consists of the following flags:

__GFP_WAIT
    The kernel is allowed to block the current process waiting for free page frames.

__GFP_HIGH
    The kernel is allowed to access the pool of free page frames left for recovering from very low memory conditions.

__GFP_IO
    The kernel is allowed to perform I/O transfers on low memory pages in order to free page frames.

__GFP_HIGHIO
    The kernel is allowed to perform I/O transfers on high memory pages in order free page frames.

__GFP_FS
    The kernel is allowed to perform low-level VFS operations.

__GFP_DMA
    The requested page frames must be included in the ZONE_DMA zone (see the earlier section "Memory Zones.")

__GFP_HIGHMEM
    The requested page frames can be included in the ZONE_HIGHMEM zone.

In practice, Linux uses the predefined combinations of flag values shown in Table 7-5; the group name is what you'll encounter as argument of the six page frame allocation functions.

Table 7-5. Groups of flag values used to request page frames

Group name	Corresponding flags
GFP_ATOMIC	__GFP_HIGH
GFP_NOIO	__GFP_HIGH __GFP_WAIT
GFP_NOHIGHIO	__GFP_HIGH __GFP_WAIT __GFP_IO
GFP_NOFS	__GFP_HIGH __GFP_WAIT __GFP_IO __GFP_HIGHIO
GFP_KERNEL	__GFP_HIGH __GFP_WAIT __GFP_IO __GFP_HIGHIO __GFP_FS
GFP_NFS	__GFP_HIGH __GFP_WAIT __GFP_IO __GFP_HIGHIO __GFP_FS

Group name	Corresponding flags
GFP_KSWAPD	__GFP_WAIT __GFP_IO __GFP_HIGHIO __GFP_FS
GFP_USER	__GFP_WAIT __GFP_IO __GFP_HIGHIO __GFP_FS
GFP_HIGHUSER	__GFP_WAIT __GFP_IO __GFP_HIGHIO __GFP_FS __GFP_HIGHMEM

The __GFP_DMA and __GFP_HIGHMEM flags are called *zone modifiers*; they specify the zones searched by the kernel while looking for free page frames. The node_zonelists field of the contig_page_data node descriptor is an array of lists of zone descriptors; each list is associated with one specific combination of the zone modifiers. Although the array includes 16 elements, only 4 are really used, since there are currently only 2 zone modifiers. They are shown in Table 7-6.

Table 7-6. Zone modifier lists

__GFP_DMA	__GFP_HIGHMEM	Zone list
0	0	ZONE_NORMAL + ZONE_DMA
0	1	ZONE_HIGHMEM + ZONE_NORMAL + ZONE_DMA
1	0	ZONE_DMA
1	1	ZONE_DMA

Page frames can be released through each of the following four functions and macros:

__free_pages(page, order)
> This function checks the page descriptor pointed to by page; if the page frame is not reserved (i.e., if the PG_reserved flag is equal to 0), it decrements the count field of the descriptor. If count becomes 0, it assumes that 2^{order} contiguous page frames starting from addr are no longer used. In this case, the function invokes __free_pages_ok( ) to insert the page frame descriptor of the first free page in the proper list of free page frames (described in the following section).

free_pages(addr, order)
> This function is similar to __free_pages( ), but it receives as an argument the linear address addr of the first page frame to be released.

__free_page(page)
> This macro releases the page frame having the descriptor pointed to by page; it expands to:
>
>   __free_pages(page, 0)

free_page(addr)
> This macro releases the page frame having the linear address addr; it expands to:
>
>   free_pages(addr, 0)

Kernel Mappings of High-Memory Page Frames

Page frames above the 896 MB boundary are not mapped in the fourth gigabyte of the kernel linear address spaces, so they cannot be directly accessed by the kernel. This implies that any page allocator function that returns the linear address of the assigned page frame doesn't work for the high memory.

For instance, suppose that the kernel invoked `__get_free_pages(GFP_HIGHMEM,0)` to allocate a page frame in high memory. If the allocator assigned a page frame in high memory, `__get_free_pages()` cannot return its linear address because it doesn't exist; thus, the function returns NULL. In turn, the kernel cannot use the page frame; even worse, the page frame cannot be released because the kernel has lost track of it.

In short, allocation of high-memory page frames must be done only through the `alloc_pages()` function and its `alloc_page()` shortcut, which both return the address of the page descriptor of the first allocated page frame. Once allocated, a high-memory page frame has to be mapped into the fourth gigabyte of the linear address space, even though the physical address of the page frame may well exceed 4 GB.

To do this, the kernel may use three different mechanisms, which are called *permanent kernel mappings*, *temporary kernel mappings*, and *noncontiguous memory allocation*. In this section, we focus on the first two techniques; the third one is discussed in the section "Noncontiguous Memory Area Management" later in this chapter.

Establishing a permanent kernel mapping may block the current process; this happens when no free Page Table entries exist that can be used as "windows" on the page frames in high memory (see the next section). Thus, a permanent kernel mapping cannot be used in interrupt handlers and deferrable functions. Conversely, establishing a temporary kernel mapping never requires blocking the current process; its drawback, however, is that very few temporary kernel mappings can be established at the same time.

Of course, none of these techniques allow addressing the whole RAM simultaneously. After all, only 128 MB of linear address space are left for mapping the high memory, while PAE supports systems having up to 64 GB of RAM.

Permanent kernel mappings

Permanent kernel mappings allow the kernel to establish long-lasting mappings of high-memory page frames into the kernel address space. They use a dedicated Page Table whose address is stored in the `pkmap_page_table` variable. The number of entries in the Page Table is yielded by the LAST_PKMAP macro. As usual, the Page Table includes either 512 or 1,024 entries, according to whether PAE is enabled or disabled (see the section "The Physical Address Extension (PAE) Paging Mechanism" in Chapter 2); thus, the kernel can access at most 2 or 4 MB of high memory at once.

The Page Table maps the linear addresses starting from PKMAP_BASE (usually 0xfe000000). The address of the descriptor corresponding to the first page frame in high memory is stored in the highmem_start_page variable.

The pkmap_count array includes LAST_PKMAP counters, one for each entry of the pkmap_page_table Page Table. We distinguish three cases:

The counter is 0
> The corresponding Page Table entry does not map any high-memory page frame and is usable.

The counter is 1
> The corresponding Page Table entry does not map any high-memory page frame, but it cannot be used because the corresponding TLB entry has not been flushed since its last usage.

The counter is n (greater than 1)
> The corresponding Page Table entry maps a high-memory page frame, which is used by exactly *n*-1 kernel components.

The kmap( ) function establishes a permanent kernel mapping. It is essentially equivalent to the following code:

```
void * kmap(struct page * page)
{
    if (page < highmem_page_start)
        return page->virtual;
    return kmap_high(page);
}
```

The virtual field of the page descriptor stores the linear address in the fourth gigabyte mapping the page frame, if any. Thus, for any page frame below the 896 MB boundary, the field always includes the physical address of the page frame plus PAGE_OFFSET. Conversely, if the page frame is in high memory, the virtual field has a non-null value only if the page frame is currently mapped, either by the permanent or the temporary kernel mapping.

The kmap_high( ) function is invoked if the page frame really belongs to the high memory. The function is essentially equivalent to the following code:

```
void * kmap_high(struct page * page)
{
    unsigned long vaddr;
    spin_lock(&kmap_lock);
    vaddr = (unsigned long) page->virtual;
    if (!vaddr)
        vaddr = map_new_virtual(page);
    pkmap_count[(vaddr-PKMAP_BASE) >> PAGE_SHIFT]++;
    spin_unlock(&kmap_lock);
    return (void *) vaddr;
}
```

The function gets the kmap_lock spin lock to protect the Page Table against concurrent accesses in multiprocessor systems. Notice that there is no need to disable the interrupts because kmap() cannot be invoked by interrupt handlers and deferrable functions. Next, the kmap_high() function checks whether the virtual field of the page descriptor already stores a non-null linear address. If not, the function invokes the map_new_virtual() function to insert the page frame physical address in an entry of pkmap_page_table. Then kmap_high() increments the counter corresponding to the linear address of the page frame by 1 because another kernel component is going to access the page frame. Finally, kmap_high() releases the kmap_lock spin lock and returns the linear address that maps the page.

The map_new_virtual() function essentially executes two nested loops:

```
for (;;) {
    int count;
    DECLARE_WAITQUEUE(wait, current);
    for (count = LAST_PKMAP; count >= 0; --count) {
        last_pkmap_nr = (last_pkmap_nr + 1) & (LAST_PKMAP - 1);
        if (!last_pkmap_nr) {
            flush_all_zero_pkmaps();
            count = LAST_PKMAP;
        }
        if (!pkmap_count[last_pkmap_nr]) {
            unsigned long vaddr = PKMAP_BASE + (last_pkmap_nr << PAGE_SHIFT);
            set_pte(&(pkmap_page_table[last_pkmap_nr]), mk_pte(page, 0x63));
            pkmap_count[last_pkmap_nr] = 1;
            page->virtual = (void *) vaddr;
            return vaddr;
        }
    }
    current->state = TASK_UNINTERRUPTIBLE;
    add_wait_queue(&pkmap_map_wait, &wait);
    spin_unlock(&kmap_lock);
    schedule();
    remove_wait_queue(&pkmap_map_wait, &wait);
    spin_lock(&kmap_lock);
    if (page->virtual)
        return (unsigned long) page->virtual;
}
```

In the inner loop, the function scans all counters in pkmap_count that are looking for a null value. The last_pkmap_nr variable stores the index of the last used entry in the pkmap_page_table Page Table. Thus, the search starts from where it was left in the last invocation of the map_new_virtual() function.

When the last counter in pkmap_count is reached, the search restarts from the counter at index 0. Before continuing, however, map_new_virtual() invokes the flush_all_zero_pkmaps() function, which starts another scanning of the counters looking for the value 1. Each counter that has value 1 denotes an entry in pkmap_page_table that is free but cannot be used because the corresponding TLB entry has not yet been flushed. flush_all_zero_pkmaps() issues the TLB flushes on such entries and resets their counters to zero.

If the inner loop cannot find a null counter in pkmap_count, the map_new_virtual() function blocks the current process until some other process releases an entry of the pkmap_page_table Page Table. This is achieved by inserting current in the pkmap_map_ wait wait queue, setting the current state to TASK_UNINTERRUPTIBLE and invoking schedule() to relinquish the CPU. Once the process is awoken, the function checks whether another process has mapped the page by looking at the virtual field of the page descriptor; if some other process has mapped the page, the inner loop is restarted.

When a null counter is found by the inner loop, the map_new_virtual() function:

1. Computes the linear address that corresponds to the counter.
2. Writes the page's physical address into the entry in pkmap_page_table. The function also sets the bits Accessed, Dirty, Read/Write, and Present (value 0x63) in the same entry.
3. Sets to 1 the pkmap_count counter.
4. Writes the linear address into the virtual field of the page descriptor.
5. Returns the linear address.

The kunmap() function destroys a permanent kernel mapping. If the page is really in the high memory zone, it invokes the kunmap_high() function, which is essentially equivalent to the following code:

```
void kunmap_high(struct page * page)
{
    spin_lock(&kmap_lock);
    if ((--pkmap_count[((unsigned long) page->virtual-PKMAP_BASE)>>PAGE_SHIFT])==1)
        wake_up(&pkmap_map_wait);
    spin_unlock(&kmap_lock);
}
```

Notice that if the counter of the Page Table entry becomes equal to 1 (free), kunmap_ high() wakes up the processes waiting in the pkmap_map_wait wait queue.

Temporary kernel mappings

Temporary kernel mappings are simpler to implement than permanent kernel mappings; moreover, they can be used inside interrupt handlers and deferrable functions because they never block the current process.

Any page frame in high memory can be mapped through a *window* in the kernel address space—namely, a Page Table entry that is reserved for this purpose. The number of windows reserved for temporary kernel mappings is quite small.

Each CPU has its own set of five windows whose linear addresses are identified by the enum km_type data structure:

```
enum km_type {
    KM_BOUNCE_READ,
```

```
        KM_SKB_DATA,
        KM_SKB_DATA_SOFTIRQ,
        KM_USER0,
        KM_USER1,
        KM_TYPE_NR
}
```

The kernel must ensure that the same window is never used by two kernel control paths at the same time. Thus, each symbol is named after the kernel component that is allowed to use the corresponding window. The last symbol, KM_TYPE_NR, does not represent a linear address by itself, but yields the number of different windows usable by every CPU.

Each symbol in km_type, except the last one, is an index of a fix-mapped linear address (see the section "Fix-Mapped Linear Addresses" in Chapter 2). The enum fixed_addresses data structure includes the symbols FIX_KMAP_BEGIN and FIX_KMAP_ END; the latter is assigned to the index FIX_KMAP_BEGIN+(KM_TYPE_NR*NR_CPUS)-1. In this manner, there are KM_TYPE_NR fix-mapped linear addresses for each CPU in the system. Furthermore, the kernel initializes the kmap_pte variable with the address of the Page Table entry corresponding to the fix_to_virt(FIX_KMAP_BEGIN) linear address.

To establish a temporary kernel mapping, the kernel invokes the kmap_atomic() function, which is essentially equivalent to the following code:

```
void * kmap_atomic(struct page * page, enum km_type type)
{
    enum fixed_addresses idx;
    if (page < highmem_start_page)
        return page->virtual;
    idx = type + KM_TYPE_NR * smp_processor_id();
    set_pte(kmap_pte-idx, mk_pte(page, 0x063));
    __flush_tlb_one(fix_to_virt(FIX_KMAP_BEGIN+idx));
}
```

The type argument and the CPU identifier specify what fix-mapped linear address has to be used to map the request page. The function returns the linear address of the page frame if it doesn't belong to high memory; otherwise, it sets up the Page Table entry corresponding to the fix-mapped linear address with the page's physical address and the bits Present, Accessed, Read/Write, and Dirty. Finally, the TLB entry corresponding to the linear address is flushed.

To destroy a temporary kernel mapping, the kernel uses the kunmap_atomic() function. In the 80×86 architecture, however, this function does nothing.

Temporary kernel mappings should be used carefully. A kernel control path using a temporary kernel mapping must never block, because another kernel control path might use the same window to map some other high memory page.

The Buddy System Algorithm

The kernel must establish a robust and efficient strategy for allocating groups of contiguous page frames. In doing so, it must deal with a well-known memory management problem called *external fragmentation*: frequent requests and releases of groups of contiguous page frames of different sizes may lead to a situation in which several small blocks of free page frames are "scattered" inside blocks of allocated page frames. As a result, it may become impossible to allocate a large block of contiguous page frames, even if there are enough free pages to satisfy the request.

There are essentially two ways to avoid external fragmentation:

- Use the paging circuitry to map groups of noncontiguous free page frames into intervals of contiguous linear addresses.

- Develop a suitable technique to keep track of the existing blocks of free contiguous page frames, avoiding as much as possible the need to split up a large free block to satisfy a request for a smaller one.

The second approach is preferred by the kernel for three good reasons:

- In some cases, contiguous page frames are really necessary, since contiguous linear addresses are not sufficient to satisfy the request. A typical example is a memory request for buffers to be assigned to a DMA processor (see Chapter 13). Since the DMA ignores the paging circuitry and accesses the address bus directly while transferring several disk sectors in a single I/O operation, the buffers requested must be located in contiguous page frames.

- Even if contiguous page frame allocation is not strictly necessary, it offers the big advantage of leaving the kernel paging tables unchanged. What's wrong with modifying the Page Tables? As we know from Chapter 2, frequent Page Table modifications lead to higher average memory access times, since they make the CPU flush the contents of the translation lookaside buffers.

- Large chunks of contiguous physical memory can be accessed by the kernel through 4 MB pages. The reduction of translation lookaside buffers misses, in comparison to the use of 4 KB pages, significantly speeds up the average memory access time (see the section "Translation Lookaside Buffers (TLB)" in Chapter 2).

The technique adopted by Linux to solve the external fragmentation problem is based on the well-known *buddy system* algorithm. All free page frames are grouped into 10 lists of blocks that contain groups of 1, 2, 4, 8, 16, 32, 64, 128, 256, and 512 contiguous page frames, respectively. The physical address of the first page frame of a block is a multiple of the group size—for example, the initial address of a 16-page-frame block is a multiple of 16×2^{12} ($2^{12} = 4,096$, which is the regular page size).

We'll show how the algorithm works through a simple example.

Assume there is a request for a group of 128 contiguous page frames (i.e., a half-megabyte). The algorithm checks first to see whether a free block in the 128-page-frame list exists. If there is no such block, the algorithm looks for the next larger block—a free block in the 256-page-frame list. If such a block exists, the kernel allocates 128 of the 256 page frames to satisfy the request and inserts the remaining 128 page frames into the list of free 128-page-frame blocks. If there is no free 256-page block, the kernel then looks for the next larger block (i.e., a free 512-page-frame block). If such a block exists, it allocates 128 of the 512 page frames to satisfy the request, inserts the first 256 of the remaining 384 page frames into the list of free 256-page-frame blocks, and inserts the last 128 of the remaining 384 page frames into the list of free 128-page-frame blocks. If the list of 512-page-frame blocks is empty, the algorithm gives up and signals an error condition.

The reverse operation, releasing blocks of page frames, gives rise to the name of this algorithm. The kernel attempts to merge pairs of free buddy blocks of size b together into a single block of size $2b$. Two blocks are considered buddies if:

- Both blocks have the same size, say b.
- They are located in contiguous physical addresses.
- The physical address of the first page frame of the first block is a multiple of $2 \times b \times 2^{12}$.

The algorithm is iterative; if it succeeds in merging released blocks, it doubles b and tries again so as to create even bigger blocks.

Data structures

Linux uses a different buddy system for each zone. Thus, in the 80×86 architecture, there are three buddy systems: the first handles the page frames suitable for ISA DMA, the second handles the "normal" page frames, and the third handles the high-memory page frames. Each buddy system relies on the following main data structures:

- The mem_map array introduced previously. Actually, each zone is concerned with a subset of the mem_map elements. The first element in the subset and its number of elements are specified, respectively, by the zone_mem_map and size fields of the zone descriptor.
- An array having 10 elements of type free_area_t, one element for each group size. The array is stored in the free_area field of the zone descriptor.
- Ten binary arrays named *bitmaps*, one for each group size. Each buddy system has its own set of bitmaps, which it uses to keep track of the blocks it allocates.

The free_area_t (or equivalently, struct free_area_struct) data structure is defined as follows:

```
typedef struct free_area_struct {
    struct list_head free_list;
    unsigned long *map;
} free_area_t;
```

The kth element of the free_area array in the zone descriptor is associated with a doubly linked circular list of blocks of size 2^k; each member of such a list is the descriptor of the first page frame of a block. The list is implemented through the list field of the page descriptor.

The map field points to a bitmap whose size depends on the number of page frames in the zone. Each bit of the bitmap of the kth entry of the free_area array describes the status of two buddy blocks of size 2^k page frames. If a bit of the bitmap is equal to 0, either both buddy blocks of the pair are free or both are busy; if it is equal to 1, exactly one of the blocks is busy. When both buddies are free, the kernel treats them as a single free block of size 2^{k+1}.

Let's consider, for sake of illustration, a zone including 128 MB of RAM. The 128 MB can be divided into 32,768 single pages, 16,384 groups of 2 pages each, or 8,192 groups of 4 pages each, and so on up to 64 groups of 512 pages each. So the bitmap corresponding to free_area[0] consists of 16,384 bits, one for each pair of the 32,768 existing page frames; the bitmap corresponding to free_area[1] consists of 8,192 bits, one for each pair of blocks of two consecutive page frames; the last bitmap corresponding to free_area[9] consists of 32 bits, one for each pair of blocks of 512 contiguous page frames.

Figure 7-2 illustrates the use of the data structures introduced by the buddy system algorithm. The array zone_mem_map contains nine free page frames grouped in one block of one (a single page frame) at the top and two blocks of four further down. The double arrows denote doubly linked circular lists implemented by the free_list field. Notice that the bitmaps are not drawn to scale.

Allocating a block

The alloc_pages() function is the core of the buddy system allocation algorithm. Any other allocator function or macro listed in the earlier section "Requesting and Releasing Page Frames" ends up invoking alloc_pages().

The function considers the list of the contig_page_data.node_zonelists array corresponding to the zone modifiers specified in the argument gfp_mask. Starting with the first zone descriptor in the list, it compares the number of free page frames in the zone (stored in the free_pages field of the zone descriptor), the number of requested page frames (argument order of alloc_pages()), and the threshold value stored in the pages_low field of the zone descriptor. If free_pages - 2^{order} is smaller than or equal to pages_low, the function skips the zone and considers the next zone in the list. If no zone has enough free page frames, alloc_pages() restarts the loop, this time looking for a zone that has at least pages_min free page frames. If such a zone doesn't exist and if the current process is allowed to wait, the function invokes balance_classzone(), which in turn invokes try_to_free_pages() to reclaim enough page frames to satisfy the memory request (see "Reclaiming Page Frame" in Chapter 16).

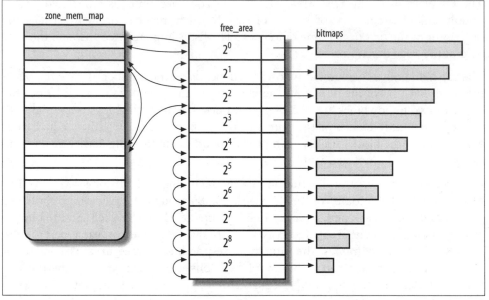

Figure 7-2. Data structures used by the buddy system

When `alloc_pages()` finds a zone with a suitable number of free page frames, it invokes the `rmqueue()` function to allocate a block in that zone. The function takes two arguments: the address of the zone descriptor, and order, which denotes the logarithm of the size of the requested block of free pages (0 for a one-page block, 1 for a two-page block, and so forth). If the page frames are successfully allocated, the `rmqueue()` function returns the address of the page descriptor of the first allocated page frame; that address is also returned by `alloc_pages()`. Otherwise, `rmqueue()` returns NULL, and `alloc_pages()` consider the next zone in the list.

The `rmqueue()` function is equivalent to the following fragments. First, a few local variables are declared and initialized:

```
free_area_t * area = &(zone->free_area[order]);
unsigned int curr_order = order;
struct list_head *head, *curr;
struct page *page;
unsigned long flags;
unsigned int index;
unsigned long size;
```

The function disables interrupts and acquires the spin lock of the zone descriptor because it will alter its fields to allocate a block. Then it performs a cyclic search through each list for an available block (denoted by an entry that doesn't point to the entry itself), starting with the list for the requested order and continuing if necessary to larger orders. This is equivalent to the following fragment:

```
spin_lock_irqsave(&zone->lock, flags);
do {
```

```
        head = &area->free_list;
        curr = head->next;
        if (curr != head)
            goto block_found;
        curr_order++;
        area++;
    } while (curr_order < 10);
    spin_unlock_irqrestore(&zone->lock, flags);
    return NULL;
```

If the loop terminates, no suitable free block has been found, so rmqueue( ) returns a NULL value. Otherwise, a suitable free block has been found; in this case, the descriptor of its first page frame is removed from the list, the corresponding bitmap is updated, and the value of free_pages in the zone descriptor is decreased:

```
block_found:
    page = list_entry(curr, struct page, list);
    list_del(curr);
    index = page - zone->zone_mem_map;
    if (curr_order != 9)
        change_bit(index>>(1+curr_order), area->map);
    zone->free_pages -= 1UL << order;
```

If the block found comes from a list of size curr_order greater than the requested size order, a while cycle is executed. The rationale behind these lines of codes is as follows: when it becomes necessary to use a block of 2^k page frames to satisfy a request for 2^h page frames ($h < k$), the program allocates the last 2^h page frames and iteratively reassigns the first $2^k - 2^h$ page frames to the free_area lists that have indexes between h and k:

```
    size = 1 << curr_order;
    while (curr_order > order) {
        area--;
        curr_order--;
        size >>= 1;
        /* insert *page as first element in the list and update the bitmap */
        list_add(&page->list, &area->free_list);
        change_bit(index >> (1+curr_order), area->map);
        /* now take care of the second half of the free block starting at *page */
        index += size;
        page += size;
    }
```

Finally, rmqueue( ) releases the spin lock, updates the count field of the page descriptor associated with the selected block, and executes the return instruction:

```
    spin_unlock_irqrestore(&zone->lock, flags);
    atomic_set(&page->count, 1);
    return page;
```

As a result, the alloc_pages( ) function returns the address of the page descriptor of the first page frame allocated.

Freeing a block

The __free_pages_ok( ) function implements the buddy system strategy for freeing page frames. It uses two input parameters:

page
> The address of the descriptor of the first page frame included in the block to be released

order
> The logarithmic size of the block

The __free_pages_ok( ) function usually inserts the block of page frames in the buddy system data structures so they can be used in subsequent allocation requests. One case is an exception: if the current process is moving pages across memory zones to rebalance them, the function does not free the page frames, but inserts the block in a special list of the process. To decide what to do with the block of page frames, __free_pages_ok( ) checks the PF_FREE_PAGES flag of the process. It is set only if the process is rebalancing the memory zones. Anyway, we discuss this special case in Chapter 16; we assume here that the PF_FREE_PAGES flag of current is not set, so __free_pages_ok( ) inserts the block in the buddy system data structures.

The function starts by declaring and initializing a few local variables:

```
unsigned long flags;
unsigned long mask = (~0UL) << order;
zone_t * zone = page->zone;
struct page * base = zone->zone_mem_map;
free_area_t * area = &zone->free_area[order];
unsigned long page_idx = page - base;
unsigned long index = page_idx >> (1 + order);
struct page * buddy;
```

The page_idx local variable contains the index of the first page frame in the block with respect to the first page frame of the zone. The index local variable contains the bit number corresponding to the block in the bitmap.

The function clears the PG_referenced and PG_dirty flags of the first page frame, then it acquires the zone spin lock and disables interrupts:

```
page->flags &= ~((1<<PG_referenced) | (1<<PG_dirty));
spin_lock_irqsave(&zone->lock, flags);
```

The mask local variable contains the two's complement of 2^{order}. It is used to increment the counter of free page frames in the zone:

```
zone->free_pages -= mask;
```

The function now starts a cycle executed at most 9 − order times, once for each possibility for merging a block with its buddy. The function starts with the smallest-sized block and moves up to the top size. The condition driving the while loop is:

```
mask + (1 << 9)
```

In the body of the loop, the bits set in mask are shifted to the left at each iteration and the buddy block of the block that has the number page_idx is checked:

```
if (!test_and_change_bit(index, area->map))
    break;
```

If the buddy block is not free, the function breaks out of the cycle; if it is free, the function detaches it from the corresponding list of free blocks. The block number of the buddy is derived from page_idx by switching a single bit:

```
buddy = &base[page_idx ^ -mask];
list_del(&buddy->list);
```

At the end of each iteration, the function updates the mask, area, index, and page_idx local variables:

```
mask <<= 1;
area++;
index >>= 1;
page_idx &= mask;
```

The function then continues the next iteration, trying to merge free blocks twice as large as the ones considered in the previous cycle. When the cycle is finished, the free block obtained cannot be merged further with other free blocks. It is then inserted in the proper list:

```
list_add(&(base[page_idx].list), &area->free_list);
```

Finally, the function releases the zone spin lock and returns:

```
spin_unlock_irqrestore(&zone->lock, flags);
return;
```

Memory Area Management

This section deals with *memory areas*—that is, with sequences of memory cells having contiguous physical addresses and an arbitrary length.

The buddy system algorithm adopts the page frame as the basic memory area. This is fine for dealing with relatively large memory requests, but how are we going to deal with requests for small memory areas, say a few tens or hundreds of bytes?

Clearly, it would be quite wasteful to allocate a full page frame to store a few bytes. A better approach instead consists of introducing new data structures that describe how small memory areas are allocated within the same page frame. In doing so, we introduce a new problem called *internal fragmentation*. It is caused by a mismatch between the size of the memory request and the size of the memory area allocated to satisfy the request.

A classical solution (adopted by early Linux versions) consists of providing memory areas whose sizes are geometrically distributed; in other words, the size depends on a power of 2 rather than on the size of the data to be stored. In this way, no matter what the memory request size is, we can ensure that the internal fragmentation is always smaller than 50 percent. Following this approach, the kernel creates 13 geometrically distributed lists of free memory areas whose sizes range from 32 to 131, 056 bytes. The buddy system is invoked both to obtain additional page frames needed to store new memory areas and, conversely, to release page frames that no longer contain memory areas. A dynamic list is used to keep track of the free memory areas contained in each page frame.

The Slab Allocator

Running a memory area allocation algorithm on top of the buddy algorithm is not particularly efficient. A better algorithm is derived from the *slab allocator* schema developed in 1994 for the Sun Microsystem Solaris 2.4 operating system. It is based on the following premises:

- The type of data to be stored may affect how memory areas are allocated; for instance, when allocating a page frame to a User Mode process, the kernel invokes the get_zeroed_page( ) function, which fills the page with zeros.

  The concept of a slab allocator expands upon this idea and views the memory areas as *objects* consisting of both a set of data structures and a couple of functions or methods called the *constructor* and *destructor*. The former initializes the memory area while the latter deinitializes it.

  To avoid initializing objects repeatedly, the slab allocator does not discard the objects that have been allocated and then released but instead saves them in memory. When a new object is then requested, it can be taken from memory without having to be reinitialized.

  In practice, the memory areas handled by Linux do not need to be initialized or deinitialized. For efficiency reasons, Linux does not rely on objects that need constructor or destructor methods; the main motivation for introducing a slab allocator is to reduce the number of calls to the buddy system allocator. Thus, although the kernel fully supports the constructor and destructor methods, the pointers to these methods are NULL.

- The kernel functions tend to request memory areas of the same type repeatedly. For instance, whenever the kernel creates a new process, it allocates memory areas for some fixed size tables such as the process descriptor, the open file object, and so on (see Chapter 3). When a process terminates, the memory areas used to contain these tables can be reused. Since processes are created and destroyed quite frequently, without the slab allocator, the kernel wastes time allocating and deallocating the page frames containing the same memory areas repeatedly; the slab allocator allows them to be saved in a cache and reused quickly.

- Requests for memory areas can be classified according to their frequency. Requests of a particular size that are expected to occur frequently can be handled most efficiently by creating a set of special-purpose objects that have the right size, thus avoiding internal fragmentation. Meanwhile, sizes that are rarely encountered can be handled through an allocation scheme based on objects in a series of geometrically distributed sizes (such as the power-of-2 sizes used in early Linux versions), even if this approach leads to internal fragmentation.

- There is another subtle bonus in introducing objects whose sizes are not geometrically distributed: the initial addresses of the data structures are less prone to be concentrated on physical addresses whose values are a power of 2. This, in turn, leads to better performance by the processor hardware cache.

- Hardware cache performance creates an additional reason for limiting calls to the buddy system allocator as much as possible. Every call to a buddy system function "dirties" the hardware cache, thus increasing the average memory access time. The impact of a kernel function on the hardware cache is called the function *footprint*; it is defined as the percentage of cache overwritten by the function when it terminates. Clearly, large footprints lead to a slower execution of the code executed right after the kernel function, since the hardware cache is by now filled with useless information.

The slab allocator groups objects into *caches*. Each cache is a "store" of objects of the same type. For instance, when a file is opened, the memory area needed to store the corresponding "open file" object is taken from a slab allocator cache named *filp* (for "file pointer"). The slab allocator caches used by Linux may be viewed at runtime by reading the */proc/slabinfo* file.

The area of main memory that contains a cache is divided into *slabs*; each slab consists of one or more contiguous page frames that contain both allocated and free objects (see Figure 7-3).

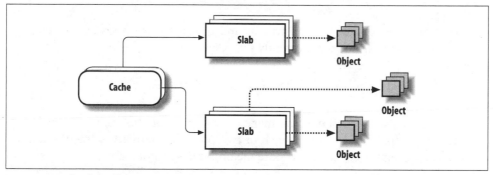

Figure 7-3. The slab allocator components

The slab allocator never releases the page frames of an empty slab on its own. It would not know when free memory is needed, and there is no benefit to releasing objects when there is still plenty of free memory for new objects. Therefore, releases occur only when the kernel is looking for additional free page frames (see the section "Releasing an Object from a Cache" later in this chapter and the section "Reclaiming Page Frame" in Chapter 16).

Cache Descriptor

Each cache is described by a table of type struct kmem_cache_s (which is equivalent to the type kmem_cache_t). The most significant fields of this table are:

name
> Character array storing the name of the cache.

slabs_full
> Doubly linked circular list of slab descriptors with no free objects.

slabs_partial
> Doubly linked circular list of slab descriptors with both free and nonfree objects.

slabs_free
> Doubly linked circular list of slab descriptors with free objects only.

spinlock
> Spin lock protecting the cache from concurrent accesses in multiprocessor systems.

num
> Number of objects packed into a single slab. (All slabs of the cache have the same size.)

objsize
> Size of the objects included in the cache. (This size may be rounded up by the slab allocator if the initial addresses of the objects must be memory-aligned.)

gfporder
> Logarithm of the number of contiguous page frames included in a single slab.

ctor, dtor
> Point, respectively, to the constructor and destructor methods associated with the cache objects. They are currently set to NULL, as stated earlier.

next
> Pointers for the doubly linked list of cache descriptors.

flags
> A set of flags that describes permanent properties of the cache. There is, for instance, a flag that specifies which of two possible alternatives (see the following section) has been chosen to store the object descriptors in memory.

dflags
> A set of flags that describe dynamic properties of the cache. There is, for instance, a flag that indicates whether the kernel is allocating new slabs to the cache. In multiprocessor systems, they must be accessed by acquiring the cache spin lock.

gfpflags

A set of flags passed to the buddy system function when allocating page frames. The field is typically used to specify the __GFP_DMA and __GFP_HIGHMEM zone modifiers. For instance, if __GFP_DMA is set in gfpflags, all objects of the cache can be used for ISA DMA.

Slab Descriptor

Each slab of a cache has its own descriptor of type struct slab_s (equivalent to the type slab_t). Slab descriptors can be stored in two possible places:

External slab descriptor

Stored outside the slab, in one of the general caches not suitable for ISA DMA pointed to by cache_sizes.

Internal slab descriptor

Stored inside the slab, at the beginning of the first page frame assigned to the slab.

The slab allocator chooses the second solution when the size of the objects is smaller than 512 or when internal fragmentation leaves enough space for the slab—and object descriptors (as described later)—inside the slab.

The most significant fields of a slab descriptor are:

inuse

Number of objects in the slab that are currently allocated.

s_mem

Points to the first object (either allocated or free) inside the slab.

free

Points to the first free object (if any) in the slab.

list

Pointers for one of the three doubly linked lists of slab descriptors (either the slabs_full, slabs_partial, or slabs_free list in the cache descriptor).

Figure 7-4 illustrates the major relationships between cache and slab descriptors. Full slabs, partially full slabs, and free slabs are linked in different lists.

General and Specific Caches

Caches are divided into two types: general and specific. *General caches* are used only by the slab allocator for its own purposes, while *specific caches* are used by the remaining parts of the kernel.

The general caches are:

- A first cache contains the cache descriptors of the remaining caches used by the kernel. The cache_cache variable contains its descriptor.

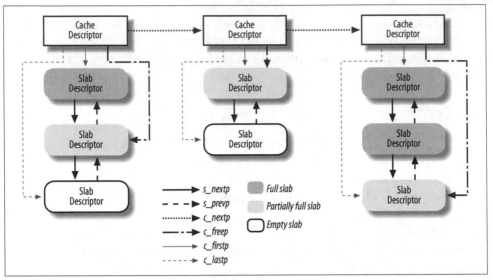

Figure 7-4. Relationship between cache and slab descriptors

- Twenty-six additional caches contain geometrically distributed memory areas. The table, called cache_sizes (whose elements are of type cache_sizes_t), points to the 26 cache descriptors associated with memory areas of size 32, 64, 128, 256, 512, 1,024, 2,048, 4,096, 8,192, 16,384, 32,768, 65,536, and 131,072 bytes, respectively. For each size, there are two caches: one suitable for ISA DMA allocations and the other for normal allocations. The table cache_sizes is used to efficiently derive the cache address corresponding to a given size.

The kmem_cache_init( ) and kmem_cache_sizes_init( ) functions are invoked during system initialization to set up the general caches.

Specific caches are created by the kmem_cache_create( ) function. Depending on the parameters, the function first determines the best way to handle the new cache (for instance, whether to include the slab descriptor inside or outside of the slab). It then creates a new cache descriptor for the new cache and inserts the descriptor in the cache_cache general cache.

It is also possible to destroy a cache by invoking kmem_cache_destroy( ). This function is mostly useful to modules that create their own caches when loaded and destroy them when unloaded. To avoid wasting memory space, the kernel must destroy all slabs before destroying the cache itself. The kmem_cache_shrink( ) function destroys all the slabs in a cache by invoking kmem_slab_destroy( ) iteratively (see the later section "Releasing a Slab from a Cache"). The growing field of the cache descriptor is used to prevent kmem_cache_shrink( ) from shrinking a cache while another kernel control path attempts to allocate a new slab for it.

The names of all general and specific caches can be obtained at runtime by reading */proc/slabinfo*; this file also specifies the number of free objects and the number of allocated objects in each cache.

Interfacing the Slab Allocator with the Buddy System

When the slab allocator creates new slabs, it relies on the buddy system algorithm to obtain a group of free contiguous page frames. For this purpose, it invokes the kmem_getpages( ) function:

```
void * kmem_getpages(kmem_cache_t *cachep, unsigned long flags)
{
    void    *addr;
    flags |= cachep->gfpflags;
    addr = (void*) __get_free_pages(flags, cachep->gfporder);
    return addr;
}
```

The parameters have the following meaning:

cachep

Points to the cache descriptor of the cache that needs additional page frames (the number of required page frames is determined by the order in the cachep->gfporder field)

flags

Specifies how the page frame is requested (see the section "Requesting and Releasing Page Frames" earlier in this chapter). This set of flags is combined with the specific cache allocation flags stored in the gfpflags of the cache descriptor.

In the reverse operation, page frames assigned to a slab allocator can be released (see the section "Releasing a Slab from a Cache" later in this chapter) by invoking the kmem_freepages( ) function:

```
void kmem_freepages(kmem_cache_t *cachep, void *addr)
{
    unsigned long i = (1<<cachep->gfporder);
    struct page *page = & mem_map[__pa(addr) >> PAGE_SHIFT];
    while (i--) {
        PageClearSlab(page);
        page++;
    }
    free_pages((unsigned long) addr, cachep->gfporder);
}
```

The function releases the page frames, starting from the one having the linear address addr, that had been allocated to the slab of the cache identified by cachep.

Allocating a Slab to a Cache

A newly created cache does not contain slab and therefore does not contain any free objects. New slabs are assigned to a cache only when both of the following are true:

- A request has been issued to allocate a new object.
- The cache does not include free object.

Under these circumstances, the slab allocator assigns a new slab to the cache by invoking kmem_cache_grow( ). This function calls kmem_getpages( ) to obtain a group of page frames from the buddy system; it then calls kmem_cache_slabmgmt( ) to get a new slab descriptor, either in the first page frame of the slab or in the general cache of order 0 pointed to by cache_sizes. Next, it calls kmem_cache_init_objs( ), which applies the constructor method (if defined) to all the objects contained in the new slab.

Then, kmem_cache_grow( ) scans all page descriptors of the page frames assigned to the new slab, and loads the next and prev subfields of the list fields in the page descriptors with the addresses of, respectively, the cache descriptor and the slab descriptor. This works correctly because the list field is used by functions of the buddy system only when the page frame is free, while page frames handled by the slab allocator functions are not free as far as the buddy system is concerned. Therefore, the buddy system is not confused by this specialized use of the page frame descriptor. The function also sets the PG_slab flag of the page frames.

The function then adds the slab descriptor *slabp at the end of the fully free slab list of the cache descriptor *cachep:

```
list_add_tail(&slabp->list, &cachep->slabs_free);
```

Releasing a Slab from a Cache

As stated previously, the slab allocator never releases the page frames of an empty slab on its own. In fact, a slab is released only if both of the following conditions are true:

- The buddy system is unable to satisfy a new request for a group of page frames (a zone is low on memory).
- The slab is empty—all the objects included in it are unused.

When the kernel looks for additional free page frames, it calls try_to_free_pages( ); this function, in turn, may invoke kmem_cache_reap( ), which selects a cache that contains at least one empty slab. The function then removes the slab from the fully free slab list and destroys it by invoking kmem_slab_destroy( ):

```
void kmem_slab_destroy(kmem_cache_t *cachep, slab_t *slabp)
{
    if (cachep->dtor) {
        int i;
        for (i = 0; i < cachep->num; i++) {
            void* objp = & slabp->s_mem[cachep->objsize*i];
            (cachep->dtor)(objp, cachep, 0);
        }
    }
    kmem_freepages(cachep, slabp->s_mem - slabp->colouroff);
    if (OFF_SLAB(cachep))
        kmem_cache_free(cachep->slabp_cache, slabp);
}
```

The function checks whether the cache has a destructor method for its objects (the dtor field is not NULL), in which case it applies the destructor to all the objects in the slab; the objp local variable keeps track of the currently examined object. Next, it calls kmem_freepages( ), which returns all the contiguous page frames used by the slab to the buddy system. Finally, if the slab descriptor is stored outside of the slab (macro OFF_SLAB returns true, as explained later in this chapter), the function releases it from the cache of slab descriptors.

Object Descriptor

Each object has a descriptor of type kmem_bufctl_t. Object descriptors are stored in an array placed after the corresponding slab descriptor. Thus, like the slab descriptors themselves, the object descriptors of a slab can be stored in two possible ways that are illustrated in Figure 7-5.

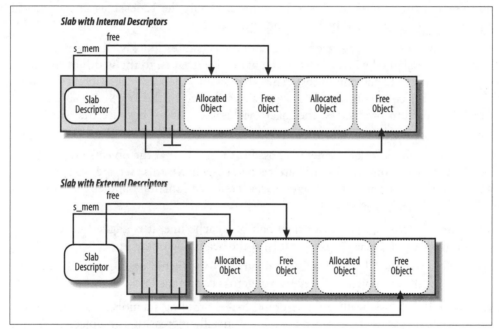

Figure 7-5. Relationships between slab and object descriptors

External object descriptors
> Stored outside the slab, in one of the general caches pointed to by cache_sizes. The size of the memory area, and thus the particular general cache used to store object descriptors, depends on the number of objects stored in the slab (num field of the cache descriptor).

Internal object descriptors
> Stored inside the slab, right after the objects they describe.

The first object descriptor in the array describes the first object in the slab, and so on. An object descriptor is simply a unsigned integer, which is meaningful only when the object is free. It contains the index of the next free object in the slab, thus implementing a simple list of free objects inside the slab. The object descriptor of the last element in the free object list is marked by the conventional value BUFCTL_END (0xffffffff).

Aligning Objects in Memory

The objects managed by the slab allocator are *aligned* in memory—that is, they are stored in memory cells whose initial physical addresses are multiples of a given constant, which is usually a power of 2. This constant is called the *alignment factor*.

The largest alignment factor allowed by the slab allocator is 4,096—the page frame size. This means that objects can be aligned by referring to either their physical addresses or their linear addresses. In both cases, only the 12 least significant bits of the address may be altered by the alignment.

Usually, microcomputers access memory cells more quickly if their physical addresses are aligned with respect to the word size (that is, to the width of the internal memory bus of the computer). Thus, by default, the kmem_cache_create( ) function aligns objects according to the word size specified by the BYTES_PER_WORD macro. For Intel Pentium processors, the macro yields the value 4 because the word is 32 bits long.

When creating a new slab cache, it's possible to specify that the objects included in it be aligned in the first-level hardware cache. To achieve this, set the SLAB_HWCACHE_ALIGN cache descriptor flag. The kmem_cache_create( ) function handles the request as follows:

- If the object's size is greater than half of a cache line, it is aligned in RAM to a multiple of L1_CACHE_BYTES—that is, at the beginning of the line.
- Otherwise, the object size is rounded up to a factor of L1_CACHE_BYTES; this ensures that an object will never span across two cache lines.

Clearly, what the slab allocator is doing here is trading memory space for access time; it gets better cache performance by artificially increasing the object size, thus causing additional internal fragmentation.

Slab Coloring

We know from Chapter 2 that the same hardware cache line maps many different blocks of RAM. In this chapter, we have also seen that objects of the same size tend to be stored at the same offset within a cache. Objects that have the same offset within different slabs will, with a relatively high probability, end up mapped in the same cache line. The cache hardware might therefore waste memory cycles transferring two objects from the same cache line back and forth to different RAM locations, while other cache lines go underutilized. The slab allocator tries to reduce this unpleasant cache behavior by a policy called *slab coloring*: different arbitrary values called *colors* are assigned to the slabs.

Before examining slab coloring, we have to look at the layout of objects in the cache. Let's consider a cache whose objects are aligned in RAM. This means that the object address must be a multiple of a given positive value, say *aln*. Even taking the alignment constraint into account, there are many possible ways to place objects inside the slab. The choices depend on decisions made for the following variables:

num
> Number of objects that can be stored in a slab (its value is in the num field of the cache descriptor).

osize
> Object size, including the alignment bytes.

dsize
> Slab descriptor size plus all object descriptors size. Its value is equal to 0 if the slab and object descriptors are stored outside of the slab.

free
> Number of unused bytes (bytes not assigned to any object) inside the slab.

The total length in bytes of a slab can then be expressed as:

> *slab length* = (*num* × *osize*) + *dsize* + *free*

free is always smaller than *osize*, since otherwise, it would be possible to place additional objects inside the slab. However, *free* could be greater than *aln*.

The slab allocator takes advantage of the *free* unused bytes to color the slab. The term "color" is used simply to subdivide the slabs and allow the memory allocator to spread objects out among different linear addresses. In this way, the kernel obtains the best possible performance from the microprocessor's hardware cache.

Slabs having different colors store the first object of the slab in different memory locations, while satisfying the alignment constraint. The number of available colors is (*free/aln*)+1. The first color is denoted as 0 and the last one (whose value is in the colour field of the cache descriptor) is denoted as *free/aln*.

If a slab is colored with color *col*, the offset of the first object (with respect to the slab initial address) is equal to *col*×*aln*+*dsize* bytes; this value is stored in the colour_off field of the cache descriptor. Figure 7-6 illustrates how the placement of objects inside the slab depends on the slab color. Coloring essentially leads to moving some of the free area of the slab from the end to the beginning.

Coloring works only when *free* is large enough. Clearly, if no alignment is required for the objects or if the number of unused bytes inside the slab is smaller than the required alignment (*free* < *aln*), the only possible slab coloring is the one that has the color 0—the one that assigns a zero offset to the first object.

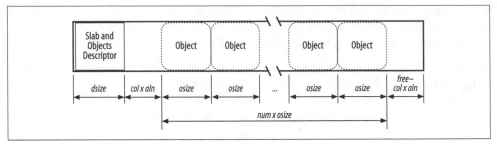

Figure 7-6. Slab with color col and alignment aln

The various colors are distributed equally among slabs of a given object type by storing the current color in a field of the cache descriptor called colour_next. The kmem_cache_grow( ) function assigns the color specified by colour_next to a new slab and then increments the value of this field. After reaching colour, it wraps around again to 0. In this way, each slab is created with a different color from the previous one, up to the maximum available colors.

Local Array of Objects in Multiprocessor Systems

The Linux 2.4 implementation of the slab allocator for multiprocessor systems differs from that of the original Solaris 2.4. To reduce spin lock contention among the processors, each cache of the slab allocator includes a small array of pointers to freed objects for each CPU in the system. Most of allocations and releases of slab objects affect the local array only; the slab data structures get involved only when the local array underflows or overflows.

The cache descriptor includes a cpudata array of pointers to cpucache_t data structures, one element for each CPU in the system. The cpucache_t data structure represents the descriptor of the local array of objects and includes the following fields:

avail
> The number of available objects in the local array. It also acts as the index of the first free slot in the array.

limit
> The size of the local array—that is, the maximum number of objects in the local array.

Notice that the local array descriptor does not include the address of the array itself; in fact, it is placed right after the descriptor. Of course, the array stores the pointers to the freed objects, not the object themselves, which are always placed inside the slabs of the cache. Nevertheless, the default size of the array depends on the size of the objects stored in the slab cache: the array size for small objects (up to 255 bytes) is 252 elements, the size for medium-size objects (between 256 and 1,023 bytes) is 124 elements, and the size for large objects (greater than 1,023 bytes) is 60 elements. Anyway, the system administrator can tune the size of the arrays for each cache by writing into the */proc/slabinfo* file.

Allocating an Object in a Cache

New objects may be obtained by invoking the kmem_cache_alloc( ) function. The parameter cachep points to the cache descriptor from which the new free object must be obtained, while the parameter flag represents the flags to be passed to the buddy system allocator functions, should all slabs of the cache be full.

The function differs for uniprocessor systems and multiprocessor ones because in the latter case, it must also cope with the local array of freed objects. Let's discuss these two cases separately.

The uniprocessor case

kmem_cache_alloc( ) first disables the local interrupts; it then looks for a slab that includes a free object:

```
void * objp;
slab_t * slabp;
struct list_head * entry;
local_irq_save(save_flags);
entry = cachep->slabs_partial.next;
if (entry == & cachep->slabs_partial) {
    entry = cachep->slabs_free.next;
    if (entry == & cachep->slabs_free)
        goto alloc_new_slab;
    list_del(entry);
    list_add(entry, & cachep->slab_partials);
}
slabp = list_entry(entry, slab_t, list);
```

The function looks into the slabs_partial doubly linked list, which links the descriptors of the slab that has at least one free object. If the list is empty (the list head points to itself), the function moves the first slab descriptor in the slabs_free list into slabs_partial. If even slabs_free is empty, the function allocates a new slab to the cache by invoking kmem_cache_grow( ), and then the whole procedure is repeated.

After obtaining a slab with a free object, the function increments the counter containing the number of objects currently allocated in the slab:

```
slabp->inuse++;
```

It then loads the objp local variable with the address of the first free object inside the slab:

```
objp = & slabp->s_mem[slabp->free * cachep->objsize];
```

The kmem_cache_alloc( ) function then updates the slabp->free field of the slab descriptor to point to the next free object:

```
slabp->free = ((kmem_bufctl_*)(slabp+1))[slabp->free];
if (slabp->free == BUFCTL_END) {
    list_del(&slabp->list);
    list_add(&slabp->list, &cachep->slabs_full);
}
```

Recall that the object descriptor of a free object stores either the index of another free object in the slab, or it stores BUFCTL_END if the free object is the last one. The array of object descriptors is placed right after the slab descriptor, so its address is computed as (slabp+1).

The function terminates by re-enabling the local interrupts and returning the address of the new object:

```
local_irq_restore(save_flags);
return objp;
```

The multiprocessor case

kmem_cache_alloc( ) first disables the local interrupts; it then looks for a free object in the cache's local array associated with the running CPU:

```
void * objp;
cpucache_t * cc;
local_irq_save(save_flags);
cc = cachep->cpudata[smp_processor_id()];
if (cc->avail)
    objp = ((void *)(cc+1))[--cc->avail];
else {
    objp = kmem_cache_alloc_batch(cachep, flags);
    if (!objp)
        goto alloc_new_slab;
}
local_irq_restore(save_flags);
return objp;
```

The cc local variable contains the address of the local array descriptor; thus, (cc+1) yields the address of the first local array element. If the avail field of the local array descriptor is positive, the function loads the address of the corresponding object into the objp local variable and decrements the counter. Otherwise, it invokes kmem_cache_alloc_batch( ) to repopulate the local array.

The kmem_cache_alloc_batch( ) function gets the cache spin lock and then allocates a predefined number of objects from the cache and inserts them into the local array:

```
count = cachep->batchcount;
cc = cachep->cpudata[smp_processor_id()];
spin_lock(&cachep->spinlock);
while (count--) {
    entry = cachep->slabs_partial.next;
    if (entry == &cachep->slabs_partial) {
        entry = cachep->slabs_free.next;
        if (entry == slabs_free)
            break;
        list_del(entry);
        list_add(entry, &cachep->slabs_partial);
    }
    slabp = list_entry(entry, slab_t, list);
    slabp->inuse++;
```

```
    objp = & slabp->s_mem[slabp->free * cachep->objsize];
    slabp->free = ((kmem_bufctl_*)(((slab_t *)slabp)+1))[slabp->free];
    if (slabp->free == BUFCTL_END) {
        list_del(&slabp->list);
        list_add(&slabp->list, &cachep->slabs_full);
    }
    ((void *)(cc+1))[cc->avail++] = objp;
}
spin_unlock(&cachep->spinlock);
if (cc->avail)
    return ((void *)(cc+1))[--cc->avail];
return NULL;
```

The number of pre-allocated objects is stored in the batchcount field of the cache descriptor; by default, it is half of the local array size, but the system administrator can modify it by writing into the /proc/slabinfo file. The code that gets the objects from the slabs is identical to that of the uniprocessor case, so we won't discuss it further.

The kmem_cache_alloc_batch() function returns NULL if the cache does not have free objects. In this case, kmem_cache_alloc() invokes kmem_cache_grow() and then repeats the whole procedure, (as in the uniprocessor case).

Releasing an Object from a Cache

The kmem_cache_free() function releases an object previously obtained by the slab allocator. Its parameters are cachep (the address of the cache descriptor) and objp (the address of the object to be released). As with kmem_cache_alloc(), we discuss the uniprocessor case separately from the multiprocessor case.

The uniprocessor case

The function starts by disabling the local interrupts and then determines the address of the descriptor of the slab containing the object. It uses the list.prev subfield of the descriptor of the page frame storing the object:

```
slab_t * slabp;
unsigned int objnr;
local_irq_save(save_flags);
slabp = (slab_t *) mem_map[__pa(objp) >> PAGE_SHIFT].list.prev;
```

Then the function computes the index of the object inside its slab, derives the address of its object descriptor, and adds the object to the head of the slab's list of free objects:

```
objnr = (objp - slabp->s_mem) / cachep->objsize;
((kmem_bufctl_t *)(slabp+1))[objnr] = slabp->free;
slabp->free = objnr;
```

Finally, the function checks whether the slab has to be moved to another list:

```
if (--slabp->inuse == 0) { /* slab is now fully free */
    list_del(&slabp->list);
```

```
        list_add(&slabp->list, &cachep->slabs_free);
    } else if (slabp->inuse+1 == cachep->num) { /* slab was full */
        list_del(&slabp->list);
        list_add(&slabp->list, &cachep->slabs_partial);
    }
    local_irq_restore(save_flags);
    return;
```

The multiprocessor case

The function starts by disabling the local interrupts; then it checks whether there is a free slot in the local array of object pointers:

```
cpucache_t * cc;
local_irq_save(save_flags);
cc = cachep->cpudata[smp_processor_id()];
if (cc->avail == cc->limit) {
    cc->avail -= cachep->batchcount;
    free_block(cachep, &((void *)(cc+1))[cc->avail], cachep->batchcount);
}
((void *)(cc+1))[cc->avail++] = objp;
local_irq_restore(save_flags);
return;
```

If there is at least one free slot in the local array, the function just sets it to the address of the object being freed. Otherwise, the function invokes free_block( ) to release a bunch of cachep->batchcount objects to the slab allocator cache.

The free_block(cachep,objpp,len) function acquires the cache spin lock and then releases len objects starting from the local array entry at address objpp:

```
spin_lock(&cachep->spinlock);
for ( ; len > 0; len--, objpp++) {
    slab_t * slabp = (slab_t *) mem_map[__pa(*objpp) >> PAGE_SHIFT].list.prev;
    unsigned int objnr = (*objpp - slabp->s_mem) / cachep->objsize;
    ((kmem_bufctl_t *)(slabp+1))[objnr] = slabp->free;
    slabp->free = objnr;
    if (--slabp->inuse == 0) { /* slab is now fully free */
        list_del(&slabp->list);
        list_add(&slabp->list, &cachep->slabs_free);
    } else if (slabp->inuse+1 == cachep->num) { /* slab was full */
        list_del(&slabp->list);
        list_add(&slabp->list, &cachep->slabs_partial);
    }
}
spin_unlock(&cachep->spinlock);
```

The code that releases the objects to the slabs is identical to that of the uniprocessor case, so we don't discuss it further.

General Purpose Objects

As stated earlier in the section "The Buddy System Algorithm," infrequent requests for memory areas are handled through a group of general caches whose objects have geometrically distributed sizes ranging from a minimum of 32 to a maximum of 131,072 bytes.

Objects of this type are obtained by invoking the kmalloc( ) function:

```
void * kmalloc(size_t size, int flags)
{
    cache_sizes_t *csizep = cache_sizes;
    kmem_cache_t * cachep;
    for (; csizep->cs_size; csizep++) {
        if (size > csizep->cs_size)
            continue;
        if (flags & __GFP_DMA)
            cachep = csizep->cs_dmacahep;
        else
            cachep = csizep->cs_cachep;
        return __kmem_cache_alloc(cachep, flags);
    }
    return NULL;
}
```

The function uses the cache_sizes table to locate the nearest power-of-2 size to the requested size. It then calls kmem_cache_alloc( ) to allocate the object, passing to it either the cache descriptor for the page frames usable for ISA DMA or the cache descriptor for the "normal" page frames, depending on whether the caller specified the __GFP_DMA flag.[*]

Objects obtained by invoking kmalloc( ) can be released by calling kfree( ):

```
void kfree(const void *objp)
{
    kmem_cache_t * c;
    unsigned long flags;
    if (!objp)
        return;
    local_irq_save(flags);
    c = (kmem_cache_t *) mem_map[__pa(objp) >> PAGE_SHIFT].list.next;
    __kmem_cache_free(c, (void *) objp);
    local_irq_restore(flags);
}
```

The proper cache descriptor is identified by reading the list.next subfield of the descriptor of the first page frame containing the memory area. The memory area is released by invoking kmem_cache_free( ).[†]

---

[*] Actually, for more efficiency, the code of kmem_cache_alloc( ) is copied inside the body of kmalloc( ). The __kmem_cache alloc( ) function, which implements kmem_cache_alloc( ), is declared inline.

[†] As for kmalloc( ), the code of kmem_cache_free( ) is copied inside kfree( ). __kmem_cache_free( ), which implements kmem_cache_free( ), is declared inline.

Noncontiguous Memory Area Management

We already know that it is preferable to map memory areas into sets of contiguous page frames, thus making better use of the cache and achieving lower average memory access times. Nevertheless, if the requests for memory areas are infrequent, it makes sense to consider an allocation schema based on noncontiguous page frames accessed through contiguous linear addresses. The main advantage of this schema is to avoid external fragmentation, while the disadvantage is that it is necessary to fiddle with the kernel Page Tables. Clearly, the size of a noncontiguous memory area must be a multiple of 4,096. Linux uses noncontiguous memory areas in several ways—for instance, to allocate data structures for active swap areas (see the section "Activating and Deactivating a Swap Area" in Chapter 16), to allocate space for a module (see Appendix B), or to allocate buffers to some I/O drivers.

Linear Addresses of Noncontiguous Memory Areas

To find a free range of linear addresses, we can look in the area starting from PAGE_ OFFSET (usually 0xc0000000, the beginning of the fourth gigabyte). Figure 7-7 shows how the fourth gigabyte linear addresses are used:

- The beginning of the area includes the linear addresses that map the first 896 MB of RAM (see the section "Process Page Tables" in Chapter 2); the linear address that corresponds to the end of the directly mapped physical memory is stored in the high_memory variable.

- The end of the area contains the fix-mapped linear addresses (see the section "Fix-Mapped Linear Addresses" in Chapter 2).

- Starting from PKMAP_BASE (0xfe000000), we find the linear addresses used for the persistent kernel mapping of high-memory page frames (see the section "Kernel Mappings of High-Memory Page Frames" earlier in this chapter).

- The remaining linear addresses can be used for noncontiguous memory areas. A safety interval of size 8 MB (macro VMALLOC_OFFSET) is inserted between the end of the physical memory mapping and the first memory area; its purpose is to "capture" out-of-bounds memory accesses. For the same reason, additional safety intervals of size 4 KB are inserted to separate noncontiguous memory areas.

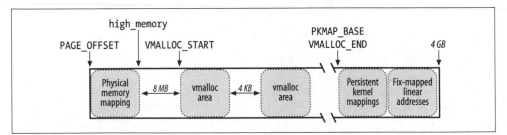

Figure 7-7. The linear address interval starting from PAGE_OFFSET

The VMALLOC_START macro defines the starting address of the linear space reserved for noncontiguous memory areas, while VMALLOC_END defines its ending address.

Descriptors of Noncontiguous Memory Areas

Each noncontiguous memory area is associated with a descriptor of type struct vm_struct:

```
struct vm_struct {
    unsigned long flags;
    void * addr;
    unsigned long size;
    struct vm_struct * next;
};
```

These descriptors are inserted in a simple list by means of the next field; the address of the first element of the list is stored in the vmlist variable. Accesses to this list are protected by means of the vmlist_lock read/write spin lock. The addr field contains the linear address of the first memory cell of the area; the size field contains the size of the area plus 4,096 (which is the size of the previously mentioned inter-area safety interval).

The get_vm_area( ) function creates new descriptors of type struct vm_struct; its parameter size specifies the size of the new memory area. The function is essentially equivalent to the following:

```
struct vm_struct * get_vm_area(unsigned long size, unsigned long flags)
{
    unsigned long addr;
    struct vm_struct **p, *tmp, *area;
    area = (struct vm_struct *) kmalloc(sizeof(*area), GFP_KERNEL);
    if (!area)
        return NULL;
    size += PAGE_SIZE;
    addr = VMALLOC_START;
    write_lock(&vmlist_lock);
    for (p = &vmlist; (tmp = *p) ; p = &tmp->next) {
        if (size + addr <= (unsigned long) tmp->addr) {
            area->flags = flags;
            area->addr = (void *) addr;
            area->size = size;
            area->next = *p;
            *p = area;
            write_unlock(&vmlist_lock);
            return area;
        }
        addr = tmp->size + (unsigned long) tmp->addr;
        if (addr + size > VMALLOC_END) {
            write_unlock(&vmlist_lock);
            kfree(area);
            return NULL;
        }
    }
}
```

The function first calls kmalloc( ) to obtain a memory area for the new descriptor. It then scans the list of descriptors of type struct vm_struct looking for an available range of linear addresses that includes at least size+4096 addresses. If such an interval exists, the function initializes the fields of the descriptor and terminates by returning the initial address of the noncontiguous memory area. Otherwise, when addr + size exceeds VMALLOC_END, get_vm_area( ) releases the descriptor and returns NULL.

Allocating a Noncontiguous Memory Area

The vmalloc( ) function allocates a noncontiguous memory area to the kernel. The parameter size denotes the size of the requested area. If the function is able to satisfy the request, it then returns the initial linear address of the new area; otherwise, it returns a NULL pointer:

```
void * vmalloc(unsigned long size)
{
    void * addr;
    struct vm_struct *area;
    size = (size + PAGE_SIZE - 1) & PAGE_MASK;
    area = get_vm_area(size, VM_ALLOC);
    if (!area)
        return NULL;
    addr = area->addr;
    if (vmalloc_area_pages((unsigned long) addr, size,
                    GFP_KERNEL|__GFP_HIGHMEM, 0x63)) {
        vfree(addr);
        return NULL;
    }
    return addr;
}
```

The function starts by rounding up the value of the size parameter to a multiple of 4,096 (the page frame size). Then vmalloc( ) invokes get_vm_area( ), which creates a new descriptor and returns the linear addresses assigned to the memory area. The flags field of the descriptor is initialized with the VM_ALLOC flag, which means that the linear address range is going to be used for a noncontiguous memory allocation (we'll see in Chapter 13 that vm_struct descriptors are also used to remap memory on hardware devices). Then the vmalloc( ) function invokes vmalloc_area_pages( ) to request noncontiguous page frames and terminates by returning the initial linear address of the noncontiguous memory area.

The vmalloc_area_pages( ) function uses four parameters:

address
    The initial linear address of the area.

size
    The size of the area.

gfp_mask

The allocation flags passed to the buddy system allocator function. It is always set to GFP_KERNEL|__GFP_HIGHMEM.

prot

The protection bits of the allocated page frames. It is always set to 0x63, which corresponds to Present, Accessed, Read/Write, and Dirty.

The function starts by assigning the linear address of the end of the area to the end local variable:

```
end = address + size;
```

The function then uses the pgd_offset_k macro to derive the entry in the master kernel Page Global Directory related to the initial linear address of the area; it then acquires the kernel Page Table spin lock:

```
dir = pgd_offset_k(address);
spin_lock(&init_mm.page_table_lock);
```

The function then executes the following cycle:

```
while (address < end) {
    pmd_t *pmd = pmd_alloc(&init_mm, dir, address);
    ret = -ENOMEM;
    if (!pmd)
        break;
    if (alloc_area_pmd(pmd, address, end - address, gfp_mask, prot))
        break;
    address = (address + PGDIR_SIZE) & PGDIR_MASK;
    dir++;
    ret = 0;
}
spin_unlock(&init_mm.page_table_lock);
return ret;
```

In each cycle, it first invokes pmd_alloc() to create a Page Middle Directory for the new area and writes its physical address in the right entry of the kernel Page Global Directory. It then calls alloc_area_pmd() to allocate all the Page Tables associated with the new Page Middle Directory. It adds the constant 2^{22}—the size of the range of linear addresses spanned by a single Page Middle Directory—to the current value of address, and it increases the pointer dir to the Page Global Directory.

The cycle is repeated until all Page Table entries referring to the noncontiguous memory area are set up.

The alloc_area_pmd() function executes a similar cycle for all the Page Tables that a Page Middle Directory points to:

```
while (address < end) {
    pte_t * pte = pte_alloc(&init_mm, pmd, address);
    if (!pte)
        return -ENOMEM;
    if (alloc_area_pte(pte, address, end - address))
```

```
        return -ENOMEM;
    address = (address + PMD_SIZE) & PMD_MASK;
    pmd++;
}
```

The pte_alloc( ) function (see the section "Page Table Handling" in Chapter 2) allocates a new Page Table and updates the corresponding entry in the Page Middle Directory. Next, alloc_area_pte( ) allocates all the page frames corresponding to the entries in the Page Table. The value of address is increased by 2^{22}—the size of the linear address interval spanned by a single Page Table—and the cycle is repeated.

The main cycle of alloc_area_pte( ) is:

```
while (address < end) {
    unsigned long page;
    spin_unlock(&init_mm.page_table_lock);
    page_alloc(gfp_mask);
    spin_lock(&init_mm.page_table_lock);
    if (!page)
        return -ENOMEM;
    set_pte(pte, mk_pte(page, prot));
    address += PAGE_SIZE;
    pte++;
}
```

Each page frame is allocated through page_alloc( ). The physical address of the new page frame is written into the Page Table by the set_pte and mk_pte macros. The cycle is repeated after adding the constant 4,096 (the length of a page frame) to address.

Notice that the Page Tables of the current process are not touched by vmalloc_area_pages( ). Therefore, when a process in Kernel Mode accesses the noncontiguous memory area, a Page Fault occurs, since the entries in the process's Page Tables corresponding to the area are null. However, the Page Fault handler checks the faulty linear address against the master kernel Page Tables (which are init_mm.pgd Page Global Directory and its child Page Tables; see the section "Kernel Page Tables" in Chapter 2). Once the handler discovers that a master kernel Page Table includes a non-null entry for the address, it copies its value into the corresponding process's Page Table entry and resumes normal execution of the process. This mechanism is described in the section "Page Fault Exception Handler" in Chapter 8.

Releasing a Noncontiguous Memory Area

The vfree( ) function releases noncontiguous memory areas. Its parameter addr contains the initial linear address of the area to be released. vfree( ) first scans the list pointed to by vmlist to find the address of the area descriptor associated with the area to be released:

```
write_lock(&vmlist_lock);
for (p = &vmlist ; (tmp = *p) ; p = &tmp->next) {
```

```
            if (tmp->addr == addr) {
                *p = tmp->next;
                vmfree_area_pages((unsigned long)(tmp->addr), tmp->size);
                write_unlock(&vmlist_lock);
                kfree(tmp);
                return;
            }
        }
    write_unlock(&vmlist_lock);
    printk("Trying to vfree() nonexistent vm area (%p)\n", addr);
```

The size field of the descriptor specifies the size of the area to be released. The area itself is released by invoking vmfree_area_pages( ), while the descriptor is released by invoking kfree( ).

The vmfree_area_pages( ) function takes two parameters: the initial linear address and the size of the area. It executes the following cycle to reverse the actions performed by vmalloc_area_pages( ):

```
dir = pgd_offset_k(address);
while (address < end) {
    free_area_pmd(dir, address, end - address);
    address = (address + PGDIR_SIZE) & PGDIR_MASK;
    dir++;
}
```

In turn, free_area_pmd( ) reverses the actions of alloc_area_pmd( ) in the cycle:

```
while (address < end) {
    free_area_pte(pmd, address, end - address);
    address = (address + PMD_SIZE) & PMD_MASK;
    pmd++;
}
```

Again, free_area_pte( ) reverses the activity of alloc_area_pte( ) in the cycle:

```
while (address < end) {
    pte_t page = *pte;
    pte_clear(pte);
    address += PAGE_SIZE;
    pte++;
    if (pte_none(page))
        continue;
    if (pte_present(page)) {
        __free_page(pte_page(page));
        continue;
    }
    printk("Whee... Swapped out page in kernel page table\n");
}
```

Each page frame assigned to the noncontiguous memory area is released by means of the buddy system __free_page( ) function. The corresponding entry in the Page Table is set to 0 by the pte_clear macro.

As for vmalloc( ), the kernel modifies the entries of the master kernel Page Global Directory and its child Page Tables (see the section "Kernel Page Tables" in Chapter 2), but it leaves unchanged the entries of the process Page Tables mapping the fourth gigabyte. This is fine because the kernel never reclaims Page Middle Directories and Page Tables rooted at the master kernel Page Global Directory.

For instance, suppose that a process in Kernel Mode accessed a noncontiguous memory area that later got released. The process's Page Global Directory entries are equal to the corresponding entries of the master kernel Page Global Directory, thanks to the mechanism explained in the section "Page Fault Exception Handler" in Chapter 8; they point to the same Page Middle Directories and Page Tables. The vmfree_area_pages( ) function clears only the entries of the Page Tables (without reclaiming the Page Tables themselves). Further accesses of the process to the released noncontiguous memory area will trigger Page Faults because of the null Page Table entries. However, the handler will consider such accesses a bug because the master kernel Page Tables do not include valid entries.

CHAPTER 8

Process Address Space

As seen in the previous chapter, a kernel function gets dynamic memory in a fairly straightforward manner by invoking one of a variety of functions: __get_free_pages( ) or pages_alloc( ) to get pages from the buddy system algorithm, kmem_cache_alloc( ) or kmalloc( ) to use the slab allocator for specialized or general-purpose objects, and vmalloc( ) to get a noncontiguous memory area. If the request can be satisfied, each of these functions returns a page descriptor address or a linear address identifying the beginning of the allocated dynamic memory area.

These simple approaches work for two reasons:

- The kernel is the highest-priority component of the operating system. If a kernel function makes a request for dynamic memory, it must have a valid reason to issue that request, and there is no point in trying to defer it.

- The kernel trusts itself. All kernel functions are assumed to be error-free, so the kernel does not need to insert any protection against programming errors.

When allocating memory to User Mode processes, the situation is entirely different:

- Process requests for dynamic memory are considered nonurgent. When a process's executable file is loaded, for instance, it is unlikely that the process will address all the pages of code in the near future. Similarly, when a process invokes malloc( ) to get additional dynamic memory, it doesn't mean the process will soon access all the additional memory obtained. Thus, as a general rule, the kernel tries to defer allocating dynamic memory to User Mode processes.

- Since user programs cannot be trusted, the kernel must be prepared to catch all addressing errors caused by processes in User Mode.

As this chapter describes, the kernel succeeds in deferring the allocation of dynamic memory to processes by using a new kind of resource. When a User Mode process asks for dynamic memory, it doesn't get additional page frames; instead, it gets the right to use a new range of linear addresses, which become part of its address space. This interval is called a *memory region*.

In the next section, we discuss how the process views dynamic memory. We then describe the basic components of the process address space in the section "Memory Regions." Next, we examine in detail the role played by the Page Fault exception handler in deferring the allocation of page frames to processes and illustrate how the kernel creates and deletes whole process address spaces. Last, we discuss the APIs and system calls related to address space management.

The Process's Address Space

The *address space* of a process consists of all linear addresses that the process is allowed to use. Each process sees a different set of linear addresses; the address used by one process bears no relation to the address used by another. As we shall see later, the kernel may dynamically modify a process address space by adding or removing intervals of linear addresses.

The kernel represents intervals of linear addresses by means of resources called *memory regions*, which are characterized by an initial linear address, a length, and some access rights. For reasons of efficiency, both the initial address and the length of a memory region must be multiples of 4,096 so that the data identified by each memory region completely fills up the page frames allocated to it. Following are some typical situations in which a process gets new memory regions:

- When the user types a command at the console, the shell process creates a new process to execute the command. As a result, a fresh address space, thus a set of memory regions, is assigned to the new process (see the section "Creating and Deleting a Process Address Space" later in this chapter; also, see Chapter 20).

- A running process may decide to load an entirely different program. In this case, the process ID remains unchanged but the memory regions used before loading the program are released and a new set of memory regions is assigned to the process (see the section "The exec Functions" in Chapter 20).

- A running process may perform a "memory mapping" on a file (or on a portion of it). In such cases, the kernel assigns a new memory region to the process to map the file (see the section "Memory Mapping" in Chapter 15).

- A process may keep adding data on its User Mode stack until all addresses in the memory region that map the stack have been used. In this case, the kernel may decide to expand the size of that memory region (see the section "Page Fault Exception Handler" later in this chapter).

- A process may create an IPC-shared memory region to share data with other cooperating processes. In this case, the kernel assigns a new memory region to the process to implement this construct (see the section "IPC Shared Memory" in Chapter 19).

- A process may expand its dynamic area (the heap) through a function such as malloc( ). As a result, the kernel may decide to expand the size of the memory region assigned to the heap (see the section "Managing the Heap" later in this chapter).

Table 8-1 illustrates some of the system calls related to the previously mentioned tasks. With the exception of brk( ), which is discussed at the end of this chapter, the system calls are described in other chapters.

Table 8-1. System calls related to memory region creation and deletion

System call	Description
brk( ),sbrk( )	Changes the heap size of the process
execve( )	Loads a new executable file, thus changing the process address space
_exit( )	Terminates the current process and destroys its address space
fork( )	Creates a new process, and thus a new address space
mmap( )	Creates a memory mapping for a file, thus enlarging the process address space
munmap( )	Destroys a memory mapping for a file, thus contracting the process address space
shmat( )	Attaches a shared memory region
shmdt( )	Detaches a shared memory region

As we shall see in the later section "Page Fault Exception Handler," it is essential for the kernel to identify the memory regions currently owned by a process (the address space of a process) since that allows the Page Fault exception handler to efficiently distinguish between two types of invalid linear addresses that cause it to be invoked:

- Those caused by programming errors.
- Those caused by a missing page; even though the linear address belongs to the process's address space, the page frame corresponding to that address has yet to be allocated.

The latter addresses are not invalid from the process's point of view; the kernel handles the Page Fault by providing the page frame and letting the process continue.

The Memory Descriptor

All information related to the process address space is included in a data structure called a *memory descriptor*. This structure of type mm_struct is referenced by the mm field of the process descriptor. The fields of a memory descriptor are listed in Table 8-2.

Table 8-2. The fields of the memory descriptor

Type	Field	Description
struct vm_area_struct *	mmap	Pointer to the head of the list of memory region objects
rb_root_t	mm_rb	Pointer to the root of the red-black tree of memory region objects
struct vm_area_struct *	mmap_cache	Pointer to the last referenced memory region object
pgd_t *	pgd	Pointer to the Page Global Directory

Table 8-2. The fields of the memory descriptor (continued)

Type	Field	Description
`atomic_t`	`mm_users`	Secondary usage counter
`atomic_t`	`mm_count`	Main usage counter
`int`	`map_count`	Number of memory regions
`struct rw_semaphore`	`mmap_sem`	Memory regions' read/write semaphore
`spinlock_t`	`page_table_lock`	Memory regions' and Page Tables' spin lock
`struct list_head`	`mmlist`	Pointers to adjacent elements in the list of memory descriptors
`unsigned long`	`start_code`	Initial address of executable code
`unsigned long`	`end_code`	Final address of executable code
`unsigned long`	`start_data`	Initial address of initialized data
`unsigned long`	`end_data`	Final address of initialized data
`unsigned long`	`start_brk`	Initial address of the heap
`unsigned long`	`brk`	Current final address of the heap
`unsigned long`	`start_stack`	Initial address of User Mode stack
`unsigned long`	`arg_start`	Initial address of command-line arguments
`unsigned long`	`arg_end`	Final address of command-line arguments
`unsigned long`	`env_start`	Initial address of environment variables
`unsigned long`	`env_end`	Final address of environment variables
`unsigned long`	`rss`	Number of page frames allocated to the process
`unsigned long`	`total_vm`	Size of the process address space (number of pages)
`unsigned long`	`locked_vm`	Number of "locked" pages that cannot be swapped out (see Chapter 16)
`unsigned long`	`def_flags`	Default access flags of the memory regions
`unsigned long`	`cpu_vm_mask`	Bit mask for lazy TLB switches (see Chapter 2)
`unsigned long`	`swap_address`	Last scanned linear address for swapping (see Chapter 16)
`unsigned int`	`dumpable`	Flag that specifies whether the process can produce a core dump of the memory
`mm_context_t`	`context`	Pointer to table for architecture-specific information (e.g., LDT's address in 80 × 86 platforms)

All memory descriptors are stored in a doubly linked list. Each descriptor stores the address of the adjacent list items in the mmlist field. The first element of the list is the mmlist field of init_mm, the memory descriptor used by process 0 in the initialization phase. The list is protected against concurrent accesses in multiprocessor systems by the mmlist_lock spin lock. The number of memory descriptors in the list is stored in the mmlist_nr variable.

The mm_users field stores the number of lightweight processes that share the mm_struct data structure (see the section "The clone( ), fork( ), and vfork( ) System Calls" in Chapter 3). The mm_count field is the main usage counter of the memory descriptor; all "users" in mm_users count as one unit in mm_count. Every time the mm_count field is decremented, the kernel checks whether it becomes zero; if so, the memory descriptor is deallocated because it is no longer in use.

We'll try to explain the difference between the use of mm_users and mm_count with an example. Consider a memory descriptor shared by two lightweight processes. Normally, its mm_users field stores the value 2, while its mm_count field stores the value 1 (both owner processes count as one).

If the memory descriptor is temporarily lent to a kernel thread (see the next section), the kernel increments the mm_count field. In this way, even if both lightweight processes die and the mm_users field becomes zero, the memory descriptor is not released until the kernel thread finishes using it because the mm_count field remains greater than zero.

If the kernel wants to be sure that the memory descriptor is not released in the middle of a lengthy operation, it might increment the mm_users field instead of mm_count (this is what the swap_out( ) function does; see the section "Swapping Out Pages" in Chapter 16). The final result is the same because the increment of mm_users ensures that mm_count does not become zero even if all lightweight processes that own the memory descriptor die.

The mm_alloc( ) function is invoked to get a new memory descriptor. Since these descriptors are stored in a slab allocator cache, mm_alloc( ) calls kmem_cache_alloc( ), initializes the new memory descriptor, and sets the mm_count and mm_users field to 1.

Conversely, the mmput( ) function decrements the mm_users field of a memory descriptor. If that field becomes 0, the function releases the Local Descriptor Table, the memory region descriptors (see later in this chapter), and the Page Tables referenced by the memory descriptor, and then invokes mmdrop( ). The latter function decrements mm_count and, if it becomes zero, releases the mm_struct data structure.

The mmap, mm_rb, mmlist, and mmap_cache fields are discussed in the next section.

Memory Descriptor of Kernel Threads

Kernel threads run only in Kernel Mode, so they never access linear addresses below TASK_SIZE (same as PAGE_OFFSET, usually 0xc0000000). Contrary to regular processes, kernel threads do not use memory regions, therefore most of the fields of a memory descriptor are meaningless for them.

Since the Page Table entries that refer to the linear address above TASK_SIZE should always be identical, it does not really matter what set of Page Tables a kernel thread uses. To avoid useless TLB and cache flushes, kernel threads use the Page Tables of a regular process in Linux 2.4. To that end, two kinds of memory descriptor pointers are included in every memory descriptor: mm and active_mm.

The mm field in the process descriptor points to the memory descriptor owned by the process, while the active_mm field points to the memory descriptor used by the process when it is in execution. For regular processes, the two fields store the same pointer. Kernel threads, however, do not own any memory descriptor, thus their mm field is always NULL. When a kernel thread is selected for execution, its active_mm field is initialized to the value of the active_mm of the previously running process (see the section "Actions performed by schedule() before a process switch" in Chapter 11).

There is, however, a small complication. Whenever a process in Kernel Mode modifies a Page Table entry for a "high" linear address (above TASK_SIZE), it should also update the corresponding entry in the sets of Page Tables of all processes in the system. In fact, once set by a process in Kernel Mode, the mapping should be effective for all other processes in Kernel Mode as well. Touching the sets of Page Tables of all processes is a costly operation; therefore, Linux adopts a deferred approach.

We already mentioned this deferred approach in the section "Noncontiguous Memory Area Management" in Chapter 7: every time a high linear address has to be remapped (typically by vmalloc() or vfree()), the kernel updates a canonical set of Page Tables rooted at the swapper_pg_dir master kernel Page Global Directory (see the section "Kernel Page Tables" in Chapter 2). This Page Global Directory is pointed to by the pgd field of a *master memory descriptor*, which is stored in the init_mm variable.*

Later, in the section "Handling Noncontiguous Memory Area Accesses," we'll describe how the Page Fault handler takes care of spreading the information stored in the canonical Page Tables when effectively needed.

Memory Regions

Linux implements a memory region by means of an object of type vm_area_struct; its fields are shown in Table 8-3.

Table 8-3. The fields of the memory region object

Type	Field	Description
struct mm_struct *	vm_mm	Pointer to the memory descriptor that owns the region
unsigned long	vm_start	First linear address inside the region
unsigned long	vm_end	First linear address after the region
struct vm_area_struct *	vm_next	Next region in the process list
pgprot_t	vm_page_prot	Access permissions for the page frames of the region
unsigned long	vm_flags	Flags of the region
rb_node_t	vm_rb	Data for the red-black tree (see later in this chapter)

---

* We mentioned in the section "Kernel Threads" in Chapter 3 that the *swapper* kernel thread uses init_mm during the initialization phase. However, swapper never uses this memory descriptor once the initialization phase completes.

Table 8-3. The fields of the memory region object (continued)

Type	Field	Description
struct vm_area_struct *	vm_next_share	Pointer to the next element in the file memory mapping list
struct vm_area_struct **	vm_pprev_share	Pointer to previous element in the file memory mapping list
struct vm_operations_struct *	vm_ops	Pointer to the methods of the memory region
unsigned long	vm_pgoff	Offset in mapped file, if any (see Chapter 15)
struct file *	vm_file	Pointer to the file object of the mapped file, if any
unsigned long	vm_raend	End of current read-ahead window of the mapped file (see the section "Demand Paging for Memory Mapping" in Chapter 15)
void *	vm_private_data	Pointer to private data of the memory region

Each memory region descriptor identifies a linear address interval. The vm_start field contains the first linear address of the interval, while the vm_end field contains the first linear address outside of the interval; vm_end - vm_start thus denotes the length of the memory region. The vm_mm field points to the mm_struct memory descriptor of the process that owns the region. We shall describe the other fields of vm_area_struct as they come up.

Memory regions owned by a process never overlap, and the kernel tries to merge regions when a new one is allocated right next to an existing one. Two adjacent regions can be merged if their access rights match.

As shown in Figure 8-1, when a new range of linear addresses is added to the process address space, the kernel checks whether an already existing memory region can be enlarged (case *a*). If not, a new memory region is created (case *b*). Similarly, if a range of linear addresses is removed from the process address space, the kernel resizes the affected memory regions (case *c*). In some cases, the resizing forces a memory region to split into two smaller ones (case *d*).[*]

The vm_ops field points to a vm_operations_struct data structure, which stores the methods of the memory region. Only three methods are defined:

open
    Invoked when the memory region is added to the set of regions owned by a process.

close
    Invoked when the memory region is removed from the set of regions owned by a process.

---

[*] Removing a linear address interval may theoretically fail because no free memory is available for a new memory descriptor.

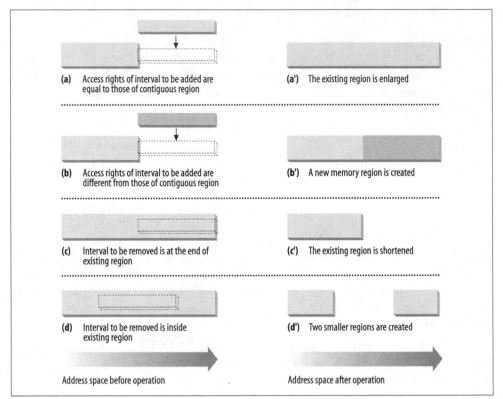

Figure 8-1. Adding or removing a linear address interval

nopage

Invoked by the Page Fault exception handler when a process tries to access a page not present in RAM whose linear address belongs to the memory region (see the later section "Page Fault Exception Handler").

Memory Region Data Structures

All the regions owned by a process are linked in a simple list. Regions appear in the list in ascending order by memory address; however, successive regions can be separated by an area of unused memory addresses. The vm_next field of each vm_area_struct element points to the next element in the list. The kernel finds the memory regions through the mmap field of the process memory descriptor, which points to the first memory region descriptor in the list.

The map_count field of the memory descriptor contains the number of regions owned by the process. A process may own up to MAX_MAP_COUNT different memory regions (this value is usually set to 65,536).

Figure 8-2 illustrates the relationships among the address space of a process, its memory descriptor, and the list of memory regions.

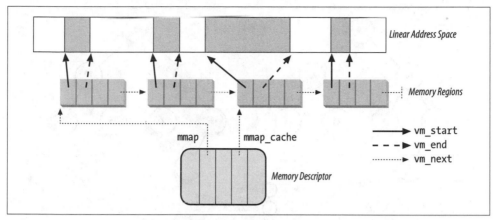

Figure 8-2. Descriptors related to the address space of a process

A frequent operation performed by the kernel is to search the memory region that includes a specific linear address. Since the list is sorted, the search can terminate as soon as a memory region that ends after the specific linear address is found.

However, using the list is convenient only if the process has very few memory regions—let's say less than a few tens of them. Searching, inserting elements, and deleting elements in the list involve a number of operations whose times are linearly proportional to the list length.

Although most Linux processes use very few memory regions, there are some large applications, such as object-oriented databases, that one might consider "pathological" because they have many hundreds or even thousands of regions. In such cases, the memory region list management becomes very inefficient, hence the performance of the memory-related system calls degrades to an intolerable point.

Therefore, Linux 2.4 stores memory descriptors in data structures called *red-black trees*.* In an red-black tree, each element (or *node*) usually has two children: a *left child* and a *right child*. The elements in the tree are sorted. For each node *N*, all elements of the subtree rooted at the left child of *N* precede *N*, while, conversely, all elements of the subtree rooted at the right child of *N* follow *N* (see Figure 8-3(*a*); the key of the node is written inside the node itself. Moreover, a red-black tree must satisfy four additional rules:

1. Every node must be either red or black.
2. The root of the tree must be black.
3. The children of a red node must be black.
4. Every path from a node to a descendant leaf must contain the same number of black nodes. When counting the number of black nodes, null pointers are counted as black nodes.

---

* Up to Version 2.4.9, the Linux kernel used another type of balanced search tree called *AVL tree*.

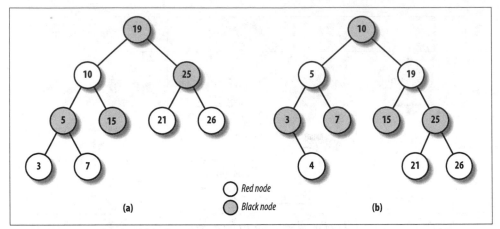

Figure 8-3. Example of red-black trees

These four rules ensure that any red-black tree with *n* internal nodes has a height of at most 2log(n + 1).

Searching an element in a red-black tree is thus very efficient because it requires operations whose execution time is linearly proportional to the logarithm of the tree size. In other words, doubling the number of memory regions adds just one more iteration to the operation.

Inserting and deleting an element in a red-black tree is also efficient because the algorithm can quickly traverse the tree to locate the position at which the element will be inserted or from which it will be removed. Any new node must be inserted as a leaf and colored red. If the operation breaks the rules, a few nodes of the tree must be moved or recolored.

For instance, suppose that an element having the value 4 must be inserted in the red-black tree shown in Figure 8-3(*a*). Its proper position is the right child of the node that has key 3, but once it is inserted, the red node that has the value 3 has a red child, thus breaking rule 3. To satisfy the rule, the color of nodes that have the values 3, 4, and 7 is changed. This operation, however, breaks rule 4, thus the algorithm performs a "rotation" on the subtree rooted at the node that has the key 19, producing the new red-black tree shown in Figure 8-3(*b*). This looks complicated, but inserting or deleting an element in a red-black tree requires a small number of operations—a number linearly proportional to the logarithm of the tree size.

Therefore, to store the memory regions of a process, Linux uses both a linked list and a red-black tree. Both data structures contain pointers to the same memory region descriptors, When inserting or removing a memory region descriptor, the kernel searches the previous and next elements through the red-black tree and uses them to quickly update the list without scanning it.

The head of the linked list is referenced by the mmap field of the memory descriptor. Any memory region object stores the pointer to the next element of the list in the vm_next field. The head of the red-black tree is referred by the mm_rb field of the memory descriptor. Any memory region object stores the color of the node, as well as the pointers to the parent, the left child, and the right child, into the vm_rb field of type rb_node_t.

In general, the red-black tree is used to locate a region including a specific address, while the linked list is mostly useful when scanning the whole set of regions.

Memory Region Access Rights

Before moving on, we should clarify the relation between a page and a memory region. As mentioned in Chapter 2, we use the term "page" to refer both to a set of linear addresses and to the data contained in this group of addresses. In particular, we denote the linear address interval ranging between 0 and 4,095 as page 0, the linear address interval ranging between 4,096 and 8,191 as page 1, and so forth. Each memory region therefore consists of a set of pages that have consecutive page numbers.

We have already discussed two kinds of flags associated with a page:

- A few flags such as Read/Write, Present, or User/Supervisor stored in each Page Table entry (see the section "Regular Paging" in Chapter 2).
- A set of flags stored in the flags field of each page descriptor (see the section "Page Frame Management" in Chapter 7).

The first kind of flag is used by the 80×86 hardware to check whether the requested kind of addressing can be performed; the second kind is used by Linux for many different purposes (see Table 7-2).

We now introduce a third kind of flags: those associated with the pages of a memory region. They are stored in the vm_flags field of the vm_area_struct descriptor (see Table 8-4). Some flags offer the kernel information about all the pages of the memory region, such as what they contain and what rights the process has to access each page. Other flags describe the region itself, such as how it can grow.

Table 8-4. The memory region flags

Flag name	Description
VM_READ	Pages can be read.
VM_WRITE	Pages can be written.
VM_EXEC	Pages can be executed.
VM_SHARED	Pages can be shared by several processes.
VM_MAYREAD	VM_READ flag may be set.
VM_MAYWRITE	VM_WRITE flag may be set.
VM_MAYEXEC	VM_EXEC flag may be set.
VM_MAYSHARE	VM_SHARE flag may be set.

Table 8-4. The memory region flags (continued)

Flag name	Description
VM_GROWSDOWN	The region can expand toward lower addresses.
VM_GROWSUP	The region can expand toward higher addresses.
VM_SHM	The region is used for IPC's shared memory.
VM_DENYWRITE	The region maps a file that cannot be opened for writing.
VM_EXECUTABLE	The region maps an executable file.
VM_LOCKED	Pages in the region are locked and cannot be swapped out.
VM_IO	The region maps the I/O address space of a device.
VM_SEQ_READ	The application accesses the pages sequentially.
VM_RAND_READ	The application accesses the pages in a truly random order.
VM_DONTCOPY	Does not copy the region when forking a new process.
VM_DONTEXPAND	Forbids region expansion through mremap( ) system call.
VM_RESERVED	Does not swap out the region.

Page access rights included in a memory region descriptor may be combined arbitrarily. It is possible, for instance, to allow the pages of a region to be executed but not read. To implement this protection scheme efficiently, the read, write, and execute access rights associated with the pages of a memory region must be duplicated in all the corresponding Page Table entries so that checks can be directly performed by the Paging Unit circuitry. In other words, the page access rights dictate what kinds of access should generate a Page Fault exception. As we shall see shortly, the job of figuring out what caused the Page Fault is delegated by Linux to the Page Fault handler, which implements several page-handling strategies.

The initial values of the Page Table flags (which must be the same for all pages in the memory region, as we have seen) are stored in the vm_page_prot field of the vm_area_struct descriptor. When adding a page, the kernel sets the flags in the corresponding Page Table entry according to the value of the vm_page_prot field.

However, translating the memory region's access rights into the page protection bits is not straightforward for the following reasons:

- In some cases, a page access should generate a Page Fault exception even when its access type is granted by the page access rights specified in the vm_flags field of the corresponding memory region. For instance, as we shall see in the section "Copy On Write" later in this chapter, the kernel may wish to store two identical, writable private pages (whose VM_SHARE flags are cleared) belonging to two different processes into the same page frame; in this case, an exception should be generated when either one of the processes tries to modify the page.

- 80×86 processors's Page Tables have just two protection bits, namely the Read/Write and User/Supervisor flags. Moreover, the User/Supervisor flag of any page included in a memory region must always be set, since the page must always be accessible by User Mode processes.

To overcome the hardware limitation of the 80×86 microprocessors, Linux adopts the following rules:

- The read access right always implies the execute access right.
- The write access right always implies the read access right.

Moreover, to correctly defer the allocation of page frames through the "Copy On Write" technique (see later in this chapter), the page frame is write-protected whenever the corresponding page must not be shared by several processes. Therefore, the 16 possible combinations of the read, write, execute, and share access rights are scaled down to the following three:

- If the page has both write and share access rights, the Read/Write bit is set.
- If the page has the read or execute access right but does not have either the write or the share access right, the Read/Write bit is cleared.
- If the page does not have any access rights, the Present bit is cleared so that each access generates a Page Fault exception. However, to distinguish this condition from the real page-not-present case, Linux also sets the Page size bit to 1.*

The downscaled protection bits corresponding to each combination of access rights are stored in the protection_map array.

Memory Region Handling

Having the basic understanding of data structures and state information that control memory handling, we can look at a group of low-level functions that operate on memory region descriptors. They should be considered auxiliary functions that simplify the implementation of do_mmap( ) and do_munmap( ). Those two functions, which are described in the sections "Allocating a Linear Address Interval" and "Releasing a Linear Address Interval" later in this chapter, enlarge and shrink the address space of a process, respectively. Working at a higher level than the functions we consider here, they do not receive a memory region descriptor as their parameter, but rather the initial address, the length, and the access rights of a linear address interval.

Finding the closest region to a given address: find_vma()

The find_vma( ) function acts on two parameters: the address mm of a process memory descriptor and a linear address addr. It locates the first memory region whose vm_end field is greater than addr and returns the address of its descriptor; if no such region exists, it returns a NULL pointer. Notice that the region selected by find_vma( ) does not necessarily include addr because addr may lie outside of any memory region.

---

* You might consider this use of the Page size bit to be a dirty trick, since the bit was meant to indicate the real page size. But Linux can get away with the deception because the 80×86 chip checks the Page size bit in Page Directory entries, but not in Page Table entries.

Each memory descriptor includes a mmap_cache field that stores the descriptor address of the region that was last referenced by the process. This additional field is introduced to reduce the time spent in looking for the region that contains a given linear address. Locality of address references in programs makes it highly likely that if the last linear address checked belonged to a given region, the next one to be checked belongs to the same region.

The function thus starts by checking whether the region identified by mmap_cache includes addr. If so, it returns the region descriptor pointer:

```
vma = mm->mmap_cache;
if (vma && vma->vm_end > addr && vma->vm_start <= addr)
    return vma;
```

Otherwise, the memory regions of the process must be scanned, and the function looks up the memory region in the red-black tree:

```
rb_node = mm->mm_rb.rb_node;
vma = NULL;
while (rb_node) {
    vma_tmp = rb_entry(rb_node, struct vm_area_struct, vm_rb);
    if (vma_tmp->vm_end > addr) {
        vma = vma_tmp;
        if (vma_tmp->vm_start <= addr)
            break;
        rb_node = rb_node->rb_left;
    } else
        rb_node = rb_node->rb_right;
}
if (vma)
    mm->mmap_cache = vma;
return vma;
```

The function uses the rb_entry macro, which derives from a pointer to a node of the red-black tree the address of the corresponding memory region descriptor.

The kernel also defines the find_vma_prev( ) function (which returns the descriptor addresses of the memory region that precedes the linear address given as parameter and of the memory region that follows it) and the find_vma_prepare( ) function (which locates the position of the new leaf in the red-black tree that corresponds to a given linear address and returns the addresses of the preceding memory region and of the parent node of the leaf to be inserted).

Finding a region that overlaps a given interval: find_vma_intersection( )

The find_vma_intersection( ) function finds the first memory region that overlaps a given linear address interval; the mm parameter points to the memory descriptor of the process, while the start_addr and end_addr linear addresses specify the interval:

```
vma = find_vma(mm,start_addr);
if (vma && end_addr <= vma->vm_start)
    vma = NULL;
return vma;
```

The function returns a NULL pointer if no such region exists. To be exact, if find_vma( ) returns a valid address but the memory region found starts after the end of the linear address interval, vma is set to NULL.

Finding a free interval: arch_get_unmapped_area()

The arch_get_unmapped_area( ) function searches the process address space to find an available linear address interval. The len parameter specifies the interval length, while the addr parameter may specify the address from which the search is started. If the search is successful, the function returns the initial address of the new interval; otherwise, it returns the error code -ENOMEM.

```
if (len > TASK_SIZE)
    return -ENOMEM;
addr = (addr + 0xfff) & 0xfffff000;
if (addr && addr + len <= TASK_SIZE) {
    vma = find_vma(current->mm, addr);
    if (!vma || addr + len <= vma->vm_start)
        return addr;
}
addr = (TASK_SIZE/3 + 0xfff) & 0xfffff000;
for (vma = find_vma(current->mm, addr); ; vma = vma->vm_next) {
    if (addr + len > TASK_SIZE)
        return -ENOMEM;
    if (!vma || addr + len <= vma->vm_start)
        return addr;
    addr = vma->vm_end;
}
```

The function starts by checking to make sure the interval length is within the limit imposed on User Mode linear addresses, usually 3 GB. If addr is different from zero, the function tries to allocate the interval starting from addr. To be on the safe side, the function rounds up the value of addr to a multiple of 4 KB. If addr is 0 or the previous search failed, the search's starting point is set to one-third of the User Mode linear address space. Starting from addr, the function then repeatedly invokes find_vma( ) with increasing values of addr to find the required free interval. During this search, the following cases may occur:

- The requested interval is larger than the portion of linear address space yet to be scanned (addr + len > TASK_SIZE). Since there are not enough linear addresses to satisfy the request, return -ENOMEM.
- The hole following the last scanned region is not large enough (vma != NULL && vma->vm_start < addr + len). Consider the next region.
- If neither one of the preceding conditions holds, a large enough hole has been found. Return addr.

Inserting a region in the memory descriptor list: insert_vm_struct( )

insert_vm_struct( ) inserts a vm_area_struct structure in the memory region object list and red-black tree of a memory descriptor. It uses two parameters: mm, which specifies the address of a process memory descriptor, and vma, which specifies the address of the vm_area_struct object to be inserted. The vm_start and vm_end fields of the memory region object must have already been initialized. The function invokes the find_vma_prepare( ) function to look up the position in the red-black tree mm->mm_rb where vma should go. Then insert_vm_struct( ) invokes the vma_link( ) function, which in turn:

1. Acquires the mm->page_table_lock spin lock.
2. Inserts the memory region in the linked list referenced by mm->mmap.
3. Inserts the memory region in the red-black tree mm->mm_rb.
4. Releases the mm->page_table_lock spin lock.
5. Increments by 1 the mm->map_count counter.

If the region contains a memory-mapped file, the vma_link( ) function performs additional tasks that are described in Chapter 16.

The kernel also defines the __insert_vm_struct( ) function, which is identical to insert_vm_struct( ) but doesn't acquire any lock before modifying the memory region data structures referenced by mm. The kernel uses it when it is sure that no concurrent accesses to the memory region data structures can happen—for instance, because it already acquired a suitable lock.

The __vma_unlink( ) function receives as parameter a memory descriptor address mm and two memory region object addresses vma and prev. Both memory regions should belong to mm, and prev should precede vma in the memory region ordering. The function removes vma from the linked list and the red-black tree of the memory descriptor.

Allocating a Linear Address Interval

Now let's discuss how new linear address intervals are allocated. To do this, the do_mmap( ) function creates and initializes a new memory region for the current process. However, after a successful allocation, the memory region could be merged with other memory regions defined for the process.

The function uses the following parameters:

file *and* offset
> File descriptor pointer file and file offset offset are used if the new memory region will map a file into memory. This topic is discussed in Chapter 15. In this section, we assume that no memory mapping is required and that file and offset are both NULL.

addr
> This linear address specifies where the search for a free interval must start.

len

The length of the linear address interval.

prot

This parameter specifies the access rights of the pages included in the memory region. Possible flags are PROT_READ, PROT_WRITE, PROT_EXEC, and PROT_NONE. The first three flags mean the same things as the VM_READ, VM_WRITE, and VM_EXEC flags. PROT_NONE indicates that the process has none of those access rights.

flag

This parameter specifies the remaining memory region flags:

MAP_GROWSDOWN, MAP_LOCKED, MAP_DENYWRITE, and MAP_EXECUTABLE

Their meanings are identical to those of the flags listed in Table 8-4.

MAP_SHARED and MAP_PRIVATE

The former flag specifies that the pages in the memory region can be shared among several processes; the latter flag has the opposite effect. Both flags refer to the VM_SHARED flag in the vm_area_struct descriptor.

MAP_ANONYMOUS

No file is associated with the memory region (see Chapter 15).

MAP_FIXED

The initial linear address of the interval must be exactly the one specified in the addr parameter.

MAP_NORESERVE

The function doesn't have to do a preliminary check on the number of free page frames.

The do_mmap( ) function performs some preliminary checks on the value of offset and then executes the do_mmap_pgoff() function. Assuming that the new interval of linear address does not map a file on disk, the latter function executes the following steps:

1. Checks whether the parameter values are correct and whether the request can be satisfied. In particular, it checks for the following conditions that prevent it from satisfying the request:

   - The linear address interval has zero length or includes addresses greater than TASK_SIZE.

   - The process has already mapped too many memory regions, so the value of the map_count field of its mm memory descriptor exceeds MAX_MAP_COUNT.

   - The flag parameter specifies that the pages of the new linear address interval must be locked in RAM, and the number of pages locked by the process exceeds the threshold stored in the rlim[RLIMIT_MEMLOCK].rlim_cur field of the process descriptor.

If any of the preceding conditions holds, do_mmap_pgoff( ) terminates by returning a negative value. If the linear address interval has a zero length, the function returns without performing any action.

2. Obtains a linear address interval for the new region; if the MAP_FIXED flag is set, a check is made on the addr value. Otherwise, the arch_get_unmapped_area( ) function is invoked to get it:

```
if (flags & MAP_FIXED) {
    if (addr + len > TASK_SIZE)
        return -ENOMEM;
    if (addr & ~PAGE_MASK)
        return -EINVAL;
} else
    addr = arch_get_unmapped_area(file, addr, len, pgoff, flags);
```

3. Computes the flags of the new memory region by combining the values stored in the prot and flags parameters:

```
vm_flags = calc_vm_flags(prot,flags) | mm->def_flags
            | VM_MAYREAD | VM_MAYWRITE | VM_MAYEXEC;
if (flags & MAP_SHARED)
    vm_flags |= VM_SHARED | VM_MAYSHARE;
```

The calc_vm_flags() function sets the VM_READ, VM_WRITE, and VM_EXEC flags in vm_flags only if the corresponding PROT_READ, PROT_WRITE, and PROT_EXEC flags in prot are set; it also sets the VM_GROWSDOWN, VM_DENYWRITE, and VM_EXECUTABLE flags in vm_flags only if the corresponding MAP_GROWSDOWN, MAP_DENYWRITE, and MAP_ EXECUTABLE flags in flags are set. A few other flags are set to 1 in vm_flags: VM_ MAYREAD, VM_MAYWRITE, VM_MAYEXEC, the default flags for all memory regions in mm-> def_flags,* and both VM_SHARED and VM_MAYSHARE if the memory region has to be shared with other processes.

4. Invokes find_vma_prepare( ) to locate the object of the memory region that shall precede the new interval, as well as the position of the new region in the red-black tree:

```
for (;;) {
    vma = find_vma_prepare(mm, addr, &prev, &rb_link, &rb_parent);
    if (!vma || vma->vm_start >= addr + len)
        break;
    if (do_munmap(mm, addr, len))
            return -ENOMEM;
}
```

The find_vma_prepare() function also checks whether a memory region that overlaps the new interval already exists. This occurs when the function returns a non-NULL address pointing to a region that starts before the end of the new interval. In this case, do_mmap_pgoff() invokes do_munmap() to remove the new interval and then repeats the whole step (see the later section "Releasing a Linear Address Interval").

---

* Actually, the def_flags field of the memory descriptor is modified only by the mlockall( ) system call, which can be used to set the VM_LOCKED flag, thus locking all future pages of the calling process in RAM.

5. Checks whether inserting the new memory region causes the size of the process address space (mm->total_vm<<PAGE_SHIFT)+len to exceed the threshold stored in the rlim[RLIMIT_AS].rlim_cur field of the process descriptor. In the affirmative case, it returns the error code -ENOMEM. Notice that the check is done here and not in Step 1 with the other checks because some memory regions could have been removed in Step 4.

6. Returns the error code -ENOMEM if the MAP_NORESERVE flag was not set in the flags parameter, the new memory region contains private writable pages, and the number of free page frames is less than the size (in pages) of the linear address interval; this last check is performed by the vm_enough_memory( ) function.

7. If the new interval is private (VM_SHARED not set) and it does not map a file on disk, invokes vma_merge( ) to check whether the preceding memory region can be expanded in such a way to include the new interval. Of course, the preceding memory region must have exactly the same flags as those memory regions stored in the vm_flags local variable. If the preceding memory region can be expanded, vma_merge( ) also tries to merge it with the following memory region (this occurs when the new interval fills the hole between two memory regions and all three have the same flags). In case it succeeds in expanding the preceding memory region, jump to Step 12.

8. Allocates a vm_area_struct data structure for the new memory region by invoking the kmem_cache_alloc( ) slab allocator function.

9. Initializes the new memory region object (pointed by vma):

```
vma->vm_mm = mm;
vma->vm_start = addr;
vma->vm_end = addr + len;
vma->vm_flags = vm_flags;
vma->vm_page_prot = protection_map[vm_flags & 0x0f];
vma->vm_ops = NULL;
vma->vm_pgoff = pgoff;
vma->vm_file = NULL;
vma->vm_private_data = NULL;
vma->vm_raend = 0;
```

10. If the MAP_SHARED flag is set (and the new memory region doesn't map a file on disk), the region is used for IPC shared memory. The function invokes shmem_zero_setup( ) to initialize it (see Chapter 19).

11. Invokes vma_link( ) to insert the new region in the memory region list and red-black tree (see the earlier section "Inserting a region in the memory descriptor list: insert_vm_struct()").

12. Increments the size of the process address space stored in the total_vm field of the memory descriptor.

13. If the VM_LOCKED flag is set, increments the counter of locked pages mm->locked_vm:

```
if (vm_flags & VM_LOCKED) {
    mm->locked_vm += len >> PAGE_SHIFT;
    make_pages_present(addr, addr + len);
}
```

The make_pages_present( ) function is invoked to allocate all the pages of the memory region in succession and lock them in RAM. The function, in turn, invokes get_user_pages( ) as follows:

```
write = (vma->vm_flags & VM_WRITE) != 0;
get_user_pages(current, current->mm, addr, len, write, 0, NULL, NULL);
```

The get_user_pages( ) function cycles through all starting linear addresses of the pages between addr and addr+len; for each of them, it invokes follow_page( ) to check whether there is a mapping to a physical page in the current's Page Tables. If no such physical page exists, get_user_pages( ) invokes handle_mm_fault( ), which, as we shall see in the section "Handling a Faulty Address Inside the Address Space," allocates one page frame and sets its Page Table entry according to the vm_flags field of the memory region descriptor.

14. Finally, terminates by returning the linear address of the new memory region.

Releasing a Linear Address Interval

The do_munmap( ) function deletes a linear address interval from the address space of the current process. The parameters are the starting address addr of the interval and its length len. The interval to be deleted does not usually correspond to a memory region; it may be included in one memory region or span two or more regions.

The function goes through two main phases. First, it scans the list of memory regions owned by the process and removes all regions that overlap the linear address interval. In the second phase, the function updates the process Page Tables and reinserts a downsized version of the memory regions that were removed during the first phase.

First phase: scanning the memory regions

The do_munmap( ) function executes the following steps:

1. Performs some preliminary checks on the parameter values. If the linear address interval includes addresses greater than TASK_SIZE, if addr is not a multiple of 4,096, or if the linear address interval has a zero length, it returns the error code -EINVAL.

2. Locates the first memory region that overlaps the linear address interval to be deleted:

```
mpnt = find_vma_prev(current->mm, addr, &prev);
if (!mpnt || mpnt->vm_start >= addr + len)
    return 0;
```

3. If the linear address interval is located inside a memory region, its deletion splits the region into two smaller ones. In this case, do_munmap( ) checks whether current is allowed to obtain an additional memory region:

```
if ((mpnt->vm_start < addr && mpnt->vm_end > addr + len) &&
    current->mm->map_count > MAX_MAP_COUNT)
    return -ENOMEM;
```

4. Attempts to get a new vm_area struct descriptor. There may be no need for it, but the function makes the request anyway so that it can terminate right away if the allocation fails. This cautious approach simplifies the code since it allows an easy error exit.

5. Builds up a list that includes all descriptors of the memory regions that overlap the linear address interval. This list is created by setting the vm_next field of the memory region descriptor (temporarily) so it points to the previous item in the list; this field thus acts as a backward link. As each region is added to this backward list, a local variable named free points to the last inserted element. The regions inserted in the list are also removed from the list of memory regions owned by the process and from the red-black tree (by means of the rb_erase() function):

```
npp = (prev ? &prev->vm_next : &current->mm->mmap);
free = NULL;
spin_lock(&current->mm->page_table_lock);
for ( ; mpnt && mpnt->vm_start < addr + len; mpnt = *npp) {
    *npp = mpnt->vm_next;
    mpnt->vm_next = free;
    free = mpnt;
    rb_erase(&mpnt->vm_rb, &current->mm->mm_rb);
}
current->mm->mmap_cache = NULL;
spin_unlock(&current->mm->page_table_lock);
```

Second phase: updating the Page Tables

A while cycle is used to scan the list of memory regions built in the first phase, starting with the memory region descriptor that free points to.

In each iteration, the mpnt local variable points to the descriptor of a memory region in the list. The map_count field of the current->mm memory descriptor is decremented (since the region has been removed in the first phase from the list of regions owned by the process) and a check is made (by means of two question-mark conditional expressions) to determine whether the mpnt region must be eliminated or simply downsized:

```
current->mm->map_count--;
st = addr < mpnt->vm_start ? mpnt->vm_start : addr;
end = addr+len;
end = end > mpnt->vm_end ? mpnt->vm_end : end;
size - end - st;
```

The st and end local variables delimit the linear address interval in the mpnt memory region that should be deleted; the size local variable specifies the length of the interval.

Next, do_munmap() releases the page frames allocated for the pages included in the interval from st to end:

```
zap_page_range(mm, st, size);
```

The zap_page_range( ) function deallocates the page frames included in the interval from st to end and updates the corresponding Page Table entries. The function invokes in nested fashion the zap_pmd_range( ) and zap_pte_range( ) functions for scanning the Page Tables; the latter function clears the Page Table entries and frees the corresponding page frames (or slot in a swap area; see Chapter 14). While doing this, zap_pte_range( ) also invalidates the TLB entries corresponding to the interval from st to end.

The last action performed in each iteration of the do_munmap( ) loop is to check whether a downsized version of the mpnt memory region must be reinserted in the list of regions of current:

```
extra = unmap_fixup(mm, mpnt, st, size, extra);
```

The unmap_fixup( ) function considers four possible cases:

1. The memory region has been totally canceled. It returns the address of the previously allocated memory region object (see Step 4 in the earlier section "First phase: scanning the memory regions"), which can be released by invoking kmem_cache_free( ).

2. Only the lower part of the memory region has been removed:

   ```
   (mpnt->vm_start < st) && (mpnt->vm_end == end)
   ```

   In this case, it updates the vm_end field of mnpt, invokes __insert_vm_struct( ) to insert the downsized region in the list of regions belonging to the process, and returns the address of the previously allocated memory region object.

3. Only the upper part of the memory region has been removed:

   ```
   (mpnt->vm_start == st) && (mpnt->vm_end > end)
   ```

   In this case, it updates the vm_start field of mnpt, invokes __insert_vm_struct( ) to insert the downsized region in the list of regions belonging to the process, and returns the address of the previously allocated memory object.

4. The linear address interval is in the middle of the memory region:

   ```
   (mpnt->vm_start < st) && (mpnt->vm_end > end)
   ```

   It updates the vm_start and vm_end fields of mnpt and of the previously allocated extra memory region object so that they refer to the linear address intervals, respectively, from mpnt->vm_start to st and from end to mpnt->vm_end. Then it invokes __insert_vm_struct( ) twice to insert the two regions in the list of regions belonging to the process and in the red-black tree, and returns NULL, thus preserving the memory region object previously allocated.

This terminates the description of what must be done in a single iteration of the second-phase loop of do_munmap( ).

After handling all the memory region descriptors in the list built during the first phase, do_munmap( ) checks if the additional extra memory descriptor has been used. If the address returned by unmap_fixup( ) is NULL, the descriptor has been used; otherwise, do_munmap( ) invokes kmem_cache_free( ) to release it. Finally, do_munmap( )

---

invokes the `free_pgtables()` function: it again scans the Page Table entries corresponding to the linear address interval just removed and reclaims the page frames that store unused Page Tables.

Page Fault Exception Handler

As stated previously, the Linux Page Fault exception handler must distinguish exceptions caused by programming errors from those caused by a reference to a page that legitimately belongs to the process address space but simply hasn't been allocated yet.

The memory region descriptors allow the exception handler to perform its job quite efficiently. The `do_page_fault()` function, which is the Page Fault interrupt service routine for the 80×86 architecture, compares the linear address that caused the Page Fault against the memory regions of the current process; it can thus determine the proper way to handle the exception according to the scheme that is illustrated in Figure 8-4.

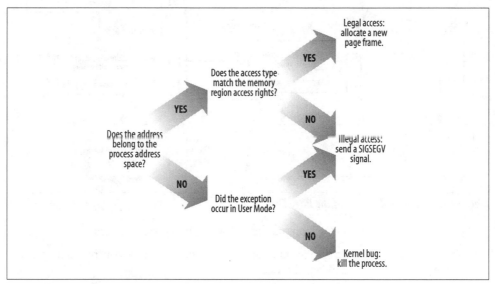

Figure 8-4. Overall scheme for the Page Fault handler

In practice, things are a lot more complex because the Page Fault handler must recognize several particular subcases that fit awkwardly into the overall scheme, and it must distinguish several kinds of legal access. A detailed flow diagram of the handler is illustrated in Figure 8-5.

The identifiers `vmalloc_fault`, `good_area`, `bad_area`, and `no_context` are labels appearing in `do_page_fault()` that should help you to relate the blocks of the flow diagram to specific lines of code.

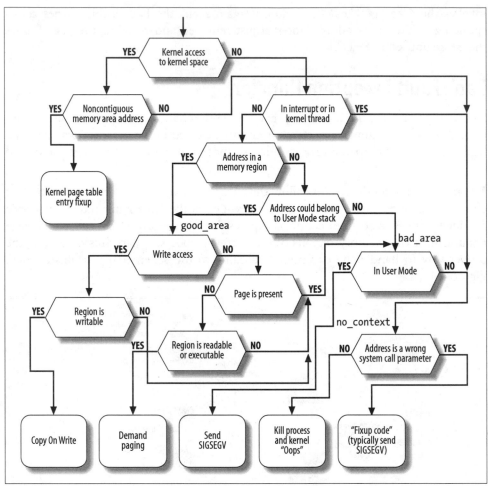

Figure 8-5. The flow diagram of the Page Fault handler

The do_page_fault( ) function accepts the following input parameters:

- The regs address of a pt_regs structure containing the values of the microprocessor registers when the exception occurred.
- A 3-bit error_code, which is pushed on the stack by the control unit when the exception occurred (see "Hardware Handling of Interrupts and Exceptions" in Chapter 4). The bits have the following meanings.
  — If bit 0 is clear, the exception was caused by an access to a page that is not present (the Present flag in the Page Table entry is clear); otherwise, if bit 0 is set, the exception was caused by an invalid access right.
  — If bit 1 is clear, the exception was caused by a read or execute access; if set, the exception was caused by a write access.
  — If bit 2 is clear, the exception occurred while the processor was in Kernel Mode; otherwise, it occurred in User Mode.

The first operation of do_page_fault( ) consists of reading the linear address that caused the Page Fault. When the exception occurs, the CPU control unit stores that value in the cr2 control register:

```
asm("movl %%cr2,%0":"=r" (address));
if (regs->eflags & 0x00000200)
    local_irq_enable();
tsk = current;
```

The linear address is saved in the address local variable. The function also ensures that local interrupts are enabled if they were enabled before the fault and saves the pointers to the process descriptor of current in the tsk local variable.

As shown at the top of Figure 8-5, do_page_fault( ) checks whether the faulty linear address belongs to the fourth gigabyte and the exception was caused by the kernel trying to access a nonexisting page frame:

```
if (address >= TASK_SIZE && !(error_code & 0x101))
    goto vmalloc_fault;
```

The code at label vmalloc_fault takes care of faults that were likely caused by accessing a noncontiguous memory area in Kernel Mode; we describe this case in the later section "Handling Noncontiguous Memory Area Accesses."

Next, the handler checks whether the exception occurred while handling an interrupt or executing a kernel thread (remember that the mm field of the process descriptor is always NULL for kernel threads):

```
info.i_code = SEGV_MAPERR;
if (in_interrupt( ) || !tsk->mm)
    goto no_context;
```

In both cases, do_page_fault( ) does not try to compare the linear address with the memory regions of current, since it would not make any sense: interrupt handlers and kernel threads never use linear addresses below TASK_SIZE, and thus never rely on memory regions. (See the next section for information on the info local variable and a description of the code at the no_context label.)

Let's suppose that the Page Fault did not occur in an interrupt handler or in a kernel thread. Then the function must inspect the memory regions owned by the process to determine whether the faulty linear address is included in the process address space:

```
down_read(&tsk->mm->mmap_sem);
vma = find_vma(tsk->mm, address);
if (!vma)
    goto bad_area;
if (vma->vm_start <= address)
    goto good_area;
```

If vma is NULL, there is no memory region ending after address, and thus the faulty address is certainly bad. On the other hand, the first memory region ending after address might not include address; if it does, the function jumps to the code at label good_area.

If none of the two "if" conditions are satisfied, the function has determined that address is not included in any memory region; however, it must perform an additional check, since the faulty address may have been caused by a push or pusha instruction on the User Mode stack of the process.

Let's make a short digression to explain how stacks are mapped into memory regions. Each region that contains a stack expands toward lower addresses; its VM_GROWSDOWN flag is set, so the value of its vm_end field remains fixed while the value of its vm_start field may be decreased. The region boundaries include, but do not delimit precisely, the current size of the User Mode stack. The reasons for the fuzz factor are:

- The region size is a multiple of 4 KB (it must include complete pages) while the stack size is arbitrary.

- Page frames assigned to a region are never released until the region is deleted; in particular, the value of the vm_start field of a region that includes a stack can only decrease; it can never increase. Even if the process executes a series of pop instructions, the region size remains unchanged.

It should now be clear how a process that has filled up the last page frame allocated to its stack may cause a Page Fault exception: the push refers to an address outside of the region (and to a nonexistent page frame). Notice that this kind of exception is not caused by a programming error; thus it must be handled separately by the Page Fault handler.

We now return to the description of do_page_fault( ), which checks for the case described previously:

```
if (!(vma->vm_flags & VM_GROWSDOWN))
    goto bad_area;
if (error_code & 4        /* User Mode */
    && address + 32 < regs->esp)
    goto bad_area;
if (expand_stack(vma, address))
    goto bad_area;
goto good_area;
```

If the VM_GROWSDOWN flag of the region is set and the exception occurred in User Mode, the function checks whether address is smaller than the regs->esp stack pointer (it should be only a little smaller). Since a few stack-related assembly language instructions (like pusha) perform a decrement of the esp register only after the memory access, a 32-byte tolerance interval is granted to the process. If the address is high enough (within the tolerance granted), the code invokes the expand_stack( ) function to check whether the process is allowed to extend both its stack and its address space; if everything is OK, it sets the vm_start field of vma to address and returns 0; otherwise, it returns 1.

Note that the preceding code skips the tolerance check whenever the VM_GROWSDOWN flag of the region is set and the exception did not occur in User Mode. These conditions mean that the kernel is addressing the User Mode stack and that the code should always run expand_stack( ).

Handling a Faulty Address Outside the Address Space

If address does not belong to the process address space, do_page_fault( ) proceeds to execute the statements at the label bad_area. If the error occurred in User Mode, it sends a SIGSEGV signal to current (see the section "Generating a Signal" in Chapter 10) and terminates:

```
bad_area:
up_read(&tsk->mm->mmap_sem);
if (error_code & 4) {    /* User Mode */
    tsk->thread.cr2 = address;
    tsk->thread.error_code = error_code;
    tsk->thread.trap_no = 14;
    info.si_signo = SIGSEGV;
    info.si_errno = 0;
    info.si_addr = (void *) address;
    force_sig_info(SIGSEGV, &info, tsk);
    return;
}
```

The force_sig_info( ) function makes sure that the process does not ignore or block the SIGSEGV signal, and sends the signal to the User Mode process while passing some additional information in the info local variable (see the section "The force_sig_info( ) and force_sig( ) Functions" in Chapter 10). The info.si_code field is already set to SEGV_MAPERR (if the exception was due to a nonexisting page frame) or to SEGV_ACCERR (if the exception was due to an invalid access to an existing page frame).

If the exception occurred in Kernel Mode (bit 2 of error_code is clear), there are still two alternatives:

- The exception occurred while using some linear address that has been passed to the kernel as parameter of a system call.
- The exception is due to a real kernel bug.

The function distinguishes these two alternatives as follows:

```
no_context:
if ((fixup = search_exception_table(regs->eip)) != 0) {
    regs->eip = fixup;
    return;
}
```

In the first case, it jumps to a "fixup code," which typically sends a SIGSEGV signal to current or terminates a system call handler with a proper error code (see the section "Dynamic Address Checking: The Fixup Code" in Chapter 9).

In the second case, the function prints a complete dump of the CPU registers, the Kernel Mode stack on the console, and on a system message buffer, and then kills the current process by invoking the do_exit( ) function (see Chapter 20). This is the so-called *"Kernel oops"* error, named after the message displayed. The dumped values can be used by kernel hackers to reconstruct the conditions that triggered the bug, and thus find and correct it.

Handling a Faulty Address Inside the Address Space

If address belongs to the process address space, do_page_fault( ) proceeds to the statement labeled good_area:

```
good_area:
info.si_code = SEGV_ACCERR;
write = 0;
if (error_code & 2) { /* write access */
    if (!(vma->vm_flags & VM_WRITE))
        goto bad_area;
    write++;
} else                  /* read access */
    if ((error_code & 1) ||
        !(vma->vm_flags & (VM_READ | VM_EXEC)))
        goto bad_area;
```

If the exception was caused by a write access, the function checks whether the memory region is writable. If not, it jumps to the bad_area code; if so, it sets the write local variable to 1.

If the exception was caused by a read or execute access, the function checks whether the page is already present in RAM. In this case, the exception occurred because the process tried to access a privileged page frame (one whose User/Supervisor flag is clear) in User Mode, so the function jumps to the bad_area code.[*] If the page is not present, the function also checks whether the memory region is readable or executable.

If the memory region access rights match the access type that caused the exception, the handle_mm_fault( ) function is invoked to allocate a new page frame:

```
survive:
ret = handle_mm_fault(tsk->mm, vma, address, write);
if (ret == 1 || ret == 2) {
    if (ret == 1) tsk->min_flt++; else tsk->maj_flt++;
    up_read(&tsk->mm->mmap_sem);
    return;
}
```

The handle_mm_fault( ) function returns 1 or 2 if it succeeded in allocating a new page frame for the process. The value 1 indicates that the Page Fault has been handled without blocking the current process; this kind of Page Fault is called *minor fault*. The value 2 indicates that the Page Fault forced the current process to sleep

---

[*] However, this case should never happen, since the kernel does not assign privileged page frames to the processes.

(most likely because time was spent while filling the page frame assigned to the process with data read from disk); a Page Fault that blocks the current process is called a *major fault*. The function can also returns −1 (for not enough memory) or 0 (for any other error).

If handle_mm_fault( ) returns the value 0, a SIGBUS signal is sent to the process:

```
if (!ret) {
    up_read(&tsk->mm->mmap_sem);
    tsk->thread.cr2 = address;
    tsk->thread.error_code = error_code;
    tsk->thread.trap_no = 14;
    info.si_signo = SIGBUS;
    info.si_errno = 0;
    info.si_code = BUS_ADRERR;
    info.si_addr = (void *) address;
    force_sig_info(SIGBUS, &info, tsk);
    if (!(error_code & 4)) /* Kernel Mode */
        goto no_context;
}
```

If handle_mm_fault( ) cannot allocate the new page frame, the kernel usually kills the current process. However, if current is the *init* process, it is just put at the end of the run queue and the scheduler is invoked; once init resumes its execution, handle_mm_fault( ) is executed again:

```
if (ret == -1) {
    up_read(&tsk->mm->mmap_sem);
    if (tsk->pid != 1) {
        if (error_code & 4) /* User Mode */
            do_exit(SIGKILL);
        goto no_context;
    }
    tsk->policy |= SCHED_YIELD;
    schedule();
    down_read(&tsk->mm->mmap_sem);
    goto survive;
}
```

The handle_mm_fault( ) function acts on four parameters:

mm

A pointer to the memory descriptor of the process that was running on the CPU when the exception occurred

vma

A pointer to the descriptor of the memory region, including the linear address that caused the exception

address

The linear address that caused the exception

write_access

Set to 1 if tsk attempted to write in address and to 0 if tsk attempted to read or execute it

The function starts by checking whether the Page Middle Directory and the Page Table used to map address exist. Even if address belongs to the process address space, the corresponding Page Tables might not have been allocated, so the task of allocating them precedes everything else:

```
spin_lock(&mm->page_table_lock);
pgd = pgd_offset(mm, address);
pmd = pmd_alloc(mm, pgd, address);
if (pmd) {
    pte = pte_alloc(mm, pmd, address);
    if (pte)
        return handle_pte_fault(mm, vma, address, write_access, pte);
}
spin_unlock(&mm->page_table_lock);
return -1;
```

The pgd local variable contains the Page Global Directory entry that refers to address; pmd_alloc( ) is invoked to allocate, if needed, a new Page Middle Directory.* pte_alloc( ) is then invoked to allocate, if needed, a new Page Table. If both operations are successful, the pte local variable points to the Page Table entry that refers to address. The handle_pte_fault( ) function is then invoked to inspect the Page Table entry corresponding to address and to determine how to allocate a new page frame for the process:

- If the accessed page is not present—that is, if it is not already stored in any page frame—the kernel allocates a new page frame and initializes it properly; this technique is called *demand paging*.

- If the accessed page is present but is marked read only—i.e., if it is already stored in a page frame—the kernel allocates a new page frame and initializes its contents by copying the old page frame data; this technique is called *Copy On Write*.

Demand Paging

The term *demand paging* denotes a dynamic memory allocation technique that consists of deferring page frame allocation until the last possible moment—until the process attempts to address a page that is not present in RAM, thus causing a Page Fault exception.

The motivation behind demand paging is that processes do not address all the addresses included in their address space right from the start; in fact, some of these addresses may never be used by the process. Moreover, the program locality principle (see the section "Hardware Cache" in Chapter 2) ensures that, at each stage of

---

* On 80×86 microprocessors, this kind of allocation never occurs since the Page Middle Directories are either included in the Page Global Directory (PAE not enabled) or allocated together with the Page Global Directory (PAE enabled).

program execution, only a small subset of the process pages are really referenced, and therefore the page frames containing the temporarily useless pages can be used by other processes. Demand paging is thus preferable to global allocation (assigning all page frames to the process right from the start and leaving them in memory until program termination) since it increases the average number of free page frames in the system and therefore allows better use of the available free memory. From another viewpoint, it allows the system as a whole to get a better throughput with the same amount of RAM.

The price to pay for all these good things is system overhead: each Page Fault exception induced by demand paging must be handled by the kernel, thus wasting CPU cycles. Fortunately, the locality principle ensures that once a process starts working with a group of pages, it sticks with them without addressing other pages for quite a while. Thus, Page Fault exceptions may be considered rare events.

An addressed page may not be present in main memory for the following reasons:

- The page was never accessed by the process. The kernel can recognize this case since the Page Table entry is filled with zeros—i.e., the pte_none macro returns the value 1.

- The page was already accessed by the process, but its content is temporarily saved on disk. The kernel can recognize this case since the Page Table entry is not filled with zeros (however, the Present flag is cleared since the page is not present in RAM).

The handle_pte_fault( ) function distinguishes the two cases by inspecting the Page Table entry that refers to address:

```
entry = *pte;
if (!pte_present(entry)) {
    if (pte_none(entry))
        return do_no_page(mm, vma, address, write_access, pte);
    return do_swap_page(mm, vma, address, pte, entry, write_access);
}
```

We'll examine the case in which the page is saved on disk (using the do_swap_page( ) function) in the section "Swapping in Pages" in Chapter 16.

In the other situation, when the page was never accessed, the do_no_page( ) function is invoked. There are two ways to load the missing page, depending on whether the page is mapped to a disk file. The function determines this by checking the nopage method of the vma memory region object, which points to the function that loads the missing page from disk into RAM if the page is mapped to a file. Therefore, the possibilities are:

- The vma->vm_ops->nopage field is not NULL. In this case, the memory region maps a disk file and the field points to the function that loads the page. This case is covered in the section "Demand Paging for Memory Mapping" in Chapter 15 and in the section "IPC Shared Memory" in Chapter 19.

- Either the vm_ops field or the vma->vm_ops->nopage field is NULL. In this case, the memory region does not map a file on disk—i.e., it is an *anonymous mapping*. Thus, do_no_page( ) invokes the do_anonymous_page( ) function to get a new page frame:

```
if (!vma->vm_ops || !vma->vm_ops->nopage)
        return do_anonymous_page(mm, vma, page_table, write_access, address);
```

The do_anonymous_page( ) function handles write and read requests separately:

```
if (write_access) {
        spin_unlock(&mm->page_table_lock);
        page = alloc_page(GFP_HIGHUSER);
        addr = kmap_atomic(page, KM_USER0);
        memset((void *)(addr), 0, PAGE_SIZE);
        kunmap_atomic(addr, KM_USER0);
        spin_lock(&mm->page_table_lock);
        mm->rss++;
        entry = pte_mkwrite(pte_mkdirty(mk_pte(page, vma->vm_page_prot)));
        lru_cache_add(page);
        mark_page_accessed(page);
        set_pte(page_table, entry);
        spin_unlock(&mm->page_table_lock);
        return 1;
}
```

When handling a write access, the function invokes alloc_page( ) and fills the new page frame with zeros by using the memset macro. The function then increments the min_flt field of tsk to keep track of the number of minor Page Faults caused by the process. Next, the function increments the rss field of the memory descriptor to keep track of the number of page frames allocated to the process.* The Page Table entry is then set to the physical address of the page frame, which is marked as writable and dirty. The lru_cache_add( ) and mark_page_accessed( ) functions insert the new page frame in the swap-related data structures; we discuss them in Chapter 16.

Conversely, when handling a read access, the content of the page is irrelevant because the process is addressing it for the first time. It is safer to give a page filled with zeros to the process rather than an old page filled with information written by some other process. Linux goes one step further in the spirit of demand paging. There is no need to assign a new page frame filled with zeros to the process right away, since we might as well give it an existing page called *zero page*, thus deferring further page frame allocation. The zero page is allocated statically during kernel initialization in the empty_zero_page variable (an array of 1,024 long integers filled with zeros); it is stored in the fifth page frame (starting from physical address 0x00004000) and can be referenced by means of the ZERO_PAGE macro.

---

* Linux records the number of minor and major Page Faults for each process. This information, together with several other statistics, may be used to tune the system.

The Page Table entry is thus set with the physical address of the zero page:

```
entry = pte_wrprotect(mk_pte(ZERO_PAGE, vma->vm_page_prot));
set_pte(page_table, entry);
spin_unlock(&mm->page_table_lock);
return 1;
```

Since the page is marked as nonwritable, if the process attempts to write in it, the Copy On Write mechanism is activated. Only then does the process get a page of its own to write in. The mechanism is described in the next section.

Copy On Write

First-generation Unix systems implemented process creation in a rather clumsy way: when a fork( ) system call was issued, the kernel duplicated the whole parent address space in the literal sense of the word and assigned the copy to the child process. This activity was quite time consuming since it required:

- Allocating page frames for the Page Tables of the child process
- Allocating page frames for the pages of the child process
- Initializing the Page Tables of the child process
- Copying the pages of the parent process into the corresponding pages of the child process

This way of creating an address space involved many memory accesses, used up many CPU cycles, and completely spoiled the cache contents. Last but not least, it was often pointless because many child processes start their execution by loading a new program, thus discarding entirely the inherited address space (see Chapter 20).

Modern Unix kernels, including Linux, follow a more efficient approach called *Copy On Write* (*COW*). The idea is quite simple: instead of duplicating page frames, they are shared between the parent and the child process. However, as long as they are shared, they cannot be modified. Whenever the parent or the child process attempts to write into a shared page frame, an exception occurs. At this point, the kernel duplicates the page into a new page frame that it marks as writable. The original page frame remains write-protected: when the other process tries to write into it, the kernel checks whether the writing process is the only owner of the page frame; in such a case, it makes the page frame writable for the process.

The count field of the page descriptor is used to keep track of the number of processes that are sharing the corresponding page frame. Whenever a process releases a page frame or a Copy On Write is executed on it, its count field is decremented; the page frame is freed only when count becomes NULL.

Let's now describe how Linux implements COW. When handle_pte_fault( ) determines that the Page Fault exception was caused by an access to a page present in memory, it executes the following instructions:

```
if (pte_present(entry)) {
    if (write_access) {
```

```
            if (!pte_write(entry))
                return do_wp_page(mm, vma, address, pte, entry);
            entry = pte_mkdirty(entry);
        }
        entry = pte_mkyoung(entry);
        set_pte(pte, entry);
        flush_tlb_page(vma, address);
        spin_unlock(&mm->page_table_lock);
        return 1;
    }
```

The handle_pte_fault( ) function is architecture-independent: it considers any possible violation of the page access rights. However, in the 80×86 architecture, if the page is present then the access was for writing and the page frame is write-protected (see the section "Handling a Faulty Address Inside the Address Space"). Thus, the do_wp_page( ) function is always invoked.

The do_wp_page( ) function starts by deriving the page descriptor of the page frame referenced by the Page Table entry involved in the Page Fault exception. Next, the function determines whether the page must really be duplicated. If only one process owns the page, Copy On Write does not apply and the process should be free to write the page. Basically, the function reads the count field of the page descriptor: if it is equal to 1, COW must not be done. Actually, the check is slightly more complicated, since the count field is also incremented when the page is inserted into the swap cache (see the section "The Swap Cache" in Chapter 16). However, when COW is not to be done, the page frame is marked as writable so that it does not cause further Page Fault exceptions when writes are attempted:

```
    set_pte(page_table, pte_mkyoung(pte_mkdirty(pte_mkwrite(pte))));
    flush_tlb_page(vma, address);
    spin_unlock(&mm->page_table_lock);
    return 1; /* minor fault */
```

If the page is shared among several processes by means of the COW, the function copies the content of the old page frame (old_page) into the newly allocated one (new_page). To avoid race conditions, the usage counter of old_page is incremented before starting the copy operation:

```
    old_page = pte_page(pte);
    atomic_inc(&old_page->count);
    spin_unlock(&mm->page_table_lock);
    new_page = alloc_page(GFP_HIGHUSER);
    vto = kmap_atomic(new_page, KM_USER0);
    if (old_page == ZERO_PAGE) {
        memset((void *)vto, 0, PAGE_SIZE);
    } else {
        vfrom = kmap_atomic(old_page, KM_USER1);
        memcpy((void *)vto, (void *)vfrom, PAGE_SIZE);
        kunmap_atomic(vfrom, KM_USER1);
    }
    kunmap_atomic(vto, KM_USER0);
```

If the old page is the zero page, the new frame is efficiently filled with zeros by using the memset macro. Otherwise, the page frame content is copied using the memcpy macro. Special handling for the zero page is not strictly required, but it improves the system performance because it preserves the microprocessor hardware cache by making fewer address references.

Since the allocation of a page frame can block the process, the function checks whether the Page Table entry has been modified since the beginning of the function (pte and *page_table do not have the same value). In this case, the new page frame is released, the usage counter of old_page is decrement (to undo the increment made previously), and the function terminates.

If everything looks OK, the physical address of the new page frame is finally written into the Page Table entry and the corresponding TLB register is invalidated:

```
set_pte(pte, pte_mkwrite(pte_mkdirty(mk_pte(new_page, vma->vm_page_prot))));
flush_tlb_page(vma, address);
lru_cache_add(new_page);
spin_unlock(&mm->page_table_lock);
```

The lru_cache_add( ) inserts the new page frame in the swap-related data structures; see Chapter 16 for its description.

Finally, do_wp_page( ) decrements the usage counter of old_page twice. The first decrement undoes the safety increment made before copying the page frame contents; the second decrement reflects the fact that the current process no longer owns the page frame.

Handling Noncontiguous Memory Area Accesses

We have seen in the section "Noncontiguous Memory Area Management" in Chapter 7 that the kernel is quite lazy in updating the Page Table entries corresponding to noncontiguous memory areas. In fact, the vmalloc( ) and vfree( ) functions limit themselves to update the master kernel Page Tables (i.e., the Page Global Directory init_mm.pgd and its child Page Tables).

However, once the kernel initialization phase ends, the master kernel Page Tables are not directly used by any process or kernel thread. Thus, consider the first time that a process in Kernel Mode accesses a noncontiguous memory area. When translating the linear address into a physical address, the CPU's memory management unit encounters a null Page Table entry and raises a Page Fault. However, the handler recognizes this special case because the exception occurred in Kernel Mode and the faulty linear address is greater than TASK_SIZE. Thus, the handler checks the corresponding master kernel Page Table entry:

```
vmalloc_fault:
asm("movl %%cr3,%0":"=r" (pgd));
pgd = __pgd_offset(address) + (pgd_t *) __va(pgd);
pgd_k = init_mm.pgd + __pgd_offset(address);
```

```
if (!pgd_present(*pgd_k))
    goto no_context;
set_pgd(pgd, *pgd_k);
pmd = pmd_offset(pgd, address);
pmd_k = pmd_offset(pgd_k, address);
if (!pmd_present(*pmd_k))
    goto no_context;
set_pmd(pmd, *pmd_k);

pte_k = pte_offset(pmd_k, address);
if (!pte_present(*pte_k))
    goto no_context;
return;
```

The pgd local variable is loaded with the Page Global Directory address of the current process, which is stored in the cr3 register,[*] while the pgd_k local variable is loaded with the master kernel Page Global Directory. If the entry corresponding to the faulty linear address is null, the function jumps to the code at the no_context label (see the earlier section "Handling a Faulty Address Outside the Address Space"). Otherwise, the entry is copied into the corresponding entry of the process Page Global Directory. Then the whole operation is repeated with the master Page Middle Directory entry and, subsequently, with the master Page Table entry.

Creating and Deleting a Process Address Space

Of the six typical cases mentioned earlier in the section "The Process's Address Space," in which a process gets new memory regions, the first one—issuing a fork( ) system call—requires the creation of a whole new address space for the child process. Conversely, when a process terminates, the kernel destroys its address space. In this section, we discuss how these two activities are performed by Linux.

Creating a Process Address Space

In the section "The clone(), fork(), and vfork() System Calls" in Chapter 3, we mentioned that the kernel invokes the copy_mm( ) function while creating a new process. This function creates the process address space by setting up all Page Tables and memory descriptors of the new process.

Each process usually has its own address space, but lightweight processes can be created by calling clone( ) with the CLONE_VM flag set. These processes share the same address space; that is, they are allowed to address the same set of pages.

---

[*] The kernel doesn't use current->mm->pgd to derive the address because this fault can occur at any instant, even during a process switch.

Following the COW approach described earlier, traditional processes inherit the address space of their parent: pages stay shared as long as they are only read. When one of the processes attempts to write one of them, however, the page is duplicated; after some time, a forked process usually gets its own address space that is different from that of the parent process. Lightweight processes, on the other hand, use the address space of their parent process. Linux implements them simply by not duplicating address space. Lightweight processes can be created considerably faster than normal processes, and the sharing of pages can also be considered a benefit so long as the parent and children coordinate their accesses carefully.

If the new process has been created by means of the clone( ) system call and if the CLONE_VM flag of the flag parameter is set, copy_mm( ) gives the clone (tsk) the address space of its parent (current):

```
if (clone_flags & CLONE_VM) {
    atomic_inc(&current->mm->mm_users);
    tsk->mm = current->mm;
    tsk->active_mm = current->mm;
    return 0;
}
```

If the CLONE_VM flag is not set, copy_mm( ) must create a new address space (even though no memory is allocated within that address space until the process requests an address). The function allocates a new memory descriptor, stores its address in the mm field of the new process descriptor tsk, and then initializes its fields:

```
tsk->mm = kmem_cache_alloc(mm_cachep, SLAB_KERNEL);
tsk->active_mm = tsk->mm;
memcpy(tsk->mm, current->mm, sizeof(*tsk->mm));
atomic_set(&tsk->mm->mm_users, 1);
atomic_set(&tsk->mm->mm_count, 1);
init_rwsem(&tsk->mm->mmap_sem);
tsk->mm->page_table_lock = SPIN_LOCK_UNLOCKED;
tsk->mm->pgd = pgd_alloc(tsk->mm);
```

Remember that the pgd_alloc( ) macro allocates a Page Global Directory for the new process.

The dup_mmap( ) function is then invoked to duplicate both the memory regions and the Page Tables of the parent process:

```
down_write(&current->mm->mmap_sem);
dup_mmap(tsk->mm);
up_write(&current->mm->mmap_sem);
copy_segments(tsk, tsk->mm);
```

The dup_mmap( ) function inserts the new memory descriptor tsk->mm in the global list of memory descriptors. Then it scans the list of regions owned by the parent process, starting from the one pointed by current->mm->mmap. It duplicates each vm_area_struct memory region descriptor encountered and inserts the copy in the list of regions owned by the child process.

Right after inserting a new memory region descriptor, dup_mmap( ) invokes copy_page_range( ) to create, if necessary, the Page Tables needed to map the group of pages included in the memory region and to initialize the new Page Table entries. In particular, any page frame corresponding to a private, writable page (VM_SHARE flag off and VM_MAYWRITE flag on) is marked as read-only for both the parent and the child, so that it will be handled with the Copy On Write mechanism. Before terminating, dup_mmap( ) also creates the red-black tree of memory regions of the child process by invoking the build_mmap_rb( ) function.

Finally, copy_mm( ) invokes copy_segments( ), which initializes the architecture-dependent portion of the child's memory descriptor. Essentially, if the parent has a custom LDT, a copy of it is also assigned to the child.

Deleting a Process Address Space

When a process terminates, the kernel invokes the exit_mm( ) function to release the address space owned by that process:

```
mm_release();
if (tsk->mm) {
    atomic_inc(&tsk->mm->mm_count);
    mm = tsk->mm;
    tsk->mm = NULL;
    enter_lazy_tlb(mm, current, smp_processor_id());
    mmput(mm);
}
```

The mm_release( ) function wakes up any process sleeping in the tsk->vfork_done completion (see the section "Completions" in Chapter 5). Typically, the corresponding wait queue is nonempty only if the exiting process was created by means of the vfork( ) system call (see the section "The clone(), fork(), and vfork() System Calls" in Chapter 3). The processor is also put in lazy TLB mode (see Chapter 2).

Managing the Heap

Each Unix process owns a specific memory region called *heap*, which is used to satisfy the process's dynamic memory requests. The start_brk and brk fields of the memory descriptor delimit the starting and ending addresses, respectively, of that region.

The following C library functions can be used by the process to request and release dynamic memory:

malloc(size)
Requests size bytes of dynamic memory; if the allocation succeeds, it returns the linear address of the first memory location.

calloc(n,size)

> Requests an array consisting of n elements of size size; if the allocation succeeds, it initializes the array components to 0 and returns the linear address of the first element.

free(addr)

> Releases the memory region allocated by malloc( ) or calloc( ) that has an initial address of addr.

brk(addr)

> Modifies the size of the heap directly; the addr parameter specifies the new value of current->mm->brk, and the return value is the new ending address of the memory region (the process must check whether it coincides with the requested addr value).

sbrk(incr)

> Is similar to brk( ), except that the incr parameter specifies the increment or decrement of the heap size in bytes.

The brk( ) function differs from the other functions listed because it is the only one implemented as a system call. All the other functions are implemented in the C library by using brk( ) and mmap( ).

When a process in User Mode invokes the brk( ) system call, the kernel executes the sys_brk(addr) function (see Chapter 9). This function first verifies whether the addr parameter falls inside the memory region that contains the process code; if so, it returns immediately:

```
mm = current->mm;
down_write(&mm->mmap_sem);
if (addr < mm->end_code) {
out:
    up_write(&mm->mmap_sem);
    return mm->brk;
}
```

Since the brk( ) system call acts on a memory region, it allocates and deallocates whole pages. Therefore, the function aligns the value of addr to a multiple of PAGE_SIZE and compares the result with the value of the brk field of the memory descriptor:

```
newbrk = (addr + 0xfff) & 0xfffff000;
oldbrk = (mm->brk + 0xfff) & 0xfffff000;
if (oldbrk == newbrk) {
    mm->brk = addr;
    goto out;
}
```

If the process asked to shrink the heap, sys_brk( ) invokes the do_munmap( ) function to do the job and then returns:

```
if (addr <= mm->brk) {
    if (!do_munmap(mm, newbrk, oldbrk-newbrk))
        mm->brk = addr;
    goto out;
}
```

If the process asked to enlarge the heap, sys_brk( ) first checks whether the process is allowed to do so. If the process is trying to allocate memory outside its limit, the function simply returns the original value of mm->brk without allocating more memory:

```
rlim = current->rlim[RLIMIT_DATA].rlim_cur;
if (rlim < RLIM_INFINITY && addr - mm->start_data > rlim)
    goto out;
```

The function then checks whether the enlarged heap would overlap some other memory region belonging to the process and, if so, returns without doing anything:

```
if (find_vma_intersection(mm, oldbrk, newbrk+PAGE_SIZE))
    goto out;
```

The last check before proceeding to the expansion consists of verifying whether the available free virtual memory is sufficient to support the enlarged heap (see the earlier section "Allocating a Linear Address Interval"):

```
if (!vm_enough_memory((newbrk-oldbrk) >> PAGE_SHIFT))
    goto out;
```

If everything is OK, the do_brk( ) function is invoked with the MAP_FIXED flag set. If it returns the oldbrk value, the allocation was successful and sys_brk( ) returns the value addr; otherwise, it returns the old mm->brk value:

```
if (do_brk(oldbrk, newbrk-oldbrk) == oldbrk)
    mm->brk = addr;
goto out;
```

The do_brk( ) function is actually a simplified version of do_mmap( ) that handles only anonymous memory regions. Its invocation might be considered equivalent to:

```
do_mmap(NULL, oldbrk, newbrk-oldbrk, PROT_READ|PROT_WRITE|PROT_EXEC,
        MAP_FIXED|MAP_PRIVATE, 0)
```

Of course, do_brk( ) is slightly faster than do_mmap( ) because it avoids several checks on the memory region object fields by assuming that the memory region doesn't map a file on disk.

CHAPTER 9

System Calls

Operating systems offer processes running in User Mode a set of interfaces to interact with hardware devices such as the CPU, disks, and printers. Putting an extra layer between the application and the hardware has several advantages. First, it makes programming easier by freeing users from studying low-level programming characteristics of hardware devices. Second, it greatly increases system security, since the kernel can check the accuracy of the request at the interface level before attempting to satisfy it. Last but not least, these interfaces make programs more portable since they can be compiled and executed correctly on any kernel that offers the same set of interfaces.

Unix systems implement most interfaces between User Mode processes and hardware devices by means of *system calls* issued to the kernel. This chapter examines in detail how Linux implements system calls that User Mode programs issue to the kernel.

POSIX APIs and System Calls

Let's start by stressing the difference between an application programmer interface (API) and a system call. The former is a function definition that specifies how to obtain a given service, while the latter is an explicit request to the kernel made via a software interrupt.

Unix systems include several libraries of functions that provide APIs to programmers. Some of the APIs defined by the *libc* standard C library refer to *wrapper routines* (routines whose only purpose is to issue a system call). Usually, each system call has a corresponding wrapper routine, which defines the API that application programs should employ.

The converse is not true, by the way—an API does not necessarily correspond to a specific system call. First of all, the API could offer its services directly in User Mode. (For something abstract like math functions, there may be no reason to make system calls.) Second, a single API function could make several system calls. Moreover, several API functions could make the same system call, but wrap extra functionality around it. For instance, in Linux, the malloc( ), calloc( ), and free( ) APIs are implemented in the *libc* library. The code in this library keeps track of the allocation and deallocation requests and uses the brk( ) system call to enlarge or shrink the process heap (see the section "Managing the Heap" in Chapter 8).

The POSIX standard refers to APIs and not to system calls. A system can be certified as POSIX-compliant if it offers the proper set of APIs to the application programs, no matter how the corresponding functions are implemented. As a matter of fact, several non-Unix systems have been certified as POSIX-compliant, since they offer all traditional Unix services in User Mode libraries.

From the programmer's point of view, the distinction between an API and a system call is irrelevant—the only things that matter are the function name, the parameter types, and the meaning of the return code. From the kernel designer's point of view, however, the distinction does matter since system calls belong to the kernel, while User Mode libraries don't.

Most wrapper routines return an integer value, whose meaning depends on the corresponding system call. A return value of −1 usually indicates that the kernel was unable to satisfy the process request. A failure in the system call handler may be caused by invalid parameters, a lack of available resources, hardware problems, and so on. The specific error code is contained in the errno variable, which is defined in the *libc* library.

Each error code is defined as a macro constant, which yields a corresponding positive integer value. The POSIX standard specifies the macro names of several error codes. In Linux, on 80×86 systems, these macros are defined in the header file *include/asm-i386/errno.h*. To allow portability of C programs among Unix systems, the *include/asm-i386/errno.h* header file is included, in turn, in the standard */usr/include/errno.h* C library header file. Other systems have their own specialized subdirectories of header files.

System Call Handler and Service Routines

When a User Mode process invokes a system call, the CPU switches to Kernel Mode and starts the execution of a kernel function. In Linux a system call must be invoked by executing the int $0x80 assembly language instruction, which raises the programmed exception that has vector 128 (see the sections "Interrupt, Trap, and System Gates" and "Hardware Handling of Interrupts and Exceptions," both in Chapter 4).

Since the kernel implements many different system calls, the process must pass a parameter called the *system call number* to identify the required system call; the eax register is used for this purpose. As we shall see in the section "Parameter Passing" later in this chapter, additional parameters are usually passed when invoking a system call.

All system calls return an integer value. The conventions for these return values are different from those for wrapper routines. In the kernel, positive or 0 values denote a successful termination of the system call, while negative values denote an error condition. In the latter case, the value is the negation of the error code that must be returned to the application program in the errno variable. The errno variable is not set or used by the kernel. Instead, the wrapper routines handles the task of setting this variable after a return from a system call.

The system call handler, which has a structure similar to that of the other exception handlers, performs the following operations:

- Saves the contents of most registers in the Kernel Mode stack (this operation is common to all system calls and is coded in assembly language).

- Handles the system call by invoking a corresponding C function called the *system call service routine*.

- Exits from the handler by means of the ret_from_sys_call( ) function (which is coded in assembly language).

The name of the service routine associated with the *xyz*( ) system call is usually sys_*xyz*( ); there are, however, a few exceptions to this rule.

Figure 9-1 illustrates the relationships between the application program that invokes a system call, the corresponding wrapper routine, the system call handler, and the system call service routine. The arrows denote the execution flow between the functions.

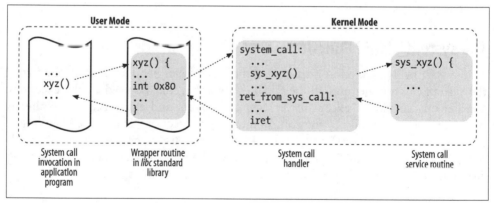

Figure 9-1. Invoking a system call

To associate each system call number with its corresponding service routine, the kernel uses a *system call dispatch table*, which is stored in the sys_call_table array and has NR_syscalls entries (usually 256). The nth entry contains the service routine address of the system call having number *n*.

The NR_syscalls macro is just a static limit on the maximum number of implementable system calls; it does not indicate the number of system calls actually implemented. Indeed, any entry of the dispatch table may contain the address of the sys_ni_syscall( ) function, which is the service routine of the "nonimplemented" system calls; it just returns the error code -ENOSYS.

Initializing System Calls

The trap_init( ) function, invoked during kernel initialization, sets up the Interrupt Descriptor Table (IDT) entry corresponding to vector 128 (i.e., 0x80) as follows:

```
set_system_gate(0x80, &system_call);
```

The call loads the following values into the gate descriptor fields (see the section "Interrupt, Trap, and System Gates" in Chapter 4):

Segment Selector
> The __KERNEL_CS Segment Selector of the kernel code segment.

Offset
> The pointer to the system_call( ) exception handler.

Type
> Set to 15. Indicates that the exception is a Trap and that the corresponding handler does not disable maskable interrupts.

DPL (Descriptor Privilege Level)
> Set to 3. This allows processes in User Mode to invoke the exception handler (see the section "Hardware Handling of Interrupts and Exceptions" in Chapter 4).

The system_call( ) Function

The system_call( ) function implements the system call handler. It starts by saving the system call number and all the CPU registers that may be used by the exception handler on the stack—except for eflags, cs, eip, ss, and esp, which have already been saved automatically by the control unit (see the section "Hardware Handling of Interrupts and Exceptions" in Chapter 4). The SAVE_ALL macro, which was already discussed in the section "Saving the registers for the interrupt handler" in Chapter 4, also loads the Segment Selector of the kernel data segment in ds and es:

```
system_call:
    pushl %eax
    SAVE_ALL
    movl %esp, %ebx
    andl $0xffffe000, %ebx
```

The function also stores the address of the process descriptor in ebx. This is done by taking the value of the kernel stack pointer and rounding it up to a multiple of 8 KB (see the section "Identifying a Process" in Chapter 3).

Next, the system_call( ) function checks whether the PT_TRACESYS flag included in the ptrace field of current is set—that is, whether the system call invocations of the executed program are being traced by a debugger. If this is the case, system_call( ) invokes the syscall_trace( ) function twice: once right before and once right after the execution of the system call service routine. This function stops current and thus allows the debugging process to collect information about it.

A validity check is then performed on the system call number passed by the User Mode process. If it is greater than or equal to NR_syscalls, the system call handler terminates:

```
cmpl $(NR_syscalls), %eax
jb nobadsys
movl $(-ENOSYS), 24(%esp)
jmp ret_from_sys_call
nobadsys:
```

If the system call number is not valid, the function stores the -ENOSYS value in the stack location where the eax register has been saved (at offset 24 from the current stack top). It then jumps to ret_from_sys_call( ). In this way, when the process resumes its execution in User Mode, it will find a negative return code in eax.

Finally, the specific service routine associated with the system call number contained in eax is invoked:

```
call *sys_call_table(0, %eax, 4)
```

Since each entry in the dispatch table is 4 bytes long, the kernel finds the address of the service routine to be invoked by multiplying the system call number by 4, adding the initial address of the sys_call_table dispatch table and extracting a pointer to the service routine from that slot in the table.

When the service routine terminates, system_call( ) gets its return code from eax and stores it in the stack location where the User Mode value of the eax register is saved. It then jumps to ret_from_sys_call( ), which terminates the execution of the system call handler (see the section "The ret_from_sys_call() Function" in Chapter 4):

```
movl %eax, 24(%esp)
jmp ret_from_sys_call
```

When the process resumes its execution in User Mode, it finds the return code of the system call in eax.

Parameter Passing

Like ordinary functions, system calls often require some input/output parameters, which may consist of actual values (i.e., numbers), addresses of variables in the address space of the User Mode process, or even addresses of data structures including pointers to User Mode functions (see the section "System Calls Related to Signal Handling" in Chapter 10).

Since the system_call( ) function is the common entry point for all system calls in Linux, each of them has at least one parameter: the system call number passed in the eax register. For instance, if an application program invokes the fork( ) wrapper routine, the eax register is set to 2 (i.e., __NR_fork) before executing the int $0x80 assembly language instruction. Because the register is set by the wrapper routines included in the *libc* library, programmers do not usually care about the system call number.

The fork( ) system call does not require other parameters. However, many system calls do require additional parameters, which must be explicitly passed by the application program. For instance, the mmap( ) system call may require up to six additional parameters (besides the system call number).

The parameters of ordinary C functions are passed by writing their values in the active program stack (either the User Mode stack or the Kernel Mode stack). Since system calls are a special kind of function that cross over from user to kernel land, neither the User Mode or the Kernel Mode stacks can be used. Rather, system call parameters are written in the CPU registers before invoking the int 0x80 assembly language instruction. The kernel then copies the parameters stored in the CPU registers onto the Kernel Mode stack before invoking the system call service routine because the latter is an ordinary C function.

Why doesn't the kernel copy parameters directly from the User Mode stack to the Kernel Mode stack? First of all, working with two stacks at the same time is complex; second, the use of registers makes the structure of the system call handler similar to that of other exception handlers.

However, to pass parameters in registers, two conditions must be satisfied:

- The length of each parameter cannot exceed the length of a register (32 bits).[*]
- The number of parameters must not exceed six (including the system call number passed in eax), since the Intel Pentium has a very limited number of registers.

The first condition is always true since, according to the POSIX standard, large parameters that cannot be stored in a 32-bit register must be passed by reference. A typical example is the settimeofday( ) system call, which must read a 64-bit structure.

However, system calls that have more than six parameters exist. In such cases, a single register is used to point to a memory area in the process address space that contains the parameter values. Of course, programmers do not have to care about this workaround. As with any C function call, parameters are automatically saved on the stack when the wrapper routine is invoked. This routine will find the appropriate way to pass the parameters to the kernel.

The six registers used to store system call parameters are, in increasing order, eax (for the system call number), ebx, ecx, edx, esi, and edi. As seen before, system_call( ) saves the values of these registers on the Kernel Mode stack by using the SAVE_ALL macro. Therefore, when the system call service routine goes to the stack, it finds the

---

[*] We refer, as usual, to the 32-bit architecture of the 80×86 processors. The discussion in this section does not apply to 64-bit architectures.

return address to system_call( ), followed by the parameter stored in ebx (the first parameter of the system call), the parameter stored in ecx, and so on (see the section "Saving the registers for the interrupt handler" in Chapter 4). This stack configuration is exactly the same as in an ordinary function call, and therefore the service routine can easily refer to its parameters by using the usual C-language constructs.

Let's look at an example. The sys_write( ) service routine, which handles the write( ) system call, is declared as:

```
int sys_write (unsigned int fd, const char * buf, unsigned int count)
```

The C compiler produces an assembly language function that expects to find the fd, buf, and count parameters on top of the stack, right below the return address, in the locations used to save the contents of the ebx, ecx, and edx registers, respectively.

In a few cases, even if the system call doesn't use any parameters, the corresponding service routine needs to know the contents of the CPU registers right before the system call was issued. For example, the do_fork( ) function that implements fork( ) needs to know the value of the registers in order to duplicate them in the child process thread field (see the section "The thread field" in Chapter 3). In these cases, a single parameter of type pt_regs allows the service routine to access the values saved in the Kernel Mode stack by the SAVE_ALL macro (see the section "The do_IRQ( ) function" in Chapter 4):

```
int sys_fork (struct pt_regs regs)
```

The return value of a service routine must be written into the eax register. This is automatically done by the C compiler when a return *n*; instruction is executed.

Verifying the Parameters

All system call parameters must be carefully checked before the kernel attempts to satisfy a user request. The type of check depends both on the system call and on the specific parameter. Let's go back to the write( ) system call introduced before: the fd parameter should be a file descriptor that describes a specific file, so sys_write( ) must check whether fd really is a file descriptor of a file previously opened and whether the process is allowed to write into it (see the section "File-Handling System Calls" in Chapter 1). If any of these conditions are not true, the handler must return a negative value—in this case, the error code -EBADF.

One type of checking, however, is common to all system calls. Whenever a parameter specifies an address, the kernel must check whether it is inside the process address space. There are two possible ways to perform this check:

- Verify that the linear address belongs to the process address space and, if so, that the memory region including it has the proper access rights.

- Verify just that the linear address is lower than PAGE_OFFSET (i.e., that it doesn't fall within the range of interval addresses reserved to the kernel).

Early Linux kernels performed the first type of checking. But it is quite time consuming since it must be executed for each address parameter included in a system call; furthermore, it is usually pointless because faulty programs are not very common.

Therefore, starting with Version 2.2, Linux employs the second type of checking. This is much more efficient because it does not require any scan of the process memory region descriptors. Obviously, this is a very coarse check: verifying that the linear address is smaller than PAGE_OFFSET is a necessary but not sufficient condition for its validity. But there's no risk in confining the kernel to this limited kind of check because other errors will be caught later.

The approach followed is thus to defer the real checking until the last possible moment—that is, until the Paging Unit translates the linear address into a physical one. We shall discuss in the section "Dynamic Address Checking: The Fixup Code," later in this chapter, how the Page Fault exception handler succeeds in detecting those bad addresses issued in Kernel Mode that were passed as parameters by User Mode processes.

One might wonder at this point why the coarse check is performed at all. This type of checking is actually crucial to preserve both process address spaces and the kernel address space from illegal accesses. We saw in Chapter 2 that the RAM is mapped starting from PAGE_OFFSET. This means that kernel routines are able to address all pages present in memory. Thus, if the coarse check were not performed, a User Mode process might pass an address belonging to the kernel address space as a parameter and then be able to read or write any page present in memory without causing a Page Fault exception.

The check on addresses passed to system calls is performed by the verify_area( ) function, which acts on two parameters: addr and size.* The function checks the address interval delimited by addr and addr + size - 1, and is essentially equivalent to the following C function:

```
int verify_area(const void * addr, unsigned long size)
{
    unsigned long a = (unsigned long) addr;
    if (a + size < a || a + size > current->addr_limit.seg)
        return -EFAULT;
    return 0;
}
```

The function first verifies whether addr + size, the highest address to be checked, is larger than $2^{32}-1$; since unsigned long integers and pointers are represented by the GNU C compiler (gcc) as 32-bit numbers, this is equivalent to checking for an

---

* A third parameter named type specifies whether the system call should read or write the referred memory locations. It is used only in systems that have buggy versions of the Intel 80486 microprocessor, in which writing in Kernel Mode to a write-protected page does not generate a Page Fault. We don't discuss this case further.

overflow condition. The function also checks whether addr + size exceeds the value stored in the addr_limit.seg field of current. This field usually has the value PAGE_OFFSET for normal processes and the value 0xffffffff for kernel threads. The value of the addr_limit.seg field can be dynamically changed by the get_fs and set_fs macros; this allows the kernel to invoke system call service routines directly and to pass addresses in the kernel data segment to them.

The access_ok macro performs the same check as verify_area( ). The only difference is its return value: it yields 1 if the specified address interval is valid and 0 otherwise. The __addr_ok macro also returns 1 if the specified linear address is valid and 0 otherwise.

Accessing the Process Address Space

System call service routines often need to read or write data contained in the process's address space. Linux includes a set of macros that make this access easier. We'll describe two of them, called get_user( ) and put_user( ). The first can be used to read 1, 2, or 4 consecutive bytes from an address, while the second can be used to write data of those sizes into an address.

Each function accepts two arguments, a value x to transfer and a variable ptr. The second variable also determines how many bytes to transfer. Thus, in get_user(x,ptr), the size of the variable pointed to by ptr causes the function to expand into a __get_user_1( ), __get_user_2( ), or __get_user_4( ) assembly language function. Let's consider one of them, __get_user_2( ):

```
__get_user_2:
    addl $1, %eax
    jc bad_get_user
    movl %esp, %edx
    andl $0xffffe000, %edx
    cmpl 12(%edx), %eax
    jae bad_get_user
2:  movzwl -1(%eax), %edx
    xorl %eax, %eax
    ret
bad_get_user:
    xorl %edx, %edx
    movl $-EFAULT, %eax
    ret
```

The eax register contains the address ptr of the first byte to be read. The first six instructions essentially perform the same checks as the verify_area( ) functions: they ensure that the 2 bytes to be read have addresses less than 4 GB as well as less than the addr_limit.seg field of the current process. (This field is stored at offset 12 in the process descriptor, which appears in the first operand of the cmpl instruction.)

If the addresses are valid, the function executes the movzwl instruction to store the data to be read in the two least significant bytes of edx register while setting the high-order bytes of edx to 0; then it sets a 0 return code in eax and terminates. If the addresses are not valid, the function clears edx, sets the -EFAULT value into eax, and terminates.

The put_user(x,ptr) macro is similar to the one discussed before, except it writes the value x into the process address space starting from address ptr. Depending on the size of x, it invokes either the __put_user_asm( ) macro (size of 1, 2, or 4 bytes) or the __put_user_u64( ) macro (size of 8 bytes). Both macros return the value 0 in the eax register if they succeed in writing the value, and -EFAULT otherwise.

Several other functions and macros are available to access the process address space in Kernel Mode; they are listed in Table 9-1. Notice that many of them also have a variant prefixed by two underscores (__). The ones without initial underscores take extra time to check the validity of the linear address interval requested, while the ones with the underscores bypass that check. Whenever the kernel must repeatedly access the same memory area in the process address space, it is more efficient to check the address once at the start and then access the process area without making any further checks.

Table 9-1. Functions and macros that access the process address space

Function	Action
get_user __get_user	Reads an integer value from user space (1, 2, or 4 bytes)
put_user __put_user	Writes an integer value to user space (1, 2, or 4 bytes)
copy_from_user __copy_from_user	Copies a block of arbitrary size from user space
copy_to_user __copy_to_user	Copies a block of arbitrary size to user space
strncpy_from_user __strncpy_from_user	Copies a null-terminated string from user space
strlen_user strnlen_user	Returns the length of a null-terminated string in user space
clear_user __clear_user	Fills a memory area in user space with zeros

Dynamic Address Checking: The Fixup Code

As seen previously, verify_area( ), access_ok, and __addr_ok make only a coarse check on the validity of linear addresses passed as parameters of a system call. Since they do not ensure that these addresses are included in the process address space, a process could cause a Page Fault exception by passing a wrong address.

Before describing how the kernel detects this type of error, let's specify the three cases in which Page Fault exceptions may occur in Kernel Mode. These cases must be distinguished by the Page Fault handler, since the actions to be taken are quite different.

1. The kernel attempts to address a page belonging to the process address space, but either the corresponding page frame does not exist or the kernel tries to write a read-only page. In these cases, the handler must allocate and initialize a new page frame (see the sections "Demand Paging" and "Copy On Write" in Chapter 8).

2. The kernel addresses a page belonging to its address space, but the corresponding Page Table entry has not yet been initialized (see the section "Handling Non-contiguous Memory Area Accesses" in Chapter 8). In this case, the kernel must properly set up some entries in the Page Tables of the current process.

3. Some kernel function includes a programming bug that causes the exception to be raised when that program is executed; alternatively, the exception might be caused by a transient hardware error. When this occurs, the handler must perform a kernel oops (see the section "Handling a Faulty Address Outside the Address Space" in Chapter 8).

4. The case introduced in this chapter: a system call service routine attempts to read or write into a memory area whose address has been passed as a system call parameter, but that address does not belong to the process address space.

The Page Fault handler can easily recognize the first case by determining whether the faulty linear address is included in one of the memory regions owned by the process. It is also able to detect the second case by checking whether the Page Tables of the process include a proper non-null entry that maps the address. Let's now explain how the handler distinguishes the remaining two cases.

The exception tables

The key to determining the source of a Page Fault lies in the narrow range of calls that the kernel uses to access the process address space. Only the small group of functions and macros described in the previous section are used to access this address space; thus, if the exception is caused by an invalid parameter, the instruction that caused it *must* be included in one of the functions, or else be generated by expanding one of the macros. The number of the instructions that address user space is fairly small.

Therefore, it does not take much effort to put the address of each kernel instruction that accesses the process address space into a structure called the *exception table*. If we succeed in doing this, the rest is easy. When a Page Fault exception occurs in Kernel Mode, the do_page_fault( ) handler examines the exception table: if it includes the address of the instruction that triggered the exception, the error is caused by a bad system call parameter; otherwise, it is caused by a more serious bug.

Linux defines several exception tables. The main exception table is automatically generated by the C compiler when building the kernel program image. It is stored in the __ex_table section of the kernel code segment, and its starting and ending

addresses are identified by two symbols produced by the C compiler: __start___ex_
table and __stop___ex_table.

Moreover, each dynamically loaded module of the kernel (see Appendix B) includes its own local exception table. This table is automatically generated by the C compiler when building the module image, and it is loaded into memory when the module is inserted in the running kernel.

Each entry of an exception table is an exception_table_entry structure that has two fields:

insn
>   The linear address of an instruction that accesses the process address space

fixup
>   The address of the assembly language code to be invoked when a Page Fault exception triggered by the instruction located at insn occurs

The fixup code consists of a few assembly language instructions that solve the problem triggered by the exception. As we shall see later in this section, the fix usually consists of inserting a sequence of instructions that forces the service routine to return an error code to the User Mode process. Such instructions are usually defined in the same macro or function that accesses the process address space; sometimes they are placed by the C compiler into a separate section of the kernel code segment called .fixup.

The search_exception_table( ) function is used to search for a specified address in all exception tables: if the address is included in a table, the function returns the corresponding fixup address; otherwise, it returns 0. Thus the Page Fault handler do_page_fault( ) executes the following statements:

```
if ((fixup = search_exception_table(regs->eip)) != 0) {
    regs->eip = fixup;
    return;
}
```

The regs->eip field contains the value of the eip register saved on the Kernel Mode stack when the exception occurred. If the value in the register (the instruction pointer) is in an exception table, do_page_fault( ) replaces the saved value with the address returned by search_exception_table( ). Then the Page Fault handler terminates and the interrupted program resumes with execution of the fixup code.

Generating the exception tables and the fixup code

The GNU Assembler .section directive allows programmers to specify which section of the executable file contains the code that follows. As we shall see in Chapter 20, an executable file includes a code segment, which in turn may be subdivided into sections. Thus, the following assembly language instructions add an entry into an exception table; the "a" attribute specifies that the section must be loaded into memory together with the rest of the kernel image:

```
.section __ex_table, "a"
    .long faulty_instruction_address, fixup_code_address
.previous
```

The .previous directive forces the assembler to insert the code that follows into the section that was active when the last .section directive was encountered.

Let's consider again the __get_user_1( ), __get_user_2( ), and __get_user_4( ) functions mentioned before. The instructions that access the process address space are those labeled as 1, 2, and 3:

```
__get_user_1:
    [...]
1:  movzbl (%eax), %edx
    [...]
__get_user_2:
    [...]
2:  movzwl -1(%eax), %edx
    [...]
__get_user_4:
    [...]
3:  movl -3(%eax), %edx
    [...]
bad_get_user:
    xorl %edx, %edx
    movl $-EFAULT, %eax
    ret
.section __ex_table,"a"
    .long 1b, bad_get_user
    .long 2b, bad_get_user
    .long 3b, bad_get_user
.previous
```

Each exception table entry consists of two labels. The first one is a numeric label with a b suffix to indicate that the label is "backward"; in other words, it appears in a previous line of the program. The fixup code is common to the three functions and is labeled as bad_get_user. If a Page Fault exception is generated by the instructions at label 1, 2, or 3, the fixup code is executed. It simply returns an -EFAULT error code to the process that issued the system call.

Other kernel functions that act in the User Mode address space use the fixup code technique. Consider, for instance, the strlen_user(string) macro. This macro returns either the length of a null-terminated string passed as a parameter in a system call or the value 0 on error. The macro essentially yields the following assembly language instructions:

```
movl $0, %eax
movl $0x7fffffff, %ecx
movl %ecx, %ebp
movl string, %edi
```

```
0:   repne; scasb
     subl %ecx, %ebp
     movl %ebp, %eax
1:
.section .fixup,"ax"
2:   movl $0, %eax
     jmp 1b
.previous
.section __ex_table,"a"
     .long 0b, 2b
.previous
```

The ecx and ebp registers are initialized with the 0x7fffffff value, which represents the maximum allowed length for the string in the User Mode address space. The repne;scasb assembly language instructions iteratively scan the string pointed to by the edi register, looking for the value 0 (the end of string \0 character) in eax. Since scasb decrements the ecx register at each iteration, the eax register ultimately stores the total number of bytes scanned in the string (that is, the length of the string).

The fixup code of the macro is inserted into the .fixup section. The "ax" attributes specify that the section must be loaded into memory and that it contains executable code. If a Page Fault exception is generated by the instructions at label 0, the fixup code is executed; it simply loads the value 0 in eax—thus forcing the macro to return a 0 error code instead of the string length—and then jumps to the 1 label, which corresponds to the instruction following the macro.

Kernel Wrapper Routines

Although system calls are used mainly by User Mode processes, they can also be invoked by kernel threads, which cannot use library functions. To simplify the declarations of the corresponding wrapper routines, Linux defines a set of seven macros called _syscall0 through _syscall6.

In the name of each macro, the numbers 0 through 6 correspond to the number of parameters used by the system call (excluding the system call number). The macros are used to declare wrapper routines that are not already included in the *libc* standard library (for instance, because the Linux system call is not yet supported by the library); however, they cannot be used to define wrapper routines for system calls that have more than six parameters (excluding the system call number) or for system calls that yield nonstandard return values.

Each macro requires exactly 2+2×n parameters, with n being the number of parameters of the system call. The first two parameters specify the return type and the name of the system call; each additional pair of parameters specifies the type and the name of the corresponding system call parameter. Thus, for instance, the wrapper routine of the fork( ) system call may be generated by:

```
_syscall0(int,fork)
```

while the wrapper routine of the write( ) system call may be generated by:

```
_syscall3(int,write,int,fd,const char *,buf,unsigned int,count)
```

In the latter case, the macro yields the following code:

```
int write(int fd,const char * buf,unsigned int count)
{
    long _ _res;
    asm("int $0x80"
        : "=a" (__res)
        : "0" (__NR_write), "b" ((long)fd),
          "c" ((long)buf), "d" ((long)count));
    if ((unsigned long)__res >= (unsigned long)-125) {
        errno = -__res;
        __res = -1;
    }
    return (int) __res;
}
```

The __NR_write macro is derived from the second parameter of _syscall3; it expands into the system call number of write( ). When compiling the preceding function, the following assembly language code is produced:

```
write:
        pushl %ebx              ; push ebx into stack
        movl 8(%esp), %ebx      ; put first parameter in ebx
        movl 12(%esp), %ecx     ; put second parameter in ecx
        movl 16(%esp), %edx     ; put third parameter in edx
        movl $4, %eax           ; put __NR_write in eax
        int $0x80               ; invoke system call
        cmpl $-126, %eax        ; check return code
        jbe .L1                 ; if no error, jump
        negl %eax               ; complement the value of eax
        movl %eax, errno        ; put result in errno
        movl $-1, %eax          ; set eax to -1
.L1:    popl %ebx               ; pop ebx from stack
        ret                     ; return to calling program
```

Notice how the parameters of the write( ) function are loaded into the CPU registers before the int $0x80 instruction is executed. The value returned in eax must be interpreted as an error code if it lies between −1 and −125 (the kernel assumes that the largest error code defined in *include/asm-i386/errno.h* is 125). If this is the case, the wrapper routine stores the value of -eax in errno and returns the value −1; otherwise, it returns the value of eax.

CHAPTER 10
Signals

Signals were introduced by the first Unix systems to allow interactions between User Mode processes; the kernel also uses them to notify processes of system events. Signals have been around for 30 years with only minor changes.

The first sections of this chapter examine in detail how signals are handled by the Linux kernel, then we discuss the system calls that allow processes to exchange signals.

The Role of Signals

A *signal* is a very short message that may be sent to a process or a group of processes. The only information given to the process is usually a number identifying the signal; there is no room in standard signals for arguments, a message, or other accompanying information.

A set of macros whose names start with the prefix SIG is used to identify signals; we have already made a few references to them in previous chapters. For instance, the SIGCHLD macro was mentioned in the section "The clone( ), fork( ), and vfork( ) System Calls" in Chapter 3. This macro, which expands into the value 17 in Linux, yields the identifier of the signal that is sent to a parent process when a child stops or terminates. The SIGSEGV macro, which expands into the value 11, was mentioned in the section "Page Fault Exception Handler" in Chapter 8; it yields the identifier of the signal that is sent to a process when it makes an invalid memory reference.

Signals serve two main purposes:

- To make a process aware that a specific event has occurred
- To force a process to execute a signal handler function included in its code

Of course, the two purposes are not mutually exclusive, since often a process must react to some event by executing a specific routine.

Table 10-1 lists the first 31 signals handled by Linux 2.4 for the 80×86 architecture (some signal numbers, such those associated with SIGCHLD or SIGSTOP, are architecture-dependent; furthermore, some signals such as SIGSTKFLT are defined only for specific architectures). The meanings of the default actions are described in the next section.

Table 10-1. The first 31 signals in Linux/i386

#	Signal name	Default action	Comment	POSIX
1	SIGHUP	Terminate	Hang up controlling terminal or process	Yes
2	SIGINT	Terminate	Interrupt from keyboard	Yes
3	SIGQUIT	Dump	Quit from keyboard	Yes
4	SIGILL	Dump	Illegal instruction	Yes
5	SIGTRAP	Dump	Breakpoint for debugging	No
6	SIGABRT	Dump	Abnormal termination	Yes
6	SIGIOT	Dump	Equivalent to SIGABRT	No
7	SIGBUS	Dump	Bus error	No
8	SIGFPE	Dump	Floating-point exception	Yes
9	SIGKILL	Terminate	Forced-process termination	Yes
10	SIGUSR1	Terminate	Available to processes	Yes
11	SIGSEGV	Dump	Invalid memory reference	Yes
12	SIGUSR2	Terminate	Available to processes	Yes
13	SIGPIPE	Terminate	Write to pipe with no readers	Yes
14	SIGALRM	Terminate	Real-timer clock	Yes
15	SIGTERM	Terminate	Process termination	Yes
16	SIGSTKFLT	Terminate	Coprocessor stack error	No
17	SIGCHLD	Ignore	Child process stopped or terminated	Yes
18	SIGCONT	Continue	Resume execution, if stopped	Yes
19	SIGSTOP	Stop	Stop process execution	Yes
20	SIGTSTP	Stop	Stop process issued from tty	Yes
21	SIGTTIN	Stop	Background process requires input	Yes
22	SIGTTOU	Stop	Background process requires output	Yes
23	SIGURG	Ignore	Urgent condition on socket	No
24	SIGXCPU	Dump	CPU time limit exceeded	No
25	SIGXFSZ	Dump	File size limit exceeded	No
26	SIGVTALRM	Terminate	Virtual timer clock	No
27	SIGPROF	Terminate	Profile timer clock	No
28	SIGWINCH	Ignore	Window resizing	No
29	SIGIO	Terminate	I/O now possible	No
29	SIGPOLL	Terminate	Equivalent to SIGIO	No
30	SIGPWR	Terminate	Power supply failure	No
31	SIGSYS	Dump	Bad system call	No
31	SIGUNUSED	Dump	Equivalent to SIGSYS	No

Besides the *regular signals* described in this table, the POSIX standard has introduced a new class of signals denoted as *real-time signals*; their signal numbers range from 32 to 63 on Linux. They mainly differ from regular signals because they are always queued so that multiple signals sent will be received. On the other hand, regular signals of the same kind are not queued: if a regular signal is sent many times in a row, just one of them is delivered to the receiving process. Although the Linux kernel does not use real-time signals, it fully supports the POSIX standard by means of several specific system calls.

A number of system calls allow programmers to send signals and determine how their processes respond to the signals they receive. Table 10-2 summarizes these calls; their behavior is described in detail in the later section "System Calls Related to Signal Handling."

Table 10-2. The most significant system calls related to signals

System call	Description
kill( )	Send a signal to a process.
sigaction( )	Change the action associated with a signal.
signal( )	Similar to sigaction( ).
sigpending( )	Check whether there are pending signals.
sigprocmask( )	Modify the set of blocked signals.
sigsuspend( )	Wait for a signal.
rt_sigaction( )	Change the action associated with a real-time signal.
rt_sigpending( )	Check whether there are pending real-time signals.
rt_sigprocmask( )	Modify the set of blocked real-time signals.
rt_sigqueueinfo( )	Send a real-time signal to a process.
rt_sigsuspend( )	Wait for a real-time signal.
rt_sigtimedwait( )	Similar to rt_sigsuspend( ).

An important characteristic of signals is that they may be sent at any time to a process whose state is usually unpredictable. Signals sent to a process that is not currently executing must be saved by the kernel until that process resumes execution. Blocking a signal (described later) requires that delivery of the signal be held off until it is later unblocked, which exacerbates the problem of signals being raised before they can be delivered.

Therefore, the kernel distinguishes two different phases related to signal transmission:

Signal generation

> The kernel updates a data structure of the destination process to represent that a new signal has been sent.

Signal delivery

> The kernel forces the destination process to react to the signal by changing its execution state, by starting the execution of a specified signal handler, or both.

Each signal generated can be delivered once, at most. Signals are consumable resources: once they have been delivered, all process descriptor information that refers to their previous existence is canceled.

Signals that have been generated but not yet delivered are called *pending signals*. At any time, only one pending signal of a given type may exist for a process; additional pending signals of the same type to the same process are not queued but simply discarded. Real-time signals are different, though: there can be several pending signals of the same type.

In general, a signal may remain pending for an unpredictable amount of time. The following factors must be taken into consideration:

- Signals are usually delivered only to the currently running process (that is, by the current process).

- Signals of a given type may be selectively *blocked* by a process (see the later section "Modifying the Set of Blocked Signals"). In this case, the process does not receive the signal until it removes the block.

- When a process executes a signal-handler function, it usually *masks* the corresponding signal—i.e., it automatically blocks the signal until the handler terminates. A signal handler therefore cannot be interrupted by another occurrence of the handled signal and the function doesn't need to be re-entrant.

Although the notion of signals is intuitive, the kernel implementation is rather complex. The kernel must:

- Remember which signals are blocked by each process.

- When switching from Kernel Mode to User Mode, check whether a signal for any process has arrived. This happens at almost every timer interrupt (roughly every 10 ms).

- Determine whether the signal can be ignored. This happens when all of the following conditions are fulfilled:
  - The destination process is not traced by another process (the PT_PTRACED flag in the process descriptor ptrace field is equal to 0).*
  - The signal is not blocked by the destination process.
  - The signal is being ignored by the destination process (either because the process explicitly ignored it or because the process did not change the default action of the signal and that action is "ignore").

- Handle the signal, which may require switching the process to a handler function at any point during its execution and restoring the original execution context after the function returns.

---

* If a process receives a signal while it is being traced, the kernel stops the process and notifies the tracing process by sending a SIGCHLD signal to it. The tracing process may, in turn, resume execution of the traced process by means of a SIGCONT signal.

Moreover, Linux must take into account the different semantics for signals adopted by BSD and System V; furthermore, it must comply with the rather cumbersome POSIX requirements.

Actions Performed upon Delivering a Signal

There are three ways in which a process can respond to a signal:

1. Explicitly ignore the signal.

2. Execute the default action associated with the signal (see Table 10-1). This action, which is predefined by the kernel, depends on the signal type and may be any one of the following:

   Terminate
   > The process is terminated (killed).

   Dump
   > The process is terminated (killed) and a core file containing its execution context is created, if possible; this file may be used for debug purposes.

   Ignore
   > The signal is ignored.

   Stop
   > The process is stopped—i.e., put in the TASK_STOPPED state (see the section "Process State" in Chapter 3).

   Continue
   > If the process is stopped (TASK_STOPPED), it is put into the TASK_RUNNING state.

3. Catch the signal by invoking a corresponding signal-handler function.

Notice that blocking a signal is different from ignoring it. A signal is not delivered as long as it is blocked; it is delivered only after it has been unblocked. An ignored signal is always delivered, and there is no further action.

The SIGKILL and SIGSTOP signals cannot be ignored, caught, or blocked, and their default actions must always be executed. Therefore, SIGKILL and SIGSTOP allow a user with appropriate privileges to terminate and to stop, respectively, any process,* regardless of the defenses taken by the program it is executing.

Data Structures Associated with Signals

For any process in the system, the kernel must keep track of what signals are currently pending or masked, as well as how to handle every signal. To do this, it uses

---

* There are two exceptions: it is not possible to send a signal to process 0 (*swapper*), and signals sent to process 1 (*init*) are always discarded unless they are caught. Therefore, process 0 never dies, while process 1 dies only when the *init* program terminates.

several data structures accessible from the processor descriptor. The most significant ones are shown in Figure 10-1.

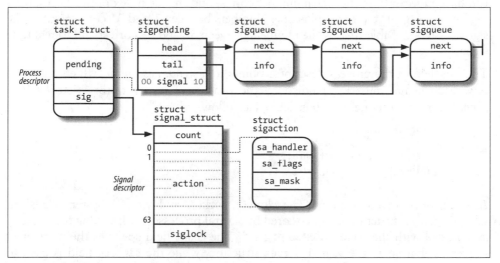

Figure 10-1. The most significant data structures related to signal handling

The fields of the process descriptor related to signal handling are listed in Table 10-3.

Table 10-3. Process descriptor fields related to signal handling

Type	Name	Description
spinlock_t	sigmask_lock	Spin lock protecting pending and blocked
struct signal_struct *	sig	Pointer to the process's signal descriptor
sigset_t	blocked	Mask of blocked signals
struct sigpending	pending	Data structure storing the pending signals
unsigned long	sas_ss_sp	Address of alternate signal handler stack
size_t	sas_ss_size	Size of alternate signal handler stack
int (*) (void *)	notifier	Pointer to a function used by a device driver to block some signals of the process
void *	notifier_data	Pointer to data that might be used by the notifier function (previous field of table)
sigset_t *	notifier_mask	Bit mask of signals blocked by a device driver through a notifier function

The blocked field stores the signals currently masked out by the process. It is a sigset_t array of bits, one for each signal type:

```
typedef struct {
    unsigned long sig[2];
} sigset_t;
```

Since each unsigned long number consists of 32 bits, the maximum number of signals that may be declared in Linux is 64 (the _NSIG macro specifies this value). No signal can have number 0, so the signal number corresponds to the index of the corresponding bit in a sigset_t variable plus one. Numbers between 1 and 31 correspond to the signals listed in Table 10-1, while numbers between 32 and 64 correspond to real-time signals.

The sig field of the process descriptor points to a *signal descriptor*, which describes how each signal must be handled by the process. The descriptor is stored in a signal_struct structure, which is defined as follows:

```
struct signal_struct {
    atomic_t          count;
    struct k_sigaction action[64];
    spinlock_t        siglock;
};
```

As mentioned in the section "The clone(), fork(), and vfork() System Calls" in Chapter 3, this structure may be shared by several processes by invoking the clone( ) system call with the CLONE_SIGHAND flag set.* The count field specifies the number of processes that share the signal_struct structure, while the siglock field is used to ensure exclusive access to its fields. The action field is an array of 64 k_sigaction structures that specify how each signal must be handled.

Some architectures assign properties to a signal that are visible only to the kernel. Thus, the properties of a signal are stored in a k_sigaction structure, which contains both the properties hidden from the User Mode process and the more familiar sigaction structure that holds all the properties a User Mode process can see. Actually, on the 80×86 platform, all signal properties are visible to User Mode processes. Thus the k_sigaction structure simply reduces to a single sa structure of type sigaction, which includes the following fields:

sa_handler *or* sa_sigaction

   Both names refer to the same field of the structure, which specifies the type of action to be performed; its value can be either a pointer to the signal handler, SIG_DFL (that is, the value 0) to specify that the default action is performed, or SIG_IGN (that is, the value 1) to specify that the signal is ignored. The two different names of this field corresponds to two different types of signal handler (see the section "Changing a Signal Action" later in this chapter).

sa_flags

   This set of flags specifies how the signal must be handled; some of them are listed in Table 10-4.

sa_mask

   This sigset_t variable specifies the signals to be masked when running the signal handler.

---

* If this is not done, about 1,300 bytes are added to the process data structures just to take care of signal handling.

Table 10-4. Flags specifying how to handle a signal

Flag Name	Description
SA_NOCLDSTOP	Do not send SIGCHLD to the parent when the process is stopped.
SA_NODEFER, SA_NOMASK	Do not mask the signal while executing the signal handler.
SA_RESETHAND, SA_ONESHOT	Reset to default action after executing the signal handler.
SA_ONSTACK	Use an alternate stack for the signal handler (see the later section "Catching the Signal").
SA_RESTART	Interrupted system calls are automatically restarted (see the later section "Reexecution of System Calls").
SA_SIGINFO	Provide additional information to the signal handler (see the later section "Changing a Signal Action").

The pending field of the process descriptor is used to keep track of what signals are currently pending. It consists of a struct sigpending data structure, which is defined as follows:

```
struct sigpending {
    struct sigqueue * head, ** tail;
    sigset_t signal;
}
```

The signal field is a bit mask specifying the pending signals for the process, while the head and tail fields point to the first and last items of a *pending signal queue*. This queue is implemented through a list of struct sigqueue data structures:

```
struct sigqueue {
    struct sigqueue * next;
    siginfo_t info;
}
```

The nr_queued_signals variable stores the number of items in the queue, while the max_queued_signals defines the maximum length of the queue (which is 1,024 by default, but the system administrator can change this value either by writing into the */proc/sys/kernel/rtsig-max* file or by issuing a suitable sysctl( ) system call).

The siginfo_t data structure is a 128-byte data structure that stores information about an occurrence of a specific signal; it includes the following fields:

si_signo
  The signal number.

si_errno
  The error code of the instruction that caused the signal to be raised, or 0 if there was no error.

si_code
  A code identifying who raised the signal (see Table 10-5).

Table 10-5. The most significant signal sender codes

Code Name	Sender
SI_USER	kill( ) and raise( ) (see the later section "System Calls Related to Signal Handling")
SI_KERNEL	Generic kernel function
SI_TIMER	Timer expiration
SI_ASYNCIO	Asynchronous I/O completion

_sifields

> A union storing information depending on the type of signal. For instance, the siginfo_t data structure relative to an occurrence of the SIGKILL signal records the PID and the UID of the sender process here; conversely, the data structure relative to an occurrence of the SIGSEGV signal stores the memory address whose access caused the signal to be raised.

Operations on Signal Data Structures

Several functions and macros are used by the kernel to handle signals. In the following description, set is a pointer to a sigset_t variable, nsig is the number of a signal, and mask is an unsigned long bit mask.

sigemptyset(set) *and* sigfillset(set)

> Sets the bits in the sigset_t variable to 0 or 1, respectively.

sigaddset(set,nsig) *and* sigdelset(set,nsig)

> Sets the bit of the sigset_t variable corresponding to signal nsig to 1 or 0, respectively. In practice, sigaddset( ) reduces to:

```
set->sig[(nsig - 1) / 32] |= 1UL << ((nsig - 1) % 32);
```

> and sigdelset( ) to:

```
set->sig[(nsig - 1) / 32] &= ~(1UL << ((nsig - 1) % 32));
```

sigaddsetmask(set,mask) *and* sigdelsetmask(set,mask)

> Sets all the bits of the sigset_t variable whose corresponding bits of mask are on 1 or 0, respectively. They can be used only with signals that are between 1 and 32. The corresponding functions reduce to:

```
set->sig[0] |= mask;
```

> and to:

```
set->sig[0] &= ~mask;
```

sigismember(set,nsig)

> Returns the value of the bit of the sigset_t variable corresponding to the signal nsig. In practice, this function reduces to:

```
return 1 & (set->sig[(nsig-1) / 32] >> ((nsig-1) % 32));
```

sigmask(nsig)

> Yields the bit index of the signal nsig. In other words, if the kernel needs to set, clear, or test a bit in an element of sigset_t that corresponds to a particular signal, it can derive the proper bit through this macro.

sigandsets(d,s1,s2), sigorsets(d,s1,s2), *and* signandsets(d,s1,s2)

> Performs a logical AND, a logical OR, and a logical NAND, respectively, between the sigset_t variables to which s1 and s2 point; the result is stored in the sigset_t variable to which d points.

sigtestsetmask(set,mask)

> Returns the value 1 if any of the bits in the sigset_t variable that correspond to the bits set to 1 in mask is set; it returns 0 otherwise. It can be used only with signals that have a number between 1 and 32.

siginitset(set,mask)

> Initializes the low bits of the sigset_t variable corresponding to signals between 1 and 32 with the bits contained in mask, and clears the bits corresponding to signals between 33 and 63.

siginitsetinv(set,mask)

> Initializes the low bits of the sigset_t variable corresponding to signals between 1 and 32 with the complement of the bits contained in mask, and sets the bits corresponding to signals between 33 and 63.

signal_pending(p)

> Returns the value 1 (true) if the process identified by the *p process descriptor has nonblocked pending signals, and returns the value 0 (false) if it doesn't. The function is implemented as a simple check on the sigpending field of the process descriptor.

recalc_sigpending(t)

> Checks whether the process identified by the process descriptor at *t has nonblocked pending signals by looking at the sig and blocked fields of the process, and then sets the sigpending field to 0 or 1 as follows:

```
ready  = t->pending.signal.sig[1] & ~t->blocked.sig[1];
ready |= t->pending.signal.sig[0] & ~t->blocked.sig[0];
t->sigpending = (ready != 0);
```

flush_signals(t)

> Deletes all signals sent to the process identified by the process descriptor at *t. This is done by clearing both the t->sigpending and the t->pending.signal fields and by emptying the queue of pending signals.

Generating a Signal

When a signal is sent to a process, either from the kernel or from another process, the kernel generates it by invoking the send_sig_info( ), send_sig( ), force_sig( ), or force_sig_info( ) functions. These accomplish the first phase of signal handling described earlier in the section "The Role of Signals," updating the process descriptor as needed. They do not directly perform the second phase of delivering the signal but, depending on the type of signal and the state of the process, may wake up the process and force it to receive the signal.

The send_sig_info( ) and send_sig( ) Functions

The send_sig_info( ) function acts on three parameters:

sig
> The signal number.

info
> Either the address of a siginfo_t table or one of two special values. 0 means that the signal has been sent by a User Mode process, while 1 means that it has been sent by the kernel.

t
> A pointer to the descriptor of the destination process.

The send_sig_info( ) function starts by checking whether the parameters are correct:

```
if (sig < 0 || sig > 64)
    return -EINVAL;
```

The function then checks if the signal is being sent by a User Mode process. This occurs when info is equal to 0 or when the si_code field of the siginfo_t table is negative or 0 (positive values of this field mean that the signal was sent by some kernel function):

```
if ((!info || ((unsigned long)info != 1 && (info->si_code <=0)))
    && ((sig != SIGCONT) || (current->session != t->session))
    && (current->euid ^ t->suid) && (current->euid ^ t->uid)
    && (current->uid ^ t->suid) && (current->uid ^ t->uid)
    && !capable(CAP_KILL))
        return -EPERM;
```

If the signal is sent by a User Mode process, the function determines whether the operation is allowed. The signal is delivered only if at least one of the following conditions holds:

- The owner of the sending process has the proper capability (usually, this simply means the signal was issued by the system administrator; see Chapter 20).
- The signal is SIGCONT and the destination process is in the same login session of the sending process.
- Both processes belong to the same user.

If the sig parameter has the value 0, the function returns immediately without generating any signal. Since 0 is not a valid signal number, it is used to allow the sending process to check whether it has the required privileges to send a signal to the destination process. The function also returns if the destination process is in the TASK_ZOMBIE state, indicated by checking whether its siginfo_t table has been released:

```
if (!sig || !t->sig)
    return 0;
```

Now the kernel has finished the preliminary checks, and it is going to fiddle with the signal-related data structures. To avoid race conditions, it disables the interrupts and acquires the signal spin lock of the destination process:

```
spin_lock_irqsave(&t->sigmask_lock, flags);
```

Some types of signals might nullify other pending signals for the destination process. Therefore, the function checks whether one of the following cases occurs:

- sig is a SIGKILL or SIGCONT signal. If the destination process is stopped, it is put in the TASK_RUNNING state so that it is able to either execute the do_exit( ) function or just continue its execution; moreover, if the destination process has SIGSTOP, SIGTSTP, SIGTTOU, or SIGTTIN pending signals, they are removed:

  ```
  if (t->state == TASK_STOPPED)
      wake_up_process(t);
  t->exit_code = 0;
  rm_sig_from_queue(SIGSTOP, t);
  rm_sig_from_queue(SIGTSTP, t);
  rm_sig_from_queue(SIGTTOU, t);
  rm_sig_from_queue(SIGTTIN, t);
  ```

  The rm_sig_from_queue( ) function clears the bit in t->pending.signal associated with the signal number passed as first argument and removes any item in the pending signal queue of the process that corresponds to that signal number.

- sig is a SIGSTOP, SIGTSTP, SIGTTIN, or SIGTTOU signal. If the destination process has a pending SIGCONT signal, it is removed:

  ```
  rm_sig_from_queue(SIGCONT, t);
  ```

Next, send_sig_info( ) checks whether the new signal can be handled immediately. In this case, the function also takes care of the delivering phase of the signal:

```
if (ignored_signal(sig, t)) {
    spin_unlock_irqrestore(&t->sigmask_lock, flags);
    return 0;
}
```

The ignored_signal( ) function returns the value 1 when all three conditions for ignoring a signal that are mentioned in the section "The Role of Signals" are satisfied. However, to fulfill a POSIX requirement, the SIGCHLD signal is handled specially. POSIX distinguishes between explicitly setting the "ignore" action for the SIGCHLD signal and leaving the default in place (even if the default is to ignore the signal). To let the kernel clean up a terminated child process and prevent it from becoming a zombie (see the section "Process Removal" in Chapter 3), the parent must explicitly set the action to "ignore" the signal. So ignored_signal( ) handles this case as follows: if the signal is explicitly ignored, ignored_signal( ) returns 0, but if the default action was "ignore" and the process didn't change that default, ignored_signal( ) returns 1.

If ignored_signal( ) returns 1, the siginfo_t table of the destination process must not be updated, and the send_sig_info( ) function terminates. Since the signal is no longer pending, it has been effectively delivered to the destination process, even if the process never sees it.

If ignored_signal( ) returns 0, the phase of signal delivering has to be deferred, therefore send_sig_info( ) may have to modify the data structures of the destination process to let it know later that a new signal has been sent to it. However, if the signal being handled was already pending, the send_sig_info( ) function can simply terminate. In fact, there can be at most one occurrence of any regular signal type in the pending signal queue of a process because regular signal occurrences are not really queued:

```
if (sig < 32 && sigismember(&t->pending.signal, sig)) {
    spin_unlock_irqrestore(&t->sigmask_lock, flags);
    return 0;
}
```

If it proceeds, the send_sig_info( ) function must insert a new item in the pending signal queue of the destination process. This is achieved by invoking the send_signal( ) function:

```
retval = send_signal(sig, info, &t->pending);
```

In turn, the send_signal( ) function checks the length of the pending signal queue and appends a new sigqueue data structure:

```
if (atomic_read(&nr_queued_signals) < max_queued_signals) {
    q = kmem_cache_alloc(sigqueue_cachep, GFP_ATOMIC);
    atomic_inc(&nr_queued_signals);
    q->next = NULL;
    *(t->pending.tail) = q;
    t->pending.tail = &q->next;
```

Then the send_sig_info( ) function fills the siginfo_t table inside the new queue item:

```
if ((unsigned long)info == 0) {
    q->info.si_signo = sig;
    q->info.si_errno = 0;
    q->info.si_code = SI_USER;
    q->info._sifields._kill._pid = current->pid;
    q->info._sifields._kill._uid = current->uid;
} else if ((unsigned long)info == 1) {
    q->info.si_signo = sig;
    q->info.si_errno = 0;
    q->info.si_code = SI_KERNEL;
    q->info._sifields._kill._pid = 0;
    q->info._sifields._kill._uid = 0;
```

```
        } else
            copy_siginfo(&q->info, info);
    }
```

The info argument passed to the send_signal( ) function either points to a previously built siginfo_t table or stores the constants 0 (for a signal sent by a User Mode process) or 1 (for a signal sent by a kernel function).

If it is not possible to add an item to the queue, either because it already includes max_queued_signals elements or because there is no free memory for the sigqueue data structure, the signal occurrence cannot be queued. If the signal is real-time and was sent through a system call that is explicitly required to queue it (like rt_sigqueueinfo( )), the send_signal( ) function returns an error code. Otherwise, it sets the corresponding bit in t->pending.signal:

```
if (sig >= 32 && info && (unsigned long)info != 1 && info->si_code != SI_USER)
    return -EAGAIN;
sigaddset(&t->pending.signal, sig);
return 0;
```

It is important to let the destination process receive the signal even if there is no room for the corresponding item in the pending signal queue. Suppose, for instance, that a process is consuming too much memory. The kernel must ensure that the kill( ) system call succeeds even if there is no free memory; otherwise, the system administrator doesn't have any chance to recover the system by terminating the offending process.

If the send_signal( ) function successfully terminated and the signal is not blocked, the destination process has a new pending signal to consider:

```
if (!retval && !sigismember(&t->blocked, sig))
    signal_wake_up(t);
```

The signal_wake_up( ) function performs three actions:

1. Sets the sigpending flag of the destination process.
2. Checks whether the destination process is already running on another CPU and, in this case, sends an interprocessor interrupt to that CPU to force a reschedule of the current process (see the section "Interprocessor Interrupt Handling" in Chapter 4). Since each process checks the existence of pending signals when returning from the schedule( ) function, the interprocessor interrupt ensures that the destination process quickly notices the new pending signal if it is already running.
3. Checks whether the destination process is in the TASK_INTERRUPTIBLE state and, in this case, wakes it up by invoking the wake_up_process( ).

Finally, the send_sig_info( ) function re-enables the interrupts, releases the spin lock, and terminates with the error code of send_signal( ):

```
spin_unlock_irqrestore(&t->sigmask_lock, flags);
return retval;
```

The send_sig( ) function is similar to send_sig_info( ). However, the info parameter is replaced by a priv flag, which is 1 if the signal is sent by the kernel and 0 if it is sent by a process. The send_sig( ) function is implemented as a special case of send_sig_info( ):

```
return send_sig_info(sig, (void*)(long)(priv != 0), t);
```

The force_sig_info( ) and force_sig( ) Functions

The force_sig_info(sig, info, t) function is used by the kernel to send signals that cannot be explicitly ignored or blocked by the destination processes. The function's parameters are the same as those of send_sig_info( ). The force_sig_info( ) function acts on the signal_struct data structure that is referenced by the sig field included in the descriptor t of the destination process:

```
spin_lock_irqsave(&t->sigmask_lock, flags);
if (t->sig->action[sig-1].sa.sa_handler == SIG_IGN)
    t->sig->action[sig-1].sa.sa_handler = SIG_DFL;
sigdelset(&t->blocked, sig);
recalc_sigpending(t);
spin_unlock_irqrestore(&t->sigmask_lock, flags);
return send_sig_info(sig, info, t);
```

force_sig( ) is similar to force_sig_info( ). Its use is limited to signals sent by the kernel; it can be implemented as a special case of the force_sig_info( ) function:

```
force_sig_info(sig, (void*)1L, t);
```

Delivering a Signal

We assume that the kernel noticed the arrival of a signal and invoked one of the functions mentioned in the previous section to prepare the process descriptor of the process that is supposed to receive the signal. But in case that process was not running on the CPU at that moment, the kernel deferred the task of delivering the signal. We now turn to the activities that the kernel performs to ensure that pending signals of a process are handled.

As mentioned in the section "Returning from Interrupts and Exceptions" in Chapter 4, the kernel checks the value of the sigpending flag of the process descriptor before allowing the process to resume its execution in User Mode. Thus, the kernel checks for the existence of pending signals every time it finishes handling an interrupt or an exception.

To handle the nonblocked pending signals, the kernel invokes the do_signal( ) function, which receives two parameters:

regs
> The address of the stack area where the User Mode register contents of the current process are saved.

oldset

The address of a variable where the function is supposed to save the bit mask array of blocked signals. It is NULL if there is no need to save the bit mask array.

The do_signal() function starts by checking whether the function itself was triggered by an interrupt; if so, it simply returns. Otherwise, if the function was triggered by an exception that was raised while the process was running in User Mode, the function continues executing:

```
if ((regs->xcs & 3) != 3)
    return 1;
```

However, as we'll see in the section "Reexecution of System Calls," this does not mean that a system call cannot be interrupted by a signal.

If the oldset parameter is NULL, the function initializes it with the address of the current->blocked field:

```
if (!oldset)
    oldset = &current->blocked;
```

The heart of the do_signal() function consists of a loop that repeatedly invokes the dequeue_signal() function until no nonblocked pending signals are left. The return code of dequeue_signal() is stored in the signr local variable. If its value is 0, it means that all pending signals have been handled and do_signal() can finish. As long as a nonzero value is returned, a pending signal is waiting to be handled. dequeue_signal() is invoked again after do_signal() handles the current signal.

The dequeue_signal() always considers the lowest-numbered pending signal. It updates the data structures to indicate that the signal is no longer pending and returns its number. This task involves clearing the corresponding bit in current->pending.signal and updating the value of current->sigpending. In the mask parameter, each bit that is set represents a blocked signal:

```
sig = 0;
if (((x = current->pending.signal.sig[0]) & ~mask->sig[0]) != 0)
    sig = 1 + ffz(~x);
else if (((x = current->pending.signal.sig[1]) & ~mask->sig[1]) != 0)
    sig = 33 + ffz(~x);
if (sig) {
    sigdelset(&current->signal, sig);
    recalc_sigpending(current);
}
return sig;
```

The collection of currently pending signals is ANDed with the blocked signals (the complement of mask). If anything is left, it represents a signal that should be delivered to the process. The ffz() function returns the index of the first 0 bit in its parameter; this value is used to compute the lowest-number signal to be delivered.

Let's see how the do_signal() function handles any pending signal whose number is returned by dequeue_signal(). First, it checks whether the current receiver process is

being monitored by some other process; in this case, do_signal( ) invokes notify_
parent( ) and schedule( ) to make the monitoring process aware of the signal
handling.

Then do_signal( ) loads the ka local variable with the address of the k_sigaction data
structure of the signal to be handled:

```
ka = &current->sig->action[signr-1];
```

Depending on the contents, three kinds of actions may be performed: ignoring the
signal, executing a default action, or executing a signal handler.

Ignoring the Signal

When a delivered signal is explicitly ignored, the do_signal( ) function normally just
continues with a new execution of the loop and therefore considers another pending
signal. One exception exists, as described earlier:

```
if (ka->sa.sa_handler == SIG_IGN) {
    if (signr == SIGCHLD)
        while (sys_wait4(-1, NULL, WNOHANG, NULL) > 0)
            /* nothing */;
    continue;
}
```

If the signal delivered is SIGCHLD, the sys_wait4( ) service routine of the wait4( ) system call is invoked to force the process to read information about its children, thus
cleaning up memory left over by the terminated child processes (see the section
"Destroying Processes" in Chapter 3).

Executing the Default Action for the Signal

If ka->sa.sa_handler is equal to SIG_DFL, do_signal( ) must perform the default
action of the signal. The only exception comes when the receiving process is *init*, in
which case the signal is discarded as described in the earlier section "Actions Performed upon Delivering a Signal":

```
if (current->pid == 1)
    continue;
```

For other processes, since the default action depends on the type of signal, the function executes a switch statement based on the value of signr.

The signals whose default action is "ignore" are easily handled:

```
case SIGCONT: case SIGCHLD: case SIGWINCH:
    continue;
```

The signals whose default action is "stop" may stop the current process. To do this,
do_signal( ) sets the state of current to TASK_STOPPED and then invokes the schedule(
) function (see the section "The schedule( ) Function" in Chapter 11). The do_signal(

) function also sends a SIGCHLD signal to the parent process of current, unless the parent has set the SA_NOCLDSTOP flag of SIGCHLD:

```
case SIGTSTP: case SIGTTIN: case SIGTTOU:
    if (is_orphaned_pgrp(current->pgrp))
        continue;
case SIGSTOP:
    current->state = TASK_STOPPED;
    current->exit_code = signr;
    if (current->p_pptr->sig && !(SA_NOCLDSTOP &
        current->p_pptr->sig->action[SIGCHLD-1].sa.sa_flags))
        notify_parent(current, SIGCHLD);
    schedule();
    continue;
```

The difference between SIGSTOP and the other signals is subtle: SIGSTOP always stops the process, while the other signals stop the process only if it is not in an "orphaned process group." The POSIX standard specifies that a process group is *not* orphaned as long as there is a process in the group that has a parent in a different process group but in the same session.

The signals whose default action is "dump" may create a core file in the process working directory; this file lists the complete contents of the process's address space and CPU registers. After the do_signal( ) creates the core file, it kills the process. The default action of the remaining 18 signals is "terminate," which consists of just killing the process:

```
exit_code = sig_nr;
case SIGQUIT: case SIGILL: case SIGTRAP:
case SIGABRT: case SIGFPE: case SIGSEGV:
case SIGBUS: case SIGSYS: case SIGXCPU: case SIGXFSZ:
    if (do_coredump(signr, regs))
        exit_code |= 0x80;
    default:
        sigaddset(&current->pending.signal, signr);
        recalc_sigpending(current);
        current->flags |= PF_SIGNALED;
        do_exit(exit_code);
```

The do_exit( ) function receives as its input parameter the signal number ORed with a flag set when a core dump has been performed. That value is used to set the exit code of the process. The function terminates the current process, and hence never returns (see Chapter 20).

Catching the Signal

If a handler has been established for the signal, the do_signal( ) function must enforce its execution. It does this by invoking handle_signal( ):

```
handle_signal(signr, ka, &info, oldset, regs);
return 1;
```

Notice how do_signal( ) returns after having handled a single signal. Other pending signals won't be considered until the next invocation of do_signal( ). This approach ensures that real-time signals will be dealt with in the proper order.

Executing a signal handler is a rather complex task because of the need to juggle stacks carefully while switching between User Mode and Kernel Mode. We explain exactly what is entailed here.

Signal handlers are functions defined by User Mode processes and included in the User Mode code segment. The handle_signal( ) function runs in Kernel Mode while signal handlers run in User Mode; this means that the current process must first execute the signal handler in User Mode before being allowed to resume its "normal" execution. Moreover, when the kernel attempts to resume the normal execution of the process, the Kernel Mode stack no longer contains the hardware context of the interrupted program because the Kernel Mode stack is emptied at every transition from User Mode to Kernel Mode.

An additional complication is that signal handlers may invoke system calls. In this case, after the service routine executes, control must be returned to the signal handler instead of to the code of the interrupted program.

The solution adopted in Linux consists of copying the hardware context saved in the Kernel Mode stack onto the User Mode stack of the current process. The User Mode stack is also modified in such a way that, when the signal handler terminates, the sigreturn( ) system call is automatically invoked to copy the hardware context back on the Kernel Mode stack and restore the original content of the User Mode stack.

Figure 10-2 illustrates the flow of execution of the functions involved in catching a signal. A nonblocked signal is sent to a process. When an interrupt or exception occurs, the process switches into Kernel Mode. Right before returning to User Mode, the kernel executes the do_signal( ) function, which in turn handles the signal (by invoking handle_signal( )) and sets up the User Mode stack (by invoking setup_frame( ) or setup_rt_frame( )). When the process switches again to User Mode, it starts executing the signal handler because the handler's starting address was forced into the program counter. When that function terminates, the return code placed on the User Mode stack by the setup_frame( ) or setup_rt_frame( ) function is executed. This code invokes the sigreturn( ) system call, whose service routine copies the hardware context of the normal program in the Kernel Mode stack and restores the User Mode stack back to its original state (by invoking restore_sigcontext( )). When the system call terminates, the normal program can thus resume its execution.

Let's now examine in detail how this scheme is carried out.

Setting up the frame

To properly set the User Mode stack of the process, the handle_signal( ) function invokes either setup_frame( ) (for signals that do not require a siginfo_t table; see

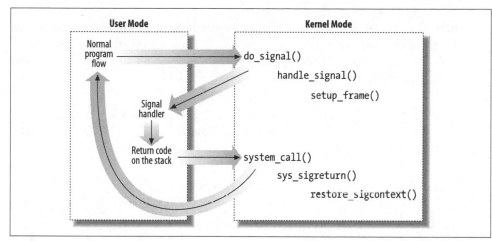

Figure 10-2. Catching a signal

the section "System Calls Related to Signal Handling" later in this chapter) or setup_
rt_frame( ) (for signals that do require a siginfo_t table). To choose among these
two functions, the kernel checks the value of the SA_SIGINFO flag in the sa_flags field
of the sigaction table associated with the signal.

The setup_frame( ) function receives four parameters, which have the following
meanings:

sig
>   Signal number

ka
>   Address of the k_sigaction table associated with the signal

oldset
>   Address of a bit mask array of blocked signals

regs
>   Address in the Kernel Mode stack area where the User Mode register contents
>   are saved

The setup_frame( ) function pushes onto the User Mode stack a data structure called
a *frame*, which contains the information needed to handle the signal and to ensure
the correct return to the sys_sigreturn( ) function. A frame is a sigframe table that
includes the following fields (see Figure 10-3):

pretcode
>   Return address of the signal handler function; it points to the retcode field (later
>   in this list) in the same table.

sig
>   The signal number; this is the parameter required by the signal handler.

sc

Structure of type `sigcontext` containing the hardware context of the User Mode process right before switching to Kernel Mode (this information is copied from the Kernel Mode stack of `current`). It also contains a bit array that specifies the blocked regular signals of the process.

fpstate

Structure of type `_fpstate` that may be used to store the floating point registers of the User Mode process (see the section "Saving the FPU, MMX, and XMM Registers" in Chapter 3).

extramask

Bit array that specifies the blocked real-time signals.

retcode

Eight-byte code issuing a `sigreturn( )` system call; this code is executed when returning from the signal handler.

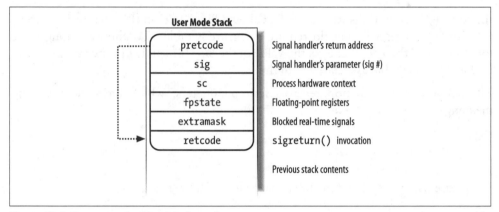

Figure 10-3. Frame on the User Mode stack

The `setup_frame( )` function starts by invoking `get_sigframe( )` to compute the first memory location of the frame. That memory location is usually* in the User Mode stack, so the function returns the value:

```
(regs->esp - sizeof(struct sigframe)) & 0xfffffff8
```

Since stacks grow toward lower addresses, the initial address of the frame is obtained by subtracting its size from the address of the current stack top and aligning the result to a multiple of 8.

---

* Linux allows processes to specify an alternate stack for their signal handlers by invoking the `sigaltstack( )` system call; this feature is also requested by the X/Open standard. When an alternate stack is present, the `get_sigframe( )` function returns an address inside that stack. We don't discuss this feature further, since it is conceptually similar to regular signal handling.

The returned address is then verified by means of the access_ok macro; if it is valid, the function repeatedly invokes __put_user( ) to fill all the fields of the frame. Once this is done, it modifies the regs area of the Kernel Mode stack, thus ensuring that control is transferred to the signal handler when current resumes its execution in User Mode:

```
regs->esp = (unsigned long) frame;
regs->eip = (unsigned long) ka->sa.sa_handler;
```

The setup_frame( ) function terminates by resetting the segmentation registers saved on the Kernel Mode stack to their default value. Now the information needed by the signal handler is on the top of the User Mode stack.

The setup_rt_frame( ) function is very similar to setup_frame( ), but it puts on the User Mode stack an *extended frame* (stored in the rt_sigframe data structure) that also includes the content of the siginfo_t table associated with the signal.

Evaluating the signal flags

After setting up the User Mode stack, the handle_signal( ) function checks the values of the flags associated with the signal.

If the received signal has the SA_ONESHOT flag set, it must be reset to its default action so that further occurrences of the same signal will not trigger the execution of the signal handler:

```
if (ka->sa.sa_flags & SA_ONESHOT)
    ka->sa.sa_handler = SIG_DFL;
```

Moreover, if the signal does not have the SA_NODEFER flag set, the signals in the sa_mask field of the sigaction table must be blocked during the execution of the signal handler:

```
if (!(ka->sa.sa_flags & SA_NODEFER)) {
    spin_lock_irq(&current->sigmask_lock);
    sigorsets(&current->blocked, &current->blocked, &ka->sa.sa_mask);
    sigaddset(&current->blocked, sig);
    recalc_sigpending(current);
    spin_unlock_irq(&current->sigmask_lock);
}
```

As described earlier, the recalc_sigpending( ) function checks whether the process has nonblocked pending signals and sets its sigpending field accordingly.

The function returns then to do_signal( ), which also returns immediately.

Starting the signal handler

When do_signal( ) returns, the current process resumes its execution in User Mode. Because of the preparation by setup_frame( ) described earlier, the eip register points to the first instruction of the signal handler, while esp points to the first memory location of the frame that has been pushed on top of the User Mode stack. As a result, the signal handler is executed.

Terminating the signal handler

When the signal handler terminates, the return address on top of the stack points to the code in the retcode field of the frame. For signals without siginfo_t table, the code is equivalent to the following assembly language instructions:

```
popl %eax
movl $__NR_sigreturn, %eax
int $0x80
```

Therefore, the signal number (that is, the sig field of the frame) is discarded from the stack, and the sigreturn( ) system call is then invoked.

The sys_sigreturn( ) function computes the address of the pt_regs data structure regs, which contains the hardware context of the User Mode process (see the section "Parameter Passing" in Chapter 9). From the value stored in the esp field, it can thus derive and check the frame address inside the User Mode stack:

```
frame = (struct sigframe *)(regs.esp - 8);
if (verify_area(VERIFY_READ, frame, sizeof(*frame)) {
    force_sig(SIGSEGV, current);
    return 0;
}
```

Then the function copies the bit array of signals that were blocked before invoking the signal handler from the sc field of the frame to the blocked field of current. As a result, all signals that have been masked for the execution of the signal handler are unblocked. The recalc_sigpending( ) function is then invoked.

The sys_sigreturn( ) function must at this point copy the process hardware context from the sc field of the frame to the Kernel Mode stack and remove the frame from the User Mode stack; it performs these two tasks by invoking the restore_sigcontext( ) function.

If the signal was sent by a system call like rt_sigqueueinfo( ) that required a siginfo_t table to be associated to the signal, the mechanism is very similar. The return code in the retcode field of the extended frame invokes the rt_sigreturn( ) system call; the corresponding sys_rt_sigreturn( ) service routine copies the process hardware context from the extended frame to the Kernel Mode stack and restores the original User Mode stack content by removing the extended frame from it.

Reexecution of System Calls

The request associated with a system call cannot always be immediately satisfied by the kernel; when this happens, the process that issued the system call is put in a TASK_INTERRUPTIBLE or TASK_UNINTERRUPTIBLE state.

If the process is put in a TASK_INTERRUPTIBLE state and some other process sends a signal to it, the kernel puts it in the TASK_RUNNING state without completing the system call (see the section "Returning from Interrupts and Exceptions" in Chapter 4).

When this happens, the system call service routine does not complete its job, but returns an EINTR, ERESTARTNOHAND, ERESTARTSYS, or ERESTARTNOINTR error code. The signal is delivered to the process while switching back to User Mode.

In practice, the only error code a User Mode process can get in this situation is EINTR, which means that the system call has not been completed. (The application programmer may check this code and decide whether to reissue the system call.) The remaining error codes are used internally by the kernel to specify whether the system call may be reexecuted automatically after the signal handler termination.

Table 10-6 lists the error codes related to unfinished system calls and their impact for each of the three possible signal actions. The terms that appear in the entries are defined in the following list:

Terminate
> The system call will not be automatically reexecuted; the process will resume its execution in User Mode at the instruction following the int $0x80 one and the eax register will contain the -EINTR value.

Reexecute
> The kernel forces the User Mode process to reload the eax register with the system call number and to reexecute the int $0x80 instruction; the process is not aware of the reexecution and the error code is not passed to it.

Depends
> The system call is reexecuted only if the SA_RESTART flag of the delivered signal is set; otherwise, the system call terminates with a -EINTR error code.

Table 10-6. Reexecution of system calls

Signal Action	Error codes and their impact on system call execution			
	EINTR	ERESTARTSYS	ERESTARTNOHAND	ERESTARTNOINTR
Default	Terminate	Reexecute	Reexecute	Reexecute
Ignore	Terminate	Reexecute	Reexecute	Reexecute
Catch	Terminate	Depends	Terminate	Reexecute

When delivering a signal, the kernel must be sure that the process really issued a system call before attempting to reexecute it. This is where the orig_eax field of the regs hardware context plays a critical role. Let's recall how this field is initialized when the interrupt or exception handler starts:

Interrupt
> The field contains the IRQ number associated with the interrupt minus 256 (see the section "Saving the registers for the interrupt handler" in Chapter 4).

0x80 exception
> The field contains the system call number (see the section "The system_call( ) Function" in Chapter 9).

Other exceptions

The field contains the value −1 (see the section "Saving the Registers for the Exception Handler" in Chapter 4).

Therefore, a non-negative value in the orig_eax field means that the signal has woken up a TASK_INTERRUPTIBLE process that was sleeping in a system call. The service routine recognizes that the system call was interrupted, and thus returns one of the previously mentioned error codes.

If the signal is explicitly ignored or if its default action is enforced, do_signal( ) analyzes the error code of the system call to decide whether the unfinished system call must be automatically reexecuted, as specified in Table 10-6. If the call must be restarted, the function modifies the regs hardware context so that, when the process is back in User Mode, eip points to the int $0x80 instruction and eax contains the system call number:

```
if (regs->orig_eax >= 0) {
    if (regs->eax == -ERESTARTNOHAND || regs->eax == -ERESTARTSYS ||
        regs->eax == -ERESTARTNOINTR) {
        regs->eax = regs->orig_eax;
        regs->eip -= 2;
    }
}
```

The regs->eax field is filled with the return code of a system call service routine (see the section "The system_call( ) Function" in Chapter 9).

If the signal is caught, handle_signal( ) analyzes the error code and, possibly, the SA_RESTART flag of the sigaction table to decide whether the unfinished system call must be reexecuted:

```
if (regs->orig_eax >= 0) {
    switch (regs->eax) {
        case -ERESTARTNOHAND:
            regs->eax = -EINTR;
            break;
        case -ERESTARTSYS:
            if (!(ka->sa.sa_flags & SA_RESTART)) {
                regs->eax = -EINTR;
                break;
            }
            /* fallthrough */
        case -ERESTARTNOINTR:
            regs->eax = regs->orig_eax;
            regs->eip -= 2;
    }
}
```

If the system call must be restarted, handle_signal( ) proceeds exactly as do_signal( ); otherwise, it returns an −EINTR error code to the User Mode process.

System Calls Related to Signal Handling

As stated in the introduction of this chapter, programs running in User Mode are allowed to send and receive signals. This means that a set of system calls must be defined to allow these kinds of operations. Unfortunately, for historical reasons, several system calls exist that serve essentially the same purpose. As a result, some of these system calls are never invoked. For instance, sys_sigaction() and sys_rt_sigaction() are almost identical, so the sigaction() wrapper function included in the C library ends up invoking sys_rt_sigaction() instead of sys_sigaction(). We shall describe some of the most significant POSIX system calls.

The kill( ) System Call

The kill(pid,sig) system call is commonly used to send signals; its corresponding service routine is the sys_kill() function. The integer pid parameter has several meanings, depending on its numerical value:

pid > 0
> The sig signal is sent to the process whose PID is equal to pid.

pid = 0
> The sig signal is sent to all processes in the same group as the calling process.

pid = −1
> The signal is sent to all processes, except *swapper* (PID 0), *init* (PID 1), and current.

pid < −1
> The signal is sent to all processes in the process group −*pid*.

The sys_kill() function sets up a minimal siginfo_t table for the signal, and then invokes kill_something_info():

```
info.si_signo = sig;
info.si_errno = 0;
info.si_code = SI_USER;
info._sifields._kill._pid = current->pid;
info._sifields._kill._uid = current->uid;
return kill_something_info(sig, &info, pid);
```

The kill_something_info() function, in turn, invokes either send_sig_info() (to send the signal to a single process), or kill_pg_info() (to scan all processes and invoke send_sig_info() for each process in the destination group).

The kill() system call is able to send any signal, even the so-called real-time signals that have numbers ranging from 32 to 63. However, as we saw in the earlier section "Generating a Signal," the kill() system call does not ensure that a new element is added to the pending signal queue of the destination process, thus multiple instances of pending signals can be lost. Real-time signals should be sent by means of a system call like rt_sigqueueinfo() (see the later section "System Calls for Real-Time Signals").

System V and BSD Unix variants also have a killpg( ) system call, which is able to explicitly send a signal to a group of processes. In Linux, the function is implemented as a library function that uses the kill( ) system call. Another variation is raise(), which sends a signal to the current process (that is, to the process executing the function). In Linux, raise() is implemented as a library function.

Changing a Signal Action

The sigaction(sig,act,oact) system call allows users to specify an action for a signal; of course, if no signal action is defined, the kernel executes the default action associated with the delivered signal.

The corresponding sys_sigaction( ) service routine acts on two parameters: the sig signal number and the act table of type sigaction that specifies the new action. A third oact optional output parameter may be used to get the previous action associated with the signal.

The function checks first whether the act address is valid. Then it fills the sa_handler, sa_flags, and sa_mask fields of a new_ka local variable of type k_sigaction with the corresponding fields of *act:

```
__get_user(new_ka.sa.sa_handler, &act->sa_handler);
__get_user(new_ka.sa.sa_flags, &act->sa_flags);
__get_user(mask, &act->sa_mask);
siginitset(&new_ka.sa.sa_mask, mask);
```

The function invokes do_sigaction( ) to copy the new new_ka table into the entry at the sig-1 position of current->sig->action (the number of the signal is one higher than the position in the array because there is no zero signal):

```
k = &current->sig->action[sig-1];
spin_lock(&current->sig->siglock);
if (act) {
    *k = *act;
    sigdelsetmask(&k->sa.sa_mask, sigmask(SIGKILL) | sigmask(SIGSTOP));
    if (k->sa.sa_handler == SIG_IGN || (k->sa.sa_handler == SIG_DFL &&
            (sig == SIGCONT || sig == SIGCHLD || sig == SIGWINCH))) {
        spin_lock_irq(&current->sigmask_lock);
        if (rm_sig_from_queue(sig, current))
            recalc_sigpending(current);
        spin_unlock_irq(&current->sigmask_lock);
    }
}
```

The POSIX standard requires that setting a signal action to either SIG_IGN or SIG_DFL when the default action is "ignore," causes any pending signal of the same type to be discarded. Moreover, notice that no matter what the requested masked signals are for the signal handler, SIGKILL and SIGSTOP are never masked.

If the oact parameter is not NULL, the contents of the previous sigaction table are copied to the process address space at the address specified by that parameter:

```
if (oact) {
    __put_user(old_ka.sa.sa_handler, &oact->sa_handler);
    __put_user(old_ka.sa.sa_flags, &oact->sa_flags);
    __put_user(old_ka.sa.sa_mask.sig[0], &oact->sa_mask);
}
```

Notice that the sigaction( ) system call also allows initialization of the sa_flags field in the sigaction table. We listed the values allowed for this field and the related meanings in Table 10-4 (earlier in this chapter).

Older System V Unix variants offered the signal( ) system call, which is still widely used by programmers. Recent C libraries implement signal( ) by means of sigaction( ). However, Linux still supports older C libraries and offers the sys_signal( ) service routine:

```
new_sa.sa.sa_handler = handler;
new_sa.sa.sa_flags = SA_ONESHOT | SA_NOMASK;
ret = do_sigaction(sig, &new_sa, &old_sa);
return ret ? ret : (unsigned long)old_sa.sa.sa_handler;
```

Examining the Pending Blocked Signals

The sigpending( ) system call allows a process to examine the set of pending blocked signals—i.e., those that have been raised while blocked. The corresponding sys_sigpending( ) service routine acts on a single parameter, set, namely, the address of a user variable where the array of bits must be copied:

```
spin_lock_irq(&current->sigmask_lock);
sigandsets(&pending, &current->blocked, &current->pending.signal);
spin_unlock_irq(&current->sigmask_lock);
copy_to_user(set, &pending, sizeof(sigset_t));
```

Modifying the Set of Blocked Signals

The sigprocmask( ) system call allows processes to modify the set of blocked signals; it applies only to regular (non-real-time) signals. The corresponding sys_sigprocmask( ) service routine acts on three parameters:

oset
: Pointer in the process address space to a bit array where the previous bit mask must be stored

set
: Pointer in the process address space to the bit array containing the new bit mask

how
: Flag that may have one of the following values:

SIG_BLOCK
: The *set bit mask array specifies the signals that must be added to the bit mask array of blocked signals.

SIG_UNBLOCK

> The *set bit mask array specifies the signals that must be removed from the bit mask array of blocked signals.

SIG_SETMASK

> The *set bit mask array specifies the new bit mask array of blocked signals.

The function invokes copy_from_user( ) to copy the value pointed to by the set parameter into the new_set local variable and copies the bit mask array of standard blocked signals of current into the old_set local variable. It then acts as the how flag specifies on these two variables:

```
if (copy_from_user(&new_set, set, sizeof(*set)))
    return -EFAULT;
new_set &= ~(sigmask(SIGKILL)|sigmask(SIGSTOP));
spin_lock_irq(&current->sigmask_lock);
old_set = current->blocked.sig[0];
if (how == SIG_BLOCK)
    sigaddsetmask(&current->blocked, new_set);
else if (how == SIG_UNBLOCK)
    sigdelsetmask(&current->blocked, new_set);
else if (how == SIG_SETMASK)
    current->blocked.sig[0] = new_set;
else
    return -EINVAL;
recalc_sigpending(current);
spin_unlock_irq(&current->sigmask_lock);
if (oset) {
    if (copy_to_user(oset, &old_set, sizeof(*oset)))
        return -EFAULT;
}
return 0;
```

Suspending the Process

The sigsuspend( ) system call puts the process in the TASK_INTERRUPTIBLE state, after having blocked the standard signals specified by a bit mask array to which the mask parameter points. The process will wake up only when a nonignored, nonblocked signal is sent to it.

The corresponding sys_sigsuspend( ) service routine executes these statements:

```
mask &= ~(sigmask(SIGKILL) | sigmask(SIGSTOP));
spin_lock_irq(&current->sigmask_lock);
saveset = current->blocked;
siginitset(&current->blocked, mask);
recalc_sigpending(current);
spin_unlock_irq(&current->sigmask_lock);
regs->eax = -EINTR;
while (1) {
    current->state = TASK_INTERRUPTIBLE;
    schedule( );
```

```
        if (do signal(regs, &saveset))
            return -EINTR;
}
```

The schedule( ) function selects another process to run. When the process that issued the sigsuspend( ) system call is executed again, sys_sigsuspend( ) invokes the do_signal( ) function to deliver the signal that has woken up the process. If that function returns the value 1, the signal is not ignored. Therefore the system call terminates by returning the error code -EINTR.

The sigsuspend( ) system call may appear redundant, since the combined execution of sigprocmask( ) and sleep( ) apparently yields the same result. But this is not true: because of interleaving of process executions, one must be conscious that invoking a system call to perform action A followed by another system call to perform action B is not equivalent to invoking a single system call that performs action A and then action B.

In the particular case, sigprocmask( ) might unblock a signal that is delivered before invoking sleep( ). If this happens, the process might remain in a TASK_INTERRUPTIBLE state forever, waiting for the signal that was already delivered. On the other hand, the sigsuspend( ) system call does not allow signals to be sent after unblocking and before the schedule( ) invocation because other processes cannot grab the CPU during that time interval.

System Calls for Real-Time Signals

Since the system calls previously examined apply only to standard signals, additional system calls must be introduced to allow User Mode processes to handle real time signals.

Several system calls for real-time signals (rt_sigaction( ), rt_sigpending( ), rt_sigprocmask( ), and rt_sigsuspend( )) are similar to those described earlier and won't be discussed further. For the same reason, we won't discuss two other system calls that deal with queues of real-time signals:

rt_sigqueueinfo( )
    Sends a real-time signal so that it is added to the pending signal queue of the destination process

rt_sigtimedwait( )
    Dequeues a blocked pending signal without delivering it and returns the signal number to the caller; if no blocked signal is pending, suspends the current process for a fixed amount of time.

CHAPTER 11
Process Scheduling

Like any time-sharing system, Linux achieves the magical effect of an apparent simultaneous execution of multiple processes by switching from one process to another in a very short time frame. Process switching itself was discussed in Chapter 3; this chapter deals with *scheduling*, which is concerned with when to switch and which process to choose.

The chapter consists of three parts. The section "Scheduling Policy" introduces the choices made by Linux to schedule processes in the abstract. The section "The Scheduling Algorithm" discusses the data structures used to implement scheduling and the corresponding algorithm. Finally, the section "System Calls Related to Scheduling" describes the system calls that affect process scheduling.

Scheduling Policy

The scheduling algorithm of traditional Unix operating systems must fulfill several conflicting objectives: fast process response time, good throughput for background jobs, avoidance of process starvation, reconciliation of the needs of low- and high-priority processes, and so on. The set of rules used to determine when and how to select a new process to run is called *scheduling policy*.

Linux scheduling is based on the *time-sharing* technique already introduced in the section "CPU's Time Sharing" in Chapter 6: several processes run in "time multiplexing" because the CPU time is divided into "slices," one for each runnable process.* Of course, a single processor can run only one process at any given instant. If a currently running process is not terminated when its time slice or *quantum* expires, a process switch may take place. Time-sharing relies on timer interrupts and is thus transparent to processes. No additional code needs to be inserted in the programs to ensure CPU time-sharing.

---

* Recall that stopped and suspended processes cannot be selected by the scheduling algorithm to run on the CPU.

The scheduling policy is also based on ranking processes according to their priority. Complicated algorithms are sometimes used to derive the current priority of a process, but the end result is the same: each process is associated with a value that denotes how appropriate it is to be assigned to the CPU.

In Linux, process priority is dynamic. The scheduler keeps track of what processes are doing and adjusts their priorities periodically; in this way, processes that have been denied the use of the CPU for a long time interval are boosted by dynamically increasing their priority. Correspondingly, processes running for a long time are penalized by decreasing their priority.

When speaking about scheduling, processes are traditionally classified as "I/O-bound" or "CPU-bound." The former make heavy use of I/O devices and spend much time waiting for I/O operations to complete; the latter are number-crunching applications that require a lot of CPU time.

An alternative classification distinguishes three classes of processes:

Interactive processes

These interact constantly with their users, and therefore spend a lot of time waiting for keypresses and mouse operations. When input is received, the process must be woken up quickly, or the user will find the system to be unresponsive. Typically, the average delay must fall between 50 and 150 milliseconds. The variance of such delay must also be bounded, or the user will find the system to be erratic. Typical interactive programs are command shells, text editors, and graphical applications.

Batch processes

These do not need user interaction, and hence they often run in the background. Since such processes do not need to be very responsive, they are often penalized by the scheduler. Typical batch programs are programming language compilers, database search engines, and scientific computations.

Real-time processes

These have very stringent scheduling requirements. Such processes should never be blocked by lower-priority processes and should have a short guaranteed response time with a minimum variance. Typical real-time programs are video and sound applications, robot controllers, and programs that collect data from physical sensors.

The two classifications we just offered are somewhat independent. For instance, a batch process can be either I/O-bound (e.g., a database server) or CPU-bound (e.g., an image-rendering program). While real-time programs are explicitly recognized as such by the scheduling algorithm in Linux, there is no way to distinguish between interactive and batch programs. To offer a good response time to interactive applications, Linux (like all Unix kernels) implicitly favors I/O-bound processes over CPU-bound ones.

Programmers may change the scheduling priorities by means of the system calls illustrated in Table 11-1. More details are given in the section "System Calls Related to Scheduling."

Table 11-1. System calls related to scheduling

System call	Description
nice( )	Change the priority of a conventional process.
getpriority( )	Get the maximum priority of a group of conventional processes.
setpriority( )	Set the priority of a group of conventional processes.
sched_getscheduler( )	Get the scheduling policy of a process.
sched_setscheduler( )	Set the scheduling policy and priority of a process.
sched_getparam( )	Get the priority of a process.
sched_setparam( )	Set the priority of a process.
sched_yield( )	Relinquish the processor voluntarily without blocking.
sched_get_priority_min( )	Get the minimum priority value for a policy.
sched_get_priority_max( )	Get the maximum priority value for a policy.
sched_rr_get_interval( )	Get the time quantum value for the Round Robin policy.

Most system calls shown in the table apply to real-time processes, thus allowing users to develop real-time applications. However, Linux does not support the most demanding real-time applications because its kernel is nonpreemptive (see the later section "Performance of the Scheduling Algorithm").

Process Preemption

As mentioned in the first chapter, Linux processes are *preemptive*. If a process enters the TASK_RUNNING state, the kernel checks whether its dynamic priority is greater than the priority of the currently running process. If it is, the execution of current is interrupted and the scheduler is invoked to select another process to run (usually the process that just became runnable). Of course, a process may also be preempted when its time quantum expires. As mentioned in the section "CPU's Time Sharing" in Chapter 6, when this occurs, the need_resched field of the current process is set, so the scheduler is invoked when the timer interrupt handler terminates.

For instance, let's consider a scenario in which only two programs—a text editor and a compiler—are being executed. The text editor is an interactive program, so it has a higher dynamic priority than the compiler. Nevertheless, it is often suspended, since the user alternates between pauses for think time and data entry; moreover, the average delay between two keypresses is relatively long. However, as soon as the user presses a key, an interrupt is raised and the kernel wakes up the text editor process. The kernel also determines that the dynamic priority of the editor is higher than the priority of current, the currently running process (the compiler), so it sets the need_ resched field of this process, thus forcing the scheduler to be activated when the kernel finishes handling the interrupt. The scheduler selects the editor and performs a process switch; as a result, the execution of the editor is resumed very quickly and the character typed by the user is echoed to the screen. When the character has been processed, the text editor process suspends itself waiting for another keypress and the compiler process can resume its execution.

Be aware that a preempted process is not suspended, since it remains in the TASK_RUNNING state; it simply no longer uses the CPU.

Some real-time operating systems feature preemptive kernels, which means that a process running in Kernel Mode can be interrupted after any instruction, just as it can in User Mode. The Linux kernel is not preemptive, which means that a process can be preempted only while running in User Mode; nonpreemptive kernel design is much simpler, since most synchronization problems involving the kernel data structures are easily avoided (see the section "When Synchronization Is Not Necessary" in Chapter 5).

How Long Must a Quantum Last?

The quantum duration is critical for system performances: it should be neither too long nor too short.

If the quantum duration is too short, the system overhead caused by process switches becomes excessively high. For instance, suppose that a process switch requires 10 milliseconds; if the quantum is also set to 10 milliseconds, then at least 50 percent of the CPU cycles will be dedicated to process switching.*

If the quantum duration is too long, processes no longer appear to be executed concurrently. For instance, let's suppose that the quantum is set to five seconds; each runnable process makes progress for about five seconds, but then it stops for a very long time (typically, five seconds times the number of runnable processes).

It is often believed that a long quantum duration degrades the response time of interactive applications. This is usually false. As described in the section "Process Preemption" earlier in this chapter, interactive processes have a relatively high priority, so they quickly preempt the batch processes, no matter how long the quantum duration is.

In some cases, a quantum duration that is too long degrades the responsiveness of the system. For instance, suppose two users concurrently enter two commands at the respective shell prompts; one command is CPU-bound, while the other is an interactive application. Both shells fork a new process and delegate the execution of the

---

* Actually, things could be much worse than this; for example, if the time required for the process switch is counted in the process quantum, all CPU time is devoted to the process switch and no process can progress toward its termination.

user's command to it; moreover, suppose such new processes have the same priority initially (Linux does not know in advance if an executed program is batch or interactive). Now if the scheduler selects the CPU-bound process to run, the other process could wait for a whole time quantum before starting its execution. Therefore, if such duration is long, the system could appear to be unresponsive to the user that launched it.

The choice of quantum duration is always a compromise. The rule of thumb adopted by Linux is choose a duration as long as possible, while keeping good system response time.

The Scheduling Algorithm

The Linux scheduling algorithm works by dividing the CPU time into *epochs*. In a single epoch, every process has a specified time quantum whose duration is computed when the epoch begins. In general, different processes have different time quantum durations. The time quantum value is the maximum CPU time portion assigned to the process in that epoch. When a process has exhausted its time quantum, it is preempted and replaced by another runnable process. Of course, a process can be selected several times from the scheduler in the same epoch, as long as its quantum has not been exhausted—for instance, if it suspends itself to wait for I/O, it preserves some of its time quantum and can be selected again during the same epoch. The epoch ends when all runnable processes have exhausted their quanta; in this case, the scheduler algorithm recomputes the time-quantum durations of all processes and a new epoch begins.

Each process has a *base time quantum*, which is the time-quantum value assigned by the scheduler to the process if it has exhausted its quantum in the previous epoch. The users can change the base time quantum of their processes by using the nice( ) and setpriority( ) system calls (see the section "System Calls Related to Scheduling" later in this chapter). A new process always inherits the base time quantum of its parent.

The INIT_TASK macro sets the value of the initial time quantum of process 0 (*swapper*) to DEF_COUNTER; that macro is defined as follows:

```
#define DEF_COUNTER (10 * HZ / 100)
```

Since HZ (which denotes the frequency of timer interrupts) is set to 100 for IBM compatible PCs (see the section "Programmable Interval Timer" in Chapter 6), the value of DEF_COUNTER is 10 ticks—that is, about 105 ms.

To select a process to run, the Linux scheduler must consider the priority of each process. Actually, there are two kinds of priorities:

Static priority

This is assigned by the users to real-time processes and ranges from 1 to 99. It is never changed by the scheduler.

Dynamic priority

This applies only to conventional processes; it is essentially the sum of the base time quantum (which is therefore also called the *base priority* of the process) and of the number of ticks of CPU time left to the process before its quantum expires in the current epoch.

Of course, the static priority of a real-time process is always higher than the dynamic priority of a conventional one. The scheduler starts running conventional processes only when there is no real-time process in a TASK_RUNNING state.

There is always at least one runnable process: the *swapper* kernel thread, which has PID 0 and executes only when the CPU cannot execute other processes. As mentioned in Chapter 3, every CPU of a multiprocessor system has its own kernel thread with PID equal to 0.

Data Structures Used by the Scheduler

Recall from the section "Process Descriptor" in Chapter 3 that the process list links all process descriptors, while the runqueue list links the process descriptors of all runnable processes—that is, of those in a TASK_RUNNING state. In both cases, the init_ task process descriptor plays the role of list header.

Process descriptor

Each process descriptor includes several fields related to scheduling:

need_resched

A flag checked by ret_from_sys_call() to decide whether to invoke the schedule() function (see the section "The ret_from_sys_call() Function" in Chapter 4).*

policy

The scheduling class. The values permitted are:

SCHED_FIFO

A First-In, First-Out real-time process. When the scheduler assigns the CPU to the process, it leaves the process descriptor in its current position in the runqueue list. If no other higher-priority real-time process is runnable, the process continues to use the CPU as long as it wishes, even if other real-time processes that have the same priority are runnable.

---

* Beside the values 0 (false) and 1 (true), the need_resched field of a *swapper* kernel thread (PID 0) in a multi-processor system can also assume the value −1; see the later section "Scheduling on multiprocessor systems" for details.

SCHED_RR

A Round Robin real-time process. When the scheduler assigns the CPU to the process, it puts the process descriptor at the end of the runqueue list. This policy ensures a fair assignment of CPU time to all SCHED_RR real-time processes that have the same priority.

SCHED_OTHER

A conventional, time-shared process.

The policy field also encodes a SCHED_YIELD binary flag. This flag is set when the process invokes the sched_yield( ) system call (a way of voluntarily relinquishing the processor without the need to start an I/O operation or go to sleep; see the later section "System Calls Related to Scheduling"). The kernel also sets the SCHED_YIELD flag and invokes the schedule( ) function whenever it is executing a long noncritical task and wishes to give other processes a chance to run.

rt_priority

The static priority of a real-time process; valid priorities range between 1 and 99. The static priority of a conventional process must be set to 0.

counter

The number of ticks of CPU time left to the process before its quantum expires; when a new epoch begins, this field contains the time-quantum duration of the process. Recall that the update_process_times( ) function decrements the counter field of the current process by 1 at every tick.

nice

Determines the length of the process time quantum when a new epoch begins. This field contains values ranging between −20 and +19; negative values correspond to "high priority" processes, positive ones to "low priority" processes. The default value 0 corresponds to normal processes.

cpus_allowed

A bit mask specifying the CPUs on which the process is allowed to run. In the 80 ×86 architecture, the maximum number of processor is set to 32, so the whole mask can be encoded in a single integer field.

cpus_runnable

A bit mask specifying the CPU that is executing the process, if any. If the process is not executed by any CPU, all bits of the field are set to 1. Otherwise, all bits of the field are set to 0, except the bit associated with the executing CPU, which is set to 1. This encoding allows the kernel to verify whether the process can be scheduled on a given CPU by simply computing the logical AND between this field, the cpus_allowed field, and the bit mask specifying the CPU.

processor

The index of the CPU that is executing the process, if any; otherwise, the index of the last CPU that executed the process.

When a new process is created, do_fork() sets the counter field of both current (the parent) and p (the child) processes in the following way:

```
p->counter = (current->counter + 1) >> 1;
current->counter >>= 1;
if (!current->counter)
    current->need_resched = 1;
```

In other words, the number of ticks left to the parent is split in two halves: one for the parent and one for the child. This is done to prevent users from getting an unlimited amount of CPU time by using the following method: the parent process creates a child process that runs the same code and then kills itself; by properly adjusting the creation rate, the child process would always get a fresh quantum before the quantum of its parent expires. This programming trick does not work since the kernel does not reward forks. Similarly, a user cannot hog an unfair share of the processor by starting lots of background processes in a shell or by opening a lot of windows on a graphical desktop. More generally speaking, a process cannot hog resources (unless it has privileges to give itself a real-time policy) by forking multiple descendents.

CPU's data structures

Besides the fields included in each process descriptor, additional information is needed to describe what each CPU is doing. To that end, the scheduler can rely on the aligned_data array of NR_CPUS structures of type schedule_data. Each such structure consists of two fields:

curr

A pointer to the process descriptor of the process running on that CPU. The field is usually accessed by means of the cpu_curr(n) macro, where n is the CPU logical number.

last_schedule

The value of the 64-bit Time Stamp Counter when the last process switch was performed on the CPU. The field is usually accessed by means of the last_schedule(n) macro, where n is the CPU logical number.

Most of the time, any CPU accesses only its own array element; it is thus convenient to align the entries of the aligned_data array so that every element falls in a different cache line. In this way, the CPUs have a better chance to find their own element in the hardware cache.

The schedule( ) Function

The schedule() function implements the scheduler. Its objective is to find a process in the runqueue list and then assign the CPU to it. It is invoked, directly or in a lazy (deferred) way, by several kernel routines.

Direct invocation

The scheduler is invoked directly when the current process must be blocked right away because the resource it needs is not available. In this case, the kernel routine that wants to block it proceeds as follows:

1. Inserts current in the proper wait queue
2. Changes the state of current either to TASK_INTERRUPTIBLE or to TASK_UNINTERRUPTIBLE
3. Invokes schedule( )
4. Checks whether the resource is available; if not, goes to Step 2
5. Once the resource is available, removes current from the wait queue

As can be seen, the kernel routine checks repeatedly whether the resource needed by the process is available; if not, it yields the CPU to some other process by invoking schedule( ). Later, when the scheduler once again grants the CPU to the process, the availability of the resource is rechecked. These steps are similar to those performed by the sleep_on( ) and interruptible_sleep_on( ) functions described in the section "How Processes Are Organized" in Chapter 3.

The scheduler is also directly invoked by many device drivers that execute long iterative tasks. At each iteration cycle, the driver checks the value of the need_resched field and, if necessary, invokes schedule( ) to voluntarily relinquish the CPU.

Lazy invocation

The scheduler can also be invoked in a lazy way by setting the need_resched field of current to 1. Since a check on the value of this field is always made before resuming the execution of a User Mode process (see the section "Returning from Interrupts and Exceptions" in Chapter 4), schedule( ) will definitely be invoked at some time in the near future.

For instance, lazy invocation of the scheduler is performed in the following cases:

- When current has used up its quantum of CPU time; this is done by the update_process_times( ) function.
- When a process is woken up and its priority is higher than that of the current process; this task is performed by the reschedule_idle( ) function, which is usually invoked by the wake_up_process( ) function (see the section "Identifying a Process" in Chapter 3).
- When a sched_setscheduler( ) or sched_yield( ) system call is issued (see the section "System Calls Related to Scheduling" later in this chapter).

Actions performed by schedule( ) before a process switch

The goal of the schedule() function consists of replacing the currently executing process with another one. Thus, the key outcome of the function is to set a local variable called next so that it points to the descriptor of the process selected to replace current. If no runnable process in the system has priority greater than the priority of current, at the end, next coincides with current and no process switch takes place.

For efficiency reasons, the schedule() function starts by initializing a few local variables:

```
prev = current;
this_cpu = prev->processor;
sched_data = & aligned_data[this_cpu];
```

As you see, the pointer returned by current is saved in prev, the logical number of the executing CPU is saved in this_cpu, and the pointer to the aligned_data array element of the CPU is saved in sched_data.

Next, schedule() makes sure that prev doesn't hold the global kernel lock or the global interrupt lock (see the sections "The Global Kernel Lock" and "Global Interrupt Disabling" in Chapter 5), and then reenables the local interrupts:

```
if (prev->lock_depth >= 0)
    spin_unlock(&kernel_flag);
release_irqlock(this_cpu);
__sti();
```

Generally speaking, a process should never hold a lock across a process switch; otherwise, the system freezes as soon as another process tries to acquire the same lock. However, notice that schedule() doesn't change the value of the lock depth field; when prev resumes its execution, it reacquires the kernel_flag spin lock if the value of this field is not negative. Thus, the global kernel lock is automatically released and reacquired across a process switch. Conversely, the global interrupt lock is not automatically reacquired.

Before starting to look at the runnable processes, schedule() must disable the local interrupts and acquire the spin lock that protects the runqueue (see section "The list of TASK_RUNNING processes" in Chapter 3):

```
spin_lock_irq(&runqueue_lock);
```

A check is then made to determine whether prev is a Round Robin real-time process (policy field set to SCHED_RR) that has exhausted its quantum. If so, schedule() assigns a new quantum to prev and puts it at the bottom of the runqueue list:

```
if (prev->policy == SCHED_RR && !prev->counter) {
    prev->counter = (20 - prev->nice) / 4 + 1;
    move_last_runqueue(prev);
}
```

Recall that the nice field of a process ranges between −20 and +19; therefore, schedule() replenishes the counter field with a number of ticks ranging from 11 to 1.

The default value of the nice field is 0, so usually the process gets a new quantum of 6 ticks, roughly 60 ms.*

Next, schedule( ) examines the state of prev. If it has nonblocked pending signals and its state is TASK_INTERRUPTIBLE, the function sets the process state to TASK_RUNNING. This action is not the same as assigning the processor to prev; it just gives prev a chance to be selected for execution:

```
if (prev->state == TASK_INTERRUPTIBLE && signal_pending(prev))
    prev->state = TASK_RUNNING;
```

If prev is not in the TASK_RUNNING state, schedule( ) was directly invoked by the process itself because it had to wait on some external resource; therefore, prev must be removed from the runqueue list:

```
if (prev->state != TASK_RUNNING)
    del_from_runqueue(prev);
```

The function also resets the need_resched field of current, just in case the scheduler was activated in the lazy way:

```
prev->need_resched = 0;
```

Now the time has come for schedule( ) to select the process to be executed in the next time quantum. To that end, the function scans the runqueue list. The objective is to store in next the process descriptor pointer of the highest priority process:

```
repeat_schedule:
    next = init_tasks[this_cpu];
    c = -1000;
    list_for_each(tmp, &runqueue_head) {
        p = list_entry(tmp, struct task_struct, run_list);
        if (p->cpus_runnable & p->cpus_allowed & (1 << this_cpu)) {
            int weight = goodness(p, this_cpu, prev->active_mm);
            if (weight > c)
                c = weight, next = p;
        }
    }
```

The function initializes next so it points to the process referenced by init_task[this_cpu]—that is, to the process 0 (*swapper*) associated with the executing CPU; the c local variable is set to −1000. As we shall see in the later section "How good is a runnable process?", the goodness( ) function returns an integer that denotes the priority of the process passed as parameter.

While scanning processes in the runqueue, schedule( ) considers only those that are both:

---

* Recall that in the 80×86 architecture, 1 tick corresponds to roughly 10 ms (see the section "Programmable Interval Timer" in Chapter 6). In all architectures, however, the formula that computes the number of ticks in a quantum is adapted so the default quantum has an order of magnitude of 50 ms.

1. Runnable on the executing CPU (cpus_allowed & (1<<this_cpu)).

2. Not already running on some other CPU. (cpus_runnable & (1<<this_cpu); see the description of cpus_runnable in the previous section.)

The loop selects the first process in the runqueue that has the maximum weight. Thus, at the end of the search, next points to the best candidate, and the c local variable contains its priority. It is possible that the runqueue list is empty; in this case, the cycle is not executed, and next points to the *swapper* kernel thread associated with the executing CPU. It is also possible that the best candidate turns out to be the old current process prev.

A particular case occurs when the local variable c is set to 0 at the exit of the loop. This happens only when all processes in the runqueue list that are runnable by the executing CPU have exhausted their quantum—i.e., all of them have a zero counter field. A new epoch must then begin, and schedule( ) assigns to all existing processes (not only to the TASK_RUNNING ones) a fresh quantum, whose duration is half the counter value plus an increment that depends on the value of nice:

```
if (!c) {
    struct task_struct *p;
    spin_unlock_irq(&runqueue_lock);
    read_lock(&tasklist_lock);
    for_each_task(p)
        p->counter = (p->counter >> 1) + (20 - p->nice) / 4 + 1;
    read_unlock(&tasklist_lock);
    spin_lock_irq(&runqueue_lock);
    goto repeat_schedule;
}
```

In this way, suspended or stopped processes have their dynamic priorities periodically increased. As stated earlier, the rationale for increasing the counter value of suspended or stopped processes is to give preference to I/O-bound processes. However, no matter how often the quantum is increased, its value can never become greater than about 230 ms.[*]

Let's assume now that schedule( ) has selected its best candidate, and that next points to its process descriptor. The function updates the aligned_data array element of the executing CPU (this element is referenced by the sched_data local variable), writes the index of the executing CPU in next's process descriptor, releases the runqueue list spin lock, and reenables local interrupts:

```
sched_data->curr = next;
next->processor = this_cpu;
next->cpus_runnable = 1UL << this_cpu;
spin_unlock_irq(&runqueue_lock);
```

---

[*] For the mathematically inclined, here is a sketch of the proof: when a new epoch starts, the value of counter is bounded by half of the previous value of counter plus P, which is the maximum value that can be added to counter. If nice is set to −20, then P is equal to 11 ticks. Solving the recurrence equation yields as upper bound the geometric series $P \times (1 + 1/2 + 1/4 + 1/8 + \dots)$, which converges to $2 \times P$ (that is, 22 ticks).

Now schedule( ) is ready to proceed with the actual process switch. But wait a moment! If the next best candidate is the previously running process prev, schedule( ) can terminate:

```
if (prev == next) {
    prev->policy &= ~SCHED_YIELD;
    if (prev->lock_depth >= 0)
        spin_lock(&kernel_flag);
    return;
}
```

Notice that schedule( ) reacquires the global kernel lock if the lock_depth field of the process is not negative, as we anticipated when we described the first actions of the function.

If a process other than prev is selected, a process switch must take place. The current value of the Time Stamp Counter, fetched by means of the rdtsc assembly language instruction, is stored in the last_schedule field of the aligned_data array element of the executing CPU:

```
asm volatile("rdtsc" : "=A" (sched_data->last_schedule));
```

The context_swtch field of kstat is also increased by 1 to update the statistics maintained by the kernel:

```
kstat.context_swtch++;
```

It is also crucial to set up the address space of next properly. We know from Chapter 8 that the active_mm field of the process descriptor points to the memory descriptor that is effectively used by the process, while the mm field points to the memory descriptor owned by the process. For normal processes, the two fields hold the same address; however, a kernel thread does not have its own address space and its mm field is always set to NULL. The schedule( ) function ensures that if next is a kernel thread, then it uses the address space used by prev:

```
if (!next->mm) {
    next->active_mm = prev->active_mm;
    atomic_inc(&prev->active_mm->mm_count);
    cpu_tlbstate[this_cpu].state == TLBSTATE_LAZY;
}
```

In earlier versions of Linux, kernel threads had their own address space. That design choice was suboptimal when the scheduler selected a kernel thread as a new process to run because changing the Page Tables was useless; since any kernel thread runs in Kernel Mode, it uses only the fourth gigabyte of the linear address space, whose mapping is the same for all processes in the system. Even worse, writing into the cr3 register invalidates all TLB entries (see "Translation Lookaside Buffers (TLB)" in Chapter 2), which leads to a significant performance penalty. Linux 2.4 is much more efficient because Page Tables aren't touched at all if next is a kernel thread. As further optimization, if next is a kernel thread, the schedule( ) function sets the process into lazy TLB mode (see the section "Translation Lookaside Buffers (TLB)" in Chapter 2).

Conversely, if next is a regular process, the schedule() function replaces the address space of prev with the one of next:

```
if (next->mm)
    switch_mm(prev->active_mm, next->mm, next, this_cpu);
```

If prev is a kernel thread, the schedule() function releases the address space used by prev and resets prev->active_mm:

```
if (!prev->mm) {
    mmdrop(prev->active_mm);
    prev->active_mm = NULL;
}
```

Recall that mmdrop() decrements the usage counter of the memory descriptor; if the counter reaches 0, it also frees the descriptor together with the associated Page Tables and virtual memory regions.

Now schedule() can finally invoke switch_to() to perform the process switch between prev and next (see the section "Performing the Process Switch" in Chapter 3):

```
switch_to(prev, next, prev);
```

Actions performed by schedule() after a process switch

The instructions of the schedule() function following the switch_to macro invocation will not be performed right away by the next process, but at a later time by prev when the scheduler selects it again for execution. However, at that moment, the prev local variable does not point to our original process that was to be replaced when we started the description of schedule(), but rather to the process that was replaced by our original prev when it was scheduled again. (If you are confused, go back and read the section "Performing the Process Switch" in Chapter 3.)

The last instructions of the schedule() function are:

```
__schedule_tail(prev);
if (prev->lock_depth >= 0)
    spin_lock(&kernel_flag);
if (current->need_resched)
    goto need_resched_back;
return;
```

As you see, schedule() invokes __schedule_tail() (described next), reacquires the global kernel lock if necessary, and checks whether some other process has set the need_resched field of prev while it was not running. In this case, the whole schedule( ) function is reexecuted from the beginning; otherwise, the function terminates.

In uniprocessor systems, the __schedule_tail() function limits itself to clear the SCHED_YIELD flag of the policy field of prev. Conversely, in multiprocessor systems, the function executes code that is essentially equivalent to the following fragment:

```
policy = prev->policy;
prev->policy = policy & ~SCHED_YIELD;
```

```
    wmb();
    spin_lock(&prev->alloc_lock);
    prev->cpus_runnable = ~0UL;
    spin_lock_irqsave(&runqueue_lock, flags);
    if (prev->state == TASK_RUNNING && prev != init_task[smp_processor_id()]
            && prev->cpus_runnable == ~0UL && !(policy & SCHED_YIELD))
        reschedule_idle(prev);
    spin_unlock_irqrestore(&runqueue_lock, flags);
    spin_unlock(&prev->alloc_lock);
```

The wmb() memory barrier is used to make sure that the processor won't reshuffle the assembly language instructions that modify the policy field with those that acquire the alloc_lock spin lock (see the section "Memory Barriers" in Chapter 5).

As you may notice, the role of __schedule_tail() is far more important in multiprocessor systems because this function checks whether the process that was replaced can be rescheduled on some other CPU. This attempt is performed only if the following conditions are satisfied:

- prev is in TASK_RUNNING state.
- prev is not the *swapper* process of the executing CPU.
- The SCHED_YIELD flag of prev->policy was not set.
- prev was not already selected by another CPU in the time frame elapsed between the assignment to the cpus_runnable field and the if statement (the if statement itself is protected by the runqueue_lock spin lock; see the code shown in the previous section).

To check whether the priority of prev is high enough to replace the current process of some other CPU, __schedule_tail() invokes reschedule_idle(). This is the same function invoked by wake_up_process() and is described in the later section "Scheduling on multiprocessor systems."

The next two sections complete the analysis of the scheduler. They describe, respectively, the goodness() and reschedule_idle() functions.

How good is a runnable process?

The heart of the scheduling algorithm includes identifying the best candidate among all processes in the runqueue list. This is what the goodness() function does. It receives as input parameters:

- p, the descriptor pointer of candidate process
- this_cpu, the logical number of the executing CPU
- this_mm, the memory descriptor address of the process being replaced

The integer value weight returned by goodness() measures the "goodness" of p and has the following meanings:

weight = *−1*

> p is the prev process, and its SCHED_YIELD flag is set. The process will be selected only if no other runnable processes (beside the *swapper* processes) are included in the runqueue.

weight = *0*

> p is a conventional process that has exhausted its quantum (p->counter is zero). Unless all runnable processes have also exhausted their quantum, it will not be selected for execution.

2 <= weight <= *77*

> p is a conventional process that has not exhausted its quantum. The weight is computed as follows:

```
weight = p->counter + 20 - p->nice;
if (p->processor == this_cpu)
    weight += 15;
if (p->mm == this_mm || !p->mm)
    weight += 1;
```

> In multiprocessor systems, a large bonus (+15) is given to the process if it was last running on the CPU that is executing the scheduler. The bonus helps in reducing the number of transfers of processes across several CPUs during their executions, thus yielding a smaller number of hardware cache misses.

> The function also gives a small bonus (+1) to the process if it is a kernel thread or it shares the memory address space with the previously running process. Again, the process is favored mainly because the TLBs must not be invalidated by writing into the cr3 register.

weight >= *1000*

> p is a real-time process. The weight is given by p->counter + 1000.

Scheduling on multiprocessor systems

With respect to earlier versions, the Linux 2.4 scheduling algorithm has been improved to enhance its performance on multiprocessor systems. It was also simplified, which is a great improvement by itself.

As we have seen, each processor runs the schedule( ) function on its own to replace the process that is currently in execution. However, processors are able to exchange information to boost system performance. In particular, right after a process switch, any processor usually checks whether the just replaced process should be executed on some other CPU running a lower priority process. This check is performed by reschedule_idle( ).

The reschedule_idle( ) function looks for some other CPU to run the process p passed as parameter and uses interprocessor interrupts to force other CPUs to perform scheduling. The function performs a series of tests in a fixed order. If one of them is successful, the function sends a RESCHEDULE_VECTOR interprocessor interrupt to the selected CPU (see the section "Interprocessor Interrupt Handling" in Chapter 4) and returns. If all tests fail, the function returns without forcing a rescheduling. The tests are performed in the following order:

1. Is the CPU that was last running p (i.e., the one having index p->processor) currently idle?

```
best_cpu = p->processor;
if ((p->cpus_allowed & p->cpus_runnable & (1 << best_cpu))
        && cpu_curr(best_cpu) == init_tasks[best_cpu]) {
send_now_idle:
    need_resched= init_tasks[best_cpu]->need_resched;
    init_tasks[best_cpu]->need_resched = 1;
    if (best_cpu != smp_processor_id() && !need_resched)
        smp_send_reschedule(best_cpu);
}
```

This is the best possible case because no process is to be preempted and the hardware cache of the processor is warm (filled with useful data). Notice that this case cannot happen when reschedule_idle() is invoked by the scheduler because schedule() never replaces a runnable process with the *swapper* kernel thread. This case may happen, however, when reschedule_idle() is invoked by wake_up_process()—that is, when p has just been woken up.

To force the rescheduling on the target processor, the need_resched field of the *swapper* kernel thread is set. If the target processor is different from the one executing the reschedule_idle() function, a RESCHEDULE_VECTOR interprocessor interrupt is also raised. In fact, the idle processor usually executes a halt assembly language instruction to save power, and it can be woken up only by an interrupt. It is also possible, however, to let the swapper kernel thread actively poll the need_resched field, waiting for its value to change from −1 to +1, in order to speed up the rescheduling and avoid the interprocessor interrupt. This much more power-consuming algorithm can be activated by passing the *"idle=poll"* parameter to the kernel in the booting phase.

2. Does an idle processor exist that can execute p?

```
oldest_idle = -1;
for (cpu=0; cpu<smp_num_cpus; cpu++) {
    if (!(p->cpus_allowed & p->cpus_runnable & (1 << cpu)))
        continue;
    if (cpu_curr(cpu) == init_tasks[cpu] && last_schedule(cpu) < oldest_idle)
            oldest_idle = last_schedule(cpu), target_tsk = cpu_curr(cpu);
}
if (oldest_idle != -1) {
    best_cpu = target_tsk->processor;
    goto send_now_idle;
}
```

Among the idle processors that can execute p, the function selects the least recently active. Recall that the Time Stamp Counter value of the last process switch of every CPU is stored in the aligned_data array (see the earlier section

"Data Structures Used by the Scheduler"). Once the function finds the oldest idle CPU, the function jumps to the code already described in the previous case to force a rescheduling. The rationale behind the "oldest idle rule" is that this CPU is likely to have the greatest number of invalid hardware cache lines.

3. Does there exist a processor that can execute p and whose current process has lower dynamic priority than p?

```
max_prio = 0;
for (cpu=0; cpu<smp_num_cpus; cpu++) {
    if (!(p->cpus_allowed & p->cpus_runnable & (1 << cpu)))
        continue;
    prio = goodness(p, cpu, cpu_curr(cpu)->active_mm) -
            goodness(cpu_curr(cpu), cpu, cpu_curr(cpu)->active_mm);
    if (prio > max_prio)
        max_prio = prio, target_tsk = cpu_curr(cpu);
}
if (max_prio > 0) {
    target_tsk->need_resched = 1;
    if (target_tsk->processor != smp_processor_id())
        smp_send_reschedule(target_tsk->processor);
}
```

reschedule_idle() finds the processor for which the difference between the goodness of replacing the current process with p and the goodness of replacing the current process with the current process itself is maximum. The function forces a rescheduling on the corresponding processor if the maximum is a positive value. Notice that the function doesn't simply look at the counter and nice fields of the processes; rather, it uses goodness(), which takes into consideration the cost of replacing the currently running process with another process that potentially uses a different address space.

The Hyper-threading Technology

Very recently, Intel introduced the hyper-threading technology. Basically, a hyper-threaded CPU is a microprocessor that executes two threads of execution at once; it includes several copies of the internal registers and quickly switches between them. Thanks to this approach, the machine cycles spent when one thread is accessing the RAM can be exploited by the second thread. A hyper-threaded CPU is seen by the kernel as two different CPUs, so Linux does not have to be explicitly made aware of it. However, Linux breaks the "oldest idle rule" and forces an immediate rescheduling when it discovers that a hyper-threaded CPU is running two idle processes.

Performance of the Scheduling Algorithm

The scheduling algorithm of Linux is both self-contained and relatively easy to follow. For this reason, many kernel hackers love to try to make improvements.

However, the scheduler is a rather mysterious component of the kernel. While you can change its performance significantly by modifying just a few key parameters, there is usually no theoretical support to justify the results obtained. Furthermore, you can't be sure that the positive (or negative) results obtained will continue to hold when the mix of requests submitted by the users (real-time, interactive, I/O-bound, background, etc.) varies significantly. Actually, for almost every proposed scheduling strategy, it is possible to derive an artificial mix of requests that yields poor system performances.

Let's try to outline some pitfalls of the Linux 2.4 scheduler. As it turns out, some of these limitations become significant on large systems with many users. On a single workstation that is running a few tens of processes at a time, the Linux 2.4 scheduler is quite efficient.

The algorithm does not scale well

If the number of existing processes is very large, it is inefficient to recompute all dynamic priorities at once.

In old traditional Unix kernels, the dynamic priorities were recomputed every second, so the problem was even worse. Linux tries instead to minimize the overhead of the scheduler. Priorities are recomputed only when all runnable processes have exhausted their time quantum. Therefore, when the number of processes is large, the recomputation phase is more expensive but executed less frequently.

This simple approach has a disadvantage: when the number of runnable processes is very large, I/O-bound processes are seldom boosted, and therefore, interactive applications have a longer response time.

The predefined quantum is too large for high system loads

The system responsiveness experienced by users depends heavily on the *system load*, which is the average number of processes that are runnable and thus waiting for CPU time.*

As mentioned before, system responsiveness also depends on the average time-quantum duration of the runnable processes. In Linux, the predefined time quantum appears to be too large for high-end machines that have a very high expected system load.

I/O-bound process boosting strategy is not optimal

The preference for I/O-bound processes is a good strategy to ensure a short response time for interactive programs, but it is not perfect. Indeed, some batch programs

---

* The uptime program returns the system load for the past 1, 5, and 15 minutes. The same information can be obtained by reading the */proc/loadavg* file.

with almost no user interaction are I/O-bound. For instance, consider a database search engine that must typically read lots of data from the hard disk, or a network application that must collect data from a remote host on a slow link. Even if these kinds of processes do not need a short response time, they are boosted by the scheduling algorithm. On the other hand, interactive programs that are also CPU-bound may appear unresponsive to the users, since the increment of dynamic priority due to I/O blocking operations may not compensate for the decrement due to CPU usage.

Support for real-time applications is weak

As stated in the first chapter, nonpreemptive kernels are not well suited for real-time applications, since processes may spend several milliseconds in Kernel Mode while handling an interrupt or exception. During this time, a real-time process that becomes runnable cannot be resumed. This is unacceptable for real-time applications, which require predictable and low response times.*

Future versions of Linux might address this problem, by either implementing SVR4's "fixed preemption points" or making the kernel fully preemptive. It remains questionable, however, whether these design choices are appropriate for a general-purpose operating systems such as Linux.

Kernel preemption, in fact, is just one of several necessary conditions for implementing an effective real-time scheduler. Several other issues must be considered. For instance, real-time processes often must use resources that are also needed by conventional processes. A real-time process may thus end up waiting until a lower-priority process releases some resource. This phenomenon is called *priority inversion*. Moreover, a real-time process could require a kernel service that is granted on behalf of another lower-priority process (for example, a kernel thread). This phenomenon is called *hidden scheduling*. An effective real-time scheduler should address and resolve such problems.

Luckily, all these shortcomings have been fixed in the brand new scheduler developed by Ingo Molnar that is included in the Linux 2.5 current development version. This scheduler is so efficient that it has been back-ported to Linux 2.4 and adopted by some commercial distributions of the GNU/Linux system.

System Calls Related to Scheduling

Several system calls have been introduced to allow processes to change their priorities and scheduling policies. As a general rule, users are always allowed to lower the priorities of their processes. However, if they want to modify the priorities of processes belonging to some other user or if they want to increase the priorities of their own processes, they must have superuser privileges.

---

* The Linux kernel has been modified in several ways so it can handle a few hard real-time jobs if they remain short. Basically, hardware interrupts are trapped and kernel execution is monitored by a kind of "superkernel." These changes do not make Linux a true real-time system, though.

The nice( ) System Call

The nice( )* system call allows processes to change their base priority. The integer value contained in the increment parameter is used to modify the nice field of the process descriptor. The *nice* Unix command, which allows users to run programs with modified scheduling priority, is based on this system call.

The sys_nice( ) service routine handles the nice( ) system call. Although the increment parameter may have any value, absolute values larger than 40 are trimmed down to 40. Traditionally, negative values correspond to requests for priority increments and require superuser privileges, while positive ones correspond to requests for priority decrements. In the case of a negative increment, the function invokes the capable( ) function to verify whether the process has a CAP_SYS_NICE capability. We discuss that function, together with the notion of capability, in Chapter 20. If the user turns out to have the capability required to change priorities, sys_nice( ) adds the value of increment to the nice field of current. If necessary, the value of this field is trimmed down so it won't be less than −20 or greater than +19.

The nice( ) system call is maintained for backward compatibility only; it has been replaced by the setpriority( ) system call described next.

The getpriority( ) and setpriority( ) System Calls

The nice( ) system call affects only the process that invokes it. Two other system calls, denoted as getpriority( ) and setpriority( ), act on the base priorities of all processes in a given group. getpriority( ) returns 20 minus the lowest nice field value among all processes in a given group—that is, the highest priority among that processes; setpriority( ) sets the base priority of all processes in a given group to a given value.

The kernel implements these system calls by means of the sys_getpriority( ) and sys_setpriority( ) service routines. Both of them act essentially on the same group of parameters:

which

> The value that identifies the group of processes; it can assume one of the following:
>
> PRIO_PROCESS
>> Selects the processes according to their process ID (pid field of the process descriptor).

---

* Since this system call is usually invoked to lower the priority of a process, users who invoke it for their processes are "nice" to other users.

PRIO_PGRP

> Selects the processes according to their group ID (pgrp field of the process descriptor).

PRIO_USER

> Selects the processes according to their user ID (uid field of the process descriptor).

who

> The value of the pid, pgrp, or uid field (depending on the value of which) to be used for selecting the processes. If who is 0, its value is set to that of the corresponding field of the current process.

niceval

> The new base priority value (needed only by sys_setpriority( )). It should range between −20 (highest priority) and +19 (lowest priority).

As stated before, only processes with a CAP_SYS_NICE capability are allowed to increase their own base priority or to modify that of other processes.

As we saw in Chapter 9, system calls return a negative value only if some error occurred. For this reason, getpriority( ) does not return a normal nice value ranging between −20 and +19, but rather a nonnegative value ranging between 1 and 40.

System Calls Related to Real-Time Processes

We now introduce a group of system calls that allow processes to change their scheduling discipline and, in particular, to become real-time processes. As usual, a process must have a CAP_SYS_NICE capability to modify the values of the rt_priority and policy process descriptor fields of any process, including itself.

The sched_getscheduler( ) and sched_setscheduler( ) system calls

The sched_getscheduler( ) system call queries the scheduling policy currently applied to the process identified by the pid parameter. If pid equals 0, the policy of the calling process is retrieved. On success, the system call returns the policy for the process: SCHED_FIFO, SCHED_RR, or SCHED_OTHER. The corresponding sys_sched_getscheduler( ) service routine invokes find_process_by_pid( ), which locates the process descriptor corresponding to the given pid and returns the value of its policy field.

The sched_setscheduler( ) system call sets both the scheduling policy and the associated parameters for the process identified by the parameter pid. If pid is equal to 0, the scheduler parameters of the calling process will be set.

The corresponding sys_sched_setscheduler( ) function checks whether the scheduling policy specified by the policy parameter and the new static priority specified by the param->sched_priority parameter are valid. It also checks whether the process has CAP_SYS_NICE capability or whether its owner has superuser rights. If everything is OK, it executes the following statements:

```
p->policy = policy;
p->rt_priority = param->sched_priority;
if (task_on_runqueue(p))
    move_first_runqueue(p);
current->need_resched = 1;
```

The sched_getparam( ) and sched_setparam( ) system calls

The sched_getparam( ) system call retrieves the scheduling parameters for the process identified by pid. If pid is 0, the parameters of the current process are retrieved. The corresponding sys_sched_getparam( ) service routine, as one would expect, finds the process descriptor pointer associated with pid, stores its rt_priority field in a local variable of type sched_param, and invokes copy_to_user( ) to copy it into the process address space at the address specified by the param parameter.

The sched_setparam( ) system call is similar to sched_setscheduler( ). The difference is that sched_setscheduler( ) does not let the caller set the policy field's value.* The corresponding sys_sched_setparam( ) service routine is almost identical to sys_sched_setscheduler( ), but the policy of the affected process is never changed.

The sched_yield( ) system call

The sched_yield( ) system call allows a process to relinquish the CPU voluntarily without being suspended; the process remains in a TASK_RUNNING state, but the scheduler puts it at the end of the runqueue list. In this way, other processes that have the same dynamic priority have a chance to run. The call is used mainly by SCHED_FIFO processes.

The corresponding sys_sched_yield( ) service routine checks first if there is some process in the system that is runnable, other than the process executing the system call and the *swapper* kernel threads. If there is no such process, sched_yield( ) returns without performing any action because no process would be able to use the freed processor. Otherwise, the function executes the following statements:

```
if (current->policy == SCHED_OTHER)
    current->policy |= SCHED_YIELD;
current->need_resched = 1;
spin_lock_irq(&runqueue_lock);
move_last_runqueue(current);
spin_unlock_irq(&runqueue_lock);
```

---

* This anomaly is caused by a specific requirement of the POSIX standard.

As a result, schedule( ) is invoked when returning from the sys_sched_yield( ) service routine (see "Returning from Interrupts and Exceptions" in Chapter 4), and the current process will most likely be replaced.

The sched_get_priority_min( ) and sched_get_priority_max( ) system calls

The sched_get_priority_min( ) and sched_get_priority_max( ) system calls return, respectively, the minimum and the maximum real-time static priority value that can be used with the scheduling policy identified by the policy parameter.

The sys_sched_get_priority_min( ) service routine returns 1 if current is a real-time process, 0 otherwise.

The sys_sched_get_priority_max( ) service routine returns 99 (the highest priority) if current is a real-time process, 0 otherwise.

The sched_rr_get_interval( ) system call

The sched_rr_get_interval( ) system writes in a structure stored in the User Mode address space the Round Robin time quantum for the real-time process identified by the pid parameter. If pid is zero, the system call writes the time quantum of the current process.

The corresponding sys_sched_rr_get_interval( ) service routine invokes, as usual, find_process_by_pid( ) to retrieve the process descriptor associated with pid. It then converts the number of ticks stored in the nice field of the selected process descriptor into seconds and nanoseconds and copies the numbers into the User Mode structure.

CHAPTER 12

The Virtual Filesystem

One of Linux's keys to success is its ability to coexist comfortably with other systems. You can transparently mount disks or partitions that host file formats used by Windows, other Unix systems, or even systems with tiny market shares like the Amiga. Linux manages to support multiple disk types in the same way other Unix variants do, through a concept called the Virtual Filesystem.

The idea behind the Virtual Filesystem is to put a wide range of information in the kernel to represent many different types of filesystems; there is a field or function to support each operation provided by any real filesystem supported by Linux. For each read, write, or other function called, the kernel substitutes the actual function that supports a native Linux filesystem, the NT filesystem, or whatever other filesystem the file is on.

This chapter discusses the aims, structure, and implementation of Linux's Virtual Filesystem. It focuses on three of the five standard Unix file types—namely, regular files, directories, and symbolic links. Device files are covered in Chapter 13, while pipes are discussed in Chapter 19. To show how a real filesystem works, Chapter 17 covers the Second Extended Filesystem that appears on nearly all Linux systems.

The Role of the Virtual Filesystem (VFS)

The *Virtual Filesystem* (also known as Virtual Filesystem Switch or VFS) is a kernel software layer that handles all system calls related to a standard Unix filesystem. Its main strength is providing a common interface to several kinds of filesystems.

For instance, let's assume that a user issues the shell command:

```
$ cp /floppy/TEST /tmp/test
```

where */floppy* is the mount point of an MS-DOS diskette and */tmp* is a normal Second Extended Filesystem (Ext2) directory. As shown in Figure 12-1(a), the VFS is an abstraction layer between the application program and the filesystem implementations. Therefore, the *cp* program is not required to know the filesystem types of */floppy/TEST* and */tmp/test*. Instead, *cp* interacts with the VFS by means of generic system calls known to anyone who has done Unix programming (see the section "File-Handling System Calls" in Chapter 1); the code executed by *cp* is shown in Figure 12-1(b).

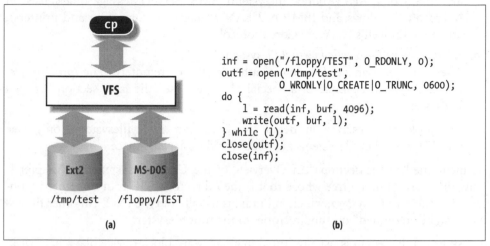

```
inf = open("/floppy/TEST", O_RDONLY, 0);
outf = open("/tmp/test",
            O_WRONLY|O_CREATE|O_TRUNC, 0600);
do {
    l = read(inf, buf, 4096);
    write(outf, buf, l);
} while (l);
close(outf);
close(inf);
```

Figure 12-1. VFS role in a simple file copy operation

Filesystems supported by the VFS may be grouped into three main classes:

Disk-based filesystems

These manage the memory space available in a local disk partition. Some of the well-known disk-based filesystems supported by the VFS are:

- Filesystems for Linux such as the widely used Second Extended Filesystem (Ext2), the recent Third Extended Filesystem (Ext3), and the Reiser Filesystems (ReiserFS)[*]

- Filesystems for Unix variants such as SYSV filesystem (System V, Coherent, XENIX), UFS (BSD, Solaris, Next), MINIX filesystem, and VERITAS VxFS (SCO UnixWare)

- Microsoft filesystems such as MS-DOS, VFAT (Windows 95 and later releases), and NTFS (Windows NT)

- ISO9660 CD-ROM filesystem (formerly High Sierra Filesystem) and Universal Disk Format (UDF) DVD filesystem

- Other proprietary filesystems such as IBM's OS/2 (HPFS), Apple's Macintosh (HFS), Amiga's Fast Filesystem (AFFS), and Acorn Disk Filing System (ADFS)

- Additional journaling file systems originating in systems other than Linux such as IBM's JFS and SGI's XFS.

[*] Although these filesystems owe their birth to Linux, they have been ported to several other operating systems.

Network filesystems

These allow easy access to files included in filesystems belonging to other networked computers. Some well-known network filesystems supported by the VFS are NFS, Coda, AFS (Andrew filesystem), SMB (Server Message Block, used in Microsoft Windows and IBM OS/2 LAN Manager to share files and printers), and NCP (Novell's NetWare Core Protocol).

Special filesystems (also called virtual filesystems)

These do not manage disk space, either locally or remotely. The */proc* filesystem is a typical example of a special filesystem (see the later section "Special Filesystems").

In this book, we describe in detail the Ext2 and Ext3 filesystems only (see Chapter 17); the other filesystems are not covered for lack of space.

As mentioned in the section "An Overview of the Unix Filesystem" in Chapter 1, Unix directories build a tree whose root is the / directory. The root directory is contained in the *root filesystem*, which in Linux, is usually of type Ext2. All other filesystems can be "mounted" on subdirectories of the root filesystem.*

A disk-based filesystem is usually stored in a hardware block device like a hard disk, a floppy, or a CD-ROM. A useful feature of Linux's VFS allows it to handle *virtual block devices* like */dev/loop0*, which may be used to mount filesystems stored in regular files. As a possible application, a user may protect his own private filesystem by storing an encrypted version of it in a regular file.

The first Virtual Filesystem was included in Sun Microsystems's SunOS in 1986. Since then, most Unix filesystems include a VFS. Linux's VFS, however, supports the widest range of filesystems.

The Common File Model

The key idea behind the VFS consists of introducing a *common file model* capable of representing all supported filesystems. This model strictly mirrors the file model provided by the traditional Unix filesystem. This is not surprising, since Linux wants to run its native filesystem with minimum overhead. However, each specific filesystem implementation must translate its physical organization into the VFS's common file model.

For instance, in the common file model, each directory is regarded as a file, which contains a list of files and other directories. However, several non-Unix disk-based

---

* When a filesystem is mounted on a directory, the contents of the directory in the parent filesystem are no longer accessible, since any pathname, including the mount point, will refer to the mounted filesystem. However, the original directory's content shows up again when the filesystem is unmounted. This somewhat surprising feature of Unix filesystems is used by system administrators to hide files; they simply mount a filesystem on the directory containing the files to be hidden.

filesystems use a File Allocation Table (FAT), which stores the position of each file in the directory tree. In these filesystems, directories are not files. To stick to the VFS's common file model, the Linux implementations of such FAT-based filesystems must be able to construct on the fly, when needed, the files corresponding to the directories. Such files exist only as objects in kernel memory.

More essentially, the Linux kernel cannot hardcode a particular function to handle an operation such as read( ) or ioctl( ). Instead, it must use a pointer for each operation; the pointer is made to point to the proper function for the particular filesystem being accessed.

Let's illustrate this concept by showing how the read( ) shown in Figure 12-1 would be translated by the kernel into a call specific to the MS-DOS filesystem. The application's call to read( ) makes the kernel invoke the corresponding sys_read( ) service routine, just like any other system call. The file is represented by a file data structure in kernel memory, as we shall see later in this chapter. This data structure contains a field called f_op that contains pointers to functions specific to MS-DOS files, including a function that reads a file. sys_read( ) finds the pointer to this function and invokes it. Thus, the application's read( ) is turned into the rather indirect call:

```
file->f_op->read(...);
```

Similarly, the write( ) operation triggers the execution of a proper Ext2 write function associated with the output file. In short, the kernel is responsible for assigning the right set of pointers to the file variable associated with each open file, and then for invoking the call specific to each filesystem that the f_op field points to.

One can think of the common file model as object-oriented, where an *object* is a software construct that defines both a data structure and the methods that operate on it. For reasons of efficiency, Linux is not coded in an object-oriented language like C++. Objects are therefore implemented as data structures with some fields pointing to functions that correspond to the object's methods.

The common file model consists of the following object types:

The superblock object
> Stores information concerning a mounted filesystem. For disk-based filesystems, this object usually corresponds to a *filesystem control block* stored on disk.

The inode object
> Stores general information about a specific file. For disk-based filesystems, this object usually corresponds to a *file control block* stored on disk. Each inode object is associated with an *inode number*, which uniquely identifies the file within the filesystem.

The file object
> Stores information about the interaction between an open file and a process. This information exists only in kernel memory during the period when each process accesses a file.

The dentry object

Stores information about the linking of a directory entry with the corresponding file. Each disk-based filesystem stores this information in its own particular way on disk.

Figure 12-2 illustrates with a simple example how processes interact with files. Three different processes have opened the same file, two of them using the same hard link. In this case, each of the three processes uses its own file object, while only two dentry objects are required—one for each hard link. Both dentry objects refer to the same inode object, which identifies the superblock object and, together with the latter, the common disk file.

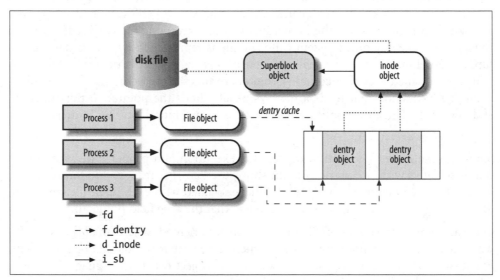

Figure 12-2. Interaction between processes and VFS objects

Besides providing a common interface to all filesystem implementations, the VFS has another important role related to system performance. The most recently used dentry objects are contained in a disk cache named the *dentry cache*, which speeds up the translation from a file pathname to the inode of the last pathname component.

Generally speaking, a *disk cache* is a software mechanism that allows the kernel to keep in RAM some information that is normally stored on a disk, so that further accesses to that data can be quickly satisfied without a slow access to the disk itself.[*]

---

[*] Notice how a disk cache differs from a hardware cache or a memory cache, neither of which has anything to do with disks or other devices. A hardware cache is a fast static RAM that speeds up requests directed to the slower dynamic RAM (see the section "Hardware Cache" in Chapter 2). A memory cache is a software mechanism introduced to bypass the Kernel Memory Allocator (see the section "The Slab Allocator" in Chapter 7).

Beside the dentry cache, Linux uses other disk caches, like the buffer cache and the page cache, which are described in forthcoming chapters.

System Calls Handled by the VFS

Table 12-1 illustrates the VFS system calls that refer to filesystems, regular files, directories, and symbolic links. A few other system calls handled by the VFS, such as ioperm( ), ioctl( ), pipe( ), and mknod( ), refer to device files and pipes. These are discussed in later chapters. A last group of system calls handled by the VFS, such as socket( ), connect( ), bind( ), and protocols( ), refer to sockets and are used to implement networking; some of them are discussed in Chapter 18. Some of the kernel service routines that correspond to the system calls listed in Table 12-1 are discussed either in this chapter or in Chapter 17.

Table 12-1. Some system calls handled by the VFS

System call name	Description
mount( ) umount( )	Mount/unmount filesystems
sysfs( )	Get filesystem information
statfs( ) fstatfs( ) ustat( )	Get filesystem statistics
chroot( ) pivot_root( )	Change root directory
chdir( ) fchdir( ) getcwd( )	Manipulate current directory
mkdir( ) rmdir( )	Create and destroy directories
getdents( ) readdir( ) link( ) unlink( ) rename( )	Manipulate directory entries
readlink( ) symlink( )	Manipulate soft links
chown( ) fchown( ) lchown( )	Modify file owner
chmod( ) fchmod( ) utime( )	Modify file attributes
stat( ) fstat( ) lstat( ) access( )	Read file status
open( ) close( ) creat( ) umask( )	Open and close files
dup( ) dup2( ) fcntl( )	Manipulate file descriptors
select( ) poll( )	Asynchronous I/O notification
truncate( ) ftruncate( )	Change file size
lseek( ) _llseek( )	Change file pointer
read( ) write( ) readv( ) writev( ) sendfile( ) readahead( )	Carry out file I/O operations
pread( ) pwrite( )	Seek file and access it
mmap( ) munmap( ) madvise( ) mincore( )	Handle file memory mapping
fdatasync( ) fsync( ) sync( ) msync( )	Synchronize file data
flock( )	Manipulate file lock

We said earlier that the VFS is a layer between application programs and specific filesystems. However, in some cases, a file operation can be performed by the VFS itself, without invoking a lower-level procedure. For instance, when a process closes an open file, the file on disk doesn't usually need to be touched, and hence the VFS simply releases the corresponding file object. Similarly, when the lseek( ) system call modifies a file pointer, which is an attribute related to the interaction between an opened file and a process, the VFS needs to modify only the corresponding file object without accessing the file on disk and therefore does not have to invoke a specific filesystem procedure. In some sense, the VFS could be considered a "generic" filesystem that relies, when necessary, on specific ones.

VFS Data Structures

Each VFS object is stored in a suitable data structure, which includes both the object attributes and a pointer to a table of object methods. The kernel may dynamically modify the methods of the object and, hence, it may install specialized behavior for the object. The following sections explain the VFS objects and their interrelationships in detail.

Superblock Objects

A superblock object consists of a super_block structure whose fields are described in Table 12-2.

Table 12-2. The fields of the superblock object

Type	Field	Description
struct list_head	s_list	Pointers for superblock list
kdev_t	s_dev	Device identifier
unsigned long	s_blocksize	Block size in bytes
unsigned char	s_blocksize_bits	Block size in number of bits
unsigned char	s_dirt	Modified (dirty) flag
unsigned long long	s_maxbytes	Maximum size of the files
struct file_system_type *	s_type	Filesystem type
struct super_operations *	s_op	Superblock methods
struct dquot_operations *	dq_op	Disk quota methods
unsigned long	s_flags	Mount flags
unsigned long	s_magic	Filesystem magic number
struct dentry *	s_root	Dentry object of mount directory
struct rw_semaphore	s_umount	Semaphore used for unmounting
struct semaphore	s_lock	Superblock semaphore
int	s_count	Reference counter
atomic_t	s_active	Secondary reference counter

Table 12-2. The fields of the superblock object (continued)

Type	Field	Description
struct list_head	s_dirty	List of modified inodes
struct list_head	s_locked_inodes	List of inodes involved in I/O
struct list_head	s_files	List of file objects assigned to the superblock
struct block_device *	s_bdev	Pointer to the block device driver descriptor
struct list_head	s_instances	Pointers for a list of superblock objects of a given filesystem type (see the section "Filesystem Type Registration")
struct quota_mount_options	s_dquot	Options for disk quota
union	u	Specific filesystem information

All superblock objects are linked in a circular doubly linked list. The first element of this list is represented by the super_blocks variable, while the s_list field of the superblock object stores the pointers to the adjacent elements in the list. The sb_lock spin lock protects the list against concurrent accesses in multiprocessor systems.

The last u union field includes superblock information that belongs to a specific filesystem; for instance, as we shall see later in Chapter 17, if the superblock object refers to an Ext2 filesystem, the field stores an ext2_sb_info structure, which includes the disk allocation bit masks and other data of no concern to the VFS common file model.

In general, data in the u field is duplicated in memory for reasons of efficiency. Any disk-based filesystem needs to access and update its allocation bitmaps in order to allocate or release disk blocks. The VFS allows these filesystems to act directly on the u union field of the superblock in memory without accessing the disk.

This approach leads to a new problem, however: the VFS superblock might end up no longer synchronized with the corresponding superblock on disk. It is thus necessary to introduce an s_dirt flag, which specifies whether the superblock is dirty—that is, whether the data on the disk must be updated. The lack of synchronization leads to the familiar problem of a corrupted filesystem when a site's power goes down without giving the user the chance to shut down a system cleanly. As we shall see in the section "Writing Dirty Buffers to Disk" in Chapter 14, Linux minimizes this problem by periodically copying all dirty superblocks to disk.

The methods associated with a superblock are called *superblock operations*. They are described by the super_operations structure whose address is included in the s_op field.

Each specific filesystem can define its own superblock operations. When the VFS needs to invoke one of them, say read_inode( ), it executes the following:

```
sb->s_op->read_inode(inode);
```

where sb stores the address of the superblock object involved. The read_inode field of the super_operations table contains the address of the suitable function, which is therefore directly invoked.

Let's briefly describe the superblock operations, which implement higher-level operations like deleting files or mounting disks. They are listed in the order they appear in the super_operations table:

read_inode(inode)
> Fills the fields of the inode object whose address is passed as the parameter from the data on disk; the i_ino field of the inode object identifies the specific filesystem inode on the disk to be read.

read_inode2(inode, p)
> Similar to the previous one, but the inode is identified by a 64-bit number pointed by p. This method should disappear as soon as the whole VFS architecture moves to 64-bit quantities; for now, it is used by the ReiserFS filesystem only.

dirty_inode(inode)
> Invoked when the inode is marked as modified (dirty). Used by filesystems like ReiserFS and Ext3 to update the filesystem journal on disk.

write_inode(inode, flag)
> Updates a filesystem inode with the contents of the inode object passed as the parameter; the i_ino field of the inode object identifies the filesystem inode on disk that is concerned. The flag parameter indicates whether the I/O operation should be synchronous.

put_inode(inode)
> Releases the inode object whose address is passed as the parameter. As usual, releasing an object does not necessarily mean freeing memory, since other processes may still use that object.

delete_inode(inode)
> Deletes the data blocks containing the file, the disk inode, and the VFS inode.

put_super(super)
> Releases the superblock object whose address is passed as the parameter (because the corresponding filesystem is unmounted).

write_super(super)
> Updates a filesystem superblock with the contents of the object indicated.

write_super_lockfs(super)
> Blocks changes to the filesystem and updates the superblock with the contents of the object indicated. The method should be implemented by journaling filesystems, and should be invoked by the Logical Volume Manager (LVM) driver. It is currently not in use.

unlockfs(super)
> Undoes the block of filesystem updates achieved by the write_super_lockfs() superblock method.

statfs(super, buf)
> Returns statistics on a filesystem by filling the buf buffer.

remount_fs(super, flags, data)
> Remounts the filesystem with new options (invoked when a mount option must be changed).

clear_inode(inode)
> Like put_inode, but also releases all pages that contain data concerning the file that corresponds to the indicated inode.

umount_begin(super)
> Interrupts a mount operation because the corresponding unmount operation has been started (used only by network filesystems).

fh_to_dentry(super, filehandle, len, filehandletype. parent)
> Used by the Network File System (NFS) kernel thread *knfsd* to return the dentry object corresponding to a given file handle. (A *file handle* is an identifier of a NFS file.)

dentry_to_fh(dentry, filehandle, lenp, need_parent)
> Used by the NFS kernel thread *knfsd* to derive the file handle corresponding to a given dentry object.

show_options(seq_file, vfsmount)
> Used to display the filesystem-specific options

The preceding methods are available to all possible filesystem types. However, only a subset of them applies to each specific filesystem; the fields corresponding to unimplemented methods are set to NULL. Notice that no read_super method to read a superblock is defined—how could the kernel invoke a method of an object yet to be read from disk? We'll find the read_super method in another object describing the filesystem type (see the later section "Filesystem Mounting").

Inode Objects

All information needed by the filesystem to handle a file is included in a data structure called an inode. A filename is a casually assigned label that can be changed, but the inode is unique to the file and remains the same as long as the file exists. An inode object in memory consists of an inode structure whose fields are described in Table 12-3.

Table 12-3. The fields of the inode object

Type	Field	Description
struct list_head	i_hash	Pointers for the hash list
struct list_head	i_list	Pointers for the inode list
struct list_head	i_dentry	Pointers for the dentry list
struct list_head	i_dirty_buffers	Pointers for the modified buffers list
struct list_head	i_dirty_data_buffers	Pointers for the modified data buffers list
unsigned long	i_ino	inode number
unsigned int	i_count	Usage counter
kdev_t	i_dev	Device identifier
umode_t	i_mode	File type and access rights
nlink_t	i_nlink	Number of hard links
uid_t	i_uid	Owner identifier
gid_t	i_gid	Group identifier
kdev_t	i_rdev	Real device identifier
off_t	i_size	File length in bytes
time_t	i_atime	Time of last file access
time_t	i_mtime	Time of last file write
time_t	i_ctime	Time of last inode change
unsigned int	i_blkbits	Block size in number of bits
unsigned long	i_blksize	Block size in bytes
unsigned long	i_blocks	Number of blocks of the file
unsigned long	i_version	Version number, automatically incremented after each use
struct semaphore	i_sem	inode semaphore
struct semaphore	i_zombie	Secondary inode semaphore used when removing or renaming the inode
struct inode_operations *	i_op	inode operations
struct file_operations *	i_fop	Default file operations
struct super_block *	i_sb	Pointer to superblock object
wait_queue_head_t	i_wait	inode wait queue
struct file_lock *	i_flock	Pointer to file lock list
struct address_space *	i_mapping	Pointer to an address_space object (see Chapter 14)
struct address_space	i_data	address_space object for block device file
struct dquot **	i_dquot	inode disk quotas
struct list_head	i_devices	Pointers of a list of block device file inodes (see Chapter 13)
struct pipe_inode_info *	i_pipe	Used if the file is a pipe (see Chapter 19)

Table 12-3. The fields of the inode object (continued)

Type	Field	Description
struct block_device *	i_bdev	Pointer to the block device driver
struct char_device *	i_cdev	Pointer to the character device driver
unsigned long	i_dnotify_mask	Bit mask of directory notify events
struct dnotify_struct *	i_dnotify	Used for directory notifications
unsigned long	i_state	inode state flags
unsigned int	i_flags	Filesystem mount flags
unsigned char	i_sock	Nonzero if file is a socket
atomic_t	i_writecount	Usage counter for writing processes
unsigned int	i_attr_flags	File creation flags
__u32	i_generation	inode version number (used by some filesystems)
union	u	Specific filesystem information

The final u union field is used to include inode information that belongs to a specific filesystem. For instance, as we shall see in Chapter 17, if the inode object refers to an Ext2 file, the field stores an ext2_inode_info structure.

Each inode object duplicates some of the data included in the disk inode—for instance, the number of blocks allocated to the file. When the value of the i_state field is equal to I_DIRTY_SYNC, I_DIRTY_DATASYNC, or I_DIRTY_PAGES, the inode is dirty—that is, the corresponding disk inode must be updated; the I_DIRTY macro can be used to check the value of these three flags at once (see later for details). Other values of the i_state field are I_LOCK (the inode object is involved in a I/O transfer), I_FREEING (the inode object is being freed), and I_CLEAR (the inode object contents are no longer meaningful).

Each inode object always appears in one of the following circular doubly linked lists:

- The list of valid unused inodes, typically those mirroring valid disk inodes and not currently used by any process. These inodes are not dirty and their i_count field is set to 0. The first and last elements of this list are referenced by the next and prev fields, respectively, of the inode_unused variable. This list acts as a disk cache.

- The list of in-use inodes, typically those mirroring valid disk inodes and used by some process. These inodes are not dirty and their i_count field is positive. The first and last elements are referenced by the inode_in_use variable.

- The list of dirty inodes. The first and last elements are referenced by the s_dirty field of the corresponding superblock object.

Each of the lists just mentioned links the i_list fields of the proper inode objects.

inode objects are also included in a hash table named inode_hashtable. The hash table speeds up the search of the inode object when the kernel knows both the inode number and the address of the superblock object corresponding to the filesystem that includes the file.* Since hashing may induce collisions, the inode object includes an i_hash field that contains a backward and a forward pointer to other inodes that hash to the same position; this field creates a doubly linked list of those inodes. The hash table also includes a special chain list for the inodes not assigned to a super-block (such as the inodes used by sockets; see Chapter 18); its first and last elements are referenced by the anon_hash_chain variable.

The methods associated with an inode object are also called *inode operations*. They are described by an inode_operations structure, whose address is included in the i_op field. Here are the inode operations in the order they appear in the inode_operations table:

create(dir, dentry, mode)
> Creates a new disk inode for a regular file associated with a dentry object in some directory.

lookup(dir, dentry)
> Searches a directory for an inode corresponding to the filename included in a dentry object.

link(old_dentry, dir, new_dentry)
> Creates a new hard link that refers to the file specified by old_dentry in the directory dir; the new hard link has the name specified by new_dentry.

unlink(dir, dentry)
> Removes the hard link of the file specified by a dentry object from a directory.

symlink(dir, dentry, symname)
> Creates a new inode for a symbolic link associated with a dentry object in some directory.

mkdir(dir, dentry, mode)
> Creates a new inode for a directory associated with a dentry object in some directory.

rmdir(dir, dentry)
> Removes from a directory the subdirectory whose name is included in a dentry object.

mknod(dir, dentry, mode, rdev)
> Creates a new disk inode for a special file associated with a dentry object in some directory. The mode and rdev parameters specify, respectively, the file type and the device's major number.

---

* Actually, a Unix process may open a file and then unlink it. The i_nlink field of the inode could become 0, yet the process is still able to act on the file. In this particular case, the inode is removed from the hash table, even if it still belongs to the in-use or dirty list.

rename(old_dir, old_dentry, new_dir, new_dentry)
> Moves the file identified by old_entry from the old_dir directory to the new_dir one. The new filename is included in the dentry object that new_dentry points to.

readlink(dentry, buffer, buflen)
> Copies into a memory area specified by buffer the file pathname corresponding to the symbolic link specified by the dentry.

follow_link(inode, dir)
> Translates a symbolic link specified by an inode object; if the symbolic link is a relative pathname, the lookup operation starts from the specified directory.

truncate(inode)
> Modifies the size of the file associated with an inode. Before invoking this method, it is necessary to set the i_size field of the inode object to the required new size.

permission(inode, mask)
> Checks whether the specified access mode is allowed for the file associated with inode.

revalidate(dentry)
> Updates the cached attributes of a file specified by a dentry object (usually invoked by the network filesystem).

setattr(dentry, iattr)
> Notifies a "change event" after touching the inode attributes.

getattr(dentry, iattr)
> Used by networking filesystems when noticing that some cached inode attributes must be refreshed.

The methods just listed are available to all possible inodes and filesystem types. However, only a subset of them applies to a specific inode and filesystem; the fields corresponding to unimplemented methods are set to NULL.

File Objects

A file object describes how a process interacts with a file it has opened. The object is created when the file is opened and consists of a file structure, whose fields are described in Table 12-4. Notice that file objects have no corresponding image on disk, and hence no "dirty" field is included in the file structure to specify that the file object has been modified.

Table 12-4. The fields of the file object

Type	Field	Description
struct list_head	f_list	Pointers for generic file object list
struct dentry *	f_dentry	dentry object associated with the file
struct vfsmount *	f_vfsmnt	Mounted filesystem containing the file

Table 12-4. *The fields of the file object (continued)*

Type	Field	Description
struct file_operations *	f_op	Pointer to file operation table
atomic_t	f_count	File object's usage counter
unsigned int	f_flags	Flags specified when opening the file
mode_t	f_mode	Process access mode
loff_t	f_pos	Current file offset (file pointer)
unsigned long	f_reada	Read-ahead flag
unsigned long	f_ramax	Maximum number of pages to be read-ahead
unsigned long	f_raend	File pointer after last read-ahead
unsigned long	f_ralen	Number of read-ahead bytes
unsigned long	f_rawin	Number of read-ahead pages
struct fown_struct	f_owner	Data for asynchronous I/O via signals
unsigned int	f_uid	User's UID
unsigned int	f_gid	User's GID
int	f_error	Error code for network write operation
unsigned long	f_version	Version number, automatically incremented after each use
void *	private_data	Needed for tty driver
struct kiobuf *	f_iobuf	Descriptor for direct access buffer (see the section "Memory Mapping" in Chapter 15)
long	f_iobuf_lock	Lock for direct I/O transfer

The main information stored in a file object is the *file pointer*—the current position in the file from which the next operation will take place. Since several processes may access the same file concurrently, the file pointer cannot be kept in the inode object. Each file object is always included in one of the following circular doubly linked lists:

- The list of "unused" file objects. This list acts both as a memory cache for the file objects and as a reserve for the superuser; it allows the superuser to open a file even if the dynamic memory in the system is exhausted. Since the objects are unused, their f_count fields are 0. The first element of the list is a dummy and it is stored in the free_list variable. The kernel makes sure that the list always contains at least NR_RESERVED_FILES objects, usually 10.

- The list of "in use" file objects not yet assigned to a superblock. The f_count field of each element in this list is set to 1. The first element of the list is a dummy and it is stored in the anon_list variable.

- Several lists of "in use" file objects already assigned to superblocks. Each super-block object stores in the s_files field the dummy first element of a list of file objects; thus, file objects of files belonging to different filesystems are included in different lists. The f_count field of each element in such a list is set to 1 plus the number of processes that are using the file object.

Regardless of which list a file object is in at the moment, the pointers of the next and previous elements in the list are stored in the f_list field of the file object. The files_lock semaphore protects the lists against concurrent accesses in multiprocessor systems.

The size of the list of "unused" file objects is stored in the nr_free_files field of the files_stat variable. The get_empty_filp( ) function is invoked when the VFS must allocate a new file object. The function checks whether the "unused" list has more than NR_RESERVED_FILES items, in which case one can be used for the newly opened file. Otherwise, it falls back to normal memory allocation.

The files_stat variable also includes the nr_files field (which stores the number of file objects included in all lists) and the max_files field (which is the maximum number of allocatable file objects—i.e., the maximum number of files that can be accessed at the same time in the system).[*]

As we explained earlier in the section "The Common File Model," each filesystem includes its own set of *file operations* that perform such activities as reading and writing a file. When the kernel loads an inode into memory from disk, it stores a pointer to these file operations in a file_operations structure whose address is contained in the i_fop field of the inode object. When a process opens the file, the VFS initializes the f_op field of the new file object with the address stored in the inode so that further calls to file operations can use these functions. If necessary, the VFS may later modify the set of file operations by storing a new value in f_op.

The following list describes the file operations in the order in which they appear in the file_operations table:

llseek(file, offset, origin)
> Updates the file pointer.

read(file, buf, count, offset)
> Reads count bytes from a file starting at position *offset; the value *offset (which usually corresponds to the file pointer) is then incremented.

write(file, buf, count, offset)
> Writes count bytes into a file starting at position *offset; the value *offset (which usually corresponds to the file pointer) is then incremented.

readdir(dir, dirent, filldir)
> Returns the next directory entry of a directory in dirent; the filldir parameter contains the address of an auxiliary function that extracts the fields in a directory entry.

---

[*] By default, max_files stores the value 8,192, but the system administrator can tune this parameter by writing into the */proc/sys/fs/file-max* file.

`poll(file, poll_table)`

Checks whether there is activity on a file and goes to sleep until something happens on it.

`ioctl(inode, file, cmd, arg)`

Sends a command to an underlying hardware device. This method applies only to device files.

`mmap(file, vma)`

Performs a memory mapping of the file into a process address space (see the section "Memory Mapping" in Chapter 15).

`open(inode, file)`

Opens a file by creating a new file object and linking it to the corresponding inode object (see the section "The open( ) System Call" later in this chapter).

`flush(file)`

Called when a reference to an open file is closed—that is, when the f_count field of the file object is decremented. The actual purpose of this method is filesystem-dependent.

`release(inode, file)`

Releases the file object. Called when the last reference to an open file is closed—that is, when the f_count field of the file object becomes 0.

`fsync(file, dentry)`

Writes all cached data of the file to disk.

`fasync(fd, file, on)`

Enables or disables asynchronous I/O notification by means of signals.

`lock(file, cmd, file_lock)`

Applies a lock to the file (see the section "File Locking" later in this chapter).

`readv(file, vector, count, offset)`

Reads bytes from a file and puts the results in the buffers described by `vector`; the number of buffers is specified by `count`.

`writev(file, vector, count, offset)`

Writes bytes into a file from the buffers described by `vector`; the number of buffers is specified by `count`.

`sendpage(file, page, offset, size, pointer, fill)`

Transfers data from this file to another file; this method is used by sockets (see Chapter 18).

`get_unmapped_area(file, addr, len, offset, flags)`

Gets an unused address range to map the file (used for frame buffer memory mappings).

The methods just described are available to all possible file types. However, only a subset of them apply to a specific file type; the fields corresponding to unimplemented methods are set to NULL.

dentry Objects

We mentioned in the section "The Common File Model" that the VFS considers each directory a file that contains a list of files and other directories. We shall discuss in Chapter 17 how directories are implemented on a specific filesystem. Once a directory entry is read into memory, however, it is transformed by the VFS into a dentry object based on the dentry structure, whose fields are described in Table 12-5. The kernel creates a dentry object for every component of a pathname that a process looks up; the dentry object associates the component to its corresponding inode. For example, when looking up the */tmp/test* pathname, the kernel creates a dentry object for the / root directory, a second dentry object for the *tmp* entry of the root directory, and a third dentry object for the *test* entry of the */tmp* directory.

Notice that dentry objects have no corresponding image on disk, and hence no field is included in the dentry structure to specify that the object has been modified. Dentry objects are stored in a slab allocator cache called dentry_cache; dentry objects are thus created and destroyed by invoking kmem_cache_alloc( ) and kmem_cache_free( ).

Table 12-5. The fields of the dentry object

Type	Field	Description
atomic_t	d_count	Dentry object usage counter
unsigned int	d_flags	Dentry flags
struct inode *	d_inode	Inode associated with filename
struct dentry *	d_parent	Dentry object of parent directory
struct list_head	d_hash	Pointers for list in hash table entry
struct list_head	d_lru	Pointers for unused list
struct list_head	d_child	Pointers for the list of dentry objects included in parent directory
struct list_head	d_subdirs	For directories, list of dentry objects of subdirectories
struct list_head	d_alias	List of associated inodes (alias)
int	d_mounted	Flag set to 1 if and only if the dentry is the mount point for a file-system
struct qstr	d_name	Filename
unsigned long	d_time	Used by d_revalidate method
struct dentry_operations*	d_op	Dentry methods
struct super_block *	d_sb	Superblock object of the file
unsigned long	d_vfs_flags	Dentry cache flags
void *	d_fsdata	Filesystem-dependent data
unsigned char *	d_iname	Space for short filename

Each dentry object may be in one of four states:

Free

> The dentry object contains no valid information and is not used by the VFS. The corresponding memory area is handled by the slab allocator.

Unused

The dentry object is not currently used by the kernel. The d_count usage counter of the object is 0, but the d_inode field still points to the associated inode. The dentry object contains valid information, but its contents may be discarded if necessary in order to reclaim memory.

In use

The dentry object is currently used by the kernel. The d_count usage counter is positive and the d_inode field points to the associated inode object. The dentry object contains valid information and cannot be discarded.

Negative

The inode associated with the dentry does not exist, either because the corresponding disk inode has been deleted or because the dentry object was created by resolving a pathname of a nonexisting file. The d_inode field of the dentry object is set to NULL, but the object still remains in the dentry cache so that further lookup operations to the same file pathname can be quickly resolved. The term "negative" is misleading since no negative value is involved.

The dentry Cache

Since reading a directory entry from disk and constructing the corresponding dentry object requires considerable time, it makes sense to keep in memory dentry objects that you've finished with but might need later. For instance, people often edit a file and then compile it, or edit and print it, or copy it and then edit the copy. In such cases, the same file needs to be repeatedly accessed.

To maximize efficiency in handling dentries, Linux uses a dentry cache, which consists of two kinds of data structures:

- A set of dentry objects in the in-use, unused, or negative state.
- A hash table to derive the dentry object associated with a given filename and a given directory quickly. As usual, if the required object is not included in the dentry cache, the hashing function returns a null value.

The dentry cache also acts as a controller for an *inode cache*. The inodes in kernel memory that are associated with unused dentries are not discarded, since the dentry cache is still using them. Thus, the inode objects are kept in RAM and can be quickly referenced by means of the corresponding dentries.

All the "unused" dentries are included in a doubly linked "Least Recently Used" list sorted by time of insertion. In other words, the dentry object that was last released is put in front of the list, so the least recently used dentry objects are always near the end of the list. When the dentry cache has to shrink, the kernel removes elements from the tail of this list so that the most recently used objects are preserved. The addresses of the first and last elements of the LRU list are stored in the next and prev fields of the dentry_unused variable. The d_lru field of the dentry object contains pointers to the adjacent dentries in the list.

Each "in use" dentry object is inserted into a doubly linked list specified by the i_ dentry field of the corresponding inode object (since each inode could be associated with several hard links, a list is required). The d_alias field of the dentry object stores the addresses of the adjacent elements in the list. Both fields are of type struct list_head.

An "in use" dentry object may become "negative" when the last hard link to the corresponding file is deleted. In this case, the dentry object is moved into the LRU list of unused dentries. Each time the kernel shrinks the dentry cache, negative dentries move toward the tail of the LRU list so that they are gradually freed (see the section "Reclaiming Page Frames from the Dentry and Inode Caches" in Chapter 16).

The hash table is implemented by means of a dentry_hashtable array. Each element is a pointer to a list of dentries that hash to the same hash table value. The array's size depends on the amount of RAM installed in the system. The d_hash field of the dentry object contains pointers to the adjacent elements in the list associated with a single hash value. The hash function produces its value from both the address of the dentry object of the directory and the filename.

The dcache_lock spin lock protects the dentry cache data structures against concurrent accesses in multiprocessor systems. The d_lookup( ) function looks in the hash table for a given parent dentry object and filename.

The methods associated with a dentry object are called *dentry operations*; they are described by the dentry_operations structure, whose address is stored in the d_op field. Although some filesystems define their own dentry methods, the fields are usually NULL and the VFS replaces them with default functions. Here are the methods, in the order they appear in the dentry_operations table:

d_revalidate(dentry, flag)
> Determines whether the dentry object is still valid before using it for translating a file pathname. The default VFS function does nothing, although network filesystems may specify their own functions.

d_hash(dentry, name)
> Creates a hash value; this function is a filesystem-specific hash function for the dentry hash table. The dentry parameter identifies the directory containing the component. The name parameter points to a structure containing both the pathname component to be looked up and the value produced by the hash function.

d_compare(dir, name1, name2)
> Compares two filenames; name1 should belong to the directory referenced by dir. The default VFS function is a normal string match. However, each filesystem can implement this method in its own way. For instance, MS-DOS does not distinguish capital from lowercase letters.

`d_delete(dentry)`

    Called when the last reference to a dentry object is deleted (d_count becomes 0). The default VFS function does nothing.

`d_release(dentry)`

    Called when a dentry object is going to be freed (released to the slab allocator). The default VFS function does nothing.

`d_iput(dentry, ino)`

    Called when a dentry object becomes "negative"—that is, it loses its inode. The default VFS function invokes iput( ) to release the inode object.

Files Associated with a Process

We mentioned in the section "An Overview of the Unix Filesystem" in Chapter 1 that each process has its own current working directory and its own root directory. These are just two examples of data that must be maintained by the kernel to represent the interactions between a process and a filesystem. A whole data structure of type fs_struct is used for that purpose (see Table 12-6) and each process descriptor has an fs field that points to the process fs_struct structure.

Table 12-6. The fields of the fs_struct structure

Type	Field	Description
atomic_t	count	Number of processes sharing this table
rwlock_t	lock	Read/write spin lock for the table fields
int	umask	Bit mask used when opening the file to set the file permissions
struct dentry *	root	Dentry of the root directory
struct dentry *	pwd	Dentry of the current working directory
struct dentry *	altroot	Dentry of the emulated root directory (always NULL for the 80 × 86 architecture)
struct vfsmount *	rootmnt	Mounted filesystem object of the root directory
struct vfsmount *	pwdmnt	Mounted filesystem object of the current working directory
struct vfsmount *	altrootmnt	Mounted filesystem object of the emulated root directory (always NULL for the 80 × 86 architecture)

A second table, whose address is contained in the files field of the process descriptor, specifies which files are currently opened by the process. It is a files_struct structure whose fields are illustrated in Table 12-7.

Table 12-7. The fields of the files_struct structure

Type	Field	Description
atomic_t	count	Number of processes sharing this table
rwlock_t	file_lock	Read/write spin lock for the table fields

Table 12-7. The fields of the files_struct structure (continued)

Type	Field	Description
int	max_fds	Current maximum number of file objects
int	max_fdset	Current maximum number of file descriptors
int	next_fd	Maximum file descriptors ever allocated plus 1
struct file **	fd	Pointer to array of file object pointers
fd_set *	close_on_exec	Pointer to file descriptors to be closed on exec( )
fd_set *	open_fds	Pointer to open file descriptors
fd_set	close_on_exec_init	Initial set of file descriptors to be closed on exec( )
fd_set	open_fds_init	Initial set of file descriptors
struct file **	fd_array	Initial array of file object pointers

The fd field points to an array of pointers to file objects. The size of the array is stored in the max_fds field. Usually, fd points to the fd_array field of the files_ struct structure, which includes 32 file object pointers. If the process opens more than 32 files, the kernel allocates a new, larger array of file pointers and stores its address in the fd fields; it also updates the max_fds field.

For every file with an entry in the fd array, the array index is the *file descriptor*. Usually, the first element (index 0) of the array is associated with the standard input of the process, the second with the standard output, and the third with the standard error (see Figure 12-3). Unix processes use the file descriptor as the main file identifier. Notice that, thanks to the dup( ), dup2( ), and fcntl( ) system calls, two file descriptors may refer to the same opened file—that is, two elements of the array could point to the same file object. Users see this all the time when they use shell constructs like 2>&1 to redirect the standard error to the standard output.

A process cannot use more than NR_OPEN (usually, 1,048,576) file descriptors. The kernel also enforces a dynamic bound on the maximum number of file descriptors in the rlim[RLIMIT_NOFILE] structure of the process descriptor; this value is usually 1,024, but it can be raised if the process has root privileges.

The open_fds field initially contains the address of the open_fds_init field, which is a bitmap that identifies the file descriptors of currently opened files. The max_fdset field stores the number of bits in the bitmap. Since the fd_set data structure includes 1,024 bits, there is usually no need to expand the size of the bitmap. However, the kernel may dynamically expand the size of the bitmap if this turns out to be necessary, much as in the case of the array of file objects.

The kernel provides an fget( ) function to be invoked when the kernel starts using a file object. This function receives as its parameter a file descriptor fd. It returns the address in current->files->fd[fd] (that is, the address of the corresponding file object), or NULL if no file corresponds to fd. In the first case, fget( ) increments the file object usage counter f_count by 1.

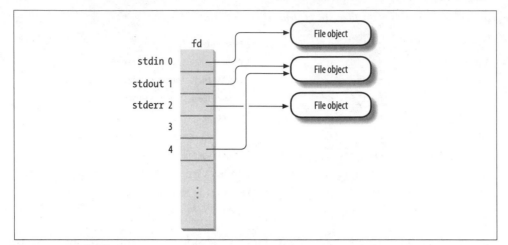

Figure 12-3. The fd array

The kernel also provides an fput( ) function to be invoked when a kernel control path finishes using a file object. This function receives as its parameter the address of a file object and decrements its usage counter, f_count. Moreover, if this field becomes 0, the function invokes the release method of the file operations (if defined), releases the associated dentry object and filesystem descriptor, decrements the i_writecount field in the inode object (if the file was opened for writing), and finally moves the file object from the "in use" list to the "unused" one.

Filesystem Types

The Linux kernel supports many different types of filesystems. In the following, we introduce a few special types of filesystems that play an important role in the internal design of the Linux kernel.

Next, we shall discuss filesystem registration—that is, the basic operation that must be performed, usually during system initialization, before using a filesystem type. Once a filesystem is registered, its specific functions are available to the kernel, so that type of filesystem can be mounted on the system's directory tree.

Special Filesystems

While network and disk-based filesystems enable the user to handle information stored outside the kernel, special filesystems may provide an easy way for system programs and administrators to manipulate the data structures of the kernel and to implement special features of the operating system. Table 12-8 lists the most common special filesystems used in Linux; for each of them, the table reports its mount point and a short description.

Notice that a few filesystems have no fixed mount point (keyword "any" in the table). These filesystems can be freely mounted and used by the users. Moreover, some other special filesystems do not have a mount point at all (keyword "none" in the table). They are not for user interaction, but the kernel can use them to easily reuse some of the VFS layer code; for instance, we'll see in Chapter 19 that, thanks to the *pipefs* special filesystem, pipes can be treated in the same way as FIFO files.

Table 12-8. Most common special filesystems

Name	Mount point	Description
bdev	none	Block devices (see Chapter 13)
binfmt_misc	any	Miscellaneous executable formats (see Chapter 20)
devfs	/dev	Virtual device files (see Chapter 13)
devpts	/dev/pts	Pseudoterminal support (Open Group's Unix98 standard)
pipefs	none	Pipes (see Chapter 19)
proc	/proc	General access point to kernel data structures
rootfs	none	Provides an empty root directory for the bootstrap phase
shm	none	IPC-shared memory regions (see Chapter 19)
sockfs	none	Sockets (see Chapter 18)
tmpfs	any	Temporary files (kept in RAM unless swapped)

Special filesystems are not bound to physical block devices. However, the kernel assigns to each mounted special filesystem a fictitious block device that has the value 0 as major number and an arbitrary value (different for each special filesystem) as a minor number. The get_unnamed_dev( ) function returns a new fictitious block device identifier, while the put_unnamed_dev( ) function releases it. The unnamed_dev_in_use array contains a mask of 256 bits that record what minor numbers are currently in use. Although some kernel designers dislike the fictitious block device identifiers, they help the kernel to handle special filesystems and regular ones in a uniform way.

We see a practical example of how the kernel defines and initializes a special filesystem in the later section "Mounting the Root Filesystem."

Filesystem Type Registration

Often, the user configures Linux to recognize all the filesystems needed when compiling the kernel for her system. But the code for a filesystem actually may either be included in the kernel image or dynamically loaded as a module (see Appendix B). The VFS must keep track of all filesystem types whose code is currently included in the kernel. It does this by performing *filesystem type registration*.

Each registered filesystem is represented as a file_system_type object whose fields are illustrated in Table 12-9.

Table 12-9. The fields of the file_system_type object

Type	Field	Description
const char *	name	Filesystem name
int	fs_flags	Filesystem type flags
struct super_block *(*)()	read_super	Method for reading superblock
struct module *	owner	Pointer to the module implementing the filesystem (see Appendix B)
struct file_system_type *	next	Pointer to the next list element
struct list_head	fs_supers	Head of a list of superblock objects

All filesystem-type objects are inserted into a simply linked list. The file_systems variable points to the first item, while the next field of the structure points to the next item in the list. The file_systems_lock read/write spin lock protects the whole list against concurrent accesses.

The fs_supers field represents the head (first dummy element) of a list of superblock objects corresponding to mounted filesystems of the given type. The backward and forward links of a list element are stored in the s_instances field of the superblock object.

The read_super field points to the filesystem-type-dependant function that reads the superblock from the disk device and copies it into the corresponding superblock object.

The fs_flags field stores several flags, which are listed in Table 12-10.

Table 12-10. The filesystem type flags

Name	Description
FS_REQUIRES_DEV	Any filesystem of this type must be located on a physical disk device.
FS_NO_DCACHE	No longer used.
FS_NO_PRELIM	No longer used.
FS_SINGLE	There can be only one superblock object for this filesystem type.
FS_NOMOUNT	Filesystem has no mount point (see the section "Special Filesystems").
FS_LITTER	Purge dentry cache after unmounting (for special filesystems).
FS_ODD_RENAME	"Rename" operations are "move" operations (for network filesystems).

During system initialization, the register_filesystem( ) function is invoked for every filesystem specified at compile time; the function inserts the corresponding file_system_type object into the filesystem-type list.

The register_filesystem( ) function is also invoked when a module implementing a filesystem is loaded. In this case, the filesystem may also be unregistered (by invoking the unregister_filesystem( ) function) when the module is unloaded.

The get_fs_type( ) function, which receives a filesystem name as its parameter, scans the list of registered filesystems looking at the name field of their descriptors, and returns a pointer to the corresponding file_system_type object, if it is present.

Filesystem Mounting

Each filesystem has its own *root directory*. The filesystem whose root directory is the root of the system's directory tree is called *root filesystem*. Other filesystems can be mounted on the system's directory tree; the directories on which they are inserted are called *mount points*. A mounted filesystem is the *child* of the mounted filesystem to which the mount point directory belongs. For instance, the */proc* virtual filesystem is a child of the root filesystem (and the root filesystem is the *parent* of */proc*).

In most traditional Unix-like kernels, each filesystem can be mounted only once. Suppose that an Ext2 filesystem stored in the */dev/fd0* floppy disk is mounted on */flp* by issuing the command:

```
mount -t ext2 /dev/fd0 /flp
```

Until the filesystem is unmounted by issuing a umount command, any other mount command acting on */dev/fd0* fails.

However, Linux 2.4 is different: it is possible to mount the same filesystem several times. For instance, issuing the following command right after the previous one will likely succeed in Linux:

```
mount -t ext2 -o ro /dev/fd0 /flp-ro
```

As a result, the Ext2 filesystem stored in the floppy disk is mounted both on */flp* and on */flp ro*; therefore, its files can be accessed through both */flp* and */flp-ro* (in this example, accesses through */flp-ro* are read-only).

Of course, if a filesystem is mounted *n* times, its root directory can be accessed through *n* mount points, one per mount operation. Although the same filesystem can be accessed by several paths, it is really unique. Thus, there is just one superblock object for all of them, no matter of how many times it has been mounted.

Mounted filesystems form a hierarchy: the mount point of a filesystem might be a directory of a second filesystem, which in turn is already mounted over a third file-system, and so on.[*]

---

[*] Quite surprisingly, the mount point of a filesystem might be a directory of the same filesystem, provided that it was already mounted before. For instance:

```
mount -t ext2 /dev/fd0 /flp; touch /flp/foo
mkdir /flp/mnt; mount -t ext2 /dev/fd0 /flp/mnt
```

Now, the empty *foo* file on the floppy filesystem can be accessed both as */flp/foo* and */flp/mnt/foo*.

It is also possible to stack multiple mounts on a single mount point. Each new mount on the same mount point hides the previously mounted filesystem, although processes already using the files and directories under the old mount can continue to do so. When the topmost mounting is removed, then the next lower mount is once more made visible.

As you can imagine, keeping track of mounted filesystems can quickly become a nightmare. For each mount operation, the kernel must save in memory the mount point and the mount flags, as well as the relationships between the filesystem to be mounted and the other mounted filesystems. Such information is stored in data structures named *mounted filesystem descriptors*; each descriptor is a data structure that has type vfsmount, whose fields are shown in Table 12-11.

Table 12-11. The fields of the vfsmount data structure

Type	Field	Description
struct list_head	mnt_hash	Pointers for the hash table list
struct vfsmount *	mnt_parent	Points to the parent filesystem on which this filesystem is mounted on
struct dentry *	mnt_mountpoint	Points to the dentry of the mount directory of this filesystem
struct dentry *	mnt_root	Points to the dentry of the root directory of this filesystem
struct super_block *	mnt_sb	Points to the superblock object of this filesystem
struct list_head	mnt_mounts	Head of the parent list of descriptors (relative to this filesystem)
struct list_head	mnt_child	Pointers for the parent list of descriptors (relative to the parent filesystem)
atomic_t	mnt_count	Usage counter
int	mnt_flags	Flags
char *	mnt_devname	Device file name
struct list_head	mnt_list	Pointers for global list of descriptors

The vfsmount data structures are kept in several doubly linked circular lists:

- A circular doubly linked "global" list including the descriptors of all mounted filesystems. The head of the list is a first dummy element, which is represented by the vfsmntlist variable. The mnt_list field of the descriptor contains the pointers to adjacent elements in the list.

- An hash table indexed by the address of the vfsmount descriptor of the parent filesystem and the address of the dentry object of the mount point directory. The hash table is stored in the mount_hashtable array, whose size depends on the amount of RAM in the system. Each item of the table is the head of a circular doubly linked list storing all descriptors that have the same hash value. The mnt_hash field of the descriptor contains the pointers to adjacent elements in this list.

- For each mounted filesystem, a circular doubly linked list including all child mounted filesystems. The head of each list is stored in the mnt_mounts field of the mounted filesystem descriptor; moreover, the mnt_child field of the descriptor stores the pointers to the adjacent elements in the list.

The mount_sem semaphore protects the lists of mounted filesystem objects from concurrent accesses.

The mnt_flags field of the descriptor stores the value of several flags that specify how some kinds of files in the mounted filesystem are handled. The flags are listed in Table 12-12.

Table 12-12. Mounted filesystem flags

Name	Description
MNT_NOSUID	Forbid setuid and setgid flags in the mounted filesystem
MNT_NODEV	Forbid access to device files in the mounted filesystem
MNT_NOEXEC	Disallow program execution in the mounted filesystem

The following functions handle the mounted filesystem descriptors:

alloc_vfsmnt( )
  Allocates and initializes a mounted filesystem descriptor

free_vfsmnt(mnt)
  Frees a mounted filesystem descriptor pointed by mnt

lookup_mnt(parent,mountpoint)
  Looks up a descriptor in the hash table and returns its address

Mounting the Root Filesystem

Mounting the root filesystem is a crucial part of system initialization. It is a fairly complex procedure because the Linux kernel allows the root filesystem to be stored in many different places, such as a hard disk partition, a floppy disk, a remote filesystem shared via NFS, or even a fictitious block device kept in RAM.

To keep the description simple, let's assume that the root filesystem is stored in a partition of a hard disk (the most common case, after all). While the system boots, the kernel finds the major number of the disk that contains the root filesystem in the ROOT_DEV variable. The root filesystem can be specified as a device file in the /dev directory either when compiling the kernel or by passing a suitable "root" option to the initial bootstrap loader. Similarly, the mount flags of the root filesystem are stored in the root_mountflags variable. The user specifies these flags either by using the rdev external program on a compiled kernel image or by passing a suitable rootflags option to the initial bootstrap loader (see Appendix A).

Mounting the root filesystem is a two-stage procedure, shown in the following list.

1. The kernel mounts the special *rootfs* filesystem, which just provides an empty directory that serves as initial mount point.

2. The kernel mounts the real root filesystem over the empty directory.

Why does the kernel bother to mount the *rootfs* filesystem before the real one? Well, the *rootfs* filesystem allows the kernel to easily change the real root filesystem. In fact, in some cases, the kernel mounts and unmounts several root filesystems, one after the other. For instance, the initial bootstrap floppy disk of a distribution might load in RAM a kernel with a minimal set of drivers, which mounts as root a minimal filesystem stored in a RAM disk. Next, the programs in this initial root filesystem probe the hardware of the system (for instance, they determine whether the hard disk is EIDE, SCSI, or whatever), load all needed kernel modules, and remount the root filesystem from a physical block device.

The first stage is performed by the init_mount_tree( ) function, which is executed during system initialization:

```
struct file_system_type root_fs_type;
root_fs_type.name = "rootfs";
root_fs_type.read_super = rootfs_read_super;
root_fs_type.fs_flags = FS_NOMOUNT;
register_filesystem(&root_fs_type);
root_vfsmnt = do_kern_mount("rootfs", 0, "rootfs", NULL);
```

The root_fs_type variable stores the descriptor object of the *rootfs* special filesystem; its fields are initialized, and then it is passed to the register_filesystem( ) function (see the earlier section "Filesystem Type Registration"). The do_kern_mount( ) function mounts the special filesystem and returns the address of a new mounted filesystem object; this address is saved by init_mount_tree( ) in the root_vfsmnt variable. From now on, root_vfsmnt represents the root of the tree of the mounted filesystems.

The do_kern_mount( ) function receives the following parameters:

type

> The type of filesystem to be mounted

flags

> The mount flags (see Table 12-13 in the later section "Mounting a Generic Filesystem")

name

> The device file name of the block device storing the filesystem (or the filesystem type name for special filesystems)

data

> Pointers to additional data to be passed to the read_super method of the filesystem

The function takes care of the actual mount operation by performing the following operations:

1. Checks whether the current process has the privileges for the mount operation (the check always succeeds when the function is invoked by init_mount_tree() because the system initialization is carried on by a process owned by root).

2. Invokes get_fs_type() to search in the list of filesystem types and locate the name stored in the type parameter; get_fs_type() returns the address of the corresponding file_system_type descriptor.

3. Invokes alloc_vfsmnt() to allocate a new mounted filesystem descriptor and stores its address in the mnt local variable.

4. Initializes the mnt->mnt_devname field with the content of the name parameter.

5. Allocates a new superblock and initializes it. do_kern_mount() checks the flags in the file_system_type descriptor to determine how to do this:

    a. If FS_REQUIRES_DEV is on, invokes get_sb_bdev() (see the later section "Mounting a Generic Filesystem")

    b. If FS_SINGLE is on, invokes get_sb_single() (see the later section "Mounting a Generic Filesystem")

    c. Otherwise, invokes get_sb_nodev()

6. If the FS_NOMOUNT flag in the file_system_type descriptor is on, sets the MS_NOUSER flag in the superblock object.

7. Initializes the mnt->mnt_sb field with the address of the new superblock object.

8. Initializes the mnt->mnt_root and mnt->mnt_mountpoint fields with the address of the dentry object corresponding to the root directory of the filesystem.

9. Initializes the mnt->mnt_parent field with the value in mnt (the newly mounted filesystem has no parent).

10. Releases the s_umount semaphore of the superblock object (it was acquired when the object was allocated in Step 5).

11. Returns the address mnt of the mounted filesystem object.

When the do_kern_mount() function is invoked by init_mount_tree() to mount the *rootfs* special filesystem, neither the FS_REQUIRES_DEV flag nor the FS_SINGLE flag are set, so the function uses get_sb_nodev() to allocate the superblock object. This function executes the following steps:

1. Invokes get_unnamed_dev() to allocate a new fictitious block device identifier (see the earlier section "Special Filesystems").

2. Invokes the read_super() function, passing to it the filesystem type object, the mount flags, and the fictitious block device identifier. In turn, this function performs the following actions:

    a. Allocates a new superblock object and puts its address in the local variable s.

    b. Initializes the s->s_dev field with the block device identifier.

c. Initializes the s->s_flags field with the mount flags (see Table 12-13).

d. Initializes the s->s_type field with the filesystem type descriptor of the file-system.

e. Acquires the sb_lock spin lock.

f. Inserts the superblock in the global circular list whose head is super_blocks.

g. Inserts the superblock in the filesystem type list whose head is s->s_type->fs_supers.

h. Releases the sb_lock spin lock.

i. Acquires for writing the s->s_umount read/write semaphore.

j. Acquires the s->s_lock semaphore.

k. Invokes the read_super method of the filesystem type.

l. Sets the MS_ACTIVE flag in s->s_flags.

m. Releases the s->s_lock semaphore.

n. Returns the address s of the superblock.

3. If the filesystem type is implemented by a kernel module, increments its usage counter.

4. Returns the address of the new superblock.

The second stage of the mount operation for the root filesystem is performed by the mount_root( ) function near the end of the system initialization. For the sake of brevity, we consider the case of a disk-based filesystem whose device files are handled in the traditional way (we briefly discuss in Chapter 13 how the *devfs* virtual filesystem offers an alternative way to handle device files). In this case, the function performs the following operations:

1. Allocates a buffer and fills it with a list of filesystem type names. This list is either passed to the kernel in the *rootfstype* boot parameter or is built by scanning the elements in the simply linked list of filesystem types.

2. Invokes the bdget( ) and blkdev_get( ) functions to check whether the ROOT_DEV root device exists and is properly working.

3. Invokes get_super( ) to search for a superblock object associated with the ROOT_DEV device in the super_blocks list. Usually none is found because the root filesystem is still to be mounted. The check is made, however, because it is possible to remount a previously mounted filesystem. Usually the root filesystem is mounted twice during the system boot: the first time as a read-only filesystem so that its integrity can be safely checked; the second time for reading and writing so that normal operations can start. We'll suppose that no superblock object associated with the ROOT_DEV device is found in the super_blocks list.

4. Scans the list of filesystem type names built in Step 1. For each name, invokes `get_fs_type()` to get the corresponding `file_system_type` object, and invokes `read_super()` to attempt to read the corresponding superblock from disk. As described earlier, this function allocates a new superblock object and attempts to fill it by using the method to which the read_super field of the `file_system_type` object points. Since each filesystem-specific method uses unique magic numbers, all `read_super()` invocations will fail except the one that attempts to fill the superblock by using the method of the filesystem really used on the root device. The `read_super()` method also creates an inode object and a dentry object for the root directory; the dentry object maps to the inode object.

5. Allocates a new mounted filesystem object and initializes its fields with the ROOT_DEV block device name, the address of the superblock object, and the address of the dentry object of the root directory.

6. Invokes the `graft_tree()` function, which inserts the new mounted filesystem object in the children list of `root_vfsmnt`, in the global list of mounted filesystem objects, and in the `mount_hashtable` hash table.

7. Sets the root and pwd fields of the `fs_struct` table of current (the *init* process) to the dentry object of the root directory.

Mounting a Generic Filesystem

Once the root filesystem is initialized, additional filesystems may be mounted. Each must have its own mount point, which is just an already existing directory in the system's directory tree.

The `mount()` system call is used to mount a filesystem; its `sys_mount()` service routine acts on the following parameters:

- The pathname of a device file containing the filesystem, or NULL if it is not required (for instance, when the filesystem to be mounted is network-based)

- The pathname of the directory on which the filesystem will be mounted (the mount point)

- The filesystem type, which must be the name of a registered filesystem

- The mount flags (permitted values are listed in Table 12-13)

- A pointer to a filesystem-dependent data structure (which may be NULL)

Table 12-13. Mount flags

Macro	Description
MS_RDONLY	Files can only be read
MS_NOSUID	Forbid setuid and setgid flags
MS_NODEV	Forbid access to device files

Table 12-13. Mount flags (continued)

Macro	Description
MS_NOEXEC	Disallow program execution
MS_SYNCHRONOUS	Write operations are immediate
MS_REMOUNT	Remount the filesystem changing the mount flags
MS_MANDLOCK	Mandatory locking allowed
MS_NOATIME	Do not update file access time
MS_NODIRATIME	Do not update directory access time
MS_BIND	Create a "bind mount," which allows making a file or directory visible at another point of the system directory tree
MS_MOVE	Atomically move a mounted filesystem on another mount point
MS_REC	Should recursively create "bind mounts" for a directory subtree (still unfinished in 2.4.18)
MS_VERBOSE	Generate kernel messages on mount errors

The sys_mount( ) function copies the value of the parameters into temporary kernel buffers, acquires the big kernel lock, and invokes the do_mount( ) function. Once do_mount( ) returns, the service routine releases the big kernel lock and frees the temporary kernel buffers.

The do_mount( ) function takes care of the actual mount operation by performing the following operations:

1. Checks whether the sixteen highest-order bits of the mount flags are set to the "magic" value 0xce0d; in this case, they are cleared. This is a legacy hack that allows the sys_mount( ) service routine to be used with old C libraries that do not handle the highest-order flags.

2. If any of the MS_NOSUID, MS_NODEV, or MS_NOEXEC flags passed as a parameter are set, clears them and sets the corresponding flag (MNT_NOSUID, MNT_NODEV, MNT_NOEXEC) in the mounted filesystem object.

3. Looks up the pathname of the mount point by invoking path_init( ) and path_walk( ) (see the later section "Pathname Lookup").

4. Examines the mount flags to determine what has to be done. In particular:

   a. If the MS_REMOUNT flag is specified, the purpose is usually to change the mount flags in the s_flags field of the superblock object and the mounted filesystem flags in the mnt_flags field of the mounted filesystem object. The do_remount( ) function performs these changes.

   b. Otherwise, checks the MS_BIND flag. If it is specified, the user is asking to make visible a file or directory on another point of the system directory tree. Usually, this is done when mounting a filesystem stored in a regular file instead of a physical disk partition (loopback). The do_loopback( ) function accomplishes this task.

c. Otherwise, checks the MS_MOVE flag. If it is specified, the user is asking to change the mount point of an already mounted filesystem. The do_move_mount( ) function does this atomically.

d. Otherwise, invokes do_add_mount( ). This is the most common case. It is triggered when the user asks to mount either a special filesystem or a regular filesystem stored in a disk partition. do_add_mount( ) performs the following actions:

 1. Invokes do_kern_mount( ) passing, to it the filesystem type, the mount flags, and the block device name. As already described in the section "Mounting the Root Filesystem," do_kern_mount( ) takes care of the actual mount operation.

 2. Acquires the mount_sem semaphore.

 3. Initializes the flags in the mnt_flags field of the new mounted filesystem object allocated by do_kern_mount( ).

 4. Invokes graft_tree( ) to insert the new mounted filesystem object in the global list, in the hash table, and in the children list of the parent-mounted filesystem.

 5. Releases the mount_sem semaphore.

5. Invokes path_release( ) to terminate the pathname lookup of the mount point (see the later section "Pathname Lookup).

The core of the mount operation is the do_kern_mount( ) function, which we already described in the earlier section "Mounting the Root Filesystem." Recall that this function checks the filesystem type flags to determine how the mount operation is to be done. For a regular disk-based filesystem, the FS_REQUIRES_DEV flag is set, so do_kern_mount( ) invokes the get_sb_bdev( ) function, which performs the following actions:

1. Invokes path_init( ) and path_walk( ) to look up the pathname of the mount point (see the section "Pathname Lookup").

2. Invokes blkdev_get( ) to open the block device storing the regular filesystem.

3. Searches the list of superblock objects; if a superblock relative to the block device is already present, returns its address. This means that the filesystem is already mounted and will be mounted again.

4. Otherwise, allocates a new superblock object, initializes its s_dev, s_bdev, s_flags, and s_type fields, and inserts it into the global lists of superblocks and the superblock list of the filesystem type descriptor.

5. Acquires the s_lock spin lock of the superblock.

6. Invokes the read_super method of the filesystem type to access the superblock information on disk and fill the other fields of the new superblock object.

7. Sets the MS_ACTIVE flag of the superblock.

8. Releases the s_lock spin lock of the superblock.

9. If the filesystem type is implemented by a kernel module, increments its usage counter.

10. Invokes path_release( ) to terminate the mount point lookup operation.

11. Returns the address of the new superblock object.

Unmounting a Filesystem

The umount( ) system call is used to unmount a filesystem. The corresponding sys_umount( ) service routine acts on two parameters: a filename (either a mount point directory or a block device filename) and a set of flags. It performs the following actions:

1. Invokes path_init( ) and path_walk( ) to look up the mount point pathname (see the next section). Once finished, the functions return the address d of the dentry object corresponding to the pathname.

2. If the resulting directory is not the mount point of a filesystem, returns the -EINVAL error code. This check is done by verifying that d->mnt->mnt_root contains the address of the dentry object d.

3. If the filesystem to be unmounted has not been mounted on the system directory tree, returns the -EINVAL error code. (Recall that some special filesystems have no mount point.) This check is done by invoking the check_mnt( ) function on d->mnt.

4. If the user does not have the privileges required to unmount the filesystem, returns the -EPERM error code.

5. Invokes do_umount( ), which performs the following operations:

   a. Retrieves the address of the superblock object from the mnt_sb field of the mounted filesystem object.

   b. If the user asked to force the unmount operation, interrupts any ongoing mount operation by invoking the umount_begin superblock operation.

   c. If the filesystem to be unmounted is the root filesystem and the user didn't ask to actually detach it, invokes do_remount_sb( ) to remount the root filesystem read-only and terminates.

   d. Acquires the mount_sem semaphore for writing and the dcache_lock dentry spin lock.

   e. If the mounted filesystem does not include mount points for any child mounted filesystem, or if the user asked to forcibly detach the filesystem, invokes umount_tree( ) to unmount the filesystem (together with all children).

   f. Releases mount_sem and dcache_lock.

Pathname Lookup

In this section, we illustrate how the VFS derives an inode from the corresponding file pathname. When a process must identify a file, it passes its file pathname to some VFS system call, such as open( ), mkdir( ), rename( ), or stat( ).

The standard procedure for performing this task consists of analyzing the pathname and breaking it into a sequence of filenames. All filenames except the last must identify directories.

If the first character of the pathname is /, the pathname is absolute, and the search starts from the directory identified by current->fs->root (the process root directory). Otherwise, the pathname is relative and the search starts from the directory identified by current->fs->pwd (the process-current directory).

Having in hand the inode of the initial directory, the code examines the entry matching the first name to derive the corresponding inode. Then the directory file that has that inode is read from disk and the entry matching the second name is examined to derive the corresponding inode. This procedure is repeated for each name included in the path.

The dentry cache considerably speeds up the procedure, since it keeps the most recently used dentry objects in memory. As we saw before, each such object associates a filename in a specific directory to its corresponding inode. In many cases, therefore, the analysis of the pathname can avoid reading the intermediate directories from the disk.

However, things are not as simple as they look, since the following Unix and VFS filesystem features must be taken into consideration.

- The access rights of each directory must be checked to verify whether the process is allowed to read the directory's content.
- A filename can be a symbolic link that corresponds to an arbitrary pathname; in this case, the analysis must be extended to all components of that pathname.
- Symbolic links may induce circular references; the kernel must take this possibility into account and break endless loops when they occur.
- A filename can be the mount point of a mounted filesystem. This situation must be detected, and the lookup operation must continue into the new filesystem.

Pathname lookup is performed by three functions: path_init(), path_walk(), and path_release(). They are always invoked in this exact order.

The path_init() function receives three parameters:

name
> A pointer to the file pathname to be resolved.

flags

   The value of flags that represent how the looked-up file is going to be accessed.
   The flags are listed in Table 12-17 in the later section "The open() System Call."*

nd

   The address of a struct nameidata data structure.

The struct nameidata data structure is filled by path_walk() with data pertaining to the pathname lookup operation. The fields of this structure are shown in Table 12-14.

Table 12-14. The fields of the nameidata data structure

Type	Field	Description
struct dentry *	dentry	Address of the dentry object
struct vfs_mount *	mnt	Address of the mounted filesystem object
struct qstr	last	Last component of the pathname (used when the LOOKUP_PARENT flag is set)
unsigned int	flags	Lookup flags
int	last_type	Type of last component of the pathname (used when the LOOKUP_PARENT flag is set)

The dentry and mnt fields point respectively to the dentry object and the mounted filesystem object of the last resolved component in the pathname. Once path_walk() successfully returns, these two fields "describe" the file that is identified by the given pathname.

The flags field stores the value of some flags used in the lookup operation; they are listed in Table 12-15.

Table 12-15. The flags of the lookup operation

Macro	Description
LOOKUP_FOLLOW	If the last component is a symbolic link, interpret (follow) it.
LOOKUP_DIRECTORY	The last component must be a directory.
LOOKUP_CONTINUE	There are still filenames to be examined in the pathname (used only by NFS).
LOOKUP_POSITIVE	The pathname must identify an existing file.
LOOKUP_PARENT	Look up the directory including the last component of the pathname.
LOOKUP_NOALT	Do not consider the emulated root directory (always set for the 80 × 86 architecture).

---

* There is, however, a small difference in how the O_RDONLY, O_WRONLY, and O_RDWR flags are encoded. The bit at index 0 (lowest-order) of the flags parameter is set only if the file access requires read privileges; similarly, the bit at index 1 is set only if the file access requires write privileges. Conversely, for the open() system call, the value of the O_WRONLY flag is stored in the bit at index 0, while the O_RDWR flag is stored in the bit at index 1; thus, the O_RDONLY flag is true when both bits are cleared. Notice that it is not possible to specify in the open() system call that a file access does not require either read or write privileges; this makes sense, however, in a pathname lookup operation involving symbolic links.

The goal of the path_init() function consists of initializing the nameidata structure, which it does in the following manner:

1. Sets the dentry field with the address of the dentry object of the directory where the pathname lookup operation starts. If the pathname is relative (it doesn't start with a slash), the field points to the dentry of the working directory (current->fs->pwd); otherwise it points to the dentry of the root directory of the process (current->fs->root).

2. Sets the mnt field with the address of the mounted filesystem object relative to the directory where the pathname lookup operation starts: either current->fs->pwdmnt or current->fs->rootmnt, according to whether the pathname is relative or absolute.

3. Initializes the flags field with the value of the flags parameter.

4. Initializes the last_type field to LAST_ROOT.

Once path_init() initializes the nameidata data structure, the path_walk() function takes care of the lookup operation, and stores in the nameidata structure the pointers to the dentry object and mounted filesystem object relative to the last component of the pathname. The function also increments the usage counters of the objects referenced by nd->dentry and nd->mnt so that the caller function may safely access them once path_walk() returns. When the caller finishes accessing them, it invokes the third function of the set, path_release(), which receives as a parameter the address of the nameidata data structure and decrements the two usage counters of nd->dentry and nd->mnt.

We are now ready to describe the core of the pathname lookup operation, namely the path_walk() function. It receives as parameters a pointer name to the pathname to be resolved and the address nd of the nameidata data structure. The function initializes to zero the total_link_count of the current process (see the later section "Lookup of Symbolic Links"), and then invokes link_path_walk(). This latter function acts on the same two parameters of path_walk().

To make things a bit easier, we first describe what link_path_walk() does when LOOKUP_PARENT is not set and the pathname does not contain symbolic links (standard pathname lookup). Next, we discuss the case in which LOOKUP_PARENT is set: this type of lookup is required when creating, deleting, or renaming a directory entry, that is, during a parent pathname lookup. Finally, we explain how the function resolves the symbolic links.

Standard Pathname Lookup

When the LOOKUP_PARENT flag is cleared, link_path_walk() performs the following steps.

1. Initializes the lookup_flags local variable with nd->flags.

2. Skips any leading slash (/) before the first component of the pathname.

3. If the remaining pathname is empty, returns the value 0. In the `nameidata` data structure, the `dentry` and `mnt` fields point to the object relative to the last resolved component of the original pathname.

4. If the `link_count` field in the descriptor of the current process is positive, sets the `LOOKUP_FOLLOW` flag in the `lookup_flags` local variable (see the section "Lookup of Symbolic Links").

5. Executes a cycle that breaks `name` into components (the intermediate slashes are treated as filename separators); for each component found, the function:

   a. Retrieves the address of the inode object of the last resolved component from `nd->dentry->d_inode`.

   b. Checks that the permissions of the last resolved component stored into the inode allow execution (in Unix, a directory can be traversed only if it is executable). If the inode has a custom `permission` method, the function executes it; otherwise, it executes the `vfs_permission()` function, which examines the access mode stored in the `i_mode` inode field and the privileges of the running process.

   c. Considers the next component to be resolved. From its name, it computes a hash value for the dentry cache hash table.

   d. Skips any trailing slash (/) after the slash that terminates the name of the component to be resolved.

   e. If the component to be resolved is the last one in the original pathname, jump to Step 6.

   f. If the name of the component is "." (a single dot), continues with the next component ("." refers to the current directory, so it has no effect inside a pathname).

   g. If the name of the component is ".." (two dots), tries to climb to the parent directory:

      1. If the last resolved directory is the process's root directory (`nd->dentry` is equal to `current->fs->root` and `nd->mnt` is equal to `current->fs->rootmnt`), continues with the next component.

      2. If the last resolved directory is the root directory of a mounted filesystem (`nd->dentry` is equal to `nd->mnt->mnt_root`), sets `nd->mnt` to `nd->mnt->mnt_parent` and `nd->dentry` to `nd->mnt->mnt_mountpoint`, and then restarts Step 5.g. (Recall that several filesystems can be mounted on the same mount point).

      3. If the last resolved directory is not the root directory of a mounted filesystem, sets `nd->dentry` to `nd->dentry->d_parent` and continues with the next component.

h. The component name is neither "." nor "..", so the function must look it up in the dentry cache. If the low-level filesystem has a custom d_hash dentry method, the function invokes it to modify the hash value already computed in Step 5.c.

 i. Invokes cached_lookup( ), passing as parameters nd->dentry, the name of the component to be resolved, the hash value, and the LOOKUP_CONTINUE flag, which specifies that this is not the last component of the pathname. The function invokes d_lookup( ) to search the dentry object of the component in the dentry cache. If cached_lookup( ) fails in finding the dentry in the cache, link_walk_path( ) invokes real_lookup( ) to read the directory from disk and create a new dentry object. In either case, we can assume at the end of this step that the dentry local variable points to the dentry object of the component name to be resolved in this cycle.

 j. Checks whether the component just resolved (dentry local variable) refers to a directory that is a mount point for some filesystem (dentry->d_mounted is set to 1). In this case, invokes lookup_mnt( ), passing to it dentry and nd->mnt, in order to get the address mounted of the child mounted filesystem object. Next, it sets dentry to mounted->mnt_root and nd->mnt to mounted. Then it repeats the whole step (several filesystems can be mounted on the same mount point).

 k. Checks whether the inode object dentry->d_inode has a custom follow_link method. If this is the case, the component is a symbolic link, which is described in the later section "Lookup of Symbolic Links."

 l. Checks that dentry points to the dentry object of a directory (dentry->d_inode >i_op >lookup method is defined). If not, returns the error -ENOTDIR, because the component is in the middle of the original pathname.

 m. Sets nd->dentry to dentry and continues with the next component of the pathname.

6. Now all components of the original pathname are resolved except the last one. If the pathname has a trailing slash, it sets the LOOKUP_FOLLOW and LOOKUP_DIRECTORY in the lookup_flags local variable to force interpretation of the last component as a directory name.

7. Checks the value of the LOOKUP_PARENT flag in the lookup_flags variable. In the following, we assume that the flag is set to 0, and we postpone the opposite case to the next section.

8. If the name of the last component is "." (a single dot), terminates the execution returning the value 0 (no error). In the nameidata structure that nd points to, the dentry and mnt fields refer to the objects relative to the next-to-last component of the pathname (any component "." has no effect inside a pathname).

9. If the name of the last component is "`..`" (two dots), tries to climb to the parent directory:

   a. If the last resolved directory is the process's root directory (nd->dentry is equal to current->fs->root and nd->mnt is equal to current->fs->rootmnt), terminates the execution returning the value 0 (no error). nd->dentry and nd->mnt refer to the objects relative to the next to the last component of the pathname—that is, to the root directory of the process.

   b. If the last resolved directory is the root directory of a mounted filesystem (nd->dentry is equal to nd->mnt->mnt_root), sets nd->mnt to nd->mnt->mnt_parent and nd->dentry to nd->mnt->mnt_mountpoint, and then restarts Step 5.j.

   c. If the last resolved directory is not the root directory of a mounted filesystem, sets nd->dentry to nd->dentry->d_parent, and terminates the execution returning the value 0 (no error). nd->dentry and nd->mnt refer to the objects relative to the next-to-last component of the pathname.

10. The name of the last component is neither "`.`" nor "`..`", so the function must look it up in the dentry cache. If the low-level filesystem has a custom d_hash dentry method, the function invokes it to modify the hash value already computed in Step 5.c.

11. Invokes cached_lookup( ), passing as parameters nd->dentry, the name of the component to be resolved, the hash value, and no flag (LOOKUP_CONTINUE is not set because this is the last component of the pathname). If cached_lookup( ) fails in finding the dentry in the cache, it also invokes real_lookup( ) to read the directory from disk and create a new dentry object. In either case, we can assume at the end of this step that the dentry local variable points to the dentry object of the component name to be resolved in this cycle.

12. Checks whether the component just resolved (dentry local variable) refers to a directory that is a mount point for some filesystem (dentry->d_mounted is set to 1). In this case, invokes lookup_mnt( ), passing to it dentry and nd->mnt, in order to get the address mounted of the child mounted filesystem object. Next, it sets dentry to mounted->mnt_root and nd->mnt to mounted. Then it repeats the whole step (because several filesystems can be mounted on the same mount point).

13. Checks whether LOOKUP_FOLLOW flag is set in lookup_flags and the inode object dentry->d_inode has a custom follow_link method. If this is the case, the component is a symbolic link that must be interpreted, as described in the later section "Lookup of Symbolic Links."

14. Sets nd->dentry with the value stored in the dentry local variable. This dentry object is "the result" of the lookup operation.

15. Checks whether nd->dentry->d_inode is NULL. This happens when there is no inode associated with the dentry object, usually because the pathname refers to a nonexisting file. In this case:

a. If either LOOKUP_POSITIVE or LOOKUP_DIRECTORY is set in lookup_flags, it terminates, returning the error code -ENOENT.

b. Otherwise, it terminates returning the value 0 (no error). nd->dentry points to the negative dentry object created by the lookup operation.

16. There is an inode associated with the last component of the pathname. If the LOOKUP_DIRECTORY flag is set in lookup_flags, checks that the inode has a custom lookup method—that is, it is a directory. If not, terminates returning the error code -ENOTDIR.

17. Terminates returning the value 0 (no error). nd->dentry and nd->mnt refer to the last component of the pathname.

Parent Pathname Lookup

In many cases, the real target of a lookup operation is not the last component of the pathname, but the next-to-last one. For example, when a file is created, the last component denotes the filename of the not yet existing file, and the rest of the pathname specifies the directory in which the new link must be inserted. Therefore, the lookup operation should fetch the dentry object of the next-to-last component. For another example, unlinking a file identified by the pathname /foo/bar consists of removing *bar* from the directory *foo*. Thus, the kernel is really interested in accessing the file directory *foo* rather than *bar*.

The LOOKUP_PARENT flag is used whenever the lookup operation must resolve the directory containing the last component of the pathname, rather than the last component itself.

When the LOOKUP_PARENT flag is set, the path_walk() function also sets up the last and last_type fields of the nameidata data structure. The last field stores the name of the last component in the pathname. The last_type field identifies the type of the last component; it may be set to one of the values shown in Table 12-16.

Table 12-16. The values of the last_type field in the nameidata data structure

Value	Description
LAST_NORM	Last component is a regular filename
LAST_ROOT	Last component is "/" (that is, the entire pathname is "/")
LAST_DOT	Last component is "."
LAST_DOTDOT	Last component is ".."
LAST_BIND	Last component is a symbolic link into a special filesystem

The LAST_ROOT flag is the default value set by path_init() when the whole pathname lookup operation starts (see the description at the beginning of the section "Pathname Lookup"). If the pathname turns out to be just "/", the kernel does not change the initial value of the last_type field. The LAST_BIND flag is set by the follow_link inode object's method of symbolic links in special filesystems (see the next section).

The remaining values of the last_type field are set by link_path_walk( ) when the LOOKUP_PARENT flag is on; in this case, the function performs the same steps described in the previous section up to Step 7. From Step 7 onward, however, the lookup operation for the last component of the pathname is different:

1. Sets nd->last to the name of the last component

2. Initializes nd->last_type to LAST_NORM

3. If the name of the last component is "." (a single dot), sets nd->last_type to LAST_DOT

4. If the name of the last component is ".." (two dots), sets nd->last_type to LAST_DOTDOT

5. Terminates by returning the value 0 (no error)

As you can see, the last component is not interpreted at all. Thus, when the function terminates, the dentry and mnt fields of the nameidata data structure point to the objects relative to the directory that includes the last component.

Lookup of Symbolic Links

Recall that a symbolic link is a regular file that stores a pathname of another file. A pathname may include symbolic links, and they must be resolved by the kernel.

For example, if */foo/bar* is a symbolic link pointing to (containing the pathname) *../dir*, the pathname */foo/bar/file* must be resolved by the kernel as a reference to the file */dir/file*. In this example, the kernel must perform two different lookup operations. The first one resolves */foo/bar*; when the kernel discovers that *bar* is the name of a symbolic link, it must retrieve its content and interpret it as another pathname. The second pathname operation starts from the directory reached by the first operation and continues until the last component of the symbolic link pathname has been resolved. Next, the original lookup operation resumes from the dentry reached in the second one and with the component following the symbolic link in the original pathname.

To further complicate the scenario, the pathname included in a symbolic link may include other symbolic links. You might think that the kernel code that resolves the symbolic links is hard to understand, but this is not true; the code is actually quite simple because it is recursive.

However, untamed recursion is intrinsically dangerous. For instance, suppose that a symbolic link points to itself. Of course, resolving a pathname including such a symbolic link may induce an endless stream of recursive invocations, which in turn quickly leads to a kernel stack overflow. The link_count field in the descriptor of the current process is used to avoid the problem: the field is incremented before each recursive execution and decremented right after. If the field reaches the value 5, the whole lookup operation terminates with an error code. Therefore, the level of nesting of symbolic links can be at most 5.

Furthermore, the total_link count field in the descriptor of the current process keeps track of how many symbolic links (even nonnested) were followed in the original lookup operation. If this counter reaches the value 40, the lookup operation aborts. Without this counter, a malicious user could create a pathological pathname including many consecutive symbolic links that freezes the kernel in a very long lookup operation.

This is how the code basically works: once the link_path_walk() function retrieves the dentry object associated with a component of the pathname, it checks whether the corresponding inode object has a custom follow_link method (see Step 5.k and Step 13 in the section "Standard Pathname Lookup"). If so, the inode is a symbolic link that must be interpreted before proceeding with the lookup operation of the original pathname.

In this case, the link_path_walk() function invokes do_follow_link(), passing to it the address of the dentry object of the symbolic link and the address of the nameidata data structure. In turn, do_follow_link() performs the following steps:

1. Checks that current->link_count is less than 5; otherwise, returns the error code -ELOOP

2. Checks that current->total_link_count is less than 40; otherwise, returns the error code -ELOOP

3. If the current->need_resched flag is set, invokes schedule() to give a chance to preempt the running process

4. Increments current->link_count and current->total_link_count

5. Updates the access time of the inode object associated with the symbolic link to be resolved

6. Invokes the follow_link method of the inode, passing to it the addresses of the dentry object and of the nameidata data structure

7. Decrements the current->link_count field

8. Returns the error code returned by the follow_link method (0 for no error)

The follow_link method is a filesystem-dependent function that reads the pathname stored in the symbolic link from the disk. Having filled a buffer with the symbolic link's pathname, most follow_link methods end up invoking the vfs_follow_link() function and returning the value taken from it. In turn, the vfs_follow_link() does the following:

1. Checks whether the first character of the symbolic link pathname is a slash; if so, the dentry and mnt fields of the nameidata data structure are set so they refer to the current process root directory.

2. Invokes link_path_walk() to resolve the symbolic link pathname, passing to it the nameidata data structure.

3. Returns the value taken from link_path_walk().

When do_follow_link() finally terminates, it returns the address of the dentry object referred to by the symbolic link to the original execution of link_path_walk(). The link_path_walk() assigns this address to the dentry local variable, and then proceeds with the next step.

Implementations of VFS System Calls

For the sake of brevity, we cannot discuss the implementation of all the VFS system calls listed in Table 12-1. However, it could be useful to sketch out the implementation of a few system calls, just to show how VFS's data structures interact.

Let's reconsider the example proposed at the beginning of this chapter: a user issues a shell command that copies the MS-DOS file */floppy/TEST* to the Ext2 file */tmp/test*. The command shell invokes an external program like *cp*, which we assume executes the following code fragment:

```
inf = open("/floppy/TEST", O_RDONLY, 0);
outf = open("/tmp/test", O_WRONLY | O_CREAT | O_TRUNC, 0600);
do {
    len = read(inf, buf, 4096);
    write(outf, buf, len);
} while (len);
close(outf);
close(inf);
```

Actually, the code of the real *cp* program is more complicated, since it must also check for possible error codes returned by each system call. In our example, we just focus our attention on the "normal" behavior of a copy operation.

The open( ) System Call

The open( ) system call is serviced by the sys_open( ) function, which receives as parameters the pathname filename of the file to be opened, some access mode flags flags, and a permission bit mask mode if the file must be created. If the system call succeeds, it returns a file descriptor—that is, the index assigned to the new file in the current->files->fd array of pointers to file objects; otherwise, it returns –1.

In our example, open( ) is invoked twice; the first time to open */floppy/TEST* for reading (O_RDONLY flag) and the second time to open */tmp/test* for writing (O_WRONLY flag). If */tmp/test* does not already exist, it is created (O_CREAT flag) with exclusive read and write access for the owner (octal 0600 number in the third parameter).

Conversely, if the file already exists, it is rewritten from scratch (O_TRUNC flag). Table 12-17 lists all flags of the open( ) system call.

Table 12-17. The flags of the open( ) system call

Flag name	Description
O_RDONLY	Open for reading
O_WRONLY	Open for writing
O_RDWR	Open for both reading and writing
O_CREAT	Create the file if it does not exist
O_EXCL	With O_CREAT, fail if the file already exists
O_NOCTTY	Never consider the file as a controlling terminal
O_TRUNC	Truncate the file (remove all existing contents)
O_APPEND	Always write at end of the file
O_NONBLOCK	No system calls will block on the file
O_NDELAY	Same as O_NONBLOCK
O_SYNC	Synchronous write (block until physical write terminates)
FASYNC	Asynchronous I/O notification via signals
O_DIRECT	Direct I/O transfer (no kernel buffering)
O_LARGEFILE	Large file (size greater than 2 GB)
O_DIRECTORY	Fail if file is not a directory
O_NOFOLLOW	Do not follow a trailing symbolic link in pathname

Let's describe the operation of the sys_open( ) function. It performs the following steps:

1. Invokes getname( ) to read the file pathname from the process address space.

2. Invokes get_unused_fd( ) to find an empty slot in current->files->fd. The corresponding index (the new file descriptor) is stored in the fd local variable.

3. Invokes the filp_open( ) function, passing as parameters the pathname, the access mode flags, and the permission bit mask. This function, in turn, executes the following steps:

    a. Copies the access mode flags into namei_flags, but encodes the access mode flags O_RDONLY, O_WRONLY, and O_RDWR with the format expected by the pathname lookup functions (see the earlier section "Pathname Lookup").

    b. Invokes open_namei( ), passing to it the pathname, the modified access mode flags, and the address of a local nameidata data structure. The function performs the lookup operation in the following manner:

        • If O_CREAT is not set in the access mode flags, starts the lookup operation with the LOOKUP_PARENT flag not set. Moreover, the LOOKUP_FOLLOW flag is set only if O_NOFOLLOW is cleared, while the LOOKUP_DIRECTORY flag is set only if the O_DIRECTORY flag is set.

        • If O_CREAT is set in the access mode flags, starts the lookup operation with the LOOKUP_PARENT flag set. Once the path_walk( ) function successfully returns, checks whether the requested file already exists. If not, allocates a new disk inode by invoking the create method of the parent inode.

The open_namei() function also executes several security checks on the file located by the lookup operation. For instance, the function checks whether the inode associated with the dentry object found really exists, whether it is a regular file, and whether the current process is allowed to access it according to the access mode flags. Also, if the file is opened for writing, the function checks that the file is not locked by other processes.

   c. Invokes the dentry_open() function, passing to it the access mode flags and the addresses of the dentry object and the mounted filesystem object located by the lookup operation. In turn, this function:

     1. Allocates a new file object.

     2. Initializes the f_flags and f_mode fields of the file object according to the access mode flags passed to the open() system call.

     3. Initializes the f_fentry and f_vfsmnt fields of the file object according to the addresses of the dentry object and the mounted filesystem object passed as parameters.

     4. Sets the f_op field to the contents of the i_fop field of the corresponding inode object. This sets up all the methods for future file operations.

     5. Inserts the file object into the list of opened files pointed to by the s_files field of the filesystem's superblock.

     6. If the O_DIRECT flag is set, preallocates a direct access buffer (see the section "Direct I/O Transfers" in Chapter 15).

     7. If the open method of the file operations is defined, invokes it.

   d. Returns the address of the file object.

  4. Sets current->files->fd[fd] to the address of the file object returned by dentry_open().

  5. Returns fd.

The read( ) and write( ) System Calls

Let's return to the code in our *cp* example. The open() system calls return two file descriptors, which are stored in the inf and outf variables. Then the program starts a loop: at each iteration, a portion of the */floppy/TEST* file is copied into a local buffer (read() system call), and then the data in the local buffer is written into the */tmp/test* file (write() system call).

The read() and write() system calls are quite similar. Both require three parameters: a file descriptor fd, the address buf of a memory area (the buffer containing the data to be transferred), and a number count that specifies how many bytes should be transferred. Of course, read() transfers the data from the file into the buffer, while write( ) does the opposite. Both system calls return either the number of bytes that were successfully transferred or −1 to signal an error condition.

A return value less than count does not mean that an error occurred. The kernel is always allowed to terminate the system call even if not all requested bytes were transferred, and the user application must accordingly check the return value and reissue, if necessary, the system call. Typically, a small value is returned when reading from a pipe or a terminal device, when reading past the end of the file, or when the system call is interrupted by a signal. The End-Of-File condition (EOF) can easily be recognized by a null return value from read( ). This condition will not be confused with an abnormal termination due to a signal, because if read( ) is interrupted by a signal before any data is read, an error occurs.

The read or write operation always takes place at the file offset specified by the current file pointer (field f_pos of the file object). Both system calls update the file pointer by adding the number of transferred bytes to it.

In short, both sys_read( ) (the read( )'s service routine) and sys_write( ) (the write( )'s service routine) perform almost the same steps:

1. Invoke fget( ) to derive from fd the address file of the corresponding file object and increment the usage counter file->f_count.

2. Check whether the flags in file->f_mode allow the requested access (read or write operation).

3. Invoke locks_verify_area( ) to check whether there are mandatory locks for the file portion to be accessed (see the section "File Locking" later in this chapter).

4. Invoke either file->f_op->read or file->f_op->write to transfer the data. Both functions return the number of bytes that were actually transferred. As a side effect, the file pointer is properly updated.

5. Invoke fput( ) to decrement the usage counter file->f_count.

6. Return the number of bytes actually transferred.

The close( ) System Call

The loop in our example code terminates when the read( ) system call returns the value 0—that is, when all bytes of */floppy/TEST* have been copied into */tmp/test*. The program can then close the open files, since the copy operation has completed.

The close( ) system call receives as its parameter fd, which is the file descriptor of the file to be closed. The sys_close( ) service routine performs the following operations:

1. Gets the file object address stored in current->files->fd[fd]; if it is NULL, returns an error code.

2. Sets current->files->fd[fd] to NULL. Releases the file descriptor fd by clearing the corresponding bits in the open_fds and close_on_exec fields of current->files (see Chapter 20 for the Close on Execution flag).

3. Invokes `filp_close( )`, which performs the following operations:

    a. Invokes the `flush` method of the file operations, if defined

    b. Releases any mandatory lock on the file

    c. Invokes `fput( )` to release the file object

4. Returns the error code of the `flush` method (usually 0).

File Locking

When a file can be accessed by more than one process, a synchronization problem occurs. What happens if two processes try to write in the same file location? Or again, what happens if a process reads from a file location while another process is writing into it?

In traditional Unix systems, concurrent accesses to the same file location produce unpredictable results. However, Unix systems provide a mechanism that allows the processes to *lock* a file region so that concurrent accesses may be easily avoided.

The POSIX standard requires a file-locking mechanism based on the `fcntl( )` system call. It is possible to lock an arbitrary region of a file (even a single byte) or to lock the whole file (including data appended in the future). Since a process can choose to lock just a part of a file, it can also hold multiple locks on different parts of the file.

This kind of lock does not keep out another process that is ignorant of locking. Like a critical region in code, the lock is considered "advisory" because it doesn't work unless other processes cooperate in checking the existence of a lock before accessing the file. Therefore, POSIX's locks are known as *advisory locks*.

Traditional BSD variants implement advisory locking through the `flock( )` system call. This call does not allow a process to lock a file region, just the whole file.

Traditional System V variants provide the `lockf( )` function, which is just an interface to `fcntl( )`. More importantly, System V Release 3 introduced *mandatory locking*: the kernel checks that every invocation of the `open( )`, `read( )`, and `write( )` system calls does not violate a mandatory lock on the file being accessed. Therefore, mandatory locks are enforced even between noncooperative processes.* A file is marked as a candidate for mandatory locking by setting its set-group bit (SGID) and clearing the group-execute permission bit. Since the set-group bit makes no sense when the group-execute bit is off, the kernel interprets that combination as a hint to use mandatory locks instead of advisory ones.

---

* Oddly enough, a process may still unlink (delete) a file even if some other process owns a mandatory lock on it! This perplexing situation is possible because when a process deletes a file hard link, it does not modify its contents, but only the contents of its parent directory.

Whether processes use advisory or mandatory locks, they can use both shared *read locks* and exclusive *write locks*. Any number of processes may have read locks on some file region, but only one process can have a write lock on it at the same time. Moreover, it is not possible to get a write lock when another process owns a read lock for the same file region, and vice versa (see Table 12-18).

Table 12-18. Whether a lock is granted

| | Grant request for | |
Current Locks	Read lock?	Write lock?
No lock	Yes	Yes
Read lock	Yes	No
Write lock	No	No

Linux File Locking

Linux supports all fashions of file locking: advisory and mandatory locks, as well as the fcntl( ), flock( ), and the lockf( ) system calls. However, the lockf( ) system call is just a library wrapper routine, and therefore is not discussed here.

fcntl( )'s mandatory locks can be enabled and disabled on a per-filesystem basis using the MS_MANDLOCK flag (the mand option) of the mount( ) system call. The default is to switch off mandatory locking. In this case, fcntl( ) creates advisory locks. When the flag is set, fcntl( ) produces mandatory locks if the file has the set-group bit on and the group-execute bit off; it produces advisory locks otherwise.

In earlier Linux versions, the flock( ) system call produced only advisory locks, without regard of the MS_MANDLOCK mount flag. This is the expected behavior of the system call in any Unix-like operating system. In Linux 2.4, however, a special kind of flock( )'s mandatory lock has been added to allow proper support for some proprietary network filesystem implementations. It is the so-called *share-mode mandatory look*; when set, no other process may open a file that would conflict with the access mode of the lock. Use of this feature for native Unix applications is discouraged, because the resulting source code will be nonportable.

Another kind of flock( )-based mandatory lock called *leases* has been introduced in Linux 2.4. When a process tries to open a file protected by a lease, it is blocked as usual. However, the process that owns the lock receives a signal. Once informed, it should first update the file so that its content is consistent, and then release the lock. If the owner does not do this in a well-defined time interval (tunable by writing a number of seconds into */proc/sys/fs/lease-break-time*, usually 45 seconds), the lease is automatically removed by the kernel and the blocked process is allowed to continue.

Beside the checks in the read( ) and write( ) system calls, the kernel takes into consideration the existence of mandatory locks when servicing all system calls that could modify the contents of a file. For instance, an open( ) system call with the O_TRUNC flag set fails if any mandatory lock exists for the file.

A lock produced by fcntl( ) is of type FL_POSIX, while a lock produced by flock( ) is of type FL_FLOCK, FL_MAND (for share-mode locks), or FL_LEASE (for leases). The types of locks produced by fcntl( ) may safely coexist with those produced by flock( ), but neither one has any effect on the other. Therefore, a file locked through fcntl( ) does not appear locked to flock( ), and vice versa.

The following section describes the main data structure used by the kernel to handle file locks. The next two sections examine the differences between the two most common lock types: FL_POSIX and FL_FLOCK.

File-Locking Data Structures

The file_lock data structure represents file locks; its fields are shown in Table 12-19. All file_lock data structures are included in a doubly linked list. The address of the first element is stored in file_lock_list, while the fields fl_nextlink and fl_prevlink store the addresses of the adjacent elements in the list.

Table 12-19. The fields of the file_lock data structure

Type	Field	Description
struct file_lock *	fl_next	Next element in inode list
struct list_head	fl_link	Pointers for global list
struct list_head	fl_block	Pointers for process list
struct files_struct *	fl_owner	Owner's files_struct
unsigned int	fl_pid	PID of the process owner
wait_queue_head_t	fl_wait	Wait queue of blocked processes
struct file *	fl_file	Pointer to file object
unsigned char	fl_flags	Lock flags
unsigned char	fl_type	Lock type
loff_t	fl_start	Starting offset of locked region
loff_t	fl_end	Ending offset of locked region
void (*)(struct file_lock *)	fl_notify	Function to call when lock is unblocked
void (*)(struct file_lock *)	fl_insert	Function to call when lock is inserted
void (*)(struct file_lock *)	fl_remove	Function to call when lock is removed
struct fasync_struct *	fl_fasync	Used for lease break notifications
union	u	Filesystem-specific information

All lock_file structures that refer to the same file on disk are collected in a simply linked list, whose first element is pointed to by the i_flock field of the inode object. The fl_next field of the lock_file structure specifies the next element in the list.

When a process tries to get an advisory or mandatory lock, it may be suspended until the previously allocated lock on the same file region is released. All processes sleeping on some lock are inserted into a wait queue, whose head is stored in the fl_wait field of the file_lock structure. Moreover, all processes sleeping on any file locks are inserted into a circular doubly linked list, whose head (first dummy element) is stored in the blocked_list variable; the fl_block field of the file_lock data structure stores the pointer to adjacent elements in the list.

FL_FLOCK Locks

An FL_FLOCK lock is always associated with a file object and is thus maintained by a particular process (or clone processes sharing the same opened file). When a lock is requested and granted, the kernel replaces any other lock that the process is holding on the same file object.

This happens only when a process wants to change an already owned read lock into a write one, or vice versa. Moreover, when a file object is being freed by the fput( ) function, all FL_FLOCK locks that refer to the file object are destroyed. However, there could be other FL_FLOCK read locks set by other processes for the same file (inode), and they still remain active.

The flock( ) system call acts on two parameters: the fd file descriptor of the file to be acted upon and a cmd parameter that specifies the lock operation. A cmd parameter of LOCK_SH requires a shared lock for reading, LOCK_EX requires an exclusive lock for writing, and LOCK_UN releases the lock. If the LOCK_NB value is ORed to the LOCK_SH or LOCK_EX operation, the system call does not block; in other words, if the lock cannot be immediately obtained, the system call returns an error code. Note that it is not possible to specify a region inside the file—the lock always applies to the whole file.

When the sys_flock( ) service routine is invoked, it performs the following steps:

1. Checks whether fd is a valid file descriptor; if not, returns an error code. Gets the address of the corresponding file object.

2. If the process has to acquire an advisory lock, checks that the process has both read and write permission on the open file; if not, returns an error code.

3. Invokes flock_lock_file( ), passing as parameters the file object pointer filp, the type type of lock operation required, and a flag wait. This last parameter is set if the system call should block (LOCK_NB clear) and cleared otherwise (LOOK_NB set). This function performs, in turn, the following actions:

    a. If the lock must be acquired, gets a new file_lock object and fills it with the appropriate lock operation.

    b. Searches the list that filp->f_dentry->d_inode->i_flock points to. If an FL_FLOCK lock for the same file object is found and an unlock operation is required, removes the file_lock element from the inode list and the global

list, wakes up all processes sleeping in the lock's wait queue, frees the file_
lock structure, and returns.

   c. Otherwise, searches the inode list again to verify that no existing FL_FLOCK
      lock conflicts with the requested one. There must be no FL_FLOCK write lock
      in the inode list, and moreover, there must be no FL_FLOCK lock at all if the
      processing is requesting a write lock. However, a process may want to
      change the type of lock it already owns; this is done by issuing a second
      flock( ) system call. Therefore, the kernel always allows the process to
      change locks that refer to the same file object. If a conflicting lock is found
      and the LOCK_NB flag was specified, the function returns an error code; other-
      wise, it inserts the current process in the circular list of blocked processes
      and suspends it.

   d. If no incompatibility exists, inserts the file_lock structure into the global
      lock list and the inode list, and then returns 0 (success).

4. Returns the return code of flock_lock_file( ).

FL_POSIX Locks

An FL_POSIX lock is always associated with a process *and* with an inode; the lock is
automatically released either when the process dies or when a file descriptor is closed
(even if the process opened the same file twice or duplicated a file descriptor). Moreover, FL_POSIX locks are never inherited by the child across a fork( ).

When used to lock files, the fcntl( ) system call acts on three parameters: the fd file
descriptor of the file to be acted upon, a cmd parameter that specifies the lock operation, and an fl pointer to a flock data structure. Version 2.4 of Linux also defines a
flock64 structure, which uses 64-bit fields for the file offset and length fields. In the
following, we focus on the flock data structure, but the description is valid for
flock64 too.

Locks of type FL_POSIX are able to protect an arbitrary file region, even a single byte.
The region is specified by three fields of the flock structure. l_start is the initial offset of the region and is relative to the beginning of the file (if field l_whence is set to
SEEK_SET), to the current file pointer (if l_whence is set to SEEK_CUR), or to the end of
the file (if l_whence is set to SEEK_END). The l_len field specifies the length of the file
region (or 0, which means that the region includes all potential writes past the current end of the file).

The sys_fcntl( ) service routine behaves differently, depending on the value of the
flag set in the cmd parameter:

F_GETLK
   Determines whether the lock described by the flock structure conflicts with
   some FL_POSIX lock already obtained by another process. In this case, the flock
   structure is overwritten with the information about the existing lock.

F_SETLK
: Sets the lock described by the flock structure. If the lock cannot be acquired, the system call returns an error code.

F_SETLKW
: Sets the lock described by the flock structure. If the lock cannot be acquired, the system call blocks; that is, the calling process is put to sleep.

F_GETLK64, F_SETLK64, F_SETLKW64
: Identical to the previous ones, but the flock64 data structure is used rather than flock.

When sys_fcntl( ) acquires a lock, it performs the following:

1. Reads the flock structure from user space.

2. Gets the file object corresponding to fd.

3. Checks whether the lock should be a mandatory one and the file has a shared memory mapping (see the section "Memory Mapping" in Chapter 15). In this case, refuses to create the lock and returns the -EAGAIN error code; the file is already being accessed by another process.

4. Initializes a new file_lock structure according to the contents of the user's flock structure.

5. Terminates returning an error code if the file does not allow the access mode specified by the type of the requested lock.

6. Invokes the lock method of the file operations, if defined.

7. Invokes the posix_lock_file( ) function, which executes the following actions:

   a. Invokes posix_locks_conflict( ) for each FL_POSIX lock in the inode's lock list. The function checks whether the lock conflicts with the requested one. Essentially, there must be no FL_POSIX write lock for the same region in the inode list, and there may be no FL_POSIX lock at all for the same region if the process is requesting a write lock. However, locks owned by the same process never conflict; this allows a process to change the characteristics of a lock it already owns.

   b. If a conflicting lock is found and fcntl( ) was invoked with the F_SETLK or F_SETLK64 flag, returns an error code. Otherwise, the current process should be suspended. In this case, invokes posix_locks_deadlock( ) to check that no deadlock condition is being created among processes waiting for FL_POSIX locks, and then inserts the current process in the circular list of blocked processes and suspends it.

   c. As soon as the inode's lock list includes no conflicting lock, checks all the FL_POSIX locks of the current process that overlap the file region that the current process wants to lock, and combines and splits adjacent areas as required. For example, if the process requested a write lock for a file region that falls inside a read-locked wider region, the previous read lock is split into two parts covering the nonoverlapping areas, while the central region is protected by the new write lock. In case of overlaps, newer locks always replace older ones.

    d. Inserts the new file_lock structure in the global lock list and in the inode list.

8. Returns the value 0 (success).

CHAPTER 13
Managing I/O Devices

The Virtual File System in the last chapter depends on lower-level functions to carry out each read, write, or other operation in a manner suited to each device. The previous chapter included a brief discussion of how operations are handled by different filesystems. In this chapter, we look at how the kernel invokes the operations on actual devices.

In the section "I/O Architecture," we give a brief survey of the 80×86 I/O architecture. In the section "Device Files," we show how the VFS associates a special file called "device file" with each different hardware device so that application programs can use all kinds of devices in the same way. Finally, in the section "Device Drivers," we illustrate the overall organization of device drivers in Linux. Readers interested in developing device drivers on their own may want to refer to Alessandro Rubini and Jonathan Corbet's *Linux Device Drivers* (O'Reilly).

I/O Architecture

To make a computer work properly, data paths must be provided that let information flow between CPU(s), RAM, and the score of I/O devices that can be connected to a personal computer. These data paths, which are denoted collectively as the *bus*, act as the primary communication channel inside the computer.

Several types of buses, such as the ISA, EISA, PCI, and MCA, are currently in use. In this section, we discuss the functional characteristics common to all PC architectures, without giving details about a specific bus type.

In fact, what is commonly denoted as a bus consists of three specialized buses:

Data bus
> A group of lines that transfer data in parallel. The Pentium has a 64-bit-wide data bus.

Address bus
> A group of lines that transmits an address in parallel. The Pentium has a 32-bit-wide address bus.

Control bus

A group of lines that transmits control information to the connected circuits. The Pentium uses control lines to specify, for instance, whether the bus is used to allow data transfers between a processor and the RAM, or alternatively, between a processor and an I/O device. Control lines also determine whether a read or a write transfer must be performed.

When the bus connects the CPU to an I/O device, it is called an *I/O bus*. In this case, 80×86 microprocessors use 16 out of the 32 address lines to address I/O devices and 8, 16, or 32 out of the 64 data lines to transfer data. The I/O bus, in turn, is connected to each I/O device by means of a hierarchy of hardware components including up to three elements: I/O ports, interfaces, and device controllers. Figure 13-1 shows the components of the I/O architecture.

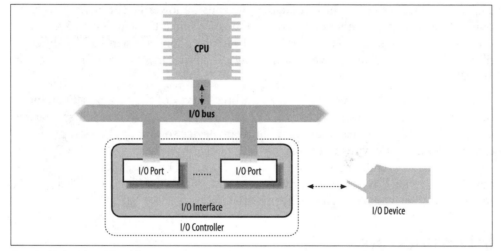

Figure 13-1. PC's I/O architecture

I/O Ports

Each device connected to the I/O bus has its own set of I/O addresses, which are usually called *I/O ports*. In the IBM PC architecture, the I/O address space provides up to 65,536 8-bit I/O ports. Two consecutive 8-bit ports may be regarded as a single 16-bit port, which must start on an even address. Similarly, two consecutive 16-bit ports may be regarded as a single 32-bit port, which must start on an address that is a multiple of 4. Four special assembly language instructions called in, ins, out, and outs allow the CPU to read from and write into an I/O port. While executing one of these instructions, the CPU uses the address bus to select the required I/O port and of the data bus to transfer data between a CPU register and the port.

I/O ports may also be mapped into addresses of the physical address space. The processor is then able to communicate with an I/O device by issuing assembly language instructions that operate directly on memory (for instance, mov, and, or, and so on).

Modern hardware devices are more suited to mapped I/O, since it is faster and can be combined with DMA.

An important objective for system designers is to offer a unified approach to I/O programming without sacrificing performance. Toward that end, the I/O ports of each device are structured into a set of specialized registers, as shown in Figure 13-2. The CPU writes the commands to be sent to the device into the *control register* and reads a value that represents the internal state of the device from the *status register*. The CPU also fetches data from the device by reading bytes from the *input register* and pushes data to the device by writing bytes into the *output register*.

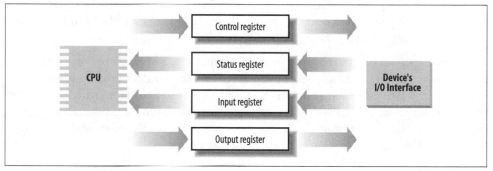

Figure 13-2. Specialized I/O ports

To lower costs, the same I/O port is often used for different purposes. For instance, some bits describe the device state, while others specify the command to be issued to the device. Similarly, the same I/O port may be used as an input register or an output register.

Accessing I/O ports

The in, out, ins, and outs assembly language instructions access I/O ports. The following auxiliary functions are included in the kernel to simplify such accesses:

inb( ), inw( ), inl( )
> Read 1, 2, or 4 consecutive bytes, respectively, from an I/O port. The suffix "b," "w," or "l" refers, respectively, to a byte (8 bits), a word (16 bits), and a long (32 bits).

inb_p( ) inw_p( ), inl_p( )
> Read 1, 2, or 4 consecutive bytes, respectively, from an I/O port, and then execute a "dummy" instruction to introduce a pause.

outb( ), outw( ), outl( )
> Write 1, 2, or 4 consecutive bytes, respectively, to an I/O port.

outb_p( ), outw_p( ), outl_p( )
> Write 1, 2, and 4 consecutive bytes, respectively, to an I/O port, and then execute a "dummy" instruction to introduce a pause.

insb( ), insw( ), insl( )
>   Read sequences of consecutive bytes in groups of 1, 2, or 4, respectively, from an
>   I/O port. The length of the sequence is specified as a parameter of the functions.

outsb( ), outsw( ), outsl( )
>   Write sequences of consecutive bytes, in groups of 1, 2, or 4, respectively, to an
>   I/O port.

While accessing I/O ports is simple, detecting which I/O ports have been assigned to
I/O devices may not be easy, in particular, for systems based on an ISA bus. Often a
device driver must blindly write into some I/O port to probe the hardware device; if,
however, this I/O port is already used by some other hardware device, a system crash
could occur. To prevent such situations, the kernel keeps track of I/O ports assigned
to each hardware device by means of "resources."

A *resource* represents a portion of some entity that can be exclusively assigned to a
device driver. In our case, a resource represents a range of I/O port addresses. The
information relative to each resource is stored in a resource data structure, whose
fields are shown in Table 13-1. All resources of the same kind are inserted in a tree-
like data structure; for instance, all resources representing I/O port address ranges
are included in a tree rooted at the node ioport_resource.

Table 13-1. The fields of the resource data structure

Type	Field	Description
const char *	name	Description of owner of the resource
unsigned long	start	Start of the resource range
unsigned long	end	End of the resource range
unsigned long	flags	Various flags
struct resource *	parent	Pointer to parent in the resource tree
struct resource *	sibling	Pointer to a sibling in the resource tree
struct resource *	child	Pointer to first child in the resource tree

The children of a node are collected in a list whose first element is pointed to by the
child field. The sibling field points to the next node in the list.

Why use a tree? Well, consider, for instance, the I/O port addresses used by an IDE
hard disk interface—let's say from 0xf000 to 0xf00f. A resource with the start field
set to 0xf000 and the end field set to 0xf00f is then included in the tree, and the conventional name of the controller is stored in the name field. However, the IDE device
driver needs to remember another bit of information, namely that the subrange from
0xf000 to 0xf007 is used for the master disk of the IDE chain, while the subrange
from 0xf008 to 0xf00f is used for the slave disk. To do this, the device driver inserts
two children below the resource corresponding to the whole range from 0xf000 to
0xf00f, one child for each subrange of I/O ports. As a general rule, each node of the
tree must correspond to a subrange of the range associated with the parent.

Any device driver may use the following three functions, passing to them the root node of the resource tree and the address of a resource data structure of interest:

request_resource( )
> Assigns a given range to an I/O device.

check_resource( )
> Checks whether a given range is free or whether some subrange has already been assigned to an I/O device

release_resource( )
> Releases a given range previously assigned to an I/O device.

The kernel also defines some shortcuts to the above functions that apply to I/O ports: request_region( ) assigns a given interval of I/O ports, check_region( ) verifies whether a given interval of I/O ports is free or (even partially) busy, and release_region( ) releases a previously assigned interval of I/O ports. The tree of all I/O addresses currently assigned to I/O devices can be obtained from the */proc/ioports* file.

I/O Interfaces

An *I/O interface* is a hardware circuit inserted between a group of I/O ports and the corresponding device controller. It acts as an interpreter that translates the values in the I/O ports into commands and data for the device. In the opposite direction, it detects changes in the device state and correspondingly updates the I/O port that plays the role of status register. This circuit can also be connected through an IRQ line to a Programmable Interrupt Controller, so that it issues interrupt requests on behalf of the device.

There are two types of interfaces:

Custom I/O interfaces
> Devoted to one specific hardware device. In some cases, the device controller is located in the same *card** that contains the I/O interface. The devices attached to a custom I/O interface can be either *internal devices* (devices located inside the PC's cabinet) or *external devices* (devices located outside the PC's cabinet).

General-purpose I/O interfaces
> Used to connect several different hardware devices. Devices attached to a general-purpose I/O interface are always external devices.

---

* Each card must be inserted in one of the available free bus slots of the PC. If the card can be connected to an external device through an external cable, the card sports a suitable connector in the rear panel of the PC.

Custom I/O interfaces

Just to give an idea of how much variety is encompassed by custom I/O interfaces—thus by the devices currently installed in a PC—we'll list some of the most commonly found:

Keyboard interface
> Connected to a keyboard controller that includes a dedicated microprocessor. This microprocessor decodes the combination of pressed keys, generates an interrupt, and puts the corresponding scan code in an input register.

Graphic interface
> Packed together with the corresponding controller in a graphic card that has its own *frame buffer*, as well as a specialized processor and some code stored in a Read-Only Memory chip (ROM). The frame buffer is an on-board memory containing a description of the current screen contents.

Disk interface
> Connected by a cable to the disk controller, which is usually integrated with the disk. For instance, the IDE interface is connected by a 40-wire flat conductor cable to an intelligent disk controller that can be found on the disk itself.

Bus mouse interface
> Connected by a cable to the corresponding controller, which is included in the mouse.

Network interface
> Packed together with the corresponding controller in a network card used to receive or transmit network packets. Although there are several widely adopted network standards, Ethernet (IEEE 802.3) is the most common.

General-purpose I/O interfaces

Modern PCs include several general-purpose I/O interfaces, which connect a wide range of external devices. The most common interfaces are:

Parallel port
> Traditionally used to connect printers, it can also be used to connect removable disks, scanners, backup units, and other computers. The data is transferred 1 byte (8 bits) at a time.

Serial port
> Like the parallel port, but the data is transferred 1 bit at a time. It includes a Universal Asynchronous Receiver and Transmitter (UART) chip to string out the bytes to be sent into a sequence of bits and to reassemble the received bits into bytes. Since it is intrinsically slower than the parallel port, this interface is mainly used to connect external devices that do not operate at a high speed, like modems, mouses, and printers.

Universal serial bus (USB)

A recent general-purpose I/O interface that is quickly gaining popularity. It operates at a high speed, and may be used for the external devices traditionally connected to the parallel port and the serial port.

PCMCIA interface

Included mostly on portable computers. The external device, which has the shape of a credit card, can be inserted into and removed from a slot without rebooting the system. The most common PCMCIA devices are hard disks, modems, network cards, and RAM expansions.

SCSI (Small Computer System Interface) interface

A circuit that connects the main PC bus to a secondary bus called the *SCSI bus*. The SCSI-2 bus allows up to eight PCs and external devices—hard disks, scanners, CD-ROM writers, and so on—to be connected. Wide SCSI-2 and the recent SCSI-3 interfaces allow you to connect 16 devices or more if additional interfaces are present. The *SCSI standard* is the communication protocol used to connect devices via the SCSI bus.

Device Controllers

A complex device may require a *device controller* to drive it. Essentially, the controller plays two important roles:

- It interprets the high-level commands received from the I/O interface and forces the device to execute specific actions by sending proper sequences of electrical signals to it.

- It converts and properly interprets the electrical signals received from the device and modifies (through the I/O interface) the value of the status register.

A typical device controller is the *disk controller*, which receives high-level commands such as a "write this block of data" from the microprocessor (through the I/O interface) and converts them into low-level disk operations such as "position the disk head on the right track" and "write the data inside the track." Modern disk controllers are very sophisticated, since they can keep the disk data in fast memory caches and can reorder the CPU high-level requests optimized for the actual disk geometry.

Simpler devices do not have a device controller; examples include the Programmable Interrupt Controller (see the section "Interrupts and Exceptions" in Chapter 4) and the Programmable Interval Timer (see the section "Programmable Interval Timer" in Chapter 6).

Several hardware devices include their own memory, which is often called *I/O shared memory*. For instance, all recent graphic cards include a few megabytes of RAM in the frame buffer, which is used to store the screen image to be displayed on the monitor.

Mapping addresses of I/O shared memory

Depending on the device and on the bus type, I/O shared memory in the PC's architecture may be mapped within three different physical address ranges:

For most devices connected to the ISA bus
> The I/O shared memory is usually mapped into the physical addresses ranging from 0xa0000 to 0xfffff; this gives rise to the "hole" between 640 KB and 1 MB mentioned in the section "Reserved Page Frames" in Chapter 2.

For some old devices using the VESA Local Bus (VLB)
> This is a specialized bus mainly used by graphic cards: the I/O shared memory is mapped into the physical addresses ranging from 0xe00000 to 0xffffff—that is, between 14 MB and 16 MB. These devices, which further complicate the initialization of the paging tables, are going out of production.

For devices connected to the PCI bus
> The I/O shared memory is mapped into very large physical addresses, well above the end of RAM's physical addresses. This kind of device is much simpler to handle.

Recently, Intel introduced the *Accelerated Graphics Port (AGP)* standard, which is an enhancement of PCI for high-performance graphic cards. Beside having its own I/O shared memory, this kind of card is capable of directly addressing portions of the motherboard's RAM by means of a special hardware circuit named *Graphics Address Remapping Table (GART)*. The GART circuitry enables AGP cards to sustain much higher data transfer rates than older PCI cards. From the kernel's point of view, however, it doesn't really matter where the physical memory is located, and GART-mapped memory is handled like the other kinds of I/O shared memory.

Accessing the I/O shared memory

How does the kernel access an I/O shared memory location? Let's start with the PC's architecture, which is relatively simple to handle, and then extend the discussion to other architectures.

Remember that kernel programs act on linear addresses, so the I/O shared memory locations must be expressed as addresses greater than PAGE_OFFSET. In the following discussion, we assume that PAGE_OFFSET is equal to 0xc0000000—that is, that the kernel linear addresses are in the fourth gigabyte.

Kernel drivers must translate I/O physical addresses of I/O shared memory locations into linear addresses in kernel space. In the PC architecture, this can be achieved simply by ORing the 32-bit physical address with the 0xc0000000 constant. For instance, suppose the kernel needs to store the value in the I/O location at physical address 0x000b0fe4 in t1 and the value in the I/O location at physical address 0xfc000000 in t2 . One might think that the following statements could do the job:

```
t1 = *((unsigned char *)(0xc00b0fe4));
t2 = *((unsigned char *)(0xfc000000));
```

During the initialization phase, the kernel maps the available RAM's physical addresses into the initial portion of the fourth gigabyte of the linear address space. Therefore, the Paging Unit maps the 0xc00b0fe4 linear address appearing in the first statement back to the original I/O physical address 0x000b0fe4, which falls inside the "ISA hole" between 640 KB and 1 MB (see the section "Paging in Linux" in Chapter 2). This works fine.

There is a problem, however, for the second statement because the I/O physical address is greater than the last physical address of the system RAM. Therefore, the 0xfc000000 linear address does not necessarily correspond to the 0xfc000000 physical address. In such cases, the kernel Page Tables must be modified to include a linear address that maps the I/O physical address. This can be done by invoking the ioremap() or ioremap_nocache() functions. These functions, which are similar to vmalloc(), invoke get_vm_area() to create a new vm_struct descriptor (see the section "Descriptors of Noncontiguous Memory Areas" in Chapter 7) for a linear address interval that has the size of the required I/O shared memory area. The functions then updates the corresponding Page Table entries of the canonical kernel Page Tables appropriately. ioremap_nocache() differs from ioremap() in that it also disables the hardware cache when referencing the remapped linear addresses properly.

The correct form for the second statement might therefore look like:

```
io_mem = ioremap(0xfb000000, 0x200000);
t2 = *((unsigned char *)(io_mem + 0x100000));
```

The first statement creates a new 2 MB linear address interval, which maps physical addresses starting from 0xfb000000; the second one reads the memory location that has the 0xfc000000 address. To remove the mapping later, the device driver must use the iounmap() function.

On some architectures other than the PC, I/O shared memory cannot be accessed by simply dereferencing the linear address pointing to the physical memory location. Therefore, Linux defines the following architecture-dependent macros, which should be used when accessing I/O shared memory:

readb, readw, readl
    Reads 1, 2, or 4 bytes, respectively, from an I/O shared memory location

writeb, writew, writel
    Writes 1, 2, or 4 bytes, respectively, into an I/O shared memory location

memcpy_fromio, memcpy_toio
    Copies a block of data from an I/O shared memory location to dynamic memory and vice versa

memset_io
    Fills an I/O shared memory area with a fixed value

The recommended way to access the 0xfc000000 I/O location is thus:

```
io_mem = ioremap(0xfb000000, 0x200000);
t2 = readb(io_mem + 0x100000);
```

Thanks to these macros, all dependencies on platform-specific ways of accessing the I/O shared memory can be hidden.

Direct Memory Access (DMA)

All PCs include an auxiliary processor called the *Direct Memory Access Controller* (*DMAC*), which can be instructed to transfer data between the RAM and an I/O device. Once activated by the CPU, the DMAC is able to continue the data transfer on its own; when the data transfer is completed, the DMAC issues an interrupt request. The conflicts that occur when both CPU and DMAC need to access the same memory location at the same time are resolved by a hardware circuit called a *memory arbiter* (see the section "Atomic Operations" in Chapter 5).

The DMAC is mostly used by disk drivers and other slow devices that transfer a large number of bytes at once. Because setup time for the DMAC is relatively high, it is more efficient to directly use the CPU for the data transfer when the number of bytes is small.

The first DMACs for the old ISA buses were complex, hard to program, and limited to the lower 16 MB of physical memory. More recent DMACs for the PCI and SCSI buses rely on dedicated hardware circuits in the buses and make life easier for device driver developers.

Until now we have distinguished three kinds of memory addresses: logical and linear addresses, which are used internally by the CPU, and physical addresses, which are the memory addresses used by the CPU to physically drive the data bus. However, there is a fourth kind of memory address: the so-called *bus address*. It corresponds to the memory addresses used by all hardware devices except the CPU to drive the data bus. In the PC architecture, bus addresses coincide with physical addresses; however, in other architectures (like Sun's SPARC and Hewlett-Packard's Alpha), these two kinds of addresses differ.

Why should the kernel be concerned at all about bus addresses? Well, in a DMA operation, the data transfer takes place without CPU intervention; the data bus is driven directly by the I/O device and the DMAC. Therefore, when the kernel sets up a DMA operation, it must write the bus address of the memory buffer involved in the proper I/O ports of the DMAC or I/O device.

Putting DMA to work

Several I/O drivers use the Direct Memory Access Controller (DMAC) to speed up operations. The DMAC interacts with the device's I/O controller to perform a data transfer and the kernel includes an easy-to-use set of routines to program the DMAC. The I/O controller signals to the CPU, via an IRQ, when the data transfer has finished.

When a device driver sets up a DMA operation for some I/O device, it must specify the memory buffer involved by using bus addresses. The kernel provides the virt_to_bus and `bus_to_virt` macros, respectively, to translate a linear address into a bus address and vice versa.

As with IRQ lines, the DMAC is a resource that must be assigned dynamically to the drivers that need it. The way the driver starts and ends DMA operations depends on the type of bus.

For recent buses, such as PCI or SCSI, there are two main steps to perform: allocating an IRQ line and triggering the DMA transfer. The IRQ line used for signaling the termination of the DMA operation is allocated when opening the device file (see the later section "Initializing a Device Driver"). To start a DMA operation, the device driver simply writes the bus address of the DMA buffer, the transfer direction, and the size of the data in an I/O port of the hardware device; the driver then suspends the current process. When the DMA transfer ends, the hardware device raises an interrupt that wakes the device driver. The release method of the device file releases the IRQ line when the file object is closed by the last process.

Device Files

As mentioned in Chapter 1, Unix-like operating systems are based on the notion of a *file*, which is just an information container structured as a sequence of characters. According to this approach, I/O devices are treated as files; thus, the same system calls used to interact with regular files on disk can be used to directly interact with I/O devices. For example, the same `write( )` system call may be used to write data into a regular file or to send it to a printer by writing to the */dev/lp0* device file.

According to the characteristics of the underlying device drivers, device files can be of two types: *block* or *character*. The difference between the two classes of hardware devices is not so clear cut. At least we can assume the following:

- The data of a block device can be addressed randomly, and the time needed to transfer any data block is small and roughly the same, at least from the point of view of the human user. Typical examples of block devices are hard disks, floppy disks, CD-ROM, and DVD players.

- The data of a character device either cannot be addressed randomly (consider, for instance, a sound card), or they can be addressed randomly, but the time required to access a random datum largely depends on its position inside the device (consider, for instance, a magnetic tape driver).

Network cards are a remarkable exception to this schema, since they are hardware devices that are not directly associated with files; we describe them in Chapter 18.

In Linux 2.4, there are two different kinds of device files: *old-style device files*, which are real files stored in the system's directory tree, and *devfs device files*, which are virtual files like those of the */proc* filesystem. Let's now discuss both types of device files in more detail.

Old-Style Device Files

Old-style device files have been in use since the early versions of the Unix operating system. An old-style device file is a real file stored in a filesystem. Its inode, however, doesn't address blocks of data on the disk. Instead, the inode includes an identifier of a hardware device. Besides its name and type (either character or block, as already mentioned), each device file has two main attributes:

Major number

> A number ranging from 1 to 254 that identifies the device type. Usually, all device files that have the same major number and the same type share the same set of file operations, since they are handled by the same device driver.

Minor number

> A number that identifies a specific device among a group of devices that share the same major number.

The mknod( ) system call is used to create old-style device files. It receives the name of the device file, its type, and the major and minor numbers as parameters. The last two parameters are merged in a 16-bit dev_t number; the eight most significant bits identify the major number, while the remaining ones identify the minor number. The MAJOR and MINOR macros extract the two values from the 16-bit number, while the MKDEV macro merges a major and minor number into a 16-bit number. Actually, dev_t is the data type specifically used by application programs; the kernel uses the kdev_t data type. In Linux 2.4, both types reduce to an unsigned short integer, but kdev_t will become a complete device file descriptor in some future Linux version.

The major and minor numbers are stored in the i_rdev field of the inode object. The type of device file (character or block) is stored in the i_mode field.

Device files are usually included in the */dev* directory. Table 13-2 illustrates the attributes of some device files.* Notice that character and block devices have independent numbering, so block device (3,0) is unique from character device (3,0).

Table 13-2. Examples of device files

Name	Type	Major	Minor	Description
/dev/fd0	block	2	0	Floppy disk
/dev/hda	block	3	0	First IDE disk
/dev/hda2	block	3	2	Second primary partition of first IDE disk
/dev/hdb	block	3	64	Second IDE disk
/dev/hdb3	block	3	67	Third primary partition of second IDE disk

---

* The official registry of allocated device numbers and */dev* directory nodes is stored in the *Documentation/ devices.txt* file. The major numbers of the devices supported may also be found in the *include/linux/major.h* file.

Table 13-2. Examples of device files (continued)

Name	Type	Major	Minor	Description
/dev/ttyp0	char	3	0	Terminal
/dev/console	char	5	1	Console
/dev/lp1	char	6	1	Parallel printer
/dev/ttyS0	char	4	64	First serial port
/dev/rtc	char	10	135	Real time clock
/dev/null	char	1	3	Null device (black hole)

Usually, a device file is associated with a hardware device (like a hard disk—for instance, */dev/hda*) or with some physical or logical portion of a hardware device (like a disk partition—for instance, */dev/hda2*). In some cases, however, a device file is not associated with any real hardware device, but represents a fictitious logical device. For instance, */dev/null* is a device file corresponding to a "black hole"; all data written into it is simply discarded, and the file always appears empty.

As far as the kernel is concerned, the name of the device file is irrelevant. If you create a device file named */tmp/disk* of type "block" with the major number 3 and minor number 0, it would be equivalent to the */dev/hda* device file shown in the table. On the other hand, device filenames may be significant for some application programs. For example, a communication program might assume that the first serial port is associated with the */dev/ttyS0* device file. But most application programs can be configured to interact with arbitrarily named device files.

Devfs Device Files

Identifying I/O devices by means of major and minor numbers has some limitations:

1. Most of the devices present in a */dev* directory don't exist; the device files have been included so that the system administrator doesn't need to create a device file before installing a new I/O driver. However, a typical */dev* directory, which includes over 1,800 device files, increases the time taken to look up an inode when first referenced.

2. The major and minor numbers are 8-bit long. Nowadays, this is a limiting factor for several hardware devices. For instance, it poses problems when identifying SCSI devices included in very large systems (the Linux workaround consists of allocating several major numbers to the SCSI disk drive; as a result, the kernel supports up to 128 SCSI disks).

The *devfs device files* have been introduced to solve these problems and other minor issues. However, at the time of this writing they are still not widely adopted; thus, we limit ourselves to sketch the main ideas behind it without describing the code.

The *devfs* virtual filesystem allows drivers to register devices by name rather than by major and minor numbers. The kernel provides a default naming scheme designed to make it easy to search for specific devices. For example, all disk devices are placed under the */dev/discs* virtual directory; */dev/hda* might become */dev/discs/disc0*, */dev/ hdb* might become */dev/discs/disc1*, and so on. Users can still refer to the old name scheme by properly configuring a device management daemon.

I/O drivers that use the *devfs* filesystem register devices by invoking devfs_register( ). Such function creates a new devfs_entry structure that includes the device file name and a pointer to a table of device driver methods. A registered device file automatically appears in a *devfs* virtual directory. The inode object of a device file in this directory is created only when the file is accessed.*

Opening a device file is also slightly more efficient because dentry objects of *devfs* files include pointers to the proper file operations (see the section "Initializing a Device Driver" later in this chapter).

There are, however, some problems with *devfs*. The most important one is that major and minor numbers are somewhat indispensable for Unix systems. First, some User Mode applications like the NFS server or the *find* command rely on the major and minor numbers to identify the physical disk partition containing a given file. Second, device numbers are required even by the POSIX standard. Thus, the *devfs* layer lets the kernel define major and minor numbers for each device driver, like the old-style device files. Currently, almost all device drivers associate the *devfs* device file with the same major and minor numbers of the corresponding old-style device file. For this reason, we mainly focus on old-style device files in the rest of this chapter.

VFS Handling of Device Files

Device files live in the system directory tree but are intrinsically different from regular files and directories. When a process accesses a regular file, it is accessing some data blocks in some disk partition through a filesystem; when a process accesses a device file, it is just driving a hardware device. For instance, a process might access a device file to read the room temperature from a digital thermometer connected to the computer. It is the VFS's responsibility to hide the differences between device files and regular files from application programs.

To do this, the VFS changes the default file operations of a device file when it is opened; as a result, each system call on the device file is translated to an invocation of a device-related function instead of the corresponding function of the hosting filesystem. The device-related function acts on the hardware device to perform the operation requested by the process.†

---

* The *devfs* filesystem is a virtual filesystem, similar to the */proc* filesystem. It does not manage disk space: inode objects are created in RAM when needed and do not have a corresponding disk inode.

† Notice that, thanks to the name-resolving mechanism explained in the section "Pathname Lookup" in Chapter 12, symbolic links to device files work just like device files.

Let's suppose that a process executes an open( ) system call on a device file (either of type block or character). The operations performed by the system call have already been described in the section "The open( ) System Call" in Chapter 12. Essentially, the corresponding service routine resolves the pathname to the device file and sets up the corresponding inode object, dentry object, and file object.

Assuming that the device file is old-style, the inode object is initialized by reading the corresponding inode on disk through a suitable function of the filesystem (usually ext2_read_inode( ); see Chapter 17). When this function determines that the disk inode is relative to a device file, it invokes init_special_inode( ), which initializes the i_rdev field of the inode object to the major and minor numbers of the device file, and sets the i_fop field of the inode object to the address of either the def_blk_fops table or the def_chr_fops table, according to the type of device file. The service routine of the open( ) system call also invokes the dentry_open( ) function, which allocates a new file object and sets its f_op field to the address stored in i_fop—that is, to the address of def_blk_fops or def_chr_fops once again. The contents of these two tables are shown in the later sections "Block Device Drivers" and "Character Device Drivers"; thanks to them, any system call issued on a device file will activate a device driver's function rather than a function of the underlying filesystem.[*]

Device Drivers

A *device driver* is a software layer that makes a hardware device respond to a well-defined programming interface. We are already familiar with this kind of interface; it consists of the canonical set of VFS functions (*open, read, lseek, ioctl,* and so forth) that control a device. The actual implementation of all these functions is delegated to the device driver. Since each device has a unique I/O controller, and thus unique commands and unique state information, most I/O devices have their own drivers.

There are many types of device drivers. They mainly differ in the level of support that they offer to the User Mode applications, as well as in their buffering strategies for the data collected from the hardware devices. Since these choices greatly influence the internal structure of a device driver, we discuss them in the sections "Levels of Kernel Support" and "Buffering Strategies of Device Drivers."

A device driver does not consist only of the functions that implement the device file operations. Before using a device driver, two activities must have taken place: registering the device driver and initializing it. Finally, when the device driver is performing a data transfer, it must also monitor the I/O operation. We see how all this is done in the sections "Registering a Device Driver," "Initializing a Device Driver," and "Monitoring I/O Operations."

---

[*] If the device file is a virtual file in the *devfs* filesystem, the mechanism is slightly different: the *devfs* filesystem layer does not invoke init_special_inode( ); rather, any *devfs* device file has a custom open method (the devfs_open( ) function), which is invoked by dentry_open( ). It is the job of devfs_open( ) function to rewrite the f_op field of the file object in such a way to customize the operations triggered by the system calls.

Levels of Kernel Support

The Linux kernel does not fully support all possible existing I/O devices. Generally speaking, in fact, there are three possible kinds of support for a hardware device:

No support at all
>   The application program interacts directly with the device's I/O ports by issuing suitable in and out assembly language instructions.

Minimal support
>   The kernel does not recognize the hardware device, but does recognize its I/O interface. User programs are able to treat the interface as a sequential device capable of reading and/or writing sequences of characters.

Extended support
>   The kernel recognizes the hardware device and handles the I/O interface itself. In fact, there might not even be a device file for the device.

The most common example of the first approach, which does not rely on any kernel device driver, is how the X Window System traditionally handles the graphic display. This is quite efficient, although it constrains the X server from using the hardware interrupts issued by the I/O device. This approach also requires some additional effort to allow the X server to access the required I/O ports. As mentioned in the section "Task State Segment" in Chapter 3, the iopl( ) and ioperm( ) system calls grant a process the privilege to access I/O ports. They can be invoked only by programs having root privileges. But such programs can be made available to users by setting the fsuid field of the executable file to 0, which is the UID of the superuser (see the section "Process Credentials and Capabilities" in Chapter 20).

Recent Linux versions support several widely used graphic cards. The /dev/fb device file provides an abstraction for the frame buffer of the graphic card and allows application software to access it without needing to know anything about the I/O ports of the graphics interface. Furthermore, Version 2.4 of the kernel supports the Direct Rendering Infrastructure (DRI) that allows application software to exploit the hardware of accelerated 3D graphics cards. In any case, the traditional do-it-yourself X Window System server is still widely adopted.

The minimal support approach is used to handle external hardware devices connected to a general-purpose I/O interface. The kernel takes care of the I/O interface by offering a device file (and thus a device driver); the application program handles the external hardware device by reading and writing the device file.

Minimal support is preferable to extended support because it keeps the kernel size small. However, among the general-purpose I/O interfaces commonly found on a PC, only the serial port and the parallel port can be handled with this approach. Thus, a serial mouse is directly controlled by an application program, like the X server, and a serial modem always requires a communication program, like Minicom, Seyon, or a Point-to-Point Protocol (PPP) daemon.

Minimal support has a limited range of applications because it cannot be used when the external device must interact heavily with internal kernel data structures. For example, consider a removable hard disk that is connected to a general-purpose I/O interface. An application program cannot interact with all kernel data structures and functions needed to recognize the disk and to mount its filesystem, so extended support is mandatory in this case.

In general, any hardware device directly connected to the I/O bus, such as the internal hard disk, is handled according to the extended support approach: the kernel must provide a device driver for each such device. External devices attached to the Universal Serial Bus (USB), the PCMCIA port found in many laptops, or the SCSI interface—in short, any general-purpose I/O interface except the serial and the parallel ports—also require extended support.

It is worth noting that the standard file-related system calls like open( ), read( ), and write( ) do not always give the application full control of the underlying hardware device. In fact, the lowest-common-denominator approach of the VFS does not include room for special commands that some devices need or let an application check whether the device is in a specific internal state.

The ioctl( ) system call was introduced to satisfy such needs. Besides the file descriptor of the device file and a second 32-bit parameter specifying the request, the system call can accept an arbitrary number of additional parameters. For example, specific ioctl( ) requests exist to get the CD-ROM sound volume or to eject the CD-ROM media. Application programs may provide the user interface of a CD player using these kinds of ioctl( ) requests.

Buffering Strategies of Device Drivers

Traditionally, Unix-like operating systems divide hardware devices into block and character devices. However, this classification does not tell the whole story. Some devices are capable of transferring sizeable amount of data in a single I/O operation, while others transfer only a few characters.

For instance, a PS/2 mouse driver gets a few bytes in each read operation—they correspond to the status of the mouse button and to the position of the mouse pointer on the screen. This kind of device is the easiest to handle. Input data is first read one character at a time from the device input register and stored in a proper kernel data structure; the data is then copied at leisure into the process address space. Similarly, output data is first copied from the process address space to a proper kernel data structure and then written one at a time into the I/O device output register. Clearly, I/O drivers for such devices do not use the DMAC because the CPU time spent to set up a DMA I/O operation is comparable to the one spent to move the data to or from the I/O ports.

On the other hand, the kernel must also be ready to deal with devices that yield a large number of bytes in each I/O operation, either sequential devices such as sound cards or network cards, or random access devices such as disks of all kinds (floppy, CDROM, SCSI disk, etc.).

Suppose, for instance, that you have set up the sound card of your computer so that you are able to record sounds coming from a microphone. The sound card samples the electrical signal coming from the microphone at a fixed rate, say 44.14 kHz, and produces a stream of 16-bit numbers divided into blocks of input data. The sound card driver must be able to cope with this avalanche of data in all possible situations, even when the CPU is temporarily busy running some other process.

This can be done by combining two different techniques:

- Use of the DMA processor (DMAC) to transfer blocks of data.
- Use of a circular buffer of two or more elements, each element having the size of a block of data. When an interrupt occurs signaling that a new block of data has been read, the interrupt handler advances a pointer to the elements of the circular buffer so that further data will be stored in an empty element. Conversely, whenever the driver succeeds in copying a block of data into user address space, it releases an element of the circular buffer so that it is available for saving new data from the hardware device.

The role of the circular buffer is to smooth out the peaks of CPU load; even if the User Mode application receiving the data is slowed down because of other higher priority tasks, the DMAC is able to continue filling elements of the circular buffer because the interrupt handler executes on behalf of the currently running process.

A similar situation occurs when receiving packets from a network card, except that in this case, the flow of incoming data is asynchronous. Packets are received independently from each other and the time interval that occurs between two consecutive packet arrivals is unpredictable.

All considered, buffer handling for sequential devices is easy because the same buffer is *never reused*: an audio application cannot ask the microphone to retransmit the same block of data; similarly, a networking application cannot ask the network card to retransmit the same packet.

On the other hand, buffering for random access devices (disks of any kind) is much more complicated. In this case, applications are entitled to ask repeatedly to read or write the same block of data. Furthermore, accesses to these devices are usually very slow. These peculiarities have a profound impact on the structure of the disk drivers.

Thus, buffers for random access devices play a different role. Instead of smoothing out the peaks of the CPU load, they are used to contain data that is no longer needed by any process, just in case some other process will require the same data at some later time. In other words, buffers are the basic components of a software cache (see Chapter 14) that reduces the number of disk accesses.

Registering a Device Driver

We know that each system call issued on a device file is translated by the kernel into an invocation of a suitable function of a corresponding device driver. To achieve this, a device driver must *register* itself. In other words, registering a device driver means linking it to the corresponding device files. Accesses to device files whose corresponding drivers have not been previously registered return the error code -ENODEV.

If a device driver is statically compiled in the kernel, its registration is performed during the kernel initialization phase. Conversely, if a device driver is compiled as a kernel module (see Appendix B), its registration is performed when the module is loaded. In the latter case, the device driver can also unregister itself when the module is unloaded.

Character device drivers using old-style device files* are described by a chrdevs array of device_struct data structures; each array index is the major number of a device file. Major numbers range between 1 (no device file can have the major number 0) and 254 (the value 255 is reserved for future extensions), thus the array contains 255 elements, but the first of them is not used. Each structure includes two fields: name points to the name of the device class and fops points to a file_operations structure (see the section "File Objects" in Chapter 12).

Similarly, block device drivers using old-style device files are described by a blkdevs array of 255 data structures (as in the chrdevs array, the first entry is not used). Each structure includes two fields: name points to the name of the device class and bdops points to a block_device_operations structure, which stores a few custom methods for crucial operations of the block device driver (see Table 13-3).

Table 13-3. The methods of block device drivers

Method	Event that triggers the invocation of the method
open	Opening the block device file
release	Closing the last reference to a block device file
ioctl	Issuing a ioctl( ) system call on the block device file
check_media_change	Checking whether the media has been changed (e.g., floppy disk)
revalidate	Checking whether the block device holds valid data

The chrdevs and blkdevs tables are initially empty. The register_chrdev( ) and register_blkdev( ) functions insert a new entry into one of the tables. If a device driver is implemented through a module, it can be unregistered when the module is unloaded by means of the unregister_chrdev( ) or unregister_blkdev( ) functions.

---

* As you might suspect, the registration procedure is quite different for the old-style device files and *devfs* device files. Unfortunately, this means that if both types are in use at the same time, a device driver must register itself twice.

For example, the descriptor for the parallel printer driver class is inserted in the chrdevs table as follows:

```
register_chrdev(6, "lp", &lp_fops);
```

The first parameter denotes the major number, the second denotes the device class name, and the last is a pointer to the table of file operations. Notice that, once registered, a device driver is linked to the major number of a device file and not to its pathname. Thus, any access to a device file activates the corresponding driver, regardless of the pathname used.

Initializing a Device Driver

Registering a device driver and initializing it are two different things. A device driver is registered as soon as possible so User Mode applications can use it through the corresponding device files. In contrast, a device driver is initialized at the last possible moment. In fact, initializing a driver means allocating precious resources of the system, which are therefore not available to other drivers.

We already have seen an example in the section "I/O Interrupt Handling" in Chapter 4: the assignment of IRQs to devices is usually made dynamically, right before using them, since several devices may share the same IRQ line. Other resources that can be allocated at the last possible moment are page frames for DMA transfer buffers and the DMA channel itself (for old non-PCI devices like the floppy disk driver).

To make sure the resources are obtained when needed but are not requested in a redundant manner when they have already been granted, device drivers usually adopt the following schema:

- A usage counter keeps track of the number of processes that are currently accessing the device file. The counter is incremented in the open method of the device file and decremented in the release method.[*]

- The open method checks the value of the usage counter before the increment. If the counter is null, the device driver must allocate the resources and enable interrupts and DMA on the hardware device.

- The release method checks the value of the usage counter after the decrement. If the counter is null, no more processes are using the hardware device. If so, the method disables interrupts and DMA on the I/O controller, and then releases the allocated resources.

---

[*] More precisely, the usage counter keeps track of the number of file objects referring to the device file, since clone processes could share the same file object.

Monitoring I/O Operations

The duration of an I/O operation is often unpredictable. It can depend on mechanical considerations (the current position of a disk head with respect to the block to be transferred), on truly random events (when a data packet arrives on the network card), or on human factors (when a user presses a key on the keyboard or when he notices that a paper jam occurred in the printer). In any case, the device driver that started an I/O operation must rely on a monitoring technique that signals either the termination of the I/O operation or a time-out.

In the case of a terminated operation, the device driver reads the status register of the I/O interface to determine whether the I/O operation was carried out successfully. In the case of a time-out, the driver knows that something went wrong, since the maximum time interval allowed to complete the operation elapsed and nothing happened.

The two techniques available to monitor the end of an I/O operation are called the *polling mode* and the *interrupt mode*.

Polling mode

According to this technique, the CPU checks (polls) the device's status register repeatedly until its value signals that the I/O operation has been completed. We have already encountered a technique based on polling in the section "Spin Locks" in Chapter 5: when a processor tries to acquire a busy spin lock, it repeatedly polls the variable until its value becomes 0. However, polling applied to I/O operations is usually more elaborate, since the driver must also remember to check for possible time-outs. A simple example of polling looks like the following:

```
for (;;) {
    if (read_status(device) & DEVICE_END_OPERATION) break;
    if (--count == 0) break;
}
```

The count variable, which was initialized before entering the loop, is decremented at each iteration, and thus can be used to implement a rough time-out mechanism. Alternatively, a more precise time-out mechanism could be implemented by reading the value of the tick counter jiffies at each iteration (see the section "PIT's interrupt service routine" in Chapter 6) and comparing it with the old value read before starting the wait loop.

If the time required to complete the I/O operation is relatively high, say in the order of milliseconds, this schema becomes inefficient because the CPU wastes precious machine cycles while waiting for the I/O completion. In such cases, it is preferable to voluntarily relinquish the CPU after each polling operation by inserting an invocation of the schedule( ) function inside the loop.

Interrupt mode

Interrupt mode can be used only if the I/O controller is capable of signaling, via an IRQ line, the end of an I/O operation.

We'll show how interrupt mode works on a simple case. Let's suppose we want to implement a driver for a simple input character device. When the user issues a read( ) system call on the corresponding device file, an input command is sent to the device's control register. After an unpredictably long time interval, the device puts a single byte of data in its input register. The device driver then returns this byte as result of the read( ) system call.

This is a typical case in which it is preferable to implement the driver using the interrupt mode; in fact, the device driver doesn't know in advance how much time it has to wait for an answer from the hardware device. Essentially, the driver includes two functions:

1. The foo_read( ) function that implements the read method of the file object

2. The foo_interrupt( ) function that handles the interrupt

The foo_read( ) function is triggered whenever the user reads the device file:

```
ssize_t foo_read(struct file *filp, char *buf, size_t count, loff_t *ppos)
{
    foo_dev_t * foo_dev = filp->private_data;
    if (down_interruptible(&foo_dev->sem)
        return -ERESTARTSYS;
    foo_dev->intr = 0;
    outb(DEV_FOO_READ, DEV_FOO_CONTROL_PORT);
    wait_event_interruptible(foo_dev->wait, (foo_dev->intr==1));
    if (put_user(foo_dev->data, buf))
        return -EFAULT;
    up(&foo_dev->sem);
    return 1;
}
```

The device driver relies on a custom descriptor of type foo_dev_t; it includes a semaphore sem that protects the hardware device from concurrent accesses, a wait queue wait, a flag intr that is set when the device issues an interrupt, and a single-byte buffer data that is written by the interrupt handler and read by the read method. In general, all I/O drivers that use interrupts rely on data structures accessed by both the interrupt handler and the read and write methods. The address of the foo_dev_t descriptor is usually stored in the private_data field of the device file's file object or in a global variable.

The main operations of the foo_read( ) function are the following:

1. Acquires the foo_dev->sem semaphore, thus ensuring that no other process is accessing the device.

2. Clears the intr flag.

3. Issues the read command to the I/O device.

4. Executes `wait_event_interruptible` to suspend the process until the `intr` flag becomes 1. This macro is described in the section "Wait queues" in Chapter 3.

After some time, our device issues an interrupt to signal that the I/O operation is completed and that the data is ready in the proper `DEV_FOO_DATA_PORT` data port. The interrupt handler sets the `intr` flag and wakes the process. When the scheduler decides to reexecute the process, the second part of `foo_read()` is executed and does the following:

1. Copies the character ready in the `foo_dev->data` variable into the user address space.

2. Terminates after releasing the `foo_dev->sem` semaphore.

For simplicity, we didn't include any time-out control. In general, time-out control is implemented through static or dynamic timers (see Chapter 6); the timer must be set to the right time before starting the I/O operation and removed when the operation terminates.

Let's now look at the code of the `foo_interrupt()` function:

```
void foo_interrupt(int irq, void *dev_id, struct pt_regs *regs)
{
    foo->data = inb(DEV_FOO_DATA_PORT);
    foo->intr = 1;
    wake_up_interruptible(&foo->wait);
}
```

The interrupt handler reads the character from the input register of the device and stores it in the data field of the `foo_dev_t` descriptor of the device driver pointed to by the `foo` global variable. It then sets the `intr` flag and invokes `wake_up_interruptible()` to wake the process blocked in the `foo->wait` wait queue.

Notice that none of the three parameters are used by our interrupt handler. This is a rather common case.

Block Device Drivers

Typical block devices like hard disks have very high average access times. Each operation requires several milliseconds to complete, mainly because the hard disk controller must move the heads on the disk surface to reach the exact position where the data is recorded. However, when the heads are correctly placed, data transfer can be sustained at rates of tens of megabytes per second.

To achieve acceptable performance, hard disks and similar devices transfer several adjacent bytes at once. In the following discussion, we say that groups of bytes are *adjacent* when they are recorded on the disk surface in such a manner that a single seek operation can access them.

The organization of Linux block device handlers is quite involved. We won't be able to discuss in detail all the functions that are included in the kernel to support the handlers. But we outline the general software architecture and introduce the main data structures. Kernel support for block device handlers includes the following features:

- A uniform interface through the VFS
- Efficient read-ahead of disk data
- Disk caching for the data

Keeping Track of Block Device Drivers

When a block device file is being opened, the kernel must determine whether the device file is already open. In fact, if the file is already open, the kernel must not initialize the corresponding block device driver.

This problem is as easy as it appears at first look. On the one hand, we stated in the earlier section "Device Files" that block device files that have the same major number are usually associated with the same block device driver. However, each block device driver that handles more than one minor number can be considered several specialized block device drivers, so this case doesn't create problems. In the rest of this section, when we use the term "block device driver," we mean the kernel layer that handles I/O data transfers from/to a hardware device specified by both a major number and a minor number.

A real complication, however, is that block device files that have the same major and minor numbers but different pathnames are regarded by the VFS as different files, but they really refer to the same block device driver. Therefore, the kernel cannot determine whether a block device driver is already in use by simply checking for the existence in the inode cache of an object for the block device file.

To keep track of which block device drivers are currently in use, the kernel uses a hash table indexed by the major and minor numbers. Every time a block device driver is being used, the kernel checks whether the corresponding block device driver identified by the major and minor numbers is already stored in the hash table. If so, the block device driver is already in use; notice that the hash function works on the major and minor numbers of the block device file, thus it doesn't matter whether the block device driver was previously activated by accessing a given block device file, or another one that has the same major and minor numbers. Conversely, if a block device driver associated with the given major and minor numbers is not found, the kernel inserts a new element into the hash table.

The hash table array is stored in bdev_hashtable variable; it includes 64 lists of block device descriptors. Each descriptor is a block_device data structure whose fields are shown in Table 13-4.

Table 13-4. The fields of the block device descriptor

Type	Field	Description
struct list_head	bd_hash	Pointers for the hash table list
atomic_t	bd_count	Usage counter for the block device descriptor
struct inode *	bd_inode	Pointer to the main inode object of the block device driver
dev_t	bd_dev	Major and minor numbers of the block device
int	bd_openers	Counter of how many times the block device driver has been opened
struct block_device_operations *	bd_op	Pointer to the block device driver operation table
struct semaphore	bd_sem	Semaphore protecting the block device driver
struct list_head	bd_inodes	List of inodes of opened block device files for this driver

The bd_inodes field of the block device descriptor stores the head (the first dummy element) of a doubly linked circular list of inodes relative to opened block device files that refer to the block device driver. The i_devices field of the inode object stores the pointers for the previous and next element in this list.

Each block device descriptor stores in the bd_inode field the address of a special *block device inode* object for the driver. This inode doesn't correspond to a disk file; rather, it belongs to the *bdev* special filesystem (see the section "Special Filesystems" in Chapter 12). Essentially, the block device inode stores the "master copy" of the information shared by all inode objects of the block device files that refer to the same block device.

Initializing a Block Device Driver

Let's now describe how a block device driver is initialized. We already described how the kernel customizes the methods of the file object when a block device file is opened in the section "VFS Handling of Device Files." Its f_op field is set to the address of the def_blk_fops variable. The contents of this table are shown in Table 13-5. The dentry_open( ) function checks whether the open method is defined; this is always true for a block device file, so the blkdev_open( ) function is executed.

Table 13-5. The default file operation methods for block device files

Method	Function for block device file
open	blkdev_open( )
release	blkdev_close( )
llseek	block_llseek( )
read	generic_file_read( )
write	generic_file_write( )
mmap	generic_file_mmap( )

Table 13-5. *The default file operation methods for block device files (continued)*

Method	Function for block device file
fsync	block_fsync( )
ioctl	blkdev_ioctl( )

This function checks whether the block device driver is already in use:

```
bd_acquire(inode);
do_open(inode->i_bdev, filp);
```

The bd_acquire( ) function essentially executes the following operations:

1. Checks whether the block device file corresponding to the inode object is already open (in this case, inode->i_bdev field points to the block device descriptor). If the file is already open, increments the usage counter of the block device descriptor (inode->i_bdev->bd_count) and returns.

2. Looks up the block device driver in the hash table using the major and minor numbers stored in inode->rdev. If the descriptor is not found because the driver is not in use, allocates a new block_device and a new inode object for the block device, and then inserts the new descriptor in the hash table.

3. Stores the address of the block device driver descriptor in inode->i_bdev.

4. Adds inode to the list of inodes of the driver descriptor.

Next, blkdev_open( ) invokes do_open( ), which executes the following main steps:

1. If the bd_op field of the block device driver descriptor is NULL, initializes it from the blkdevs table's element corresponding to the major number of the block device file

2. Invokes the open method of the block device driver descriptor (bd_op->open) if it is defined

3. Increments the bd_openers counter of the block device driver descriptor

4. Sets the i_size and i_blkbits fields of the block device inode object (bd_inode)

The open method of the block device driver descriptor can further customize the methods of the block device driver, allocate resources, and take other measures based on the minor number of the block device file.

Among other things, the device driver initialization function must determine the size of the physical block device corresponding to the device file. This length, represented in 1,024-byte units, is stored in the blk_size global array indexed by both the major and minor number of the device file.

Sectors, Blocks, and Buffers

Each data transfer operation for a block device acts on a group of adjacent bytes called a *sector*. In most disk devices, the size of a sector is 512 bytes, although there are devices that use larger sectors (1,024 and 2,048 bytes). Notice that the sector should be considered the basic unit of data transfer; it is never possible to transfer less than a sector, although most disk devices are capable of transferring several adjacent sectors at once.

The kernel stores the sector size of each hardware block device in a table named hardsect_size. Each element in the table is indexed by the major number and the minor number of the corresponding block device file. Thus, hardsect_size[3][2] represents the sector size of */dev/hda2*, which is the second primary partition of the first IDE disk (see Table 13-2). If hardsect_size[*maj*] is NULL, all block devices sharing the major number *maj* have a standard sector size of 512 bytes.

Block device drivers transfer a large number of adjacent bytes called a *block* in a single operation. A block should not be confused with a sector. The sector is the basic unit of data transfer for the hardware device, while the block is simply a group of adjacent bytes involved in an I/O operation requested by a device driver.

In Linux, the block size must be a power of 2 and cannot be larger than a page frame. Moreover, it must be a multiple of the sector size, since each block must include an integral number of sectors. Therefore, on PC architecture, the permitted block sizes are 512, 1,024, 2,048, and 4,096 bytes. The same block device driver may operate with several block sizes, since it has to handle a set of device files sharing the same major number, while each block device file has its own predefined block size. For instance, a block device driver could handle a hard disk with two partitions containing an Ext2 filesystem and a swap area (see Chapter 16 and Chapter 17). In this case, the device driver uses two different block sizes: 1,024 bytes for the Ext2 partition and 4,096 bytes for the swap partition.

The kernel stores the block size in a table named blksize_size; each element in the table is indexed by the major number and the minor number of the corresponding block device file. If blksize_size[*maj*] is NULL, all block devices sharing the major number *maj* have a standard block size of 1,024 bytes. (You should not confuse blk_size with the blksize_size array, which stores the block size of the block devices rather than the size of the block device themselves.)

Each block requires its own *buffer*, which is a RAM memory area used by the kernel to store the block's content. When a device driver reads a block from disk, it fills the corresponding buffer with the values obtained from the hardware device; similarly, when a device driver writes a block on disk, it updates the corresponding group of adjacent bytes on the hardware device with the actual values of the associated buffer. The size of a buffer always matches the size of the corresponding block.

Buffer Heads

The *buffer head* is a descriptor of type buffer_head associated with each buffer. It contains all the information needed by the kernel to know how to handle the buffer; thus, before operating on each buffer, the kernel checks its buffer head.

The buffer head fields are listed in Table 13-6. The b_data field of each buffer head stores the starting address of the corresponding buffer. Since a page frame may store several buffers, the b_this_page field points to the buffer head of the next buffer in the page. This field facilitates the storage and retrieval of entire page frames (see the section "Page I/O operations" later in this chapter). The b_blocknr field stores the *logical block number* (i.e., the index of the block inside the disk partition).

Table 13-6. The fields of a buffer head

Type	Field	Description
struct buffer_head *	b_next	Next item in collision hash list
unsigned long	b_blocknr	Logical block number
unsigned short	b_size	Block size
unsigned short	b_list	LRU list including the buffer head
kdev_t	b_dev	Virtual device identifier
atomic_t	b_count	Block usage counter
kdev_t	b_rdev	Real device identifier
unsigned long	b_state	Buffer status flags
unsigned long	b_flushtime	Flushing time for buffer
struct buffer_head *	b_next_free	Next item in list of buffer heads
struct buffer_head *	b_prev_free	Previous item in list of buffer heads
struct buffer_head *	b_this_page	Per-page buffer list
struct buffer_head *	b_reqnext	Next item in the request queue
struct buffer_head **	b_pprev	Previous item in collision hash list
char *	b_data	Pointer to buffer
struct page *	b_page	Pointer to the descriptor of the page that stores the buffer
void (*)( )	b_end_io	I/O completion method
void (*)	b_private	Specialized device driver data
unsigned long	b_rsector	Block number on real device
wait_queue_head_t	b_wait	Buffer wait queue
struct inode *	b_inode	Pointer to inode object to which the buffer belongs
struct list_head	b_inode_buffers	Pointers for list of inode buffers

The b_state field stores the following flags:

BH_Uptodate
    Set if the buffer contains valid data. The value of this flag is returned by the buffer_uptodate( ) macro.

BH_Dirty
    Set if the buffer is dirty—that is, if it contains data that must be written to the block device. The value of this flag is returned by the buffer_dirty( ) macro.

BH_Lock

Set if the buffer is locked, which happens if the buffer is involved in a disk transfer. The value of this flag is returned by the buffer_locked( ) macro.

BH_Req

Set if the corresponding block is requested (see the next section) and has valid (up-to-date) data. The value of this flag is returned by the buffer_req( ) macro.

BH_Mapped

Set if the buffer is mapped to disk—that is, if the b_dev and b_blocknr fields of the corresponding buffer head are significant. The value of this flag is returned by the buffer_mapped( ) macro.

BH_New

Set if the corresponding file block has just been allocated and has never been accessed. The value of this flag is returned by the buffer_new( ) macro.

BH_Async

Set if the buffer is being processed by end_buffer_io_async( ) (described in the later section "Page I/O operations"). The value of this flag is returned by the buffer_async( ) macro.

BH_Wait_IO

Used to delay flushing the buffer to disk when reclaiming memory (see Chapter 16).

BH_launder

Set when the buffer is being flushed to disk when reclaiming memory (see Chapter 16).

BH_JBD

Set if the buffer is used by a journaling filesystem (see Chapter 17).

The b_dev field identifies the virtual device containing the block stored in the buffer, while the b_rdev field identifies the real device. This distinction, which is meaningless for simple hard disks, has been introduced to model Redundant Array of Independent Disks (RAID) storage units consisting of several disks operating in parallel. For reasons of safety and efficiency, files stored in a RAID array are scattered across several disks that the applications think of as a single logical disk. Besides the b_blocknr field representing the logical block number, it is necessary to specify the specific disk unit in the b_rdev field and the corresponding sector number in the b_rsector field.

An Overview of Block Device Driver Architecture

Although block device drivers are able to transfer a single block at a time, the kernel does not perform an individual I/O operation for each block to be accessed on disk; this would lead to poor disk performances, since locating the physical position of a block on the disk surface is quite time-consuming. Instead, the kernel tries, whenever possible, to cluster several blocks and handle them as a whole, thus reducing the average number of head movements.

When a process, the VFS layer, or any other kernel component wishes to read or write a disk block, it actually creates a *block device request*. That request essentially describes the requested block and the kind of operation to be performed on it (read or write). However, the kernel does not satisfy a request as soon as it is created—the I/O operation is just scheduled and will be performed at a later time. This artificial delay is paradoxically the crucial mechanism for boosting the performance of block devices. When a new block data transfer is requested, the kernel checks whether it can be satisfied by slightly enlarging a previous request that is still waiting (i.e., whether the new request can be satisfied without further seek operations). Since disks tend to be accessed sequentially, this simple mechanism is very effective.

Deferring requests complicates block device handling. For instance, suppose a process opens a regular file and, consequently, a filesystem driver wants to read the corresponding inode from disk. The block device driver puts the request on a queue and the process is suspended until the block storing the inode is transferred. However, the block device driver itself cannot be blocked because any other process trying to access the same disk would be blocked as well.

To keep the block device driver from being suspended, each I/O operation is processed asynchronously. Thus, no kernel control path is forced to wait until a data transfer completes. In particular, block device drivers are interrupt-driven (see the section "Monitoring I/O Operations" earlier in this chapter): a *high-level driver* creates a new block device request or enlarges an already existing block device request and then terminates. A *low-level driver*, which is activated at a later time, invokes a so-called *strategy routine*, which takes the request from a queue and satisfies it by issuing suitable commands to the disk controller. When the I/O operation terminates, the disk controller raises an interrupt and the corresponding handler invokes the strategy routine again, if necessary, to process another request in the queue.

Each block device driver maintains its own *request queues*; there should be one request queue for each physical block device, so that the requests can be ordered in such a way as to increase disk performance. The strategy routine can thus sequentially scan the queue and service all requests with the minimum number of head movements.

Request descriptors

Each block device request is represented by a *request descriptor*, which is stored in the request data structure illustrated in Table 13-7. The direction of the data transfer is stored in the cmd field; it is either READ (from block device to RAM) or WRITE (from RAM to block device). The rq_status field is used to specify the status of the request; for most block devices, it is simply set either to RQ_INACTIVE (for a request descriptor not in use) or to RQ_ACTIVE (for a valid request that is to be serviced or is already being serviced by the low-level driver).

Table 13-7. The fields of a request descriptor

Type	Field	Description
struct list_head	queue	Pointers for request queue list
int	elevator_sequence	The "age" of the request for the elevator algorithm
volatile int	rq_status	Request status
kdev_t	rq_dev	Device identifier
int	cmd	Requested operation
int	errors	Success or failure code
unsigned long	sector	First sector number on the (virtual) block device
unsigned long	nr_sectors	Number of sectors of the request on the (virtual) block device
unsigned long	hard_sector	First sector number of the (real) block device
unsigned long	hard_nr_sectors	Number of sectors of the request on the (real) block device
unsigned int	nr_segments	Number of segments in the request on the (virtual) block device
unsigned int	nr_hw_segments	Number of segments in the request on the (real) block device
unsigned long	current_nr_sectors	Number of sectors in the block currently transferred
void *	special	Used only by drivers of SCSI devices
char *	buffer	Memory area for I/O transfer
struct completion *	waiting	Wait queue associated with request
struct buffer_head *	bh	First buffer descriptor of the request
struct buffer_head *	bhtail	Last buffer descriptor of the request
request_queue_t *	q	Pointer to request queue descriptor

The request may encompass many adjacent blocks on the same device. The rq_dev field identifies the block device, while the sector field specifies the number of the first sector of the first block in the request. The nr_sector field specifies the number of sectors in the request yet to be transferred. The current_nr_sector field stores the number of sectors in first block of the request. As we'll later see in the section "Low-Level Request Handling," the sector, nr_sector, and current_nr_sector fields could be dynamically updated while the request is being serviced.

The nr_segments field store the number of segments in the request. Although all blocks in the requests must be adjacent on the block device, their corresponding buffers are not necessarily contiguous in RAM. A *segment* is a sequence of adjacent blocks in the request whose corresponding buffers are also contiguous in memory. Of course, a low-level device driver could program the DMA controller so as to transfer all blocks in the same segment in a single operation.

The hard_sector, hard_nr_sectors, and nr_hw_segments fields usually have the same value as the sector, nr_sectors, and nr_segments fields, respectively. They differ, however, when the request refers to a driver that handles several physical block devices at once. A typical example of such a driver is the Logical Volume Manager

(LVM), which is able to handle several disks and disk partitions as a single virtual disk partition. In this case, the two series of fields differ because the former refers to the real physical block device, while the latter refers to the virtual device. Another example is software RAID, a driver that duplicates data on several disks to enhance reliability.

All buffer heads of the blocks in the request are collected in a simply linked list. The b_reqnext field of each buffer head points to the next element in the list, while the bh and bhtail fields of the request descriptor point, respectively, to the first element and the last element in the list.

The buffer field of the request descriptor points to the memory area used for the actual data transfer. If the request involves a single block, buffer is just a copy of the b_data field of the buffer head. However, if the request encompasses several blocks whose buffers are not consecutive in memory, the buffers are linked through the b_reqnext fields of their buffer heads as shown in Figure 13-3. On a read, the low-level driver could choose to allocate a large memory area referred by buffer, read all sectors of the request at once, and then copy the data into the various buffers. Similarly, for a write, the low-level device driver could copy the data from many nonconsecutive buffers into a single memory area referred by buffer and then perform the whole data transfer at once.

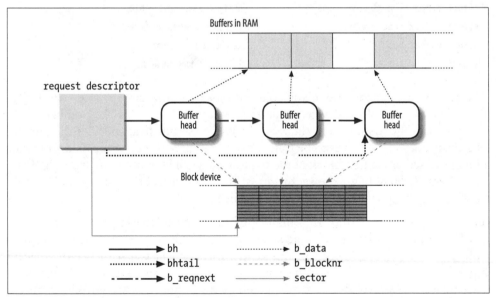

Figure 13-3. A request descriptor and its buffers and sectors

Figure 13-3 illustrates a request descriptor encompassing three blocks. The buffers of two of them are consecutive in RAM, while the third buffer is by itself. The corresponding buffer heads identify the logical blocks on the block device; the blocks must necessarily be adjacent. Each logical block includes two sectors. The sector field of the request descriptor points to the first sector of the first block on disk, and the b_reqnext field of each buffer head points to the next buffer head.

During the initialization phase, each block device driver usually allocates a fixed number of request descriptors to handle its forthcoming I/O requests. The blk_init_queue( ) function sets up two equally sized lists of free request descriptors: one for the READ operation and another for the WRITE operations. The size of these lists is set to 64 if the RAM size is greater than 32 MB, or to 32 if the RAM size is less than or equal to 32 MB. The status of all request descriptors is set initially to RQ_INACTIVE.

The fixed number of request descriptors may become, under very heavy loads and high disk activity, a bottleneck. A dearth of free descriptors may force processes to wait until an ongoing data transfer terminates. Thus, a wait queue is used to queue processes waiting for a free request element. The get_request_wait( ) tries to get a free request descriptor and puts the current process to sleep in the wait queue if none is found; the get_request( ) function is similar but simply returns NULL if no free request descriptor is available.

A threshold value known as batch_requests (set to 32 or to 16, depending on the RAM size) is used to cut down kernel overhead; when releasing a request descriptor, processes waiting for free request descriptors are not woken up unless there are at least batch_requests free descriptors. Conversely, when looking for a free request descriptor, get_request_wait( ) relinquishes the CPU if there are fewer than batch_requests free descriptors.

Request queue descriptors

Request queues are represented by means of request queue descriptors; each of them is a request_queue_t data structure whose fields are listed in Table 13-8.

Table 13-8. The fields of a request queue descriptor

Type	Field	Description
struct request_list []	rq	READ and WRITE free lists of requests
struct list_head	queue_head	List of pending requests
elevator_t	elevator	Methods of the elevator algorithm
request_fn_proc *	request_fn	Strategy routine of the driver
merge_request_fn *	back_merge_fn	Method to append a block to the request
merge_request_fn *	front_merge_fn	Method to insert a block in front of the request
merge_requests_fn *	merge_requests_fn	Method to attempt merging an enlarged request with the adjacent ones
make_request_fn *	make_request_fn	Method that passes a request to a driver (usually it inserts the request in the proper queue)
plug_device_fn *	plug_device_fn	Method to plug the driver
void *	queuedata	Private data of the device driver

Table 13-8. The fields of a request queue descriptor (continued)

Type	Field	Description
`struct tq_struct`	`plug_tq`	Task queue element for the plugging mechanism
`char`	`plugged`	Flag denoting whether the driver is currently plugged
`char`	`head_active`	Flag denoting whether the first request in queue is active when the driver is unplugged
`spinlock_t`	`queue_lock`	Request queue lock
`wait_queue_head_t`	`wait_for_request`	Wait queue for lack of request descriptors

When the kernel initializes a device driver, it creates and fills a request queue descriptor for each request queue handled by the driver.

Essentially, a request queue is a doubly linked list whose elements are request descriptors (that is, request data structures). The queue_head field of the request queue descriptor stores the head (the first dummy element) of the list, while the pointers in the queue field of the request descriptor link any request to the previous and next elements in the list. The ordering of the elements in the queue list is specific to each block device driver; the Linux kernel offers, however, two predefined ways of ordering elements, which are discussed in the later section "Extending the request queue."

Block device low-level driver descriptor

Each block device driver may define one or more request queues. To keep track of the request queues of each driver, a *low-level driver descriptor* is used. The descriptor is a data structure of type `blk_dev_struct`, whose fields are listed in Table 13-9. The descriptors for all the block devices are stored in the `blk_dev` table, which is indexed by the major number of the block device.

Table 13-9. The fields of a block device driver descriptor

Type	Field	Description
`request_queue_t`	`request_queue`	Common request queue (for drivers that do not define per-device queues)
`queue_proc *`	`queue`	Method returning the address of a per-device queue
`void *`	`data`	Data (e.g., minor number) used by queue

If the block device driver has a unique request queue for all physical block devices, its address is stored in the request_queue field. Conversely, if the block device driver maintains several queues, the queue field points to a custom driver method that receives the identifier of the block device file, selects one of the queues according to the value of the data field, then returns the address of the proper request queue.

The ll_rw_block( ) Function

The `ll_rw_block( )` function creates a block device request. It is invoked from several places in the kernel to trigger the I/O data transfer of one or more blocks. The function receives the following parameters:

- The type of operation, rw, whose value can be READ, WRITE, or READA. The last operation type differs from the former in that the function does not block when a request descriptor is not available.

- The number, nr, of blocks to be transferred.

- A bhs array of nr pointers to buffer heads describing the blocks (all of them must have the same block size and must refer to the same block device).

The buffer heads were previously initialized, so each specifies the block number, the block size, and the virtual device identifier (see the earlier section "Buffer Heads").

The function performs the following actions:

1. Checks that the block size b_size matches the block size of the virtual device b_dev for each buffer head in the bhs array.

2. If the operation is WRITE, checks that the block device is not read-only.

3. For each buffer head in the bhs array, performs the following steps:

   a. Sets the BH_Lock flag of the buffer head. If it is already set by some other kernel thread, it skips that buffer.

   b. Increments the b_count field of the buffer head.

   c. Sets the b_end_io field of the buffer head to end_buffer_io_sync( ); that is, to the function that updates the buffer head when the data transfer is completed (see the section "Low-Level Request Handling" later in this chapter.)

   d. If the block must be written, tests the BH_Dirty flag of the buffer head in one of the following ways:

      - If BH_Dirty is reset, executes the b_end_io method (the end_buffer_io_sync( ) function) and continues with the next buffer because there is no need to write this block.

      - If BH_Dirty is set, resets it and places the buffer head in the list of locked buffer heads.

      As a general rule, the caller of ll_rw_block( ) must set the BH_Dirty flag for each block that is going to be written. Therefore, if ll_rw_block( ) finds that the flag is clear, then the block is already involved in a write operation, so nothing has to be done.

   e. If the block must be read, tests the BH_Uptodate flag of the buffer head. If it is set, executes the b_end_io method (the end_buffer_io_sync( ) function) and continues with the next buffer. The kernel never rereads a block from disk when its buffer contains valid (up-to-date) data.

f. Invokes the submit_bh( ) function, which:

1. Determines the number of the first block's sector on the disk—that is, the value of the b_rsector field—from the fields b_blocknr (the logical block number) and b_size (the block size). This field could be later modified by the block device driver if it handles the Logical Volume Manager (LVM) or a RAID disk.

2. Sets the BH_Req flag in b_state to denote that the block has been requested.

3. Initializes the b_rdev field from the b_dev field. As before, this field could be modified later by the block device driver if it handles the LVM or a RAID disk.

4. Invokes generic_make_request( ).

The generic_make_request( ) function posts the request to the low-level driver. It receives as parameters the buffer head bh and the type of operation rw (READ, WRITE, or READA), and performs the following operations:

1. Checks that bh->b_rsector does not exceed the number of sectors of the block device. If it does, prints a kernel error message, invokes the b_end_io method of the buffer head, and terminates.

2. Extracts the major number maj of the block device driver from bh->b_rdev.

3. Gets the descriptor of the device driver request queue from the low-level driver descriptor blk_dev[maj]. To do this, it invokes the blk_dev[maj].queue method, if it is defined (the driver makes use of several queues); otherwise, it reads the blk_dev[maj].request_queue field (the driver uses a single queue).

4. Invokes the make_request_fn method of the request queue descriptor identified in the previous step.

In most cases, block device drivers implement the make_request_fn method with the __make_request( ) function. It receives as parameters the queue descriptor, the buffer head bh, and the type of operation rw, and performs the following operations:

1. Checks whether the type of the operation rw is READA; in this case, it sets the local flag rw_ahead to 1 and sets rw to READ.

2. Invokes the create_bounce( ) function, which looks at the PG_highmem flag in bh->b_page->flags and determines whether the bh->b_data buffer is stored in high memory or not (see the section "Kernel Mappings of High-Memory Page Frames" in Chapter 7). If the buffer is in high memory, the low-level driver might not be able to handle it. Therefore, create_bounce( ) temporarily allocates a new buffer in low memory and a new buffer head pointing to it. The new buffer head is almost identical to bh, except for the b_data field, which points to the new buffer, the b_private field, which points to the original buffer head bh, and the b_end_io method, which points to a custom method that releases the low-memory

buffer when the I/O operation terminates. If rw is WRITE, then the low-memory buffer is filled with the high memory buffer contents by create_bounce(); otherwise, if rw is READ, the low memory buffer is copied into the high-memory buffer by the b_end_io custom method.

3. Checks whether the request queue is empty:

- If the request queue is empty, inserts a new request descriptor in it and schedules activation of the strategy routine of the low-level driver at a later time.

- If the request queue is not empty, inserts a new request descriptor in it, trying to cluster it with other requests that are already queued. As we'll see shortly, there is no need to schedule the activation of the strategy routine.

Let's look closer at these two cases.

Scheduling the activation of the strategy routine

As we saw earlier, it's expedient to delay activation of the strategy routine in order to increase the chances of clustering requests for adjacent blocks. The delay is accomplished through a technique known as device plugging and unplugging. As long as a block device driver is plugged, its strategy routine is not activated even if there are requests to be processed in the driver's queues.

If the real device's request queue is empty and the device isn't already plugged, __make_request() carries out a *device plugging*. The plug_device_fn method that performs this task is usually implemented by means of the generic_plug_device() function. This function sets the plugged field of the request queue descriptor to 1 and inserts the plug_tq task queue element (statically included in the request queue descriptor) in the tq_disk task queue (see the section "Extending a bottom half" in Chapter 4) to cause the device's strategy routine to be activated later.

The __make_request() function then allocates a new request descriptor by invoking get_request(). If no request descriptor is available, the function checks the value of the rw_ahead flag. If it is set, then the function is handling a relatively unimportant read-ahead operation, thus it invokes the b_end_io method and terminates without performing the I/O data transfer. Otherwise, the function invokes the get_request_wait() function to force the process to sleep until a request descriptor is freed.

Next, __make_request() initializes the new request descriptor with the information read from the buffer head, inserts it into the proper real device's request queue, and terminates.

How is the actual I/O data transfer started? The kernel checks periodically whether the tq_disk task queue contains any elements. This occurs in a kernel thread such as *kswapd*, or when the kernel must wait for some resource related to block device drivers, such as buffers or request descriptors. During the tq_disk check, the kernel removes any element in the queue and executes the corresponding function.

Usually, the function stored in any `plug_tq` task queue points to the `generic_unplug_device( )` function, which resets the `plugged` field of the request queue descriptor and invokes its `request_fn` method, thus executing the low-level driver's strategy routine. This activity is referred to as *unplugging* the device. As a result, the requests included in the queues of the driver are processed, and the corresponding I/O data transfers take place.

Extending the request queue

If the request queue is not empty, the driver was already plugged when the kernel inserted the first request in the queue. Therefore, there is no need to schedule the activation of the strategy routine again. Either the low-level driver is already unplugged, or it soon will be.

Notice that if `__make_request( )` finds that the queue is not empty, the low-level driver could be actively handling the requests of the queue. Nevertheless, the function can safely modify the queue because the low-level driver usually removes the requests from the queue *before* processing them. As a particular case, however, the function never touches the first request in the queue when the `head_active` field of the request queue descriptor is set. This flag is set when the low-level driver's policy is always to process the first request in the queue and not to remove the request from the queue until the I/O data transfer completes.

The `__make_request( )` function must either add a new element in the queue or include the new block in an existing request; the second case is known as *block clustering*.

Block clustering requires that all the following conditions be satisfied:

- The block to be inserted belongs to the same block device as the other blocks in the request and is adjacent to them: it either immediately precedes the first block in the request or immediately follows the last block in the request.
- The blocks in the request have the same I/O operation type (READ or WRITE) as the block to be inserted.
- The extended request does not exceed the allowed maximum number of sectors. This value is stored in the `max_sectors` table, which is indexed by the major and minor number of the block device. The default value is 255 sectors.
- The extended request does not exceed the allowed maximum number of segments (see the section "Request descriptors" earlier in this chapter), which is usually 128.
- No process is waiting for the completion of request—i.e., the `waiting` field of the request descriptor is NULL.

When the `__make_request( )` function must determine how to insert the requested block in the queue, it uses a program that is traditionally called an *elevator algorithm*. The elevator algorithm basically defines the ordering of the elements in the queue; usually, this ordering is also followed by the low-level driver when it is handling the requests.

Although each block device driver may define its own elevator algorithm, most block device drivers use either one of the following:

ELEVATOR_NOOP *algorithm*

New requests descriptors are inserted at the end of the queue. Therefore, older requests precede younger ones. Notice that block clustering enlarges a request but doesn't make it younger. This algorithm favors fairness of servicing time among the various requests.

ELEVATOR_LINUS *algorithm*

The queue elements tend to be ordered by the position of the corresponding sectors on the block device. This algorithm tries to minimize the number and extent of seek operations on the physical device. However, the algorithm must also rely on an ageing mechanism to avoid making requests in the last positions of the queue to remain unhanded for long periods of time. When searching for a request that might include the block, the algorithm starts from the bottom of the queue and interrupts the scanning as soon as it finds a very old request.

The elevator algorithm is implemented by three methods included in the elevator field of the request queue descriptor:

elevator_merge_fn

Scans the queue and searches a candidate request for the block clustering. If block clustering is not possible, it also returns the position where the new request should be inserted. Otherwise, it returns the request that has to be enlarged in order to include the blocks in the new request.

elevator_merge_cleanup_fn

Invoked after a successful block clustering operation. It should increase the age of all requests in the queue that follow the enlarged request. (The method does nothing in the ELEVATOR_NOOP algorithm).

elevator_merge_req_fn

Invoked when the kernel merges two existing requests of the queue. It should assign the age of the new enlarged request. (The method does nothing in the ELEVATOR_NOOP algorithm).

To add an existing request to the front or the back of a request, the __make_request() function uses back_merge_fn and front_merge_fn methods of the request queue descriptor, respectively. After a successful block clustering operation, __make_request() also checks whether the enlarged request can be merged with the previous or the next request in the queue by invoking the merge_requests_fn method of the request queue descriptor.

Low-Level Request Handling

We have now reached the lowest level in Linux's block device handling. This level is implemented by the strategy routine, which interacts with the physical block device to satisfy the requests collected in the queue.

As mentioned earlier, the strategy routine is usually started after inserting a new request in an empty request queue. Once activated, the low-level driver should handle all requests in the queue and terminate when the queue is empty.

A naïve implementation of the strategy routine could be the following: for each element in the queue, interact with the block device controller to service the request and wait until the data transfer completes. Then remove the serviced request from the queue and proceed with the next one.

Such an implementation is not very efficient. Even assuming that data can be transferred using DMA, the strategy routine must suspend itself while waiting for I/O completion; hence, an unrelated user process would be heavily penalized. (The strategy routine does not necessarily execute on behalf of the process that has requested the I/O operation but at a random, later time, since it is activated by means of the tq_disk task queue.)

Therefore, many low-level drivers adopt the following strategy:

• The strategy routine handles the first request in the queue and sets up the block device controller so that it raises an interrupt when the data transfer completes. Then the strategy routine terminates.

• When the block device controller raises the interrupt, the interrupt handler activates a bottom half. The bottom half handler removes the request from the queue and reexecutes the strategy routine to service the next request in the queue.

Basically, low-level drivers can be further classified into the following:

• Drivers that service each block in a request separately

• Drivers that service several blocks in a request together

Drivers of the second type are much more complicated to design and implement than drivers of the first type. Indeed, although the sectors are adjacent on the physical block devices, the buffers in RAM are not necessarily consecutive. Therefore, any such driver may have to allocate a temporary area for the DMA data transfer, and then perform a memory-to-memory copy of the data between the temporary area and each buffer in the request's list.

Since requests handled by both types of drivers consist of adjacent blocks, disk performance is enhanced because fewer seek commands are issued. However, the second type of drivers do not further reduce the number of seek commands, so transferring several blocks from disk together is not as effective in boosting disk performance.

The kernel doesn't offer any support for the second type of drivers: they must handle the request queues and the buffer head lists on their own. The choice to leave the job up to the driver is not capricious or lazy. Each physical block device is inherently different from all others (for example, a floppy driver groups blocks in disk tracks and transfers a whole track in a single I/O operation), so making general assumptions on how to service each clustered request makes very little sense.

However, the kernel offers a limited degree of support for the low-level drivers in the first class. We'll spend a little more time describing such drivers.

A typical strategy routine should perform the following actions:

1. Get the current request from a request queue. If all request queues are empty, terminate the routine.

2. Check that the current request has consistent information. In particular, compare the major number of the block device with the value stored in the rq_rdev field of the request descriptor. Moreover, check that the first buffer head in the list is locked (the BH_Lock flag should have been set by ll_rw_block()).

3. Program the block device controller for the data transfer of the first block. The data transfer direction can be found in the cmd field of the request descriptor and the address of the buffer in the buffer field, while the initial sector number and the number of sectors to be transferred are stored in the sector and current_nr_sectors fields, respectively.* Also, set up the block device controller so that an interrupt is raised when the DMA data transfer completes.

4. If the routine is handling a block device file for which ll_rw_block() accomplishes block clustering, increment the sector field and decrement the nr_sectors field of the request descriptor to keep track of the blocks to be transferred.

The interrupt handler associated with the termination of the DMA data transfer for the block device should invoke (either directly or via a bottom half) the end_request function (or a custom function of the block device driver that does the same things). The function, which receives as parameters the value 1 if the data transfer succeeds or the value 0 if an error occurs, performs the following operations:

1. If an error occurred (parameter value is 0), updates the sector and nr_sectors fields so as to skip the remaining sectors of the block. In Step 3a, the buffer content is also marked as not up-to-date.

2. Removes the buffer head of the transferred block from the request's list.

3. Invokes the b_end_io method of the buffer head. When the ll_rw_block() function allocates the buffer head, it loads this field with the address of the end_buffer_io_sync() function, which essentially performs two operations:

   a. Sets the BH_Uptodate flag of the buffer head to 1 or 0, according to the success or failure of the data transfer

   b. Clears the BH_Lock, BH_Wait_IO, and BH_launder flags of the buffer head and wakes up all processes sleeping in the wait queue to which the b_wait field of the buffer head points

---

* Recall that current_nr_sectors contains the number of sectors in the first block of the request, while nr_sectors contains the total number of sectors in the request.

The b_end_io field could also point to other functions. For instance, if the create_bounce() function created a temporary buffer in low memory, the b_end_io field points to a suitable function that updates the original buffer in high memory and then invokes the b_end_io method of the original buffer head.

4. If there is another buffer head on the request's list, sets the current_nr_sectors field of the request descriptor to the number of sectors of the new block.

5. Sets the buffer field with the address of the new buffer (from the b_data field of the new buffer head).

6. Otherwise, if the request's list is empty, all blocks have been processed. Therefore, it performs the following operations:

    a. Removes the request descriptor from the request queue

    b. Wakes up any process waiting for the request to complete (waiting field in the request descriptor)

    c. Sets the rq_status field of the request to RQ_INACTIVE

    d. Puts the request descriptor in the list of free requests

After invoking end_request, the low-level driver checks whether the request queue is empty. If it is not, the strategy routine is executed again. Notice that end_request actually performs two nested iterations: the outer one on the elements of the request queue and the inner one on the elements in the buffer head list of each request. The strategy routine is thus invoked once for each block in the request queue.

Block and Page I/O Operations

We'll discuss in the forthcoming chapters how the kernel uses the block device drivers. We'll see that there are a number of cases in which the kernel activates disk I/O data transfers. However, let's describe here the two fundamental kinds of I/O data transfer for block devices:

Block I/O operations

   Here the I/O operation transfers a single block of data, so the transferred data can be kept in a single RAM buffer. The disk address consists of a device number and a block number. The buffer is associated with a specific disk block, which is identified by the major and minor numbers of the block device and by the logical block number.

Page I/O operations

   Here the I/O operation transfers as many blocks of data as needed to fill a single page frame (the exact number depends both on the disk block size and on the page frame size). If the size of a page frame is a multiple of the block size, several disk blocks are transferred in a single I/O operation. Each page frame contains data belonging to a file. Since this data is not necessarily stored in adjacent disk blocks, it is identified by the file's inode and by an offset within the file.

Block I/O operations are most often used when the kernel reads or writes single blocks in a filesystem (for example, a block containing an inode or a superblock). Conversely, page I/O operations are used mainly for reading and writing files (both regular files and block device files), for accessing files through the memory mapping, and for swapping.

Both kinds of I/O operations rely on the same functions to access a block device, but the kernel uses different algorithms and buffering techniques with them.

Block I/O operations

The bread( ) function reads a single block from a block device and stores it in a buffer. It receives as parameters the device identifier, the block number, and the block size, and returns a pointer to the buffer head of the buffer containing the block.

The function performs the following operations:

1. Invokes the getblk( ) function to search for the block in a software cache called the buffer cache (see Chapter 14). If the block is not included in the cache, getblk( ) allocates a new buffer for it.

2. Invokes mark_page_accessed( ) on the buffer page containing the data (see the section "The Least Recently Used (LRU) Lists" in Chapter 16).

3. If the buffer already contains valid data, it terminates.

4. Invokes ll_rw_block( ) to start the READ operation (see the section "The ll_rw_block( ) Function" earlier in this chapter).

5. Waits until the data transfer completes. This is done by invoking a function named wait_on_buffer( ), which inserts the current process in the b_wait wait queue and suspends the process until the buffer is unlocked.

6. Checks whether the buffer contains valid data. If so, it returns the address of the buffer head; otherwise, it returns a NULL pointer.

No function exists to directly write a block to disk. Declaring a buffer dirty is sufficient to force its flushing to disk at some later time. In fact, write operations are not considered critical for system performance, so they are deferred whenever possible (see the section "Writing Dirty Buffers to Disk" in Chapter 14).

Page I/O operations

Block devices transfer information one block at a time, while process address spaces (or to be more precise, memory regions allocated to the process) are defined as sets of pages. This mismatch can be hidden to some extent by using page I/O operations. They may be activated in the following cases:

- A process issues a read( ) or write( ) system call on a file (see Chapter 15).

- A process reads a location of a page that maps a file in memory (see the section "Memory Mapping" in Chapter 15).

- The kernel flushes some dirty pages related to a file memory mapping to disk (see the section "Flushing Dirty Memory Mapping Pages to Disk" in Chapter 15).

- When swapping in or swapping out, the kernel loads from or saves to disk the contents of whole page frames (see Chapter 16).

Page I/O operations can be activated by several kernel functions. In this section, we'll present the brw_page( ) function used to read or write swap pages (see Chapter 16). Other functions that start page I/O operations are discussed in Chapter 15.

The brw_page( ) function receives the following parameters:

rw
> Type of I/O operation (READ, WRITE, or READA)

page
> Address of a page descriptor

dev
> Block device number (major and minor numbers)

b
> Array of logical block numbers

size
> Block size

The page descriptor refers to the page involved in the page I/O operation. It must already be locked (PG_locked flag on) before invoking brw_page( ) so that no other kernel control path can access it. The page is considered as split into 4096/size buffers; the ith buffer in the page is associated with the block b[i] of device dev.

The function performs the following operations:

1. Checks the page->buffers field; if it is NULL, invokes create_empty_buffers( ) to allocate temporary buffer heads for all buffers included in the page (such buffer heads are called asynchronous; they are discussed in the section "Buffer Head Data Structures" in Chapter 14). The address of the buffer head for the first buffer in the page is stored in the page->buffers field. The b_this_page field of each buffer head points to the buffer head of the next buffer in the page.

   Conversely, if the page->buffers field is not NULL, the kernel does not need to allocate temporary buffer heads. In fact, in this case, the page stores some buffers already included in the buffer cache, presumably because some of them were previously involved in block I/O operations (see the section "Buffer Pages" in Chapter 14 for further details).

2. For each buffer head in the page, performs the following substeps:

   a. Sets the BH_Lock (locks the buffer for the I/O data transfer) and the BH_Mapped (the buffer maps a file on disk) flags of the buffer head.

---

b. Stores in the b_blocknr field the value of the corresponding element of the array b.

c. Since it is an asynchronous buffer head, sets the BH_Async flag, and in the b_end_io field, stores a pointer to end_buffer_io_async( ) (described next).

3. For each buffer head in the page, invokes submit_bh( ) to request the buffer (see the section "The ll_rw_block( ) Function" earlier in this chapter.)

The submit_bh( ) function activates the device driver of the block device being accessed. As described in the earlier section "Low-Level Request Handling," the device driver performs the actual data transfer and then invokes the b_end_io method of all asynchronous buffer heads that have been transferred. The b_end_io field points to the end_buffer_io_async( ) function, which performs the following operations:

1. Sets the BH_Uptodate flag of the asynchronous buffer head according to the result of the I/O operation.

2. If the BH_Uptodate flag is off, sets the PG_error flag of the page descriptor because an error occurred while transferring the block. The function gets the page descriptor address from the b_page field of the buffer head.

3. Gets the page_update_lock spin lock.

4. Clears both the BH_Async and the BH_Lock flags of the buffer head, and awakens each process waiting for the buffer.

5. If any of the buffer heads in the page are still locked (i.e., the I/O data transfer is not yet terminated), releases the page_update_lock spin lock and returns.

6. Otherwise, releases the page_update_lock spin lock and checks the PG_error flag of the page descriptor. If it is cleared, then all data transfers on the page have successfully completed, so the function sets the PG_uptodate flag of the page descriptor.

7. Unlocks the page, clears the PG_locked flag, and wakes any process sleeping on page->wait wait queue.

Notice that once the page I/O operation terminates, the temporary buffer heads allocated by create_empty_buffers( ) are not automatically released. As we shall see in Chapter 16, the temporary buffer heads are released only when the kernel tries to reclaim some memory.

Character Device Drivers

Handling a character device is relatively easy, since usually sophisticated buffering strategies are not needed and disk caches are not involved. Of course, character devices differ in their requirements: some of them must implement a sophisticated communication protocol to drive the hardware device, while others just have to read a few values from a couple of I/O ports of the hardware devices. For instance, the device driver of a multiport serial card device (a hardware device offering many serial ports) is much more complicated than the device driver of a bus mouse.

A small complication, however, comes from the fact that the same major number might be allocated to several different device drivers. For instance, the major number 10 is used by many different device drivers, such as a real-time clock and a PS/2 mouse.

To keep track of which character device drivers are currently in use, the kernel uses a hash table indexed by the major and minor numbers.* The hash table array is stored in cdev_hashtable variable; it includes 64 lists of character device descriptors. Each descriptor is a char_device data structure, whose fields are shown in Table 13-10.

Table 13-10. The fields of the character device descriptor

Type	Field	Description
struct list_head	hash	Pointers for the hash table list
atomic_t	count	Usage counter for the character device descriptor
dev_t	dev	Major and minor numbers of the character device
atomic_t	openers	Not used
struct semaphore	sem	Semaphore protecting the character device

As for block device drivers, a hash table is required because the kernel cannot determine whether a character device driver is in use by simply checking whether a character device file has been already opened. In fact, the system directory tree might include several character device files having different pathnames but equal major and minor numbers, and they all refer to the very same device driver.

A character device descriptor is inserted into the hash table whenever a device file referring to it is opened for the first time. This job is performed by the init_special_inode() function, which is invoked by the low-level filesystem layer when it determines that a disk inode represents a device file. init_special_inode() looks up the character device descriptor in the hash table; if the descriptor is not found, the function allocates a new descriptor and inserts that into the hash table. The function also stores the descriptor address into the i_cdev field of the inode object of the device file.

We mentioned in the section "VFS Handling of Device Files" that the dentry_open() function triggered by the open() system call service routine customizes the f_op field in the file object of the character device file so that it points to the def_chr_fops table. This table is almost empty; it only defines the chrdev_open() function as the open method of the device file. This method is immediately invoked by dentry_open().

---

* A character device driver registered with the *devfs* device file might not have major and minor numbers. In this case, the kernel assumes that its major and minor numbers are equal to zero.

The chrdev_open() function rewrites the f_op field of the file object with the address stored in the chrdevs table element that corresponds to the major number of the character device file. Then the function invokes the open method again.

If the major number is assigned to a unique device driver, the method initializes the device driver. Otherwise, if the major number is shared among several device drivers, the method rewrites once more the f_op field of the file object with an address found in the data structure indexed by the minor number of the device file. For instance, the file_operations data structures for the device file that has the major number 10 are stored in the simply linked list misc_list. Finally, the open method is invoked for the last time to initialize the device driver.

Once opened, the character device file usually can be accessed for reading and/or for writing; to do this, the read and write methods of the file object points to suitable functions of the device driver. Most device drivers also support the ioctl() system call through the ioctl file object method; it allows special commands to be sent to the underlying hardware device.

CHAPTER 14
Disk Caches

This chapter deals with disk caches. It shows how Linux uses sophisticated techniques to improve system performances by reducing disk accesses as much as possible.

As mentioned in the section "The Common File Model" in Chapter 12, a disk cache is a software mechanism that allows the system to keep in RAM some data that is normally stored on a disk, so that further accesses to that data can be satisfied quickly without accessing the disk.

Besides the dentry cache, which is used by the VFS to speed up the translation of a file pathname to the corresponding inode, two main disk caches—the buffer cache and the page cache—are used by Linux.

As suggested by its name, the *buffer cache* is a disk cache consisting of buffers; as we know from the section "Sectors, Blocks, and Buffers" in Chapter 13, each buffer stores a single disk block. The block I/O operations (described in the section "Block I/O operations" in the same chapter) rely on the buffer cache to reduce the number of disk accesses.

Conversely, the *page cache* is a disk cache consisting of pages; each page in the cache corresponds to several blocks of a regular file or a block device file. Of course, the exact number of blocks contained in a page depends on the size of the block. All such blocks are logically contiguous—that is, they represent an integral portion of a regular file or of a block device file. To reduce the number of disk accesses, before activating a page I/O operation (described in the section "Page I/O operations" in Chapter 13), the kernel should check whether the wanted data is already stored in the page cache.

Table 14-1 shows how some widely used I/O operations use the buffer and page caches. Some of the examples given refer to the Ext2 filesystem, but they can apply to almost all disk-based filesystems.

Table 14-1. Use of the buffer cache and page cache

Kernel function	System call	Cache	I/O operation
bread( )	None	Buffer	Read an Ext2 superblock
bread( )	None	Buffer	Read an Ext2 inode
generic_file_read( )	getdents( )	Page	Read an Ext2 directory
generic_file_read( )	read( )	Page	Read an Ext2 regular file
generic_file_write( )	write( )	Page	Write an Ext2 regular file
generic_file_read( )	read( )	Page	Read a block device file
generic_file_write( )	write( )	Page	Write a block device file
filemap_nopage( )	None	Page	Access a memory-mapped file
brw_page( )	None	Page	Access to swapped-out page

Each operation in this table appears in subsequent chapters:

Read an Ext2 superblock
　　See the section "Block I/O operations" in Chapter 13. See also Chapter 17.

Read an Ext2 inode
　　See the section "Writing to a File" in Chapter 15. See also Chapter 17 for the Ext2 filesystem.

Read an Ext2 directory
　　See the section "Reading from a File" in Chapter 15. See also Chapter 17 for the Ext2 filesystem.

Read an Ext2 regular file
　　See the section "Reading from a File" in Chapter 15.

Write an Ext2 regular file
　　See the section "Writing to a File" in Chapter 15. See also Chapter 17 for the Ext2 filesystem.

Read a block device file
　　See the section "Reading from a File" in Chapter 15.

Write a block device file
　　See the section "Writing to a File" in Chapter 15.

Access a memory-mapped file
　　See the section "Memory Mapping" in Chapter 15.

Access to swapped-out page
　　See the section "Page I/O operations" in Chapter 13. See also Chapter 16.

For each type of I/O activity, the table also shows the system call required to start it (if any) and the main corresponding kernel function that handles it.

The table shows that accesses to memory-mapped files and swapped-out pages do not require system calls; they are transparent to the programmer. Once a file memory mapping is set up and swapping is activated, the application program can access the mapped file or the swapped-out page as if it were present in memory. It is the kernel's responsibility to delay the process until the required page is located on disk and brought into RAM.

You'll also notice that the same kernel function, namely `generic_file_read()`, is used to read from block device files and from regular files. Similarly, `generic_file_write()` is used to write both into block device files and into regular files. We describe these functions in Chapter 15.

The Page Cache

To avoid unnecessary disk accesses, the kernel never tries to read a page from disk without looking into the page cache and verifying that it does not already include the requested data. To take the maximum advantage from the page cache, searching into it should be a very fast operation.

The unit of information kept in the page cache is, of course, a whole page of data. A page does not necessarily contain physically adjacent disk blocks, so it cannot be identified by a device number and a block number. Instead, a page in the page cache is identified by an address of a special data structure named `address_space`, and by an offset within the file (or whatever) referenced by the `address_space` data structure.

The address_space Object

Table 14-1 suggests that the Linux page cache speeds up several different kinds of I/O operations. In fact, the page cache may include the following types of pages:

- Pages containing data of regular files and directories of disk-based filesystems; in Chapter 15, we describe how the kernel handles read and write operations on them.

- Pages containing data of a memory-mapped file; see Chapter 15 for details.

- Pages containing data directly read from block device files (skipping the filesystem layer); as discussed in Chapter 15, the kernel handles them using the same set of functions as for pages containing data of regular files.

- Pages containing data of User Mode processes that have been swapped out on disk. As we shall see in Chapter 16, the kernel could be forced to keep in the page cache some pages whose contents have been already written on a swap area.

- Pages belonging to an Interprocess Communication (IPC) shared memory region; we describe IPC resources in Chapter 19.

So far, so good, but how is the kernel supposed to keep track of how every page in the page cache should be handled? For instance, suppose the kernel wishes to update the content of a page included in the page cache—reading the page contents from a regular file, from a directory, from a block device file, or from a swap area are quite different operations, and the kernel must execute the proper operation according to the type of page.

The key data structure that establishes the relationship between pages and methods that operate on the pages is the address_space object. Formally, each address_space object establishes a link between a generic kernel object (the so-called *owner*) and a set of methods that operate on the pages belonging to the owner.

As stated before, the page cache includes five kinds of pages, so a page may belong to five possible kinds of owners.

For instance, if a page belongs to a regular file that is stored in an Ext2 filesystem, the owner of the page is an inode object. The i_mapping field of this object points to an address_space object. In turn, the address_space object defines a set of methods that allow the kernel to act on the pages containing the data of our regular file.

Specifically, the address_space object includes the fields shown in Table 14-2.

Table 14-2. The fields of the address_space object

Type	Field	Description
struct list_head	clean_pages	List of owner's clean pages
struct list_head	dirty_pages	List of owner's nonlocked dirty pages
struct list_head	locked_pages	List of owner's locked dirty pages
unsigned long	nrpages	Total number of owner's pages
struct address_space_operations *	a_ops	Methods that operate on the owner's pages
struct inode *	host	Pointer to the owning inode
struct vm_area_struct *	i_mmap	List of memory regions for private memory mapping
struct vm_area_struct *	i_mmap_shared	List of memory regions for shared memory mapping
spinlock_t	i_shared_lock	Spin lock for the lists of memory regions
int	gfp_mask	Memory allocator flags for the owner's pages

The clean_pages, dirty_pages, and locked_pages fields represent the heads of three lists of page descriptors. Together, these lists include all pages that belong to the owner of the address_space object. We discuss the role of each list in the next section. The nrpages field stores the total number of pages inserted in the three lists.

Although the owner of the address_space object could be any generic kernel object, usually it is a VFS inode object. (After all, the page cache was introduced to speed up disk accesses!) In this case, the host field points to the inode that owns the address_space object.

The i_mmap, i_mmap_shared, i_shared_lock, and gfp_mask fields are used whenever the owner of the address_space object is an inode of a memory-mapped file. We discuss them in the section "Memory Mapping Data Structures" in Chapter 15.

The most important field of the address_space object is a_ops, which points to a table of type address_space_operations containing the methods that define how the owner's pages are handled. These methods are shown in Table 14-3.

Table 14-3. The methods of the address_space object

Method	Description
writepage	Write operation (from the page to the owner's disk image)
readpage	Read operation (from the owner's disk image to the page)
sync_page	Start the I/O data transfer of already scheduled operations on the page
prepare_write	Prepare the write operation (used by disk-based filesystems)
commit_write	Complete the write operation (used by disk-based filesystems)
bmap	Get a logical block number from a file block index
flushpage	Prepare to delete the page from the owner's disk image
releasepage	Used by journaling filesystems to prepare the release of a page
direct_IO	Direct I/O transfer of the data of the page

The most important methods are readpage, writepage, prepare_write, and commit_write. We discuss them in Chapter 15. In most cases, the methods link the owner inode objects with the low-level drivers that access the physical devices. For instance, the function that implements the readpage method for an inode of a regular file "knows" how to locate the positions on the physical disk device of the blocks corresponding to any page of the file. In this chapter, however, we don't have to discuss the address_space methods further.

Page Cache Data Structures

The page cache uses the following main data structures:

A page hash table
> This lets the kernel quickly derive the page descriptor address for the page associated with a specified address_space object and a specified offset (presumably, a file offset)

Page descriptor lists in the address_space object
> This lets the kernel quickly retrieve all pages in a given state owned by a particular inode object (or other kernel object) referenced by an address_space object

Manipulation of the page cache involves adding and removing entries from these data structures, as well as updating the fields in all objects that reference the cached pages. The pagecache_lock spin lock protects the page cache data structures against concurrent accesses in multiprocessor systems.

The page hash table

When a process reads a large file, the page cache may become filled with pages related to that file. In such cases, scanning a long list of page descriptors to find the page that maps the required file portion could become a time-consuming operation.

For this reason, Linux uses a hash table of page descriptor pointers named page_ hash_table. Its size depends on the amount of available RAM; for example, for systems having 128 MB of RAM, page_hash_table is stored in 32 page frames and includes 32,768 page descriptor pointers.

The page_hash macro uses the address of an address_space object and an offset value to derive the address of the corresponding entry in the hash table. As usual, chaining is introduced to handle entries that cause a collision: the next_hash and pprev_hash fields of the page descriptors are used to implement doubly circular lists of entries that have the same hash value. The page_cache_size variable specifies the number of page descriptors included in the collision lists of the page hash table (and therefore in the whole page cache).

The add_page_to_hash_queue( ) and remove_page_from_hash_queue( ) functions add an element into the hash table and remove an element from it, respectively.

The lists of page descriptors in the address_space object

As we have seen, the address_space object includes three lists of page descriptors, whose heads are stored in the clean_pages, dirty_pages, and locked_pages fields. The lists allow the kernel to quickly find all pages of a file (or whatever) in a specific state:

clean_pages
> Includes the pages not locked and not dirty (the PG_locked and PG_dirty flags in the page descriptor are equal to 0). The PG_uptodate flag indicates whether the data in the pages is up to date. Typically, a page is not up to date when its contents have yet to be read from the corresponding image on disk.

dirty_pages
> Includes the pages that contain up-to-date data, but whose image on disk have yet to be updated. The PG_uptodate and PG_dirty flags in the page descriptor are set, while the PG_locked flag is clear.

locked_pages
> Includes the pages whose contents are being transferred to or from disk, so the pages cannot currently accessed. The PG_locked flag is set.

The add_page_to_inode_queue( ) function is used to insert a page descriptor into the clean_pages list of an address_space object. Conversely, the remove_page_from_inode_ queue( ) is used to remove a page descriptor from the list that is currently including it.[*] The kernel moves a page descriptor from a list to another one whenever the page changes its state.

Page descriptor fields related to the page cache

When a page is included in the page cache, some fields of the corresponding page descriptor have special meanings:

list
>   Depending on the state of the page, includes pointers for the next and previous elements in the doubly linked list of clean, dirty, or locked pages of the address_ space object.

mapping
>   Points to the address_space object to which the page belongs. If the page does not belong to the page cache, this field is NULL.

index
>   When the page's owner is an inode object, specifies the position of the data contained in the page within the disk image. The value is in page-size units.

next_hash
>   Points to the next colliding page descriptor in the page hash list.

pprev_hash
>   Points to the next_hash field of the previous colliding page descriptor in the page hash list.

In addition, when a page is inserted into the page cache, the usage counter (count field) of the corresponding page descriptor is incremented. If the count field is exactly 1, the page belongs to the cache but is not being accessed by any process; it can thus be removed from the page cache whenever free memory becomes scarce, as described in Chapter 16.

Page Cache Handling Functions

The high-level functions that use the page cache involve finding, adding, and removing a page.

The find_get_page macro receives as parameters the address of an address_space object and an offset value. It uses the page_hash macro to derive the address of the hash table entry corresponding to the values of the parameters, and invokes the __find_get_ page( ) function to search for the requested page descriptor in the proper collision list. In turn, __find_get_page( ) acquires the pagecache_lock spin lock, scans the list of entries that have the same hash value, then releases the spin lock. If the page is found,

---

[*] The names of these functions are inherited from the old Version 2.2 of the kernel.

the function increments the count field of the corresponding page descriptor and returns its address; otherwise, it returns NULL.

The add_to_page_cache( ) function inserts a new page descriptor (whose address is passed as a parameter) in the page cache. This is achieved by performing the following operations:

1. Acquires the pagecache_lock spin lock.
2. Clears the PG_uptodate, PG_error, PG_dirty, PG_referenced, PG_arch_1, and PG_checked flags, and sets the PG_locked flag of the page frame to indicate that the page is locked and present in the cache, but not yet filled with data.
3. Increments the count field of the page descriptor.
4. Initializes the index field of the page descriptor with a value passed as a parameter, which specifies the position of the data contained in the page within the page's disk image.
5. Invokes add_page_to_inode_queue( ) to insert the page descriptor in the clean_pages list of an address_space object, whose address is passed as a parameter.
6. Invokes add_page_to_hash_queue( ) to insert the page descriptor in the hash table, using the address_space object address and the value of page's index field as hash keys.
7. Releases the pagecache_lock spin lock.
8. Invokes lru_cache_add( ) to add the page descriptor in the inactive list (see Chapter 16).

The find_or_create_page( ) function is similar to find_get_page; however, if the requested page is not in the cache, the function invokes alloc_page( ) to get a new page frame, then invokes add_to_page_cache( ) to insert the page descriptor in the page cache.

The remove_inode_page( ) function removes a page descriptor from the page cache. This is achieved by acquiring the pagecache_lock spin lock, invoking remove_page_from_inode_queue( ) and remove_page_from_hash_queue( ), and then releasing the spin lock.

The Buffer Cache

The whole idea behind the buffer cache is to relieve processes from having to wait for relatively slow disks to retrieve or store data. Thus, it would be counterproductive to write a lot of data at once; instead, data should be written piecemeal at regular intervals so that I/O operations have a minimal impact on the speed of the user processes and on response time experienced by human users.

The kernel maintains a lot of information about each buffer to help it pace the writes, including a "dirty" bit to indicate the buffer has been changed in memory and needs to be written, and a timestamp to indicate how long the buffer should be kept in memory before being flushed to disk. Information on buffers is kept in buffer heads (introduced in the previous chapter), so these data structures require maintenance along with the buffers of user data themselves.

The size of the buffer cache may vary. Page frames are allocated on demand when a new buffer is required and one is not available. When free memory becomes scarce, as we shall see in Chapter 16, buffers are released and the corresponding page frames are recycled.

The buffer cache consists of two kinds of data structures:

- A set of buffer heads describing the buffers in the cache
- A hash table to help the kernel quickly derive the buffer head that describes the buffer associated with a given pair of device and block numbers

Buffer Head Data Structures

As mentioned in the section "Buffer Heads" in Chapter 13, each buffer head is stored in a data structure of type buffer_head. These data structures have their own slab allocator cache called bh_cachep, which should not be confused with the buffer cache itself. The slab allocator cache is a memory cache (see the section "Identifying a Process" in Chapter 3) for the buffer head objects, meaning that it has no interaction with disks and is simply a way of managing memory efficiently. In contrast, the buffer cache is a disk cache for the data in the buffers.

Each buffer used by a block device driver must have a corresponding buffer head that describes the buffer's current status. The converse is not true: a buffer head may be unused, which means it is not bound to any buffer. The kernel keeps a certain number of unused buffer heads to avoid the overhead of constantly allocating and deallocating memory.

In general, a buffer head may be in any one of the following states:

Unused buffer head
> The object is available; the values of its fields are meaningless, except for the b_ dev field that stores the value B_FREE (0xffff).

Buffer head for a cached buffer
> Its b_data field points to a buffer stored in the buffer cache. The b_dev field identifies a block device, and the BH_Mapped flag is set. Moreover, the buffer could be one of the following:
>
> *Not up-to-date (BH_Uptodate flag is clear)*
> > The data in the buffer is not valid (for instance, the data has yet to be read from disk).

Dirty (BH_Dirty *flag set*)

> The data in the buffer has been modified, and the corresponding block on disk needs to be updated.

Locked (BH_Lock *flag set*)

> An I/O data transfer on the buffer contents is in progress.

Asynchronous buffer head

> Its b_data field points to a buffer inside a page that is involved in a page I/O operation (see the section "Page I/O operations" in Chapter 13); in this case, the BH_Async flag is set. As soon as the page I/O operation terminates, the BH_Async flag is cleared, but the buffer head is not freed; rather, it remains allocated and inserted into a simply linked circular list of the page (see the later section "Buffer Pages"). Thus, it can be reused without the overhead of always allocating new ones. Asynchronous buffer heads are released whenever the kernel tries to reclaim some memory (see Chapter 16).

Strictly speaking, the buffer cache data structures include only pointers to buffer heads for a cached buffer. For the sake of completeness, we shall examine the data structures and the methods used by the kernel to handle all kinds of buffer heads, not just those in the buffer cache.

The list of unused buffer heads

All unused buffer heads are collected in a simply linked list, whose first element is addressed by the unused_list variable. Each buffer head stores the address of the next list element in the b_next_free field. The current number of elements in the list is stored in the nr_unused_buffer_heads variable. The unused_list_lock spin lock protects the list against concurrent accesses in multiprocessor systems.

The list of unused buffer heads acts as a primary memory cache for the buffer head objects, while the bh_cachep slab allocator cache is a secondary memory cache. When a buffer head is no longer needed, it is inserted into the list of unused buffer heads. Buffer heads are released to the slab allocator (a preliminary step to letting the kernel free the memory associated with them altogether) only when the number of list elements exceeds MAX_UNUSED_BUFFERS (usually 100 elements). In other words, a buffer head in this list is considered an allocated object by the slab allocator and an unused data structure by the buffer cache.

A subset of NR_RESERVED (usually 80) elements in the list is reserved for page I/O operations. This is done to prevent nasty deadlocks caused by the lack of free buffer heads. As we shall see in Chapter 16, if free memory is scarce, the kernel can try to free a page frame by swapping out some page to disk. To do this, it requires at least one additional buffer head to perform the page I/O file operation. If the swapping algorithm fails to get a buffer head, it simply keeps waiting and lets writes to files proceed to free up buffers, since at least NR_RESERVED buffer heads are going to be released as soon as the ongoing file operations terminate.

The get_unused_buffer_head( ) function is invoked to get a new buffer head. It essentially performs the following operations:

1. Acquires the unused_list_lock spin lock.
2. If the list of unused buffer heads has more than NR_RESERVED elements, removes one of them from the list, releases the spin lock, and returns the address of the buffer head.
3. Otherwise, releases the spin lock and invokes kmem_cache_alloc( ) to allocate a new buffer head from the bh_cachep slab allocator cache with priority GFP_NOFS (see the section "Requesting and Releasing Page Frames" in Chapter 7); if the operation succeeds, returns its address.
4. No free memory is available. If the buffer head has been requested for a block I/O operation, returns NULL (failure).
5. If this point is reached, the buffer head has been requested for a page I/O operation. If the list of unused buffer heads is not empty, acquires the unused_list_lock spin lock, removes one element from the list, releases the spin lock, and returns the address of the buffer head.
6. Otherwise (if the list is empty), returns NULL (failure).

The put_unused_buffer_head( ) function performs the reverse operation, releasing a buffer head. It inserts the object in the list of unused buffer heads if that list has fewer than MAX_UNUSED_BUFFERS elements; otherwise, it releases the object to the slab allocator by invoking kmem_cache_free( ) on the buffer head.

Lists of buffer heads for cached buffers

When a buffer belongs to the buffer cache, the flags of the corresponding buffer head describe its current status (see the section "Buffer Heads" in Chapter 13). For instance, when a block not present in the cache must be read from disk, a new buffer is allocated and the BH_Uptodate flag of the buffer head is cleared because the buffer's contents are meaningless. While filling the buffer by reading from disk, the BH_Lock flag is set to protect the buffer from being reclaimed. If the read operation terminates successfully, the BH_Uptodate flag is set and the BH_Lock flag is cleared. If the block must be written to disk, the buffer content is modified and the BH_Dirty flag is set; the flag is cleared only after the buffer is successfully written to disk.

Any buffer head associated with a used buffer is contained in a doubly linked list, implemented by means of the b_next_free and b_prev_free fields. There are three different lists, identified by an index defined as a macro (BUF_CLEAN, BUF_LOCKED, and BUF_DIRTY). We'll define these lists in a moment.

The three lists are introduced to speed up the functions that flush dirty buffers to disk (see the section "Writing Dirty Buffers to Disk" later in this chapter). For reasons of efficiency, a buffer head is not moved right away from one list to another when it changes status; this makes the following description a bit murky.

BUF_CLEAN

This list collects buffer heads of nondirty buffers (BH_Dirty flag is off). Notice that buffers in this list are not necessarily up to date—that is, they don't necessarily contain valid data. If the buffer is not up to date, it could even be locked (BH_Lock is on) and selected to be read from the physical device while being on this list. The buffer heads in this list are guaranteed only to be not dirty; in other words, the corresponding buffers are ignored by the functions that flush dirty buffers to disk.

BUF_DIRTY

This list mainly collects buffer heads of dirty buffers that have not been selected to be written into the physical device—that is, dirty buffers that have not yet been included in a block request for a block device driver (BH_Dirty is on and BH_Lock is off). However, this list could also include nondirty buffers, since in a few cases, the BH_Dirty flag of a dirty buffer is cleared without flushing it to disk and without removing the buffer head from the list (for instance, whenever a floppy disk is removed from its drive without unmounting—an event that most likely leads to data loss, of course).

BUF_LOCKED

This list mainly collects buffer heads of buffers that have been selected to be read from or written to the block device (BH_Lock is on; BH_Dirty is clear because the add_request( ) function resets it before including the buffer head in a block request). However, when a block I/O operation for a locked buffer is completed, the low-level block device handler clears the BH_Lock flag without removing the buffer head from the list (see the section "Low-Level Request Handling" in Chapter 13). The buffer heads in this list are guaranteed only to be not dirty, or dirty but selected to be written.

For any buffer head associated with a used buffer, the b_list field of the buffer head stores the index of the list containing the buffer. The lru_list array* stores the address of the first element in each list, the nr_buffers_type array stores the number of elements in each list, and the size_buffers_type array stores the total capacity of the buffers in each list (in byte). The lru_list_lock spin lock protects these arrays from concurrent accesses in multiprocessor systems.

The mark_buffer_dirty( ) and mark_buffer_clean( ) functions set and clear, respectively, the BH_Dirty flag of a buffer head. To keep the number of dirty buffers in the system bounded, mark_buffer_dirty( ) invokes the balance_dirty( ) function (see the later section "Writing Dirty Buffers to Disk"). Both functions also invoke the refile_buffer( ) function, which moves the buffer head into the proper list according to the value of the BH_Dirty and BH_Lock flags.

---

* The name of the array derives from the abbreviation for Least Recently Used. In earlier versions of Linux, these lists were ordered according to the time each buffer was last accessed.

Beside the BUF_DIRTY list, the kernel manages two doubly linked lists of dirty buffers for every inode object. They are used whenever the kernel must flush all dirty buffers of a given file—for instance, when servicing the fsync() or fdatasync() service calls (see the section "The sync(), fsync(), and fdatasync() system calls" later in this chapter).

The first of the two lists includes buffers containing the file's control data (like the disk inode itself), while the other list includes buffers containing the file's data. The heads of these lists are stored in the i_dirty_buffers and i_dirty_data_buffers fields of the inode object, respectively. The b_inode_buffers field of any buffer head stores the pointers to the next and previous elements of these lists. Both of them are protected by the lru_list_lock spin lock just mentioned. The buffer_insert_inode_queue() and buffer_insert_inode_data_queue() functions are used, respectively, to insert a buffer head in the i_dirty_buffers and i_dirty_data_buffers lists. The inode_remove_queue() function removes a buffer head from the list that includes it.

The hash table of cached buffer heads

The addresses of the buffer heads belonging to the buffer cache are inserted into a hash table. Given a device identifier and a block number, the kernel can use the hash table to quickly derive the address of the corresponding buffer head, if one exists. The hash table noticeably improves kernel performance because checks on buffer heads are frequent. Before starting a block I/O operation, the kernel must check whether the required block is already in the buffer cache; in this situation, the hash table lets the kernel avoid a lengthy sequential scan of the lists of cached buffers.

The hash table is stored in the hash_table array, which is allocated during system initialization and whose size depends on the amount of RAM installed on the system. For example, for systems having 128 MB of RAM, hash_table is stored in 4 page frames and includes 4,096 buffer head pointers. As usual, entries that cause a collision are chained in doubly linked lists implemented by means of the b_next and b_pprev fields of each buffer head. The hash_table_lock read/write spin lock protects the hash table data structures from concurrent accesses in multiprocessor systems.

The get_hash_table() function retrieves a buffer head from the hash table. The buffer head to be located is identified by three parameters: the device number, the block number, and the size of the corresponding data block. The function hashes the values of the device number and the block number, and looks into the hash table to find the first element in the collision list; then it checks the b_dev, b_blocknr, and b_size fields of each element in the list and returns the address of the requested buffer head. If the buffer head is not in the cache, the function returns NULL.

Buffer usage counter

The b_count field of the buffer head is a usage counter for the corresponding buffer. The counter is incremented right before each operation on the buffer and decremented right after. It acts mainly as a safety lock, since the kernel never destroys a

---

buffer (or its contents) as long as it has a non-null usage counter. Instead, the cached buffers are examined either periodically or when the free memory becomes scarce, and only those buffers that have null counters may be destroyed (see Chapter 16). In other words, a buffer with a null usage counter may belong to the buffer cache, but it cannot be determined how long the buffer will stay in the cache.

When a kernel control path wishes to access a buffer, it should increment the usage counter first. This task is performed by the getblk( ) function, which is usually invoked to locate the buffer, so that the increment need not be done explicitly by higher-level functions. When a kernel control path stops accessing a buffer, it may invoke either brelse( ) or bforget( ) to decrement the corresponding usage counter. The difference between these two functions is that bforget( ) also marks the buffer as clean, thus forcing the kernel to forget any change in the buffer that has yet to be written on disk.

Buffer Pages

Although the page cache and the buffer cache are different disk caches, in Version 2.4 of Linux, they are somewhat intertwined.

In fact, for reasons of efficiency, buffers are not allocated as single memory objects; instead, buffers are stored in dedicated pages called *buffer pages*. All the buffers within a single buffer page must have the same size; hence, on the 80×86 architecture, a buffer page can include from one to eight buffers, depending on the block size.

A stronger constraint, however, is that all the buffers in a buffer page must refer to adjacent blocks of the underlying block device. For instance, suppose that the kernel wants to read a 1,024-byte inode block of a regular file. Instead of allocating a single 1,024-byte buffer for the inode, the kernel must reserve a whole page storing four buffers; these buffers will contain the data of a group of four adjacent blocks on the block device, including the requested inode block.

It is easy to understand that a buffer page can be regarded in two different ways. On one hand, it is the "container" for some buffers, which can be individually addressed by means of the buffer cache. On the other hand, each buffer page contains a 4,096-byte portion of a block device file, hence, it can be included in the page cache. In other words, the portion of RAM cached by the buffer cache is always a subset of the portion of RAM cached by the page cache. The benefit of this mechanism consists of dramatically reducing the synchronization problems between the buffer cache and the page cache.

In the 2.2 version of the kernel, the two disk caches were not intertwined. A given physical block could have two images in RAM: one in the page cache and the other in the buffer cache. To avoid data loss, whenever one of the two block's memory images is modified, the 2.2 kernel must also find and update the other memory image. As you might imagine, this is a costly operation.

By way of contrast, in Linux 2.4, modifying a buffer implies modifying the page that contains it, and vice versa. The kernel must only pay attention to the "dirty" flags of both the buffer heads and the page descriptors. For instance, whenever a buffer head is marked as "dirty," the kernel must also set the PG_dirty flag of the page that contains the corresponding buffer.

Buffer heads and page descriptors include a few fields that define the link between a buffer page and the corresponding buffers. If a page acts as a buffer page, the buffers field of its page descriptor points to the buffer head of the first buffer included in the page; otherwise the buffers field is NULL. In turn, the b_this_page field of each buffer head implements a simply linked circular list that includes all buffer heads of the buffers stored in the buffer page. Moreover, the b_page field of each buffer head points to the page descriptor of the corresponding buffer page. Figure 14-1 shows a buffer page containing four buffers and the corresponding buffer heads.

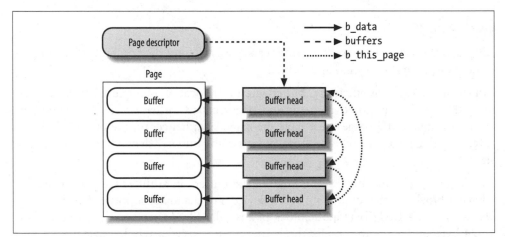

Figure 14-1. A buffer page including four buffers and their buffer heads

There is a special case: if a page has been involved in a page I/O operation (see the section "Page I/O operations" in Chapter 13), the kernel might have allocated some asynchronous buffer heads and linked them to the page by means of the buffers and b_this_page fields. Thus, a page could act as a buffer page under some circumstances, even though the corresponding buffer heads are not in the buffer cache.

Allocating buffer pages

The kernel allocates a new buffer page when it discovers that the buffer cache does not include data for a given block. In this case, the kernel invokes the grow_buffers() function, passing to it three parameters that identify the block:

- The block device number—the major and minor numbers of the device
- The logical block number—the position of the block inside the block device
- The block size

The function essentially performs the following actions:

1. Computes the offset index of the page of data within the block device that includes the requested block.

2. Gets the address bdev of the block device descriptor (see the section "Keeping Track of Block Device Drivers" in Chapter 13).

3. Invokes grow_dev_page() to create a new buffer page, if necessary. In turn, this function performs the following substeps:

   a. Invokes find_or_create_page(), passing to it the address_space object of the block device (bdev->bd_inode->i_mapping) and the page offset index. As described in the earlier section "Page Cache Handling Functions," find_or_create_page() looks for the page in the page cache and, if necessary, inserts a new page in the cache.

   b. Now the page cache is known to include a descriptor for our page. The function checks its buffers field; if it is NULL, the page has not yet been filled with buffers and the function jumps to Step 3e.

   c. Checks whether the size of the buffers on the page is equal to the size of the requested block; if so, returns the address of the page descriptor (the page found in the page cache is a valid buffer page).

   d. Otherwise, checks whether the buffers found in the page can be released by invoking try_to_free_buffers().* If the function fails, presumably because some process is using the buffers, grow_dev_page() returns NULL (it was not able to allocate the buffer page for the requested block).

   e. Invokes the create_buffers() function to allocate the buffer heads for the blocks of the requested size within the page. The address of the buffer head for the first buffer in the page is stored in the buffers field of the page descriptor, and all buffer heads are inserted into the simply linked circular list implemented by the b_this_page fields of the buffer heads. Moreover, the b_page fields of the buffer heads are initialized with the address of the page descriptor.

   f. Returns the page descriptor address.

4. If grow_dev_page() returned NULL, returns 0 (failure).

5. Invokes the hash_page_buffers() function to initialize the fields of all buffer heads in the simply linked circular list of the buffer page and insert them into the buffer cache.

6. Unlocks the page (the page was locked by find_or_create_page())

7. Decrements the page's usage counter (again, the counter was incremented by find_or_create_page())

---

* This can happen when the page was previously involved in a page I/O operation using a different block size, and the corresponding asynchronous buffer heads are still allocated.

8. Increments the `buffermem_pages` variable, which stores the total number of buffer pages—that is, the memory currently cached by the buffer cache in page-size units.

9. Returns 1 (success).

The getblk( ) Function

The `getblk()` function is the main service routine for the buffer cache. When the kernel needs to read or write the contents of a block of a physical device, it must check whether the buffer head for the required buffer is already included in the buffer cache. If the buffer is not there, the kernel must create a new entry in the cache. To do this, the kernel invokes `getblk()`, specifying as parameters the device identifier, the block number, and the block size. This function returns the address of the buffer head associated with the buffer.

Remember that having a buffer head in the cache does not imply that the data in the buffer is valid. (For instance, the buffer has yet to be read from disk.) Any function that reads blocks must check whether the buffer obtained from `getblk()` is up to date; if not, it must read the block first from disk before using the buffer.

The `getblk()` function looks deceptively simple:

```
struct buffer_head * getblk(kdev_t dev, int block, int size)
{
    for (;;) {
        struct buffer_head * bh;
        bh = get_hash_table(dev, block, size);
        if (bh)
            return bh;
        if (!grow_buffers(dev, block, size))
            free_more_memory();
    }
}
```

The function first invokes `get_hash_table()` (see the earlier section "The hash table of cached buffer heads") to check whether the required buffer head is already in the cache. If so, `getblk()` returns the buffer head address.

Otherwise, if the required buffer head is not in the cache, `getblk()` invokes `grow_buffers()` to allocate a new buffer page that contains the buffer for the requested block. If `grow_buffers()` fails in allocating such a page, `getblk()` tries to reclaim some memory (see Chapter 16). These actions are repeated until `get_hash_table()` succeeds in finding the requested buffer in the buffer cache.

Writing Dirty Buffers to Disk

Unix systems allow the deferred writes of dirty buffers into block devices, since this noticeably improves system performance. Several write operations on a buffer could be satisfied by just one slow physical update of the corresponding disk block. Moreover, write operations are less critical than read operations, since a process is usually not suspended because of delayed writings, while it is most often suspended because of delayed reads. Thanks to deferred writes, each physical block device will service, on the average, many more read requests than write ones.

A dirty buffer might stay in main memory until the last possible moment—that is, until system shutdown. However, pushing the delayed-write strategy to its limits has two major drawbacks:

- If a hardware or power supply failure occurs, the contents of RAM can no longer be retrieved, so many file updates that were made since the system was booted are lost.
- The size of the buffer cache, and hence of the RAM required to contain it, would have to be huge—at least as big as the size of the accessed block devices.

Therefore, dirty buffers are *flushed* (written) to disk under the following conditions:

- The buffer cache gets too full and more buffers are needed, or the number of dirty buffers becomes too large; when one of these conditions occurs, the *bdflush* kernel thread is activated.
- Too much time has elapsed since a buffer has stayed dirty; the *kupdate* kernel thread regularly flushes old buffers.
- A process requests all the buffers of block devices or of particular files to be flushed; it does this by invoking the sync( ), fsync( ), or fdatasync( ) system call.

As explained in the earlier section "Buffer Pages," a buffer page is dirty (PG_DIRTY flag set) if some of its buffers are dirty. As soon as the kernel flushes all dirty buffers in a buffer page to disk, it resets the PG_DIRTY flag of the page.

The bdflush kernel thread

The *bdflush* kernel thread (also called *kflushd*) is created during system initialization. It executes the bdflush( ) function, which selects some dirty buffers and forces an update of the corresponding blocks on the physical block devices.

Some system parameters control the behavior of *bdflush*; they are stored in the b_un field of the bdf_prm table and are accessible either by means of the */proc/sys/vm/bdflush* file or by invoking the bdflush( ) system call. Each parameter has a default standard value, although it may vary within a minimum and a maximum value stored in the bdflush_min and bdflush_max tables, respectively. The parameters are listed in Table 14-4.*

---

* The bdf_prm table also includes several other unused fields.

Table 14-4. Buffer cache tuning parameters

Parameter	Default	Min	Max	Description
nfract	40	0	100	Threshold percentage of dirty buffers for waking up *bdflush*
nfract_sync	60	0	100	Threshold percentage of dirty buffers for waking up *bdflush* in blocking mode
age_buffer	3000	100	600,000	Time-out in ticks of a dirty buffer for being written to disk
interval	500	0	1,000,000	Delay in ticks between *kupdate* activations

The most typical cases that cause the kernel thread to be woken up are:

- The balance_dirty() function verifies that the number of buffer pages in the BUF_DIRTY and BUF_LOCKED lists exceeds the threshold:

$P \times$ bdf_prm.b_un.nfract_sync / 100

where P represents the number of pages in the system that can be used as buffer pages (essentially, this is all the pages in the "DMA" and "Normal" memory zones; see the section "Memory Zones" in Chapter 7). Actually, the computation is done by the balance_dirty_state() helper function, which returns −1 if the number of dirty or locked buffers is below the nfract threshold, 0 if it is between nfract and nfract_sync, and 1 if it is above nfract_sync. The balance_dirty() function is usually invoked whenever a buffer is marked as "dirty" and the function moves its buffer head into the BUF_DIRTY list.

- When the try_to_free_buffers() function fails to release the buffer heads of some buffer page (see the earlier section "Allocating buffer pages").

- When the grow_buffers() function fails to allocate a new buffer page, or the create_buffers() function fails to allocate a new buffer head (see the earlier section "Allocating buffer pages").

- When a user presses some specific combinations of keys on the console (usually ALT+SysRq+U and ALT+SysRq+S). These key combinations, which are enabled only if the Linux kernel has been compiled with the Magic SysRq Key option, allow Linux hackers to have some explicit control over kernel behavior.

To wake up *bdflush*, the kernel invokes the wakeup_bdflush() function, which simply executes:

```
wake_up_interruptible(&bdflush_wait);
```

to wake up the process suspended in the bdflush_wait task queue. There is just one process in this wait queue, namely *bdflush* itself.

The core of the bdflush() function is the following endless loop:

```
for (;;) {
    if (emergency_sync_scheduled) /* Only if the kernel has been compiled */
        do_emergency_sync();      /*   with Magic SysRq Key support       */
    spin_lock(&lru_list_lock);
    if (!write_some_buffers(0) || balance_dirty_state() < 0) {
```

```
          wait_for_some_buffers(0);
          interruptible_sleep_on(&bdflush_wait);
     }
 }
```

If the Linux kernel has been compiled with the Magic SysRq Key option, bdflush() checks whether the user has requested an emergency sync. If so, the function invokes do_emergency_sync() to execute fsync_dev() on all existing block devices, flushing all dirty buffers (see the later section "The sync(), fsync(), and fdatasync() system calls").

Next, the function acquires the lru_list_lock spin lock, and invokes the write_some_buffers() function, which tries to activate block I/O write operations for up to 32 unlocked dirty buffers. Once the write operations have been activated, write_some_buffers() releases the lru_list_lock spin lock and returns 0 if less than 32 unlocked dirty buffers have been found; it returns a negative value otherwise.

If write_some_buffers() didn't find 32 buffers to flush, or the number of dirty or locked buffers falls below the percentage threshold given by the *bdflush*'s parameter nfract, the *bdflush* kernel thread goes to sleep. To do this, it first invokes the wait_for_some_buffers() function so that it sleeps until all I/O data transfers of the buffers in the BUF_LOCKED list terminate. During this time interval, the kernel thread is not woken up even if the kernel executes the wakeup_bdflush() function. Once data transfers terminate, the bdflush() function invokes interruptible_sleep_on() on the bdflush_wait wait queue to sleep until the next wakeup_bdflush() invocation.

The kupdate kernel thread

Since the *bdflush* kernel thread is usually activated only when there are too many dirty buffers or when more buffers are needed and available memory is scarce, some dirty buffers might stay in RAM for an arbitrarily long time before being flushed to disk. The *kupdate* kernel thread is thus introduced to flush the older dirty buffers.[*]

As shown in Table 14-4, age_buffer is a time-out parameter that specifies the time for buffers to age before *kupdate* writes them to disk (usually 30 seconds), while the interval field of the bdf_prm table stores the delay in ticks between two activations of the *kupdate* kernel thread (usually five seconds). If this field is null, the kernel thread is normally stopped, and is activated only when it receives a SIGCONT signal.

When the kernel modifies the contents of some buffer, it sets the b_flushtime field of the corresponding buffer head to the time (in jiffies) when it should later be flushed to disk. The *kupdate* kernel thread selects only the dirty buffers whose b_flushtime field is smaller than the current value of jiffies.

---

[*] In an earlier version of Linux 2.2, the same task was achieved by means of the bdflush() system call, which was invoked every five seconds by a User Mode system process launched at system startup and which executed the */sbin/update* program. In more recent kernel versions, the bdflush() system call is used only to allow users to modify the system parameters in the bdf_prm table.

The *kupdate* kernel thread runs the kupdate( ) function; it keeps executing the following endless loop:

```
for (;;) {
    wait_for_some_buffers(0);
    if (bdf_prm.b_un.interval) {
        tsk->state = TASK_INTERRUPTIBLE;
        schedule_timeout(bdf_prm.b_un.interval);
    } else {
            tsk->state = TASK_STOPPED;
            schedule(); /* wait for SIGCONT */
    }
    sync_old_buffers();
}
```

First of all, the kernel thread suspends itself until the I/O data transfers have been completed for all buffers in the BUF_LOCKED list. Then, if bdf.prm.b_un.interval interval is not null, the thread goes to sleep for the specified amount of ticks (see the section "An Application of Dynamic Timers" in Chapter 6); otherwise, the thread stops itself until a SIGCONT signal is received (see the section "The Role of Signals" in Chapter 10).

The core of the kupdate( ) function consists of the sync_old_buffers( ) function. The operations to be performed are very simple for standard filesystems used with Unix; all the function has to do is write dirty buffers to disk. However, some nonnative filesystems introduce complexities because they store their superblock or inode information in complicated ways. sync_old_buffers( ) executes the following steps:

1. Acquires the big kernel lock.

2. Invokes sync_unlocked_inodes( ), which scans the superblocks of all currently mounted filesystems and, for each superblock, the list of dirty inodes to which the s_dirty field of the superblock object points. For each inode, the function flushes the dirty pages that belong to memory mappings of the corresponding file (see the section "Flushing Dirty Memory Mapping Pages to Disk" in Chapter 15), then invokes the write_inode superblock operation if it is defined. (The write_inode method is defined only by non-Unix filesystems that do not store all the inode data inside a single disk block—for instance, the MS-DOS filesystem).

3. Invokes sync_supers( ), which takes care of superblocks used by filesystems that do not store all the superblock data in a single disk block (an example is Apple Macintosh's HFS). The function accesses the superblocks list of all currently mounted filesystems (see the section "Filesystem Mounting" in Chapter 12). It then invokes, for each superblock, the corresponding write_super superblock operation, if one is defined (see the section "Superblock Objects" in Chapter 12). The write_super method is not defined for any Unix filesystem.

4. Releases the big kernel lock.

5. Starts a loop consisting of the following steps:

a. Gets the `lru_list_lock` spin lock.

b. Gets the `bh` pointer to the first buffer head in the `BUF_DIRTY` list.

c. If the pointer is null or if the `b_flushtime` buffer head field has a value greater than `jiffies` (young buffer), releases the `lru_list_lock` spin lock and terminates.

d. Invokes `write_some_buffers()`, which tries to activate block I/O write operations for up to 32 unlocked dirty buffers in the `BUF_DIRTY` list. Once the write activations have been performed, `write_some_buffers()` releases the `lru_list_lock` spin lock and returns 0 if less than 32 unlocked dirty buffers have been found; it returns a negative value otherwise.

e. If `write_some_buffers()` flushed to disk exactly 32 unlocked dirty buffers, jumps to Step 5a; otherwise, terminates the execution.

The sync( ), fsync( ), and fdatasync( ) system calls

Three different system calls are available to user applications to flush dirty buffers to disk:

sync( )
> Usually issued before a shutdown, since it flushes all dirty buffers to disk

fsync( )
> Allows a process to flush all blocks that belong to a specific open file to disk

fdatasync( )
> Very similar to fsync( ), but doesn't flush the inode block of the file

The core of the `sync()` system call is the `fsync_dev()` function, which performs the following actions:

1. Invokes `sync_buffers()`, which essentially executes the following code:

```
do {
    spin_lock(&lru_list_lock);
} while (write_some_buffers(0));
run_task_queue(&tq_disk);
```

As you see, the function keeps invoking the `write_some_buffers()` function until it succeeds in finding 32 unlocked, dirty buffers. Then, the block device drivers are unplugged to start real I/O data transfers (see the section "Scheduling the activation of the strategy routine" in Chapter 13).

2. Acquires the big kernel lock.

3. Invokes `sync_inodes()`, which is quite similar to the `sync_unlocked_inodes()` function discussed in the previous section.

4. Invokes `sync_supers()` to write the dirty superblocks to disk, if necessary, by using the `write_super` methods (see earlier in this section).

5. Releases the big kernel lock.

6. Invokes sync_buffers( ) once again. This time, it waits until all locked buffers have been transferred.

The fsync( ) system call forces the kernel to write to disk all dirty buffers that belong to the file specified by the fd file descriptor parameter (including the buffer containing its inode, if necessary). The system service routine derives the address of the file object and then invokes the fsync method. Usually, this method simply invokes the fsync_inode_buffers( ) function, which scans the two lists of dirty buffers of the inode object (see the earlier section "Lists of buffer heads for cached buffers"), and invokes ll_rw_block( ) on each element present in the lists. The function then suspends the calling process until all dirty buffers of the file have been written to disk by invoking wait_on_buffer( ) on each locked buffer. Moreover, the service routine of the fsync( ) system call flushes the dirty pages that belong to the memory mapping of the file, if any (see the section "Flushing Dirty Memory Mapping Pages to Disk" in Chapter 15).

The fdatasync( ) system call is very similar to fsync( ), but writes to disk only the buffers that contain the file's data, not those that contain inode information. Since Linux 2.4 does not have a specific file method for fdatasync( ), this system call uses the fsync method and is thus identical to fsync( ).

Accessing Files

Accessing a file is a complex activity that involves the VFS abstraction (Chapter 12), handling block devices (Chapter 13), and the use of disk caches (Chapter 14). This chapter shows how the kernel builds on all those facilities to carry out file reads and writes. The topics covered in this chapter apply both to regular files stored in disk-based filesystems and to block device files; these two kinds of files will be referred to simply as "files."

The stage we are working at in this chapter starts after the proper read or write method of a particular file has been called (as described in Chapter 12). We show here how each read ends with the desired data delivered to a User Mode process and how each write ends with data marked ready for transfer to disk. The rest of the transfer is handled by the facilities described in Chapter 13 and Chapter 14.

In particular, in the section "Reading and Writing a File," we describe how files are accessed by means of the read( ) and write( ) system calls. When a process reads from a file, data is first moved from the disk itself to a set of buffers in the kernel's address space. This set of buffers is included in a set of pages in the page cache (see the section "Page I/O operations" in Chapter 13). Next, the pages are copied into the process's user address space. A write is basically the opposite, although some stages are different from reads in important ways.

In the section "Memory Mapping," we discuss how the kernel allows a process to directly map a regular file into its address space, because that activity also has to deal with pages in kernel memory.

Finally, in the section "Direct I/O Transfers," we discuss the kernel support to self-caching applications.

Reading and Writing a File

The section "The read( ) and write( ) System Calls" in Chapter 12, described how the read( ) and write( ) system calls are implemented. The corresponding service routines end up invoking the file object's read and write methods, which may be filesystem-dependent. For disk-based filesystems, these methods locate the physical blocks that contain the data being accessed, and activate the block device driver to start the data transfer.

Reading a file is page-based: the kernel always transfers whole pages of data at once. If a process issues a read( ) system call to get a few bytes, and that data is not already in RAM, the kernel allocates a new page frame, fills the page with the suitable portion of the file, adds the page to the page cache, and finally copies the requested bytes into the process address space. For most filesystems, reading a page of data from a file is just a matter of finding what blocks on disk contain the requested data. Once this is done, the kernel can use one or more page I/O operations to fill the pages. The read method of most filesystems is implemented by a common function named generic_file_read( ).

Write operations on disk-based files are slightly more complicated to handle, since the file size could change, and therefore the kernel might allocate or release some physical blocks on the disk. Of course, how this is precisely done depends on the filesystem type. However, many disk-based filesystems implement their write methods by means of a common function named generic_file_write( ). Examples of such filesystems are Ext2, System V/Coherent/Xenix, and Minix. On the other hand, several other filesystems, such as journaling and network filesystems, implement the write method by means of custom functions.

Reading from a File

The read method of the regular files that belong to almost all disk-based filesystems, as well as the read method of any block device file, is implemented by the generic_file_read( ) function. It acts on the following parameters:

filp
> Address of the file object

buf
> Linear address of the User Mode memory area where the characters read from the file must be stored

count
> Number of characters to be read

ppos
> Pointer to a variable that stores the offset from which reading must start (usually the f_pos field of the filp file object)

As a first step, the function checks whether the O_DIRECT flag of the file object is set. If so, the read access should bypass the page cache; we discuss this special case in the later section "Direct I/O Transfers."

Let's assume that the O_DIRECT flag is not set. The function invokes access_ok() to verify that the buf and count parameters received from the system call service routine sys_read() are correct, and returns the -EFAULT error code if they aren't (see the section "Verifying the Parameters" in Chapter 9).

If everything is ok, generic_file_read() allocates a *read operation descriptor*— namely, a data structure of type read_descriptor_t that stores the current status of the ongoing file read operation. The fields of this descriptor are shown in Table 15-1.

Table 15-1. The fields of the read operation descriptor

Type	Field	Description
size_t	written	How many bytes have been transferred
size_t	count	How many bytes are yet to be transferred
char *	buf	Current position in User Mode buffer
int	error	Error code of the read operation (0 for no error)

Then the function invokes do_generic_file_read(), passing to it the file object pointer filp, the pointer to the file offset ppos, the address of the just allocated read operation descriptor desc, and the address of the file_read_actor() function (see later). The do_generic_file_read() function performs the following actions:[*]

1. Gets the address_space object corresponding to the file being read; its address is stored in filp->f_dentry->d_inode->i_mapping.

2. Gets the inode object that owns the address space; its address is stored in the host field of the address_space object. Notice that this object could be different from the inode pointed to by filp->f_dentry->d_inode (see "Keeping Track of Block Device Drivers" in Chapter 13).

3. Considers the file as subdivided in pages of data (4,096 bytes per page) and derives, from the file pointer *ppos, the logical number index of the page including the first requested byte. Also stores in offset the displacement inside the page of the first requested byte.

4. Checks whether the file pointer is inside the read-ahead window of the file. We defer discussing read-ahead until the later section "Read-Ahead of Files."

5. Starts a cycle to read all pages that include the requested desc->count bytes. During a single iteration, the function transfers a page of data by performing the following substeps:

   a. If index*4096+offset exceeds the file size stored in the i_size field of the inode object, it exits from the cycle and goes to Step 6.

   b. Looks up the page cache to find the page that stores the requested data. Remember that the page cache is essentially a hash table indexed by the address of the address_space object and the displacement of the page inside the file (index).

---

[*] As usual, for the sake of simplicity, we do not discuss how errors and anomalous conditions are handled.

c. If the page is not found inside the page cache, allocates a new page frame and inserts it into the page cache by invoking add_to_page_cache( ) (see the section "Page Cache Handling Functions" in Chapter 14). Remember that the PG_uptodate flag of the page is cleared, while the PG_locked flag is set. The function jumps to Step 5h.

d. Here the page has been found in the page cache. The function increments the usage counter of the page descriptor.

e. Checks the PG_uptodate flag of the page; if it is set, the data stored in the page is up-to-date. The function jumps to Step 5j.

f. Invokes generic_file_readahead( ) to consider activating further read-ahead operations on the file. As we'll see in the later section "Read-Ahead of Files," this function could trigger I/O data transfers for some other blocks in the page. However, we may safely ignore the issue right now.

g. The data on the page is not valid, so it must be read from disk. The function gains exclusive access to the page by setting the PG_locked flag. Of course, the page might be already locked if a previously started I/O data transfer is not yet terminated; in this case, it sleeps until the page is unlocked, and then checks the PG_uptodate flag again in case another data transfer has performed the necessary read. If the flag is now set to 1, the function jumps to Step 5j. Otherwise, the function continues to perform the read.

h. Invokes the readpage method of the address_space object of the file. The corresponding function takes care of activating the I/O data transfer from the disk to the page. We discuss later what this function does for regular files and block device files.

i. Checks the PG_uptodate flag of the page. If the I/O data transfer is not already completed, the flag is still cleared, so the function invokes again the generic_file_readahead( ) function and waits until the I/O data transfer completes.

j. The page contains up-to-date data. The function invokes generic_file_readahead( ) to consider activating further read-ahead operations on the file. As we'll see in the later section "Read-Ahead of Files," this function could trigger I/O data transfers for some other blocks in the page.

k. Invokes mark_page_accessed( ) to set the PG_referenced flag, which denotes that the page is actively used and should not be swapped out (see Chapter 16). This is done only if the page has been explicitly requested by the user (the kernel is not performing read-ahead).

l. Now it is time to copy the data on the page in the User Mode buffer. To do this, do_generic_file_read( ) invokes the file_read_actor( ) function, whose address has been passed as a parameter of the function. In turn, file_read_actor( ) takes one of the steps shown in the following list.

1. Invokes kmap( ), which establishes a permanent kernel mapping for the page if it is in high memory (see the section "Kernel Mappings of High-Memory Page Frames" in Chapter 7).

2. Invokes __copy_to_user( ), which copies the data on the page in the User Mode address space (see the section "Accessing the Process Address Space" in Chapter 9). Notice that this operation might block the process.

3. Invokes kunmap( ) to release any permanent kernel mapping of the page.

4. Updates the count, written, and buf fields of the read_descriptor_t descriptor.

m. Updates the index and offset local variables according to the number of bytes effectively transferred in the User Mode buffer.

n. Decrements the page descriptor usage counter.

o. If the count field of the read_descriptor_t descriptor is not null and all requested bytes in the page have been successfully transferred into the User Mode address space, continues the loop, with the next page of data in the file jumping to Step 5a.

6. Assigns to *ppos the value index*4096+offset, thus storing the next position where a read is to occur for a future invocation of this function.

7. Sets the f_reada field of the file descriptor to 1 to record the fact that data is being read sequentially from the file (see the later section "Read-Ahead of Files").

8. Invokes update_atime( ) to store the current time in the i_atime field of the file's inode and to mark the inode as dirty.

The readpage method for regular files

As we saw in the previous section, the readpage method is used repeatedly by do_generic_file_read( ) to read individual pages from disk into memory.

The readpage method of the address_space object stores the address of the function that effectively activates the I/O data transfer from the physical disk to the page cache. For regular files, this field typically points to a wrapper that invokes the block_read_full_page( ) function. For instance, the readpage method of the Ext2 filesystem is implemented by the following function:

```
int ext2_readpage(struct file *file, struct page *page)
{
    return block_read_full_page(page, ext2_get_block);
}
```

The wrapper is needed because the block_read_full_page( ) function receives as parameters the descriptor page of the page to be filled and the address get_block of a function that helps block_read_full_page( ) find the right block. This function translates the block numbers relative to the beginning of the file into logical block numbers relative to positions of the block in the disk partition (for an example, see Chapter 17). Of course, the latter parameter depends on the type of filesystem to which the regular file belongs; in the previous example, the parameter is the address of the ext2_get_block( ) function.

The block_read_full_page( ) function starts a page I/O operation on the buffers included in the page. It allocates any necessary buffer heads, finds the buffers on disk using the get_block method described earlier, and transfers the data. Specifically, it performs the following steps:

1. Checks the page->buffers field; if it is NULL, invokes create_empty_buffers( ) to allocate asynchronous buffer heads for all buffers included in the page (see the section "Page I/O operations" in Chapter 13). The address of the buffer head for the first buffer in the page is stored in the page->buffers field. The b_this_page field of each buffer head points to the buffer head of the next buffer in the page.

2. Derives from the file offset relative to the page (page->index field) the file block number of the first block in the page.

3. For each buffer head of the buffers in the page, performs the following substeps:

   a. If the BH_Uptodate flag is set, skips the buffer and continues with the next buffer in the page.

   b. If the BH_Mapped flag is not set, invokes the filesystem-dependent function whose address has been passed as a parameter called get_block. The function looks in the on-disk data structures of the filesystem and finds the logical block number of the buffer (relative to the beginning of the disk partition rather than the beginning of the regular file). The filesystem-dependent function stores this number in the b_blocknr field of the corresponding buffer head, and sets its BH_Mapped flag. In rare cases, the filesystem-dependent function might not find the block, even if the block belongs to the regular file, because the application might have left a hole in that location (see the section "File Holes" in Chapter 17). In this case, block_read_full_page( ) fills the buffer with 0's, sets the BH_Uptodate flag of the corresponding buffer head, and continues with the next buffer in the page.

   c. Tests again the BH_Uptodate flag because the filesystem-dependent function could have triggered a block I/O operation that updated the buffer. If BH_Uptodate is set, continues with the next buffer in the page.

   d. Stores the address of the buffer head in the arr local array, and continues with the next buffer in the page.

4. Now the arr local array stores the addresses of the buffer heads that correspond to the buffers whose content is not up-to-date. If the array is empty, all buffers in the page are valid. So the function sets the PG_uptodate flag of the page descriptor, unlocks the page, and terminates.

5. The `arr` local array is not empty. For each buffer head in the array, `block_read_full_page()` performs the following substeps:

   a. Sets the `BH_Lock` flag. If the flag was already set, the function waits until the buffer is released.

   b. Sets the `b_end_io` field of the buffer head to the address of the `end_buffer_io_async()` function (see the section "Page I/O operations" in Chapter 13).

   c. Sets the `BH_Async` flag of the buffer head.

6. For each buffer head in the `arr` local array, invokes the `submit_bh()` function on it, specifying the operation type `READ`. As we saw in the section "The ll_rw_block() Function" in Chapter 13, this function triggers the I/O data transfer of the corresponding block.

The readpage method for block device files

In the sections "VFS Handling of Device Files" and "Block Device Drivers" in Chapter 13, we discussed how the kernel handles requests to open a block device file. We saw how the kernel allocates a descriptor of type `block_device` for any newly opened device driver and inserts it into a hash table. The `bd_inode` field of the descriptor points to a block device inode that belongs to the *bdev* special filesystem (see the section "Keeping Track of Block Device Drivers" in Chapter 13). Each I/O operation on the block device refers to this inode, rather than to the inode of the block device file that was specified in the `open()` system call. (Remember that different device files might refer to the same block device.)

Block devices use an `address_space` object that is stored in the `i_data` field of the corresponding block device inode. Unlike regular files—whose readpage method in the `address_space` object depends on the filesystem type to which the file belongs—the readpage method of block device files is always the same. It is implemented by the `blkdev_readpage()` function, which calls `block_read_full_page()`:

```
int blkdev_readpage(struct file * file, struct * page page)
{
    return block_read_full_page(page, blkdev_get_block);
}
```

As you see, the function is once again a wrapper for the `block_read_full_page()` function described in the previous section. This time the second parameter points to a function that must translate the file block number relative to the beginning of the file into a logical block number relative to the beginning of the block device. For block device files, however, the two numbers coincide; therefore, the `blkdev_get_block()` function performs the following steps:

1. Checks whether the number of the first block in the page exceeds the size of the block device (stored in `blk_size[MAJOR(inode->i_rdev)][MINOR(inode->i_rdev)]`, see the section "Initializing a Block Device Driver" in Chapter 13). If so, returns the error code `-EIO`.

2. Sets the `b_dev` field of the buffer head to `inode->r_dev`.

3. Sets the b_blocknr field of the buffer head to the file block number of the first block in the page.

4. Sets the BH_Mapped flag of the buffer head to state that the b_dev and b_blocknr fields of the buffer head are significant.

Read-Ahead of Files

Many disk accesses are sequential. As we shall see in Chapter 17, regular files are stored on disk in large groups of adjacent sectors, so that they can be retrieved quickly with few moves of the disk heads. When a program reads or copies a file, it often accesses it sequentially, from the first byte to the last one. Therefore, many adjacent sectors on disk are likely to be fetched in several I/O operations.

Read-ahead is a technique that consists of reading several adjacent pages of data of a regular file or block device file, before they are actually requested. In most cases, read-ahead significantly enhances disk performance, since it lets the disk controller handle fewer commands, each of which refers to a larger chunk of adjacent sectors. Moreover, it improves system responsiveness. A process that is sequentially reading a file does not usually wait for the requested data because it is already available in RAM.

However, read-ahead is of no use to random accesses to files; in this case, it is actually detrimental since it tends to waste space in the page cache with useless information. Therefore, the kernel stops read-ahead when it determines that the most recently issued I/O access is not sequential to the previous one.

Read-ahead of files requires a sophisticated algorithm for several reasons:

- Since data is read page by page, the read-ahead algorithm does not have to consider the offsets inside the page, but only the positions of the accessed pages inside the file. A series of accesses to pages of the same file is considered sequential if the related pages are close to each other. We'll define the word "close" more precisely in a moment.

- Read-ahead must be restarted from scratch when the current access is not sequential with respect to the previous one (random access).

- Read-ahead should be slowed down or even stopped when a process keeps accessing the same pages over and over again (only a small portion of the file is being used).

- If necessary, the read-ahead algorithm must activate the low-level I/O device driver to make sure that the new pages will ultimately be read.

The read-ahead algorithm identifies a set of pages that correspond to a contiguous portion of the file as the *read-ahead window*. If the next read operation issued by a process falls inside this set of pages, the kernel considers the file access "sequential" to the previous one. The read-ahead window consists of pages requested by the process or read in advance by the kernel and included in the page cache. The read-ahead window always includes the pages requested in the last read-ahead operation; they arc called the *read-ahead group*. If the next operation issued by a process falls inside the read-ahead group, the kernel might read in advance some of the pages following the read-ahead window just to ensure that the kernel will be "ahead" of the reading process. Not all the pages in the read-ahead window or group are necessarily up to date. They are invalid (i.e., their PG_uptodate flags are cleared) if their transfer from disk is not yet completed.

The file object includes the following fields related to read-ahead:

f_raend
   Position of the first byte after the read-ahead group and the read-ahead window

f_rawin
   Length in bytes of the current read-ahead window

f_ralen
   Length in bytes of the current read-ahead group

f_ramax
   Maximum number of characters to get in the next read-ahead operation

f_reada
   Flag specifying whether the file pointer has been set explicitly by a lseek() system call (if value is 0) or implicitly by a previous read() system call (if value is 1)

When a file is opened, all these fields are set to 0. Figure 15-1 illustrates how some of the fields arc used to delimit the read-ahead window and the read-ahead group.

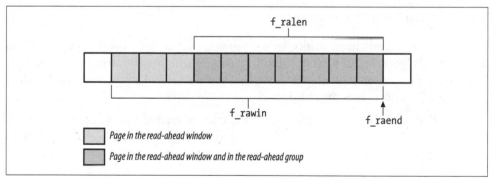

Figure 15-1. Read-ahead window and read-ahead group

The kernel distinguishes two kinds of read-ahead operations:

Synchronous read-ahead operation
   Performed whenever a read access falls outside the current read-ahead window of a file. The synchronous read-ahead operation usually affects all pages requested by the user in the read operation plus one. After the operation, the read-ahead window coincides with the read-ahead group (see Figure 15-2).

Asynchronous read-ahead operation

Performed whenever a read access falls inside the current read-ahead group of a file. The asynchronous read-ahead operation usually tries to shift forward and to enlarge the read-ahead window of the file by reading from disk twice as many pages as the length of the previous read-ahead group. The new read-ahead window spans the old read-ahead group and the new one (see Figure 15-2).

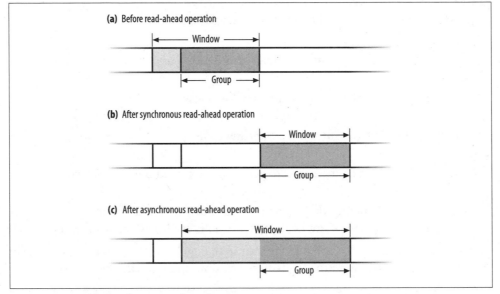

Figure 15-2. Read-ahead group and window

To explain how read-ahead works, let's suppose a user issues a read( ) system call on a file. The do_generic_file_read( ) function checks whether the first page to be read falls inside the current read-ahead window of the file (Step 4 in the section "Reading from a File"). Three cases are considered:

- The first page to be read falls outside the current read-ahead window. The function sets the f_raend, f_ralen, f_ramax, and f_rawin fields of the file object to 0. Moreover, it disables asynchronous read-ahead operations by setting the reada_ ok local variable to 0.

- The first page to be read falls inside the current read-ahead window. This means that the user is accessing the file sequentially. The function enables asynchronous read-ahead operations by setting the reada_ok local variable to 1.

- The current read-ahead window and groups are empty because the file was never accessed before; moreover, the first page to be read is the initial page of the file. In this special case, the function enables asynchronous read-ahead operations by setting the reada_ok local variable to 1.

The do_generic_file_read() function also adjusts the value stored in the f_ramax field of the file object, which represents the number of pages to be requested in the next read-ahead operation. Although its value is determined by the previous read-ahead operation on the file (if any), do_generic_file_read() ensures that f_ramax is always greater than the number of pages requested in the read() system call plus 1. Moreover, the function ensures that f_ramax is always greater than the value stored in the vm_min_readahead global variable (usually three pages) and smaller than a per-device upper bound. Each block device may define this upper bound by storing a value into the max_readahead array, which is indexed by the major and minor number of the device. If the driver does not specify an upper bound, the kernel uses the upper bound stored in the vm_max_readahead global variable (usually 31 pages). System administrators may tune the values in vm_min_readahead and vm_max_readahead by writing into the */proc/sys/vm/min-readahead* and */proc/sys/vm/max-readahead* files, respectively.*

We saw in the earlier section "Reading from a File" that the do_generic_file_read() function invokes the generic_file_readahead() function several times, at least once for each page involved in the read request. The function receives as parameters the file and inode objects, the descriptor of the page currently considered by do_generic_file_read(), and the value of the reada_ok flag, which enables or disables asynchronous read-ahead operations.

To read ahead a page, the generic_file_readahead() function invokes page_cache_read(), which looks up (and optionally inserts) the page in the page cache and then invokes the readpage method of the corresponding address_space object to request the I/O data transfer.

The overall scheme of generic_file_readahead() is shown in Figure 15-3. Basically, the function distinguishes two cases: synchronous and asynchronous. It checks the page descriptor passed as its parameter. If the PG_locked flag in this descriptor is set, the page is most likely still involved in the I/O data transfer triggered by the do_generic_file_read() function and any read-ahead must be synchronous. Otherwise, asynchronous read-ahead is possible. We examine the actions based on the PG_locked flag in the following sections.

The accessed page is locked (synchronous read-ahead)

In this case, generic_file_readahead() may take three different courses of action:

- When the read access is not sequential with respect to the previous one (that is, either the read-ahead group is empty, or the accessed page is outside the read-ahead window) and f_ramax is not null, the function performs a synchronous read-ahead operation as follows:

---

* A special heuristic applies for read() system calls that affect only the first half of the initial page of the file. In this case, the do_generic_file_read() function sets the f_ramax field to 0. The idea is that if a user reads only a small number of characters at the beginning of the file, then she is not really interested in sequentially accessing the whole file, so read-ahead operations are useless.

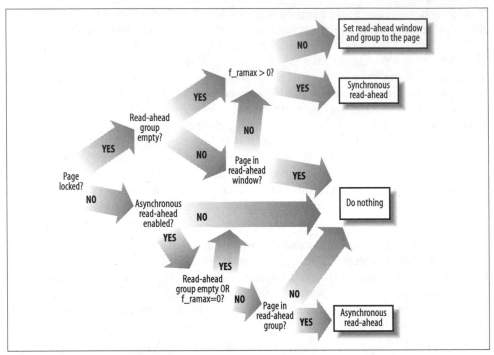

Figure 15-3. Overall scheme of the generic_file_readahead() function

— Reads f_ramax pages starting from the page following the accessed one.

— Sets the new read-ahead window and the new read-ahead group to contain the f_ramax pages just read and the page referenced by the do_generic_file_read( ) function.

— Doubles the value stored in f_ramax (but allows it to become no larger than the upper bound defined by the block device).

• When a synchronous read-ahead operation is likely to be performed, but the f_ramax field is set to 0, the generic_file_readahead( ) function resets the read-ahead window and the read-ahead group as follows:

— The read-ahead window includes just the accessed page, so its size is set to 1.

— The read-ahead group is set to be the same as the read-ahead window.

Remember that do_generic_file_read( ) sets f_ramax to 0 when the user requests the first few characters of a file.

• If the accessed page falls inside the non-null read-ahead window, the function does nothing. Since the page is locked, the corresponding I/O data transfers are still to be finished, so it is pointless to start an additional read operation.

The accessed page is unlocked (asynchronous read-ahead)

If the page accessed by the caller do_generic_file_read( ) function is unlocked, the corresponding I/O data transfers have most likely finished. In this case, generic_file_readahead( ) may take two different courses of action:

- When several conditions are satisfied, the function performs an asynchronous read-ahead operation. These conditions are as follows: asynchronous read-ahead operations are enabled, the read-head group is not empty and the accessed page falls into it, and the f_ramax field is not null. The function does the following:

  — Reads f_ramax+1 pages starting from f_raend

  — Sets the new read-ahead window to include the previous read-ahead group and the f_ramax+1 pages just read

  — Sets the new read-ahead group to include the f_ramax+1 pages just read

  — Doubles the value stored in f_ramax (but allows it to become no larger than the upper bound defined by the block device)

- The function does nothing whenever the function cannot start an asynchronous read-ahead operation—for instance, when the read operation is not sequential with respect to the previous one (the asynchronous read-ahead is disabled by do_generic_file_read( )), or when the access is sequential but the accessed page falls inside the read-ahead window and outside the read-ahead group (i.e., the process is lagging with respect to read-ahead).

Writing to a File

Recall that the write( ) system call involves moving data from the User Mode address space of the calling process into the kernel data structures, and then to disk. The write method of the file object permits each filesystem type to define a specialized write operation. In Linux 2.4, the write method of each disk-based filesystem is a procedure that basically identifies the disk blocks involved in the write operation, copies the data from the User Mode address space into some pages belonging to the page cache, and marks the buffers in those pages as dirty.

Several filesystems (such as Ext2) implement the write method of the file object by means of the generic_file_write( ) function, which acts on the following parameters:

file
> File object pointer

buf
> Address where the characters to be written into the file must be fetched

count
> Number of characters to be written

ppos
> Address of a variable storing the file offset from which writing must start

The function performs the following operations:

1. Verifies that the parameters count and buf are valid (they must refer to the User Mode address space); if not, returns the error code -EFAULT.

2. Determines the address inode of the inode object that corresponds to the file to be written (file->f_dentry->d_inode->i_mapping->host).

3. Acquires the semaphore inode->i_sem. Thanks to this semaphore, only one process at a time can issue a write( ) system call on the file.

4. If the O_APPEND flag of file->flags is on and the file is regular (not a block device file), sets *ppos to the end of the file so that all new data is appended to it.

5. Performs several checks on the size of the file. For instance, the write operation must not enlarge a regular file so much as to exceed the per-user limit stored in current->rlim[RLIMIT_FSIZE] (see the section "Process Resource Limits" in Chapter 3) and the filesystem limit stored in inode->i_sb->s_maxbytes.

6. Stores the current time of day in the inode->mtime field (the time of last file write operation) and in the inode->mtime field (the time of last inode change), and marks the inode object as dirty.

7. Checks the value of the O_DIRECT flag of the file object. If it is set, the write operation bypasses the page cache. We discuss this case later in this chapter. In the rest of this section, we assume that O_DIRECT is not set.

8. Starts a cycle to update all the pages of the file involved in the write operation. During each iteration, performs the following substeps:

   a. Tries to find the page in the page cache. If it isn't there, allocates a free page and adds it to the page cache.

   b. Locks the page—that is, sets its PG_locked flag.

   c. Increments the page usage counter as a fail-safe mechanism.

   d. Invokes kmap( ) to get the starting linear address of the page (see the section "Kernel Mappings of High-Memory Page Frames" in Chapter 7).

   e. Invokes the prepare_write method of the address_space object of the inode (file->f_dentry->d_inode->i_mapping). The corresponding function takes care of allocating asynchronous buffer heads for the page and of reading some buffers from disk, if necessary. We'll discuss in subsequent sections what this function does for regular files and block device files.

   f. Invokes __copy_from_user( ) to copy the characters from the buffer in User Mode to the page.

   g. Invokes the commit_write method of the address_space object of the inode (file->f_dentry->d_inode->i_mapping). The corresponding function marks the underlying buffers as dirty so they are written to disk later. We discuss what this function does for regular files and block device files in the next two sections.

h. Invokes `kunmap()` to release any permanent high-memory mapping established in Step 8d.

i. Sets the `PG_referenced` flag of the page; it is used by the memory reclaiming algorithm described in Chapter 16.

j. Clears the `PG_locked` flag, and wakes up any process that is waiting for the page to unlock.

k. Decrements the page usage counter to undo the increment in Step 8c.

9. Now all pages of the file involved in the write operation have been handled. Updates the value of *ppos to point right after the last character written.

10. Checks whether the O_SYNC flag of the file is set. If so, invokes generic_osync_inode() to force the kernel to flush all dirty buffers of the page to disk, blocking the current process until the I/O data transfers terminate. In Version 2.4.18 of Linux, this function over-ices the cake because it flushes to disk all dirty buffers of the file, not just those belonging to the file portion just written.

11. Releases the `inode->i_sem` semaphore.

12. Returns the number of characters written into the file.

The prepare_write and commit_write methods for regular files

The prepare_write and commit_write methods of the address_space object specialize the generic write operation implemented by generic_file_write() for regular files and block device files. Both of them are invoked once for every page of the file that is affected by the write operation.

Each disk-based filesystem defines its own prepare_write method. As with read operations, this method is simply a wrapper for a common function. For instance, the Ext2 filesystem implements the prepare_write method by means of the following function:

```
int ext2_prepare_write(struct file *file, struct page *page, unsigned from, unsigned to)
{
    return block_prepare_write(page,from,to,ext2_get_block);
}
```

The ext2_get_block() function was already mentioned in the earlier section "Reading from a File"; it translates the block number relative to the file into a logical block number, which represents the position of the data on the physical block device.

The block_prepare_write() function takes care of preparing the buffers and the buffer heads of the file's page by performing the following steps:

1. Checks the page->buffers field; if it is NULL, the function invokes create_empty_buffers() to allocate buffer heads for all buffers included in the page (see the section "Page I/O operations" in Chapter 13). The address of the buffer head for the first buffer in the page is stored in the page->buffers field. The b_this_page field of each buffer head points to the buffer head of the next buffer in the page.

2. For each buffer head relative to a buffer included in the page and affected by the write operation, the following is performed:

   a. If the BH_Mapped flag is not set, the function performs the following substeps:

      1. Invokes the filesystem-dependent function whose address was passed as a parameter. The function looks in the on-disk data structures of the filesystem and finds the logical block number of the buffer (relative to the beginning of the disk partition rather than the beginning of the regular file). The filesystem-dependent function stores this number in the b_blocknr field of the corresponding buffer head and sets its BH_Mapped flag. The filesystem-specific function could allocate a new physical block for the file (for instance, if the accessed block falls inside a "hole" of the regular file, see section "File Holes" in Chapter 17). In this case, it sets the BH_New flag.

      2. Checks the value of the BH_New flag; if it is set, invokes unmap_underlying_metadata() to make sure that the buffer cache does not include a dirty buffer referencing the same block on disk.* Moreover, if the write operation does not rewrite the whole buffer, the function fills it with 0's. Then considers the next buffer in the page.

   b. If the write operation does not rewrite the whole buffer and its BH_Uptodate flag is not set, the function invokes ll_rw_block() on the block to read its content from disk (see the section "The ll_rw_block() Function" in Chapter 13).

3. Blocks the current process until all read operations triggered in Step 2b have been completed.

Once the prepare_write method returns, the generic_file_write() function updates the page with the data stored in the User Mode address space. Next, it invokes the commit_write method of the address_space object. This method is implemented by the generic_commit_write() function for almost all disk-based filesystems.

The generic_commit_write() function performs the following steps:

1. Invokes the block_commit_write() function. In turn, this function considers all buffers in the page that are affected by the write operation; for each of them, it sets the BH_Uptodate and BH_Dirty flags and inserts the buffer head in the BUF_DIRTY list and in the list of dirty buffers of the inode (if it is not already in the list). The function also invokes the balance_dirty() function to keep the number of dirty buffers in the system bounded (see the section "Writing Dirty Buffers to Disk" in Chapter 14).

---

* Although unlikely, this case might happen if another block in the same buffer page was previously accessed by means of a block I/O operation (which caused our buffer head to be inserted in the buffer cache; see the section "Buffer Pages" in Chapter 14), and if in addition a user wrote into our block by accessing the corresponding block device file, thus making it dirty.

2. Checks whether the write operation enlarged the file. In this case, the function
   updates the i_size field of the file's inode and marks the inode object as dirty.

The prepare_write and commit_write methods for block device files

Write operations into block device files are very similar to the corresponding operations on regular files. In fact, the prepare_write method of the address_space object
of block device files is usually implemented by the following function:

```
int blkdev_prepare_write(struct file *file, struct page *page,
                         unsigned from, unsigned to)
{
    return block_prepare_write(page, from, to, blkdev_get_block);
}
```

As you see, the function is simply a wrapper to the block_prepare_write() function
already discussed in the previous section. The only difference, of course, is in the second parameter, which points to the function that must translate the file block number relative to the beginning of the file to a logical block number relative to the
beginning of the block device. Remember that for block device files, the two numbers coincide. (See the earlier section "The readpage method for block device files"
for a discussion of the blkdev_get_block() function.)

The commit_write method for block device files is implemented by the following simple wrapper function:

```
int blkdev_commit_write(struct file *file, struct page *page, unsigned from, unsigned
to)
{
    return block_commit_write(page, from, to);
}
```

As you see, the commit_write method for block device files does essentially the same
things as the commit_write method for regular files (we described the block_commit_
write() function in the previous section). The only difference is that the method
does not check whether the write operation has enlarged the file; you simply cannot
enlarge a block device file by appending characters to its last position.

Memory Mapping

As already mentioned in the section "Memory Regions" in Chapter 8, a memory
region can be associated with some portion of either a regular file in a disk-based filesystem or a block device file. This means that an access to a byte within a page of the
memory region is translated by the kernel into an operation on the corresponding
byte of the file. This technique is called *memory mapping*.

Two kinds of memory mapping exist:

Shared

> Any write operation on the pages of the memory region changes the file on disk; moreover, if a process writes into a page of a shared memory mapping, the changes are visible to all other processes that map the same file.

Private

> Meant to be used when the process creates the mapping just to read the file, not to write it. For this purpose, private mapping is more efficient than shared mapping. But any write operation on a privately mapped page will cause it to stop mapping the page in the file. Thus, a write does not change the file on disk, nor is the change visible to any other processes that access the same file.

A process can create a new memory mapping by issuing an mmap( ) system call (see the section "Creating a Memory Mapping" later in this chapter). Programmers must specify either the MAP_SHARED flag or the MAP_PRIVATE flag as a parameter of the system call; as you can easily guess, in the former case the mapping is shared, while in the latter it is private. Once the mapping is created, the process can read the data stored in the file by simply reading from the memory locations of the new memory region. If the memory mapping is shared, the process can also modify the corresponding file by simply writing into the same memory locations. To destroy or shrink a memory mapping, the process may use the munmap( ) system call (see the later section "Destroying a Memory Mapping").

As a general rule, if a memory mapping is shared, the corresponding memory region has the VM_SHARED flag set; if it is private, the VM_SHARED flag is cleared. As we'll see later, an exception to this rule exists for read-only shared memory mappings.

Memory Mapping Data Structures

A memory mapping is represented by a combination of the following data structures:

- The inode object associated with the mapped file
- The address_space object of the mapped file
- A file object for each different mapping performed on the file by different processes
- A vm_area_struct descriptor for each different mapping on the file
- A page descriptor for each page frame assigned to a memory region that maps the file

Figure 15-4 illustrates how the data structures are linked. In the upper-left corner, we show the inode, which identifies the file. The i_mapping field of each inode object points to the address_space object of the file. In turn, the i_mmap or i_mmap_shared fields of each address_space object point to the first element of a doubly linked list that includes all memory regions that currently map the file; if both fields are NULL, the file is not mapped by any memory region. The list contains vm_area_struct descriptors that represent memory regions, and is implemented by means of the vm_next_share and vm_pprev_share fields.

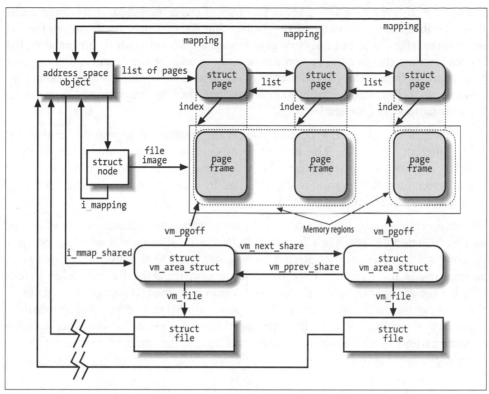

Figure 15-4. Data structures for file memory mapping

The vm_file field of each memory region descriptor contains the address of a file object for the mapped file; if that field is null, the memory region is not used in a memory mapping. The file object contains fields that allow the kernel to identify both the process that owns the memory mapping and the file being mapped.

The position of the first mapped location is stored into the vm_pgoff field of the memory region descriptor; it represents the file offset as a number of page-size units. The length of the mapped file portion is simply the length of the memory region, which can be computed from the vm_start and vm_end fields.

Pages of shared memory mappings are always included in the page cache; pages of private memory mappings are included in the page cache as long as they are unmodified. When a process tries to modify a page of a private memory mapping, the kernel duplicates the page frame and replaces the original page frame with the duplicate in the process Page Table; this is one of the applications of the Copy On Write mechanism that we discussed in Chapter 8. The original page frame still remains in the page cache, although it no longer belongs to the memory mapping since it is replaced by the duplicate. In turn, the duplicate is not inserted into the page cache since it no longer contains valid data representing the file on disk.

Figure 15-4 also shows a few page descriptors of pages included in the page cache that refer to the memory-mapped file. Notice that the first memory region in the figure is three pages long, but only two page frames are allocated for it; presumably, the process owning the memory region has never accessed the third page. Although not shown in the figure, the page descriptors are inserted into the clean_pages, dirty_pages, and locked_pages doubly linked lists described in the section "Page Cache Data Structures" in Chapter 14.

The kernel offers several hooks to customize the memory mapping mechanism for every different filesystem. The core of memory mapping implementation is delegated to a file object's method named mmap. For most disk-based filesystems and for block device files, this method is implemented by a general function called generic_file_mmap( ), which is described in the next section.

File memory mapping depends on the demand paging mechanism described in the section "Demand Paging" in Chapter 8. In fact, a newly established memory mapping is a memory region that doesn't include any page; as the process references an address inside the region, a Page Fault occurs and the Page Fault handler checks whether the nopage method of the memory region is defined. If nopage is not defined, the memory region doesn't map a file on disk; otherwise, it does, and the method takes care of reading the page by accessing the block device. Almost all disk-based filesystems and block device files implement the nopage method by means of the filemap_nopage( ) function.

Creating a Memory Mapping

To create a new memory mapping, a process issues an mmap( ) system call, passing the following parameters to it:

- A file descriptor identifying the file to be mapped.
- An offset inside the file specifying the first character of the file portion to be mapped.
- The length of the file portion to be mapped.
- A set of flags. The process must explicitly set either the MAP_SHARED flag or the MAP_PRIVATE flag to specify the kind of memory mapping requested.[*]

---

[*] The process could also set the MAP_ANONYMOUS flag to specify that the new memory region is anonymous— that is, not associated with any disk-based file (see the section "Demand Paging" in Chapter 8). This flag is supported by some Unix operating systems, including Linux, but it is not defined by the POSIX standard. In Linux 2.4, a process can also create a memory region that is both MAP_SHARED and MAP_ANONYMOUS. In this case, the region maps a special file in the *shm* filesystem (see the section "IPC Shared Memory" in Chapter 19), which can be accessed by all the process's descendants.

- A set of permissions specifying one or more types of access to the memory region: read access (PROT_READ), write access (PROT_WRITE), or execution access (PROT_EXEC).

- An optional linear address, which is taken by the kernel as a hint of where the new memory region should start. If the MAP_FIXED flag is specified and the kernel cannot allocate the new memory region starting from the specified linear address, the system call fails.

The mmap() system call returns the linear address of the first location in the new memory region. For compatibility reasons, in the 80×86 architecture, the kernel reserves two entries in the system call table for mmap(): one at index 90 and the other at index 192. The former entry corresponds to the old_mmap() service routine (used by older C libraries), while the latter one corresponds to the sys_mmap2() service routine (used by recent C libraries). The two service routines differ only in how the six parameters of the system call are passed. Both of them end up invoking the do_mmap_pgoff() function described in the section "Allocating a Linear Address Interval" in Chapter 8. We now complete that description by detailing the steps performed only when creating a memory region that maps a file.

1. Checks whether the mmap file operation for the file to be mapped is defined; if not, it returns an error code. A NULL value for mmap in the file operation table indicates that the corresponding file cannot be mapped (for instance, because it is a directory).

2. Checks whether the get_unmapped_area method of the file object is defined. If so, invokes it; otherwise, invokes the arch_get_unmapped_area() function already described in Chapter 8. On the 80×86 architecture, a custom method is used only by the frame buffer layer, so we don't discuss the case further. Remember that the arch_get_unmapped_area() allocates an interval of linear addresses for the new memory region.

3. In addition to the usual consistency checks, compares the kind of memory mapping requested and the flags specified when the file was opened. The flags passed as a parameter of the system call specify the kind of mapping required, while the value of the f_mode field of the file object specifies how the file was opened. Depending on these two sources of information, it performs the following checks:

   a. If a shared writable memory mapping is required, checks that the file was opened for writing and that it was not opened in append mode (O_APPEND flag of the open() system call)

   b. If a shared memory mapping is required, checks that there is no mandatory lock on the file (see the section "File Locking" in Chapter 12)

   c. For any kind of memory mapping, checks that the file was opened for reading

   If any of these conditions is not fulfilled, an error code is returned.

4. When initializing the value of the vm_flags field of the new memory region descriptor, sets the VM_READ, VM_WRITE, VM_EXEC, VM_SHARED, VM_MAYREAD, VM_MAYWRITE, VM_MAYEXEC, and VM_MAYSHARE flags according to the access rights of the file and the kind of requested memory mapping (see the section "Memory Region Access Rights" in Chapter 8). As an optimization, the VM_SHARED flag is cleared for nonwritable shared memory mapping. This can be done because the process is not allowed to write into the pages of the memory region, so the mapping is treated the same as a private mapping; however, the kernel actually allows other processes that share the file to access the pages in this memory region.

5. Initializes the vm_file field of the memory region descriptor with the address of the file object and increments the file's usage counter.

6. Invokes the mmap method for the file being mapped, passing as parameters the address of the file object and the address of the memory region descriptor. For most filesystems, this method is implemented by the generic_file_mmap( ) function, which performs the following operations:

   a. If a shared writable memory mapping is required, checks that the writepage method of the address_space object of the file is defined; if not, it returns the error code -EINVAL.

   b. Checks that the readpage method of the address_space object of the file is defined; if not, it returns the error code -ENOEXEC.

   c. Stores the current time in the i_atime field of the file's inode and marks the inode as dirty.

   d. Initializes the vm_ops field of the memory region descriptor with the address of the generic_file_vm_ops table. All methods in this table are null, except the nopage method, which is implemented by the filemap_nopage( ) function.

7. Recall from the section "Allocating a Linear Address Interval" in Chapter 8 that do_mmap( ) invokes vma_link( ). This function inserts the memory region descriptor into either the i_mmap list or the i_mmap_shared list of the address_space object, according to whether the requested memory mapping is private or shared, respectively.

Destroying a Memory Mapping

When a process is ready to destroy a memory mapping, it invokes the munmap( ) system call, passing the following parameters to it:

* The address of the first location in the linear address interval to be removed
* The length of the linear address interval to be removed

Notice that the munmap( ) system call can be used to either remove or reduce the size of each kind of memory region. Indeed, the sys_munmap( ) service routine of the system call essentially invokes the do_munmap( ) function already described in the section

"Releasing a Linear Address Interval" in Chapter 8. However, if the memory region maps a file, the following additional steps are performed for each memory region included in the range of linear addresses to be released:

1. Invokes remove_shared_vm_struct( ) to remove the memory region descriptor from the address_space object list (either i_mmap or i_mmap_shared).

2. When executing the unmap_fixup( ) function, decrements the file usage counter if an entire memory region is destroyed, and increments the file usage counter if a new memory region is created—that is, if the unmapping created a hole inside a region. If the region has just been shrunken, it leaves the file usage counter unchanged.

Notice that there is no need to flush to disk the contents of the pages included in a writable shared memory mapping to be destroyed. In fact, these pages continue to act as a disk cache because they are still included in the page cache (see the next section).

Demand Paging for Memory Mapping

For reasons of efficiency, page frames are not assigned to a memory mapping right after it has been created at the last possible moment—that is, when the process attempts to address one of its pages, thus causing a Page Fault exception.

We saw in the section "Page Fault Exception Handler" in Chapter 8 how the kernel verifies whether the faulty address is included in some memory region of the process; if so, the kernel checks the Page Table entry corresponding to the faulty address and invokes the do_no_page( ) function if the entry is null (see the section "Demand Paging" in Chapter 8).

The do_no_page( ) function performs all the operations that are common to all types of demand paging, such as allocating a page frame and updating the Page Tables. It also checks whether the nopage method of the memory region involved is defined. In the section "Demand Paging" in Chapter 8, we described the case in which the method is undefined (anonymous memory region); now we complete the description by discussing the actions performed by the function when the method is defined:

1. Invokes the nopage method, which returns the address of a page frame that contains the requested page.

2. If the process is trying to write into the page and the memory mapping is private, avoids a future Copy On Write fault by making a copy of the page just read and inserting it into the inactive list of pages (see Chapter 16). In the following steps, the function uses the new page instead of the page returned by the nopage method so that the latter is not modified by the User Mode process.

3. Increments the rss field of the process memory descriptor to indicate that a new page frame has been assigned to the process.

4. Sets up the Page Table entry corresponding to the faulty address with the address of the page frame and the page access rights included in the memory region vm_page_prot field.

5. If the process is trying to write into the page, forces the Read/Write and Dirty bits of the Page Table entry to 1. In this case, either the page frame is exclusively assigned to the process, or the page is shared; in both cases, writing to it should be allowed.

The core of the demand paging algorithm consists of the memory region's nopage method. Generally speaking, it must return the address of a page frame that contains the page accessed by the process. Its implementation depends on the kind of memory region in which the page is included.

When handling memory regions that map files on disk, the nopage method must first search for the requested page in the page cache. If the page is not found, the method must read it from disk. Most filesystems implement the nopage method by means of the filemap_nopage( ) function, which receives three parameters:

area
:   Descriptor address of the memory region, including the required page.

address
:   Linear address of the required page.

unused
:   Parameter of the nopage method that is not used by filemap_nopage( ).

The filemap_nopage( ) function executes the following steps:

1. Gets the file object address file from area->vm_file field. Derives the address_ space object address from file->f_dentry->d_inode->i_mapping. Derives the inode object address from the host field of the address_space object.

2. Uses the vm_start and vm_pgoff fields of area to determine the offset within the file of the data corresponding to the page starting from address.

3. Checks whether the file offset exceeds the file size. When this happens, returns NULL, which means failure in allocating the new page, unless the Page Fault was caused by a debugger tracing another process through the ptrace( ) system call. We are not going to discuss this special case.

4. Invokes find_get_page( ) to look in the page cache for the page identified by the address_space object and the file offset.

5. If the page is not in the page cache, checks the value of the VM_RAND_READ flag of the memory region. The value of this flag can be changed by means of the madvise( ) system call; when the flag is set, it indicates that the user application is not going to read more pages of the file than those just accessed.

- If the VM_RAND_READ flag is set, invokes page_cache_read( ) to read just the requested page from disk (see the earlier section "Reading from a File").

- If the VM_RAND_READ flag is cleared, invokes page_cache_read( ) several times to read a cluster of adjacent pages inside the memory region, including the requested page. The length of the cluster is stored in the page_request variable; its default value is three pages, but the system administrator may tune its value by writing into the /proc/sys/vm/page-cluster special file.

Then the function jumps back to Step 4 and repeats the page cache lookup operation (the process might have been blocked while executing the page_cache_read( ) function).

6. The page is inside the page cache. Checks its PG_uptodate flag. If the flag is not set (page not up to date), the function performs the following substeps:

    a. Locks up the page by setting the PG_locked flag, sleeping if necessary.

    b. Invokes the readpage method of the address_space object to trigger the I/O data transfer.

    c. Invokes wait_on_page( ) to sleep until the I/O transfer completes.

7. The page is up to date. The function checks the VM_SEQ_READ flag of the memory region. The value of this flag can be changed by means of the madvise( ) system call; when the flag is set, it indicates that the user application is going to reference the pages of the mapped file sequentially, thus the pages should be aggressively read in advance and freed after they are accessed. If the flag is set, it invokes nopage_sequential_readahead( ). This function uses a large, fixed-size read-ahead window, whose length is approximately the maximum read-ahead window size of the underlying block device (see the earlier section "Read-Ahead of Files"). The vm_raend field of the memory region descriptor stores the ending position of the current read-ahead window. The function shifts the read-ahead windows forward (by reading in advance the corresponding pages) whenever the requested page falls exactly in the middle point of the current read-ahead window. Moreover, the function should release the pages in the memory region that are far behind the requested page; if the function reads the nth read-ahead window of the memory region, it flushes to disk the pages belonging to the $(n-3)$th window (however, the kernel Version 2.4.18 doesn't release them; see the next section).

8. Invokes mark_page_accessed( ) to mark the requested page as accessed (see Chapter 16).

9. Returns the address of the requested page.

Flushing Dirty Memory Mapping Pages to Disk

The msync( ) system call can be used by a process to flush to disk dirty pages belonging to a shared memory mapping. It receives as parameters the starting address of an interval of linear addresses, the length of the interval, and a set of flags that have the following meanings:

MS_SYNC

Asks the system call to suspend the process until the I/O operation completes. In this way, the calling process can assume that when the system call terminates, all pages of its memory mapping have been flushed to disk.

MS_ASYNC

Asks the system call to return immediately without suspending the calling process.

MS_INVALIDATE

Asks the system call to remove all pages included in the memory mapping from the process address space (not really implemented).

The sys_msync() service routine invokes msync_interval() on each memory region included in the interval of linear addresses. In turn, the latter function performs the following operations:

1. If the vm_file field of the memory region descriptor is NULL, or if the VM_SHARED flag is clear, returns 0 (the memory region is not a writable shared memory mapping of a file).

2. Invokes the filemap_sync() function, which scans the Page Table entries corresponding to the linear address intervals included in the memory region. For each page found, it invokes flush_tlb_page() to flush the corresponding translation lookaside buffers, and marks the page as dirty.

3. If the MS_SYNC flag is not set, returns. Otherwise, continues with the following steps to flush the pages in the memory region to disk, sleeping until all I/O data transfers terminate. Notice that, at least in the last stable version of the kernel at the time of this writing, the function does not take the MS_INVALIDATE flag into consideration.

4. Acquires the i_sem semaphore of the file's inode.

5. Invokes the filemap_fdatasync() function, which receives the address of the file's address_space object. For every page belonging to the dirty pages list of the address_space object, the function performs the following substeps:

    a. Moves the page from the dirty pages list to the locked pages list.

    b. If the PG_Dirty flag is not set, continues with the next page in the list (the page is already being flushed by another process).

    c. Increments the usage counter of the page and locks it, sleeping if necessary.

    d. Clears the PG_dirty flag of the page.

    e. Invokes the writepage method of the address_space object on the page (described following this list).

    f. Releases the usage counter of the page

The `writepage` method for block device files and almost all disk-based filesystems is just a wrapper for the `block_write_full_page()` function; it is used to pass to `block_write_full_page()` the address of a filesystem-dependent function that translates the block numbers relative to the beginning of the file into logical block numbers relative to positions of the block in the disk partition. (This is the same mechanism that is already described in the earlier section "Reading from a File" and that is used for the readpage method). In turn, `block_write_full_page( )` is very similar to `block_read_full_page()` described earlier: it allocates asynchronous buffer heads for the page, and invokes the `submit_bh( )` function on each of them specifying the `WRITE` operation.

6. Checks whether the `fsync` method of the file object is defined; if so, executes it. For regular files, this method usually limits itself to flushing the inode object of the file to disk. For block device files, however, the method invokes `sync_buffers( )`, which activates the I/O data transfer of all dirty buffers of the device.

7. Executes the `filemap_fdatawait( )` function. For each page in the locked pages list of the `address_space` object, the function waits until the page becomes unlocked—when the ongoing I/O data transfer on the page terminates.

8. Releases the `i_sem` semaphore of the file.

Direct I/O Transfers

As we have seen, in Version 2.4 of Linux, there is no substantial difference between accessing a regular file through the filesystem, accessing it by referencing its blocks on the underlying block device file, or even establishing a file memory mapping. There are, however, some highly sophisticated programs (*self-caching applications*) that would like to have full control of the whole I/O data transfer mechanism. Consider, for example, high-performance database servers: most of them implement their own caching mechanisms that exploit the peculiar nature of the queries to the database. For these kinds of programs, the kernel page cache doesn't help; on the contrary, it is detrimental for the following reasons:

- Lots of page frames are wasted to duplicate disk data already in RAM (in the user-level disk cache)

- The `read( )` and `write( )` system calls are slowed down by the redundant instructions that handle the page cache and the read-ahead; ditto for the paging operations related to the file memory mappings

- Rather than transferring the data directly between the disk and the user memory, the `read( )` and `write( )` system calls make two transfers: between the disk and a kernel buffer and between the kernel buffer and the user memory

Since block hardware devices *must* be handled through interrupts and Direct Memory Access (DMA), and this can be done only in Kernel Mode, some sort of kernel support is definitely required to implement self-caching applications.

Version 2.4 of Linux offers a simple way to bypass the page cache: *direct I/O transfers*. In each I/O direct transfer, the kernel programs the disk controller to transfer the data directly from/to pages belonging to the User Mode address space of a self-caching application.

As we know, any data transfer proceeds asynchronously. While it is in progress, the kernel may switch the current process, the CPU may return to User Mode, the pages of the process that raised the data transfer might be swapped out, and so on. This works just fine for ordinary I/O data transfers because they involve pages of the disk caches. Disk caches are owned by the kernel, cannot be swapped out, and are visible to all processes in Kernel Mode.

On the other hand, direct I/O transfers should move data within pages that belong to the User Mode address space of a given process. The kernel must take care that these pages are accessible by any process in Kernel Mode and that they are not swapped out while the data transfer is in progress. This is achieved thanks to the "direct access buffers."

A *direct access buffer* consists of a set of physical page frames reserved for direct I/O data transfers, which are mapped both by the User Mode Page Tables of a self-caching application and by the kernel Page Tables (the Kernel Mode Page Tables of each process). Each direct access buffer is described by a kiobuf data structure, whose fields are shown in Table 15-2.

Table 15-2. The fields of the direct access buffer descriptor

Type	Field	Description
int	nr_pages	Number of pages in the direct access buffer
int	array_len	Number of free elements in the map_array field
int	offset	Offset to valid data inside the first page of the direct access buffer
int	length	Length of valid data inside the direct access buffer
struct page **	maplist	List of page descriptor pointers referring to pages in the direct access buffer (usually points to the map_array field)
unsigned int	locked	Lock flag for all pages in the direct access buffer
struct page * []	map_array	Array of 129 page descriptor pointers
struct buffer_head * []	bh	Array of 1,024 preallocated buffer head pointers
unsigned long []	blocks	Array of 1,024 logical block numbers
atomic_t	io_count	Atomic flag that indicates whether I/O is in progress
int	errno	Error number of last I/O operation
void (*) (struct kiobuf *)	end_io	Completion method
wait_queue_head_t	wait_queue	Queue of processes waiting for I/O to complete

Suppose a self-caching application wishes to directly access a file. As a first step, the application opens the file specifying the O_DIRECT flag (see the section "The open() System Call" in Chapter 12). While servicing the open() system call, the dentry_ open() function checks the value of this flag; if it is set, the function invokes alloc_ kiovec(), which allocates a new direct access buffer descriptor and stores its address into the f_iobuf field of the file object. Initially the buffer includes no page frames, so the nr_pages field of the descriptor stores the value 0. The alloc_kiovec(), however, preallocates 1,024 buffer heads, whose addresses are stored in the bh array of the descriptor. These buffer heads ensure that the self-caching application is not blocked while directly accessing the file (recall that ordinary data transfers block if no free buffer heads are available). A drawback of this approach, however, is that data transfers must be done in chunks of at most 512 KB.

Next, suppose the self-caching application issues a read() or write() system call on the file opened with O_DIRECT. As mentioned earlier in this chapter, the generic_ file_read() and generic_file_write() functions check the value of the flag and handle the case in a special way. For instance, the generic_file_read() function executes a code fragment essentially equivalent to the following:

```
if (filp->f_flags & O_DIRECT) {
    inode = filp->f_dentry->d_inode->i_mapping->host;
    if (count == 0 || *ppos >= inode->i_size)
        return 0;
    if (*ppos + count > inode->i_size)
        count = inode->i_size - *ppos;
    retval = generic_file_direct_IO(READ, filp, buf, count, *ppos);
    if (retval > 0)
        *ppos += retval;
    UPDATE_ATIME(filp->f_dentry->d_inode);
    return retval;
}
```

The function checks the current values of the file pointer, the file size, and the number of requested characters, and then invokes the generic_file_direct_IO() function, passing to it the READ operation type, the file object pointer, the address of the User Mode buffer, the number of requested bytes, and the file pointer. The generic_ file_write() function is similar, but of course it passes the WRITE operation type to the generic_file_direct_IO() function.

The generic_file_direct_IO() function performs the following steps:

1. Tests and sets the f_iobuf_lock lock in the file object. If it was already set, the direct access buffer descriptor stored in f_iobuf is already in use by a concurrent direct I/O transfer, so the function allocates a new direct access buffer descriptor and uses it in the following steps.

2. Checks that the file pointer offset and the number of requested characters are multiples of the block size of the file; returns -EINVAL if they are not.

3. Checks that the direct_IO method of the address_space object of the file (filp-> f_dentry->d_inode->i_mapping) is defined; returns -EINVAL if it isn't.

4. Even if the self-caching application is accessing the file directly, there could be other applications in the system that access the file through the page cache. To avoid data loss, the disk image is synchronized with the page cache before starting the direct I/O transfer. The function flushes the dirty pages belonging to memory mappings of the file to disk by invoking the `filemap_fdatasync()` function (see the previous section).

5. Flushes to disk the dirty pages updated by `write()` system calls by invoking the `fsync_inode_data_buffers()` function, and waits until the I/O transfer terminates.

6. Invokes the `filemap_fdatawait()` function to wait until the I/O operations started in the Step 4 complete (see the previous section).

7. Starts a loop, and divides the data to be transferred in chunks of 512 KB. For every chunk, the function performs the following substeps:

   a. Invokes `map_user_kiobuf()` to establish a mapping between the direct access buffer and the portion of the user-level buffer corresponding to the chunk. To achieve this, the function:

      1. Invokes `expand_kiobuf()` to allocate a new array of page descriptor addresses in case the array embedded in the direct access buffer descriptor is too small. This is not the case here, however, because the 129 entries in the `map_array` field suffice to map the chunk of 512 KB (notice that the additional page is required when the buffer is not page-aligned).

      2. Accesses all user pages in the chunk (allocating them when necessary by simulating Page Faults) and stores their addresses in the array pointed to by the `maplist` field of the direct access buffer descriptor.

      3. Properly initializes the `nr_pages`, `offset`, and `length` fields, and resets the `locked` field to 0.

   b. Invokes the `direct_IO` method of the `address_space` object of the file (explained next).

   c. If the operation type was READ, invokes `mark_dirty_kiobuf()` to mark the pages mapped by the direct access buffer as dirty.

   d. Invokes `unmap_kiobuf()` to release the mapping between the chunk and the direct access buffer, and then continues with the next chunk.

8. If the function allocated a temporary direct access buffer descriptor in Step 1, it releases it. Otherwise, it releases the `f_iobuf_lock` lock in the file object.

In almost all cases, the `direct_IO` method is a wrapper for the `generic_direct_IO()` function, passing it the address of the usual filesystem-dependent function that computes the position of the physical blocks on the block device (see the earlier section "Reading from a File"). This function executes the following steps:

1. For each block of the file portion corresponding to the current chunk, invokes the filesystem-dependent function to determine its logical block number, and stores this number in an entry of the blocks array in the direct access buffer descriptor. The 1,024 entries of the array suffice because the minimum block size in Linux is 512 bytes.

2. Invokes the brw_kiovec( ) function, which essentially calls the submit_bh( ) function on each block in the blocks array using the buffer heads stored in the bh array of the direct access buffer descriptor. The direct I/O operation is similar to a buffer or page I/O operation, but the b_end_io method of the buffer heads is set to the special function end_buffer_io_kiobuf( ) rather than to end_buffer_io_sync( ) or end_buffer_io_async( ) (see the section "Block and Page I/O Operations" in Chapter 13). The method deals with the fields of the kiobuf data structure. brw_kiovec( ) does not return until the I/O data transfers are completed.

CHAPTER 16

Swapping: Methods for Freeing Memory

The disk caches examined in previous chapters used RAM as an extension of the disk; the goal was to improve system response time and the solution was to reduce the number of disk accesses. In this chapter, we introduce an opposite approach called *swapping*, in which the kernel uses some space on disk as an extension of RAM. Swapping is transparent to the programmer: once the swapping areas are properly installed and activated, the processes may run under the assumption that they have all the physical memory available that they can address, never knowing that some of their pages are stored away and retrieved again as needed.

Disk caches enhance system performance at the expense of free RAM, while swapping extends the amount of addressable memory at the expense of access speed. Thus, disk caches are "good" and desirable, while swapping should be regarded as some sort of last resort to be used whenever the amount of free RAM becomes too scarce.

We start by defining swapping in the section "What Is Swapping?". Then we describe in the section "Swap Area" the main data structures introduced by Linux to implement swapping. We discuss the swap cache and the low-level functions that transfer pages between RAM and swap areas, and vice versa. The two crucial sections are "Swapping Out Pages," where we describe the procedure used to select a page to be swapped out to disk, and "Swapping in Pages," where we explain how a page stored in a swap area is read back into RAM when the need occurs.

This chapter effectively concludes our discussion of memory management. Just one topic remains to be covered—namely, page frame reclaiming; this is done in the last section, which is related only in part to swapping. With so many disk caches around, including the swap cache, all the available RAM could eventually end up in these caches and no more free RAM would be left. We shall see how the kernel prevents this by monitoring the amount of free RAM and by freeing pages from the caches or from the process address spaces, as the need occurs.

What Is Swapping?

Swapping serves two main purposes:

- To expand the address space that is effectively usable by a process
- To expand the amount of dynamic RAM (i.e., what is left of the RAM once the kernel code and static data structures have been initialized) to load processes

Let's give a few examples of how swapping benefits the user. The simplest is when a program's data structures take up more space than the size of the available RAM. A swap area will allow this program to be loaded without any problem, and thus to run correctly. A more subtle example involves users who issue several commands that try to simultaneously run large applications that require a lot of memory. If no swap area is active, the system might reject requests to launch a new application. In contrast, a swap area allows the kernel to launch it, since some memory can be freed at the expense of some of the already existing processes without killing them.

These two examples illustrate the benefits, but also the drawbacks, of swapping. Simulation of RAM is not like RAM in terms of performance. Every access by a process to a page that is currently swapped out increases the process execution time by several orders of magnitude. In short, if performance is of great importance, swapping should be used only as a last resort; adding RAM chips still remains the best solution to cope with increasing computing needs. It is fair to say, however, that in some cases, swapping may be beneficial to the system as a whole. Long-running processes typically access only half of the page frames obtained. Even when some RAM is available, swapping unused pages out and using the RAM for disk cache can improve overall system performance.

Swapping has been around for many years. The first Unix system kernels monitored the amount of free memory constantly. When it became less than a fixed threshold, they performed some swapping out. This activity consisted of copying the entire address space of a process to disk. Conversely, when the scheduling algorithm selected a swapped-out process, the whole process was swapped in from disk.

This approach was abandoned by modern Unix kernels, including Linux, mainly because process switches are quite expensive when they involve swapping in swapped-out processes. To compensate for the burden of such swapping activity, the scheduling algorithm must be very sophisticated: it must favor in-RAM processes without completely shutting out the swapped-out ones.

In Linux, swapping is currently performed at the page level rather than at the process address space level. This finer level of granularity has been reached thanks to the inclusion of a hardware paging unit in the CPU. Recall from the section "Regular Paging" in Chapter 2 that each Page Table entry includes a Present flag; the kernel can take advantage of this flag to signal to the hardware that a page belonging to a process address space has been swapped out. Besides that flag, Linux also takes advantage of the remaining bits of the Page Table entry to store the location of the swapped-out page on disk. When a Page Fault exception occurs, the corresponding exception handler can detect that the page is not present in RAM and invoke the function that swaps the missing page in from the disk.

Much of the algorithm's complexity is thus related to swapping out. In particular, four main issues must be considered:

- Which kind of page to swap out
- How to distribute pages in the swap areas
- How to select the page to be swapped out
- When to perform page swap out

Let's give a short preview of how Linux handles these four issues before describing the main data structures and functions related to swapping.

Which Kind of Page to Swap Out

Swapping applies only to the following kinds of pages:

- Pages that belong to an anonymous memory region of a process (for instance, a User Mode stack)
- Modified pages that belong to a private memory mapping of a process
- Pages that belong to an IPC shared memory region (see the section "IPC Shared Memory" in Chapter 19)

The remaining kinds of pages are either used by the kernel or used to map files on disk. In the first case, they are ignored by swapping because this simplifies the kernel design; in the second case, the best swap areas for the pages are the files themselves.

How to Distribute Pages in the Swap Areas

Each swap area is organized into *slots*, where each slot contains exactly one page. When swapping out, the kernel tries to store pages in contiguous slots to minimize disk seek time when accessing the swap area; this is an important element of an efficient swapping algorithm.

If more than one swap area is used, things become more complicated. Faster swap areas—swap areas stored in faster disks—get a higher priority. When looking for a free slot, the search starts in the swap area that has the highest priority. If there are several of them, swap areas of the same priority are cyclically selected to avoid overloading one of them. If no free slot is found in the swap areas that have the highest priority, the search continues in the swap areas that have a priority next to the highest one, and so on.

How to Select the Page to Be Swapped Out

When choosing pages for swap out, it would be nice to be able to rank them according to some criterion. Several Least Recently Used (LRU) replacement algorithms have been proposed and used in some kernels. The main idea is to associate a counter storing the age of the page with each page in RAM—that is, the interval of time elapsed since the last access to the page. The oldest page of the process can then be swapped out.

Some computer platforms provide sophisticated support for LRU algorithms; for instance, the CPUs of some mainframes automatically update the value of a counter included in each Page Table entry to specify the age of the corresponding page. But 80×86 processors do not offer such a hardware feature, so Linux cannot use a true LRU algorithm. However, when selecting a candidate for swap out, Linux takes advantage of the Accessed flag included in each Page Table entry, which is automatically set by the hardware when the page is accessed. As we'll see later, this flag is set and cleared in a rather simplistic way to keep pages from being swapped in and out too much.

When to Perform Page Swap Out

Swapping out is useful when the kernel is dangerously low on memory. As the kernel's first defense against critically low memory, it keeps a small reserve of free page frames that can be used only by the most critical functions. This turns out to be essential to avoid system crashes, which might occur when a kernel routine invoked to free resources is unable to obtain the memory area it needs to complete its task. To protect this reserve of free page frames, Linux may perform a swap out on the following occasions:

- By a kernel thread denoted as *kswapd* that is activated periodically whenever the number of free page frames falls below a predefined threshold.
- When a memory request to the buddy system (see the section "The Buddy System Algorithm" in Chapter 7) cannot be satisfied because the number of free page frames would fall below a predefined threshold.

Swap Area

The pages swapped out from memory are stored in a *swap area*, which may be implemented either as a disk partition of its own or as a file included in a larger partition. Several different swap areas may be defined, up to a maximum number specified by the MAX_SWAPFILES macro (usually set to 32).

Having multiple swap areas allows a system administrator to spread a lot of swap space among several disks so that the hardware can act on them concurrently; it also lets swap space be increased at runtime without rebooting the system.

Each swap area consists of a sequence of *page slots*: 4,096-byte blocks used to contain a swapped-out page. The first page slot of a swap area is used to persistently store some information about the swap area; its format is described by the swap_ header union composed of two structures, info and magic. The magic structure provides a string that marks part of the disk unambiguously as a swap area; it consists of just one field, magic.magic, which contains a 10-character "magic" string. The magic structure essentially allows the kernel to unambiguously identify a file or a partition as a swap area; the text of the string depends on the swapping algorithm version: SWAP-SPACE for Version 1 or SWAPSPACE2 for Version 2. The field is always located at the end of the first page slot.

The info structure includes the following fields:

info.bootbits
> Not used by the swapping algorithm; this field corresponds to the first 1,024 bytes of the swap area, which may store partition data, disk labels, and so on.

info.version
> Swapping algorithm version.

info.last_page
> Last page slot that is effectively usable.

info.nr_badpages
> Number of defective page slots.

info.padding[125]
> Padding bytes.

info.badpages[1]
> Up to 637 numbers specifying the location of defective page slots.

The data stored in a swap area is meaningful as long as the system is on. When the system is switched off, all processes are killed, so all data stored by processes in swap areas is discarded. For this reason, swap areas contain very little control information; essentially, the swap area type and the list of defective page slots. This control information easily fits in a single 4 KB page.

Usually, the system administrator creates a swap partition when creating the other partitions on the Linux system, and then uses the *mkswap* command to set up the disk area as a new swap area. That command initializes the fields just described within the first page slot. Since the disk may include some bad blocks, the program also examines all other page slots to locate the defective ones. But executing the *mkswap* command leaves the swap area in an inactive state. Each swap area can be activated in a script file at system boot or dynamically after the system is running. An initialized swap area is considered *active* when it effectively represents an extension of the system RAM (see the section "Activating and Deactivating a Swap Area" later in this chapter).

Swap Area Descriptor

Each active swap area has its own `swap_info_struct` descriptor in memory. The fields of the descriptor are illustrated in Table 16-1.

Table 16-1. Fields of a swap area descriptor

Type	Field	Description
unsigned int	flags	Swap area flags
kdev_t	swap_device	Device number of the swap disk partition
spinlock_t	sdev_lock	Swap area descriptor spin lock
struct dentry *	swap_file	Dentry of the file or device file
struct vfsmount *	swap_vfsmnt	Mounted filesystem descriptor of the file or device file
unsigned short *	swap_map	Pointer to array of counters, one for each swap area page slot
unsigned int	lowest_bit	First page slot to be scanned when searching for a free one
unsigned int	highest_bit	Last page slot to be scanned when searching for a free one
unsigned int	cluster_next	Next page slot to be scanned when searching for a free one
unsigned int	cluster_nr	Number of free page slot allocations before restarting from the beginning
int	prio	Swap area priority
int	pages	Number of usable page slots
unsigned long	max	Size of swap area in pages
int	next	Pointer to next swap area descriptor

The `flags` field includes two overlapping subfields:

SWP_USED

> 1 if the swap area is active; 0 if it is nonactive.

SWP_WRITEOK

> This 2-bit field is set to 3 if it is possible to write into the swap area and to 0 otherwise; since the least-significant bit of this field coincides with the bit used to implement SWP_USED, a swap area can be written only if it is active. The kernel is not allowed to write in a swap area when it is being activated or deactivated.

The `swap_map` field points to an array of counters, one for each swap area page slot. If the counter is equal to 0, the page slot is free; if it is positive, the page slot is filled with a swapped-out page (the exact meaning of positive values is discussed later in the section "The Swap Cache"). If the counter has the value SWAP_MAP_MAX (equal to 32,767), the page stored in the page slot is "permanent" and cannot be removed from the corresponding slot. If the counter has the value SWAP_MAP_BAD (equal to 32,768), the page slot is considered defective, and thus unusable.[*]

---

[*] "Permanent" page slots protect against overflows of swap_map counters. Without them, valid page slots could become "defective" if they are referenced too many times, thus leading to data losses. However, no one really expects that a page slot counter could reach the value 32,768. It's just a "belt and suspenders" approach.

The prio field is a signed integer that denotes the order in which the swap subsystem should consider each swap area. Swap areas implemented on faster disks should have a higher priority so they will be used first. Only when they are filled does the swapping algorithm consider lower-priority swap areas. Swap areas that have the same priority are cyclically selected to distribute swapped-out pages among them. As we shall see in the section "Activating and Deactivating a Swap Area," the priority is assigned when the swap area is activated.

The sdev_lock field is a spin lock that protects the descriptor against concurrent accesses in SMP systems.

The swap_info array includes MAX_SWAPFILES swap area descriptors. Of course, not all of them are necessarily used, only those having the SWP_USED flag set. Figure 16-1 illustrates the swap_info array, one swap area, and the corresponding array of counters.

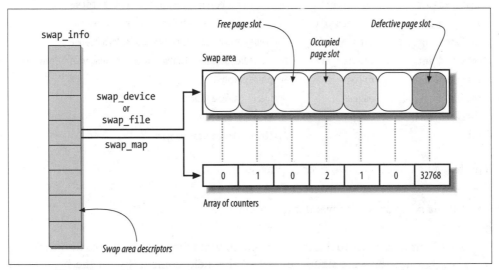

Figure 16-1. Swap area data structures

The nr_swapfiles variable stores the index of the last array element that contains, or that has contained, a used swap area descriptor. Despite its name, the variable *does not* contain the number of active swap areas.

Descriptors of active swap areas are also inserted into a list sorted by the swap area priority. The list is implemented through the next field of the swap area descriptor, which stores the index of the next descriptor in the swap_info array. This use of the field as an index is different from most fields with the name next, which are usually pointers.

The swap_list variable, of type swap_list_t, includes the following fields:

head
    Index in the swap_info array of the first list element.

next

Index in the swap_info array of the descriptor of the next swap area to be selected for swapping out pages. This field is used to implement a round-robin algorithm among maximum-priority swap areas with free slots.

The swaplock spin lock protects the list against concurrent accesses in multiprocessor systems.

The max field of the swap area descriptor stores the size of the swap area in pages, while the pages field stores the number of usable page slots. These numbers differ because pages does not take the first page slot and the defective page slots into consideration.

Finally, the nr_swap_pages variable contains the number of available (free and nondefective) page slots in all active swap areas, while the total_swap_pages variable contains the total number of nondefective page slots.

Swapped-Out Page Identifier

A swapped-out page is uniquely identified quite simply by specifying the index of the swap area in the swap_info array and the page slot index inside the swap area. Since the first page (with index 0) of the swap area is reserved for the swap_header union discussed earlier, the first useful page slot has index 1. The format of a *swapped-out page identifier* is illustrated in Figure 16-2.

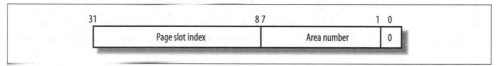

Figure 16-2. Swapped-out page identifier

The SWP_ENTRY(type,offset) macro constructs a swapped-out page identifier from the swap area index type and the page slot index offset. Conversely, the SWP_TYPE and SWP_OFFSET macros extract from a swapped-out page identifier the swap area index and the page slot index, respectively.

When a page is swapped out, its identifier is inserted as the page's entry into the Page Table so the page can be found again when needed. Notice that the least-significant bit of such an identifier, which corresponds to the Present flag, is always cleared to denote the fact that the page is not currently in RAM. However, at least one of the remaining 31 bits has to be set because no page is ever stored in slot 0 of swap area 0. It is therefore possible to identify three different cases from the value of a Page Table entry:

Null entry
    The page does not belong to the process address space.

First 31 most-significant bits not all equal to 0, last bit equal to 0
> The page is currently swapped out.

Least-significant bit equal to 1
> The page is contained in RAM.

Notice that the maximum size of a swap area is determined by the number of bits available to identify a slot. On the 80×86 architecture, the 24 bits available limit the size of a swap area to 2^{24} slots (that is, to 64 GB).

Since a page may belong to the address spaces of several processes (see the later section "The Swap Cache"), it may be swapped out from the address space of one process and still remain in main memory; therefore, it is possible to swap out the same page several times. A page is physically swapped out and stored just once, of course, but each subsequent attempt to swap it out increments the swap_map counter.

The swap_duplicate( ) function is usually invoked while trying to swap out an already swapped-out page. It just verifies that the swapped-out page identifier passed as its parameter is valid and increments the corresponding swap_map counter. More precisely, it performs the following actions:

1. Uses the SWP_TYPE and SWP_OFFSET macros to extract the swap area number type and the page slot index offset from the parameter.

2. Checks whether the swap area is activated; if not, it returns 0 (invalid identifier).

3. Checks whether the page slot is valid and not free (its swap_map counter is greater than 0 and less than SWAP_MAX_BAD); if not, returns 0 (invalid identifier).

4. Otherwise, the swapped-out page identifier locates a valid page. Increments the swap_map counter of the page slot if it has not already reached the value SWAP_MAP_MAX.

5. Returns 1 (valid identifier).

Activating and Deactivating a Swap Area

Once a swap area is initialized, the superuser (or, more precisely, any user having the CAP_SYS_ADMIN capability, as described in the section "Process Credentials and Capabilities" in Chapter 20) may use the *swapon* and *swapoff* programs to activate and deactivate the swap area, respectively. These programs use the swapon( ) and swapoff( ) system calls; we'll briefly sketch out the corresponding service routines.

The sys_swapon( ) service routine

The sys_swapon( ) service routine receives the following as parameters:

specialfile
> This parameter points to the pathname (in the User Mode address space) of the device file (partition) or plain file used to implement the swap area.

swap_flags

> This parameter consists of a single SWAP_FLAG_PREFER bit plus 15 bits of priority of the swap area (these bits are significant only if the SWAP_FLAG_PREFER bit is on).

The function checks the fields of the swap_header union that was put in the first slot when the swap area was created. The function performs these main steps:

1. Checks that the current process has the CAP_SYS_ADMIN capability.

2. Searches for the first element in the swap_info array of swap area descriptors that have the SWP_USED flag cleared, meaning that the corresponding swap area is inactive. If there is none, there are already MAX_SWAPFILES active swap areas, so the function returns an error code.

3. A descriptor for the swap area has been found. The function initializes the descriptor's fields (setting flags to SWP_USED, setting lowest_bit and highest_bit to 0, and so on). Moreover, if the descriptor's index is greater than nr_swapfiles, the function updates that variable.

4. If the swap_flags parameter specifies a priority for the new swap area, the function sets the prio field of the descriptor. Otherwise, it initializes the field with the lowest priority among all active swap areas minus 1 (thus assuming that the last activated swap area is on the slowest block device). If no other swap areas are already active, the function assigns the value −1.

5. Copies the string pointed to by the specialfile parameter from the User Mode address space.

6. Invokes path_init() and path_walk() to perform a pathname lookup on the string copied from the User Mode address space (see the section "Pathname Lookup" in Chapter 12).

7. Stores the addresses of the dentry object and of the mounted filesystem descriptor returned by path_walk() in the swap_file and swap_vfsmnt fields of the swap area descriptor, respectively.

8. If the specialfile parameter identifies a block device file, the function performs the following substeps:

    a. Stores the device number in the swap_device field of the descriptor.

    b. Sets the block size of the device to 4 KB—that is, sets its blksize_size entry to PAGE_SIZE.

    c. Initializes the block device driver by invoking the bd_acquire() and do_open( ) functions, described in the section "Initializing a Block Device Driver" in Chapter 13.

9. Checks to make sure that the swap area was not already activated by looking at the address_space objects of the other active swap areas in swap_info (given an address q of a swap area descriptor, the corresponding address_space object is obtained by q->swap_file->d_inode->i_mapping). If the swap area is already active, it returns an error code.

10. Allocates a page frame and invokes `rw_swap_page_nolock( )` (see the section "Transferring Swap Pages" later in this chapter) to fill it with the `swap_header` union stored in the first page of the swap area.

11. Checks that the magic string in the last ten characters of the first page in the swap area is equal to `SWAP-SPACE` or to `SWAPSPACE2` (there are two slightly different versions of the swapping algorithm). If not, the `specialfile` parameter does not specify an already initialized swap area, so the function returns an error code. For the sake of brevity, we'll suppose that the swap area has the `SWAPSPACE2` magic string.

12. Initializes the `lowest_bit` and `highest_bit` fields of the swap area descriptor according to the size of the swap area stored in the `info.last_page` field of the `swap_header` union.

13. Invokes `vmalloc( )` to create the array of counters associated with the new swap area and store its address in the `swap_map` field of the swap descriptor. Initializes the elements of the array to 0 or to `SWAP_MAP_BAD`, according to the list of defective page slots stored in the `info.bad_pages` field of the `swap_header` union.

14. Computes the number of useful page slots by accessing the `info.last_page` and `info.nr_badpages` fields in the first page slot.

15. Sets the `flags` field of the swap descriptor to `SWP_WRITEOK`, sets the `pages` field to the number of useful page slots, and updates the `nr_swap_pages` and `total_swap_pages` variables.

16. Inserts the new swap area descriptor in the list to which the `swap_list` variable points.

17. Releases the page frame that contains the data of the first page of the swap area and returns 0 (success).

The sys_swapoff( ) service routine

The `sys_swapoff( )` service routine deactivates a swap area identified by the parameter `specialfile`. It is much more complex and time-consuming than `sys_swapon( )`, since the partition to be deactivated might still contain pages that belong to several processes. The function is thus forced to scan the swap area and to swap in all existing pages. Since each swap in requires a new page frame, it might fail if there are no free page frames left. In this case, the function returns an error code. All this is achieved by performing the following major steps:

1. Checks that the current process has the `CAP_SYS_ADMIN` capability.

2. Copies the string pointed to by `specialfile`, and invokes `path_init( )` and `path_walk( )` to perform a pathname lookup.

3. Scans the list to which `swap_list` points and locates the descriptor whose `swap_file` field points to the dentry object found by the pathname lookup. If no such descriptor exists, an invalid parameter was passed to the function, so it returns an error code.

4. Otherwise, if the descriptor exists, checks that its SWP_WRITE flag is set; if not, returns an error code because the swap area is already being deactivated by another process.

5. Removes the descriptor from the list and sets its flags field to SWP_USED so the kernel doesn't store more pages in the swap area before this function deactivates it.

6. Subtracts the swap area size stored in the pages field of the swap area descriptor from the values of nr_swap_pages and total_swap_pages.

7. Invokes the try_to_unuse( ) function (see below) to successively force all pages left in the swap area into RAM and to correspondingly update the Page Tables of the processes that use these pages.

8. If try_to_unuse( ) fails in allocating all requested page frames, the swap area cannot be deactivated. Therefore, the function executes the following substeps:

   a. Reinserts the swap area descriptor in the swap_list list and sets its flags field to SWP_WRITEOK (see Step 5)

   b. Adds the content of the pages field to the nr_swap_pages and total_swap_ pages variables (see Step 6)

   c. Invokes path_release( ) to release the VFS objects allocated by path_walk( ) in Step 2.

   d. Finally, returns an error code.

9. Otherwise, all used page slots have been successfully transferred to RAM. Therefore, the function executes the following substeps:

   a. If specialfile identifies a block device file, releases the corresponding block device driver.

   b. Invokes path_release( ) to release the VFS objects allocated by path_walk( ) in Step 2.

   c. Releases the memory area used to store the swap_map array.

   d. Invokes path_release( ) again because the VFS objects that refer to specialfile have been allocated by the path_walk( ) function invoked by sys_swapon( ) (see Step 6 in the previous section).

   e. Returns 0 (success).

The try_to_unuse( ) function

As stated previously, the try_to_unuse( ) function swaps in pages and updates all the Page Tables of processes that have swapped out pages. To that end, the function visits the address spaces of all kernel threads and processes, starting with the init_mm memory descriptor that is used as a marker. It is a time-consuming function that runs mostly with the interrupts enabled. Synchronization with other processes is therefore critical.

The try_to_unuse( ) function scans the swap_map array of the swap area. When the function finds a in-use page slot, it first swaps in the page, and then starts looking for the processes that reference the page. The ordering of these two operations is crucial to avoid race conditions. While the I/O data transfer is ongoing, the page is locked, so no process can access it. Once the I/O data transfer completes, the page is locked again by try_to_unuse( ), so it cannot be swapped out again by another kernel control path. Race conditions are also avoided because each process looks up the page cache before starting a swap in or swap out operation (see the later section "The Swap Cache"). Finally, the swap area considered by try_to_unuse( ) is marked as nonwritable (SWP_WRITE flag is not set), so no process can perform a swap out on a page slot of this area.

However, try_to_unuse( ) might be forced to scan the swap_map array of usage counters of the swap area several times. This is because memory regions that contain references to swapped-out pages might disappear during one scan and later reappear in the process lists.

For instance, recall the description of the do_munmap( ) function (in the section "Releasing a Linear Address Interval" in Chapter 8): whenever a process releases an interval of linear addresses, do_munmap( ) removes from the process list all memory regions that include the affected linear addresses; later, the function reinserts the memory regions that have been only partially unmapped in the process list. do_munmap( ) takes care of freeing the swapped-out pages that belong to the interval of released linear addresses; however, it commendably doesn't free the swapped-out pages that belong to the memory regions that have to be reinserted in the process list.

Hence, try_to_unuse( ) might fail in finding a process that references a given page slot because the corresponding memory region is temporarily not included in the process list. To cope with this fact, try_to_unuse( ) keeps scanning the swap_map array until all reference counters are null. Eventually, the ghost memory regions referencing the swapped-out pages will reappear in the process lists, so try_to_unuse( ) will succeed in freeing all page slots.

Let's describe now the major operations executed by try_to_unuse( ). It executes a continuous loop on the reference counters in the swap_map array of the swap area passed as its parameter. For each reference counter, the function performs the following steps:

1. If the counter is equal to 0 (no page is stored there) or to SWAP_MAP_BAD, it continues with the next page slot.

2. Otherwise, it invokes the read_swap_cache_async( ) function (see the section "Transferring Swap Pages" later in this chapter) to swap in the page. This consists of allocating, if necessary, a new page frame, filling it with the data stored in the page slot, and putting the page in the swap cache.

3. Waits until the new page has been properly updated from disk and locks it.

4. While the function was executing the previous step, the process could have been suspended. Therefore, it checks again whether the reference counter of the page slot is null; if so, it continues with the next page slot (this swap page has been freed by another kernel control path).

5. Invokes unuse_process( ) on every memory descriptor in the doubly linked list whose head is init_mm (see the section "The Memory Descriptor" in Chapter 8). This time-consuming function scans all Page Table entries of the process that owns the memory descriptor, and replaces each occurrence of the swapped-out page identifier with the physical address of the page frame. To reflect this move, the function also decrements the page slot counter in the swap_map array (unless it is equal to SWAP_MAP_MAX) and increments the usage counter of the page frame.

6. Invokes shmem_unuse( ) to check whether the swapped-out page is used for an IPC shared memory resource and to properly handle that case (see the section "IPC Shared Memory" in Chapter 19).

7. Checks the value of the reference counter of the page. If it is equal to SWAP_MAP_MAX, the page slot is "permanent." To free it, it forces the value 1 into the reference counter.

8. The swap cache might own the page as well (it contributes to the value of the reference counter). If the page belongs to the swap cache, it invokes the rw_swap_page( ) function to flush its contents on disk (if the page is dirty), invokes delete_from_swap_cache( ) to remove the page from the swap cache, and decrements its reference counter.

9. Sets the PG_dirty flag of the page descriptor and unlocks the page.

10. Checks the need_resched field of the current process; if it is set, it invokes schedule( ) to relinquish the CPU. Deactivating a swap area is a long job, and the kernel must ensure that the other processes in the system still continue to execute. The try_to_unuse( ) function continues from this step whenever the process is selected again by the scheduler.

11. Proceeds with the next page slot. starting at Step 1.

The function continues until every reference counter in the swap_map array is null. Recall that even if the function starts examining the next page slot, the reference counter of the previous page slot could still be positive. In fact, a "ghost" process could still reference the page, typically because some memory regions have been temporarily removed from the process list scanned in Step 5. Eventually, try_to_unuse( ) catches every reference. In the meantime, however, the page is no longer in the swap cache, it is unlocked, and a copy is still included in the page slot of the swap area being deactivated.

One might expect that this situation could lead to data loss. For instance, suppose that some "ghost" process accesses the page slot and starts swapping the page in. Since the page is no longer in the swap cache, the process fills a new page frame with the data read from disk. However, this page frame would be different from the page frames owned by the processes that are supposed to share the page with the "ghost" process.

This problem does not arise when deactivating a swap area because interference from a ghost process could happen only if a swapped-out page belongs to a private anonymous memory mapping.* In this case, the page frame is handled by means of the Copy on Write mechanism described in Chapter 8, so it is perfectly legal to assign different page frames to the processes that reference the page. However, the try_to_unuse( ) function marks the page as "dirty" (Step 9); otherwise, the try_to_swap_out( ) function might later drop the page from the Page Table of some process without saving it in an another swap area (see the later section "Swapping Out Pages").

Allocating and Releasing a Page Slot

As we shall see later, when freeing memory, the kernel swaps out many pages in a short period of time. It is therefore important to try to store these pages in contiguous slots to minimize disk seek time when accessing the swap area.

A first approach to an algorithm that searches for a free slot could choose one of two simplistic, rather extreme strategies:

- Always start from the beginning of the swap area. This approach may increase the average seek time during swap-out operations because free page slots may be scattered far away from one another.

- Always start from the last allocated page slot. This approach increases the average seek time during swap-in operations if the swap area is mostly free (as is usually the case) because the handful of occupied page slots may be scattered far away from one another.

Linux adopts a hybrid approach. It always starts from the last allocated page slot unless one of these conditions occurs:

- The end of the swap area is reached

- SWAPFILE_CLUSTER (usually 256) free page slots were allocated after the last restart from the beginning of the swap area

The cluster_nr field in the swap_info_struct descriptor stores the number of free page slots allocated. This field is reset to 0 when the function restarts allocation from the beginning of the swap area. The cluster_next field stores the index of the first page slot to be examined in the next allocation.†

---

* Actually, the page might also belong to an IPC shared memory region; Chapter 19 has a discussion of this case.

† As you may have noticed, the names of Linux data structures are not always appropriate. In this case, the kernel does not really "cluster" page slots of a swap area.

To speed up the search for free page slots, the kernel keeps the lowest_bit and highest_bit fields of each swap area descriptor up to date. These fields specify the first and the last page slots that could be free; in other words, any page slot below lowest_bit and above highest_bit is known to be occupied.

The scan_swap_map() function

The scan_swap_map() function is used to find a free page slot in a given swap area. It acts on a single parameter, which points to a swap area descriptor and returns the index of a free page slot. It returns 0 if the swap area does not contain any free slots. The function performs the following steps:

1. It tries first to use the current cluster. If the cluster_nr field of the swap area descriptor is positive, it scans the swap_map array of counters starting from the element at index cluster_next and looks for a null entry. If a null entry is found, it decrements the cluster_nr field and goes to Step 4.

2. If this point is reached, either the cluster_nr field is null or the search starting from cluster_next didn't find a null entry in the swap_map array. It is time to try the second stage of the hybrid search. It reinitializes cluster_nr to SWAPFILE_CLUSTER and restarts scanning the array from the lowest_bit index that is trying to find a group of SWAPFILE_CLUSTER free page slots. If such a group is found, it goes to Step 4.

3. No group of SWAPFILE_CLUSTER free page slots exists. It restarts scanning the array from the lowest_bit index that is trying to find a single free page slot. If no null entry is found, it sets the lowest_bit field to the maximum index in the array, the highest_bit field to 0, and returns 0 (the swap area is full).

4. A null entry is found. Puts the value 1 in the entry, decrements nr_swap_pages, updates the lowest_bit and highest_bit fields if necessary, and sets the cluster_next field to the index of the page slot just allocated plus 1.

5. Returns the index of the allocated page slot.

The get_swap_page() function

The get_swap_page() function is used to find a free page slot by searching all the active swap areas. The function, which returns the index of a newly allocated page slot or 0 if all swap areas are filled, takes into consideration the different priorities of the active swap areas.

Two passes are necessary. The first pass is partial and applies only to areas that have a single priority; the function searches such areas in a round-robin fashion for a free slot. If no free page slot is found, a second pass is made starting from the beginning of the swap area list; during this second pass, all swap areas are examined. More precisely, the function performs the following steps:

1. If nr_swap_pages is null or if there are no active swap areas, returns 0.

2. Starts by considering the swap area pointed to by swap_list.next (recall that the swap area list is sorted by decreasing priorities).

3. If the swap area is active and not being deactivated, invokes scan_swap_map( ) to allocate a free page slot. If scan_swap_map( ) returns a page slot index, the function's job is essentially done, but it must prepare for its next invocation. Thus, it updates swap_list.next to point to the next swap area in the swap area list, if the latter has the same priority (thus continuing the round-robin use of these swap areas). If the next swap area does not have the same priority as the current one, the function sets swap_list.next to the first swap area in the list (so that the next search will start with the swap areas that have the highest priority). The function finishes by returning the identifier corresponding to the page slot just allocated.

4. Either the swap area is not writable, or it does not have free page slots. If the next swap area in the swap area list has the same priority as the current one, the function makes it the current one and goes to Step 3.

5. At this point, the next swap area in the swap area list has a lower priority than the previous one. The next step depends on which of the two passes the function is performing.

    a. If this is the first (partial) pass, it considers the first swap area in the list and goes to Step 3, thus starting the second pass.

    b. Otherwise, it checks if there is a next element in the list; if so, it considers it and goes to Step 3.

6. At this point the list is completely scanned by the second pass and no free page slot has been found; it returns 0.

The swap_free( ) function

The swap_free( ) function is invoked when swapping in a page to decrement the corresponding swap_map counter (see Table 16-1). When the counter reaches 0, the page slot becomes free since its identifier is no longer included in any Page Table entry. We'll see in the later section "The Swap Cache," however, that the swap cache counts as an owner of the page slot.

The function acts on a single entry parameter that specifies a swapped-out page identifier and performs the following steps:

1. Derives the swap area index and the offset page slot index from the entry parameter and gets the address of the swap area descriptor.

2. Checks whether the swap area is active and returns right away if it is not.

3. If the swap_map counter corresponding to the page slot being freed is smaller than SWAP_MAP_MAX, decrements it. Recall that entries that have the SWAP_MAP_MAX value are considered persistent (undeletable).

4. If the `swap_map` counter becomes 0, increments the value of `nr_swap_pages` and updates, if necessary, the `lowest_bit` and `highest_bit` fields of the swap area descriptor.

The Swap Cache

The swap cache is crucial to avoid race conditions among processes trying to access pages that are being swapped.

If a page is owned by a single process (or better, if the page belongs to an address space that is owned by one or more clone processes), there is just one race condition to be considered: the process attempts to address a page that is being swapped out. An array of semaphores, one per each page slot, could be used to block the process until the I/O data transfer completes.

In many cases, however, a page is owned by several processes. Again, the same array of semaphores could suffice to avoid race conditions, provided that the kernel is able to locate quickly all Page Table entries that refer to the page to be swapped out. Therefore, the kernel could ensure that either all processes see the same page frame or all of them see the swapped-out page identifier.

Unfortunately, there is no quick way in Linux 2.4 to derive from the page frame the list of processes that own it.* Scanning all Page Table entries of all processes looking for an entry with a given physical address is very costly, and it is done only in rare occasions (for instance, when deactivating a swap area).

As a result, the same page may be swapped out for some processes and present in memory for others. The kernel avoids the race conditions induced by this peculiar scenario by means of the swap cache.

Before describing how the swap cache works, let's recall when a page frame may be shared among several processes:

- The page frame is associated with a shared nonanonymous memory mapping (see the section "Memory Mapping" in Chapter 15).

- The page frame is handled by means of Copy On Write, typically because a new process has been forked or because the page frame belongs to a private memory mapping (see the section "Copy On Write" in Chapter 8).

- The page frame is allocated to an IPC shared memory resource (see the section "IPC Shared Memory" in Chapter 19) or to a shared anonymous memory mapping.

---

* One of the hot features of Linux 2.5 consists of a data structure that allows the kernel to quickly get a list of all processes that share a given page.

Of course, a page frame is also shared by several processes if they share the memory descriptor and thus the whole set of Page Tables. Recall that such processes are created by passing the CLONE_VM flag to the clone() system call (see the section "The clone(), fork(), and vfork() System Calls" in Chapter 3). All clone processes, however, count as a single process as far as the swapping algorithm is concerned. Therefore, here we use the term "processes" to mean "processes owning different memory descriptors."

As we shall see later in this chapter, page frames used for shared nonanonymous memory mappings are never swapped out. Instead, they are handled by another kernel function that writes their data to the proper files and discards them. However, the other two kinds of shared page frames must be carefully handled by the swapping algorithm by means of the swap cache.

The swap cache collects shared page frames that have been copied to swap areas. It does not exist as a data structure on its own; instead, the pages in the regular page cache are considered to be in the swap cache if certain fields are set.

Shared page swapping works in the following manner: consider a page P that is shared among two processes, A and B. Suppose that the swapping algorithm scans the page frames of process A and selects P for swapping out: it allocates a new page slot and copies the data stored in P into the new page slot. It then puts the swapped-out page identifier in the corresponding Page Table entry of process A. Finally, it invokes __free_page() to release the page frame. However, the page's usage counter does not become 0 since P is still owned by B. Thus, the swapping algorithm succeeds in transferring the page into the swap area, but fails to reclaim the corresponding page frame.

Suppose now that the swapping algorithm scans the page frames of process B at a later time and selects P for swapping out. The kernel must recognize that P has already been transferred into a swap area so the page won't be swapped out a second time. Moreover, it must be able to derive the swapped-out page identifier so it can increase the page slot usage counter.

Figure 16-3 illustrates schematically the actions performed by the kernel on a shared page that is swapped out from multiple processes at different times. The numbers inside the swap area and inside P represent the page slot usage counter and the page usage counter, respectively. Notice that each usage count includes every process that is using the page or page slot, plus the swap cache if the page is included in it. Four stages are shown:

1. In (a), P is present in the Page Tables of both A and B.
2. In (b), P has been swapped out from A's address space.
3. In (c), P has been swapped out from both the address spaces of A and B, but is still included in the swap cache.
4. Finally, in (d), P has been released to the buddy system.

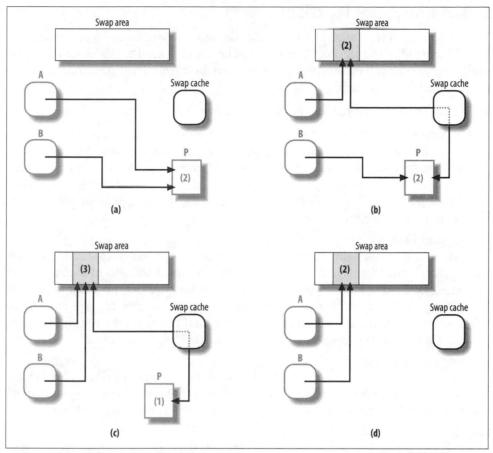

Figure 16-3. The role of the swap cache

The swap cache is implemented by the page cache data structures and procedures, which are described in the section "The Page Cache" in Chapter 14. Recall that the core of the page cache is a hash table that allows the algorithm to quickly derive the address of a page descriptor from the address of an address_space object identifying the owner of the page as well as from an offset value.

Pages in the swap cache are stored like any other page in the page cache, with the following special treatment:

- The mapping field of the page descriptor points to an address_space object stored in the swapper_space variable.
- The index field stores the swapped-out page identifier associated with the page.

Moreover, when the page is put in the swap cache, both the count field of the page descriptor and the page slot usage counters are incremented, since the swap cache uses both the page frame and the page slot.

Swap Cache Helper Functions

The kernel uses several functions to handle the swap cache; they are based mainly on those discussed in the section "The Page Cache" in Chapter 14. We show later how these relatively low-level functions are invoked by higher-level functions to swap pages in and out as needed.

The main functions that handle the swap cache are:

lookup_swap_cache( )

Finds a page in the swap cache through its swapped-out page identifier passed as a parameter and returns the page address. It returns 0 if the page is not present in the cache. It invokes find_get_page( ), passing as parameters the address of the swapper_space page address space object and the swapped-out page identifier to find the required page.

add_to_swap_cache( )

Inserts a page into the swap cache. It essentially invokes swap_duplicate() to check whether the page slot passed as a parameter is valid and to increment the page slot usage counter; find_get_page() to make sure that no other page with the same address_space object and offset already exists; add_to_page_cache() to insert the page into the cache; and lru_cache_add() to insert the page in the inactive list (see the later section "The Least Recently Used (LRU) Lists").

delete_from_swap_cache( )

Removes a page from the swap cache by flushing its content to disk, clearing the PG_dirty flag, and invoking remove_page_from_inode_queue( ) and remove_page_from_hash_queue( ) (see the section "Page Cache Data Structures" in Chapter 14).

free_page_and_swap_cache( )

Releases a page by invoking __free_page( ). If the caller is the only process that owns the page, this function also removes the page from the active or inactive list (see the later section "The Least Recently Used (LRU) Lists"), removes the page from the swap cache by invoking delete_from_swap_cache(), and frees the page slot on the swap area by flushing the page contents to disk and invoking swap_free( ).

Transferring Swap Pages

Transferring swap pages wouldn't be so complicated if there weren't so many race conditions and other potential hazards to guard against. Here are some of the things that have to be checked regularly:

- The process that owns a page may terminate while the page is being swapped in or out.

- Another process may be in the middle of swapping in a page that the current one is trying to swap out (or vice versa).

Like any other disk access type, I/O data transfers for swap pages are blocking operations. Therefore, the kernel must take care to avoid simultaneous transfers involving the same page frame, the same page slot, or both.

Race conditions can be avoided on the page frame through the mechanisms discussed in Chapter 13. Specifically, before starting an I/O operation on the page frame, the kernel waits until its PG_locked flag is off. When the function returns, the page frame lock has been acquired, and therefore no other kernel control path can access the page frame's contents during the I/O operation.

But the state of the page slot must also be tracked. The PG_locked flag of the page descriptor is used once again to ensure exclusive access to the page slot involved in the I/O data transfer. Before starting an I/O operation on a swap page, the kernel checks that the page frame involved is included in the swap cache; if not, it adds the page frame into the swap cache. Let's suppose some process tries to swap in a page while the same page is currently being transferred. Before doing any work related to the swap in, the kernel looks in the swap cache for a page frame associated with the given swapped-out page identifier. Since the page frame is found, the kernel knows that it must not allocate a new page frame, but must simply use the cached page frame. Moreover, since the PG_locked flag is set, the kernel suspends the kernel control path until the bit becomes 0, so that both the page frame's contents and the page slot in the swap area are preserved until the I/O operation terminates.

In short, thanks to the swap cache, the PG_locked flag of the page frame also acts as a lock for the page slot in the swap area.

The rw_swap_page( ) Function

The rw_swap_page( ) function is used to swap in or swap out a page. It receives the following parameters:

rw

> A flag specifying the direction of data transfer: READ for swapping in, WRITE for swapping out.

page

> The address of a descriptor of a page in the swap cache.

Before invoking the function, the caller must ensure that the page is included in the swap cache and lock the page to prevent race conditions due to concurrent accesses to the page frame or to the page slot in the swap area, as described in the previous section. To be on the safe side, the rw_swap_page( ) function checks that these two conditions effectively hold, and then gets the swapped-out page identifier from page->index and invokes the rw_swap_page_base( ) function, passing to it the page identifier, the page descriptor address page, and the direction flag rw.

The rw_swap_page_base( ) function is the core of the swapping algorithm; it performs the following steps:

1. If the data transfer is for a swap-in operation (rw set to READ), it clears the PG_ uptodate flag of the page frame. The flag is set again only if the swap-in operation terminates successfully.

2. Gets the proper swap area descriptor and the slot index from the swapped-out page identifier.

3. If the swap area is a disk partition, gets the corresponding block device number from the swap_device field of the swap area descriptor. In this case, the slot index also represents the logical block number of the requested data because the block size of any swap disk partition is always equal to the page size (PAGE_SIZE).

4. Otherwise, if the swap area is a regular file, it executes the following substeps:

   a. Gets the number of the block device that stores the file from the i_dev field of its inode object (the swap_files->d_inode field in the swap area descriptor).

   b. Gets the block size of the device (the i_sb->s_blocksize field of the inode).

   c. Computes the file block number corresponding to the given slot index.

   d. Fills a local array with the logical block numbers of the blocks in the page slot; every logical block number is obtained by invoking the bmap method of the address_space object whose address is stored in the i_mapping field of the inode. If the bmap method fails, rw_swap_page_base( ) returns 0 (failure).

5. Invokes the brw_page( ) function to start a page I/O operation on the block (or blocks) identified in the previous steps and returns 1 (success).

Since the page I/O operation activated by brw_page( ) is asynchronous, the rw_swap_ page( ) function might terminate before the actual I/O data transfer completes. However, as described in the section "Page I/O operations" in Chapter 13, the kernel eventually executes the end_buffer_io_async( ) function (which verifies that all data transfers successfully completed), unlocks the page, and sets its PG_uptodate flag.

The read_swap_cache_async( ) Function

The read_swap_cache_async( ) function, which receives as a parameter a swapped-out page identifier, is invoked whenever the kernel must swap in a page. As we know, before accessing the swap partition, the function must check whether the swap cache already includes the desired page frame. Therefore, the function essentially executes the following operations:

1. Invokes find_get_page( ) to search for the page in the swap cache. If the page is found, it returns the address of its descriptor.

2. The page is not included in the swap cache. Invokes alloc_page( ) to allocate a new page frame. If no free page frame is available, it returns 0 (indicating the system is out of memory).

3. Invokes add_to_swap_cache( ) to insert the new page frame into the swap cache. As mentioned in the earlier section "Swap Cache Helper Functions," this function also locks the page.

4. The previous step might fail if add_to_swap_cache( ) finds a duplicate of the page in the swap cache. For instance, the process could block in Step 2, thus allowing another process to start a swap-in operation on the same page slot. In this case, the function releases the page frame allocated in Step 3 and restarts from Step 1.

5. Otherwise, the new page frame is inserted into the swap cache. Invokes rw_swap_page( ) to read the page's contents from the swap area, passing the READ parameter and the page descriptor to that function.

6. Returns the address of the page descriptor.

The rw_swap_page_nolock( ) Function

There is just one case in which the kernel wants to read a page from a swap area without putting it in the swap cache. This happens when servicing the swapon( ) system call: the kernel reads the first page of a swap area, which contains the swap_header union, and then immediately discards the page frame. Since the kernel is activating the swap area, no process can swap in or swap out a page on it, so there is no need to protect the access to the page slot.

The rw_swap_page_nolock( ) function receives as parameters the type of I/O operation (READ or WRITE), a swapped-out page identifier, and the address of a page frame (already locked). It performs the following operations:

1. Gets the page descriptor of the page frame passed as a parameter.

2. Initializes the swapping field of the page descriptor with the address of the swapper_space object; this is done because the sync_page method is executed in Step 4.

3. Invokes rw_swap_page_base( ) to start the I/O swap operation.

4. Waits until the I/O data transfer completes by invoking wait_on_page( ).

5. Unlocks the page.

6. Sets the mapping field of the page descriptor to NULL and returns.

Swapping Out Pages

The later section "Reclaiming Page Frame" explains what happens when pages are swapped out. As we indicated at the beginning of this chapter, swapping out pages is a last resort and appears as part of a general strategy to free memory that uses other tactics as well. In this section, we show how the kernel performs a swap out. This is achieved by a series of functions called in cascading fashion. Let's start with the functions at the higher level.

The swap_out() function acts on a single classzone parameter that specifies the memory zone from which pages should be swapped out (see the section "Memory Zones" in Chapter 7). Two other parameters, priority and gfp_mask, are not used.

The swap_out() function scans existing memory descriptors and tries to swap out the pages referenced in each process's Page Tables. It terminates as soon as one of the following conditions occurs:

- The function succeeds in releasing SWAP_CLUSTER_MAX page frames (by default, 32). A page frame is considered released when it is removed from the Page Tables of all processes that share it.

- The function scans *n* memory descriptors, where *n* is the length of the memory descriptor list when the function starts.*

To ensure that all processes are evenly penalized by swap_out(), the function starts scanning the list from the memory descriptor that was last analyzed in the previous invocation; the address of this memory descriptor is stored in the swap_mm global variable.

For each memory descriptor mm to be considered, the swap_out() function increments the usage counter mm->mm_users, thus ensuring that the memory descriptor cannot disappear from the list while the swapping algorithm is working on it. Then, swap_out() invokes the swap_out_mm() function, passing to it the memory descriptor address mm, the memory zone classzone, and the number of page frames still to be released. Once swap_out_mm() returns, swap_out() decrements the usage counter mm->mm_users, and then decides whether it should analyze the next memory descriptor in the list or just terminate.

swap_out_mm() returns the number of pages of the process that owns the memory descriptor that the function has released. The swap_out() function uses this value to update a counter of how many pages have been released since the beginning of its execution; if the counter reaches the value SWAP_CLUSTER_MAX, swap_out() terminates.

The swap_out_mm() function scans the memory regions of the process that owns the memory descriptor mm passed as a parameter. Usually, the function starts analyzing the first memory region object in the mm->mmap list (remember that they are ordered by starting linear addresses). However, if mm is the memory descriptor that was analyzed last in the previous invocation of swap_out(), swap_out_mm() does not restart from the first memory region, but from the memory region that includes the linear address last analyzed in the previous invocation. This linear address is stored in the swap_address field of the memory descriptor; if all memory regions of the process have been analyzed, then the field stores the conventional value TASK_SIZE.

---

* The swap_out() function can block, so memory descriptors might appear and disappear on the list during a single invocation of the function.

For each memory region of the process that owns the memory descriptor mm, swap_out_mm( ) invokes the swap_out_vma( ) function, passing to it the number of pages yet to be released, the first linear address to analyze, the memory region object, and the memory descriptor. Again, swap_out_vma( ) returns the number of released pages belonging to the memory region. The loop of swap_out_mm( ) continues until either the requested number of pages is released or all memory regions are considered.

The swap_out_vma( ) function checks that the memory region is swappable (e.g., the flag VM_RESERVED is cleared). It then starts a sequence in which it considers all entries in the process's Page Global Directory that refer to linear addresses in the memory region. For each such entry, the function invokes the swap_out_pgd( ) function, which in turn considers all entries in a Page Middle Directory corresponding to address intervals in the memory region. For each such entry, swap_out_pgd( ) invokes the swap_out_pmd( ) function, which considers all entries in a Page Table referencing pages in the memory region. Also, swap_out_pmd( ) invokes the try_to_swap_out( ) function, which finally attempts to swap out the page. As usual, this chain of function invocations breaks as soon as the requested number of released page frames is reached.

The try_to_swap_out( ) Function

The try_to_swap_out( ) function attempts to free a given page frame, either discarding or swapping out its contents. The function returns the value 1 if it succeeds in releasing the page, and 0 otherwise. Remember that by "releasing the page," we mean that the references to the page frame are removed from the Page Tables of all processes that share the page. In this case, however, the page frame is not necessarily released to the buddy system; for instance, it could be referenced by the swap cache.

The parameters of the function are:

mm
    Memory descriptor address

vma
    Memory region object address

address
    Initial linear address of the page

page_table
    Address of the Page Table entry that maps address

page
    Page descriptor address

classzone
    The memory zone from which pages should be swapped out

The try_to_swap_out() function uses the Accessed and Dirty flags included in the Page Table entry. We stated in the section "Regular Paging" in Chapter 2 that the Accessed flag is automatically set by the CPU's paging unit at every read or write access, while the Dirty flag is automatically set at every write access. These two flags offer a limited degree of hardware support that allows the kernel to use a primitive LRU replacement algorithm.

try_to_swap_out() must recognize many different situations demanding different responses, but the responses all share many of the same basic operations. In particular, the function performs the following steps:

1. Checks the Accessed flag of the page_table entry. If it is set, the page must be considered "young"; in this case, the function clears the flag, invokes mark_page_accessed() (see the section "The Least Recently Used (LRU) Lists" later in this chapter), and returns 0. This check ensures that a page can be swapped out only if it was not accessed since the previous invocation of try_to_swap_out() on it.

2. If the memory region is locked (VM_LOCKED flag set), invokes mark_page_accessed() on it, and returns 0.

3. If the PG_active flag in the page->flags field is set, the page is considered actively used and shouldn't be swapped out; the function returns 0.

4. If the page does not belong to the memory zone specified by the classzone parameter, returns 0.

5. Tries to lock the page; if it is already locked (PG_locked flag set), it is not possible to swap out the page because it is involved in an I/O data transfer; the function returns 0.

6. At this point, the function knows that the page can be swapped out. Forces the value zero into the Page Table entry addressed by page_table and invokes flush_tlb_page() to invalidate the corresponding TLB entries.

7. If the Dirty flag in the Page Table entry was set, invokes the set_page_dirty() function to set the PG_dirty flag in the page descriptor. Moreover, this function moves the page in the dirty_pages list of the address_space object referenced by page->mapping, if any, and marks the inode page->mapping->host as dirty (see the section "The lists of page descriptors in the address_space object" in Chapter 14).

8. If the page belongs to the swap cache, it performs the following substeps:

   a. Gets the swapped-out page identifier from page->index.

   b. Invokes swap_duplicate() to verify whether the page slot index is valid and to increment the corresponding usage counter in swap_map.

   c. Stores the swapped-out page identifier in the Page Table entry addressed by page_table.

   d. Decrements the rss field of the memory descriptor mm.

e. Unlocks the page.

f. Decrements the page usage counter page->count.

g. If the page is no longer referenced by any process, it returns 1; otherwise, it returns 0.*

Notice that the function does not have to allocate a new page slot, because the page frame has already been swapped out when scanning the Page Tables of some other process.

9. The page is not inserted into the swap cache. Checks whether the page belongs to an address_space object (the page->mapping field is not null); in this case, the page belongs to a shared file memory mapping, so the function jumps to Step 8d to release the page frame, leaving the corresponding Page Table entry null.

   Notice that the page frame reference of the process is released even if the page is not saved into a swap area. This is because the page has an image on disk, and the function has already triggered, if necessary, the update of this image in Step 7. Moreover, notice also that the page frame is not released to the buddy system because the page is still owned by the page cache (see the section "Page descriptor fields related to the page cache" in Chapter 14).

10. If the function reaches this point, the page is not inserted into the swap cache, and it does not belong to an address_space object. The function checks the status of the PG_dirty flag; if it is cleared, the function jumps to Step 8d to release the page frame, leaving the corresponding Page Table entry null.

    There is no need to save the page contents on a swap area because the process never wrote into the page frame. The kernel recognizes this case because the PG_dirty flag is cleared, and this flag is never reset if the page has no image on disk or if it belongs to a private memory mapping. When the process accesses the same page again, the kernel handles the Page Fault through the demand paging technique (see the section "Demand Paging" in Chapter 8); then the new page frame is filled with exactly the same data as that stored in this released page frame.

11. If the function reaches this point, the page is not inserted into the swap cache, it does not have an image on disk, and it is dirty; here the function checks whether the page contains buffers (it is a buffer page, its page->buffers field is not null). In this case, the function restores the original contents of the Page Table entry, unlocks the page, and returns 0.

    How could the page host some buffers if the page doesn't belong to an address_space object—that is, it has no image on disk? Actually, this might occur in rare circumstances—for instance, if the page maps a portion of a file that has just been truncated. In these cases, try_to_swapout( ) does nothing.

---

* The check is easily done by looking at the value of the page->count usage counter. Of course, the function must consider that the counter is incremented when the page is inserted into the swap cache (or the page cache), and when there are buffers allocated on the page (i.e., when the page->buffers field is not null).

12. At this point, the page is not inserted into the swap cache, it does not have an image on disk, and it is dirty; the function must definitively swap it out in a new page slot. It invokes the get_swap_page( ) function to allocate a free page slot in an active swap area. If there are none, it restores the original content of the Page Table entry, unlocks the page, and returns 0.

13. Invokes add_to_swap_cache( ) to insert the page in the swap cache. The function might fail if another kernel control path is trying to swap in the page. As we shall see in the next section, this can happen even if the page slot is not referenced by any process. In this case, it invokes swap_free( ) to release the page slot and restarts from Step 12.

14. Sets the PG_uptodate flag of the page.

15. Invokes the set_page_dirty( ) function again (see Step 7 above) because add_to_swap_cache( ) resets the PG_dirty flag.

16. Jumps to Step 8c to store the swapped-out page identifier in the Page Table entry and to release the page frame.

The try_to_swap_out( ) function does not directly invoke rw_swap_page( ) to trigger the activation of the I/O data transfer. Rather, the function limits itself to inserting the page in the swap cache, if necessary, and to marking the page as dirty. However, we'll see in the later section "The shrink_caches() Function" that the kernel periodically flushes the disk caches to disk by invoking the writepage methods of the address_space objects that own the dirty pages.

As mentioned in the earlier section "The Swap Cache," the address_space object of the pages that belong to the swap cache is a special object stored in swapper_space. Its writepage method is implemented by the swap_writepage( ) function, which executes the following steps:

1. Checks whether the page is not included in the Page Tables of any process; in this case, it removes the page from the swap cache and releases the swap page slot.

2. Otherwise, it invokes rw_swap_page( ) on the page, specifying the WRITE command (see the earlier section "The rw_swap_page( ) Function").

Swapping in Pages

Swap in must take place when a process attempts to address a page within its address space that has been swapped out to disk. The Page Fault exception handler triggers a swap-in operation when the following conditions occur (see the section "Handling a Faulty Address Inside the Address Space" in Chapter 8):

• The page including the address that caused the exception is a valid one—that is, it belongs to a memory region of the current process.

• The page is not present in memory—that is, the Present flag in the Page Table entry is cleared.

- The Page Table entry associated with the page is not null, which means it contains a swapped-out page identifier.

As described in the section "Demand Paging" in Chapter 8, the handle_pte_fault( ) function, invoked by the do_page_fault( ) exception handler, checks whether the Page Table entry is non-null. If so, it invokes a quite handy do_swap_page( ) function to swap in the page required.

The do_swap_page( ) Function

This do_swap_page( ) function acts on the following parameters:

mm
   Memory descriptor address of the process that caused the Page Fault exception

vma
   Memory region descriptor address of the region that includes address

address
   Linear address that causes the exception

page_table
   Address of the Page Table entry that maps address

orig_pte
   Content of the Page Table entry that maps address

write_access
   Flag denoting whether the attempted access was a read or a write

Contrary to other functions, do_swap_page( ) never returns 0. It returns 1 if the page is already in the swap cache (minor fault), 2 if the page was read from the swap area (major fault), and −1 if an error occurred while performing the swap in. It essentially executes the following steps:

1. Releases the page_table_lock spin lock of the memory descriptor (it was acquired by the caller function handle_pte_fault( )).

2. Gets the swapped-out page identifier from orig_pte.

3. Invokes lookup_swap_cache( ) to check whether the swap cache already contains a page corresponding to the swapped-out page identifier; if the page is already in the swap cache, it jumps to Step 6.

4. Invokes the swapin_readahead( ) function to read from the swap area a group of at most 2^n pages, including the requested one. The value n is stored in the page_cluster variable, and is usually equal to 3.* Each page is read by invoking the read_swap_cache_async( ) function.

---

* The system administrator may tune this value by writing into the */proc/sys/vm/page_cluster* file. Swap-in read-ahead can be disabled by setting page_cluster to 0.

5. Invokes `read_swap_cache_async()` once more to swap in precisely the page accessed by the process that caused the Page Fault. This step might appear redundant, but it isn't really. The `swapin_readahead()` function might fail in reading the requested page—for instance, because `page_cluster` is set to 0 or the function tried to read a group of pages including a defective page slot (`SWAP_MAP_BAD`). On the other hand, if `swapin_readahead()` succeeded, this invocation of `read_swap_cache_async()` terminates quickly because it finds the page in the swap cache.

6. If, despite all efforts, the requested page was not added to the swap cache, another kernel control path might have already swapped in the requested page on behalf of a clone of this process. This case is checked by temporarily acquiring the `page_table_lock` spin lock and comparing the entry to which `page_table` points with `orig_pte`. If they differ, the page has already been swapped in by some other kernel thread, so the function returns 1 (minor fault); otherwise, it returns −1 (failure).

7. At this point, we know that the page is in the swap cache. Invokes `mark_page_accessed()` (see the later section "The Least Recently Used (LRU) Lists") and locks the page.

8. Acquires the `page_table_lock` spin lock.

9. Checks whether another kernel control path has swapped in the requested page on behalf of a clone of this process. In this case, releases the `page_table_lock` spin lock, unlocks the page, and returns 1 (minor fault).

10. Invokes `swap_free()` to decrement the usage counter of the page slot corresponding to `entry`.

11. Checks whether the swap cache is at least 50 percent full (`nr_swap_pages` is smaller than a half of `total_swap_pages`). If so, checks whether the page is owned only by the process that caused the fault (or one of its clones); if this is the case, removes the page from the swap cache.

12. Increments the `rss` field of the process's memory descriptor.

13. Unlocks the page.

14. Updates the Page Table entry so the process can find the page. The function accomplishes this by writing the physical address of the requested page and the protection bits found in the `vm_page_prot` field of the memory region into the Page Table entry addressed by `page_table`. Moreover, if the access that caused the fault was a write and the faulting process is the unique owner of the page, the function also sets the `Dirty` flag and the `Read/Write` flag to prevent a useless Copy on Write fault.

15. Releases the `mm->page_table_lock` spin lock and returns 1 (minor fault) or 2 (major fault).

Reclaiming Page Frame

The virtual memory subsystem of Linux is, without any doubt, the most complex and performance-critical component of the whole kernel.

In previous chapters, we explained how the kernel handles dynamic memory by keeping track of free and busy page frames. We have also discussed how every process in User Mode has its own linear address space so that page frames can be assigned to the process at the very last possible moment. Finally, we have also described how dynamic memory is used to cache the data of the slow block devices.

In this chapter, we complete our description of the virtual memory subsystem by discussing *page frame reclaiming*. As we saw in Chapter 14, the cache systems grab more and more page frames but never release any of them. This is reasonable because cache systems don't know if and when processes will reuse some of the cached data and are therefore unable to identify the portions of cache that should be released. Moreover, thanks to the demand paging mechanism described in Chapter 8, User Mode processes get page frames as long as they proceed with their execution; however, demand paging has no way to force processes to release the page frames whenever they are no longer used. Page frame reclaiming is a remedy for this problem.

The kernel developers' worst nightmare is to encounter a situation in which no free page frame exists. When this happens, the kernel might be easily trapped in a deadly chain of memory requests—to free a page frame, the kernel must write its data to disk. However, to accomplish this operation, the kernel requires another page frame (for instance, to allocate the buffer heads for the I/O data transfer). Since no free page frame exists, no page frame can be freed. In this situation, there is just one solution: kill a victim User Mode process to reclaim the page frames it was using. Of course, even if this solution avoids a system crash, it is not very satisfying for the end users.

The goal of page frame reclaiming is to conserve a minimal pool of free page frames so that the kernel may safely recover from "low on memory" conditions. To do this, it must neither trash the disk caches nor penalize User Mode processes too much, otherwise system performances will be greatly reduced. As a matter of fact, the hardest job of a developer working on the virtual memory subsystem consists of finding an algorithm that ensures acceptable performances both to desktop machines (on which memory requests are quite limited) and to high-level machines like large database servers (on which memory requests tend to be huge).

Unfortunately, finding a good page frame reclaiming algorithm is a rather empirical job, with very little support from theory. The situation is somewhat similar to evaluating the factors that determine the dynamic priority of a process: the main objective is to tune the parameters that achieve good system performance, without asking too many questions about why it works well. Often, it's just a matter of "let's try this approach and see what happens..." An unpleasant side effect of this empirical approach is the code changes quickly, even in the even-numbered versions of Linux, which are supposed to be stable. The description that follows refers to Linux 2.4.18.

Outline of the Page Frame Reclaiming Algorithm

Before plunging into details, let's give a brief overview of Linux page frame reclaiming. (Looking too close to the trees' leaves might lead us to miss the whole forest!)

Page frames can be freed in two ways:

- By reclaiming an unused page frame within a cache (either a memory cache or a disk cache)
- By reclaiming a page that belongs to a memory region of a process or to an IPC shared memory region (see the section "IPC Shared Memory" in Chapter 19)

Of course, the algorithm should take into consideration the various different kinds of page frames. For instance, it is preferable to reclaim page frames from a memory cache rather than from a disk cache because the latter pages include precious data obtained by costly accesses to block disk devices.

Moreover, the algorithm should keep track of the number of accesses to every page frame. If a page has not been accessed for a long time, the probability that it will be accessed in the near future is low; on the other hand, if a page has been accessed recently, the probability that it will continue to be accessed is high. This is just another application of the locality principle mentioned in the section "Hardware Cache" in Chapter 2.

Therefore, the page frame reclaiming algorithm is a blend of several heuristics:

- Careful selection of the order in which caches are examined
- Ordering of pages based on ageing (least recently used pages should be freed before pages accessed recently)
- Distinction of pages based on the page state (for example, nondirty pages are better candidates than dirty pages for swapping out because they don't have to be written to disk)

The main function that triggers page frame reclaiming is try_to_free_pages(). It is invoked every time the kernel fails in allocating memory. For instance:

- When the grow_buffers() function fails to allocate a new buffer page, or the create_buffers() function fails to allocate the buffer heads for a buffer page (see the sections "Buffer Pages" and "The getblk() Function" in Chapter 14). In these cases, the kernel executes free_more_memory(), which in turn invokes try_to_free_pages().
- When the pages_alloc() function fails in allocating a group of page frames in a given list of memory zones (see the section "The Buddy System Algorithm" in

Chapter 7). Recall that every memory zone descriptor includes the pages_min watermark, which specifies the number of page frames that should remain free to cope with the "low on memory" emergencies. If no zone in the list has enough free memory to satisfy the request while preserving the minimal pool of free page frames, the kernel invokes the balance_classzone() function, which in turn invokes try_to_free_pages().

- When the *kswapd* kernel thread discovers that the number of free page frames in some memory zone falls below the pages_low watermark (see the later section "The kswapd Kernel Thread").

The core of the try_to_free_pages() function is the shrink_caches() function: it receives as a parameter a "goal"—namely, a given number of page frames to be reclaimed—and it terminates as soon as it has reached the goal, if possible.

To help shrink_caches() do its job, all pages in dynamic memory are grouped into two lists called the "active list" and the "inactive list"; they are also collectively denoted as *LRU lists*. The former list tends to include the pages that have been accessed recently, while the latter tends to include the pages that have not been accessed for some time. Clearly, pages should be stolen from the inactive list, although some percolation between the two lists is performed from time to time.

The shrink_caches() function invokes, in turn, the following functions:

kmem_cache_reap()
:   Removes empty slabs from the slab cache

refill_inactive()
:   Moves pages from the active list to the inactive list, and vice versa.

shrink_cache()
:   Tries to free page frames by writing to disk inactive pages included in the page cache.

shrink_dcache_memory()
:   Removes entries from the dentry cache

shrink_icache_memory()
:   Removes entries from the inode cache

Let's now discuss in greater detail the various components of the page frame reclaiming algorithm.

The Least Recently Used (LRU) Lists

The *active list* and the *inactive list* of pages are the core data structures of the page frame reclaiming algorithm. The heads of these two doubly linked lists are stored, respectively, in the active_list and inactive_list variables. The nr_active_pages and nr_inactive_pages variables store the number of pages in the two lists. The pagemap_lru_lock spin lock protects the two lists against concurrent accesses in SMP systems.

If a page belongs to an LRU list, its PG_lru flag in the page descriptor is set. Moreover, if the page belongs to the active list, the PG_active flag is set, while if it belongs to the inactive list, the PG_active flag is cleared. The lru field of the page descriptor stores the pointers to the next and previous elements in the LRU list.

Several auxiliary functions and macros are available to handle the LRU lists:

add_page_to_active_list
> Sets the PG_active flag, adds the page to the head of the active list, and increases nr_active_pages.

add_page_to_inactive_list
> Adds the page to the head of the inactive list and increases nr_inactive_pages.

del_page_from_active_list
> Removes the page from the active list, clears the PG_active flag, and decreases nr_active_pages.

del_page_from_inactive_list
> Removes the page from the inactive list and decreases nr_inactive_pages.

activate_page_nolock() *and* activate_page()
> If the page is in the inactive list, moves it in the active list by executing del_page_from_inactive_list and then add_page_to_active_list. The activate_page() function also acquires the pagemap_lru_lock spin lock before moving the page.

lru_cache_add()
> If the page is not included in a LRU list, sets the PG_lru flag, acquires the pagemap_lru_lock spin lock, and executes add_page_to_inactive_list to insert the page in the inactive list.

__lru_cache_del() *and* lru_cache_del()
> If the page is included in a LRU list, clears the PG_lru flag and executes either del_page_from_active_list or del_page_from_inactive_list, according to the value of the PG_active flag. The lru_cache_del() function also acquires the pagemap_lru_lock spin lock before removing the page.

Moving pages across the LRU lists

The kernel collects the pages that were recently accessed in the active list so that it will not scan them when looking for a page frame to reclaim. Conversely, the kernel collects the pages that have not been accessed for a long time in the inactive list. Of course, pages should move from the inactive list to the active list and back, according to whether they are being accessed.

Clearly, two page states ("active" and "inactive") are not sufficient to describe all possible access patterns. For instance, suppose a logger process writes some data in a page once every hour. Although the page is "inactive" for most of the time, the access makes it "active," thus denying the reclaiming of the corresponding page frame, even if it is not going to be accessed for an entire hour. Of course, there is no general solution to this problem because the kernel has no way to predict the behavior of User Mode processes; however, it seems reasonable that pages should not change their status on every single access.

The PG_referenced flag in the page descriptor is used to double the number of accesses required to move a page from the inactive list to the active list; it is also used to double the number of "missing accesses" required to move a page from the active list to the inactive list (see below). For instance, suppose that a page in the inactive list has the PG_referenced flag set to 0. The first page access sets the value of the flag to 1, but the page remains in the inactive list. The second page access finds the flag set and causes the page to be moved in the active list. If, however, the second access does not occur within a given time interval after the first one, the page frame reclaiming algorithm may reset the PG_referenced flag.

As shown in Figure 16-4, the kernel uses the mark_page_accessed() and refill_inactive() functions to move the pages across the LRU lists. In the figure, the LRU list including the page is specified by the status of the PG_active flag.

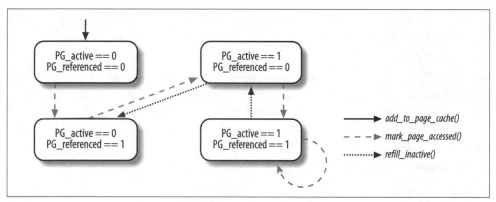

Figure 16-4. Moving pages across the LRU lists

Whenever the kernel must mark a page as accessed, it invokes the mark_page_accessed() function. This happens every time the kernel determines that a page is being referenced either by a User Mode process, a filesystem layer, or a device driver. For instance, mark_page_accessed() is invoked in the following cases:

- When loading an anonymous page of a process on demand (performed by the do_anonymous_page() function in the section "Demand Paging" in Chapter 8).

- When reading a block from disk (performed by the bread() function in the section "Block and Page I/O Operations" in Chapter 13).

- When loading on demand a page of a memory mapped file (performed by the filemap_nopage() function in the section "Demand Paging for Memory Mapping" in Chapter 15).

- When reading a page of data from a file (performed by the do_generic_file_ read() function in the section "Reading from a File" in Chapter 15).

- When swapping in a page (see the earlier section "The do_swap_page() Function").

- When the kernel finds the Accessed flag set in the Page Table entry while searching for a page to be swapped out (see the earlier section "The try_to_swap_out() Function").

- When the kernel reads a page of data from a disk device (performed by the ext2_ get_page() function in Chapter 17).

The mark_page_accessed() function executes the following code fragment:

```
if (PageActive(page) || !PageReferenced(page))
    SetPageReferenced(page);
else {
    activate_page(page);
    ClearPageReferenced(page);
}
```

As shown in Figure 16-4, the function moves the page from the inactive list to the active list only if the PG_referenced flag is set before the invocation.

The kernel periodically checks the status of the pages in the active list by executing the refill_inactive() function. Starting from the bottom of the active list (the older pages in the list), the function checks whether the PG_referenced flag of each page is set. If it is, the function clears the flag and moves the page into the first position of the active list; if it isn't, the function moves the page into the first position of the inactive list. The logic in the function is as follows:

```
if (PageReferenced(page)) {
    ClearPageReferenced(page);
    list_del(&page->lru);
    list_add(&page->lru, &active_list);
} else {
    del_page_from_active_list(page);
    add_page_to_inactive_list(page);
    SetPageReferenced(page);
}
```

The refill_inactive() function does not scan the pages in the inactive list; hence, the PG_referenced flag of a page is never cleared as long as the page remains in the inactive list.

The try_to_free_pages( ) Function

The try_to_free_pages() function is the main function that triggers the reclaiming of page frames. It receives as parameters:

classzone
    The memory zone containing the page frames to be reclaimed

gfp_mask

A set of flags whose meaning is exactly the same as the corresponding parameter of the alloc_pages() function (see the section "Requesting and Releasing Page Frames" in Chapter 7)

order

Not used

The goal of the function is to free SWAP_CLUSTER_MAX page frames (usually, 32) by repeatedly invoking the shrink_caches() function, each time with a higher priority than the previous invocation. The try_to_free_pages() function is thus essentially equivalent to the following code fragment:

```
int priority = DEF_PRIORITY;
int nr_pages = SWAP_CLUSTER_MAX;

if (current->flags & PF_NOIO)
    gfp_mask &= ~(__GFP_IO | __GFP_HIGHIO | __GFP_FS);

do {
    nr_pages = shrink_caches(classzone, priority, gfp_mask, nr_pages);
    if (nr_pages <= 0)
        return 1;
} while (--priority);
out_of_memory();
```

try_to_free_pages() clears the __GFP_IO, __GFP_HIGHIO, and __GFP_FS bits in the gfp_mask parameter if the current process has the PF_NOIO flag set. This flag is set whenever the kernel must ensure that the page frame reclaiming algorithm never triggers I/O data transfers; it is currently used only by kernel threads of the *loop* device driver, which allows User Mode processes to handle regular files as if they were disk block partitions.

The loop is repeated at most DEF_PRIORITY times (usually six times). The value of the decreasing priority loop index is passed to the shrink_caches() function. Each time shrink_caches() tries harder to reclaim a page frame because lower values correspond to higher priorities.

If DEF_PRIORITY iterations are not enough to reclaim SWAP_CLUSTER_MAX page frames, the kernel is in serious trouble. It has just one last resort: killing a User Mode process to free all its page frames. This operation is performed by the out_of_memory() function. Loosely speaking, the victim process is selected from those that have the smallest runtimes, ruling out those that have superuser privileges and those that perform direct I/O operations (see the section "Direct I/O Transfers" in Chapter 15).

The shrink_caches() Function

The shrink_caches() function invokes several auxiliary functions in a fixed order to reclaim page frames in different memory subsystems. One of the functions invoked is called shrink_cache() and should not be confused with the parent function shink_caches(). The function shrink_caches() acts on the following parameters:

classzone
> The memory zone that contains the page frames to be freed.

priority
> The "priority" of this trial: it tells how drastic page frame reclaiming must be.

gfp_mask
> Memory allocator flags, specifying the type of page frames to be freed, as well as what the kernel is allowed to do in pursuit of its goal (block the current process, trigger I/O transfers, and so on).

nr_pages
> The goal—i.e., the number of page frames to be freed.

The function returns the difference between nr_pages and the number of page frames that have been effectively reclaimed; if more than nr_pages page frames have been freed, the function returns 0. It executes the following actions:

1. Invokes kmem_cache_reap() to reclaim page frames from the slab allocator caches (see the section "Releasing a Slab from a Cache" in Chapter 7).

2. If kmem_cache_reap() succeeds in freeing at least nr_pages page frames, returns 0.

3. Invokes the refill_inactive() function to move some pages from the active list to the inactive list. As described in the earlier section "The Least Recently Used (LRU) Lists," refill_inactive() clears the PG_referenced flags of the pages at the bottom of the active list, and moves the pages that have not been accessed since the previous execution of shrink_caches(). The number of pages to be moved is passed as a parameter to refill_inactive(); it is computed as:

    ratio = nr_pages * nr_active_pages / ((nr_inactive_pages + 1) * 2);

    The rationale behind the formula is to keep the size of active list roughly equal to two-thirds of the page cache size (that's another rule of thumb, of course).

4. Invokes shrink_cache() to try to reclaim nr_pages from the inactive list (see the next section). If the function succeeds in freeing all the required page frames, it returns 0 (all requested page frame have been freed).

5. At this point, shrink_caches() has lost any hope of reaching its target in the current execution. However, it tries to free small objects in several disk caches so that the future invocations of the function will likely succeed in releasing the page frames storing them. Thus, the function invokes shrink_dcache_memory() to remove dentry objects from the dentry cache (see the later section "Reclaiming Page Frames from the Dentry and Inode Caches").

6. Invokes shrink_icache_memory() to remove inode objects from the inode cache (see the section "Reclaiming Page Frames from the Dentry and Inode Caches" later in this chapter)

7. If the kernel has support for disk quota, the function invokes shrink_dqcache_memory( ) to remove objects from the disk quota cache. (We won't discuss disk quota for lack of space.)

8. Returns the number of page frames still to be freed.

The shrink_cache( ) Function

The shrink_cache( ) function acts on the same parameters as shrink_caches( ): nr_pages, classzone, gfp_mask, and priority. It looks for page frames to be reclaimed in the inactive list. Since the last inserted elements are placed near the head of the list, the function starts scanning from the tail of the list and moves backward.

The function achieves its goal by:

- Freeing to the buddy system the page frames that do not belong to any process
- Swapping out pages belonging to processes if there are too many of them in the scanned portion of the inactive list

The priority parameter controls the size of the portion of the inactive list to be scanned in this invocation of shrink_cache( ). If priority is equal to 6 (DEF_PRIORITY, the lowest priority), the function scans at most one-sixth of the list; as priority decreases, the function scans more and more of the list until it reaches 1 (the highest priority), whereupon it scans the whole list.

The function starts by acquiring the pagemap_lru_lock spin lock and then loops over the pages of the inactive list backwards until either the chosen portion of the list is scanned or the number of elements specified by priority is reached. For every scanned page, the function performs the following actions:

1. If the need_resched field of the current process is set, temporarily relinquishes the CPU by releasing the pagemap_lru_lock spin lock and invoking schedule( ). When executing again, the function reacquires the spin lock and continues.

2. Moves the page from the tail to the head of the inactive list. This ensures that inactive pages are considered in a round-robin fashion in successive invocations of shrink_cache( ).

3. Checks whether the usage counter of the page is null; if so, it continues with the next page at the tail of the list. Ideally, any page with a null usage counter should belong to the buddy system; however, to free a page frame, first its usage counter is decremented and then the page frame is released to the buddy system. Therefore, there is a small time window in which the page frame reclaiming algorithm may see the page freed.

4. Checks whether the page belongs to the memory zone specified by the classzone parameter; if not, the function stops working on this page and continues with the next page at the tail of the list.

5. Checks whether the page is not a buffer page and whether its usage counter is greater than one or the page doesn't have an image on disk (mapping field set to NULL). In this case, the page frame cannot be released to the buddy system because the usage counter indicates that there are processes that still reference the page. The function performs the following substeps:

   a. Increments a local counter storing the number of scanned pages that cannot be freed.

   b. If the counter exceeds a threshold value, releases the pagemap_lru_lock spin lock, invokes swap_out() to swap out some process pages (see the earlier section "Swapping Out Pages"), and returns the number of pages frames yet to be freed. The threshold value is equal to the smaller of two values: one-tenth of the number of pages to be scanned and 2^{10}-priority times the number of page frames to be released (the nr_pages parameter).

   c. Otherwise, if the counter does not exceed the threshold value, the function continues with the next page at the tail of the inactive list.

6. If the function reaches this point, the page frame can be released to the buddy system. The function tries to lock the page. If the PG_locked flag of the page is already set, it executes the following substeps:

   a. If both the PG_launder flag of the page and the __GFP_FS bit in the gfp_mask parameter are set, invokes wait_on_page() to sleep until the page is unlocked. The PG_launder flag is set whenever the page is involved in an I/O data transfer triggered by the shrink_cache() function itself.

   b. Continues with the next page at the tail of the inactive list.

7. Now the page is locked. Checks whether the page is dirty (PG_dirty flag set), the page has an image on disk (mapping field not NULL), and it is owned only by the page cache—that is, whether the underlying page frame is effectively freeable. If all these conditions hold, and moreover, the __GFP_FS bit in the gfp_mask parameter is set, the function updates the disk image by performing the following actions:

   a. Clears the PG_dirty flag.

   b. Sets the PG_launder flag so that a future invocation of shrink_cache() waits for the completion of the I/O data transfer.

   c. Increments the page usage counter (fail-safe mechanism) and releases the pagemap_lru_lock spin lock.

   d. Invokes the writepage method of the address_space object of the page. As described in the section "Flushing Dirty Memory Mapping Pages to Disk" in Chapter 15, the method activates the I/O data transfer of the page contents to the disk.

   e. Decrements the page usage counter and acquires the pagemap_lru_lock spin lock again.

   f. Continues with the next page at the tail of the inactive list.

8. If the page is a buffer page (the buffers field is not NULL), the function tries to free the buffers contained in the page. In particular, it performs the following substeps:

  a. Releases the pagemap_lru_lock spin lock and increments the page usage counter (a fail-safe mechanism).

  b. Invokes the try_to_release_page() function. In turn, this function:

    1. Executes the releasepage method of the corresponding address_space object, if it is defined, to release the metadata associated with the buffers in journaling filesystems.

    2. Invokes the try_to_free_buffers() function to free the buffers in the page, provided they are referenced only by the buffer cache (see the section "Buffer Pages" in Chapter 14).

  c. If try_to_release_page() failed in releasing all the buffers in the page, the function unlocks the page, decrements its usage counter to undo the increment done in Step 8a, and continues with the next page at the tail of the inactive list.

  d. Otherwise, if try_to_release_page() succeeded in releasing all the buffers in the page, the function tries to release the page frame itself. In particular, if the page is anonymous (i.e., has no image on disk), the function acquires the pagemap_lru_lock spin lock, unlocks the page, removes the page from the inactive list, and releases the page frame to the buddy system. If the function has released the number of page frames that was its goal, it also releases the spin lock and returns the value 0; otherwise, it continues with Step 9.

  e. The buffer page is included in the page cache because it has an image on disk. It decrements its usage counter to undo the increment in Step 8a and acquires the pagemap_lru_lock spin lock. It then continues with the following step.

9. Acquires the pagecache_lock spin lock.

10. If the page has no image on disk or if the page is still referenced by some process, the function releases the pagecache_lock spin lock, unlocks the page, and jumps back to Step 5a.

11. If the function reaches this point, the page has an image on disk and is freeable because no process references it and it no longer includes any buffers. Checks whether the page is dirty (i.e., the PG_dirty flag is set); in this case, the page frame cannot be freed; otherwise, the data is lost. The function releases the pagecache_lock spin lock, unlocks the page, and continues with the next page at the tail of the inactive list.

12. If the function reaches this point, the page has an image on disk, is freeable, and is clean, so the page frame can effectively be reclaimed. If the page belongs to the swap cache, the function gets the swapped-out page identifier from the index

field, invokes `delete_from_swap_cache()` to remove the page descriptor from the swap cache, releases the `pagecache_lock` spin lock, and then invokes `swap_free()` to decrement the usage counter of the page slot.

13. Otherwise, it checks whether the page belongs to the swap cache. If not, it invokes `remove_inode_page()` to remove it from the page cache (see the section "Page Cache Handling Functions" in Chapter 14) and releases the `pagecache_lock` spin lock.

14. Invokes `__lru_cache_del()` to remove the page from the inactive list.

15. Unlocks the page.

16. Releases the page frame to the buddy system.

17. If the goal on the number of page frames to be freed is reached, the function releases the spin lock and returns the value 0; otherwise, it continues with the next page at the tail of the inactive list.

Reclaiming Page Frames from the Dentry and Inode Caches

Dentry and inode objects themselves aren't big, but freeing one of them has a cascading effect that can ultimately free a lot of memory by releasing several data structures. For this reason, the `shrink_caches()` function invokes two special purpose functions to reclaim page frames from the dentry and inode caches.

Reclaiming page frames from the dentry cache

The `shrink_dcache_memory()` function is invoked to remove dentry objects from the dentry cache. Clearly, only dentry objects not referenced by any process (defined as unused dentries in the section "dentry Objects" in Chapter 12) can be removed.

Since the dentry cache objects are allocated through the slab allocator, the `shrink_dcache_memory()` function may lead some slabs to become free, causing some page frames to be consequently reclaimed by `kmem_cache_reap()`. Moreover, the dentry cache acts as a controller of the inode cache. Therefore, when a dentry object is released, the buffer storing the corresponding inode becomes unused and the `shrink_mmap()` function may release the corresponding buffer page.

The `shrink_dcache_memory()` function, which acts on the two well-known parameters `priority` and `gfp_mask`, performs the following steps:

1. Returns 0 if the kernel is not allowed to trigger operations on filesystem on-disk data structures (the `__GFP_IO` bit is cleared in the `gfp_mask` parameter).

2. Otherwise, invokes `prune_dcache()`, passing it a parameter that is the ratio between the number of unused dentries and the value of `priority`.

3. Invokes `kmem_cache_shrink()` on the dentry cache to release frames that contained objects freed in the previous step.

4. Returns 0.

The prune_dcache( ) function receives a parameter that specifies the number of objects to free. It scans the list of unused dentries until it reaches the requested number of freed objects or until the whole list is scanned. On each object that wasn't recently referenced, the function calls prune_one_dentry( ).

The prune_one_dentry( ) function, in turn, performs the following operations.

1. Removes the dentry object from the dentry hash table, from the list of dentry objects in its parent directory, and from the list of dentry objects of the owner inode.

2. Decrements the usage counter of the dentry's inode by invoking the d_iput dentry method, if defined, or the iput( ) function.

3. Invokes the d_release method of the dentry object, if defined.

4. Invokes kmem_cache_free( ) to release the object to the slab allocator (see the section "Releasing an Object from a Cache" in Chapter 7).

5. Decrements the usage counter of the parent directory.

Reclaiming page frames from the inode cache

The shrink_icache_memory( ) function is invoked to remove inode objects from the inode cache. It is very similar to the shrink_dcache_memory( ) just described. It checks the __GFP_FS bit in the gfp_mask parameter, and then invokes prune_icache( ), passing to it the number of inodes to be freed—namely the ratio between the number of unused inodes and the value of the priority parameter. Finally, it invokes the kmem_cache_shrink( ) function to release to the buddy system each page frame that has been completely freed by prune_icache( ).

The prune_icache( ) function, in turn, scans the inode_unused list (see the section "Inode Objects" in Chapter 12), looking for inodes that can be freed. Basically, a good inode should be clean, it should have a null usage counter, its I_FREEING, I_CLEAR, and I_LOCK flags should be cleared, and it should not include any buffer head in its lists of dirty buffers. Any such inode is freed by invoking the clear_inode( ) and kmem_cache_free( ) functions.

If prune_icache( ) fails in releasing the requested number of inode objects, it schedules the execution of the try_to_sync_unused_inodes( ) function, which flushes some unused inodes to disk. Since this function might block, it is executed by the *keventd* kernel thread (see the section "Kernel Threads" in Chapter 3).

The kswapd Kernel Thread

The *kswapd* kernel thread is another kernel mechanism that activates the reclamation of memory. Why is it necessary? Is it not sufficient to invoke try_to_free_pages( ) when free memory becomes really scarce and another memory allocation request is issued?

Unfortunately, this is not the case. Some memory allocation requests are performed by interrupt and exception handlers, which cannot block the current process waiting for a page frame to be freed; moreover, some memory allocation requests are done by kernel control paths that have already acquired exclusive access to critical resources and that, therefore, cannot activate I/O data transfers. In the infrequent case in which all memory allocation requests are done by such sorts of kernel control paths, the kernel is never able to free memory.

kswapd also has a beneficial effect on system performances by keeping memory free in what would otherwise be idle time for the machine; processes can thus get their pages much faster.

The *kswapd* kernel thread is activated when a zone includes a number of free page frames that is below a "warning" threshold. Essentially, the kernel starts to reclaim some page frames in order to avoid much more dramatic "low on memory" conditions.

The "warning" threshold is stored into the pages_low field of the memory zone descriptor. Recall from the section "Memory Zones" in Chapter 7 that this descriptor also includes the pages_min field (a threshold that specifies the minimum number of free page frames that should always be preserved) and the pages_high field (a threshold that specifies the "safe" number of free page frames above which page frame reclaiming should be stopped). Usually, the pages_min field is set to the ratio between the size of the memory zone in pages and the number 128, the pages_low field is set to twice pages_min, and the pages_high field is set to three times the value of pages_min.*

The *kswapd* kernel thread is usually inserted into the kswapd_wait wait queue. As mentioned in the section "Requesting and Releasing Page Frames" in Chapter 7, if the alloc_pages() function fails to find a memory zone that has more than pages_low page frames, it sets the need_balance field of the first checked memory zone and wakes up *kswapd*.

The *kswapd* kernel thread executes the kswapd() function, which at each activation performs the following operations:

1. Sets the state of current to TASK_RUNNING and removes it from the kswapd_wait wait queue.

2. Invokes kswapd_balance() (see below).

3. Invokes run_task_queue() on the tq_disk task queue to activate the strategy routines of the block device drivers (see the section "The ll_rw_block() Function" in Chapter 13). This relieves pressure on memory by starting scheduled I/O operations and thus eventually allowing the kernel to free asynchronous buffer heads and pages in the page cache.

---

* A system administrator may set new values for the pages_min fields, and hence also new values for the pages_ low and pages_high fields, by passing ad-hoc ratios for every memory zone with the *memfrac* kernel boot option. However, the minimal allowed value for pages_min is 20 and the maximum allowed value is 255.

4. Sets the state of current to TASK_INTERRUPTIBLE and adds it to the kswapd_wait wait queue.

5. Checks the need_balance flags of every memory zone descriptor (see the section "Memory Zones" in Chapter 7). If none are set, invokes schedule() to put the *kswapd* kernel thread to sleep. When executed again, it jumps to Step 1.

The kswapd_balance() function checks the need_balance flag of all existing memory zones. For any memory zone having the flag set, the function invokes try_to_free_pages() to start reclaiming page frames. As we know, the latter function might not succeed in freeing SWAP_CLUSTER_MAX page frames; in this case, a process is killed. When this happens, kswapd_balance() suspends itself for one second, thus letting the kernel reclaim the page frames owned by the victim.

The kswapd_balance() function keeps invoking try_to_free_pages() on a memory zone until the number of free page frames in the zone (or in one of the other zones in the node) rises above the threshold stored in the pages_high field of the memory zone descriptor.

CHAPTER 17

The Ext2 and Ext3 Filesystems

In this chapter, we finish our extensive discussion of I/O and filesystems by taking a look at the details the kernel has to take care of when interacting with a particular filesystem. Since the Second Extended Filesystem (Ext2) is native to Linux and is used on virtually every Linux system, it is a natural choice for this discussion. Furthermore, Ext2 illustrates a lot of good practices in its support for modern filesystem features with fast performance. To be sure, other filesystems will embody new and interesting requirements because they are designed for other operating systems, but we cannot examine the oddities of various filesystems and platforms in this book.

After introducing Ext2 in the section "General Characteristics of Ext2," we describe the data structures needed, just as in other chapters. Since we are looking at a particular way to store data on a disk, we have to consider two versions of data structures. The section "Ext2 Disk Data Structures" shows the data structures stored by Ext2 on the disk, while "Ext2 Memory Data Structures" shows how they are duplicated in memory.

Then we get to the operations performed on the filesystem. In the section "Creating the Ext2 Filesystem," we discuss how Ext2 is created in a disk partition. The next sections describe the kernel activities performed whenever the disk is used. Most of these are relatively low-level activities dealing with the allocation of disk space to inodes and data blocks.

In the last section, we give a short description of the Ext3 filesystem, which is the next step in the evolution of the Ext2 filesystem.

General Characteristics of Ext2

Unix-like operating systems use several filesystems. Although the files of all such filesystems have a common subset of attributes required by a few POSIX APIs like stat( ), each filesystem is implemented in a different way.

The first versions of Linux were based on the Minix filesystem. As Linux matured, the *Extended Filesystem (Ext FS)* was introduced; it included several significant extensions, but offered unsatisfactory performance. The *Second Extended Filesystem (Ext2)* was introduced in 1994; besides including several new features, it is quite efficient and robust and has become the most widely used Linux filesystem.

The following features contribute to the efficiency of Ext2:

- When creating an Ext2 filesystem, the system administrator may choose the optimal block size (from 1,024 to 4,096 bytes), depending on the expected average file length. For instance, a 1,024-block size is preferable when the average file length is smaller than a few thousand bytes because this leads to less internal fragmentation—that is, less of a mismatch between the file length and the portion of the disk that stores it (see the section "Memory Area Management" in Chapter 7, where internal fragmentation for dynamic memory was discussed). On the other hand, larger block sizes are usually preferable for files greater than a few thousand bytes because this leads to fewer disk transfers, thus reducing system overhead.

- When creating an Ext2 filesystem, the system administrator may choose how many inodes to allow for a partition of a given size, depending on the expected number of files to be stored on it. This maximizes the effectively usable disk space.

- The filesystem partitions disk blocks into groups. Each group includes data blocks and inodes stored in adjacent tracks. Thanks to this structure, files stored in a single block group can be accessed with a lower average disk seek time.

- The filesystem *preallocates* disk data blocks to regular files before they are actually used. Thus, when the file increases in size, several blocks are already reserved at physically adjacent positions, reducing file fragmentation.

- Fast symbolic links are supported. If the pathname of the symbolic link (see the section "Hard and Soft Links" in Chapter 1) has 60 bytes or less, it is stored in the inode and can thus be translated without reading a data block.

Moreover, the Second Extended File System includes other features that make it both robust and flexible:

- A careful implementation of the file-updating strategy that minimizes the impact of system crashes. For instance, when creating a new hard link for a file, the counter of hard links in the disk inode is incremented first, and the new name is added into the proper directory next. In this way, if a hardware failure occurs after the inode update but before the directory can be changed, the directory is consistent, even if the inode's hard link counter is wrong. Deleting the file does not lead to catastrophic results, although the file's data blocks cannot be automatically reclaimed. If the reverse were done (changing the directory before updating the inode), the same hardware failure would produce a dangerous inconsistency: deleting the original hard link would remove its data blocks from disk, yet the new directory entry would refer to an inode that no longer exists. If that inode number were used later for another file, writing into the stale directory entry would corrupt the new file.

- Support for automatic consistency checks on the filesystem status at boot time. The checks are performed by the *e2fsck* external program, which may be activated not only after a system crash, but also after a predefined number of filesystem mountings (a counter is incremented after each mount operation) or after a predefined amount of time has elapsed since the most recent check.

- Support for immutable files (they cannot be modified, deleted, or renamed) and for append-only files (data can be added only to the end of them).

- Compatibility with both the Unix System V Release 4 and the BSD semantics of the Group ID for a new file. In SVR4, the new file assumes the Group ID of the process that creates it; in BSD, the new file inherits the Group ID of the directory containing it. Ext2 includes a mount option that specifies which semantic is used.

The Ext2 filesystem is a mature, stable program, and it has not evolved significantly in recent years. Several additional features, however, have been considered for inclusion. Some of them have already been coded and are available as external patches. Others are just planned, but in some cases, fields have already been introduced in the Ext2 inode for them. The most significant features being considered are:

Block fragmentation
: System administrators usually choose large block sizes for accessing disks because computer applications often deal with large files. As a result, small files stored in large blocks waste a lot of disk space. This problem can be solved by allowing several files to be stored in different fragments of the same block.

Access Control Lists (ACL)
: Instead of classifying the users of a file under three classes—owner, group, and others—this list is associated with each file to specify the access rights for any specific users or combinations of users.

Handling of transparently compressed and encrypted files
: These new options, which must be specified when creating a file, allow users to transparently store compressed and/or encrypted versions of their files on disk.

Logical deletion
: An *undelete* option allows users to easily recover, if needed, the contents of a previously removed file.

Journaling
: Journaling avoids the time-consuming check that is automatically performed on a filesystem when it is abruptly unmounted—for instance, as a consequence of a system crash.

In practice, none of these features has been officially included in the Ext2 filesystem. One might say that Ext2 is victim of its success; it is still the preferred filesystem adopted by most Linux distribution companies, and the millions of users who use it every day would look suspiciously at any attempt to replace Ext2 with some other filesystem that has not been so heavily tested and used.

A self-evident example of this phenomenon is journaling, which is the most compelling feature required by high-availability servers. Journaling has not been introduced in the Ext2 filesystem; rather, as we shall discuss in the later section "The Ext3 Filesystem," a new filesystem that is fully compatible with Ext2 has been created, which also offers journaling. Users who do not really require journaling may continue to use the good old Ext2 filesystem, while the others will likely adopt the new filesystem.

Ext2 Disk Data Structures

The first block in any Ext2 partition is never managed by the Ext2 filesystem, since it is reserved for the partition boot sector (see Appendix A). The rest of the Ext2 partition is split into *block groups*, each of which has the layout shown in Figure 17-1. As you will notice from the figure, some data structures must fit in exactly one block, while others may require more than one block. All the block groups in the filesystem have the same size and are stored sequentially, thus the kernel can derive the location of a block group in a disk simply from its integer index.

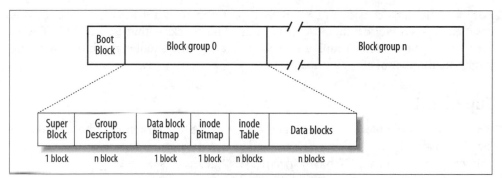

Figure 17-1. Layouts of an Ext2 partition and of an Ext2 block group

Block groups reduce file fragmentation, since the kernel tries to keep the data blocks belonging to a file in the same block group, if possible. Each block in a block group contains one of the following pieces of information:

- A copy of the filesystem's superblock
- A copy of the group of block group descriptors
- A data block bitmap
- A group of inodes
- An inode bitmap
- A chunk of data that belongs to a file; i.e., a data block

If a block does not contain any meaningful information, it is said to be free.

As can be seen from Figure 17-1, both the superblock and the group descriptors are duplicated in each block group. Only the superblock and the group descriptors included in block group 0 are used by the kernel, while the remaining superblocks and group descriptors are left unchanged; in fact, the kernel doesn't even look at them. When the *e2fsck* program executes a consistency check on the filesystem status, it refers to the superblock and the group descriptors stored in block group 0, and then copies them into all other block groups. If data corruption occurs and the main superblock or the main group descriptors in block group 0 becomes invalid, the system administrator can instruct *e2fsck* to refer to the old copies of the superblock and the group descriptors stored in a block groups other than the first. Usually, the redundant copies store enough information to allow *e2fsck* to bring the Ext2 partition back to a consistent state.

How many block groups are there? Well, that depends both on the partition size and the block size. The main constraint is that the block bitmap, which is used to identify the blocks that are used and free inside a group, must be stored in a single block. Therefore, in each block group, there can be at most $8 \times b$ blocks, where b is the block size in bytes. Thus, the total number of block groups is roughly $s/(8 \times b)$, where s is the partition size in blocks.

For example, let's consider an 8 GB Ext2 partition with a 4-KB block size. In this case, each 4-KB block bitmap describes 32K data blocks—that is, 128 MB. Therefore, at most 64 block groups are needed. Clearly, the smaller the block size, the larger the number of block groups.

Superblock

An Ext2 disk superblock is stored in an ext2_super_block structure, whose fields are listed in Table 17-1. The __u8, __u16, and __u32 data types denote unsigned numbers of length 8, 16, and 32 bits respectively, while the __s8, __s16, __s32 data types denote signed numbers of length 8, 16, and 32 bits.

Table 17-1. The fields of the Ext2 superblock

Type	Field	Description
__u32	s_inodes_count	Total number of inodes
__u32	s_blocks_count	Filesystem size in blocks
__u32	s_r_blocks_count	Number of reserved blocks
__u32	s_free_blocks_count	Free blocks counter
__u32	s_free_inodes_count	Free inodes counter
__u32	s_first_data_block	Number of first useful block (always 1)
__u32	s_log_block_size	Block size
__s32	s_log_frag_size	Fragment size
__u32	s_blocks_per_group	Number of blocks per group
__u32	s_frags_per_group	Number of fragments per group
__u32	s_inodes_per_group	Number of inodes per group

Table 17-1. The fields of the Ext2 superblock (continued)

Type	Field	Description
__u32	s_mtime	Time of last mount operation
__u32	s_wtime	Time of last write operation
__u16	s_mnt_count	Mount operations counter
__u16	s_max_mnt_count	Number of mount operations before check
__u16	s_magic	Magic signature
__u16	s_state	Status flag
__u16	s_errors	Behavior when detecting errors
__u16	s_minor_rev_level	Minor revision level
__u32	s_lastcheck	Time of last check
__u32	s_checkinterval	Time between checks
__u32	s_creator_os	OS where filesystem was created
__u32	s_rev_level	Revision level
__u16	s_def_resuid	Default UID for reserved blocks
__u16	s_def_resgid	Default GID for reserved blocks
__u32	s_first_ino	Number of first nonreserved inode
__u16	s_inode_size	Size of on-disk inode structure
__u16	s_block_group_nr	Block group number of this superblock
__u32	s_feature_compat	Compatible features bitmap
__u32	s_feature_incompat	Incompatible features bitmap
__u32	s_feature_ro_compat	Read-only compatible features bitmap
__u8 [16]	s_uuid	128-bit filesystem identifier
char [16]	s_volume_name	Volume name
char [64]	s_last_mounted	Pathname of last mount point
__u32	s_algorithm_usage_bitmap	Used for compression
__u8	s_prealloc_blocks	Number of blocks to preallocate
__u8	s_prealloc_dir_blocks	Number of blocks to preallocate for directories
__u16	s_padding1	Alignment to word
__u32 [204]	s_reserved	Nulls to pad out 1,024 bytes

The s_inodes_count field stores the number of inodes, while the s_blocks_count field stores the number of blocks in the Ext2 filesystem.

The s_log_block_size field expresses the block size as a power of 2, using 1,024 bytes as the unit. Thus, 0 denotes 1,024-byte blocks, 1 denotes 2,048-byte blocks, and so on. The s_log_frag_size field is currently equal to s_log_block_size, since block fragmentation is not yet implemented.

The s_blocks_per_group, s_frags_per_group, and s_inodes_per_group fields store the number of blocks, fragments, and inodes in each block group, respectively.

Some disk blocks are reserved to the superuser (or to some other user or group of users selected by the s_def_resuid and s_def_resgid fields). These blocks allow the system administrator to continue to use the filesystem even when no more free blocks are available for normal users.

The s_mnt_count, s_max_mnt_count, s_lastcheck, and s_checkinterval fields set up the Ext2 filesystem to be checked automatically at boot time. These fields cause *e2fsck* to run after a predefined number of mount operations has been performed, or when a predefined amount of time has elapsed since the last consistency check. (Both kinds of checks can be used together.) The consistency check is also enforced at boot time if the filesystem has not been cleanly unmounted (for instance, after a system crash) or when the kernel discovers some errors in it. The s_state field stores the value 0 if the filesystem is mounted or was not cleanly unmounted, 1 if it was cleanly unmounted, and 2 if it contains errors.

Group Descriptor and Bitmap

Each block group has its own group descriptor, an ext2_group_desc structure whose fields are illustrated in Table 17-2.

Table 17-2. The fields of the Ext2 group descriptor

Type	Field	Description
__u32	bg_block_bitmap	Block number of block bitmap
__u32	bg_inode_bitmap	Block number of inode bitmap
__u32	bg_inode_table	Block number of first inode table block
__u16	bg_free_blocks_count	Number of free blocks in the group
__u16	bg_free_inodes_count	Number of free inodes in the group
__u16	bg_used_dirs_count	Number of directories in the group
__u16	bg_pad	Alignment to word
__u32 [3]	bg_reserved	Nulls to pad out 24 bytes

The bg_free_blocks_count, bg_free_inodes_count, and bg_used_dirs_count fields are used when allocating new inodes and data blocks. These fields determine the most suitable block in which to allocate each data structure. The bitmaps are sequences of bits, where the value 0 specifies that the corresponding inode or data block is free and the value 1 specifies that it is used. Since each bitmap must be stored inside a single block and since the block size can be 1,024, 2,048, or 4,096 bytes, a single bitmap describes the state of 8,192, 16,384, or 32,768 blocks.

Inode Table

The inode table consists of a series of consecutive blocks, each of which contains a predefined number of inodes. The block number of the first block of the inode table is stored in the bg_inode_table field of the group descriptor.

All inodes have the same size: 128 bytes. A 1,024-byte block contains 8 inodes, while a 4,096-byte block contains 32 inodes. To figure out how many blocks are occupied by the inode table, divide the total number of inodes in a group (stored in the s_inodes_per_group field of the superblock) by the number of inodes per block.

Each Ext2 inode is an ext2_inode structure whose fields are illustrated in Table 17-3.

Table 17-3. The fields of an Ext2 disk inode

Type	Field	Description
__u16	i_mode	File type and access rights
__u16	i_uid	Owner identifier
__u32	i_size	File length in bytes
__u32	i_atime	Time of last file access
__u32	i_ctime	Time that inode last changed
__u32	i_mtime	Time that file contents last changed
__u32	i_dtime	Time of file deletion
__u16	i_gid	Group identifier
__u16	i_links_count	Hard links counter
__u32	i_blocks	Number of data blocks of the file
__u32	i_flags	File flags
union	osd1	Specific operating system information
__u32 [EXT2_N_BLOCKS]	i_block	Pointers to data blocks
__u32	i_generation	File version (used when the file is accessed by a network filesystem)
__u32	i_file_acl	File access control list
__u32	i_dir_acl	Directory access control list
__u32	i_faddr	Fragment address
union	osd2	Specific operating system information

Many fields related to POSIX specifications are similar to the corresponding fields of the VFS's inode object and have already been discussed in the section "Inode Objects" in Chapter 12. The remaining ones refer to the Ext2-specific implementation and deal mostly with block allocation.

In particular, the i_size field stores the effective length of the file in bytes, while the i_blocks field stores the number of data blocks (in units of 512 bytes) that have been allocated to the file.

The values of i_size and i_blocks are not necessarily related. Since a file is always stored in an integer number of blocks, a nonempty file receives at least one data block (since fragmentation is not yet implemented) and i_size may be smaller than 512×i_blocks. On the other hand, as we shall see in the section "File Holes" later in this chapter, a file may contain holes. In that case, i_size may be greater than 512×i_blocks.

The i_block field is an array of EXT2_N_BLOCKS (usually 15) pointers to blocks used to identify the data blocks allocated to the file (see the section "Data Blocks Addressing" later in this chapter).

The 32 bits reserved for the i_size field limit the file size to 4 GB. Actually, the highest-order bit of the i_size field is not used, so the maximum file size is limited to 2 GB. However, the Ext2 filesystem includes a "dirty trick" that allows larger files on 64-bit architectures like Hewlett-Packard's Alpha. Essentially, the i_dir_acl field of the inode, which is not used for regular files, represents a 32-bit extension of the i_size field. Therefore, the file size is stored in the inode as a 64-bit integer. The 64-bit version of the Ext2 filesystem is somewhat compatible with the 32-bit version because an Ext2 filesystem created on a 64-bit architecture may be mounted on a 32-bit architecture, and vice versa. On a 32-bit architecture, a large file cannot be accessed, unless opening the file with the O_LARGEFILE flag set (see the section "The open() System Call" in Chapter 12).

Recall that the VFS model requires each file to have a different inode number. In Ext2, there is no need to store on disk a mapping between an inode number and the corresponding block number because the latter value can be derived from the block group number and the relative position inside the inode table. For example, suppose that each block group contains 4,096 inodes and that we want to know the address on disk of inode 13,021. In this case, the inode belongs to the third block group and its disk address is stored in the 733rd entry of the corresponding inode table. As you can see, the inode number is just a key used by the Ext2 routines to retrieve the proper inode descriptor on disk quickly.

How Various File Types Use Disk Blocks

The different types of files recognized by Ext2 (regular files, pipes, etc.) use data blocks in different ways. Some files store no data and therefore need no data blocks at all. This section discusses the storage requirements for each type, which are listed in Table 17-4.

Table 17-4. Ext2 file types

File_type	Description
0	Unknown
1	Regular file
2	Directory
3	Character device
4	Block device
5	Named pipe
6	Socket
7	Symbolic link

Regular file

Regular files are the most common case and receive almost all the attention in this chapter. But a regular file needs data blocks only when it starts to have data. When first created, a regular file is empty and needs no data blocks; it can also be emptied by the truncate( ) or open( ) system calls. Both situations are common; for instance, when you issue a shell command that includes the string >*filename*, the shell creates an empty file or truncates an existing one.

Directory

Ext2 implements directories as a special kind of file whose data blocks store filenames together with the corresponding inode numbers. In particular, such data blocks contain structures of type ext2_dir_entry_2. The fields of that structure are shown in Table 17-5. The structure has a variable length, since the last name field is a variable length array of up to EXT2_NAME_LEN characters (usually 255). Moreover, for reasons of efficiency, the length of a directory entry is always a multiple of 4 and, therefore, null characters (\0) are added for padding at the end of the filename, if necessary. The name_len field stores the actual file name length (see Figure 17-2).

Table 17-5. The fields of an Ext2 directory entry

Type	Field	Description
__u32	inode	Inode number
__u16	rec_len	Directory entry length
__u8	name_len	Filename length
__u8	file_type	File type
char [EXT2_NAME_LEN]	name	Filename

The file_type field stores a value that specifies the file type (see Table 17-4). The rec_len field may be interpreted as a pointer to the next valid directory entry: it is the offset to be added to the starting address of the directory entry to get the starting address of the next valid directory entry. To delete a directory entry, it is sufficient to set its inode field to 0 and suitably increment the value of the rec_len field of the previous valid entry. Read the rec_len field of Figure 17-2 carefully; you'll see that the *oldfile* entry was deleted because the rec_len field of *usr* is set to 12+16 (the lengths of the *usr* and *oldfile* entries).

Symbolic link

As stated before, if the pathname of the symbolic link has up to 60 characters, it is stored in the i_block field of the inode, which consists of an array of 15 4-byte integers; no data block is therefore required. If the pathname is longer than 60 characters, however, a single data block is required.

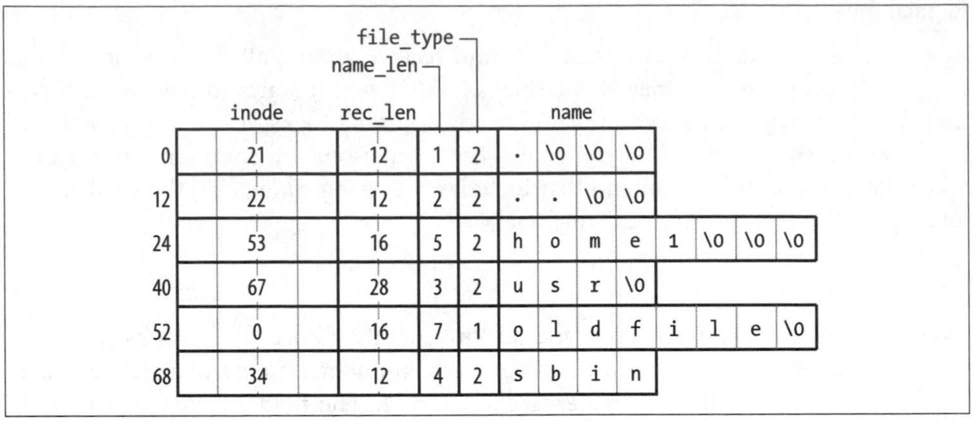

	inode	rec_len	name_len	file_type	name							
0	21	12	1	2	.	\0	\0	\0				
12	22	12	2	2	.	.	\0	\0				
24	53	16	5	2	h	o	m	e	1	\0	\0	\0
40	67	28	3	2	u	s	r	\0				
52	0	16	7	1	o	l	d	f	i	l	e	\0
68	34	12	4	2	s	b	i	n				

Figure 17-2. An example of the EXT2 directory

Device file, pipe, and socket

No data blocks are required for these kinds of files. All the necessary information is stored in the inode.

Ext2 Memory Data Structures

For the sake of efficiency, most information stored in the disk data structures of an Ext2 partition are copied into RAM when the filesystem is mounted, thus allowing the kernel to avoid many subsequent disk read operations. To get an idea of how often some data structures change, consider some fundamental operations:

- When a new file is created, the values of the s_free_inodes_count field in the Ext2 superblock and of the bg_free_inodes_count field in the proper group descriptor must be decremented.

- If the kernel appends some data to an existing file so that the number of data blocks allocated for it increases, the values of the s_free_blocks_count field in the Ext2 superblock and of the bg_free_blocks_count field in the group descriptor must be modified.

- Even just rewriting a portion of an existing file involves an update of the s_wtime field of the Ext2 superblock.

Since all Ext2 disk data structures are stored in blocks of the Ext2 partition, the kernel uses the buffer cache and the page cache to keep them up to date (see the section "Writing Dirty Buffers to Disk" in Chapter 14).

Table 17-6 specifies, for each type of data related to Ext2 filesystems and files, the data structure used on the disk to represent its data, the data structure used by the kernel in memory, and a rule of thumb used to determine how much caching is used. Data that is updated very frequently is always cached; that is, the data is permanently stored in memory and included in the buffer cache or in the page cache until the corresponding Ext2 partition is unmounted. The kernel gets this result by keeping the buffer's usage counter greater than 0 at all times.

Table 17-6. VFS images of Ext2 data structures

Type	Disk data structure	Memory data structure	Caching mode
Superblock	ext2_super_block	ext2_sb_info	Always cached
Group descriptor	ext2_group_desc	ext2_group_desc	Always cached
Block bitmap	Bit array in block	Bit array in buffer	Fixed limit
Inode bitmap	Bit array in block	Bit array in buffer	Fixed limit
Inode	ext2_inode	ext2_inode_info	Dynamic
Data block	Unspecified	Buffer page	Dynamic
Free inode	ext2_inode	None	Never
Free block	Unspecified	None	Never

The never-cached data is not kept in any cache since it does not represent meaningful information.

In between these extremes lie two other modes: *fixed-limit* and *dynamic*. In the fixed-limit mode, a specific number of data structures can be kept in the buffer cache; older ones are flushed to disk when the number is exceeded. In the dynamic mode, the data is kept in a cache as long as the associated object (an inode or data block) is in use; when the file is closed or the data block is deleted, the shrink_mmap( ) function may remove the associated data from the cache and write it back to disk.

The ext2_sb_info and ext2_inode_info Structures

When an Ext2 filesystem is mounted, the u field of the VFS superblock, which contains filesystem-specific data, is loaded with a structure of type ext2_sb_info so that the kernel can find out things related to the filesystem as a whole. This structure includes the following information:

- Most of the disk superblock fields
- The block bitmap cache, tracked by the s_block_bitmap and s_block_bitmap_number arrays (see the next section)
- The inode bitmap cache, tracked by the s_inode_bitmap and s_inode_bitmap_number arrays (see the next section)
- An s_sbh pointer to the buffer head of the buffer containing the disk superblock
- An s_es pointer to the buffer containing the disk superblock
- The number of group descriptors, s_desc_per_block, that can be packed in a block

- An `s_group_desc` pointer to an array of buffer heads of buffers containing the group descriptors (usually, a single entry is sufficient)
- Other data related to mount state, mount options, and so on

Similarly, when an inode object pertaining to an Ext2 file is initialized, the u field is loaded with a structure of type `ext2_inode_info`, which includes this information:

- Most of the fields found in the disk's inode structure that are not kept in the generic VFS inode object (see Table 12-3 in Chapter 12)
- The fragment size and the fragment number (not yet used)
- The `block_group` block group index at which the inode belongs (see the section "Ext2 Disk Data Structures" earlier in this chapter)
- The `i_prealloc_block` and `i_prealloc_count` fields, which are used for data block preallocation (see the section "Allocating a Data Block" later in this chapter)
- The `i_osync` field, which is a flag specifying whether the disk inode should be synchronously updated

Bitmap Caches

When the kernel mounts an Ext2 filesystem, it allocates a buffer for the Ext2 disk superblock and reads its contents from disk. The buffer is released only when the Ext2 filesystem is unmounted. When the kernel must modify a field in the Ext2 superblock, it simply writes the new value in the proper position of the corresponding buffer and then marks the buffer as dirty.

Unfortunately, this approach cannot be adopted for all Ext2 disk data structures. The tenfold increase in disk capacity reached in recent years has induced a tenfold increase in the size of inode and data block bitmaps, so we have reached the point at which it is no longer convenient to keep all the bitmaps in RAM at the same time.

For instance, consider a 4-GB disk with a 1-KB block size. Since each bitmap fills all the bits of a single block, each of them describes the status of 8,192 blocks—that is, of 8 MB of disk storage. The number of block groups is 4,096 MB/8 MB=512. Since each block group requires both an inode bitmap and a data block bitmap, 1 MB of RAM would be required to store all 1,024 bitmaps in memory.

The solution adopted to limit the memory requirements of the Ext2 descriptors is to use, for any mounted Ext2 filesystem, two caches of size `EXT2_MAX_GROUP_LOADED` (usually 8). One cache stores the most recently accessed inode bitmaps, while the other cache stores the most recently accessed block bitmaps. Buffers that contain bitmaps included in a cache have a usage counter greater than 0, therefore they are never freed by `shrink_mmap()` (see the section "Reclaiming Page Frame" in Chapter 16). Conversely, buffers that contain bitmaps not included in a bitmap cache have a null usage counter, so they can be freed if free memory becomes scarce.

Each cache is implemented by means of two arrays of EXT2_MAX_GROUP_LOADED elements. One array contains the indexes of the block groups whose bitmaps are currently in the cache, while the other array contains pointers to the buffer heads that refer to those bitmaps.

The ext2_sb_info structure stores the arrays pertaining to the inode bitmap cache; indexes of block groups are found in the s_inode_bitmap field and pointers to buffer heads are found in the s_inode_bitmap_number field. The corresponding arrays for the block bitmap cache are stored in the s_block_bitmap and s_block_bitmapnumber fields.

The load_inode_bitmap( ) function loads the inode bitmap of a specified block group and returns the cache position in which the bitmap can be found.

If the bitmap is not already in the bitmap cache, load_inode_bitmap( ) invokes read_inode_bitmap( ). The latter function gets the number of the block containing the bitmap from the bg_inode_bitmap field of the group descriptor, and then invokes bread( ) to allocate a new buffer and read the block from disk if it is not already included in the buffer cache.

If the number of block groups in the Ext2 partition is less than or equal to EXT2_MAX_GROUP_LOADED, the index of the cache array position in which the bitmap is inserted always matches the block group index passed as the parameter to the load_inode_bitmap( ) function.

Otherwise, if there are more block groups than cache positions, a bitmap is removed from the cache, if necessary, by using a Least Recently Used (LRU) policy, and the requested bitmap is inserted in the first cache position. Figure 17-3 illustrates the three possible cases in which the bitmap in block group 5 is referenced: where the requested bitmap is already in cache, where the bitmap is not in cache but there is a free position, and where the bitmap is not in cache and there is no free position.

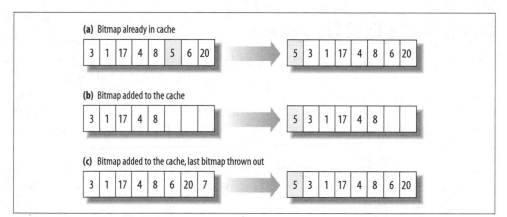

Figure 17-3. Adding a bitmap to the cache

The load_block_bitmap( ) and read_block_bitmap( ) functions are very similar to load_inode_bitmap( ) and read_inode_bitmap( ), but they refer to the block bitmap cache of an Ext2 partition.

Figure 17-4 illustrates the memory data structures of a mounted Ext2 filesystem. In our example, there are three block groups whose descriptors are stored in three blocks on disk; therefore, the s_group_desc field of the ext2_sb_info points to an array of three buffer heads. We have shown just one inode bitmap having index 2 and one block bitmap having index 4, although the kernel may keep 2×EXT2_MAX_GROUP_LOADED bitmaps in the bitmap caches, and even more may be stored in the buffer cache.

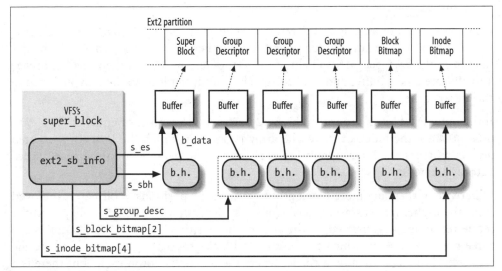

Figure 17-4. Ext2 memory data structures

Creating the Ext2 Filesystem

There are generally two stages to creating a filesystem on a disk. The first step is to format it so that the disk driver can read and write blocks on it. Modern hard disks come preformatted from the factory and need not be reformatted; floppy disks may be formatted on Linux using the *superformat* utility program. The second step involves creating a filesystem, which means setting up the structures described in detail earlier in this chapter.

Ext2 filesystems are created by the *mke2fs* utility program; it assumes the following default options, which may be modified by the user with flags on the command line:

- Block size: 1,024 bytes
- Fragment size: block size (block fragmentation is not implemented)

- Number of allocated inodes: one for each group of 4,096 bytes
- Percentage of reserved blocks: 5 percent

The program performs the following actions:

1. Initializes the superblock and the group descriptors.
2. Optionally, checks whether the partition contains defective blocks; if so, it creates a list of defective blocks.
3. For each block group, reserves all the disk blocks needed to store the superblock, the group descriptors, the inode table, and the two bitmaps.
4. Initializes the inode bitmap and the data map bitmap of each block group to 0.
5. Initializes the inode table of each block group.
6. Creates the /root directory.
7. Creates the lost+found directory, which is used by e2fsck to link the lost and found defective blocks.
8. Updates the inode bitmap and the data block bitmap of the block group in which the two previous directories have been created.
9. Groups the defective blocks (if any) in the lost+found directory.

Let's consider how an Ext2 1.4 MB floppy disk is initialized by *mke2fs* with the default options.

Once mounted, it appears to the VFS as a volume consisting of 1,390 blocks; each one is 1,024 bytes in length. To examine the disk's contents, we can execute the Unix command:

```
$ dd if=/dev/fd0 bs=1k count=1440 | od -tx1 -Ax > /tmp/dump_hex
```

to get a file containing the hexadecimal dump of the floppy disk contents in the /tmp directory.[*]

By looking at that file, we can see that, due to the limited capacity of the disk, a single group descriptor is sufficient. We also notice that the number of reserved blocks is set to 72 (5 percent of 1,440) and, according to the default option, the inode table must include 1 inode for each 4,096 bytes—that is, 360 inodes stored in 45 blocks.

Table 17-7 summarizes how the Ext2 filesystem is created on a floppy disk when the default options are selected.

Table 17-7. Ext2 block allocation for a floppy disk

Block	Content
0	Boot block
1	Superblock

---

[*] Some information on an Ext2 filesystem could also be obtained by using the *dumpe2fs* and *debugfs* utility programs.

Table 17-7. Ext2 block allocation for a floppy disk (continued)

Block	Content
2	Block containing a single block group descriptor
3	Data block bitmap
4	Inode bitmap
5–49	Inode table: inodes up to 10: reserved; inode 11: *lost+found*; inodes 12–360: free
50	Root directory (includes ., .., and *lost+found*)
51	*lost+found* directory (includes . and ..)
52–62	Reserved blocks preallocated for *lost+found* directory
63–1439	Free blocks

Ext2 Methods

Many of the VFS methods described in Chapter 12 have a corresponding Ext2 implementation. Since it would take a whole book to describe all of them, we limit ourselves to briefly reviewing the methods implemented in Ext2. Once the disk and the memory data structures are clearly understood, the reader should be able to follow the code of the Ext2 functions that implement them.

Ext2 Superblock Operations

Many VFS superblock operations have a specific implementation in Ext2, namely read_inode, write_inode, put_inode, delete_inode, put_super, write_super, statfs, and remount_fs. The addresses of the superblock methods are stored into the ext2_sops array of pointers.

Ext2 Inode Operations

Some of the VFS inode operations have a specific implementation in Ext2, which depends on the type of the file to which the inode refers.

If the inode refers to a regular file, all inode operations listed in the ext2_file_inode_operations table have a NULL pointer, except for the truncate operation that is implemented by the ext2_truncate( ) function. Recall that the VFS uses its own generic functions when the corresponding Ext2 method is undefined (a NULL pointer).

If the inode refers to a directory, most inode operations listed in the ext2_dir_inode_operations table are implemented by specific Ext2 functions (see Table 17-8).

Table 17-8. Ext2 inode operations for directory files

VFS inode operation	Ext2 directory inode method
create	ext2_create( )
lookup	ext2_lookup( )
link	ext2_link( )

Table 17-8. Ext2 inode operations for directory files (continued)

VFS inode operation	Ext2 directory inode method
unlink	ext2_unlink( )
symlink	ext2_symlink( )
mkdir	ext2_mkdir( )
rmdir	ext2_rmdir( )
mknod	ext2_mknod( )
rename	ext2_rename( )

If the inode refers to a symbolic link that can be fully stored inside the inode itself, all inode methods are NULL except for readlink and follow_link, which are implemented by ext2_readlink( ) and ext2_follow_link( ), respectively. The addresses of those methods are stored in the ext2_fast_symlink_inode_operations table. On the other hand, if the inode refers to a long symbolic link that has to be stored inside a data block, the readlink and follow_link methods are implemented by the generic page_readlink( ) and page_follow_link( ) functions, whose addresses are stored in the page_symlink_inode_operations table.

If the inode refers to a character device file, to a block device file, or to a named pipe (see "FIFOs" in Chapter 19), the inode operations do not depend on the filesystem. They are specified in the chrdev_inode_operations, blkdev_inode_operations, and fifo_inode_operations tables, respectively.

Ext2 File Operations

The file operations specific to the Ext2 filesystem are listed in Table 17-9. As you can see, several VFS methods are implemented by generic functions that are common to many filesystems. The addresses of these methods are stored in the ext2_file_operations table.

Table 17-9. Ext2 file operations

VFS file operation	Ext2 method
llseek	generic_file_llseek( )
read	generic_file_read( )
write	generic_file_write( )
ioctl	ext2_ioctl( )
mmap	generic_file_mmap( )
open	generic_file_open( )
release	ext2_release_file( )
fsync	ext2_sync_file( )

Notice that the Ext2's read and write methods are implemented by the `generic_file_read()` and `generic_file_write()` functions, respectively. These are described in the sections "Reading from a File" and "Writing to a File" in Chapter 15.

Managing Ext2 Disk Space

The storage of a file on disk differs from the view the programmer has of the file in two ways: blocks can be scattered around the disk (although the filesystem tries hard to keep blocks sequential to improve access time), and files may appear to a programmer to be bigger than they really are because a program can introduce holes into them (through the `lseek()` system call).

In this section, we explain how the Ext2 filesystem manages the disk space—how it allocates and deallocates inodes and data blocks. Two main problems must be addressed:

- Space management must make every effort to avoid *file fragmentation*—the physical storage of a file in several, small pieces located in nonadjacent disk blocks. File fragmentation increases the average time of sequential read operations on the files, since the disk heads must be frequently repositioned during the read operation.* This problem is similar to the external fragmentation of RAM discussed in the section "The Buddy System Algorithm" in Chapter 7.

- Space management must be time-efficient; that is, the kernel should be able to quickly derive from a file offset the corresponding logical block number in the Ext2 partition. In doing so, the kernel should limit as much as possible the number of accesses to addressing tables stored on disk, since each such intermediate access considerably increases the average file access time.

Creating Inodes

The `ext2_new_inode()` function creates an Ext2 disk inode, returning the address of the corresponding inode object (or NULL, in case of failure). It acts on two parameters: the address `dir` of the inode object that refers to the directory into which the new inode must be inserted and a `mode` that indicates the type of inode being created. The latter argument also includes an `MS_SYNCHRONOUS` flag that requires the current process to be suspended until the inode is allocated. The function performs the following actions:

1. Invokes `new_inode()` to allocate a new inode object and initializes its `i_sb` field to the superblock address stored in `dir->i_sb`.

2. Invokes `down()` on the `s_lock` semaphore included in the parent superblock. As we know, the kernel suspends the current process if the semaphore is already busy.

---

* Please note that fragmenting a file across block groups (A Bad Thing) is quite different from the not-yet-implemented fragmentation of blocks to store many files in one block (A Good Thing).

3. If the new inode is a directory, tries to place it so that directories are evenly scattered through partially filled block groups. In particular, allocates the new directory in the block group that has the maximum number of free blocks among all block groups that have a greater than average number of free inodes. (The average is the total number of free inodes divided by the number of block groups).

4. If the new inode is not a directory, allocates it in a block group having a free inode. The function selects the group by starting from the one that contains the parent directory and moving farther away from it; to be precise:

   a. Performs a quick logarithmic search starting from the block group that includes the parent directory dir. The algorithm searches $\log(n)$ block groups, where n is the total number of block groups. The algorithm jumps further ahead until it finds an available block group—for example, if we call the number of the starting block group i, the algorithm considers block groups $i \bmod (n)$, $i+1 \bmod (n)$, $i+1+2 \bmod (n)$, $i+1+2+4 \bmod (n)$, etc.

   b. If the logarithmic search failed in finding a block group with a free inode, the function performs an exhaustive linear search starting from the block group that includes the parent directory dir.

5. Invokes load_inode_bitmap( ) to get the inode bitmap of the selected block group and searches for the first null bit into it, thus obtaining the number of the first free disk inode.

6. Allocates the disk inode: sets the corresponding bit in the inode bitmap and marks the buffer containing the bitmap as dirty. Moreover, if the filesystem has been mounted specifying the MS_SYNCHRONOUS flag, invokes ll_rw_block( ) and waits until the write operation terminates (see the section "Mounting a Generic Filesystem" in Chapter 12).

7. Decrements the bg_free_inodes_count field of the group descriptor. If the new inode is a directory, increments the bg_used_dirs_count field. Marks the buffer containing the group descriptor as dirty.

8. Decrements the s_free_inodes_count field of the disk superblock and marks the buffer containing it as dirty. Sets the s_dirt field of the VFS's superblock object to 1.

9. Initializes the fields of the inode object. In particular, sets the inode number i_no and copies the value of xtime.tv_sec into i_atime, i_mtime, and i_ctime. Also loads the i_block_group field in the ext2_inode_info structure with the block group index. Refer to Table 17-3 for the meaning of these fields.

10. Inserts the new inode object into the hash table inode_hashtable and invokes mark_inode_dirty( ) to move the inode object into the superblock's dirty inode list (see the section "Inode Objects" in Chapter 12).

11. Invokes up( ) on the s_lock semaphore included in the parent superblock.

12. Returns the address of the new inode object.

Deleting Inodes

The ext2_free_inode( ) function deletes a disk inode, which is identified by an inode object whose address is passed as the parameter. The kernel should invoke the function after a series of cleanup operations involving internal data structures and the data in the file itself. It should come after the inode object has been removed from the inode hash table, after the last hard link referring to that inode has been deleted from the proper directory and after the file is truncated to 0 length to reclaim all its data blocks (see the section "Releasing a Data Block" later in this chapter). It performs the following actions:

1. Invokes down( ) on the s_lock semaphore included in the parent superblock to get exclusive access to the superblock object.

2. Invokes clear_inode( ) to perform the following operations:

    a. Invokes invalidate_inode_buffers() to remove the dirty buffers that belong to the inode from its i_dirty_buffers and i_dirty_data_buffers lists (see the section "Buffer Head Data Structures" in Chapter 14).

    b. If the I_LOCK flag of the inode is set, some of the inode's buffers are involved in I/O data transfers; the function suspends the current process until these I/O data transfers terminate.

    c. Invokes the clear_inode method of the superblock object, if defined; the Ext2 filesystem does not define it.

    d. Sets the state of the inode to I_CLEAR (the inode object contents are no longer meaningful).

3. Computes the index of the block group containing the disk inode from the inode number and the number of inodes in each block group.

4. Invokes load_inode_bitmap( ) to get the inode bitmap.

5. Increments the bg_free_inodes_count field of the group descriptor. If the deleted inode is a directory, decrements the bg_used_dirs_count field. Marks the buffer that contains the group descriptor as dirty.

6. Increments the s_free_inodes_count field of the disk superblock and marks the buffer that contains it as dirty. Also sets the s_dirt field of the superblock object to 1.

7. Clears the bit corresponding to the disk inode in the inode bitmap and marks the buffer that contains the bitmap as dirty. Moreover, if the filesystem has been mounted with the MS_SYNCHRONIZE flag, invokes ll_rw_block( ) and waits until the write operation on the bitmap's buffer terminates.

8. Invokes up( ) on the s_lock semaphore included in the parent superblock object.

Data Blocks Addressing

Each nonempty regular file consists of a group of data blocks. Such blocks may be referred to either by their relative position inside the file (their *file block number*) or by their position inside the disk partition (their logical block number, explained in the section "Buffer Heads" in Chapter 13).

Deriving the logical block number of the corresponding data block from an offset f inside a file is a two-step process:

1. Derive from the offset f the file block number—the index of the block that contains the character at offset f.

2. Translate the file block number to the corresponding logical block number.

Since Unix files do not include any control characters, it is quite easy to derive the file block number containing the fth character of a file: simply take the quotient of f and the filesystem's block size and round down to the nearest integer.

For instance, let's assume a block size of 4 KB. If f is smaller than 4,096, the character is contained in the first data block of the file, which has file block number 0. If f is equal to or greater than 4,096 and less than 8,192, the character is contained in the data block that has file block number 1, and so on.

This is fine as far as file block numbers are concerned. However, translating a file block number into the corresponding logical block number is not nearly as straightforward, since the data blocks of an Ext2 file are not necessarily adjacent on disk.

The Ext2 filesystem must therefore provide a method to store the connection between each file block number and the corresponding logical block number on disk. This mapping, which goes back to early versions of Unix from AT&T, is implemented partly inside the inode. It also involves some specialized blocks that contain extra pointers, which are an inode extension used to handle large files.

The i_block field in the disk inode is an array of EXT2_N_BLOCKS components that contain logical block numbers. In the following discussion, we assume that EXT2_N_BLOCKS has the default value, namely 15. The array represents the initial part of a larger data structure, which is illustrated in Figure 17-5. As can be seen in the figure, the 15 components of the array are of 4 different types:

- The first 12 components yield the logical block numbers corresponding to the first 12 blocks of the file—to the blocks that have file block numbers from 0 to 11.

- The component at index 12 contains the logical block number of a block that represents a second-order array of logical block numbers. They correspond to the file block numbers ranging from 12 to $b/4+11$, where b is the filesystem's block size (each logical block number is stored in 4 bytes, so we divide by 4 in the formula). Therefore, the kernel must look in this component for a pointer to a block, and then look in that block for another pointer to the ultimate block that contains the file contents.

- The component at index 13 contains the logical block number of a block containing a second-order array of logical block numbers; in turn, the entries of this second-order array point to third-order arrays, which store the logical block numbers that correspond to the file block numbers ranging from $b/4+12$ to $(b/4)^2+(b/4)+11$.

- Finally, the component at index 14 uses triple indirection: the fourth-order arrays store the logical block numbers corresponding to the file block numbers ranging from $(b/4)^2+(b/4)+12$ to $(b/4)^3+(b/4)^2+(b/4)+11$ upward.

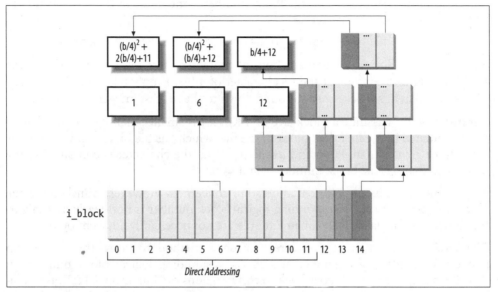

Figure 17-5. Data structures used to address the file's data blocks

In Figure 17-5, the number inside a block represents the corresponding file block number. The arrows, which represent logical block numbers stored in array components, show how the kernel finds its way to reach the block that contains the actual contents of the file.

Notice how this mechanism favors small files. If the file does not require more than 12 data blocks, any data can be retrieved in two disk accesses: one to read a component in the i_block array of the disk inode and the other to read the requested data block. For larger files, however, three or even four consecutive disk accesses may be needed to access the required block. In practice, this is a worst-case estimate, since dentry, buffer, and page caches contribute significantly to reduce the number of real disk accesses.

Notice also how the block size of the filesystem affects the addressing mechanism, since a larger block size allows the Ext2 to store more logical block numbers inside a single block. Table 17-10 shows the upper limit placed on a file's size for each block size and each addressing mode. For instance, if the block size is 1,024 bytes and the file contains up to 268 kilobytes of data, the first 12 KB of a file can be accessed through direct mapping and the remaining 13–268 KB can be addressed through simple indirection. Files larger than 2 GB must be opened on 32-bit architectures by specifying the O_LARGEFILE opening flag. In any case, the Ext2 filesystem puts an upper limit on the file size equal to 2 TB minus 4,096 bytes.

Table 17-10. File size upper limits for data block addressing

Block Size	Direct	1-Indirect	2-Indirect	3-Indirect
1,024	12 KB	268 KB	64.26 MB	16.06 GB
2,048	24 KB	1.02 MB	513.02 MB	256.5 GB
4,096	48 KB	4.04 MB	4 GB	~2 TB

File Holes

A *file hole* is a portion of a regular file that contains null characters and is not stored in any data block on disk. Holes are a long-standing feature of Unix files. For instance, the following Unix command creates a file in which the first bytes are a hole:

```
$ echo -n "X" | dd of=/tmp/hole bs=1024 seek=6
```

Now */tmp/hole* has 6,145 characters (6,144 null characters plus an X character), yet the file occupies just one data block on disk.

File holes were introduced to avoid wasting disk space. They are used extensively by database applications and, more generally, by all applications that perform hashing on files.

The Ext2 implementation of file holes is based on dynamic data block allocation: a block is actually assigned to a file only when the process needs to write data into it. The i_size field of each inode defines the size of the file as seen by the program, including the hole, while the i_blocks field stores the number of data blocks effectively assigned to the file (in units of 512 bytes).

In our earlier example of the dd command, suppose the */tmp/hole* file was created on an Ext2 partition that has blocks of size 4,096. The i_size field of the corresponding disk inode stores the number 6,145, while the i_blocks field stores the number 8 (because each 4,096-byte block includes eight 512-byte blocks). The second element of the i_block array (corresponding to the block having file block number 1) stores the logical block number of the allocated block, while all other elements in the array are null (see Figure 17-6).

Allocating a Data Block

When the kernel has to locate a block holding data for an Ext2 regular file, it invokes the ext2_get_block( ) function. If the block does not exist, the function automatically allocates the block to the file. Remember that this function is invoked every

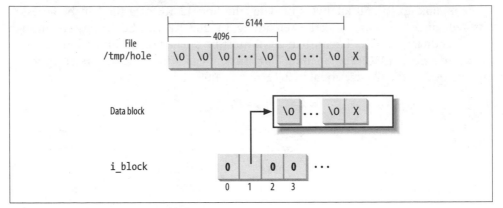

Figure 17-6. A file with an initial hole

time the kernel issues a read or write operation on a Ext2 regular file (see the sections "Reading from a File" and "Writing to a File" in Chapter 15).

The ext2_get_block( ) function handles the data structures already described in the section "Data Blocks Addressing," and when necessary, invokes the ext2_alloc_block( ) function to actually search for a free block in the Ext2 partition.

To reduce file fragmentation, the Ext2 filesystem tries to get a new block for a file near the last block already allocated for the file. Failing that, the filesystem searches for a new block in the block group that includes the file's inode. As a last resort, the free block is taken from one of the other block groups.

The Ext2 filesystem uses preallocation of data blocks. The file does not get just the requested block, but rather a group of up to eight adjacent blocks. The i_prealloc_count field in the ext2_inode_info structure stores the number of data blocks preallocated to a file that are still unused, and the i_prealloc_block field stores the logical block number of the next preallocated block to be used. Any preallocated blocks that remain unused are freed when the file is closed, when it is truncated, or when a write operation is not sequential with respect to the write operation that triggered the block preallocation.

The ext2_alloc_block( ) function receives as parameters a pointer to an inode object and a *goal*. The goal is a logical block number that represents the preferred position of the new block. The ext2_getblk( ) function sets the goal parameter according to the following heuristic:

1. If the block that is being allocated and the previously allocated block have consecutive file block numbers, the goal is the logical block number of the previous block plus 1; it makes sense that consecutive blocks as seen by a program should be adjacent on disk.

2. If the first rule does not apply and at least one block has been previously allocated to the file, the goal is one of these blocks' logical block numbers. More precisely, it is the logical block number of the already allocated block that precedes the block to be allocated in the file.

3. If the preceding rules do not apply, the goal is the logical block number of the first block (not necessarily free) in the block group that contains the file's inode.

The ext2_alloc_block( ) function checks whether the goal refers to one of the preallocated blocks of the file. If so, it allocates the corresponding block and returns its logical block number; otherwise, the function discards all remaining preallocated blocks and invokes ext2_new_block( ).

This latter function searches for a free block inside the Ext2 partition with the following strategy:

1. If the preferred block passed to ext2_alloc_block( ), the goal, is free, and the function allocates the block.

2. If the goal is busy, the function checks whether one of the next 64 blocks after the preferred block is free.

3. If no free block is found in the near vicinity of the preferred block, the function considers all block groups, starting from the one including the goal. For each block group, the function does the following:

    a. Looks for a group of at least eight adjacent free blocks.

    b. If no such group is found, looks for a single free block.

The search ends as soon as a free block is found. Before terminating, the ext2_new_block( ) function also tries to preallocate up to eight free blocks adjacent to the free block found and sets the i_prealloc_block and i_prealloc_count fields of the disk inode to the proper block location and number of blocks.

Releasing a Data Block

When a process deletes a file or truncates it to 0 length, all its data blocks must be reclaimed. This is done by ext2_truncate( ), which receives the address of the file's inode object as its parameter. The function essentially scans the disk inode's i_block array to locate all data blocks and all blocks used for the indirect addressing. These blocks are then released by repeatedly invoking ext2_free_blocks( ).

The ext2_free_blocks( ) function releases a group of one or more adjacent data blocks. Besides its use by ext2_truncate( ), the function is invoked mainly when discarding the preallocated blocks of a file (see the earlier section "Allocating a Data Block"). Its parameters are:

inode
    The address of the inode object that describes the file

block
    The logical block number of the first block to be released

count
    The number of adjacent blocks to be released

The function invokes down( ) on the s_lock superblock's semaphore to get exclusive access to the filesystem's superblock, and then performs the following actions for each block to be released:

1. Gets the block bitmap of the block group, including the block to be released

2. Clears the bit in the block bitmap that corresponds to the block to be released and marks the buffer that contains the bitmap as dirty

3. Increments the bg_free_blocks_count field in the block group descriptor and marks the corresponding buffer as dirty

4. Increments the s_free_blocks_count field of the disk superblock, marks the corresponding buffer as dirty, and sets the s_dirt flag of the superblock object

5. If the filesystem has been mounted with the MS_SYNCHRONOUS flag set, invokes ll_rw_block( ) and waits until the write operation on the bitmap's buffer terminates

Finally, the function invokes up( ) to release the superblock's s_lock semaphore.

The Ext3 Filesystem

In this section we'll briefly describe the enhanced filesystem that has evolved from Ext2, named *Ext3*. The new filesystem has been designed with two simple concepts in mind:

- To be a journaling filesystem (see the next section)
- To be, as much as possible, compatible with the old Ext2 filesystem

Ext3 achieves both the goals very well. In particular, it is largely based on Ext2, so its data structures on disk are essentially identical to those of an Ext2 filesystem. As a matter of fact, if an Ext3 filesystem has been cleanly unmounted, it can be remounted as an Ext2 filesystem; conversely, creating a journal of an Ext2 filesystem and remounting it as an Ext3 filesystem is a simple, fast operation.

Thanks to the compatibility between Ext3 and Ext2, most descriptions in the previous sections of this chapter apply to Ext3 as well. Therefore, in this section, we focus on the new feature offered by Ext3—"the journal."

Journaling Filesystems

As disks became larger, one design choice of traditional Unix filesystems (like Ext2) turns out to be inappropriate. As we know from Chapter 14, updates to filesystem blocks might be kept in dynamic memory for long period of time before being flushed to disk. A dramatic event like a power-down failure or a system crash might thus leave the filesystem in an inconsistent state. To overcome this problem, each traditional Unix filesystem is checked before being mounted; if it has not been properly unmounted, then a specific program executes an exhaustive, time-consuming check and fixes all filesystem's data structures on disk.

For instance, the Ext2 filesystem status is stored in the s_mount_state field of the superblock on disk. The *e2fsck* utility program is invoked by the boot script to check the value stored in this field; if it is not equal to EXT2_VALID_FS, the filesystem was not properly unmounted, and therefore *e2fsck* starts checking all disk data structures of the filesystem.

Clearly, the time spent checking the consistency of a filesystem depends mainly on the number of files and directories to be examined; therefore, it also depends on the disk size. Nowadays, with filesystems reaching hundreds of gigabytes, a single consistency check may take hours. The involved downtime is unacceptable for any production environment or high-availability server.

The goal of a *journaling filesystem* is to avoid running time-consuming consistency checks on the whole filesystem by looking instead in a special disk area that contains the most recent disk write operations named *journal*. Remounting a journaling filesystem after a system failure is a matter of few seconds.

The Ext3 Journaling Filesystem

The idea behind Ext3 journaling is to perform any high-level change to the filesystem in two steps. First, a copy of the blocks to be written is stored in the journal; then, when the I/O data transfer to the journal is completed (in short, data is *committed to the journal*), the blocks are written in the filesystem. When the I/O data transfer to the filesystem terminates (data is *committed to the filesystem*), the copies of the blocks in the journal are discarded.

While recovering after a system failure, the *e2fsck* program distinguishes the following two cases:

The system failure occurred before a commit to the journal.   Either the copies of the blocks relative to the high-level change are missing from the journal or they are incomplete; in both cases, *e2fsck* ignores them.

The system failure occurred after a commit to the journal.   The copies of the blocks are valid and *e2fsck* writes them into the filesystem.

In the first case, the high-level change to the filesystem is lost, but the filesystem state is still consistent. In the second case, *e2fsck* applies the whole high-level change, thus fixing any inconsistency due to unfinished I/O data transfers into the filesystem.

Don't expect too much from a journaling filesystem; it ensures consistency only at the system call level. For instance, a system failure that occurs while you are copying a large file by issuing several write( ) system calls will interrupt the copy operation, thus the duplicated file will be shorter than the original one.

Furthermore, journaling filesystems do not usually copy all blocks into the journal. In fact, each filesystem consists of two kinds of blocks: those containing the so-called *metadata* and those containing regular data. In the case of Ext2 and Ext3, there are six kinds of metadata: superblocks, group block descriptors, inodes, blocks used for indirect addressing (indirection blocks), data bitmap blocks, and inode bitmap blocks. Other filesystems may use different metadata.

Most journaling filesystems, like ReiserFS, SGI's XFS, and IBM's JFS, limit themselves to log the operations affecting metadata. In fact, metadata's log records are sufficient to restore the consistency of the on-disk filesystem data structures. However, since operations on blocks of file data are not logged, nothing prevents a system failure from corrupting the contents of the files.

The Ext3 filesystem, however, can be configured to log the operations affecting both the filesystem metadata and the data blocks of the files. Since logging every kind of write operation leads to a significant performance penalty, Ext3 lets the system administrator decide what has to be logged; in particular, it offers three different journaling modes:

Journal
> All filesystem data and metadata changes are logged into the journal. This mode minimizes the chance of losing the updates made to each file, but it requires many additional disk accesses. For example, when a new file is created, all its data blocks must be duplicated as log records. This is the safest and slowest Ext3 journaling mode.

Ordered
> Only changes to filesystem metadata are logged into the journal. However, the Ext3 filesystem groups metadata and relative data blocks so that data blocks are written to disk *before* the metadata. This way, the chance to have data corruption inside the files is reduced; for instance, any write access that enlarges a file is guaranteed to be fully protected by the journal. This is the default Ext3 journaling mode.

Writeback
> Only changes to filesystem metadata are logged; this is the method found on the other journaling filesystems and is the fastest mode.

The journaling mode of the Ext3 filesystem is specified by an option of the *mount* system command. For instance, to mount an Ext3 filesystem stored in the */dev/sda2* partition on the */jdisk* mount point with the "writeback" mode, the system administrator can type the command:

```
# mount -t ext3 -o data=writeback /dev/sda2 /jdisk
```

The Journaling Block Device Layer

The Ext3 journal is usually stored in a hidden file named *.journal* located in the root directory of the filesystem.

The Ext3 filesystem does not handle the journal on its own; rather, it uses a general kernel layer named *Journaling Block Device*, or *JBD*. Right now, only Ext3 uses the JBD layer, but other filesystems might use it in the future.

The JBD layer is a rather complex piece of software. The Ext3 filesystem invokes the JBD routines to ensure that its subsequent operations don't corrupt the disk data structures in case of system failure. However, JBD typically uses the same disk to log the changes performed by the Ext3 filesystem, and it is therefore vulnerable to system failures as much as Ext3. In other words, JBD must also protect itself from any system failure that could corrupt the journal.

Therefore, the interaction between Ext3 and JBD is essentially based on three fundamental units:

Log record
> Describes a single update of a disk block of the journaling filesystem.

Atomic operation handle
> Includes log records relative to a single high-level change of the filesystem; typically, each system call modifying the filesystem gives rise to a single atomic operation handle.

Transaction
> Includes several atomic operation handles whose log records are marked valid for *e2fsck* at the same time.

Log records

A *log record* is essentially the description of a low-level operation that is going to be issued by the filesystem. In some journaling filesystems, the log record consists of exactly the span of bytes modified by the operation, together with the starting position of the bytes inside the filesystem. The JBD layer, however, uses log records consisting of the whole buffer modified by the low-level operation. This approach may waste a lot of journal space (for instance, when the low-level operation just changes the value of a bit in a bitmap), but it is also much faster because the JBD layer can work directly with buffers and their buffer heads.

Log records are thus represented inside the journal as normal blocks of data (or metadata). Each such block, however, is associated with a small tag of type journal_block_tag_t, which stores the logical block number of the block inside the filesystem and a few status flags.

Later, whenever a buffer is being considered by the JBD, either because it belongs to a log record or because it is a data block that should be flushed to disk before the corresponding metadata block (in the "ordered" journaling mode), the kernel attaches a journal_head data structure to the buffer head. In this case, the b_private field of the buffer head stores the address of the journal_head data structure and the BH_JBD flag is set (see the section "Buffer Heads" in Chapter 13).

Atomic operation handles

Any system call modifying the filesystem is usually split into a series of low-level operations that manipulate disk data structures.

For instance, suppose that Ext3 must satisfy a user request to append a block of data to a regular file. The filesystem layer must determine the last block of the file, locate a free block in the filesystem, update the data block bitmap inside the proper block group, store the logical number of the new block either in the file's inode or in an indirect addressing block, write the contents of the new block, and finally, update several fields of the inode. As you see, the append operation translates into many lower-level operations on the data and metadata blocks of the filesystem.

Now, just imagine what could happen if a system failure occurred in the middle of an append operation, when some of the lower-level manipulations have already been executed while others have not. Of course, the scenario could be even worse, with high-level operations affecting two or more files (for example, moving a file from one directory to another).

To prevent data corruption, the Ext3 filesystem must ensure that each system call is handled in an atomic way. An *atomic operation handle* is a set of low-level operations on the disk data structures that correspond to a single high-level operation. When recovering from a system failure, the filesystem ensures that either the whole high-level operation is applied or none of its low-level operations is.

Any atomic operation handle is represented by a descriptor of type handle_t. To start an atomic operation, the Ext3 filesystem invokes the journal_start( ) JBD function, which allocates, if necessary, a new atomic operation handle and inserts it into the current transactions (see the next section). Since any low-level operation on the disk might suspend the process, the address of the active handle is stored in the journal_info field of the process descriptor. To notify that an atomic operation is completed, the Ext3 filesystem invokes the journal_stop( ) function.

Transactions

For reasons of efficiency, the JBD layer manages the journal by grouping the log records that belong to several atomic operation handles into a single *transaction*. Furthermore, all log records relative to a handle must be included in the same transaction.

All log records of a transaction are stored in consecutive blocks of the journal. The JBD layer handles each transaction as a whole. For instance, it reclaims the blocks used by a transaction only after all data included in its log records is committed to the filesystem.

As soon as it is created, a transaction may accept log records of new handles. The transaction stops accepting new handles when either of the following occurs:

- A fixed amount of time has elapsed, typically 5 seconds.
- There are no free blocks in the journal left for a new handle

A transaction is represented by a descriptor of type transaction_t. The most important field is t_state, which describes the current status of the transaction.

Essentially, a transaction can be:

Complete

All log records included in the transaction have been physically written onto the journal. When recovering from a system failure, *e2fsck* considers every complete transaction of the journal and writes the corresponding blocks into the filesystem. In this case, the i_state field stores the value T_FINISHED.

Incomplete

At least one log record included in the transaction has not yet been physically written to the journal, or new log records are still being added to the transaction. In case of system failure, the image of the transaction stored in the journal is likely not up to date. Therefore, when recovering from a system failure, *e2fsck* does not trust the incomplete transactions in the journal and skips them. In this case, the i_state field stores one of the following values:

T_RUNNING

Still accepting new atomic operation handles.

T_LOCKED

Not accepting new atomic operation handles, but some of them are still unfinished.

T_FLUSH

All atomic operation handles have finished, but some log records are still being written to the journal.

T_COMMIT

All log records of the atomic operation handles have been written to disk, and the transaction is marked as completed on the journal.

At any given instance, the journal may include several transactions. Just one of them is in the T_RUNNING state—it is the *active transaction* that is accepting the new atomic operation handle requests issued by the Ext3 filesystem.

Several transactions in the journal might be incomplete because the buffers containing the relative log records have not yet been written to the journal.

A complete transaction is deleted from the journal only when the JBD layer verifies that all buffers described by the log records have been successfully written onto the Ext3 filesystem. Therefore, the journal can include at most one incomplete transaction and several complete transactions. The log records of a complete transaction have been written to the journal but some of the corresponding buffers have yet to be written onto the filesystem.

How Journaling Works

Let's try to explain how journaling works with an example: the Ext3 filesystem layer receives a request to write some data blocks of a regular file.

As you might easily guess, we are not going to describe in detail every single operation of the Ext3 filesystem layer and of the JBD layer. There would be far too many issues to be covered! However, we describe the essential actions:

1. The service routine of the write() system call triggers the write method of the file object associated with the Ext3 regular file. For Ext3, this method is implemented by the generic_file_write() function, already described in the section "Writing to a File" in Chapter 15.

2. The generic_file_write() function invokes the prepare_write method of the address_space object several times, once for every page of data involved by the write operation. For Ext3, this method is implemented by the ext3_prepare_write() function.

3. The ext3_prepare_write() function starts a new atomic operation by invoking the journal_start() JBD function. The handle is added to the active transaction. Actually, the atomic operation handle is created only when executing the first invocation of the journal_start() function. Following invocations verify that the journal_info field of the process descriptor is already set and use the referenced handle.

4. The ext3_prepare_write() function invokes the block_prepare_write() function already described in Chapter 15, passing to it the address of the ext3_get_block() function. Remember that block_prepare_write() takes care of preparing the buffers and the buffer heads of the file's page.

5. When the kernel must determine the logical number of a block of the Ext3 filesystem, it executes the ext3_get_block() function. This function is actually similar to ext2_get_block(), which is described in the earlier section "Allocating a Data Block." A crucial difference, however, is that the Ext3 filesystem invokes functions of the JBD layer to ensure that the low-level operations are logged:

   - *Before* issuing a low-level write operation on a metadata block of the filesystem, the function invokes journal_get_write_access(). Basically, this latter function adds the metadata buffer to a list of the active transaction. However, it must also check whether the metadata is included in an older incomplete transaction of the journal; in this case, it duplicates the buffer to make sure that the older transactions are committed with the old content.

   - *After* updating the buffer containing the metadata block, the Ext3 filesystem invokes journal_dirty_metadata() to move the metadata buffer to the proper dirty list of the active transaction and to log the operation in the journal.

   Notice that metadata buffers handled by the JBD layer are not usually included in the dirty lists of buffers of the inode, so they are not written to disk by the normal disk cache flushing mechanisms described in Chapter 14.

6. If the Ext3 filesystem has been mounted in "journal" mode, the ext3_prepare_write() function also invokes journal_get_write_access() on every buffer touched by the write operation.

7. Control returns to the generic_file_write() function, which updates the page with the data stored in the User Mode address space and then invokes the commit_write method of the address_space object. For Ext3, this method is implemented by the ext3_commit_write() function.

8. If the Ext3 filesystem has been mounted in "journal" mode, the ext3_commit_write() function invokes journal_dirty_metadata() on every buffer of data (not metadata) in the page. This way, the buffer is included in the proper dirty list of the active transaction and not in the dirty list of the owner inode; moreover, the corresponding log records are written to the journal.

9. If the Ext3 filesystem has been mounted in "ordered" mode, the ext3_commit_write() function invokes the journal_dirty_data() function on every buffer of data in the page to insert the buffer in a proper list of the active transactions. The JBD layer ensures that all buffers in this list are written to disk before the metadata buffers of the transaction. No log record is written onto the journal.

10. If the Ext3 filesystem has been mounted in "ordered" or "writeback" mode, the ext3_commit_write() function executes the normal generic_commit_write() function described in Chapter 15, which inserts the data buffers in the list of the dirty buffers of the owner inode.

11. Finally, ext3_commit_write() invokes journal_stop() to notify the JBD layer that the atomic operation handle is closed.

12. The service routine of the write() system call terminates here. However, the JBD layer has not finished its work. Eventually, our transaction becomes complete when all its log records have been physically written to the journal. Then journal_commit_transaction() is executed.

13. If the Ext3 filesystem has been mounted in "ordered" mode, the journal_commit_transaction() function activates the I/O data transfers for all data buffers included in the list of the transaction and waits until all data transfers terminate.

14. The journal_commit_transaction() function activates the I/O data transfers for all metadata buffers included in the transaction (and also for all data buffers, if Ext3 was mounted in "journal" mode).

15. Periodically, the kernel activates a checkpoint activity for every complete transaction in the journal. The checkpoint basically involves verifying whether the I/O data transfers triggered by journal_commit_transaction() have successfully terminated. If so, the transaction can be deleted from the journal.

Of course, the log records in the journal never play an active role until a system failure occurs. Only in this case, in fact, does the *e2fsck* utility program scan the journal stored in the filesystem and reschedule all write operations described by the log records of the complete transactions.

CHAPTER 18
Networking

The Linux kernel supports many different network architectures (TCP/IP being just one of them), implements several alternative algorithms for scheduling the network packets, and includes programs that make it easy for system administrators to set up routers, gateways, firewalls, and even a simple World Wide Web server, directly at the kernel level.

The current code, inspired from the original Berkeley Unix implementation, is referred to as Net-4. As the name suggests, it is the fourth major version of Linux networking. Similar to VFS, the code uses objects to provide a common interface to the large number of available architectures. However, contrary to VFS, the networking code is organized into layers, each of which has a well-defined interface with the adjacent layers. Since data transmitted along the network is not reusable, there is no need to cache it. For the sake of efficiency, Linux avoids copying the data across layers; the original data is stored in a memory buffer, which is large enough to contain the control information requested by each layer.

Packing a detailed description of the Linux networking code in a single chapter of a book would be a truly impossible mission. In fact, nearly 20 percent of all kernel source code is devoted to networking. Therefore, we couldn't even succeed, within the space constraints of a single chapter, in mentioning the names of all the features, components, and data structures of the Linux network subsystem.

Our objective is more limited. We concentrate on the well-known TCP/IP stack of protocols and consider only the data link layer, the network layer, and the transport layer. Furthermore, for the sake of simplicity, we focus our attention on the UDP protocol and attempt to give a succinct description of how the kernel succeeds in sending or receiving a single datagram. Finally, we assume that our computer is connected to a local area network by means of an Ethernet card.

The first section of the chapter covers the main data structures used by Linux networking, while the second one illustrates the system calls needed to send or receive a single datagram and describes sketchily the corresponding service routines. The last two sections describe how the kernel interacts with the network card to send or receive a packet.

We assume that you already have some background in network protocols, layers, and applications. There are many good books on these topics, some of which are listed in the Bibliography at the end of this book.

One final remark: writing programs for the network subsystem is quite a hard task. While you have to stick to the documented standards, following them is not enough because they do not specify the smallest, most cumbersome details of the protocols. Thus you have to take into account the implementations of the already existing network programs, even those in other operating systems (bugs included). And, of course, you must write fast and efficient programs; otherwise your server will not keep up with the highest network loads.

Main Networking Data Structures

In this section, we shall give a general idea of how Linux implements the lower layers of networking.

Network Architectures

A *network architecture* describe how a specific computer network is made. The architecture defines a set of *layers*, each of which should have a well-defined purpose; programs in each layer communicate by using a shared set of rules and conventions (a so-called *protocol*).

Generally speaking, Linux supports a large number of different network architectures; some of them are listed in Table 18-1.

Table 18-1. Some network architectures supported by Linux

Name	Network architecture and/or protocol family
PF_APPLETALK	Appletalk
PF_BLUETOOTH	Bluetooth
PF_BRIDGE	Multiprotocol bridge
PF_DECnet	DECnet
PF_INET	IPS's IPv4 protocol
PF_INET6	IPS's IPv6 protocol
PF_IPX	Novell IPX
PF_LOCAL, PF_UNIX	Unix domain sockets (local communication)
PF_PACKET	IPS's IPv4/IPv6 protocol low-level access
PF_X25	X25

IPS (Internet Protocol Suite) is the network architecture of *Internet*, the well-known internetwork that collects hundreds of thousands of local computer networks all around the world. Sometimes it is also called *TCP/IP network architecture* from the names of the two main protocols that it defines.

Network Interface Cards

A *network interface card* (NIC) is a special kind of I/O device that does not have a corresponding device file. Essentially, a network card places outgoing data on a line going to remote computer systems and receives packets from those systems into kernel memory.

Starting with BSD, all Unix systems assign a different symbolic name to each network card included in the computer; for instance, the first Ethernet card gets the eth0 name. However, the name does not correspond to any device file and has no corresponding inode in the system directory tree.

Instead of using the filesystem, the system administrator has to set up a relationship between the device name and a network address. Therefore, as we shall see in the later section "System Calls Related to Networking," BSD Unix introduced a new group of system calls, which has become the standard programming model for network devices.

BSD Sockets

Generally speaking, any operating system must define a common Application Programming Interface (API) between the User Mode program and the networking code. The Linux networking API is based on *BSD sockets*. They were introduced in Berkeley's Unix 4.1cBSD and are available in almost all Unix-like operating systems, either natively or by means of a User Mode helper library.[*]

A *socket* is a communication endpoint—the terminal gate of a channel that links two processes. Data is pushed on a terminal gate, and after some delay, shows up at the other gate. The communicating processes may be on different computers; it's up to the kernel's networking code to forward the data between the two endpoints.

Linux implements BSD sockets as files that belong to the *sockfs* special filesystem (see the section "Special Filesystems" in Chapter 12). More precisely, for every new BSD socket, the kernel creates a new inode in the *sockfs* special filesystem. The attributes of the BSD socket are stored in a socket data structure, which is an object included in the filesystem-specific u.socket_i field of the *sockfs*'s inode.

The most important fields of the BSD socket object are:

inode
    Points to the *sockfs*'s inode object

file
    Points to the file object of the *sockfs*'s file

---

[*] An alternative API between User Mode programs and networking code is provided by the Transport Layer Interface (TLI), introduced by System V Release 3.0. In general, TLI is implemented as a User Mode library that uses the STREAMS I/O subsystem. As mentioned in the section "Linux Versus Other Unix-Like Kernels" in Chapter 1, the Linux kernel does not implement the STREAMS I/O subsystem.

state

Stores the connection status of the socket: SS_FRFF (not allocated), SS_ UNCONNECTED (not yet connected), SS_CONNECTING (in process of connecting), SS_ CONNECTED (connected), SS_DISCONNECTING (in process of disconnecting).

ops

Points to a proto_ops data structure, which stores the methods of the socket object; they are listed in Table 18-2. Most of the methods refer to system calls that operate on sockets. Each network architecture implements the methods by means of its own functions; hence, the same system call acts differently according to the networking architecture to which the target socket belongs.

Table 18-2. The methods of the BSD socket object

Method	Description
release	Close the socket
bind	Assign a local address (a name)
connect	Either establish a connection (TCP) or assign a remote address (UDP)
socketpair	Create a pair of sockets for two-way data flow
accept	Wait for connection requests
getname	Return the local address
ioctl	Implement ioctl( )'s commands
listen	Initialize the socket to accept connection requests
shutdown	Close a half or both halves of a full-duplex connection
setsockopt	Set the value of the socket flags
getsockopt	Get the value of the socket flags
sendmsg	Send a packet on the socket
recvmsg	Receive a packet from the socket
mmap	File memory-mapping (not used by network sockets)
sendpage	Copy data directly from/to a file (sendfile( ) system call)

sk

Points to the low-level struct sock socket descriptor (see the next section).

INET Sockets

INET sockets are data structures of type struct sock. Any BSD socket that belongs to the IPS network architecture stores the address of an INET socket in the sk field of the socket object.

INET sockets are required because the socket objects (describing BSD sockets) include only fields that are meaningful to all network architectures. However, the kernel must also keep track of several other bits of information for any socket of every specific network architecture. For instance, in each INET socket, the kernel records the local and remote IP addresses, the local and remote port numbers, the relative transport protocol, the queue of packets that were received from the socket, the queue of packets waiting to be sent to the socket, and several tables of methods that handle the packets traveling on the socket. These attributes are stored, together with many others, in the INET socket.

The INET socket object also defines some methods specific to the type of transport protocol adopted (TCP or UDP). The methods are stored in a data structure of type proto and are listed in Table 18-3.

Table 18-3. The methods of the INET socket object

Method	Description
close	Close the socket
connect	Either establish a connection or assign a remote address
disconnect	Relinquish an established connection
accept	Wait for connection request
ioctl	Implement ioctl()'s commands
init	INET socket object constructor
destroy	INET socket object destructor
shutdown	Close a half or both halves of a full-duplex connection
setsockopt	Set the value of the socket flags
getsockopt	Get the value of the socket flags
sendmsg	Send a packet on the socket
recvmsg	Receive a packet from the socket
bind	Assign a local address (a name)
backlog_rcv	Callback function invoked when receiving a packet
hash	Add the INET socket to the per-protocol hash table
unhash	Remove the INET socket from the per-protocol hash table
get_port	Assign a port number to the INET socket

As you may notice, many methods replicate the methods of the BSD socket object (Table 18-2). Actually, a BSD socket method usually invokes the corresponding INET socket method, if it is defined.

The sock object includes no less than 80 fields; many of them are pointers to other objects, tables of methods, or other data structures that deserve a detailed description by themselves. Rather than including a boring list of field names, we introduce a few fields of the sock object whenever we encounter them in the rest of the chapter.

The Destination Cache

As we shall see in the later section "The bind() System Call," processes usually "assign names" to sockets—that is, they specify the remote IP address and port number of the host that should receive the data written onto the socket. The kernel shall also make available to the processes reading the sockets every packet received from the remote host carrying the proper port number.

Actually, the kernel has to keep in memory a bunch of data about the remote host identified by an in-use socket. To speed up the networking code, this data is stored in a so-called *destination cache*, whose entries are objects of type dst_entry. Each INET socket stores in the dst_cache field a pointer to a single dst_entry object, which corresponds to the destination host bound to the socket.

A dst_entry object stores a lot of data used by the kernel whenever it sends a packet to the corresponding remote host. For instance, it includes:

- A pointer to a net_device object describing the network device (for instance, a network card) that transmits or receives the packets
- A pointer to a neighbour structure relative to the router that forwards the packets to their final destination, if any (see the later section "The neighbor cache")
- A pointer to a hh_cache structure, which describes the common header to be attached to every packet to be transmitted (see the later section "The neighbor cache")
- The pointer to a function invoked whenever a packet is received from the remote host
- The pointer to a function invoked whenever a packet is to be transmitted

Routing Data Structures

The most important function of the IP layer consists of ensuring that packets originated by the host or received by the network interface cards are forwarded toward their final destinations. As you might easily guess, this task is really crucial because the routing algorithm should be fast enough to keep up with the highest network loads.

The IP routing mechanism is fairly simple. Each 32-bit integer representing an IP address encodes both a *network address*, which specifies the network the host is in, and a *host identifier*, which specifies the host inside the network. To properly interpret the IP address, the kernel must know the *network mask* of a given IP address—that is, what bits of the IP address encode the network address. For instance, suppose the network mask of the IP address 192.160.80.110 is 255.255.255.0; then 192.160.80.0 represents the network address, while 110 identifies the host inside its network. Nowadays, the network address is almost always stored in the most significant bits of the IP address, so each network mask can also be represented by the number of bits set to 1 (24 in our example).

The key property of IP routing is that any host in the internetwork needs only to know the address of a computer inside its local area network (a so-called *router*), which is able to forward the packets to the destination network.

For instance, consider the following routing table shown by the *netstat -rn* system command:

```
Destination     Gateway         Genmask          Flags   MSS  Window   irtt Iface
192.160.80.0    0.0.0.0         255.255.255.0    U        40  0           0 eth1
192.160.0.0     0.0.0.0         255.255.0.0      U        40  0           0 eth0
192.160.50.0    192.160.11.1    255.255.0.0      UG       40  0           0 eth0
0.0.0.0         192.160.1.1     0.0.0.0          UG       40  0           0 eth0
```

This computer is linked to two networks. One of them has the IP address 192.160. 80.0 and a netmask of 24 bits, and it is served by the Network Interface Card (NIC) associated with the network device *eth1*. The other network has the IP address 192. 160.0.0 and a netmask of 16 bits, and it is served by the NIC associated with *eth0*.

Suppose that a packet must be sent to a host that belongs to the local area network 192.160.80.0 and that has the IP address 192.160.80.110. The kernel examines the static routing table starting with the higher entry (the one including the greater number of bits set to 1 in the netmask). For each entry, it performs a logical AND between the destination host's IP address and the netmask; if the results are equal to the network destination address, the kernel uses the entry to route the packet. In our case, the first entry wins and the packet is sent to the *eth1* network device.

In this case, the "gateway" field of the static routing table entry is null ("0.0.0.0"). This means the address is on the local network of the sender, so the computer sends packets directly to hosts in the network; it encapsulates the packet in a frame carrying the Ethernet address of the destination host. The frame is physically broadcast to all hosts in the network, but any NIC automatically ignores frames carrying Ethernet addresses different from its own.

Suppose now that a packet must be sent to a host that has the IP address 209.204. 146.22. This address belongs to a remote network (not directly linked to our computer). The last entry in the table is a catch-all entry, since the AND logical operation with the netmask 0.0.0.0 always yields the network address 0.0.0.0. Thus, in our case, any IP address still not resolved by higher entries is sent through the *eth0* network device to the *default router* that has the IP address 192.160.1.1, which hopefully knows how to forward the packet toward its final destination. The packet is encapsulated in a frame carrying the Ethernet address of the default router.

The Forwarding Information Base (FIB)

The *Forwarding Information Base* (FIB), or *static routing table*, is the ultimate reference used by the kernel to determine how to forward packets to their destinations. As a matter of fact, if the destination network of a packet is not included in the FIB, then the kernel cannot transmit that packet. As mentioned previously, however, the FIB usually includes a default entry that catches any IP address not resolved by the other entries.

The kernel data structures that implement the FIB are quite sophisticated. In fact, routers might include several hundred lines, most of which refer to the same network devices or to the same gateway. Figure 18-1 illustrates a simplified view of the FIB's data structures when the table includes the four entries of the routing table just shown. You can get a low-level view of the data included in the FIB data structures by reading the */proc/net/route* file.

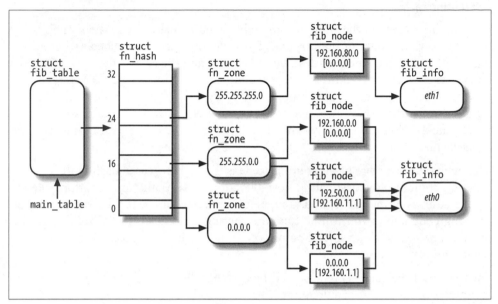

Figure 18-1. FIB's main data structures

The main_table global variable points to an fib_table object that represents the static routing table of the IPS architecture. Actually, it is possible to define secondary routing tables, but the table referenced by main_table is the most important one. The fib_table object includes the addresses of some methods that operate on the FIB, and stores the pointer to a fn_hash data structure.

The fn_hash data structure is essentially an array of 33 pointers, one for every FIB zone. A *zone* includes routing information for destination networks that have a given number of bits in the network mask. For instance, zone 24 includes entries for networks that have the mask 255.255.255.0.

Each zone is represented by a fn_zone descriptor. It references, through a hash table, the set of entries of the routing table that have the given netmask. For instance, in Figure 18-1, zone 16 references the entries 192.160.0.0 and 192.50.0.0.

The data relative to each routing table entry is stored in a fib_node descriptor. A router might have several entries, but it usually has very few network devices. Thus, to avoid wasting space, the fib_node descriptor does not include information about the network interface, but rather a pointer to a fib_info descriptor shared by several entries.

The routing cache

Looking up a route in the static routing table is quite a slow task: the kernel has to walk the various zones in the FIB and, for each entry in a zone, check whether the logical AND between the host destination address and the entry's netmask yields the entry's exact network address. To speed up routing, the kernel keeps the most recently discovered routes in a *routing cache*. Typically, the cache includes several hundreds of entries; they are sorted so that more frequently used routes are retrieved more quickly. You can easily get the contents of the cache by reading the */proc/net/rt_cache* file.

The main data structure of the routing cache is the rt_hash_table hash table; its hash function combines the destination host's IP address with other information, like the source address of the packet and the type of service required. In fact, the Linux networking code allows you to fine tune the routing process so that a packet can, for instance, be routed along several paths according to where the packet came from and what kind of data it is carrying.

Each entry of the cache is represented by a rtable data structure, which stores several pieces of information; among them:

- The source and destination IP addresses
- The gateway IP address, if any
- Data relative to the route identified by the entry, stored in a dst_entry embedded in the rtable data structure (see the earlier section "The Destination Cache")

The neighbor cache

Another core component of the networking code is the so-called "neighbor cache," which includes information relative to hosts that belong to the networks directly linked to the computer.

We know that IP addresses are the main host identifiers of the network layer; unfortunately, they are meaningless for the lower data-link layer, whose protocols are essentially hardware-dependent. In practice, when the kernel has to transmit a packet by means of a given network card device, it must encapsulate the data in a *frame* carrying, among other things, the hardware-dependent identifiers of the source and destination network card devices.

Most local area networks are based on the IEEE 802 standards, and in particular, on the 802.3 standard, which is commercially known as "Ethernet."[*] The network card identifiers of the 802 standards are 48-bit numbers, which are usually written as 6 bytes separated by colons (such as "00:50:DA:61:A7:83"). There are no two network card devices sharing the same identifier (although it would be sufficient to ensure that all network card devices in the same local area network have different identifiers).

How can the kernel know the identifier of a remote device? It uses an IPS protocol named Address Resolution Protocol (ARP). Basically, the kernel sends a broadcast packet into the local area network carrying the question: "What is the identifier of the network card device associated with IP address X?" As a result, the host identified by the specified IP address sends an answer packet carrying the network card device identifier.

It is a waste of time and bandwidth to repeat the whole process for every packet to be sent. Thus, the kernel keeps the network card device identifier, together with other precious data concerning the physical connection to the remote device, in the *neighbor cache* (often also called *arp cache*). You might get the contents of this cache by reading the */proc/net/arp* file. System administrators may also explicitly set the entries of this cache by means of the *arp* command.

Each entry of the neighbor cache is an object of type neighbour; the most important field is certainly ha, which stores the network card device identifier. The entry also stores a pointer to a hh_cache object belonging to the *hardware header cache*; since all packets sent to the same remote network card device are encapsulated in frames having the same header (essentially carrying the source and destination device identifiers), the kernel keeps a copy of the header in memory to avoid having to reconstruct it from scratch for every packet.

The Socket Buffer

Each single packet transmitted through a network device is composed of several pieces of information. Besides the *payload*—that is, the data whose transmission caused the creation of the packet itself—all network layers, starting from the data link layer and ending at the transport layer, add some control information. The format of a packet handled by a network card device is shown in Figure 18-2.

The whole packet is built by different functions in several stages. For instance, the UDP/TCP header and the IP header are composed of functions belonging, respectively, to the transport layer and the network layer of the IPS architecture, while the hardware header and trailer, which build the frame encapsulating the IP datagram, are written by a suitable method specific to the network card device.

---

[*] Actually, Ethernet local area networks sprang up before IEEE published its standards; unfortunately, Ethernet and IEEE standards disagree in small but nevertheless crucial details—for instance, in the format of the data link packets. Every host in the Internet is able to operate with both standards, though.

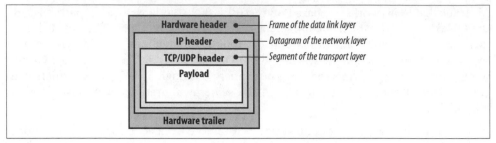

Figure 18-2. The packet format

The Linux networking code keeps each packet in a large memory area called a *socket buffer*. Each socket buffer is associated with a descriptor, which is a data structure of type sk_buff that stores, among other things, pointers to the following data structures:

- The socket buffer
- The *payload*—that is, the user data (inside the socket buffer)
- The data link trailer (inside the socket buffer)
- The INET socket (sock object)
- The network device's net_device object
- A descriptor of the transport layer header
- A descriptor of the network layer header
- A descriptor of the data link layer header
- The destination cache entry (dst_entry object)

The sk_buff data structure includes many other fields, like an identifier of the network protocol used for transmitting the packet, a checksum field, and the arrival time for received packets.

As a general rule, the kernel avoids copying data, but simply passes the sk_buff descriptor pointer, and thus the socket buffer, to each networking layer in turn. For instance, when preparing a packet to send, the transport layer starts copying the payload from the User Mode buffer into the higher portion of the socket buffer; then the transport layer adds its TCP or UDP header before the payload. Next, the control is transferred to the network layer, which receives the socket buffer descriptor and adds the IP header before the transport header. Eventually, the data link layer adds its header and trailer, and enqueues the packet for transmission.

System Calls Related to Networking

We won't be able to discuss all system calls related to networking. However, we shall examine the basic ones, namely those needed to send a UDP datagram.

In most Unix-like systems, the User Mode code fragment that sends a datagram looks like the following:

```
int sockfd; /* socket descriptor */
struct sockaddr_in addr_local, addr_remote; /* IPv4 address descriptors */
const char *mesg[] = "Hello, how are you?";

sockfd = socket(PF_INET, SOCK_DGRAM, 0);

addr_local.sin_family = AF_INET;
addr.sin_port = htons(50000);
addr.sin_addr.s_addr = htonl(0xc0a050f0); /* 192.160.80.240 */
bind(sockfd, (struct sockaddr *) & addr_local, sizeof(struct sockaddr_in));

addr_remote.sin_family = AF_INET;
addr_remote.sin_port = htons(49152);
inet_pton(AF_INET, "192.160.80.110", &addr_remote.sin_addr);
connect(sockfd, (struct sockaddr *) &addr_remote, sizeof(struct sockaddr_in));

write(sockfd, mesg, strlen(mesg)+1);
```

Obviously, this listing does not represent the complete source code of the program. For instance, we have not defined a main() function, we have omitted the proper #include directives for loading the header files, and we have not checked the return values of the system calls. However, the listing includes all network-related system calls issued by the program to send a UDP datagram.

Let's describe the system calls in the order the program uses them.

The socket() System Call

The socket() system call creates a new endpoint for a communication between two or more processes. In our example program, it is invoked in this way:

```
sockfd = socket(PF_INET, SOCK_DGRAM, 0);
```

The socket() system call returns a file descriptor. In fact, a socket is similar to an opened file because it is possible to read and write data on it by means of the usual read() and write() system calls.

The first parameter of the socket() system call represents the network architecture that will be used for the communication, as well as a particular network layer protocol adopted by the network architecture. The PF_INET macro denotes both the IPS architecture and Version 4 of the IP protocol (IPv4). Linux supports several different network architectures; a few of them are shown in Table 18-1 earlier in this chapter.

The second parameter of the socket() system call specifies the basic model of communication inside the network architecture. As we already know, the IPS architecture offers essentially two alternative models of communication:

SOCK_STREAM

> Reliable, connection-oriented, stream-based communication implemented by the TCP transport protocol

SOCK_DGRAM

> Unreliable, connection-less, datagram-based communication implemented by the UDP transport protocol

Moreover, the special SOCK_RAW value creates a socket that can be used to directly access the network layer protocol (in our case, the IPv4 protocol).

In general, a network architecture might offer other models of communication. For instance, SOCK_SEQPACKET specifies a reliable, connection-oriented, datagram-based communication, while SOCK_RDM specifies a reliable, connection-less, datagram-based communication; however, neither of them is available in the IPS.

The third parameter of the socket( ) system call specifies the transport protocol to be used in the communication; in general, for any model of communication, the network architecture might offer several different protocols. Passing the value 0 selects the default protocol for the specified communication model. Of course, when using the IPS, the value 0 selects the TCP transport protocol (IPPROTO_TCP) for the SOCK_STREAM model and the UDP protocol (IPPROTO_IP) for the SOCK_DGRAM model. On the other hand, the SOCK_RAW model allows the programmer to specify any one of the network-layer service protocols of the IPS—for instance, the Internet Control Message Protocol (IPPROTO_ICMP), the Exterior Gateway Protocol (IPPROTO_EGP), or the Internet Group Management Protocol (IPPROTO_IGMP).

The socket( ) system call is implemented by means of the sys_socket( ) service routine, which essentially performs three actions:

1. Allocates a descriptor for the new BSD socket (see the later section "BSD Sockets").
2. Initializes the new descriptor according to the specified network architecture, communication model, and protocol.
3. Allocates the first available file descriptor of the process and associates a new file object with that file descriptor and with the socket object.

Socket initialization

Let's return to the service routine of the socket( ) system call. After having allocated a new BSD socket, the function must initialize it according to the given network architecture, communication model, and protocol.

For every known network architecture, the kernel stores a pointer to an object of type net_proto_family in the net_families array. Essentially, the object just defines the create method, which is invoked whenever the kernel initializes a new socket of that network architecture.

The create method corresponding to the PF_INET architecture is implemented by inet_create( ). This function checks whether the communication model and the protocol specified as parameters of the socket( ) system call are compatible with the IPS network architecture; then it allocates and initializes a new INET socket and links it to the parent BSD socket.

Socket's files

Before terminating, the socket( )'s service routine allocates a new file object and a new dentry object for the *sockfs*'s file of the socket; then it associates these objects with the process that raised the system call through a new file descriptor (see the section "Files Associated with a Process" in Chapter 12).

As far as the VFS is concerned, any file associated with a socket is in no way special. The corresponding dentry object and inode object are included in the dentry cache and in the inode cache, respectively. The process that created the socket can access the file by means of the system calls that act on already opened files—that is, the system calls that receive a file descriptor as a parameter. Of course, the file object methods are implemented by functions that operate on the socket rather than on the file.

As far as the User Mode process is concerned, however, the socket's file is somewhat peculiar. In fact, a process can never issue an open( ) system call on such a file because it never appears on the system directory tree (remember that the *sockfs* special filesystem has no visible mount point). For the same reason, it is not possible to remove a socket file through the unlink( ) system call: the inodes belonging to the *sockfs* filesystem are automatically destroyed by the kernel whenever the socket is closed (released).

The bind( ) System Call

Once the socket( ) system call completes, a new socket is created and initialized. It represents a new communication channel that can be identified by the following five elements: protocol, local IP address, local port number, remote IP address, and remote port number.

Only the "protocol" element has been set so far. Hence, the next action of the User Mode process consists of setting the "local IP address" and the "local port number." These two elements identify the process that is sending packets onto the socket so the receiving process on the remote machine can determine who is talking and where the answers should be sent.[*]

The corresponding instructions in our simple program are the following:

---

[*] Actually, when a process uses the UDP protocol, it can omit the invocation of the bind( ) system call. In this case, the kernel automatically assigns a local address and a local port number to the socket as soon as the program issues a connect( ) or listen( ) system call.

```
struct sockaddr_in addr_local;
addr_local.sin_family = AF_INET;
addr.sin_port = htons(50000);
addr.sin_addr.s_addr = htonl(0xc0a050f0); /* 192.160.80.240 */
bind(sockfd, (struct sockaddr *) & addr_local, sizeof(struct sockaddr_in));
```

The addr_local local variable is of type struct sockaddr_in and represents an IPS identifier for a socket. It includes three significant fields:

sin_family
> The protocol family (AF_INET, AF_INET6, or AF_PACKET; this is the same as the macros in Table 18-1).

sin_port
> The port number.

sin_addr
> The network address. In the IPS architecture, it is composed of a single 32-bit field s_addr storing the IP address.

Therefore, our program sets the fields of the addr_local variable to the protocol family AF_INET, the port number 50,000, and the IP address 192.160.80.240. Notice how the dotted notation of the IP address is translated into a hexadecimal number.

In the 80 × 86 architecture, the numbers are represented in the "little endian" format (the byte at lower address is the less significant one) while the IPS architecture requires that the numbers be represented in the "big endian" format (the byte at lower address is the most significant one). Several functions, such as htons() and htonl(), are used to ensure that data is sent in the network byte order; other functions, such as ntohs() and ntohl(), ensure that received data is converted from the network to the host byte order.

The bind() system call receives as parameters the socket file descriptor and the address of addr_local. It also receives the length of the struct sockaddr_in data structure; in fact, bind() can be used for sockets of any network architecture, as well as for Unix sockets and any different type of socket that has addresses of different length.

The sys_bind() service routine copies the data of the sock_addr variable into the kernel address space, retrieves the address of the BSD socket object (struct socket) that corresponds to the file descriptor, and invokes its bind method. In the IPS architecture, this method is implemented by the inet_bind() function.

The inet_bind() function performs essentially the following operations:

1. Invokes the inet_addr_type() function to check whether the IP address passed to the bind() system call corresponds to the address of some network card device of the host; if not, it returns an error code. However, the User Mode program may pass the special IP address INADDR_ANY (0.0.0.0), which essentially delegates to the kernel the task of assigning the IP sender address.

---

2. If the port number passed to the bind( ) system call is smaller than 1,024, checks whether the User Mode process has superuser privileges (this is the CAP_NET_BIND_SERVICE capability; see the section "Process Credentials and Capabilities" in Chapter 20). However, the User Mode process may pass the value 0 as the port number; the kernel assigns a random, unused port number (see below).

3. Sets the rcv_saddr and saddr fields of the INET socket object with the IP address passed to the system call (the former field is used when looking in the routing table, while the latter is included in the header of outgoing packets). Usually, the fields hold the same value, except for special transmission modes like broadcast and multicasting.

4. Invokes the get_port protocol method of the INET socket object to check whether there already exists an INET socket for the transport protocol using the same local port number and IP address as the one being initialized. For IPv4 sockets using the UDP transport protocol, the method is implemented by the udp_v4_get_port( ) function. To speed up the lookup operation, the function uses a per-protocol hash table. Moreover, if the User Mode program specified a value of 0 for the port, the function assigns an unused number to the socket.

5. Stores the local port number in the sport field of the INET socket object.

The connect( ) System Call

The next operation of the User Mode process consists of setting the "remote IP address" and the "remote port number," so the kernel knows where datagrams written to the socket have to be sent. This is achieved by invoking the connect( ) system call.

It is important to observe that a User Mode program is in no way obliged to connect a UDP socket to a destination host. In fact, the program may use the sendto( ) and sendmsg( ) system calls to transmit datagrams over the socket, each time specifying the destination host's IP address and port number. Similarly, the program may receive datagrams from a UDP socket by invoking the recvfrom( ) and recvmsg( ) system calls. However, the connect( ) system call is required if the User Mode program transfers data on the socket by means of the read( ) and write( ) system call.

Since our program is going to use the write( ) system call to send its datagram, it invokes connect( ) to set up the destination of the message. The relevant instructions are:

```
struct sockaddr_in addr_remote;
addr_remote.sin_family = AF_INET;
addr_remote.sin_port = htons(49152);
inet_pton(AF_INET, "192.160.80.110", &addr_remote.sin_addr);
connect(sockfd, (struct sockaddr *) &addr_remote, sizeof(struct sockaddr_in));
```

The program initializes the addr_remote local variable by writing into it the IP address 192.160.80.110 and the port number 49,152. This is very similar to the initialization of the addr_local variable discussed in the previous section; however, this time the program invoked the inet_pton( ) library helper function to convert a string representing the IP address in dotted notation into a number in the network order format.

The connect( ) system call receives the same parameters as the bind( ) system call. It copies the data of the addr_remote variable into the kernel address space, retrieves the address of the BSD socket object (struct socket) corresponding to the file descriptor, and invokes its connect method. In IPS architecture, this method is implemented by either the inet_dgram_connect( ) function for UDP or the inet_stream_connect( ) function for TCP.

Our simple program uses a UDP socket, so let's describe what the inet_dgram_connection( ) function does:

1. If the socket does not have a local port number, invokes inet_autobind( ) to automatically assign a unused value. In our case, the program issued a bind( ) system call before invoking collect( ), but an application using UDP is not really obliged to do so.

2. Invokes the connect method of the INET socket object.

The UDP protocol implements the INET socket's connect method by means of the udp_connect( ) function, which executes the following actions:

1. If the INET socket already has a destination host, removes it from the destination cache (which is the dst_cache field of the sock object; see the earlier section "The Destination Cache").

2. Invokes the ip_route_connect( ) function to establish a route to the host identified by the IP address passed as a parameter of connect( ). In turn, this function invokes ip_route_output_key( ) to search an entry corresponding to the route in the route cache (see the earlier section "The routing cache"). If the route cache does not include the desired entry, ip_route_output_key( ) invokes ip_route_output_slow( ) to look up a suitable entry in the FIB (see the earlier section "The Forwarding Information Base (FIB)"). Let's assume that, once this step terminates, a route is found, so the address of a suitable rtable object is determined.

3. Initializes the daddr field of the INET socket object with the remote IP address found in the rtable object. Usually, it coincides with the IP address specified by the user as a parameter of the connect( ) system call.

4. Initializes the dport field of the INET socket object with the remote port number specified as a parameter of the connect( ) system call.

5. Puts the value TCP_ESTABLISHED in the state field of the INET socket object (when used by UDP, the flag indicates that the INET socket is "connected" to a destination host).

6. Sets the dst_cache entry of the sock object to the address of the dst_entry object embedded in the rtable object (see the earlier section "The Destination Cache").

Writing Packets to a Socket

Finally, our example program is ready to send messages to the remote host; it simply writes the data onto the socket:

```
write(sockfd, mesg, strlen(mesg)+1);
```

The write() system call triggers the write method of the file object associated with the sockfd file descriptor. For socket files, this method is implemented by the sock_write() function, which performs the following actions:

1. Determines the address of the socket object embedded in the file's inode.

2. Allocates and initializes a "message header"; namely, a msghdr data structure, which stores various control information.

3. Invokes the sock_sendmsg() function, passing to it the addresses of the socket object and the msghdr data structure. In turn, this function performs the following actions:

   a. Invokes scm_send() to check the contents of the message header and allocate a scm_cookie (*socket control message*) data structure, storing into it a few fields of control information distilled from the message header.

   b. Invokes the sendmsg method of the socket object, passing to it the addresses of the socket object, message header, and scm_cookie data structure.

   c. Invokes scm_destroy() to release the scm_cookie data structure.

Since the BSD socket has been set up specifying the UDP protocol, the addresses of the socket object's methods are stored in the inet_dgram_ops table. In particular, the sendmsg method is implemented by the inet_sendmsg() function, which extracts the address of the INET socket stored in the BSD socket and invokes the sendmsg method of the INET socket.

Again, since the INET socket has been set up specifying the UDP protocol, the addresses of the sock object's methods are stored in the udp_prot table. In particular, the sendmsg method is implemented by the udp_sendmsg() function.

Transport layer: the udp_sendmsg() function

The udp_sendmsg() function receives as parameters the addresses of the sock object and the message header (msghdr data structure), and performs the following actions:

1. Allocates a udpfakehdr data structure, which contains the UDP header of the packet to be sent.

2. Determines the address of the rtable describing the route to the destination host from the dst_cache field of the sock object.

3. Invokes ip_build_xmit(), passing to it the addresses of all relevant data structures, like the sock object, the UDP header, the rtable object, and the address of a UDP-specific function that constructs the packet to be transmitted.

Transport and network layers: the ip_build_xmit() function

The `ip_build_xmit()` function is used to transmit an IP datagram. It performs the following actions:

1. Invokes `sock_alloc_send_skb()` to allocate a new socket buffer together with the corresponding socket buffer descriptor (see the earlier section "The Socket Buffer").

2. Determines the position inside the socket buffer where the payload shall go (the payload is placed near the end of the socket buffer, so its position depends on the payload size).

3. Writes the IP header on the socket buffer, leaving space for the UDP header.

4. Invokes either `udp_getfrag_nosum()` or `udp_getfrag()` to copy the data of the UDP datagram from the User Mode buffer; the latter function also computes, if required, the checksum of the data and of the UDP header (the UDP standard specifies that this checksum computation be optional).*

5. Invokes the `output` method of the `dst_entry` object, passing to it the address of the socket buffer descriptor.

Data link layer: composing the hardware header

The `output` method of the `dst_entry` object invokes the function of the data link layer that writes the hardware header (and trailer, if required) of the packet in the buffer.

The `output` method of the IP's `dst_entry` object is usually implemented by the `ip_output()` function, which receives as a parameter the address `skb` of the socket buffer descriptor. In turn, this function essentially performs the following actions:

- Checks whether there is already a suitable hardware header descriptor in the cache by looking at the `hh` field of the `skb->dst` destination cache object (see the earlier section "The Destination Cache"). If the field is not `NULL`, the cache includes the header, so it copies the hardware header into the socket buffer, and then invokes the `hh_output` method of the `hh_cache` object.

- Otherwise, if the `skb->dst->hh` field is `NULL`, the header must be prepared from scratch. Thus, the function invokes the `output` method of the `neighbour` object pointed to by the `neighbour` field of `skb->dst`, which is implemented by the `neigh_resolve_output()` function. To compose the header, the latter function invokes a suitable method of the `net_device` object relative to the network card device that shall transmit the packet, and then inserts the new hardware header in the cache.

---

* You might wonder why the IP header is written in the socket buffer before the UDP header. Well, the UDP standard dictates that the checksum, if used, has to be computed on the payload, the UDP header, and the last 12 bytes of the IP header (including the source and destination IP addresses). The simplest way to compute the UDP checksum is thus to write the IP header before the UDP header.

Both the hh_output method of the hh_cache object and the output method of the neighbour object end up invoking the dev_queue_xmit() function.

Data link layer: enqueueing the socket buffer for transmission

The dev_queue_xmit() function takes care of queueing the socket buffer for later transmission. In general, network cards are slow devices, and at any given instant there can be many packets waiting to be transmitted. They are usually processed with a First-In, First-Out policy (hence the queue of packets), even if the Linux kernel offers several sophisticated packet scheduling algorithms to be used in high-performance routers. As a general rule, all network card devices define their own queue of packets waiting to be transmitted. Exceptions are virtual devices like the loopback device (*lo*) and the devices offered by various tunneling protocols, but we don't discuss these further.

A queue of socket buffers is implemented through a complex Qdisc object. Thanks to this data structure, the packet scheduling functions can efficiently manipulate the queue and quickly select the "best" packet to be sent. However, for the purpose of our simple description, the queue is just a list of socket buffer descriptors.

Essentially, dev_queue_xmit() performs the following actions:

1. Checks whether the driver of the network device (whose descriptor is stored in the dev field of the socket buffer descriptor) defines its own queue of packets waiting to be transmitted (the address of the Qdisc object is stored in the qdisc field of the net_device object).

2. Invokes the enqueue method of the corresponding Qdisc object to append the socket buffer to the queue.

3. Invokes the qdisc_run() function to ensure that the network device is actively sending the packets in the queue.

The chain of functions executed by the sys_write() system call service routine ends here. As you see, the final result consists of a new packet that is appended to the transmit queue of a network card device.

In the next section, we look at how our packet is processed by the network card.

Sending Packets to the Network Card

A network card device driver is usually started either when the kernel inserts a packet in its transmit queue (as described in the previous section), or when a packet is received from the communication channel. Let's focus here on packet transmission.

As we have seen, the qdisc_run() function is invoked whenever the kernel wishes to activate a network card device driver; it is also executed by the NET_TX_SOFTIRQ softirq, which is implemented by the net_tx_action() function (see the section "Softirqs, Tasklets, and Bottom Halves" in Chapter 4).

Essentially, the qdisc_run() function checks whether the network card device is idle and can thus transmit the packets in the queue. If the device cannot do this—for instance, because the card is already busy in transmitting or receiving a packet, the queue has been stopped to avoid flooding the communication channel, or for whatever other reason—the NET_TX_SOFTIRQ softirq is activated and the current execution of qdisc_run() is terminated. At a later time, when the scheduler selects a *ksoftirqd_CPUn* kernel thread, the net_tx_action() function invokes qdisc_run() again to retry the packet transmission.

In particular, qdisc_run() performs the following actions:

1. Checks whether the packet queue is "stopped"—that is, whether a suitable bit in the state field of the net_device network card object is set. If it is stopped, the function returns immediately.

2. Invokes the qdisc_restart() function, which in turn performs the following actions:

   a. Invokes the dequeue method of the Qdisc packet queue to extract a packet from the queue. If the queue is empty, it terminates.

   b. Checks whether a packet sniffing policy is enforced on the kernel, telling it to pass a copy of each outgoing packet to a local socket; in this case, the function invokes the dev_queue_xmit_nit() function to do the job. We won't discuss this further.

   c. Invokes the hard_start_xmit method of the net_device object that describes the network card device.

   d. If the hard_start_xmit method fails in transmitting the packet, it reinserts the packet in the queue and invokes cpu_raise_softirq() to schedule the activation of the NET_TX_SOFTIRQ softirq.

3. If the queue is now empty, or the hard_start_xmit method fails in transmitting the packet, the function terminates. Otherwise, it jumps to Step 1 to process another packet in the queue.

The hard_start_xmit method is specific to the network card device and takes care of transferring the packet from the socket buffer to the device's memory. Typically, the method limits itself to activate a DMA transfer. In PCI-based network cards, moreover, a small number of DMA transfers may usually be booked in advance: they are automatically activated by the card whenever it finishes the ongoing DMA transfers. If the card is not able to accept further packets because the device's memory is full, the method stops the packet queue by setting the proper bit in the state field of the net_device object. Therefore, the qdisc_run() function terminates and is presumably executed again later by the softirq.

When a DMA transfer ends, the card raises an interrupt. The corresponding interrupt handler, in turn, performs the following actions:

1. Acknowledges the interrupt issued by the card.

2. Checks for transmission errors, updates driver statistics, and so on.

3. Invokes, if necessary, the cpu_raise_softirq( ) function to schedule the activation of the softirq.

4. If the queue is stopped, resets the bit in the state field of the net_device object and restarts packet processing.

As you see, network card device drivers work like disk device drivers: the real work is mostly done in interrupt handlers and deferrable functions, so that usual processes are not blocked waiting for packet transmissions.

Receiving Packets from the Network Card

This chapter is mostly focused on how the kernel handles the transmission of network packets. We have already glimpsed at many crucial data structures of the networking code, so we will just give a brief description of the other side of the story; namely, how a network packet is received.

The main difference between transmitting and receiving is that the kernel cannot predict when a packet will arrive at a network card device. Therefore, the networking code that takes care of receiving the packets runs in interrupt handlers and deferrable functions.

Let's sketch a typical chain of events occurring when a packet carrying the right hardware address (card identifier) arrives to the network device.

1. The network device saves the packet in a buffer in the device's memory (the card usually keeps several packets at once in a circular buffer).

2. The network device raises an interrupt.

3. The interrupt handler allocates and initializes a new socket buffer for the packet.

4. The interrupt handler copies the packet from the device's memory to the socket buffer.

5. The interrupt handler invokes a function (such as eth_type_trans( ) function for Ethernet and IEEE 802.3) to determine the protocol of the packet encapsulated in the data link frame.

6. The interrupt handler invokes the netif_rx( ) function to notify the Linux networking code that a new packet is arrived and should be processed.

Of course, the interrupt handler is specific to the network card device. Many device drivers try to be nice to the other devices in the system and move lengthy tasks, such as allocating a socket buffer or copying a packet to deferrable functions.

The netif_rx( ) function is the main entry point of the receiving code of the networking layer (above the network card device driver). The kernel uses a per-CPU queue for the packets that have been received from the network devices and are waiting to be processed by the various protocol stack layers. The function essentially appends the new packet in this queue and invokes cpu_raise_softirq() to schedule the activation of the NET_RX_SOFTIRQ softirq. (Remember that the same softirq can be executed concurrently on several CPUs, hence the reason for the per-CPU queue of received packets.)

The NET_RX_SOFTIRQ softirq is implemented by the net_rx_action() function, which essentially executes the following operations:[*]

1. Extracts the first packet from the queue. If the queue is empty, it terminates.
2. Determines the network layer protocol number encoded in the data link layer.
3. Invokes a suitable function of the network layer protocol.

The corresponding function for the IP protocol is named ip_rcv(), which essentially executes the following actions:

1. Checks the length and the checksum of the packet and discards it if it is corrupted or truncated.
2. Invokes ip_route_input(), which initializes the destination cache (dst_entry field) of the socket buffer descriptor. To determine the route followed by the packet, the function looks the route up first in the route cache, and then in the FIB (if the route cache doesn't include a relevant entry). In this way, the kernel determines whether the packet must be forwarded to another host or simply passed to a protocol of the transport layer.
3. Checks to see whether any packet sniffing or other input policy is enforced. In the affirmative case, it handles the packet accordingly; we don't discuss these topics further.
4. Invokes the input method of the dst_entry object of the packet.

If the packet has to be forwarded to another host, the input method is implemented by the ip_forward() function; otherwise, it is implemented by the ip_local_delivery() function. Let's follow the latter path.

The ip_local_delivery() function takes care of reassembling the original IP datagram, if the datagram has been fragmented along its way. Then the function reads the IP header and determines the type of transport protocol to which the packet belongs. If the transport protocol is TCP, the function ends up invoking tcp_v4_rcv(); if the transport protocol is UDP, the function ends up invoking udp_rcv().

Let's continue following the UDP path. The udp_rcv() function essentially executes the following actions:

1. Invokes the udp_v4_lookup() function to find the INET socket to which the UDP datagram has been sent (by looking at the port number inside the UDP header). The kernel keeps the INET socket in a hash table so that the lookup operation is reasonably fast. If the UDP datagram is not associated with a socket, the function discards the packet and terminates.

---

[*] We omit discussing several special cases, such as when the packet has to be quickly forwarded to another network card device or when the host is acting as a bridge that links two local area network as if they were a single one.

2. Invokes `udp_queue_rcv_skb()`, which in turn invokes `sock_queue_rcv_skb()`, to append the packet into a queue of the INET socket (`receive_queue` field of the `sock` object) and to invoke the `data_ready` method of the `sock` object.

3. Releases the socket buffer and the socket buffer descriptor.

INET sockets implement the `data_ready` method by means of the `sock_def_readable()` function, which essentially wakes up any process sleeping in the socket's wait queue (listed in the `sleep` field of the `sock` object).

There is one final step to describe what happens when a process reads from the BSD socket owning our INET socket. The `read()` system call triggers the read method of the file object associated with the socket's special file. This method is implemented by the `sock_read()` function, which in turn invokes the `sock_recvmsg()` function. The latter function is similar to `sock_sendmsg()` described earlier. Essentially, it invokes the `recvmsg` method of the BSD socket. In turn, this method (`inet_recvmsg()`) invokes the `recvmsg` method of the INET socket; that is, either the `tcp_recvmsg()` or the `udp_recvmsg()` function.

Finally, the `udp_recvmsg()` function executes the following actions:

1. Invokes the `skb_recv_datagram()` function to extract the first packet from the `receive_queue` queue of the INET socket and return the address of the corresponding socket buffer descriptor. If the queue is empty, the function blocks the current process (unless the read operation was not blocking).

2. If the UDP datagram carries a valid checksum and checks that the message has not been corrupted during the transmission (actually, this step is performed at the same time as Step 3).

3. Copies the payload of the UDP datagram into the User Mode buffer.

CHAPTER 19
Process Communication

This chapter explains how User Mode processes can synchronize their actions and exchange data. We already covered several synchronization topics in Chapter 5, but the actors there were kernel control paths, not User Mode programs. We are now ready, after having discussed I/O management and filesystems at length, to extend the discussion to User Mode processes. These processes must rely on the kernel to facilitate interprocess synchronization and communication.

As we saw in the section "Linux File Locking" in Chapter 12, a form of synchronization among User Mode processes can be achieved by creating a (possibly empty) file and using suitable VFS system calls to lock and unlock it. While processes can similarly share data via temporary files protected by locks, this approach is costly because it requires accesses to the disk filesystem. For this reason, all Unix kernels include a set of system calls that supports process communication without interacting with the filesystem; furthermore, several wrapper functions were developed and inserted in suitable libraries to expedite how processes issue their synchronization requests to the kernel.

As usual, application programmers have a variety of needs that call for different communication mechanisms. Here are the basic mechanisms that Unix systems offer to allow interprocess communication:

Pipes and FIFOs (named pipes)
> Best suited to implement producer/consumer interactions among processes. Some processes fill the pipe with data, while others extract data from the pipe.

Semaphores
> Represent, as the name implies, the User Mode version of the kernel semaphores discussed in the section "Semaphores" in Chapter 5.

Messages
> Allow processes to exchange messages (short blocks of data) by reading and writing them in predefined message queues.

Shared memory regions

Allow processes to exchange information via a shared block of memory. In applications that must share large amounts of data, this can be the most efficient form of process communication.

Sockets

Allow processes on different computers to exchange data through a network, as described in Chapter 18. Sockets can also be used as a communication tool for processes located on the same host computer; the X Window System graphic interface, for instance, uses a socket to allow client programs to exchange data with the X server.

Pipes

Pipes are an interprocess communication mechanism that is provided in all flavors of Unix. A *pipe* is a one-way flow of data between processes: all data written by a process to the pipe is routed by the kernel to another process, which can thus read it.

In Unix command shells, pipes can be created by means of the | operator. For instance, the following statement instructs the shell to create two processes connected by a pipe:

```
$ ls | more
```

The standard output of the first process, which executes the *ls* program, is redirected to the pipe; the second process, which executes the *more* program, reads its input from the pipe.

Note that the same results can also be obtained by issuing two commands such as the following:

```
$ ls > temp
$ more < temp
```

The first command redirects the output of *ls* into a regular file; then the second command forces *more* to read its input from the same file. Of course, using pipes instead of temporary files is usually more convenient due to the following reasons:

• The shell statement is much shorter and simpler.

• There is no need to create temporary regular files, which must be deleted later.

Using a Pipe

Pipes may be considered open files that have no corresponding image in the mounted filesystems. A process creates a new pipe by means of the pipe( ) system call, which returns a pair of file descriptors; the process may then pass these descriptors to its descendants through fork( ), thus sharing the pipe with them. The processes can read from the pipe by using the read( ) system call with the first file descriptor; likewise, they can write into the pipe by using the write( ) system call with the second file descriptor.

POSIX defines only half-duplex pipes, so even though the pipe( ) system call returns two file descriptors, each process must close one before using the other. If a two-way flow of data is required, the processes must use two different pipes by invoking pipe( ) twice.

Several Unix systems, such as System V Release 4, implement full-duplex pipes. In a *full-duplex pipe*, both descriptors can be written into and read from, thus there are two bidirectional channels of information. Linux adopts yet another approach: each pipe's file descriptors are still one-way, but it is not necessary to close one of them before using the other.

Let's resume the previous example. When the command shell interprets the ls|more statement, it essentially performs the following actions:

1. Invokes the pipe( ) system call; let's assume that pipe( ) returns the file descriptors 3 (the pipe's *read channel*) and 4 (the *write channel*).
2. Invokes the fork( ) system call twice.
3. Invokes the close( ) system call twice to release file descriptors 3 and 4.

The first child process, which must execute the *ls* program, performs the following operations:

1. Invokes dup2(4,1) to copy file descriptor 4 to file descriptor 1. From now on, file descriptor 1 refers to the pipe's write channel.
2. Invokes the close( ) system call twice to release file descriptors 3 and 4.
3. Invokes the execve( ) system call to execute the *ls* program (see the section "The exec Functions" in Chapter 20). The program writes its output to the file that has file descriptor 1 (the standard output); i.e., it writes into the pipe.

The second child process must execute the *more* program; therefore, it performs the following operations:

1. Invokes dup2(3,0) to copy file descriptor 3 to file descriptor 0. From now on, file descriptor 0 refers to the pipe's read channel.
2. Invokes the close( ) system call twice to release file descriptors 3 and 4.
3. Invokes the execve( ) system call to execute *more*. By default, that program reads its input from the file that has file descriptor 0 (the standard input); i.e., it reads from the pipe.

In this simple example, the pipe is used by exactly two processes. Because of its implementation, though, a pipe can be used by an arbitrary number of processes.[*]

---

[*] Since most shells offer pipes that connect only two processes, applications requiring pipes used by more than two processes must be coded in a programming language such as C.

Clearly, if two or more processes read or write the same pipe, they must explicitly synchronize their accesses by using file locking (see the section "Linux File Locking" in Chapter 12) or IPC semaphores (see the section "IPC Semaphores" later in this chapter).

Many Unix systems provide, besides the pipe( ) system call, two wrapper functions named popen( ) and pclose( ) that handle all the dirty work usually done when using pipes. Once a pipe has been created by means of the popen( ) function, it can be used with the high-level I/O functions included in the C library (fprintf( ), fscanf( ), and so on).

In Linux, popen( ) and pclose( ) are included in the C library. The popen( ) function receives two parameters: the filename pathname of an executable file and a type string specifying the direction of the data transfer. It returns the pointer to a FILE data structure. The popen( ) function essentially performs the following operations:

1. Creates a new pipe by using the pipe( ) system call
2. Forks a new process, which in turn executes the following operations:
   a. If type is r, duplicates the file descriptor associated with the pipe's write channel as file descriptor 1 (standard output); otherwise, if type is w, duplicates the file descriptor associated with the pipe's read channel as file descriptor 0 (standard input)
   b. Closes the file descriptors returned by pipe( )
   c. Invokes the execve( ) system call to execute the program specified by filename
3. If type is r, closes the file descriptor associated with the pipe's write channel; otherwise, if type is w, closes the file descriptor associated with the pipe's read channel
4. Returns the address of the FILE file pointer that refers to whichever file descriptor for the pipe is still open

After the popen( ) invocation, parent and child can exchange information through the pipe: the parent can read (if type is r) or write (if type is w) data by using the FILE pointer returned by the function. The data is written to the standard output or read from the standard input, respectively, by the program executed by the child process.

The pclose( ) function (which receives the file pointer returned by popen( ) as its parameter) simply invokes the wait4( ) system call and waits for the termination of the process created by popen( ).

Pipe Data Structures

We now have to start thinking again on the system call level. Once a pipe is created, a process uses the read( ) and write( ) VFS system calls to access it. Therefore, for each pipe, the kernel creates an inode object plus two file objects—one for reading and the other for writing. When a process wants to read from or write to the pipe, it must use the proper file descriptor.

When the inode object refers to a pipe, its i_pipe field points to a pipe_inode_info structure shown in Table 19-1.

Table 19-1. The pipe_inode_info structure

Type	Field	Description
struct wait_queue *	wait	Pipe/FIFO wait queue
char *	base	Address of kernel buffer
unsigned int	len	Number of bytes written into the buffer and yet to be read
unsigned int	start	Read position in kernel buffer
unsigned int	readers	Flag for (or number of) reading processes
unsigned int	writers	Flag for (or number of) writing processes
unsigned int	waiting_readers	Number of reading processes sleeping in the wait queue
unsigned int	waiting_writers	Number of writing processes sleeping in the wait queue
unsigned int	r_counter	Like readers, but used when waiting for a process that reads from the FIFO
unsigned int	w_counter	Like writers, but used when waiting for a process that writes into the FIFO

Besides one inode and two file objects, each pipe has its own *pipe buffer*—a single page frame containing the data written into the pipe and yet to be read. The address of this page frame is stored in the base field of the pipe_inode_info structure. The len field of the structure stores the number of bytes written into the pipe buffer that are yet to be read; in the following, we call that number the current *pipe size*.

The pipe buffer is circular and it is accessed both by reading and writing processes, so the kernel must keep track of two current positions in the buffer:

- The offset of the next byte to be read, which is stored in the start field of the pipe_inode_info structure
- The offset of the next byte to be written, which is derived from start and the pipe size (the len field of the structure)

To avoid race conditions on the pipe's data structures, the kernel prevents concurrent accesses to the pipe buffer through the use of the i_sem semaphore included in the inode object.

The pipefs special filesystem

A pipe is implemented as a set of VFS objects, which have no corresponding disk image. In Linux 2.4, these VFS objects are organized into the *pipefs* special filesystem to expedite their handling (see the section "Special Filesystems" in Chapter 12). Since this filesystem has no mount point in the system directory tree, users never see it. However, thanks to *pipefs*, the pipes are fully integrated in the VFS layer, and the kernel can handle them in the same way as named pipes or FIFOs, which truly exist as files recognizable to end users (see the later section "FIFOs").

The init_pipe_fs( ) function, typically executed during kernel initialization, registers the *pipefs* filesystem and mounts it (refer to the discussion in the section "Mounting the Root Filesystem" in Chapter 12):

```
struct file_system_type pipe_fs_type;
root_fs_type.name = "pipefs";
root_fs_type.read_super = pipefs_read_super;
root_fs_type.fs_flags = FS_NOMOUNT;
register_filesystem(&pipe_fs_type);
pipe_mnt = do_kern_mount("pipefs", 0, "pipefs", NULL);
```

The mounted filesystem object that represents the root directory of *pipefs* is stored in the pipe_mnt variable.

Creating and Destroying a Pipe

The pipe( ) system call is serviced by the sys_pipe( ) function, which in turn invokes the do_pipe( ) function. To create a new pipe, do_pipe( ) performs the following operations:

1. Invokes the get_pipe_inode( ) function, which allocates and initializes an inode object for the pipe in the *pipefs* filesystem. In particular, this function executes the following actions:

    a. Allocates a pipe_inode_info data structure and stores its address in the i_pipe field of the inode.

    b. Allocates a page frame for the pipe buffer and stores its starting address in the base field of the pipe inode info structure.

    c. Initializes the start, len, waiting_readers, and waiting_writers fields of the pipe_inode_info structure to 0.

    d. Initializes the r_counter and w_counter fields of the pipe_inode_info structure to 1.

2. Sets the readers and writers fields of the pipe_inode_info structure to 1.

3. Allocates a file object and a file descriptor for the read channel of the pipe, sets the flag field of the file object to O_RDONLY, and initializes the f_op field with the address of the read_pipe_fops table.

4. Allocates a file object and a file descriptor for the write channel of the pipe, sets the flag field of the file object to O_WRONLY, and initializes the f_op field with the address of the write_pipe_fops table.

5. Allocates a dentry object and uses it to link the two file objects and the inode object (see the section "The Common File Model" in Chapter 12); then inserts the new inode in the *pipefs* special filesystem.

6. Returns the two file descriptors to the User Mode process.

The process that issues a pipe( ) system call is initially the only process that can access the new pipe, both for reading and writing. To represent that the pipe has both a reader and a writer, the readers and writers fields of the pipe_inode_info data structure are initialized to 1. In general, each of these two fields is set to 1 only if the corresponding pipe's file object is still opened by a process; the field is set to 0 if the corresponding file object has been released, since it is no longer accessed by any process.

Forking a new process does not increase the value of the readers and writers fields, so they never rise above 1;[*] however, it does increase the value of the usage counters of all file objects still used by the parent process (see the section "The clone( ), fork( ), and vfork( ) System Calls" in Chapter 3). Thus, the objects are not released even when the parent dies, and the pipe stays open for use by the children.

Whenever a process invokes the close( ) system call on a file descriptor associated with a pipe, the kernel executes the fput( ) function on the corresponding file object, which decrements the usage counter. If the counter becomes 0, the function invokes the release method of the file operations (see the sections "The close( ) System Call" and "Files Associated with a Process" in Chapter 12).

According to whether the file is associated with the read or write channel, the release method is implemented by either pipe_read_release( ) or pipe_write_release( ); both functions invoke pipe_release( ), which sets either the readers field or the writers field of the pipe_inode_info structure to 0. The function checks whether both the readers and writers fields are equal to 0; in this case, it releases the page frame containing the pipe buffer. Otherwise, the function wakes up any processes sleeping in the pipe's wait queue so they can recognize the change in the pipe state.

Reading from a Pipe

A process wishing to get data from a pipe issues a read( ) system call, specifying the file descriptor associated with the pipe's reading end. As described in the section "The read( ) and write( ) System Calls" in Chapter 12, the kernel ends up invoking the read method found in the file operation table associated with the proper file object. In the case of a pipe, the entry for the read method in the read_pipe_fops table points to the pipe_read( ) function.

The pipe_read( ) function is quite involved, since the POSIX standard specifies several requirements for the pipe's read operations. Table 19-2 summarizes the expected behavior of a read( ) system call that requests n bytes from a pipe that has a pipe size (number of bytes in the pipe buffer yet to be read) equal to p.

---

[*] As we'll see, the readers and writers fields act as counters instead of flags when associated with FIFOs.

The system call might block the current process in two cases:

- The pipe buffer is empty when the system call starts.
- The pipe buffer does not include all requested bytes, and a writing process was previously put to sleep while waiting for space in the buffer.

Notice that the read operation can be nonblocking: in this case, it completes as soon as all available bytes (even none) are copied into the user address space.[*]

Notice also that the value 0 is returned by the read( ) system call only if the pipe is empty and no process is currently using the file object associated with the pipe's write channel.

Table 19-2. Reading n bytes from a pipe

| Pipe Size p | At least one writing process | | | No writing process |
| | Blocking read | | Nonblocking read | |
	Sleeping writer	No sleeping writer		
p = 0	Copy n bytes and return n, waiting for data when the pipe buffer is empty.	Wait for some data, copy it, and return its size.	Return -EAGAIN.	Return 0.
0 < p < n		Copy p bytes and return p: 0 bytes are left in the pipe buffer.		
p ≥ n	Copy n bytes and return n: p-n bytes are left in the pipe buffer.			

The function performs the following operations:

1. Acquires the i_sem semaphore of the inode.
2. Determines whether the pipe size, which is stored into the len field of the pipe_inode_info structure, is 0. In this case, determines whether the function must return or whether the process must be blocked while waiting until another process writes some data in the pipe (see Table 19-2). The type of I/O operation (blocking or nonblocking) is specified by the O_NONBLOCK flag in the f_flags field of the file object. If the current process must be blocked, the function performs the following actions:

    a. Adds 1 to the waiting_readers field of the pipe_inode_info structure.

    b. Adds current to the wait queue of the pipe (the wait field of the pipe_inode_info structure).

    c. Releases the inode semaphore.

    d. Sets the process status to TASK_INTERRUPTIBLE and invokes schedule( ).

    e. Once awake, removes current from the wait queue, acquires again the i_sem inode semaphore, decrements the waiting_readers field, and then jumps back to Step 2.

---

[*] Nonblocking operations are usually requested by specifying the O_NONBLOCK flag in the open( ) system call. This method does not work for pipes, since they cannot be opened. A process can, however, require a nonblocking operation on a pipe by issuing a fcntl( ) system call on the corresponding file descriptor.

3. Copies the requested number of bytes (or the number of available bytes, if the buffer size is too small) from the pipe's buffer to the user address space.

4. Updates the start and len fields of the pipe_inode_info structure.

5. Invokes wake_up_interruptible( ) to wake up all processes sleeping on the pipe's wait queue.

6. If not all requested bytes have been copied, there is at least one writing process currently sleeping (waiting_writers field greater than 0) and the read operation is nonblocking, so the function jumps back to Step 2.

7. Releases the i_sem semaphore of the inode.

8. Returns the number of bytes copied into the user address space.

Writing into a Pipe

A process wishing to put data into a pipe issues a write( ) system call, specifying the file descriptor for the writing end of the pipe. The kernel satisfies this request by invoking the write method of the proper file object; the corresponding entry in the write_pipe_fops table points to the pipe_write( ) function.

Table 19-3 summarizes the behavior, specified by the POSIX standard, of a write( ) system call that requested to write n bytes into a pipe having u unused bytes in its buffer. In particular, the standard requires that write operations involving a small number of bytes must be atomically executed. More precisely, if two or more processes are concurrently writing into a pipe, each write operation involving fewer than 4,096 bytes (the pipe buffer size) must finish without being interleaved with write operations of other processes to the same pipe. However, write operations involving more than 4,096 bytes may be nonatomic and may also force the calling process to sleep.

Table 19-3. Writing n bytes to a pipe

	At least one reading process		
Available buffer space u	Blocking write	Nonblocking write	No reading process
$u<n\leq 4096$	Wait until $n-u$ bytes are freed, copy n bytes, and return n.	Return -EAGAIN.	Send SIGPIPE signal and return -EPIPE.
$n>4096$	Copy n bytes (waiting when necessary) and return n.	If $u>0$, copy u bytes and return u; else return -EAGAIN.	
$u\geq n$	Copy n bytes and return n.		

Moreover, each write operation to a pipe must fail if the pipe does not have a reading process (that is, if the readers field of the pipe's inode object has the value 0). In this case, the kernel sends a SIGPIPE signal to the writing process and terminates the write( ) system call with the -EPIPE error code, which usually leads to the familiar "Broken pipe" message.

The pipe_write( ) function performs the following operations:

1. Acquires the i_sem semaphore of the inode.

2. Checks whether the pipe has at least one reading process. If not, it sends a SIGPIPE signal to the current process, releases the inode semaphore, and returns an -EPIPE value.

3. Checks whether the number of bytes to be written is within the pipe's buffer size:

   a. If so, the write operation must be atomic. Therefore, checks whether the buffer has enough free space to store all bytes to be written.

   b. Otherwise, if the number of bytes is greater than the buffer size, the operation can start as long as there is any free space at all. Therefore, the function checks for at least one free byte.

4. If the buffer does not have enough free space and the write operation is non-blocking, releases the inode semaphore and returns the -EAGAIN error code.

5. If the buffer does not have enough free space and the write operation is blocking, performs the following actions:

   a. Adds 1 to the waiting_writers field of the pipe_inode_info structure.

   b. Adds current to the wait queue of the pipe (the wait field of the pipe_inode_info structure).

   c. Releases the inode semaphore.

   d. Sets the process status to TASK_INTERRUPTIBLE and invokes schedule( ).

   e. Once awake, removes current from the wait queue, again acquires the inode semaphore, decrements the waiting_writers field, and then jumps back to Step 5.

6. Now the pipe buffer has enough free space to either copy the requested number of bytes (if the write operation must be atomic) or copy at least one byte; notice that other writers cannot steal free space because this writer owns the inode semaphore. Copies the requested number of bytes (or the number of free bytes if the pipe size is too small) from the user address space to the pipe's buffer.

7. Wakes up all processes sleeping on the pipe's wait queue.

8. If the write operation was blocking and not all requested bytes were written in the pipe buffer, jumps back to Step 5. Notice that this case may occur only when the write operation is nonatomic; hence the current process remains blocked until one or more bytes of the pipe buffer are freed.

9. Releases the inode semaphore.

10. Returns the number of bytes written into the pipe's buffer.

FIFOs

Although pipes are a simple, flexible, and efficient communication mechanism, they have one main drawback—namely, that there is no way to open an already existing pipe. This makes it impossible for two arbitrary processes to share the same pipe, unless the pipe was created by a common ancestor process.

This drawback is substantial for many application programs. Consider, for instance, a database engine server, which continuously polls client processes wishing to issue some queries and which sends the results of the database lookups back to them. Each interaction between the server and a given client might be handled by a pipe. However, client processes are usually created on demand by a command shell when a user explicitly queries the database; server and client processes thus cannot easily share a pipe.

To address such limitations, Unix systems introduce a special file type called a *named pipe* or *FIFO* (which stands for "first in, first out"; the first byte written into the special file is also the first byte that is read). Any FIFO is much like a pipe: rather than owning disk blocks in the filesystems, an opened FIFO is associated with a kernel buffer that temporarily stores the data exchanged by two or more processes.

Thanks to the disk inode, however, a FIFO can be accessed by any process, since the FIFO filename is included in the system's directory tree. Thus, in our example, the communication between server and clients may be easily established by using FIFOs instead of pipes. The server creates, at startup, a FIFO used by client programs to make their requests. Each client program creates, before establishing the connection, another FIFO to which the server program can write the answer to the query and includes the FIFO's name in the initial request to the server.

In Linux 2.4, FIFOs and pipes are almost identical and use the same `pipe_inode_info` structures. As a matter of fact, the `read` and `write` file operation methods of a FIFO are implemented by the same `pipe_read()` and `pipe_write()` functions described in the earlier sections "Reading from a Pipe" and "Writing into a Pipe." Actually, there are only two significant differences:

- FIFO inodes appear on the system directory tree rather than on the *pipefs* special filesystem.
- FIFOs are a bidirectional communication channel; that is, it is possible to open a FIFO in read/write mode.

To complete our description, therefore, we just have to explain how FIFOs are created and opened.

Creating and Opening a FIFO

A process creates a FIFO by issuing a mknod( )[*] system call (see the section "Device Files" in Chapter 13), passing to it as parameters the pathname of the new FIFO and the value S_IFIFO (0x1000) logically ORed with the permission bit mask of the new file. POSIX introduces a function named mkfifo( ) specifically to create a FIFO. This call is implemented in Linux, as in System V Release 4, as a C library function that invokes mknod( ).

Once created, a FIFO can be accessed through the usual open( ), read( ), write( ), and close( ) system calls, but the VFS handles it in a special way because the FIFO inode and file operations are customized and do not depend on the filesystems in which the FIFO is stored.

The POSIX standard specifies the behavior of the open( ) system call on FIFOs; the behavior depends essentially on the requested access type, the kind of I/O operation (blocking or nonblocking), and the presence of other processes accessing the FIFO.

A process may open a FIFO for reading, for writing, or for reading and writing. The file operations associated with the corresponding file object are set to special methods for these three cases.

When a process opens a FIFO, the VFS performs the same operations as it does for device files (see the section "VFS Handling of Device Files" in Chapter 13). The inode object associated with the opened FIFO is initialized by a filesystem-dependent read_inode superblock method; this method always checks whether the inode on disk represents a special file, and invokes if necessary the init_special_inode( ) function. It turn, this function sets the i_fop field of the inode object to the address of the def_fifo_fops table. Later, the kernel sets the file operation table of the file object to def_fifo_fops, and executes its open method, which is implemented by fifo_open( ).

The fifo_open( ) function initializes the data structures specific to the FIFO; in particular, it performs the following operations:

1. Acquires the i_sem inode semaphore.
2. Checks the i_pipe field of the inode object; if it is NULL, it allocates and initializes a new pipe_inode_info structure, as in Step 1 in the earlier section "Creating and Destroying a Pipe."
3. Depending on the access mode specified as the parameter of the open( ) system call, it initializes the f_op field of the file object with the address of the proper file operation table (see Table 19-4).

---

[*] In fact, mknod( ) can be used to create nearly any kind of file, such as block and character device files, FIFOs, and even regular files (it cannot create directories or sockets, though).

Table 19-4. FIFO's file operations

Access type	File operations	read method	write method
Read-only	`read_fifo_fops`	`pipe_read( )`	`bad_pipe_w( )`
Write-only	`write_fifo_fops`	`bad_pipe_r( )`	`pipe_write( )`
Read/write	`rdwr_fifo_fops`	`pipe_read( )`	`pipe_write( )`

4. If the access mode is either read-only or read/write, it adds one to the `readers` and `r_counter` fields of the `pipe_inode_info` structure. Moreover, if the access mode is read-only and there is no other reading process, it wakes up any writing process sleeping in the wait queue.

5. If the access mode is either write-only or read/write, it adds one to the `writers` and `w_counter` fields of the `pipe_inode_info` structure. Moreover, if the access mode is write-only and there is no other writing process, it wakes up any reading process sleeping in the wait queue.

6. If there are no readers or no writers, it decides whether the function should block or terminate returning an error code (see Table 19-5).

Table 19-5. Behavior of the fifo_open() function

Access type	Blocking	Nonblocking
Read-only, with writers	Successfully return	Successfully return
Read-only, no writer	Wait for a writer	Successfully return
Write-only, with readers	Successfully return	Successfully return
Write-only, no reader	Wait for a reader	Return -ENXIO
Read/write	Successfully return	Successfully return

7. Releases the inode semaphore, and terminates, returning 0 (success).

The FIFO's three specialized file operation tables differ mainly in the implementation of the `read` and `write` methods. If the access type allows read operations, the `read` method is implemented by the `pipe_read( )` function. Otherwise, it is implemented by `bad_pipe_r( )`, which just returns an error code. Similarly, if the access type allows write operations, the `write` method is implemented by the `pipe_write( )` function; otherwise, it is implemented by `bad_pipe_w( )`, which also returns an error code.

System V IPC

IPC is an abbreviation for Interprocess Communication, and commonly refers to a set of mechanisms that allow a User Mode process to do the following:

- Synchronize itself with other processes by means of semaphores
- Send messages to other processes or receive messages from them
- Share a memory area with other processes

System V IPC first appeared in a development Unix variant called "Columbus Unix" and later was adopted by AT&T's System III. It is now found in most Unix systems, including Linux.

IPC data structures are created dynamically when a process requests an *IPC resource* (a semaphore, a message queue, or a shared memory region). An IPC resource is persistent: unless explicitly removed by a process, it is kept in memory and remains available until the system is shut down. An IPC resource may be used by any process, including those that do not share the ancestor that created the resource.

Since a process may require several IPC resources of the same type, each new resource is identified by a 32-bit *IPC key*, which is similar to the file pathname in the system's directory tree. Each IPC resource also has a 32-bit *IPC identifier*, which is somewhat similar to the file descriptor associated with an open file. IPC identifiers are assigned to IPC resources by the kernel and are unique within the system, while IPC keys can be freely chosen by programmers.

When two or more processes wish to communicate through an IPC resource, they all refer to the IPC identifier of the resource.

Using an IPC Resource

IPC resources are created by invoking the semget( ), msgget( ), or shmget( ) functions, depending on whether the new resource is a semaphore, a message queue, or a shared memory region.

The main objective of each of these three functions is to derive from the IPC key (passed as the first parameter) the corresponding IPC identifier, which is then used by the process for accessing the resource. If there is no IPC resource already associated with the IPC key, a new resource is created. If everything goes right, the function returns a positive IPC identifier; otherwise, it returns one of the error codes listed in Table 19-6.

Table 19-6. Error codes returned while requesting an IPC identifier

Error code	Description
EACCESS	Process does not have proper access rights.
EEXIST	Process tried to create an IPC resource with the same key as one that already exists.
EIDRM	Resource is marked to be deleted.
ENOENT	No IPC resource with the requested key exists and the process did not ask to create it.
ENOMEM	No more storage is left for an additional IPC resource.
ENOSPC	Maximum limit on the number of IPC resources has been exceeded.

Assume that two independent processes want to share a common IPC resource. This can be achieved in two possible ways:

- The processes agree on some fixed, predefined IPC key. This is the simplest case, and it works quite well for any complex application implemented by many processes. However, there's a chance that the same IPC key is chosen by another unrelated program. In this case, the IPC functions might be successfully invoked and still return the IPC identifier of the wrong resource.[*]

- One process issues a semget( ), msgget( ), or shmget( ) function by specifying IPC_PRIVATE as its IPC key. A new IPC resource is thus allocated, and the process can either communicate its IPC identifier to the other process in the application[†] or fork the other process itself. This method ensures that the IPC resource cannot be used accidentally by other applications.

The last parameter of the semget( ), msgget( ), and shmget( ) functions can include two flags. IPC_CREAT specifies that the IPC resource must be created, if it does not already exist; IPC_EXCL specifies that the function must fail if the resource already exists and the IPC_CREAT flag is set.

Even if the process uses the IPC_CREAT and IPC_EXCL flags, there is no way to ensure exclusive access to an IPC resource, since other processes may always refer to the resource by using its IPC identifier.

To minimize the risk of incorrectly referencing the wrong resource, the kernel does not recycle IPC identifiers as soon as they become free. Instead, the IPC identifier assigned to a resource is almost always larger than the identifier assigned to the previously allocated resource of the same type. (The only exception occurs when the 32-bit IPC identifier overflows.) Each IPC identifier is computed by combining a *slot usage sequence number* relative to the resource type, an arbitrary *slot index* for the allocated resource, and an arbitrary value chosen in the kernel that is greater than the maximum number of allocatable resources. If we choose s to represent the slot usage sequence number, M to represent the upper bound on the number of allocatable resources, and i to represent the slot index, where $0 \le i < M$, each IPC resource's ID is computed as follows:

$$\text{IPC identifier} = s \times M + i$$

In Linux 2.4, the value of M is set to 32,768 (IPCMNI macro). The slot usage sequence number s is initialized to 0 and is incremented by 1 at every resource allocation. When s reaches a predefined threshold, which depends on the type of IPC resource, it restarts from 0.

Every type of IPC resource (semaphores, message queues, and shared memory areas) owns an ipc_ids data structure, which includes the fields shown in Table 19-7.

---

[*] The ftok( ) function attempts to create a new key from a file pathname and an 8-bit project identifier passed as parameters. It does not guarantee, however, a unique key number, since there is a small chance that it will return the same IPC key to two different applications using different pathnames and project identifiers.

[†] This implies, of course, the existence of another communication channel between the processes not based on IPC.

Table 19-7. The fields of the ipc_ids data structure

Type	Field	Description
int	size	Current maximum number of IPC resources
int	in_use	Number of allocated IPC resources
int	max_id	Maximum slot index in use
unsigned short	seq	Slot usage sequence number for the next allocation
unsigned short	seq_max	Maximum slot usage sequence number
struct semaphore	sem	Semaphore protecting the ipc_ids data structure
spinlock_t	ary	Spin lock protecting the IPC resource descriptors
struct ipc_id *	entries	Array of IPC resource descriptors

The size field stores the maximum number of allocatable IPC resources of the given type. The system administrator may increase this value for any resource type by writing into the */proc/sys/kernel/sem*, */proc/sys/kernel/msgmni*, and */proc/sys/kernel/shmmni* special files, respectively.

The entries field points to an array of pointers to kern_ipc_perm data structures, one for every allocatable resource (the size field is also the size of the array). Each kern_ipc_perm data structure is associated with an IPC resource and contains the fields shown in Table 19-8. The uid, gid, cuid, and cgid fields store the user and group identifiers of the resource's creator and the user and group identifiers of the current resource's owner, respectively. The mode bit mask includes six flags, which store the read and write access permissions for the resource's owner, the resource's group, and all other users. IPC access permissions are similar to file access permissions described in the section "Access Rights and File Mode" in Chapter 1, except that the Execute permission flag is not used.

Table 19-8. The fields in the kern_ipc_perm structure

Type	Field	Description
int	key	IPC key
unsigned int	uid	Owner user ID
unsigned int	gid	Owner group ID
unsigned int	cuid	Creator user ID
unsigned int	cgid	Creator group ID
unsigned short	mode	Permission bit mask
unsigned long	seq	Slot usage sequence number

The kern_ipc_perm data structure also includes a key field (which contains the IPC key of the corresponding resource) and a seq field (which stores the slot usage sequence number *s* used to compute the IPC identifier of the resource).

The `semctl()`, `msgctl()`, and `shmctl()` functions may be used to handle IPC resources. The `IPC_SET` subcommand allows a process to change the owner's user and group identifiers and the permission bit mask in the `ipc_perm` data structure. The `IPC_STAT` and `IPC_INFO` subcommands retrieve some information concerning a resource. Finally, the `IPC_RMID` subcommand releases an IPC resource. Depending on the type of IPC resource, other specialized subcommands are also available.*

Once an IPC resource is created, a process may act on the resource by means of a few specialized functions. A process may acquire or release an IPC semaphore by issuing the `semop()` function. When a process wants to send or receive an IPC message, it uses the `msgsnd()` and `msgrcv()` functions, respectively. Finally, a process attaches and detaches an IPC shared memory region in its address space by means of the `shmat()` and `shmdt()` functions, respectively.

The ipc( ) System Call

All IPC functions must be implemented through suitable Linux system calls. Actually, in the 80×86 architecture, there is just one IPC system call named `ipc()`. When a process invokes an IPC function, let's say `msgget()`, it really invokes a wrapper function in the C library. This in turn invokes the `ipc()` system call by passing to it all the parameters of `msgget()` plus a proper subcommand code—in this case, `MSGGET`. The `sys_ipc()` service routine examines the subcommand code and invokes the kernel function that implements the requested service.

The `ipc()` "multiplexer" system call is a legacy from older Linux versions, which included the IPC code in a dynamic module (see Appendix B). It did not make much sense to reserve several system call entries in the `system_call` table for a kernel component that could be missing, so the kernel designers adopted the multiplexer approach.

Nowadays, System V IPC can no longer be compiled as a dynamic module, and there is no justification for using a single IPC system call. As a matter of fact, Linux provides one system call for each IPC function on Hewlett-Packard's Alpha architecture and on Intel's IA-64.

IPC Semaphores

IPC semaphores are quite similar to the kernel semaphores introduced in Chapter 5; they are counters used to provide controlled access to shared data structures for multiple processes.

The semaphore value is positive if the protected resource is available, and 0 if the protected resource is currently not available. A process that wants to access the

---

* Another IPC design flaw is that a User Mode process cannot atomically create and initialize an IPC semaphore, since these two operations are performed by two different IPC functions.

resource tries to decrement the semaphore value; the kernel, however, blocks the process until the operation on the semaphore yields a positive value. When a process relinquishes a protected resource, it increments its semaphore value; in doing so, any other process waiting for the semaphore is woken up.

Actually, IPC semaphores are more complicated to handle than kernel semaphores for two main reasons:

- Each IPC semaphore is a set of one or more semaphore values, not just a single value like a kernel semaphore. This means that the same IPC resource can protect several independent shared data structures. The number of semaphore values in each IPC semaphore must be specified as a parameter of the semget( ) function when the resource is being allocated. From now on, we'll refer to the counters inside an IPC semaphore as *primitive semaphores*. There are bounds both on the number of IPC semaphore resources (by default, 128) and on the number of primitive semaphores inside a single IPC semaphore resource (by default, 250); however, the system administrator can easily modify these bounds by writing into the */proc/sys/kernel/sem* file.

- System V IPC semaphores provide a fail-safe mechanism for situations in which a process dies without being able to undo the operations that it previously issued on a semaphore. When a process chooses to use this mechanism, the resulting operations are called *undoable* semaphore operations. When the process dies, all of its IPC semaphores can revert to the values they would have had if the process had never started its operations. This can help prevent other processes that use the same semaphores from remaining blocked indefinitely as a consequence of the terminating process failing to manually undo its semaphore operations.

First, we'll briefly sketch the typical steps performed by a process wishing to access one or more resources protected by an IPC semaphore:

1. Invokes the semget( ) wrapper function to get the IPC semaphore identifier, specifying as the parameter the IPC key of the IPC semaphore that protects the shared resources. If the process wants to create a new IPC semaphore, it also specifies the IPC_CREATE or IPC_PRIVATE flag and the number of primitive semaphores required (see the section "Using an IPC Resource" earlier in this chapter).

2. Invokes the semop( ) wrapper function to test and decrement all primitive semaphore values involved. If all the tests succeed, the decrements are performed, the function terminates, and the process is allowed to access the protected resources. If some semaphores are in use, the process is usually suspended until some other process releases the resources. The function receives as parameters the IPC semaphore identifier, an array of integers specifying the operations to be atomically performed on the primitive semaphores, and the number of such operations. Optionally, the process may specify the SEM_UNDO flag, which instructs the kernel to reverse the operations, should the process exit without releasing the primitive semaphores.

3. When relinquishing the protected resources, invokes the semop( ) function again to atomically increment all primitive semaphores involved.

4. Optionally, invokes the semctl( ) wrapper function, specifying the IPC_RMID command to remove the IPC semaphore from the system.

Now we can discuss how the kernel implements IPC semaphores. The data structures involved are shown in Figure 19-1. The sem_ids variable stores the ipc_ids data structure of the IPC semaphore resource type; its entries field is an array of pointers to sem_array data structures, one item for every IPC semaphore resource.

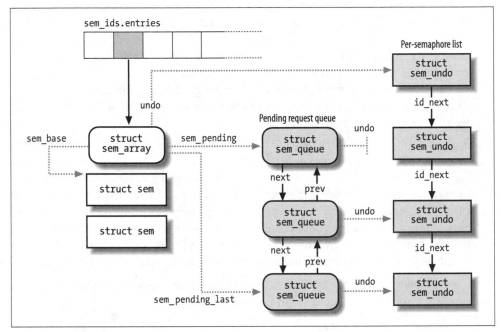

Figure 19-1. IPC semaphore data structures

Formally, the array stores pointers to kern_ipc_perm data structures, but each structure is simply the first field of the sem_array data structure. All fields of the sem_array data structure are shown in Table 19-9.

Table 19-9. The fields in the sem_array data structure

Type	Field	Description
struct kern_ipc_perm	sem_perm	kern_ipc_perm data structure
long	sem_otime	Timestamp of last semop( )
long	sem_ctime	Timestamp of last change
struct sem *	sem_base	Pointer to first sem structure
struct sem_queue *	sem_pending	Pending operations

Table 19-9. The fields in the sem_array data structure (continued)

Type	Field	Description
struct sem_queue **	sem_pending_last	Last pending operation
struct sem_undo *	undo	Undo requests
unsigned short	sem_nsems	Number of semaphores in array

The sem_base field points to an array of struct sem data structures, one for every IPC primitive semaphore. The latter data structure includes only two fields:

semval
> The value of the semaphore's counter.

sempid
> The PID of the last process that accessed the semaphore. This value can be queried by a process through the semctl( ) wrapper function.

Undoable semaphore operations

If a process aborts suddenly, it cannot undo the operations that it started (for instance, release the semaphores it reserved); so by declaring them undoable, the process lets the kernel return the semaphores to a consistent state and allow other processes to proceed. Processes can request undoable operations by specifying the SEM_UNDO flag in the semop( ) function.

Information to help the kernel reverse the undoable operations performed by a given process on a given IPC semaphore resource is stored in a sem_undo data structure. It essentially contains the IPC identifier of the semaphore and an array of integers representing the changes to the primitive semaphore's values caused by all undoable operations performed by the process.

A simple example can illustrate how such sem_undo elements are used. Consider a process that uses an IPC semaphore resource containing four primitive semaphores. Suppose that it invokes the semop( ) function to increment the first counter by 1 and decrement the second by 2. If it specifies the SEM_UNDO flag, the integer in the first array element in the sem_undo data structure is decremented by 1, the integer in the second element is incremented by 2, and the other two integers are left unchanged. Further undoable operations on the IPC semaphore performed by the same process change the integers stored in the sem_undo structure accordingly. When the process exits, any nonzero value in that array corresponds to one or more unbalanced operations on the corresponding primitive semaphore; the kernel reverses these operations, simply adding the nonzero value to the corresponding semaphore's counter. In other words, the changes made by the aborted process are backed out while the changes made by other processes are still reflected in the state of the semaphores.

For each process, the kernel keeps track of all semaphore resources handled with undoable operations so that it can roll them back if the process unexpectedly exits.

Furthermore, for each semaphore, the kernel has to keep track of all its sem_undo structures so it can quickly access them whenever a process uses semctl( ) to force an explicit value into a primitive semaphore's counter or to destroy an IPC semaphore resource.

The kernel is able to handle these tasks efficiently, thanks to two lists, which we denote as the *per-process* and the *per-semaphore* lists. The first list keeps track of all semaphores operated upon by a given process with undoable operations. The second list keeps track of all processes that are acting on a given semaphore with undoable operations. More precisely:

- The per-process list includes all sem_undo data structures corresponding to IPC semaphores on which the process has performed undoable operations. The semundo field of the process descriptor points to the first element of the list, while the proc_next field of each sem_undo data structure points to the next element in the list.

- The per-semaphore list includes all sem_undo data structures corresponding to the processes that performed undoable operations on the semaphore. The undo field of the semid_ds data structure points to the first element of the list, while the id_next field of each sem_undo data structure points to the next element in the list.

The per-process list is used when a process terminates. The sem_exit( ) function, which is invoked by do_exit( ), walks through the list and reverses the effect of any unbalanced operation for every IPC semaphore touched by the process. By contrast, the per-semaphore list is mainly used when a process invokes the semctl( ) function to force an explicit value into a primitive semaphore. The kernel sets the corresponding element to 0 in the arrays of all sem_undo data structures referring to that IPC semaphore resource, since it would no longer make any sense to reverse the effect of previous undoable operations performed on that primitive semaphore. Moreover, the per-semaphore list is also used when an IPC semaphore is destroyed; all related sem_undo data structures are invalidated by setting the semid field to −1.[*]

The queue of pending requests

The kernel associates a *queue of pending requests* with each IPC semaphore to identify processes that are waiting on one (or more) of the semaphores in the array. The queue is a doubly linked list of sem_queue data structures whose fields are shown in Table 19-10. The first and last pending requests in the queue are referenced, respectively, by the sem_pending and sem_pending_last fields of the sem_array structure. This last field allows the list to be handled easily as a FIFO; new pending requests are added to the end of the list so they will be serviced later. The most important fields of a pending request are nsops (which stores the number of primitive semaphores

---

[*] Notice that they are just invalidated and not freed, since it would be too costly to remove the data structures from the per-process lists of all processes.

involved in the pending operation) and sops (which points to an array of integer values describing each semaphore operation). The sleeper field stores the descriptor address of the sleeping process that requested the operation.

Table 19-10. The fields in the sem_queue data structure

Type	Field	Description
struct sem_queue *	next	Pointer to next queue element
struct sem_queue **	prev	Pointer to previous queue element
struct task_struct *	sleeper	Pointer to the sleeping process that requested the semaphore operation
struct sem_undo *	undo	Pointer to sem_undo structure
int	pid	Process identifier
int	status	Completion status of operation
struct sem_array *	sma	Pointer to IPC semaphore descriptor
int	id	Slot index of the IPC semaphore resource
struct sembuf *	sops	Pointer to array of pending operations
int	nsops	Number of pending operations
int	alter	Flag indicating that the operation sets the semaphore value

Figure 19-1 illustrates an IPC semaphore that has three pending requests. Two of them refer to undoable operations, so the undo field of the sem_queue data structure points to the corresponding sem_undo structure; the third pending request has a NULL undo field since the corresponding operation is not undoable.

IPC Messages

Processes can communicate with one another by means of IPC messages. Each message generated by a process is sent to an *IPC message queue*, where it stays until another process reads it.

A message is composed of a fixed-size *header* and a variable-length *text*; it can be labeled with an integer value (the *message type*), which allows a process to selectively retrieve messages from its message queue.[*] Once a process has read a message from an IPC message queue, the kernel destroys the message; therefore, only one process can receive a given message.

To send a message, a process invokes the msgsnd( ) function, passing the following as parameters:

- The IPC identifier of the destination message queue
- The size of the message text

---

[*] As we'll see, the message queue is implemented by means of a linked list. Since messages can be retrieved in an order different from "first in, first out," the name "message queue" is not appropriate. However, new messages are always put at the end of the linked list.

- The address of a User Mode buffer that contains the message type immediately followed by the message text

To retrieve a message, a process invokes the msgrcv( ) function, passing to it:

- The IPC identifier of the IPC message queue resource
- The pointer to a User Mode buffer to which the message type and message text should be copied
- The size of this buffer
- A value t that specifies what message should be retrieved

If the value t is 0, the first message in the queue is returned. If t is positive, the first message in the queue with its type equal to t is returned. Finally, if t is negative, the function returns the first message whose message type is the lowest value less than or equal to the absolute value of t.

To avoid resource exhaustion, there are some limits on the number of IPC message queue resources allowed (by default, 16), on the size of each message (by default, 8,192 bytes), and on the maximum total size of the messages in a queue (by default, 16,384 bytes). As usual, however, the system administrator can tune these values by writing into the */proc/sys/kernel/msgmni*, */proc/sys/kernel/msgmnb*, and */proc/sys/kernel/msgmax* files, respectively.

The data structures associated with IPC message queues are shown in Figure 19-2. The msg_ids variable stores the ipc_ids data structure of the IPC message queue resource type; its entries field is an array of pointers to msg_queue data structures—one item for every IPC message queue resource. Formally, the array stores pointers to kern_ipc_perm data structures, but each such structure is simply the first field of the msg_queue data structure. All fields of the msg_queue data structure are shown in Table 19-11.

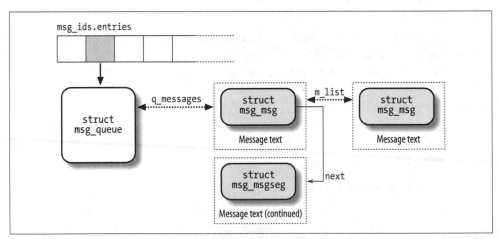

Figure 19-2. IPC message queue data structures

Table 19-11. The msg_queue data structure

Type	Field	Description
struct ipc_perm	q_perm	kern_ipc_perm data structure
long	q_stime	Time of last msgsnd( )
long	q_rtime	Time of last msgrcv( )
long	q_ctime	Last change time
unsigned long	q_qcbytes	Number of bytes in queue
unsigned long	q_qnum	Number of messages in queue
unsigned long	q_qbytes	Maximum number of bytes in queue
int	q_lspid	PID of last msgsnd( )
int	q_lrpid	PID of last msgrcv( )
struct list_head	q_messages	List of messages in queue
struct list_head	q_receivers	List of processes receiving messages
struct list_head	q_senders	List of processes sending messages

The most important field is q_messages, which represents the head (i.e., the first dummy element) of a doubly linked circular list containing all messages currently in the queue.

Each message is broken in one or more pages, which are dynamically allocated. The beginning of the first page stores the message header, which is a data structure of type msg_msg; its fields are listed in Table 19-12. The m_list field stores the pointers to the previous and next messages in the queue. The message text starts right after the msg_msg descriptor; if the message is longer than 4,072 bytes (the page size minus the size of the msg_msg descriptor), it continues on another page, whose address is stored in the next field of the msg_msg descriptor. The second page frame starts with a descriptor of type msg_msgseg, which just includes a next pointer storing the address of an optional third page, and so on.

Table 19-12. The msg_msg data structure

Type	Field	Description
struct list_head	m_list	Pointers for message list
long	m_type	Message type
int	m_ts	Message text size
struct msg_msgseg *	next	Next portion of the message

When the message queue is full (either the maximum number of messages or the maximum total size has been reached), processes that try to enqueue new messages may be blocked. The q_senders field of the msg_queue data structure is the head of a list that includes the pointers to the descriptors of all blocked sending processes.

Even receiving processes may be blocked when the message queue is empty (or the process specified a type of message not present in the queue). The q_receivers field of the msg_queue data structure is the head of a list of msg_receiver data structures, one for every blocked receiving process. Each of these structures essentially includes a pointer to the process descriptor, a pointer to the msg_msg structure of the message, and the type of the requested message.

IPC Shared Memory

The most useful IPC mechanism is shared memory, which allows two or more processes to access some common data structures by placing them in an *IPC shared memory region*. Each process that wants to access the data structures included in an IPC shared memory region must add to its address space a new memory region (see the section "Memory Regions" in Chapter 8), which maps the page frames associated with the IPC shared memory region. Such page frames can then be easily handled by the kernel through demand paging (see the section "Demand Paging" in Chapter 8).

As with semaphores and message queues, the shmget( ) function is invoked to get the IPC identifier of a shared memory region, optionally creating it if it does not already exist.

The shmat( ) function is invoked to "attach" an IPC shared memory region to a process. It receives as its parameter the identifier of the IPC shared memory resource and tries to add a shared memory region to the address space of the calling process. The calling process can require a specific starting linear address for the memory region, but the address is usually unimportant, and each process accessing the shared memory region can use a different address in its own address space. The process's Page Tables are left unchanged by shmat( ). We describe later what the kernel does when the process tries to access a page that belongs to the new memory region.

The shmdt( ) function is invoked to "detach" an IPC shared memory region specified by its IPC identifier—that is, to remove the corresponding memory region from the process's address space. Recall that an IPC shared memory resource is persistent: even if no process is using it, the corresponding pages cannot be discarded, although they can be swapped out.

As for the other types of IPC resources, in order to avoid overuse of memory by User Mode processes, there are some limits on the allowed number of IPC shared memory regions (by default, 4,096), on the size of each segment (by default, 32 megabytes), and on the maximum total size of all segments (by default, 8 gigabytes). As usual, however, the system administrator can tune these values by writing into the */proc/sys/kernel/shmmni*, */proc/sys/kernel/shmmax*, and */proc/sys/kernel/shmall* files, respectively.

The data structures associated with IPC shared memory regions are shown in Figure 19-3. The shm_ids variable stores the ipc_ids data structure of the IPC shared

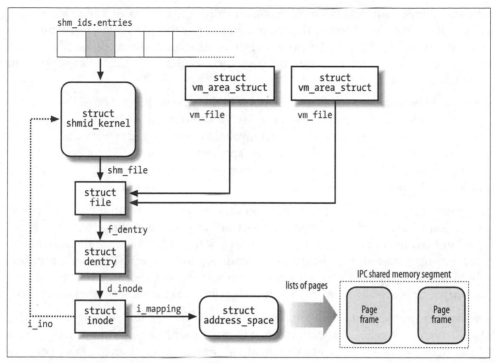

Figure 19-3. IPC shared memory data structures

memory resource type; its entries field is an array of pointers to shmid_kernel data structures, one item for every IPC shared memory resource. Formally, the array stores pointers to kern_ipc_perm data structures, but each such structure is simply the first field of the msg_queue data structure. All fields of the shmid_kernel data structure are shown in Table 19-13.

Table 19-13. The fields in the shmid_kernel data structure

Type	Field	Description
struct kern_ipc_perm	shm_perm	kern_ipc_perm data structure
struct file *	shm_file	Special file of the segment
int	id	Slot index of the segment
unsigned long	shm_nattch	Number of current attaches
unsigned long	shm_segsz	Segment size in bytes
long	shm_atime	Last access time
long	shm_dtime	Last detach time
long	shm_ctime	Last change time
int	shm_cprid	PID of creator
int	shm_lprid	PID of last accessing process

The most important field is shm_file, which stores the address of a file object. This reflects the tight integration of IPC shared memory with the VFS layer in Linux 2.4. In particular, each IPC shared memory region is associated with a regular file belonging to the *shm* special filesystem (see the section "Special Filesystems" in Chapter 12).

Since the *shm* filesystem has no mount point in the system directory tree, no user can open and access its files by means of regular VFS system calls. However, whenever a process "attaches" a segment, the kernel invokes do_mmap( ) and creates a new shared memory mapping of the file in the address space of the process. Therefore, files that belong to the *shm* special filesystem have just one file object method, mmap, which is implemented by the shm_mmap( ) function.

As shown in Figure 19-3, a memory region that corresponds to an IPC shared memory region is described by a vm_area_struct object (see the section "Memory Mapping" in Chapter 15); its vm_file field points back to the file object of the special file, which in turn references a dentry object and an inode object. The inode number, stored in the i_ino field of the inode, is actually the slot index of the IPC shared memory region, so the inode object indirectly references the shmid_kernel descriptor.

As usual, for any shared memory mapping, page frames that belong to the IPC shared memory region are included in the page cache through an address_space object referenced by the i_mapping field of the inode (you might also refer to Figure 15-4).

Swapping out pages of IPC shared memory regions

The kernel has to be careful when swapping out pages included in shared memory regions, and the role of the swap cache is crucial (this topic was already discussed in the section "The Swap Cache" in Chapter 16).

As explained in the section "The try_to_swap_out( ) Function" in Chapter 16, to swap out a page owned by an address_space object, the kernel essentially marks the page as dirty, thus triggering a data transfer to disk, and then removes the page from the process's Page Table. If the page belongs to a shared file memory mapping, eventually the page is no longer referenced by any process, and the shrink_cache( ) function will release it to the Buddy system (see the section "The shrink_cache( ) Function" in Chapter 16). This is fine because the data in the page is just a duplicate of some data on disk.

However, pages of an IPC shared memory region map a special inode that has no image on disk. Moreover, an IPC shared memory region is persistent—that is, its pages must be preserved even when the segment is not attached to any process. Therefore, the kernel cannot simply discard the pages when reclaiming the corresponding page frames; rather, the pages have to be swapped out.

The try_to_swap_out() function includes no check for this special case, so a page belonging to the region is marked as dirty and removed from the process address space. Even the shrink_cache() function, which periodically prunes the page cache from the least recently used pages, has no check for this special case, so it ends up invoking the writepage method of the owner address_space object (see the section "The shrink_cache() Function" in Chapter 16).

How, then, are IPC shared memory regions preserved when their pages are swapped out? Pages belonging to IPC shared memory regions implement the writepage method by means of a custom shmem_writepage() function, which essentially allocates a new page slot in a swap area and moves the page from the page cache to the swap cache (it's just a matter of changing the owner address_space object of the page). The function also stores the swapped-out page identifier in a shmem_inode_info structure embedded in the filesystem-specific portion of the inode object. Notice that the page is not immediately written onto the swap area: this is done when the shrink_cache() is invoked again.

Demand paging for IPC shared memory regions

The pages added to a process by shmat() are dummy pages; the function adds a new memory region into a process's address space, but it doesn't modify the process's Page Tables. Moreover, as we have seen, pages of an IPC shared memory region can be swapped out. Therefore, these pages are handled through the demand paging mechanism.

As we know, a Page Fault occurs when a process tries to access a location of an IPC shared memory region whose underlying page frame has not been assigned. The corresponding exception handler determines that the faulty address is inside the process address space and that the corresponding Page Table entry is null; therefore, it invokes the do_no_page() function (see the section "Demand Paging" in Chapter 8). In turn, this function checks whether the nopage method for the memory region is defined. That method is invoked, and the Page Table entry is set to the address returned from it (see also the section "Demand Paging for Memory Mapping" in Chapter 15).

Memory regions used for IPC shared memory always define the nopage method. It is implemented by the shmem_nopage() function, which performs the following operations:

1. Walks the chain of pointers in the VFS objects and derives the address of the inode object of the IPC shared memory resource (see Figure 19-3).

2. Computes the logical page number inside the segment from the vm_start field of the memory region descriptor and the requested address.

3. Checks whether the page is already included in the swap cache (see the section "The Swap Cache" in Chapter 16); if so, it terminates by returning its address.

4. Checks whether the `shmem_inode_info` embedded in the inode object stores a swapped-out page identifier for the logical page number. If so, it performs a swap-in operation by invoking `swapin_readahead( )` (see the section "The do_swap_page() Function" in Chapter 16), waits until the data transfer completes, and terminates by returning the address of the page.

5. Otherwise, the page is not stored in a swap area; therefore, the function allocates a new page from the Buddy system, inserts into the page cache, and returns its address.

The `do_no_page( )` function sets the entry that corresponds to the faulty address in the process's Page Table so that it points to the page frame returned by the method.

CHAPTER 20
Program Execution

The concept of a "process," described in Chapter 3, was used in Unix from the beginning to represent the behavior of groups of running programs that compete for system resources. This final chapter focuses on the relationship between program and process. We specifically describe how the kernel sets up the execution context for a process according to the contents of the program file. While it may not seem like a big problem to load a bunch of instructions into memory and point the CPU to them, the kernel has to deal with flexibility in several areas:

Different executable formats
Linux is distinguished by its ability to run binaries that were compiled for other operating systems.

Shared libraries
Many executable files don't contain all the code required to run the program but expect the kernel to load in functions from a library at runtime

Other information in the execution context
This includes the command-line arguments and environment variables familiar to programmers.

A program is stored on disk as an *executable file*, which includes both the object code of the functions to be executed and the data on which these functions will act. Many functions of the program are service routines available to all programmers; their object code is included in special files called "libraries." Actually, the code of a library function may either be statically copied in the executable file (static libraries) or linked to the process at runtime (shared libraries, since their code can be shared by several independent processes).

When launching a program, the user may supply two kinds of information that affect the way it is executed: command-line arguments and environment variables. *Command-line arguments* are typed in by the user following the executable filename at the shell prompt. *Environment variables*, such as HOME and PATH, are inherited from the shell, but the users may modify the values of any such variables before they launch the program.

In the section "Executable Files," we explain what a program execution context is. In the section "Executable Formats," we mention some of the executable formats supported by Linux and show how Linux can change its "personality" to execute programs compiled for other operating systems. Finally, in the section "The exec Functions," we describe the system call that allows a process to start executing a new program.

Executable Files

Chapter 1 defined a process as an "execution context." By this we mean the collection of information needed to carry on a specific computation; it includes the pages accessed, the open files, the hardware register contents, and so on. An *executable file* is a regular file that describes how to initialize a new execution context (i.e., how to start a new computation).

Suppose a user wants to list the files in the current directory; he knows that this result can be simply achieved by typing the filename of the */bin/ls** external command at the shell prompt. The command shell forks a new process, which in turn invokes an execve( ) system call (see the section "The exec Functions" later in this chapter), passing as one of its parameters a string that includes the full pathname for the *ls* executable file—*/bin/ls*, in this case. The sys_execve( ) service routine finds the corresponding file, checks the executable format, and modifies the execution context of the current process according to the information stored in it. As a result, when the system call terminates, the process starts executing the code stored in the executable file, which performs the directory listing.

When a process starts running a new program, its execution context changes drastically since most of the resources obtained during the process's previous computations are discarded. In the preceding example, when the process starts executing */bin/ ls*, it replaces the shell's arguments with new ones passed as parameters in the execve( ) system call and acquires a new shell environment (see the later section "Command-Line Arguments and Shell Environment"). All pages inherited from the parent (and shared with the Copy On Write mechanism) are released so that the new computation starts with a fresh User Mode address space; even the privileges of the process could change (see the later section "Process Credentials and Capabilities"). However, the process PID doesn't change, and the new computation inherits from the previous one all open file descriptors that were not closed automatically while executing the execve( ) system call.[†]

---

* The pathnames of executable files are not fixed in Linux; they depend on the distribution used. Several standard naming schemes, such as FHS, have been proposed for all Unix systems.

† By default, a file already opened by a process stays open after issuing an execve( )system call. However, the file is automatically closed if the process has set the corresponding bit in the close_on_exec field of the files_ struct structure (see Table 12-7 in Chapter 12); this is done by means of the fcntl( )system call.

Process Credentials and Capabilities

Traditionally, Unix systems associate with each process some *credentials*, which bind the process to a specific user and a specific user group. Credentials are important on multiuser systems because they determine what each process can or cannot do, thus preserving both the integrity of each user's personal data and the stability of the system as a whole.

The use of credentials requires support both in the process data structure and in the resources being protected. One obvious resource is a file. Thus, in the Ext2 filesystem, each file is owned by a specific user and is bound to a group of users. The owner of a file may decide what kind of operations are allowed on that file, distinguishing among herself, the file's user group, and all other users. When a process tries to access a file, the VFS always checks whether the access is legal, according to the permissions established by the file owner and the process credentials.

The process's credentials are stored in several fields of the process descriptor, listed in Table 20-1. These fields contain identifiers of users and user groups in the system, which are usually compared with the corresponding identifiers stored in the inodes of the files being accessed.

Table 20-1. Traditional process credentials

Name	Description
uid, gid	User and group real identifiers
euid, egid	User and group effective identifiers
fsuid, fsgid	User and group effective identifiers for file access
groups	Supplementary group identifiers
suid, sgid	User and group saved identifiers

A UID of 0 specifies the superuser (root), while a GID of 0 specifies the root group. If a process credential stores a value of 0, the kernel bypasses the permission checks and allows the privileged process to perform various actions, such as those referring to system administration or hardware manipulation, that are not possible to unprivileged processes.

When a process is created, it always inherits the credentials of its parent. However, these credentials can be modified later, either when the process starts executing a new program or when it issues suitable system calls. Usually, the uid, euid, fsuid, and suid fields of a process contain the same value. When the process executes a *setuid program*—that is, an executable file whose *setuid* flag is on—the euid and fsuid fields are set to the identifier of the file's owner. Almost all checks involve one of these two fields: fsuid is used for file-related operations, while euid is used for all other operations. Similar considerations apply to the gid, egid, fsgid, and sgid fields that refer to group identifiers.

As an illustration of how the fsuid field is used, consider the typical situation when a user wants to change his password. All passwords are stored in a common file, but he cannot directly edit this file because it is protected. Therefore, he invokes a system program named */usr/bin/passwd*, which has the *setuid* flag set and whose owner is the superuser. When the process forked by the shell executes such a program, its euid and fsuid fields are set to 0—to the PID of the superuser. Now the process can access the file, since, when the kernel performs the access control, it finds a 0 value in fsuid. Of course, the */usr/bin/passwd* program does not allow the user to do anything but change his own password.

Unix's long history teaches the lesson that *setuid* programs are quite dangerous: malicious users could trigger some programming errors (bugs) in the code to force *setuid* programs to perform operations that were never planned by the program's original designers. In the worst case, the entire system's security can be compromised. To minimize such risks, Linux, like all modern Unix systems, allows processes to acquire *setuid* privileges only when necessary and drop them when they are no longer needed. This feature may turn out to be useful when implementing user applications with several protection levels. The process descriptor includes an suid field, which stores the values of the effective identifiers (euid and fsuid) right after the execution of the *setuid* program. The process can change the effective identifiers by means of the setuid( ), setresuid( ), setfsuid( ), and setreuid( ) system calls.[*]

Table 20-2 shows how these system calls affect the process's credentials. Be warned that if the calling process does not already have superuser privileges—that is, if its euid field is not null—these system calls can be used only to set values already included in the process's credential fields. For instance, an average user process can store the value 500 into its fsuid field by invoking the setfsuid( ) system call, but only if one of the other credential fields already holds the same value.

Table 20-2. Semantics of the system calls that set process credentials

| Field | setuid (e) | | setresuid (u,e,s) | setreuid (u,e) | setfsuid (f) |
	euid=0	euid≠0			
uid	Set to e	Unchanged	Set to u	Set to u	Unchanged
euid	Set to e	Set to e	Set to e	Set to e	Unchanged
fsuid	Set to e	Set to e	Set to e	Set to e	Set to f
suid	Set to e	Unchanged	Set to s	Set to e	Unchanged

To understand the sometimes complex relationships among the four user ID fields, consider for a moment the effects of the setuid( ) system call. The actions are different, depending on whether the calling process's euid field is set to 0 (that is, the process has superuser privileges) or to a normal UID.

---

[*] GID effective credentials can be changed by issuing the corresponding setgid( ), setresgid( ), setfsgid( ), and setregid( ) system calls.

If the euid field is 0, the system call sets all credential fields of the calling process (uid, euid, fsuid, and suid) to the value of the parameter e. A superuser process can thus drop its privileges and become a process owned by a normal user. This happens, for instance, when a user logs in: the system forks a new process with superuser privileges, but the process drops its privileges by invoking the setuid( ) system call and then starts executing the user's login shell program.

If the euid field is not 0, the system call modifies only the value stored in euid and fsuid, leaving the other two fields unchanged. This allows a process executing a *setuid* program to have its effective privileges stored in euid and fsuid set alternately to uid (the process acts as the user who launched the executable file) and to suid (the process acts as the user who owns the executable file).

Process capabilities

Linux is moving toward another model of process credentials based on the notion of "capabilities." A *capability* is simply a flag that asserts whether the process is allowed to perform a specific operation or a specific class of operations. This model is different from the traditional "superuser versus normal user" model in which a process can either do everything or do nothing, depending on its effective UID. As illustrated in Table 20-3, several capabilities have already been included in the Linux kernel.

Table 20-3. Linux capabilities

Name	Description
CAP_CHOWN	Ignore restrictions on file user and group ownership changes.
CAP_DAC_OVERRIDE	Ignore file access permissions.
CAP_DAC_READ_SEARCH	Ignore file/directory read and search permissions.
CAP_FOWNER	Generally ignore permission checks on file ownership.
CAP_FSETID	Ignore restrictions on setting the *setuid* and *setgid* flags for files.
CAP_KILL	Bypass permission checks when generating signals.
CAP_IPC_LOCK	Allow locking of pages and of shared memory segments.
CAP_IPC_OWNER	Skip IPC ownership checks.
CAP_LEASE	Allow taking of leases on files (see "Linux File Locking" in Chapter 12).
CAP_LINUX_IMMUTABLE	Allow modification of append-only and immutable Ext2/Ext3 files.
CAP_MKNOD	Allow privileged mknod( ) operations.
CAP_NET_ADMIN	Allow general networking administration.
CAP_NET_BIND_SERVICE	Allow binding to TCP/UDP sockets below 1,024.
CAP_NET_BROADCAST	Currently unused.
CAP_NET_RAW	Allow use of RAW and PACKET sockets.
CAP_SETGID	Ignore restrictions on group's process credentials manipulations.
CAP_SETPCAP	Allow capability manipulations.
CAP_SETUID	Ignore restrictions on user's process credentials manipulations.

Table 20-3. Linux capabilities (continued)

Name	Description
CAP_SYS_ADMIN	Allow general system administration.
CAP_SYS_BOOT	Allow use of reboot( ).
CAP_SYS_CHROOT	Allow use of chroot( ).
CAP_SYS_MODULE	Allow inserting and removing of kernel modules.
CAP_SYS_NICE	Skip permission checks of the nice( ) and setpriority( ) system calls, and allow creation of real-time processes.
CAP_SYS_PACCT	Allow configuration of process accounting.
CAP_SYS_PTRACE	Allow use of ptrace( ) on any process.
CAP_SYS_RAWIO	Allow access to I/O ports through ioperm( ) and iopl( ).
CAP_SYS_RESOURCE	Allow resource limits to be increased.
CAP_SYS_TIME	Allow manipulation of system clock and real-time clock.
CAP_SYS_TTY_CONFIG	Allow execution of the vhangup( ) system call to configure the terminal.

The main advantage of capabilities is that, at any time, each program needs a limited number of them. Consequently, even if a malicious user discovers a way to exploit a buggy program, she can illegally perform only a limited set of operations.

Assume, for instance, that a buggy program has only the CAP_SYS_TIME capability. In this case, the malicious user who discovers an exploitation of the bug can succeed only in illegally changing the real-time clock and the system clock. She won't be able to perform any other kind of privileged operations.

Neither the VFS nor the Ext2 filesystem currently supports the capability model, so there is no way to associate an executable file with the set of capabilities that should be enforced when a process executes that file. Nevertheless, a process can explicitly get and set its capabilities by using, respectively, the capget( ) and capset( ) system calls, provided that the process already owns the CAP_SETPCAP capability. For instance, it is possible to modify the *login* program to retain a subset of the capabilities and drop the others.

The Linux kernel already takes capabilities into account. Let's consider, for instance, the nice( ) system call, which allows users to change the static priority of a process. In the traditional model, only the superuser can raise a priority; the kernel should therefore check whether the euid field in the descriptor of the calling process is set to 0. However, the Linux kernel defines a capability called CAP_SYS_NICE, which corresponds exactly to this kind of operation. The kernel checks the value of this flag by invoking the capable( ) function and passing the CAP_SYS_NICE value to it.

This approach works thanks to some "compatibility hacks" that have been added to the kernel code: each time a process sets the euid and fsuid fields to 0 (either by invoking one of the system calls listed in Table 20-2 or by executing a *setuid* program owned by the superuser), the kernel sets all process capabilities so that all checks will succeed. When the process resets the euid and fsuid fields to the real UID of the process owner, the kernel checks the keep_capabilities flag in the process descriptor and drops all capabilities of the process if the flag is set. A process can set and reset the keep_capabilities flag by means of the Linux-specific prctl( ) system call.

Command-Line Arguments and Shell Environment

When a user types a command, the program that is loaded to satisfy the request may receive some *command-line arguments* from the shell. For example, when a user types the command:

```
$ ls -l /usr/bin
```

to get a full listing of the files in the */usr/bin* directory, the shell process creates a new process to execute the command. This new process loads the */bin/ls* executable file. In doing so, most of the execution context inherited from the shell is lost, but the three separate arguments ls, -l, and /usr/bin are kept. Generally, the new process may receive any number of arguments.

The conventions for passing the command-line arguments depend on the high-level language used. In the C language, the main( ) function of a program may receive as parameters an integer specifying how many arguments have been passed to the program and the address of an array of pointers to strings. The following prototype formalizes this standard:

```
int main(int argc, char *argv[])
```

Going back to the previous example, when the */bin/ls* program is invoked, argc has the value 3, argv[0] points to the ls string, argv[1] points to the -l string, and argv[2] points to the /usr/bin string. The end of the argv array is always marked by a null pointer, so argv[3] contains NULL.

A third optional parameter that may be passed in the C language to the main( ) function is the parameter containing *environment variables*. They are used to customize the execution context of a process, to provide general information to a user or other processes, or to allow a process to keep some information across an execve( ) system call.

To use the environment variables, main( ) can be declared as follows:

```
int main(int argc, char *argv[], char *envp[])
```

The envp parameter points to an array of pointers to environment strings of the form:

```
VAR_NAME=something
```

where VAR_NAME represents the name of an environment variable, while the substring following the = delimiter represents the actual value assigned to the variable. The end of the envp array is marked by a null pointer, like the argv array. The address of the envp array is also stored in the environ global variable of the C library.

Command-line arguments and environment strings are placed on the User Mode stack, right before the return address (see the section "Parameter Passing" in Chapter 9). The bottom locations of the User Mode stack are illustrated in Figure 20-1. Notice that the environment variables are located near the bottom of the stack, right after a 0 long integer.

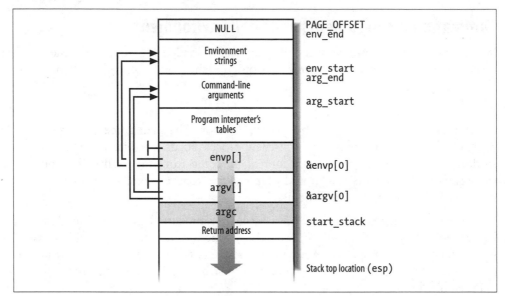

Figure 20-1. The bottom locations of the User Mode stack

Libraries

Each high-level source code file is transformed through several steps into an *object file*, which contains the machine code of the assembly language instructions corresponding to the high-level instructions. An object file cannot be executed, since it does not contain the linear address that corresponds to each reference to a name of a global symbol external to the source code file, such as functions in libraries or other source code files of the same program. The assigning, or *resolution*, of such addresses is performed by the linker, which collects all the object files of the program and constructs the executable file. The linker also analyzes the library's functions used by the program and glues them into the executable file in a manner described later in this chapter.

Most programs, even the most trivial ones, use libraries. Consider, for instance, the following one-line C program:

```
void main(void) { }
```

Although this program does not compute anything, a lot of work is needed to set up the execution environment (see the section "The exec Functions" later in this chapter) and to kill the process when the program terminates (see the section "Destroying Processes" in Chapter 3). In particular, when the main( ) function terminates, the C compiler inserts an exit( ) function call in the object code.

We know from Chapter 9 that programs usually invoke system calls through wrapper routines in the C library. This holds for the C compiler too. Besides including the code directly generated by compiling the program's statements, each executable file also includes some "glue" code to handle the interactions of the User Mode process with the kernel. Portions of such glue code are stored in the C library.

Many other libraries of functions, besides the C library, are included in Unix systems. A generic Linux system could easily have 50 different libraries. Just to mention a couple of them: the math library *libm* includes advanced functions for floating point operations, while the X11 library *libX11* collects together the basic low-level functions for the X11 Window System graphics interface.

All executable files in traditional Unix systems were based on *static libraries*. This means that the executable file produced by the linker includes not only the code of the original program but also the code of the library functions that the program refers to. One big disadvantage of static libraries is that they eat lots of space on disk. Indeed, each statically linked executable file duplicates some portion of library code.

Modern Unix systems use *shared libraries*. The executable file does not contain the library object code, but only a reference to the library name. When the program is loaded in memory for execution, a suitable program called the *program interpreter* (or *ld.so*) takes care of analyzing the library names in the executable file, locating the library in the system's directory tree and making the requested code available to the executing process. A process can also load additional shared libraries at runtime by using the dlopen( ) library function.

Shared libraries are especially convenient on systems that provide file memory mapping, since they reduce the amount of main memory requested for executing a program. When the program interpreter must link some shared library to a process, it does not copy the object code, but just performs a memory mapping of the relevant portion of the library file into the process's address space. This allows the page frames containing the machine code of the library to be shared among all processes that are using the same code.

Shared libraries also have some disadvantages. The startup time of a dynamically linked program is usually longer than that of a statically linked one. Moreover, dynamically linked programs are not as portable as statically linked ones, since they may not execute properly in systems that include a different version of the same library.

A user may always require a program to be linked statically. For example, the GCC compiler offers the -static option, which tells the linker to use the static libraries instead of the shared ones.

Program Segments and Process Memory Regions

The linear address space of a Unix program is traditionally partitioned, from a logical point of view, in several linear address intervals called segments:*

Text segment

Includes the executable code

Initialized data segment

Contains the initialized data—that is, the static variables and the global variables whose initial values are stored in the executable file (because the program must know their values at startup).

Uninitialized data segment (bss)

Contains the uninitialized data—that is, all global variables whose initial values are not stored in the executable file (because the program sets the values before referencing them); it is historically called a *bss segment*.

Stack segment

Contains the program stack, which includes the return addresses, parameters, and local variables of the functions being executed.

Each `mm_struct` memory descriptor (see the section "The Memory Descriptor" in Chapter 8) includes some fields that identify the role of particular memory regions of the corresponding process:

`start_code, end_code`

Store the initial and final linear addresses of the memory region that includes the native code of the program—the code in the executable file. Since the text segment includes shared libraries but the executable file does not, the memory region demarcated by these fields is a subset of the text segment.

`start_data, end_data`

Store the initial and final linear addresses of the memory region that includes the native initialized data of the program, as specified in the executable file. The fields identify a memory region that roughly corresponds to the data segment. Actually, `start_data` should almost always be set to the address of the first page right after `end_code`, and thus the field is unused. The `end_data` field is used, though.

`start_brk, brk`

Store the initial and final linear addresses of the memory region that includes the dynamically allocated memory areas of the process (see the section "Managing the Heap" in Chapter 8). This memory region is sometimes called the *heap*.

---

* The word "segment" has historical roots, since the first Unix systems implemented each linear address interval with a different segment register. Linux, however, does not rely on the segmentation mechanism of the 80×86 microprocessors to implement program segments.

---

start_stack

> Stores the address right above that of main( )'s return address; as illustrated in Figure 20-1, higher addresses are reserved (recall that stacks grow toward lower addresses).

arg_start, arg_end

> Store the initial and final addresses of the stack portion containing the command-line arguments.

env_start, env_end

> Store the initial and final addresses of the stack portion containing the environment strings.

Notice that shared libraries and file memory mapping have made the classification of the process's address space based on program segments a bit obsolete, since each of the shared libraries is mapped into a different memory region from those discussed in the preceding list.

Now we'll describe, by means of a simple example, how the Linux kernel maps shared libraries into the process's address space. We assume as usual that the User Mode address space ranges from 0x00000000 and 0xbfffffff. We consider the */sbin/ init* program, which creates and monitors the activity of all the processes that implement the outer layers of the operating system (see the section "Kernel Threads" in Chapter 3). The memory regions of the corresponding *init* process are shown in Table 20-4 (this information can be obtained from the */proc/1/maps* file; you might see a different table, of course, depending on the version of the *init* program and how it has been compiled and linked). Notice that all regions listed are implemented by means of private memory mappings (the letter p in the Permissions column). This is not surprising because these memory regions exist only to provide data to a process. While executing instructions, a process may modify the contents of these memory regions; however, the files on disk associated with them stay unchanged. This is precisely how private memory mappings act.

Table 20-4. Memory regions of the init process

Address range	Perms	Mapped file
0x08048000-0x0804cfff	r-xp	*/sbin/init* at offset 0
0x0804d000-0x0804dfff	rw-p	*/sbin/init* at offset 0x4000
0x0804e000-0x0804efff	rwxp	Anonymous
0x40000000-0x40014fff	r-xp	*/lib/ld-2.2.3.so* at offset 0
0x40015000-0x40015fff	rw-p	*/lib/ld-2.2.3.so* at offset 0x14000
0x40016000-0x40016fff	rw-p	Anonymous
0x40020000-0x40126fff	r-xp	*/lib/libc.2.2.3.so* at offset 0
0x40127000-0x4012cfff	rw-p	*/lib/libc.2.2.3.so* at offset 0x106000
0x4012d000-0x40130fff	rw-p	Anonymous
0xbfffd000-0xbfffffff	rwxp	Anonymous

The memory region starting from 0x8048000 is a memory mapping associated with the portion of the */sbin/init* file ranging from byte 0 to byte 20,479 (only the start and end of the region are shown in the */proc/1/maps* file, but the region size can easily be derived from them). The permissions specify that the region is executable (it contains object code), read only (it's not writable because the instructions don't change during a run), and private, so we can guess that the region maps the text segment of the program.

The memory region starting from 0x804d000 is a memory mapping associated with another portion of */sbin/init* ranging from byte 16384 (corresponding to offset 0x4000 shown in Table 20-4) to 20,479. Since the permissions specify that the private region may be written, we can conclude that it maps the data segment of the program.

The next one-page memory region starting from 0x0804e000 is anonymous, that is, it is not associated with any file and includes the bss segment of *init*.

Similarly, the next three memory regions starting from 0x40000000, 0x40015000, and 0x40016000 correspond to the text segment, the data segment, and the bss segment, respectively, of the */lib/ld.2.2.3.so* library, which is the program interpreter for the ELF shared libraries. The program interpreter is never executed alone: it is always memory-mapped inside the address space of a process executing another program.

On this system, the C library happens to be stored in the */lib/libc.2.2.3.so* file. The text segment, data segment, and bss segment of the C library are mapped into the next three memory regions, starting from address 0x40020000. Remember that page frames included in private regions can be shared among several processes with the Copy On Write mechanism, as long as they are not modified. Thus, since the text segment is read-only, the page frames containing the executable code of the C library are shared among almost all currently executing processes (all except the statically linked ones).

Finally, the last anonymous memory region from 0xbfffd000 to 0xbfffffff is associated with the User Mode stack. We already explained in the section "Page Fault Exception Handler" in Chapter 8 how the stack is automatically expanded toward lower addresses whenever necessary.

Execution Tracing

Execution tracing is a technique that allows a program to monitor the execution of another program. The traced program can be executed step by step, until a signal is received, or until a system call is invoked. Execution tracing is widely used by debuggers, together with other techniques like the insertion of breakpoints in the debugged program and run-time access to its variables. We focus on how the kernel supports execution tracing rather than discussing how debuggers work.

In Linux, execution tracing is performed through the ptrace( ) system call, which can handle the commands listed in Table 20-5. Processes having the CAP_SYS_PTRACE capability flag set are allowed to trace any process in the system except *init*. Conversely, a process *P* with no CAP_SYS_PTRACE capability is allowed to trace only processes having the same owner as *P*. Moreover, a process cannot be traced by two processes at the same time.

Table 20-5. The ptrace commands

Command	Description
PTRACE_TRACEME	Start execution tracing for the current process
PTRACE_PEEKTEXT	Read a 32-bit value from the text segment
PTRACE_PEEKDATA	Read a 32-bit value from the data segment
PTRACE_PEEKUSR	Read the CPU's normal and debug registers
PTRACE_POKETEXT	Write a 32-bit value into the text segment
PTRACE_POKEDATA	Write a 32-bit value into the data segment
PTRACE_POKEUSR	Write the CPU's normal and debug registers
PTRACE_CONT	Resume execution
PTRACE_KILL	Kill the traced process
PTRACE_SINGLESTEP	Resume execution for a single assembly language instruction
PTRACE_GETREGS	Read privileged CPU's registers
PTRACE_SETREGS	Write privileged CPU's registers
PTRACE_GETFPREGS	Read floating point registers
PTRACE_SETFPREGS	Write floating point registers
PTRACE_GETFPXREGS	Read MMX and XMM registers
PTRACE_SETFPXREGS	Write MMX and XMM registers
PTRACE_ATTACH	Start execution tracing for another process
PTRACE_DETACH	Terminate execution tracing
PTRACE_SETOPTIONS	Modify ptrace( ) behavior
PTRACE_SYSCALL	Resume execution until the next system call boundary

The ptrace( ) system call modifies the p_pptr field in the descriptor of the traced process so that it points to the tracing process; therefore, the tracing process becomes the effective parent of the traced one. When execution tracing terminates—i.e., when ptrace( ) is invoked with the PTRACE_DETACH command—the system call sets p_pptr to the value of p_opptr, thus restoring the original parent of the traced process (see the section "Parenthood Relationships Among Processes" in Chapter 3).

Several monitored events can be associated with a traced program:

- End of execution of a single assembly language instruction
- Entering a system call
- Exiting from a system call
- Receiving a signal

When a monitored event occurs, the traced program is stopped and a SIGCHLD signal is sent to its parent. When the parent wishes to resume the child's execution, it can use one of the PTRACE_CONT, PTRACE_SINGLESTEP, and PTRACE_SYSCALL commands, depending on the kind of event it wants to monitor.

The PTRACE_CONT command just resumes execution; the child executes until it receives another signal. This kind of tracing is implemented by means of the PT_PTRACED flag in the ptrace field of the process descriptor, which is checked by the do_signal( ) function (see the section "Delivering a Signal" in Chapter 10).

The PTRACE_SINGLESTEP command forces the child process to execute the next assembly language instruction, and then stops it again. This kind of tracing is implemented on 80×86-based machines by means of the TF trap flag in the eflags register: when it is on, a "Debug" exception is raised right after any assembly language instruction. The corresponding exception handler just clears the flag, forces the current process to stop, and sends a SIGCHLD signal to its parent. Notice that setting the TF flag is not a privileged operation, so User Mode processes can force single-step execution even without the ptrace( ) system call. The kernel checks the PT_DTRACE flag in the process descriptor to keep track of whether the child process is being single-stepped through ptrace( ).

The PTRACE_SYSCALL command causes the traced process to resume execution until a system call is invoked. The process is stopped twice: the first time when the system call starts, and the second time when the system call terminates. This kind of tracing is implemented by means of the PT_TRACESYS flag in the processor descriptor, which is checked in the system_call( ) assembly language function (see the section "The system_call( ) Function" in Chapter 9).

A process can also be traced using some debugging features of the Intel Pentium processors. For example, the parent could set the values of the dr0,...dr7 debug registers for the child by using the PTRACE_POKEUSR command. When an event monitored by a debug register occurs, the CPU raises the "Debug" exception; the exception handler can then suspend the traced process and send the SIGCHLD signal to the parent.

Executable Formats

The standard Linux executable format is named *Executable and Linking Format (ELF)*. It was developed by Unix System Laboratories and is now the most widely used format in the Unix world. Several well-known Unix operating systems, such as System V Release 4 and Sun's Solaris 2, have adopted ELF as their main executable format.

Older Linux versions supported another format named *Assembler OUTput Format (a.out)*; actually, there were several versions of that format floating around the Unix world. It is seldom used now, since ELF is much more practical.

Linux supports many other different formats for executable files; in this way, it can run programs compiled for other operating systems, such as MS-DOS EXE programs or BSD Unix's COFF executables. A few executable formats, like Java or *bash* scripts, are platform-independent.

An executable format is described by an object of type linux_binfmt, which essentially provides three methods:

load_binary
> Sets up a new execution environment for the current process by reading the information stored in an executable file.

load_shlib
> Dynamically binds a shared library to an already running process; it is activated by the uselib( ) system call.

core_dump
> Stores the execution context of the current process in a file named core. This file, whose format depends on the type of executable of the program being executed, is usually created when a process receives a signal whose default action is "dump" (see the section "Actions Performed upon Delivering a Signal" in Chapter 10).

All linux_binfmt objects are included in a simply linked list, and the address of the first element is stored in the formats variable. Elements can be inserted and removed in the list by invoking the register_binfmt( ) and unregister_binfmt( ) functions. The register_binfmt( ) function is executed during system startup for each executable format compiled into the kernel. This function is also executed when a module implementing a new executable format is being loaded, while the unregister_binfmt( ) function is invoked when the module is unloaded.

The last element in the formats list is always an object describing the executable format for *interpreted scripts*. This format defines only the load_binary method. The corresponding load_script( ) function checks whether the executable file starts with the #! pair of characters. If so, it interprets the rest of the first line as the pathname of another executable file and tries to execute it by passing the name of the script file as a parameter.[*]

Linux allows users to register their own custom executable formats. Each such format may be recognized either by means of a magic number stored in the first 128 bytes of the file, or by a filename extension that identifies the file type. For example, MS-DOS extensions consist of three characters separated from the filename by a dot: the *.exe* extension identifies executable programs, while the *.bat* extension identifies shell scripts.

---

[*] It is possible to execute a script file even if it doesn't start with the #! characters, as long as the file is written in the language recognized by a command shell. In this case, however, the script is interpreted either by the shell on which the user types the command or by the default Bourne shell *sh*; therefore, the kernel is not directly involved.

Each custom format is associated with an interpreter program, which is automatically invoked by the kernel with the original custom executable filename as a parameter. The mechanism is similar to the script's format, but it's more powerful since it doesn't impose any restrictions on the custom format. To register a new format, the user writes into the */proc/sys/fs/binfmt_misc/register* file a string with the following format:

```
:name:type:offset:string:mask:interpreter:
```

where each field has the following meaning:

name
>   An identifier for the new format

type
>   The type of recognition (M for magic number, E for extension)

offset
>   The starting offset of the magic number inside the file

string
>   The byte sequence to be matched either in the magic number or in the extension

mask
>   The string to mask out some bits in string

interpreter
>   The full pathname of the program interpreter

For example, the following command performed by the superuser enables the kernel to recognize the Microsoft Windows executable format:

```
$ echo ':DOSWin:M:0:MZ:0xff:/usr/local/bin/wine:' > /proc/sys/fs/binfmt_misc/register
```

A Windows executable file has the MZ magic number in the first two bytes, and it is executed by the */usr/local/bin/wine* program interpreter.

Execution Domains

As mentioned in Chapter 1, a neat feature of Linux is its ability to execute files compiled for other operating systems. Of course, this is possible only if the files include machine code for the same computer architecture on which the kernel is running. Two kinds of support are offered for these "foreign" programs:

• Emulated execution: necessary to execute programs that include system calls that are not POSIX-compliant

• Native execution: valid for programs whose system calls are totally POSIX-compliant

Microsoft MS-DOS and Windows programs are emulated: they cannot be natively executed, since they include APIs that are not recognized by Linux. An emulator like

DOSemu or Wine (which appeared in the example at the end of the previous section) is invoked to translate each API call into an emulating wrapper function call, which in turn uses the existing Linux system calls. Since emulators are mostly implemented as User Mode applications, we don't discuss them further.

On the other hand, POSIX-compliant programs compiled on operating systems other than Linux can be executed without too much trouble, since POSIX operating systems offer similar APIs. (Actually, the APIs should be identical, although this is not always the case.) Minor differences that the kernel must iron out usually refer to how system calls are invoked or how the various signals are numbered. This information is stored in *execution domain descriptors* of type exec_domain.

A process specifies its execution domain by setting the personality field of its descriptor and storing the address of the corresponding exec_domain data structure in the exec_domain field. A process can change its personality by issuing a suitable system call named personality( ); typical values assumed by the system call's parameter are listed in Table 20-6. The C library does not include a corresponding wrapper routine because programmers are not expected to directly change the personality of their programs. Instead, the personality( ) system call should be issued by the glue code that sets up the execution context of the process (see the next section).

Table 20-6. Main personalities supported by the Linux kernel

Personality	Operating system
PER_LINUX	Standard execution domain
PER_SVR4	System V Release 4
PER_SVR3	System V Release 3
PER_SCOSVR3	SCO Unix Version 3.2
PER_OSR5	SCO OpenServer Release 5
PER_WYSEV386	Unix System V/386 Release 3.2.1
PER_ISCR4	Interactive Unix
PER_BSD	BSD Unix
PER_SUNOS	SunOS
PER_XENIX	Xenix
PER_IRIX32	SGI Irix-5 32 bit
PER_IRIXN32	SGI Irix-6 32 bit
PER_IRIX64	SGI Irix-6 64 bit
PER_RISCOS	RISC OS
PER_SOLARIS	Sun's Solaris
PER_UW7	Caldera's UnixWare 7

The exec Functions

Unix systems provide a family of functions that replace the execution context of a process with a new context described by an executable file. The names of these functions start with the prefix exec, followed by one or two letters; therefore, a generic function in the family is usually referred to as an exec function.

The exec functions are listed in Table 20-7; they differ in how the parameters are interpreted.

Table 20-7. The exec functions

Function name	PATH search	Command-line arguments	Environment array
execl( )	No	List	No
execlp( )	Yes	List	No
execle( )	No	List	Yes
execv( )	No	Array	No
execvp( )	Yes	Array	No
execve( )	No	Array	Yes

The first parameter of each function denotes the pathname of the file to be executed. The pathname can be absolute or relative to the process's current directory. Moreover, if the name does not include any / characters, the execlp( ) and execvp( ) functions search for the executable file in all directories specified by the PATH environment variable.

Besides the first parameter, the execl( ), execlp( ), and execle( ) functions include a variable number of additional parameters. Each points to a string describing a command-line argument for the new program; as the "l" character in the function names suggests, the parameters are organized in a list terminated by a NULL value. Usually, the first command-line argument duplicates the executable filename. Conversely, the execv( ), execvp( ), and execve( ) functions specify the command-line arguments with a single parameter; as the v character in the function names suggests, the parameter is the address of a vector of pointers to command-line argument strings. The last component of the array must be NULL.

The execle( ) and execve( ) functions receive as their last parameter the address of an array of pointers to environment strings; as usual, the last component of the array must be NULL. The other functions may access the environment for the new program from the external environ global variable, which is defined in the C library.

All exec functions, with the exception of execve( ), are wrapper routines defined in the C library and use execve( ), which is the only system call offered by Linux to deal with program execution.

The sys_execve( ) service routine receives the following parameters:

- The address of the executable file pathname (in the User Mode address space).
- The address of a NULL-terminated array (in the User Mode address space) of pointers to strings (again in the User Mode address space); each string represents a command-line argument.
- The address of a NULL-terminated array (in the User Mode address space) of pointers to strings (again in the User Mode address space); each string represents an environment variable in the NAME=value format.

The function copies the executable file pathname into a newly allocated page frame. It then invokes the do_execve( ) function, passing to it the pointers to the page frame, to the pointer's arrays, and to the location of the Kernel Mode stack where the User Mode register contents are saved. In turn, do_execve( ) performs the following operations:

1. Statically allocates a linux_binprm data structure, which will be filled with data concerning the new executable file.

2. Invokes path_init( ), path_walk( ), and dentry_open( ) to get the dentry object, the file object, and the inode object associated with the executable file. On failure, returns the proper error code.

3. Verifies that the executable file is not being written by checking the i_writecount field of the inode; stores –1 in that field to forbid further write accesses.

4. Invokes the prepare_binprm( ) function to fill the linux_binprm data structure. This function, in turn, performs the following operations:

   a. Checks whether the permissions of the file allow its execution; if not, returns an error code.

   b. Initializes the e_uid and e_gid fields of the linux_binprm structure, taking into account the values of the *setuid* and *setgid* flags of the executable file. These fields represent the effective user and group IDs, respectively. Also checks process capabilities (a compatibility hack explained in the earlier section "Process Credentials and Capabilities").

   c. Fills the buf field of the linux_binprm structure with the first 128 bytes of the executable file. These bytes include the magic number of the executable format and other information suitable for recognizing the executable file.

5. Copies the file pathname, command-line arguments, and environment strings into one or more newly allocated page frames. (Eventually, they are assigned to the User Mode address space.)

6. Invokes the search_binary_handler( ) function, which scans the formats list and tries to apply the load_binary method of each element, passing to it the linux_binprm data structure. The scan of the formats list terminates as soon as a load_binary method succeeds in acknowledging the executable format of the file.

7. If the executable file format is not present in the formats list, releases all allocated page frames and returns the error code -ENOEXEC. Linux cannot recognize the executable file format.

8. Otherwise, returns the code obtained from the load_binary method associated with the executable format of the file.

The load_binary method corresponding to an executable file format performs the following operations (we assume that the executable file is stored on a filesystem that allows file memory mapping and that it requires one or more shared libraries):

1. Checks some magic numbers stored in the first 128 bytes of the file to identify the executable format. If the magic numbers don't match, returns the error code -ENOEXEC.

2. Reads the header of the executable file. This header describes the program's segments and the shared libraries requested.

3. Gets from the executable file the pathname of the program interpreter, which is used to locate the shared libraries and map them into memory.

4. Gets the dentry object (as well as the inode object and the file object) of the program interpreter.

5. Checks the execution permissions of the program interpreter.

6. Copies the first 128 bytes of the program interpreter into a buffer.

7. Performs some consistency checks on the program interpreter type.

8. Invokes the flush_old_exec( ) function to release almost all resources used by the previous computation; in turn, this function performs the following operations:

    a. If the table of signal handlers is shared with other processes, allocates a new table and decrements the usage counter of the old one; this is done by invoking the make_private_signals( ) function.

    b. Invokes the exec_mmap( ) function to release the memory descriptor, all memory regions, and all page frames assigned to the process and to clean up the process's Page Tables.

    c. Updates the table of signal handlers by resetting each signal to its default action. This is done by invoking the release_old_signals( ) and flush_signal_handlers( ) functions.

    d. Sets the comm field of the process descriptor with the executable file pathname.

    e. Invokes the flush_thread( ) function to clear the values of the floating point registers and debug registers saved in the TSS segment.

    f. Invokes the de_thread( ) function to detach the process from the old thread group (see the section "Identifying a Process" in Chapter 3).

g. Invokes the `flush_old_files()` function to close all open files having the corresponding flag in the `files->close_on_exec` field of the process descriptor set (see the section "Files Associated with a Process" in Chapter 12).*

Now we have reached the point of no return: the function cannot restore the previous computation if something goes wrong.

9. Sets up the new personality of the process—that is, the `personality` field in the process descriptor.

10. Clears the `PF_FORKNOEXEC` flag in the process descriptor. This flag, which is set when a process is forked and cleared when it executes a new program, is required for process accounting.

11. Invokes the `setup_arg_pages()` function to allocate a new memory region descriptor for the process's User Mode stack and to insert that memory region into the process's address space. `setup_arg_pages()` also assigns the page frames containing the command-line arguments and the environment variable strings to the new memory region.

12. Invokes the `do_mmap()` function to create a new memory region that maps the text segment (that is, the code) of the executable file. The initial linear address of the memory region depends on the executable format, since the program's executable code is usually not relocatable. Therefore, the function assumes that the text segment is loaded starting from some specific logical address offset (and thus from some specified linear address). ELF programs are loaded starting from linear address 0x08048000.

13. Invokes the `do_mmap()` function to create a new memory region that maps the data segment of the executable file. Again, the initial linear address of the memory region depends on the executable format, since the executable code expects to find its variables at specified offsets (that is, at specified linear addresses). In an ELF program, the data segment is loaded right after the text segment.

14. Allocates additional memory regions for any other specialized segments of the executable file. Usually, there are none.

15. Invokes a function that loads the program interpreter. If the program interpreter is an ELF executable, the function is named `load_elf_interp()`. In general, the function performs the operations in Steps 11 through 13, but for the program interpreter instead of the file to be executed. The initial addresses of the memory regions that will include the text and data of the program interpreter are specified by the program interpreter itself; however, they are very high (usually above 0x40000000) to avoid collisions with the memory regions that map the text and data of the file to be executed (see the earlier section "Program Segments and Process Memory Regions").

* These flags can be read and modified by means of the `fcntl()` system call.

16. Stores in the `binfmt` field of the process descriptor the address of the `linux_binfmt` object of the executable format.

17. Determines the new capabilities of the process.

18. Creates specific program interpreter tables and stores them on the User Mode stack between the command-line arguments and the array of pointers to environment strings (see Figure 20-1).

19. Sets the values of the `start_code`, `end_code`, `end_data`, `start_brk`, `brk`, and `start_stack` fields of the process's memory descriptor.

20. Invokes the `do_brk()` function to create a new anonymous memory region mapping the bss segment of the program. (When the process writes into a variable, it triggers demand paging, and thus the allocation of a page frame.) The size of this memory region was computed when the executable program was linked. The initial linear address of the memory region must be specified, since the program's executable code is usually not relocatable. In an ELF program, the bss segment is loaded right after the data segment.

21. Invokes the `start_thread()` macro to modify the values of the User Mode registers eip and esp saved on the Kernel Mode stack, so that they point to the entry point of the program interpreter and to the top of the new User Mode stack, respectively.

22. If the process is being traced, sends the SIGTRAP signal to it.

23. Returns the value 0 (success).

When the execve( ) system call terminates and the calling process resumes its execution in User Mode, the execution context is dramatically changed: the code that invoked the system call no longer exists. In this sense, we could say that execve( ) never returns on success. Instead, a new program to be executed is mapped in the address space of the process.

However, the new program cannot yet be executed, since the program interpreter must still take care of loading the shared libraries.*

Although the program interpreter runs in User Mode, we briefly sketch out here how it operates. Its first job is to set up a basic execution context for itself, starting from the information stored by the kernel in the User Mode stack between the array of pointers to environment strings and `arg_start`. Then the program interpreter must examine the program to be executed to identify which shared libraries must be loaded and which functions in each shared library are effectively requested. Next, the interpreter issues several mmap( ) system calls to create memory regions mapping the pages that will hold the library functions (text and data) actually used by the

---

* Things are much simpler if the executable file is statically linked—that is, if no shared library is requested. The load_binary method just maps the text, data, bss, and stack segments of the program into the process memory regions, and then sets the User Mode eip register to the entry point of the new program.

program. Then the interpreter updates all references to the symbols of the shared library, according to the linear addresses of the library's memory regions. Finally, the program interpreter terminates its execution by jumping to the main entry point of the program to be executed. From now on, the process will execute the code of the executable file and of the shared libraries.

As you may have noticed, executing a program is a complex activity that involves many facets of kernel design, such as process abstraction, memory management, system calls, and filesystems. It is the kind of topic that makes you realize what a marvelous piece of work Linux is!

System Startup

This appendix explains what happens right after users switch on their computers—that is, how a Linux kernel image is copied into memory and executed. In short, we discuss how the kernel, and thus the whole system, is "bootstrapped."

Traditionally, the term *bootstrap* refers to a person who tries to stand up by pulling his own boots. In operating systems, the term denotes bringing at least a portion of the operating system into main memory and having the processor execute it. It also denotes the initialization of kernel data structures, the creation of some user processes, and the transfer of control to one of them.

Computer bootstrapping is a tedious, long task, since initially, nearly every hardware device, including the RAM, is in a random, unpredictable state. Moreover, the bootstrap process is highly dependent on the computer architecture; as usual, we refer to IBM's PC architecture in this appendix.

Prehistoric Age: The BIOS

The moment after a computer is powered on, it is practically useless because the RAM chips contain random data and no operating system is running. To begin the boot, a special hardware circuit raises the logical value of the RESET pin of the CPU. After RESET is asserted, some registers of the processor (including cs and eip) are set to fixed values, and the code found at physical address 0xfffffff0 is executed. This address is mapped by the hardware to a certain read-only, persistent memory chip that is often called Read-Only Memory (ROM). The set of programs stored in ROM is traditionally called Basic Input/Output System (BIOS), since it includes several interrupt-driven low-level procedures used by some operating systems, including Microsoft's MS-DOS, to handle the hardware devices that make up the computer.

Once initialized, Linux does not use BIOS, but provides its own device driver for every hardware device on the computer. In fact, the BIOS procedures must be executed in real mode, while the kernel executes in protected mode (see the section "Segmentation in Hardware" in Chapter 2), so they cannot share functions even if that would be beneficial.

The BIOS uses Real Mode addresses because they are the only ones available when the computer is turned on. A Real Mode address is composed of a *seg* segment and an *off* offset; the corresponding physical address is given by *seg**16+*off*. As a result, no Global Descriptor Table, Local Descriptor Table, or paging table is needed by the CPU addressing circuit to translate a logical address into a physical one. Clearly, the code that initializes the GDT, LDT, and paging tables must run in Real Mode.

Linux is forced to use BIOS in the bootstrapping phase, when it must retrieve the kernel image from disk or from some other external device. The BIOS bootstrap procedure essentially performs the following four operations:

1. Executes a series of tests on the computer hardware to establish which devices are present and whether they are working properly. This phase is often called Power-On Self-Test (POST). During this phase, several messages, such as the BIOS version banner, are displayed.

2. Initializes the hardware devices. This phase is crucial in modern PCI-based architectures, since it guarantees that all hardware devices operate without conflicts on the IRQ lines and I/O ports. At the end of this phase, a table of installed PCI devices is displayed.

3. Searches for an operating system to boot. Actually, depending on the BIOS setting, the procedure may try to access (in a predefined, customizable order) the first sector (*boot sector*) of any floppy disk, hard disk, and CD-ROM in the system.

4. As soon as a valid device is found, copies the contents of its first sector into RAM, starting from physical address 0x00007c00, and then jumps into that address and executes the code just loaded.

The rest of this appendix takes you from the most primitive starting state to the full glory of a running Linux system.

Ancient Age: The Boot Loader

The *boot loader* is the program invoked by the BIOS to load the image of an operating system kernel into RAM. Let's briefly sketch how boot loaders work in IBM's PC architecture.

To boot from a floppy disk, the instructions stored in its first sector are loaded in RAM and executed; these instructions copy all the remaining sectors containing the kernel image into RAM.

Booting from a hard disk is done differently. The first sector of the hard disk, named the Master Boot Record (MBR), includes the partition table[*] and a small program,

---

[*] Each partition table entry typically includes the starting and ending sectors of a partition and the kind of operating system that handles it.

which loads the first sector of the partition containing the operating system to be started. Some operating systems, such as Microsoft Windows 98, identify this partition by means of an *active* flag included in the partition table;[*] following this approach, only the operating system whose kernel image is stored in the active partition can be booted. As we shall see later, Linux is more flexible because it replaces the rudimentary program included in the MBR with a sophisticated program such as LILO or GRand Unified Bootloader (GRUB) that allows users to select the operating system to be booted.

Booting Linux from Floppy Disk

The only way to store a Linux kernel on a single floppy disk is to compress the kernel image. As we shall see, compression is done at compile time and decompression is done by the loader.

If the Linux kernel is loaded from a floppy disk, the boot loader is quite simple. It is coded in the *arch/i386/boot/bootsect.S* assembly language file. When a new kernel image is produced by compiling the kernel source, the executable code yielded by this assembly language file is placed at the beginning of the kernel image file. Thus, it is very easy to produce a bootable floppy by copying the Linux kernel image to the floppy disk starting from the first sector of the disk. When the BIOS loads the first sector of the floppy disk into memory, it actually copies the code of the boot loader.

The boot loader, which is invoked by the BIOS by jumping to physical address 0x00007c00, performs the following operations:

1. Moves itself from address 0x00007c00 to address 0x00090000.
2. Sets up the Real Mode stack from address 0x00003ff4. As usual, the stack grows toward lower addresses.
3. Sets up the disk parameter table, used by the BIOS to handle the floppy device driver.
4. Invokes a BIOS procedure to display a "Loading" message.
5. Invokes a BIOS procedure to load the setup( ) code of the kernel image from the floppy disk and puts it in RAM starting from address 0x00090200.
6. Invokes a BIOS procedure to load the rest of the kernel image from the floppy disk and puts the image in RAM starting from either low address 0x00010000 (for small kernel images compiled with make zImage) or high address 0x00100000 (for big kernel images compiled with make bzImage). In the following discussion, we say that the kernel image is "loaded low" or "loaded high" in RAM, respectively. Support for big kernel images uses essentially the same booting scheme as the other one, but it places data in different physical memory addresses to avoid

---

[*] The active flag may be set through programs like MS-DOS's FDISK.

problems with the ISA hole mentioned in the section "Reserved Page Frames" in Chapter 2.

7. Jumps to the setup( ) code.

Booting Linux from Hard Disk

In most cases, the Linux kernel is loaded from a hard disk, and a two-stage boot loader is required. The most commonly used Linux boot loader on 80×86 systems is named LInux LOader (LILO); corresponding programs exist for other architectures. LILO may be installed either on the MBR (replacing the small program that loads the boot sector of the active partition) or in the boot sector of a (usually active) disk partition. In both cases, the final result is the same: when the loader is executed at boot time, the user may choose which operating system to load.

The LILO boot loader is broken into two parts, since otherwise it is too large to fit into the MBR. The MBR or the partition boot sector includes a small boot loader, which is loaded into RAM starting from address 0x00007c00 by the BIOS. This small program moves itself to the address 0x0009a000, sets up the Real Mode stack (ranging from 0x0009b000 to 0x0009a200), and loads the second part of the LILO boot loader into RAM starting from address 0x0009b000. In turn, this latter program reads a map of available operating systems from disk and offers the user a prompt so she can choose one of them. Finally, after the user has chosen the kernel to be loaded (or let a time-out elapse so that LILO chooses a default), the boot loader may either copy the boot sector of the corresponding partition into RAM and execute it or directly copy the kernel image into RAM.

Assuming that a Linux kernel image must be booted, the LILO boot loader, which relies on BIOS routines, performs essentially the same operations as the boot loader integrated into the kernel image described in the previous section about floppy disks. The loader displays the "Loading Linux" message; then it copies the integrated boot loader of the kernel image to address 0x00090000, the setup( ) code to address 0x00090200, and the rest of the kernel image to address 0x00010000 or 0x00100000. Then it jumps to the setup( ) code.

Middle Ages: The setup( ) Function

The code of the setup( ) assembly language function is placed by the linker immediately after the integrated boot loader of the kernel—that is, at offset 0x200 of the kernel image file. The boot loader can therefore easily locate the code and copy it into RAM, starting from physical address 0x00090200.

The setup( ) function must initialize the hardware devices in the computer and set up the environment for the execution of the kernel program. Although the BIOS already initialized most hardware devices, Linux does not rely on it, but reinitializes the devices in its own manner to enhance portability and robustness. setup( ) performs the following operations:

1. Invokes a BIOS procedure to find out the amount of RAM available in the system.

2. Sets the keyboard repeat delay and rate. (When the user keeps a key pressed past a certain amount of time, the keyboard device sends the corresponding keycode over and over to the CPU.)

3. Initializes the video adapter card.

4. Reinitializes the disk controller and determines the hard disk parameters.

5. Checks for an IBM Micro Channel bus (MCA).

6. Checks for a PS/2 pointing device (bus mouse).

7. Checks for Advanced Power Management (APM) BIOS support.

8. If the kernel image was loaded low in RAM (at physical address 0x00010000), moves it to physical address 0x00001000. Conversely, if the kernel image was loaded high in RAM, the function does not move it. This step is necessary because to be able to store the kernel image on a floppy disk and to save time while booting, the kernel image stored on disk is compressed, and the decompression routine needs some free space to use as a temporary buffer following the kernel image in RAM.

9. Sets up a provisional Interrupt Descriptor Table (IDT) and a provisional Global Descriptor Table (GDT).

10. Resets the floating-point unit (FPU), if any.

11. Reprograms the Programmable Interrupt Controller (PIC) and maps the 16 hardware interrupts (IRQ lines) to the range of vectors from 32 to 47. The kernel must perform this step because the BIOS erroneously maps the hardware interrupts in the range from 0 to 15, which is already used for CPU exceptions (see the section "Exceptions" in Chapter 4).

12. Switches the CPU from Real Mode to Protected Mode by setting the PE bit in the cr0 status register. The PG bit in the cr0 register is cleared, so paging is still disabled.

13. Jumps to the startup_32( ) assembly language function.

Renaissance: The startup_32( ) Functions

There are two different startup_32( ) functions; the one we refer to here is coded in the *arch/i386/boot/compressed/head.S* file. After setup( ) terminates, the function has been moved either to physical address 0x00100000 or to physical address 0x00001000, depending on whether the kernel image was loaded high or low in RAM.

This function performs the following operations:

1. Initializes the segmentation registers and a provisional stack.

2. Fills the area of uninitialized data of the kernel identified by the _edata and _end symbols with zeros (see the section "Reserved Page Frames" in Chapter 2).

3. Invokes the decompress_kernel( ) function to decompress the kernel image. The "Uncompressing Linux..." message is displayed first. After the kernel image is decompressed, the "OK, booting the kernel." message is shown. If the kernel image was loaded low, the decompressed kernel is placed at physical address 0x00100000. Otherwise, if the kernel image was loaded high, the decompressed kernel is placed in a temporary buffer located after the compressed image. The decompressed image is then moved into its final position, which starts at physical address 0x00100000.

4. Jumps to physical address 0x00100000.

The decompressed kernel image begins with another startup_32( ) function included in the *arch/i386/kernel/head.S* file. Using the same name for both the functions does not create any problems (besides confusing our readers), since both functions are executed by jumping to their initial physical addresses.

The second startup_32( ) function sets up the execution environment for the first Linux process (process 0). The function performs the following operations:

1. Initializes the segmentation registers with their final values.

2. Sets up the Kernel Mode stack for process 0 (see the section "Kernel Threads" in Chapter 3).

3. Initializes the provisional kernel Page Tables contained in swapper_pg_dir and pg0 to identically map the linear addresses to the same physical addresses, as explained in the section "Kernel Page Tables" in Chapter 2.

4. Stores the address of the Page Global Directory in the cr3 register, and enables paging by setting the PG bit in the cr0 register.

5. Fills the bss segment of the kernel (see the section "Program Segments and Process Memory Regions" in Chapter 20) with zeros.

6. Invokes setup_idt( ) to fill the IDT with null interrupt handlers (see the section "Preliminary Initialization of the IDT" in Chapter 4).

7. Puts the system parameters obtained from the BIOS and the parameters passed to the operating system into the first page frame (see the section "Reserved Page Frames" in Chapter 2).

8. Identifies the model of the processor.

9. Loads the gdtr and idtr registers with the addresses of the GDT and IDT tables.

10. Jumps to the start_kernel( ) function.

Modern Age: The start_kernel( ) Function

The start_kernel( ) function completes the initialization of the Linux kernel. Nearly every kernel component is initialized by this function; we mention just a few of them:

- The Page Tables are initialized by invoking the paging_init( ) function (see the section "Kernel Page Tables" in Chapter 2).

- The page descriptors are initialized by the kmem_init( ), free_area_init( ), and mem_init( ) functions (see the section "Initialization of the Memory Handling Data Structures" in Chapter 7).

- The final initialization of the IDT is performed by invoking trap_init( ) (see the section "Exception Handling" in Chapter 4) and init_IRQ( ) (see the section "IRQ data structures" in Chapter 4).

- The slab allocator is initialized by the kmem_cache_init( ) and kmem_cache_sizes_init( ) functions (see the section "General and Specific Caches" in Chapter 7).

- The system date and time are initialized by the time_init( ) function (see the section "Real Time Clock" in Chapter 6).

- The kernel thread for process 1 is created by invoking the kernel_thread( ) function. In turn, this kernel thread creates the other kernel threads and executes the /sbin/init program, as described in the section "Kernel Threads" in Chapter 3.

Besides the "Linux version 2.4.18…" message, which is displayed right after the beginning of start_kernel( ), many other messages are displayed in this last phase, both by the *init* functions and by the kernel threads. At the end, the familiar login prompt appears on the console (or in the graphical screen, if the X Window System is launched at startup), telling the user that the Linux kernel is up and running.

Modules

As stated in Chapter 1, *modules* are Linux's recipe for effectively achieving many of the theoretical advantages of microkernels without introducing performance penalties.

To Be (a Module) or Not to Be?

When system programmers want to add new functionality to the Linux kernel, they are faced with a basic decision: should they write the new code so that it will be compiled as a module, or should they statically link the new code to the kernel?

As a general rule, system programmers tend to implement new code as a module. Because modules can be linked on demand (as we see later), the kernel does not have to be bloated with hundreds of seldom-used programs. Nearly every higher-level component of the Linux kernel—filesystems, device drivers, executable formats, network layers, and so on—can be compiled as a module.

However, some Linux code must necessarily be linked statically, which means that either the corresponding component is included in the kernel or it is not compiled at all. This happens typically when the component requires a modification to some data structure or function statically linked in the kernel.

For example, suppose the component has to introduce new fields into the process descriptor. Linking a module cannot change an already defined data structure like task_struct since, even if the module uses its modified version of the data structure, all statically linked code continues to see the old version. Data corruption easily occurs. A partial solution to the problem consists of "statically" adding the new fields to the process descriptor, thus making them available to the kernel component no matter how it has been linked. However, if the kernel component is never used, such extra fields replicated in every process descriptor are a waste of memory. If the new kernel component increases the size of the process descriptor a lot, one would get better system performance by adding the required fields in the data structure only if the component is statically linked to the kernel.

As a second example, consider a kernel component that has to replace statically linked code. It's pretty clear that no such component can be compiled as a module because the kernel cannot change the machine code already in RAM when linking the module. For instance, it is not possible to link a module that changes the way page frames are allocated, since the Buddy system functions are always statically linked to the kernel.*

The kernel has two key tasks to perform in managing modules. The first task is making sure the rest of the kernel can reach the module's global symbols, such as the entry point to its main function. A module must also know the addresses of symbols in the kernel and in other modules. Thus, references are resolved once and for all when a module is linked. The second task consists of keeping track of the use of modules, so that no module is unloaded while another module or another part of the kernel is using it. A simple reference count keeps track of each module's usage.

Module Implementation

Modules are stored in the filesystem as ELF object files and are linked to the kernel by executing the *insmod* program (see the later section, "Linking and Unlinking Modules"). For each module, the kernel allocates a memory area containing the following data:

- A module object
- A null-terminated string that represents the name of the module (all modules should have unique names)
- The code that implements the functions of the module

The module object describes a module; its fields are shown in Table B-1. A simply linked list collects all module objects, where the next field of each object points to the next element in the list. The first element of the list is addressed by the module_list variable. But actually, the first element of the list is always the same: it is named kernel_module and refers to a fictitious module representing the statically linked kernel code.

Table B-1. The module object

Type	Name	Description
unsigned long	size_of_struct	Size of module object
struct module *	next	Next list element
const char *	name	Pointer to module name
unsigned long	size	Module size

---

* You might wonder why not all kernel components have been modularized. Actually, there is no strong technical reason because it is essentially a software license issue. Kernel developers want to make sure that core components will never be replaced by proprietary code released through binary-only "black-box" modules.

Table B-1. The module object (continued)

Type	Name	Description
atomic_t	uc.usecount	Module usage counter
unsigned long	flags	Module flags
unsigned int	nsyms	Number of exported symbols
unsigned int	ndeps	Number of referenced modules
struct module_symbol *	syms	Table of exported symbols
struct module_ref *	deps	List of referenced modules
struct module_ref *	refs	List of referencing modules
int (*)(void)	init	Initialization method
void (*)(void)	cleanup	Cleanup method
struct exception_table_entry *	ex_table_start	Start of exception table
struct exception_table_entry *	ex_table_end	End of exception table
struct module_persist *	persist_start	Start of area containing module's persistent data
struct module_persist *	persist_end	End of area containing module's persistent data
int (*)(void)	can_unload	Return 1 if the module is currently unused
int	runsize	Not used
char *	kallsyms_start	Start of area storing kernel symbols for debugging
char *	kallsyms_end	End of area storing kernel symbols for debugging
char *	archdata_start	Start of architecture-dependent data area
char *	archdata_end	End of architecture-dependent data area
char *	kernel_data	Not used

The total size of the memory area allocated for the module (including the module object and the module name) is contained in the size field.

As already mentioned in the section "Dynamic Address Checking: The Fixup Code" in Chapter 9, each module has its own exception table. The table includes the addresses of the fixup code of the module, if any. The table is copied into RAM when the module is linked, and its starting and ending addresses are stored in the ex_table_start and ex_table_end fields of the module object.

The fields below ex_table_end were introduced in Linux 2.4 and implement some advanced features of modules. For instance, it is now possible to record in a disk file data that should be preserved across loading and unloading of a module. New module support also offers a lot of debugging data to kernel debuggers, so catching a bug hidden in the code of a module is now a lot easier.

Module Usage Counter

Each module has a usage counter, stored in the uc.usecount field of the corresponding module object. The counter is incremented when an operation involving the module's functions is started and decremented when the operation terminates. A module can be unlinked only if its usage counter is 0.

For example, suppose that the MS-DOS filesystem layer is compiled as a module and the module is linked at runtime. Initially, the module usage counter is 0. If the user mounts an MS-DOS floppy disk, the module usage counter is incremented by 1. Conversely, when the user unmounts the floppy disk, the counter is decremented by 1.

Besides this simple mechanism, Linux 2.4's modules may also define·a custom function whose address is stored in the can_unload field of the module object. The function is invoked when the module is being unlinked; it should check whether it is really safe to unload the module, and return 0 or 1 accordingly. If the function returns 0, the unloading operation is aborted, much as if the usage counter were not equal to 0.

Exporting Symbols

When linking a module, all references to global kernel symbols (variables and functions) in the module's object code must be replaced with suitable addresses. This operation, which is very similar to that performed by the linker while compiling a User Mode program (see the section "Libraries" in Chapter 20), is delegated to the *insmod* external program (described later in the section, "Linking and Unlinking Modules").

A special table is used by the kernel to store the symbols that can be accessed by modules together with their corresponding addresses. This *kernel symbol table* is contained in the __ksymtab section of the kernel code segment, and its starting and ending addresses are identified by two symbols produced by the C compiler: __start___ksymtab and __stop___ksymtab. The EXPORT_SYMBOL macro, when used inside the statically linked kernel code, forces the C compiler to add a specified symbol to the table.

Only the kernel symbols actually used by some existing module are included in the table. Should a system programmer need, within some module, to access a kernel symbol that is not already exported, he can simply add the corresponding EXPORT_SYMBOL macro into the *kernel/ksyms.c* file of the Linux source code.

Linked modules can also export their own symbols so that other modules can access them. The *module symbol table* is contained in the __ksymtab section of the module code segment. If the module source code includes the EXPORT_NO_SYMBOLS macro, symbols from that module are not added to the table. To export a subset of symbols from the module, the programmer must define the EXPORT_SYMTAB macro before including the *include/linux/module.h* header file. Then he may use the EXPORT_SYMBOL macro to export a specific symbol. If neither EXPORT_NO_SYMBOLS nor EXPORT_SYMTAB appears in the module source code, all nonstatic global symbols of the modules are exported.

The symbol table in the __ksymtab section is copied into a memory area when the module is linked, and the address of the area is stored in the syms field of the module object. The symbols exported by the statically linked kernel and all linked-in modules can be retrieved by reading the */proc/ksyms* file or using the query_module( ) system call (described in the later section, "Linking and Unlinking Modules").

Recently, a new EXPORT_SYMBOL_GPL macro was added. It is functionally equivalent to EXPORT_SYMBOL, but it marks the exported symbol as usable only in modules licensed through either the General Public License (GPL) license or a compatible one. This way, the author of a kernel component may forbid using his work in binary-only modules that do not comply with the standard requirements of the GPL. The license of a module is specified by a MODULE_LICENSE macro inserted into its source code, whose argument is usually "GPL" or "Proprietary."

Module Dependency

A module (B) can refer to the symbols exported by another module (A); in this case, we say that B is loaded on top of A, or equivalently that A is used by B. To link module B, module A must have already been linked; otherwise, the references to the symbols exported by A cannot be properly linked in B. In short, there is a *dependency* between modules.

The deps field of the module object of B points to a list describing all modules that are used by B; in our example, A's module object would appear in that list. The ndeps field stores the number of modules used by B. Conversely, the refs field of A points to a list describing all modules that are loaded on top of A (thus, B's module object is included when it is loaded). The refs list must be updated dynamically whenever a module is loaded on top of A. To ensure that module A is not removed before B, A's usage counter is incremented for each module loaded on top of it.

Beside A and B there could be, of course, another module (C) loaded on top of B, and so on. Stacking modules is an effective way to modularize the kernel source code to speed up its development and improve its portability.

Linking and Unlinking Modules

A user can link a module into the running kernel by executing the *insmod* external program. This program performs the following operations:

1. Reads from the command line the name of the module to be linked.
2. Locates the file containing the module's object code in the system directory tree. The file is usually placed in some subdirectory below */lib/modules*.
3. Computes the size of the memory area needed to store the module code, its name, and the module object.

4. Invokes the create_module( ) system call, passing to it the name and size of the new module. The corresponding sys_create_module( ) service routine performs the following operations:

   a. Checks whether the user is allowed to link the module (the current process must have the CAP_SYS_MODULE capability). In any situation where one is adding functionality to a kernel, which has access to all data and processes on the system, security is a paramount concern.

   b. Invokes the find_module( ) function to scan the module_list list of module objects looking for a module with the specified name. If it is found, the module has already been linked, so the system call terminates.

   c. Invokes vmalloc( ) to allocate a memory area for the new module.

   d. Initializes the fields of the module object at the beginning of the memory area and copies the name of the module right below the object.

   e. Inserts the module object into the list pointed to by module_list.

   f. Returns the starting address of the memory area allocated to the module.

5. Invokes the query_module( ) system call with the QM_MODULES subcommand to get the name of all already linked modules.

6. Invokes the query_module( ) system call with the QM_INFO subcommand repeatedly, to get the starting address and the size of all modules that are already linked in.

7. Invokes the query_module( ) system call with the QM_SYMBOLS subcommand repeatedly, to get the kernel symbol table and the symbol tables of all modules that are already linked in.

8. Using the kernel symbol table, the module symbol tables, and the address returned by the create_module( ) system call, the program relocates the object code included in the module's file. This means replacing all occurrences of external and global symbols with the corresponding logical address offsets.

9. Allocates a memory area in the User Mode address space and loads it with a copy of the module object, the module's name, and the module's code relocated for the running kernel. The address fields of the object point to the relocated code.

   In particular, the init field is set to the relocated address of the module's function named init_module( ), or equivalently to the address of the module's function marked by the module_init macro. Similarly, the cleanup field is set to the relocated address of the module's cleanup_module( ) function or, equivalently, to the address of the module's function marked by the module_exit macro. Each module should implement these two functions.

10. Invokes the `init_module()` system call, passing to it the address of the User Mode memory area set up in the previous step. The `sys_init_module()` service routine performs the following operations:

   a. Checks whether the user is allowed to link the module (the current process must have the `CAP_SYS_MODULE` capability).

   b. Invokes `find_module()` to find the proper `module` object in the list to which `module_list` points.

   c. Overwrites the `module` object with the contents of the corresponding object in the User Mode memory area.

   d. Performs a series of sanity checks on the addresses in the `module` object.

   e. Copies the remaining part of the User Mode memory area into the memory area allocated to the module.

   f. Scans the module list and initializes the `ndeps` and `deps` fields of the `module` object.

   g. Sets the module usage counter to 1.

   h. Executes the `init` method of the module to initialize the module's data structures properly.

   i. Sets the module usage counter to 0 and returns.

11. Releases the User Mode memory area and terminates.

To unlink a module, a user invokes the *rmmod* external program, which performs the following operations:

1. From the command line, reads the name of the module to be unlinked.

2. Invokes the `query_module()` system call with the `QM_MODULES` subcommand to get the list of linked modules.

3. Invokes the `query_module()` system call with the `QM_SYMBOLS` subcommand repeatedly, to get the kernel symbol table and the symbol tables of all modules that are already linked in.

4. If the option *-r* has been passed to *rmmod*, invokes the `query_module()` system call with the `QM_REFS` subcommand several times to retrieve dependency information on the linked modules.

5. Builds a list of modules to be unloaded: if the option *-r* has not been specified, the list includes only the module passed as argument to *rmmod*; otherwise, it includes the module passed as argument and all loaded modules that ultimately depend on it.

6. Invokes the `delete_module()` system call, passing the name of a module to be unloaded. The corresponding `sys_delete_module()` service routine performs these operations:

a. Checks whether the user is allowed to remove the module (the current process must have the `CAP_SYS_MODULE` capability).

b. Invokes `find_module( )` to find the corresponding `module` object in the list to which `module_list` points.

c. Checks whether the `refs` field is null; otherwise, returns an error code.

d. If defined, invokes the `can_unload` method; otherwise, checks whether the `uc.usecount` fields of the `module` object is null. If the module is busy, returns an error code.

e. If defined, invokes the `cleanup` method to perform the operations needed to cleanly shut down the module. The method is usually implemented by the `cleanup_module( )` function defined inside the module.

f. Scans the `deps` list of the module and removes the module from the `refs` list of any element found.

g. Removes the module from the list to which `module_list` points.

h. Invokes `vfree( )` to release the memory area used by the module and returns 0 (success).

7. If the list of modules to be unloaded is not empty, jumps back to Step 6; otherwise, terminates.

Linking Modules on Demand

A module can be automatically linked when the functionality it provides is requested and automatically removed afterward.

For instance, suppose that the MS-DOS filesystem has not been linked, either statically or dynamically. If a user tries to mount an MS-DOS filesystem, the `mount( )` system call normally fails by returning an error code, since MS-DOS is not included in the `file_systems` list of registered filesystems. However, if support for automatic linking of modules has been specified when configuring the kernel, Linux makes an attempt to link the MS-DOS module, and then scans the list of registered filesystems again. If the module is successfully linked, the `mount( )` system call can continue its execution as if the MS-DOS filesystem were present from the beginning.

The modprobe Program

To automatically link a module, the kernel creates a kernel thread to execute the *modprobe* external program,[*] which takes care of possible complications due to module dependencies. The dependencies were discussed earlier: a module may require one or more other modules, and these in turn may require still other modules. For

[*] This is one of the few examples in which the kernel relies on an external program.

instance, the MS-DOS module requires another module named *fat* containing some code common to all filesystems based on a File Allocation Table (FAT). Thus, if it is not already present, the *fat* module must also be automatically linked into the running kernel when the MS-DOS module is requested. Resolving dependencies and finding modules is a type of activity that's best done in User Mode because it requires locating and accessing module object files in the filesystem.

The *modprobe* external program is similar to *insmod*, since it links in a module specified on the command line. However, *modprobe* also recursively links in all modules used by the module specified on the command line. For instance, if a user invokes *modprobe* to link the MS-DOS module, the program links the *fat* module, if necessary, followed by the MS-DOS module. Actually, *modprobe* just checks for module dependencies; the actual linking of each module is done by forking a new process and executing *insmod*.

How does *modprobe* know about module dependencies? Another external program named *depmod* is executed at system startup. It looks at all the modules compiled for the running kernel, which are usually stored inside the */lib/modules* directory. Then it writes all module dependencies to a file named *modules.dep*. The *modprobe* program can thus simply compare the information stored in the file with the list of linked modules produced by the query_module( ) system call.

The request_module( ) Function

In some cases, the kernel may invoke the request_module( ) function to attempt automatic linking for a module.

Consider again the case of a user trying to mount an MS-DOS filesystem. If the get_fs_type( ) function discovers that the filesystem is not registered, it invokes the request_module( ) function in the hope that MS-DOS has been compiled as a module.

If the request_module( ) function succeeds in linking the requested module, get_fs_type( ) can continue as if the module were always present. Of course, this does not always happen; in our example, the MS-DOS module might not have been compiled at all. In this case, get_fs_type( ) returns an error code.

The request_module( ) function receives the name of the module to be linked as its parameter. It invokes kernel_thread( ) to create a new kernel thread that executes the exec_modprobe( ) function. Then it simply waits until that kernel thread terminates.

The exec_modprobe( ) function, in turn, also receives the name of the module to be linked as its parameter. It invokes the execve( ) system call and executes the *modprobe* external program,[*] passing the module name to it. In turn, the *modprobe* program actually links the requested module, along with any that it depends on.

Each module automatically linked into the kernel has the MOD_AUTOCLEAN flag in the flags field of the module object set. This flag allows automatic unlinking of the module when it is no longer used.

To automatically unlink the module, a system process (like *crond*) periodically executes the *rmmod* external program, passing the *–a* option to it. The latter program executes the delete_module( ) system call with a NULL parameter. The corresponding service routine scans the list of module objects and removes all unused modules having the MOD_AUTOCLEAN flag set.

---

[*] The name and path of the program executed by exec_modprobe( ) can be customized by writing into the */proc/sys/kernel/modprobe* file.

APPENDIX C

Source Code Structure

To help you to find your way through the files of the source code, we briefly describe the organization of the kernel directory tree. As usual, all pathnames refer to the main directory of the Linux kernel, which is, in most Linux distributions, */usr/src/ linux*.

Linux source code for all supported architectures is contained in about 8750 C and Assembly files stored in about 530 subdirectories; it consists of about 4 million lines of code, which occupy more than 144 megabytes of disk space.

The following list illustrates the directory tree containing the Linux source code. Please notice that only the subdirectories somehow related to the target of this book have been expanded.

Directory	Description
Documentation	Text files with general explanations and hints about kernel components
arch	Platform-dependent code
└ i386	IBM's PC architecture
└ kernel	Kernel core
└ mm	Memory management
└ math-emu	Software emulator for floating-point unit
└ lib	Hardware-dependent utility functions
└ boot	Bootstrapping
└ compressed	Compressed kernel handling
└ tools	Programs to build compressed kernel image
└ alpha	Hewlett-Packard's Alpha architecture
└ arm	Architectures based on ARM processors
└ cris	Axis Communication AB's Code Reduced Instruction Set architecture used by thin-servers
└ ia64	Workstations based on Intel's 64-bit Itanium microprocessor
└ m68k	Motorola's MC680x0-based architecture

Directory	Description
└ mips	MIPS architecture adopted by Silicon Graphics and other computer manufacturers
└ mips64	64-bit MIPS architecture
└ parisc	HP 9000 parisc workstations
└ ppc	Motorola-IBM's PowerPC-based architectures
└ s390	IBM's ESA/390 and 32-bit zSeries architectures
└ s390x	IBM's 64-bit zSeries architectures
└ sh	SuperH-based embedded computers
└ sparc	Sun's SPARC architecture
└ sparc64	Sun's Ultra-SPARC architecture
drivers	Device drivers
└ acorn	Acorn's devices
└ acpi	Advanced Configuration Power Interface (a power management standard that provides more features than APM)
└ atm	Support for ATM network architecture
└ block	Block device drivers
└ paride	Support for accessing IDE devices from parallel port
└ bluetooth	Drivers for devices connected through the Bluetooth wireless protocol
└ cdrom	Proprietary CD-ROM devices (neither ATAPI nor SCSI)
└ char	Character device drivers
└ agp	Drivers for AGP video cards
└ drm	Driver that supports the Xfree86 Direct Rendering Infrastructure
└ drm-4.0	Another driver that supports the Xfree86 Direct Rendering Infrastructure
└ ftape	Tape-streaming devices
⎸ ip2	Computone Intelliport II multiport serial controllers
└ joystick	Joysticks
└ mwave	IBM's Winmodem-like driver for Linux
└ pcmcia	Driver for PCMCIA serial device
└ rio	Driver for the Specialix Rio multiport serial card
└ dio	Hewlett-Packard's HP300 DIO bus support
└ fc4	Fibre Channel devices
└ hotplug	Support for hotplugging of PCI devices
└ i2c	Driver for Philips' I2C 2-wire bus
└ ide	Drivers for IDE disks
└ ieee1394	Driver for IEEE1394 high-speed serial bus
└ input	Input layer module for joysticks, keyboards, and mouses
└ isdn	ISDN devices
└ macintosh	Apple's Macintosh devices

Directory	Description
└─ md	Layer for "multiple devices" (disk arrays and Logical Volume Manager)
└─ media	Drivers for radio and video devices
└─ message	High performance SCSI + LAN/Fibre Channel drivers
└─ misc	Miscellaneous devices
└─ mtd	Support for Memory Technology Devices (especially flash devices)
└─ net	Network card devices
└─ nubus	Apple's Macintosh Nubus support
└─ parport	Parallel port support
└─ pci	PCI bus support
└─ pcmcia	PCMCIA card support
└─ pnp	Plug-and-play support
└─ s390	IBM's ESA/390 and zSeries device support
└─ sbus	Sun's SPARC SBus support
└─ scsi	SCSI device drivers
└─ sgi	Silicon Graphics' devices
└─ sound	Audio card devices
└─ tc	Hewlett-Packard (formerly DEC) TURBOChannel bus support
└─ telephony	Support for voice-over-IP devices
└─ usb	Universal Serial Bus (USB) support
└─ video	Video card devices
└─ zorro	Amiga's Zorro bus support
fs	Filesystems
└─ adfs	Acorn Disc Filing System
└─ affs	Amiga's Fast File System (FFS)
└─ autofs	Support for kernel-based filesystem automounter daemon
└─ autofs4	Another version of support for kernel-based filesystem automounter daemon (Version 4)
└─ bfs	SCO UnixWare Boot File System
└─ coda	Coda network filesystem
└─ cramfs	Data compressing filesystem for MTD devices
└─ devfs	Device filesystem
└─ devpts	Pseudoterminal support (Open Group's Unix98 standard)
└─ efs	SGI IRIX's EFS filesystem
└─ ext2	Linux native Ext2 filesystem
└─ ext3	Linux native Ext3 filesystem
└─ fat	Common code for FAT-based filesystems
└─ freevxfs	Veritas VxFS filesystem used by SCO UnixWare
└─ hfs	Apple's Macintosh filesystem

Directory	Description
└ hpfs	IBM's OS/2 filesystem
└ inflate_fs	Layer for decompressing files in cramfs and iso9660 filesystems
└ intermezzo	InterMezzo high-availability distributed filesystem
└ isofs	ISO9660 filesystem (CD-ROM)
└ jbd	Journaling filesystem layer used by Ext3
└ jffs	Journaling filesystems for MTD devices
└ jffs2	Another journaling filesystems for MTD devices
└ lockd	Remote file locking support
└ minix	MINIX filesystem
└ msdos	Microsoft's MS-DOS filesystem
└ ncpfs	Novell's Netware Core Protocol (NCP)
└ nfs	Network File System (NFS)
└ nfsd	Integrated Network filesystem server
└ nls	Native Language Support
└ ntfs	Microsoft's Windows NT filesystem
└ openpromfs	Special filesystem for SPARC's OpenPROM device tree
└ partitions	Code for reading several disk partition formats
└ proc	*/proc* virtual filesystem
└ qnx4	Filesystem for QNX 4 OS
└ ramfs	Simple RAM filesystem
└ reiserfs	Reiser filesystem
└ romfs	Small read-only filesystem
└ smbfs	Microsoft's Windows Server Message Block (SMB) filesystem
└ sysv	System V, SCO, Xenix, Coherent, and Version 7 filesystem
└ udf	Universal Disk Format filesystem (DVD)
└ ufs	Unix BSD, SunOS, FreeBSD, OpenBSD, and NeXTStep filesystem
└ umsdos	UMSDOS filesystem
└ vfat	Microsoft's Windows filesystem (VFAT)
include	Header files (*.h*)
└ asm-generic	Platform-independent low-level header files
└ asm-i386	IBM's PC architecture
└ asm-xxx	Header files for other architecture
└ linux	Kernel core
└ byteorder	Byte-swapping functions
└ isdn	ISDN functions
└ lockd	Remote file locking

Directory	Description
└ mtd	MTD devices
└ netfilter_ipv4	Filtering for TCP/IPv4
└ netfilter_ipv6	Filtering for TCP/IPv6
└ nfsd	Integrated Network File Server
└ raid	RAID disks
└ sunrpc	Sun's Remote Procedure Call
└ math-emu	Mathematical coprocessor emulation
└ net	Networking
└ pcmcia	PCMCIA support
└ scsi	SCSI support
└ video	Frame buffer support
init	Kernel initialization code
ipc	System V's Interprocess Communication
kernel	Kernel core: processes, timing, program execution, signals, modules, etc.
lib	General-purpose kernel functions
mm	Memory handling
net	A bunch of networking protocols
scripts	External programs for building the kernel image

Bibliography

This bibliography is broken down by subject area and lists some of the most common and, in our opinion, useful books and online documentation on the topic of kernels.

Books on Unix Kernels

Bach, M. J. *The Design of the Unix Operating System*. Prentice Hall International, Inc., 1986. A classic book describing the SVR2 kernel.

Goodheart, B. and J. Cox. *The Magic Garden Explained: The Internals of the Unix System V Release 4*. Prentice Hall International, Inc., 1994. An excellent book on the SVR4 kernel.

McKusick. M. K., M. J. Karels, and K. Bostic. *The Design and Implementation of the 4.4 BSD Operating System*. Addison Wesley, 1986. Perhaps the most authoritative book on the 4.4 BSD kernel.

Vahalia, U. *Unix Internals: The New Frontiers*. Prentice Hall, Inc., 1996. A valuable book that provides plenty of insight on modern Unix kernel design issues. It includes a rich bibliography.

Books on the Linux Kernel

Beck, M., H. Boehme, M. Dziadzka, U. Kunitz, R. Magnus, C. Schroter, and D. Verworner. *Linux Kernel Programming* (3rd ed.). Addison Wesley, 2002. A hardware-independent book covering the Linux 2.4 kernel.

Maxwell, S. *Linux Core Kernel Commentary*. The Coriolis Group, LLC, 1999. A listing of part of the Linux kernel source code with some interesting comments at the end of the book.

Mosberger, D., S. Eranian, and B. Perens. *IA-64 Linux Kernel: Design and Implementation*. Prentice Hall, Inc., 2002. An excellent description of the hardware-dependent Linux kernel for the Itanium IA-64 microprocessor.

Rubini, A., J. Corbet. *Linux Device Drivers (2nd ed.)*. O'Reilly & Associates, Inc., 2001. A valuable book that is somewhat complementary to this one. It gives plenty of information on how to develop drivers for Linux.

Satchell S., H. Clifford. *Linux IP Stacks Commentary*. The Coriolis Group, LLC, 2000. A listing of part of the Linux kernel networking source code with some comments at the end of the book.

Books on PC Architecture and Technical Manuals on Intel Microprocessors

Intel, *Intel Architecture Software Developer's Manual, vol. 3: System Programming*. 1999. Describes the Intel Pentium microprocessor architecture. It can be downloaded from *http://developer.intel.com/design/pentiumii/manuals/24319202.pdf*.

Intel, *MultiProcessor Specification, Version 1.4*. 1997. Describes the Intel multiprocessor architecture specifications. It can be downloaded from *http://www.intel.com/design/pentium/datashts/242016.htm*.

Messmer, H. P. *The Indispensable PC Hardware Book (3rd ed.)*. Addison Wesley Longman Limited, 1997. A valuable reference that exhaustively describes the many components of a PC.

Other Online Documentation Sources

Linux source code

The official site for getting kernel source can be found at *http://www.kernel.org*.

Many mirror sites are also available all over the world.

A valuable search engine for the Linux 2.4 source code is available at *http://www.tamacom.com/tour/linux/*.

GCC manuals

All distributions of the GNU C compiler should include full documentation for all its features, stored in several info files that can be read with the Emacs program or an info reader. By the way, the information on Extended Inline Assembly is quite hard to follow, since it does not refer to any specific architecture. Some pertinent information about 80 × 86 GCC's Inline Assembly and *gas*, the GNU assembler invoked by GCC, can be found at:

http://www.delorie.com/djgpp/doc/brennan/brennan_att_inline_djgpp.html
http://www.ibm.com/developerworks/linux/library/l-ia.html
http://www.gnu.org/manual/gas-2.9.1/as.html

The Linux Documentation Project

The web site (*http://www.tldp.org*) contains the home page of the Linux Documentation Project, which, in turn, includes several interesting references to guides, FAQs, and HOWTOs.

Linux kernel development forum

The newsgroup *comp.os.linux.development.system* is dedicated to discussions about development of the Linux system.

The linux-kernel mailing list

This fascinating mailing list contains much noise as well as a few pertinent comments about the current development version of Linux and about the rationale for including or not including in the kernel some proposals for changes. It is a living laboratory of new ideas that are taking shape. The name of the mailing list is *linux-kernel@vger.kernel.org.*

The Linux Kernel online book

Authored by David A. Rusling, this 200-page book can be viewed at *http://www.tldp.org/LDP/tlk/tlk.html*, and describes some fundamental aspects of the Linux 2.0 kernel.

Linux Virtual File System

The page at *http://www.atnf.csiro.au/~rgooch/linux/docs/vfs.txt* is an introduction to the Linux Virtual File System. The author is Richard Gooch.

Source Code Index

A

access_ok
 include/asm-i386/uaccess.h   311
activate_page
 mm/swap.c   562
activate_page_nolock
 mm/swap.c   562
active_list
 mm/page_alloc.c   561
add_page_to_active_list
 include/linux/swap.h   562
add_page_to_hash_queue
 mm/filemap.c   479
add_page_to_inactive_list
 include/linux/swap.h   562
add_page_to_inode_queue
 mm/filemap.c   479
address_space
 include/linux/fs.h   477
address_space_operations
 include/linux/fs.h   478
__addr_ok
 include/asm-i386/uaccess.h   311
add_timer
 kernel/timer.c   208
add_to_page_cache
 mm/filemap.c   481
add_to_runqueue
 kernel/sched.c   81
add_to_swap_cache
 mm/swap_state.c   548
add_wait_queue
 kernel/fork.c   85

add_wait_queue_exclusive
 kernel/fork.c   85
aligned_data
 kernel/sched.c   355
alignment_check
 arch/i386/kernel/entry.S   118
alloc_area_pmd
 mm/vmalloc.c   259
alloc_area_pte
 mm/vmalloc.c   260
alloc_kiovec
 fs/iobuf.c   525
alloc_page
 include/linux/mm.h   225
alloc_pages
 include/linux/mm.h   235
alloc_task_struct
 include/asm-i386/processor.h   78
alloc_vfsmnt
 fs/namespace.c   399
anon_hash_chain
 fs/inode.c   384
anon_list
 fs/file_table.c   386
apic_timer_interrupt
 include/asm-i386/hw_irq.h   201
apic_timer_irqs
 arch/i386/kernel/apic.c   206
arch_get_unmapped_area
 mm/mmap.c   277
atomic_add
 include/asm-i386/atomic.h   165
atomic_add_negative
 include/asm-i386/atomic.h   165

We'd like to hear your suggestions for improving our indexes. Send email to *index@oreilly.com*.

atomic_clear_mask
   include/asm-i386/atomic.h   166
atomic_dec
   include/asm-i386/atomic.h   165
atomic_dec_and_test
   include/asm-i386/atomic.h   165
atomic_inc
   include/asm-i386/atomic.h   165
atomic_inc_and_test
   include/asm-i386/atomic.h   165
atomic_read
   include/asm-i386/atomic.h   165
atomic_set
   include/asm-i386/atomic.h   165
atomic_set_mask
   include/asm-i386/atomic.h   166
atomic_sub
   include/asm-i386/atomic.h   165
atomic_sub_and_test
   include/asm-i386/atomic.h   165
atomic_t
   include/asm-i386/atomic.h   165
AURORA_BH
   include/linux/interrupt.h   154

B

bad_pipe_r
   fs/pipe.c   644
bad_pipe_w
   fs/pipe.c   644
balance_classzone
   mm/page_alloc.c   561
balance_dirty
   fs/buffer.c   492
balance_dirty_state
   fs/buffer.c   492
batch_requests
   drivers/block/ll_rw_blk.c   459
bd_acquire
   fs/block_dev.c   452
bdev_hashtable
   fs/block_dev.c   450
bdflush
   fs/buffer.c   491
bdflush_max
   fs/buffer.c   491
bdflush_min
   fs/buffer.c   491
bdflush_wait
   fs/buffer.c   492

bdf_prm
   fs/buffer.c   491
bforget
   include/linux/fs.h   487
B_FREE
   include/linux/kdev_t.h   482
BH   455
bh_action
   kernel/softirq.c   154
BH_Async
   include/linux/fs.h   455
bh_base
   kernel/softirq.c   153
bh_cachep
   fs/dcache.c   482
BH_Dirty
   include/linux/fs.h   454
BH_JBD
   include/linux/fs.h   455, 603
BH_launder
   include/linux/fs.h   455
BH_Lock
   include/linux/fs.h   455
BH_Mapped
   include/linux/fs.h   455
BH_New
   include/linux/fs.h   455
BH_Req
   include/linux/fs.h   455
bh_task_vec
   kernel/softirq.c   154
BH_Uptodate
   include/linux/fs.h   454
BH_Wait_IO
   include/linux/fs.h   455
blk_dev
   drivers/block/ll_rw_blk.c   460
blkdev_commit_write
   fs/block_dev.c   513
blkdev_get_block
   fs/block_dev.c   503
blkdev_open
   fs/block_dev.c   451
blkdev_prepare_write
   fs/block_dev.c   513
blkdev_readpage
   fs/block_dev.c   503
blkdevs
   fs/block_dev.c   445
blk_dev_struct
   include/linux/blk_dev.h   460

blk_init_queue
  drivers/block/ll_rw_blk.c   459
blk_size
  drivers/block/ll_rw_blk.c   452
blksize_size
  drivers/block/ll_rw_blk.c   453
block_commit_write
  fs/buffer.c   512
block_device
  include/linux/fs.h   450
block_device_operations
  include/linux/fs.h   445
blocked_list
  fs/locks.c   423
block_prepare_write
  fs/buffer.c   511
block_read_full_page
  fs/buffer.c   502
bounds
  arch/i386/kernel/entry.S   117
bread
  fs/buffer.c   469
brelse
  include/linux/fs.h   487
__brlock_array
  lib/brlock.c   173
br_read_lock
  include/linux/brlock.h   173
br_read_unlock
  include/linux/brlock.h   173
brw_kiovec
  fs/buffer.c   527
brw_page
  fs/buffer.c   470
br_write_lock
  include/linux/brlock.h   173
br_write_unlock
  include/linux/brlock.h   173
BUF_CLEAN
  include/linux/fs.h   484
BUFCTL_END
  mm/slab.c   248
BUF_DIRTY
  include/linux/fs.h   484
BUFDIRTY
  include/fs.h   484
buffer_async
  include/linux/fs.h   455
buffer_dirty
  include/linux/fs.h   454
buffer_head
  include/linux/fs.h   453

buffer_insert_inode_data_queue
  fs/buffer.c   486
buffer_insert_inode_queue
  fs/buffer.c   486
buffer_locked
  include/linux/fs.h   455
buffer_mapped
  include/linux/fs.h   455
buffermem_pages
  fs/buffer.c   490
buffer_new
  include/linux/fs.h   455
buffer_req
  include/linux/fs.h   455
buffer_uptodate
  include/linux/fs.h   454
BUF_LOCKED
  include/linux/fs.h   484
BUILD_COMMON_IRQ
  include/asm-i386/hw_irq.h   137
BUILD_IRQ
  include/asm-i386/hw_irq.h   137
build_mmap_rb
  mm/mmap.c   300
BUILD_SMP_INTERRUPT
  include/asm-i386/hw_irq.h   145
bus_to_virt
  include/asm-i386/io.h   437
BYTES_PER_WORD
  mm/slab.c   248

C

cache_cache
  mm/slab.c   243
cache_chain_sem
  mm/slab.c   191
cached_lookup
  fs/namei.c   411, 412
cache_sizes
  mm/slab.c   244
cache_sizes_t
  mm/slab.c   244
calc_load
  kernel/timer.c   205
calc_vm_flags
  mm/mmap.c   280
calibrate_APIC_clock
  arch/i386/kernel/apic.c   200
calibrate_tsc
  arch/i386/kernel/time.c   195
call_function_interrupt
  arch/i386/kernel/i8259.c   144

CALL_FUNCTION_VECTOR
   include/asm-i386/hw_irq.h   144
capable
   include/linux/sched.h   666
CAP_CHOWN
   include/linux/capability.h   665
CAP_DAC_OVERRIDE
   include/linux/capability.h   665
CAP_DAC_READ_SEARCH
   include/linux/capability.h   665
CAP_FOWNER
   include/linux/capability.h   665
CAP_FSETID
   include/linux/capability.h   665
CAP_IPC_LOCK
   include/linux/capability.h   665
CAP_IPC_OWNER
   include/linux/capability.h   665
CAP_KILL
   include/linux/capability.h   665
CAP_LEASE
   include/linux/capability.h   665
CAP_LINUX_IMMUTABLE
   include/linux/capability.h   665
CAP_MKNOD
   include/linux/capability.h   665
CAP_NET_ADMIN
   include/linux/capability.h   665
CAP_NET_BIND_SERVICE
   include/linux/capability.h   665
CAP_NET_BROADCAST
   include/linux/capability.h   665
CAP_NET_RAW
   include/linux/capability.h   665
CAP_SETGID
   include/linux/capability.h   665
CAP_SETPCAP
   include/linux/capability.h   665
CAP_SETUID
   include/linux/capability.h   665
CAP_SYS_ADMIN
   include/linux/capability.h   666
CAP_SYS_BOOT
   include/linux/capability.h   666
CAP_SYS_CHROOT
   include/linux/capability.h   666
CAP_SYS_MODULE
   include/linux/capability.h   666
CAP_SYS_NICE
   include/linux/capability.h   666

CAP_SYS_PACCT
   include/linux/capability.h   666
CAP_SYS_PTRACE
   include/linux/capability.h   666
CAP_SYS_RAWIO
   include/linux/capability.h   666
CAP_SYS_RESOURCE
   include/linux/capability.h   666
CAP_SYS_TIME
   include/linux/capability.h   666
CAP_SYS_TTY_CONFIG
   include/linux/capability.h   666
cascade_timers
   kernel/timer.c   212
cdev_hashtable
   fs/char_dev.c   472
chained lists   82
change_bit
   include/asm-i386/bitops.h   166
char_device
   include/linux/fs.h   472
check_region
   include/linux/ioport.h   431
check_resource
   kernel/resource.c   431
chrdev_open
   fs/devices.c   473
chrdevs
   fs/devices.c   445
clear_bit
   include/asm-i386/bitops.h   166
clear_inode
   fs/inode.c   594
ClearPageActive
   include/linux/mm.h   219
ClearPageDecrAfter
   include/linux/mm.h   219
ClearPageDirty
   include/linux/mm.h   219
ClearPageError
   include/linux/mm.h   219
ClearPageReferenced
   include/linux/mm.h   219
ClearPageReserved
   include/linux/mm.h   219
clear_page_tables
   mm/memory.c   61
ClearPageUptodate
   include/linux/mm.h   219
__clear_user
   arch/i386/lib/usercopy.c   312

clear_user
  arch/i386/lib/usercopy.c   312
__cli()
  include/asm-i386/system.h   180
cli()
  include/asm-i386/system.h   181
CLOCK_TICK_RATE
  include/asm-i386/timex.h   196
CLONE_FILES
  include/linux/sched.h   100
CLONE_FS
  include/linux/sched.h   100
CLONE_PARENT
  include/linux/sched.h   100
CLONE_PID
  include/linux/sched.h   100
CLONE_PTRACE
  include/linux/sched.h   101
CLONE_SIGHAND
  include/linux/sched.h   101
CLONE_SIGNAL
  include/linux/sched.h   101
CLONE_THREAD
  include/linux/sched.h   101
CLONE_VFORK
  include/linux/sched.h   101
CLONE_VM
  include/linux/sched.h   100
CM206_BH
  include/linux/interrupt.h   154
complete
  kernel/sched.c   179
completion
  include/linux/completion.h   179
contig_page_data
  mm/numa.c   222
coprocessor_error
  arch/i386/kernel/entry.S   118
coprocessor_segment_overrun
  arch/i386/kernel/entry.S   117
copy_files
  kernel/fork.c   102
__copy_from_user
  include/asm-i386/uaccess.h   312
copy_from_user
  include/asm-i386/uaccess.h   312
copy_fs
  kernel/fork.c   102
copy_mm
  kernel/fork.c   298
copy_page_range
  mm/memory.c   300

copy_segments
  arch/i386/kernel/process.c   300
copy_sighand
  kernel/fork.c   102
copy_thread
  arch/i386/kernel/process.c   103
__copy_to_user
  include/asm-i386/uaccess.h   312
copy_to_user
  include/asm-i386/uaccess.h   312
cpucache_t
  mm/slab.c   250
cpu_curr
  kernel/sched.c   355
cpu_idle
  arch/i386/kernel/process.c   105
__cpu_raise_softirq
  include/linux/interrupt.h   149
cpu_raise_softirq
  kernel/softirq.c   149
cpu_tlbstate
  arch/i386/kernel/smp.c   71
create_buffers
  fs/buffer.c   489
create_empty_buffers
  fs/buffer.c   470
current
  include/asm-i386/current.h   78
CYCLADES_BH
  include/linux/interrupt.h   154

D

dcache_lock
  fs/dcache.c   391
debug
  arch/i386/kernel/entry.S   117
DECLARE_TASK_QUEUE
  include/linux/tqueue.h   155
DECLARE_WAIT_QUEUE_HEAD
  include/linux/wait.h   85
decompress_kernel
  arch/i386/boot/compressed/misc.c   690
default_ldt
  arch/i386/kernel/traps.c   42
def_chr_fops
  fs/devices.c   472
DEF_COUNTER
  include/linux/sched.h   352
def_fifo_fops
  fs/fifo.c   643
DEF_PRIORITY
  mm/vmscan.c   565

delay_at_last_interrupt
  arch/i386/kernel/time.c   198

delete_from_swap_cache
  mm/swap_state.c   548

del_from_runqueue
  include/linux/sched.h   81

del_page_from_active_list
  include/linux/swap.h   562

del_page_from_inactive_list
  include/linux/swap.h   562

del_timer
  kernel/timer.c   208

del_timer_sync
  kernel/timer.c   208

dentry
  include/linux/dcache.h   389

dentry_cache
  fs/dcache.c   389

dentry_hashtable
  fs/dcache.c   391

dentry_operations
  include/linux/dcache.h   391

dentry_unused
  fs/dcache.c   390

dequeue_signal
  kernel/signal.c   333

detach_timer
  kernel/timer.c   212

de_thread
  fs/exec.c   680

devfs_entry
  fs/devfs/base.c   440

devfs_open
  fs/devfs/base.c   441

devfs_register
  fs/devfs/base.c   440

device_not_available
  arch/i386/kernel/entry.S   117

device_struct
  fs/devices.c   445

dev_queue_xmit
  net/core/dev.c   627

dev_queue_xmit_nit
  net/core/dev.c   628

dev_t
  include/linux/types.h   438

die
  arch/i386/kernel/traps.c   127

DIGI_BH
  include/linux/interrupt.h   154

disable_8259A_irq
  arch/i386/kernel/i8259.c   134

disable_irq
  arch/i386/kernel/irq.c   133

disable_irq_nosync
  arch/i386/kernel/irq.c   133

divide_error
  arch/i386/kernel/entry.S   117

d_lookup
  fs/dcache.c   391

do_anonymous_page
  mm/memory.c   294

do_brk
  mm/mmap.c   302

do_coredump
  fs/exec.c   335

do_emergency_sync
  drivers/char/sysreq.c   493

do_execve
  fs/exec.c   679

do_exit
  kernel/exit.c   107

do_fast_gettimeoffset
  arch/i386/kernel/time.c   214

do_follow_link
  fs/namei.c   415

do_fork
  kernel/fork.c   101

do_generic_file_read
  mm/filemap.c   499

do_gettimeofday
  arch/i386/kernel/time.c   214

do_gettimeoffset
  arch/i386/kernel/time.c   214

do_IRQ
  arch/i386/kernel/irq.c   138

do_it_prof
  kernel/timer.c   216

do_it_virt
  kernel/timer.c   216

do_kern_mount
  fs/super.c   400

do_loopback
  fs/namespace.c   404

do_mmap
  include/linux/mm.h   278

do_mmap_pgoff
  mm/mmap.c   279

do_mount
  fs/namespace.c   404

do_move_mount
  fs/namespace.c 405
do_munmap
  mm/mmap.c 282
do_nmi
  arch/i386/kernel/traps.c 206
do_no_page
  mm/memory.c 293
do_open
  fs/block_dev.c 452
do_page_fault
  arch/i386/mm/fault.c 285
do_pipe
  fs/pipe.c 637
do_process_times
  kernel/timer.c 204
do_remount
  fs/super.c 404
do_remount_sb
  fs/super.c 406
do_settimeofday
  arch/i386/kernel/time.c 215
do_sigaction
  kernel/signal.c 344
do_signal
  arch/i386/kernel/signal.c 332
do_slow_gettimeoffset
  arch/i386/kernel/time.c 214
do_softirq
  kernel/softirq.c 149
do_swap_page
  mm/memory.c 557
do_timer
  kernel/timer.c 198
do_timer_interrupt
  arch/i386/kernel/time.c 198
double_fault
  arch/i386/kernel/entry.S 117
do_umount
  fs/namespace.c 406
__down
  arch/i386/kernel/semaphore.c 175
down
  include/asm-i386/semaphore.h 175
down_interruptible
  include/asm-i386/semaphore.h 177
down_read
  include/linux/rwsem.h 178
down_trylock
  include/asm-i386/semaphore.h 177

down_write
  include/linux/rwsem.h 178
do_wp_page
  mm/memory.c 296
dst_entry
  include/net/dst.h 613
dup2
  fs/fcntl.c 393
dup_mmap
  kernel/fork.c 299

E

EINTR
  include/asm-i386/errno.h 341
ELEVATOR_LINUS
  include/linux/elevator.h 465
ELEVATOR_NOOP
  include/linux/elevator.h 465
empty_zero_page
  arch/i386/kernel/head.S 294
enable_8259A_irq
  arch/i386/kernel/i8259.c 134
enable_irq
  arch/i386/kernel/irq.c 133
end_8259A_irq
  arch/i386/kernel/i8259.c 134
end_buffer_io_async
  fs/buffer.c 471
end_buffer_io_kiobuf
  fs/buffer.c 527
end_buffer_io_sync
  fs/buffer.c 461, 467
end_request
  include/linux/blk.h 467
ENOSYS
  include/asm-i386/errno.h 306
ERESTARTNOHAND
  include/linux/errno.h 341
ERESTARTNOINTR
  include/linux/errno.h 341
ERESTARTSYS
  include/linux/errno.h 341
ERROR_APIC_VECTOR
  include/asm-i386/hw_irq.h 145
ESP_BH
  include/linux/interrupt.h 154
eth_type_trans
  net/ethernet/eth.c 629
exception_table_entry
  include/asm-i386/uaccess.h 314

exec_domain
    include/linux/personality.h   677
exec_mmap
    fs/exec.c   680
exec_modprobe
    kernel/kmod.c   700
__exit_files
    kernel/exit.c   107
__exit_fs
    kernel/exit.c   107
__exit_mm
    kernel/exit.c   107
exit_mm
    kernel/exit.c   300
exit_notify
    kernel/exit.c   107
exit_sighand
    kernel/signal.c   107
expand_kiobuf
    fs/iobuf.c   526
expand_stack
    include/linux/mm.h   288
EXPORT_NO_SYMBOLS
    include/linux/module.h   695
EXPORT_SYMBOL
    include/linux/module.h   695
EXPORT_SYMBOL_GPL
    include/linux/module.h   696
EXT2   586
ext2_alloc_block
    fs/ext2/inode.c   598
ext2_create
    fs/ext2/namei.c   590
ext2_dir_entry_2
    include/linux/ext2_fs.h   583
ext2_dir_inode_operations
    fs/ext2/namei.c   590
ext2_fast_symlink_inode_operations
    fs/ext2/symlink.c   591
ext2_file_inode_operations
    fs/ext2/file.c   590
ext2_file_operations
    fs/ext2/file.c   591
ext2_follow_link
    fs/ext2/symlink.c   591
ext2_free_blocks
    fs/ext2/balloc.c   599
ext2_free_inode
    fs/ext2/ialloc.c   594
ext2_get_block
    fs/ext2/inode.c   597

ext2_group_desc
    include/linux/ext2_fs.h   580
ext2_inode
    include/linux/ext2_fs.h   581
ext2_inode_info
    include/linux/ext2_fs_i.h   586
ext2_ioctl
    fs/ext2/ioctl.c   591
ext2_link
    fs/ext2/namei.c   590
ext2_lookup
    fs/ext2/namei.c   590
EXT2_MAX_GROUP_LOADED
    include/linux/ext2_fs_sb.h   586
ext2_mkdir
    fs/ext2/namei.c   591
ext2_mknod
    fs/ext2/namei.c   591
EXT2_NAME_LEN
    include/linux/ext2_fs.h   583
EXT2_N_BLOCKS
    include/linux/ext2_fs.h   582
ext2_new_block
    fs/ext2/balloc.c   599
ext2_new_inode
    fs/ext2/ialloc.c   592
ext2_prepare_write
    fs/ext2/inode.c   511
ext2_readlink
    fs/ext2/symlink.c   591
ext2_release_file
    fs/ext2/file.c   591
ext2_rename
    fs/ext2/namei.c   591
ext2_rmdir
    fs/ext2/namei.c   591
ext2_sb_info
    include/linux/ext2_fs_sb.h   585
ext2_sops
    fs/ext2/super.c   590
ext2_super_block
    include/linux/ext2_fs.h   578
ext2_symlink
    fs/ext2/namei.c   591
ext2_sync_file
    fs/ext2/fsync.c   591
ext2_truncate
    fs/ext2/inode.c   590, 599
ext2_unlink
    fs/ext2/namei.c   591

EXT2_VALID_FS
  include/linux/ext2_fs.h   601
ext3_commit_write
  fs/ext3/inode.c   607
ext3_get_block
  fs/ext3/inode.c   606
ext3_prepare_write
  fs/ext3/inode.c   606

F

FASYNC
  include/asm-i386/fcntl.h   417
fd_set
  include/linux/types.h   393
ffz
  include/asm-i386/bitops.h   333
fget
  fs/file_table.c   393
F_GETLK
  include/asm-i386/fcntl.h   424
F_GETLK64
  include/asm-i386/fcntl.h   425
fib_info
  include/net/ip_fib.h   616
fib_node
  net/ipv4/fib_hash.c   615
fib_table
  include/net/ip_fib.h   615
fifo_open
  fs/fifo.c   643
file
  include/linux/fs.h   385
file_lock
  include/linux/fs.h   422
file_lock_list
  fs/locks.c   422
filemap_fdatasync
  mm/filemap.c   522
filemap_nopage
  mm/filemap.c   520
filemap_sync
  mm/filemap.c   522
file_operations
  include/linux/fs.h   387
file_read_actor
  mm/filemap.c   500
files_lock
  fs/file_table.c   387
files_stat
  fs/file_table.c   387
files_struct
  include/linux/sched.h   392

file_systems
  fs/super.c   396
file_systems_lock
  fs/super.c   396
file_system_type
  include/linux/fs.h   395
filp_close
  fs/open.c   420
filp_open
  fs/open.c   417
__find_get_page
  mm/filemap.c   480
find_get_page
  include/linux/pagemap.h   480
find_module
  kernel/module.c   697
find_or_create_page
  mm/filemap.c   481
find_task_by_pid
  include/linux/sched.h   83
find_vma
  mm/mmap.c   275
find_vma_intersection
  include/linux/mm.h   276
find_vma_prepare
  mm/mmap.c   276
find_vma_prev
  mm/mmap.c   276
fixed_addresses
  include/asm-i386/fixmap.h   68
fix_to_virt
  include/asm-i386/fixmap.h   68
FL_FLOCK
  include/linux/fs.h   422
FL_LEASE
  include/linux/fs.h   422
FL_MAND
  include/linux/fs.h   422
flock
  include/asm-i386/fcntl.h   424
flock64
  include/asm-i386/fcntl.h   424
flock_lock_file
  fs/locks.c   423
FL_POSIX
  include/linux/fs.h   422
flush_all_zero_pkmaps
  mm/highmem.c   230
flush_old_exec
  fs/exec.c   680
flush_old_files
  fs/exec.c   681

flush_signal_handlers
kernel/signal.c   680

flush_signals
kernel/signal.c   327

flush_thread
arch/i386/kernel/process.c   680

__flush_tlb
include/asm-i386/pgtable.h   70

flush_tlb
include/asm-i386/pgalloc.h   70

__flush_tlb_all
include/asm-i386/pgtable.h   70

flush_tlb_all
include/asm-i386/pgalloc.h   70

flush_tlb_mm
include/asm-i386/pgalloc.h   70

__flush_tlb_one
include/asm-i386/pgtable.h   69

flush_tlb_page
include/asm-i386/pgalloc.h   69

flush_tlb_range
include/asm-i386/pgalloc.h   70

fn_hash
net/ipv4/fib_hash.c   615

fn_zone
net/ipv4/fib_hash.c   615

follow_page
mm/memory.c   282

force_sig
kernel/signal.c   332

force_sig_info
kernel/signal.c   332

for_each_task
include/linux/sched.h   80

formats
fs/exec.c   675

_fpstate
include/asm-i386/sigcontext.h   338

fput
fs/file_table.c   394

free_area_init
mm/page_alloc.c   223

free_area_pmd
mm/vmalloc.c   261

free_area_pte
mm/vmalloc.c   261

free_area_struct
include/linux/mmzone.h   234

free_area_t
include/linux/mmzone.h   234

free_block
mm/slab.c   254

free_irq
arch/i386/kernel/irq.c   143

free_list
fs/file_table.c   386

free_more_memory
fs/buffer.c   560

free_one_pgd
mm/memory.c   61

free_one_pmd
mm/memory.c   61

__free_page
include/linux/mm.h   227

free_page
include/linux/mm.h   227

free_page_and_swap_cache
mm/swap_state.c   548

__free_pages
mm/page_alloc.c   227

free_pages
mm/page_alloc.c   227

__free_pages_ok
mm/page_alloc.c   238

free_pgtables
mm/mmap.c   285

free_task_struct
include/asm-i386/processor.h   78

free_uid
kernel/user.c   108

free_vfsmnt
fs/namespace.c   399

F_SETLK
include/asm-i386/fcntl.h   425

F_SETLK64
include/asm-i386/fcntl.h   425

F_SETLKW
include/asm-i386/fcntl.h   425

F_SETLKW64
include/asm-i386/fcntl.h   425

FS_LITTER
include/linux/fs.h   396

FS_NO_DCACHE
include/linux/fs.h   396

FS_NOMOUNT
include/linux/fs.h   396

FS_NO_PRELIM
include/linux/fs.h   396

FS_ODD_RENAME
include/linux/fs.h   396

FS_REQUIRES_DEV
  include/linux/fs.h   396
FS_SINGLE
  include/linux/fs.h   396
fs_struct
  include/linux/fs_struct.h   392
fsync_dev
  fs/buffer.c   495
fsync_inode_data_buffers
  fs/buffer.c   526

G

gdt
  arch/i386/kernel/head.S   40
gdt_table
  arch/i386/kernel/head.S   40
general_protection
  arch/i386/kernel/entry.S   117
generic_commit_write
  fs/buffer.c   512
generic_direct_IO
  fs/buffer.c   526
generic_file_direct_IO
  mm/filemap.c   525
generic_file_mmap
  fs/filemap.c   518
  mm/filemap.c   518
generic_file_read
  mm/filemap.c   498
generic_file_readahead
  mm/filemap.c   507
generic_file_vm_ops
  mm/filemap.c   518
generic_file_write
  mm/filemap.c   509
generic_make_request
  drivers/block/ll_rw_blk.c   462
generic_osync_inode
  fs/inode.c   511
generic_plug_device
  ll_rw_blk.c   463
generic_unplug_device
  drivers/block/ll_rw_blk.c   464
getblk
  fs/buffer.c   490
get_cmos_time
  arch/i386/kernel/time.c   203
__get_dma_pages
  include/linux/mm.h   226
get_empty_filp
  fs/file_table.c   387

__get_free_page
  include/linux/mm.h   225
get_free_page
  include/linux/mm.h   226
__get_free_pages
  mm/page_alloc.c   225
get_fs
  include/asm-i386/uaccess.h   311
get_fs_type
  fs/super.c   397, 403
get_hash_table
  fs/buffer.c   486
get_irqlock
  arch/i386/kernel/irq.c   181
getname
  fs/namei.c   417
get_pgd_slow
  include/asm-i386/pgalloc.h   60
get_pid
  kernel/fork.c   102
get_pipe_inode
  fs/pipe.c   637
get_request
  drivers/block/ll_rw_blk.c   459
get_request_wait
  drivers/block/ll_rw_blk.c   459
get_sb_bdev
  fs/super.c   405
get_sb_nodev
  fs/super.c   401
get_sigframe
  arch/i386/kernel/signal.c   338
get_super
  fs/super.c   402
get_swap_page
  mm/swapfile.c   543
get_unnamed_dev
  fs/super.c   395
get_unused_buffer_head
  fs/buffer.c   484
get_unused_fd
  fs/open.c   417
__get_user
  include/asm-i386/uaccess.h   312
get_user
  include/asm-i386/uaccess.h   311
__get_user_1
  arch/i386/lib/getuser.S   311
__get_user_2
  arch/i386/lib/getuser.S   311
__get_user_4
  arch/i386/lib/getuser.S   311

get_user_pages
   mm/memory.c 282
get_vm_area
   mm/vmalloc.c 257
get_zeroed_page
   mm/page_alloc.c 226
GFP_ATOMIC
   include/linux/mm.h 226
__GFP_DMA
   include/linux/mm.h 226
__GFP_FS
   include/linux/mm.h 226
__GFP_HIGH
   include/linux/mm.h 226
__GFP_HIGHIO
   include/linux/mm.h 226
__GFP_HIGHMEM
   include/linux/mm.h 226
GFP_HIGHUSER
   include/linux/mm.h 227
__GFP_IO
   include/linux/mm.h 226
GFP_KERNEL
   include/linux/mm.h 226
GFP_KSWAPD
   include/linux/mm.h 227
GFP_NFS
   include/linux/mm.h 226
GFP_NOFS
   include/linux/mm.h 226
GFP_NOHIGHIO
   include/linux/mm.h 226
GFP_NOIO
   include/linux/mm.h 226
GFP_USER
   include/linux/mm.h 227
__GFP_WAIT
   include/linux/mm.h 226
global_bh_lock
   kernel/softirq.c 153
__global_cli
   arch/i386/kernel/irq.c 181
global_irq_holder
   arch/i386/kernel/irq.c 181
__global_sti
   arch/i386/kernel/irq.c 182
goodness
   kernel/sched.c 362
graft_tree
   fs/namespace.c 403

grow_buffers
   fs/buffer.c 488
grow_dev_page
   fs/buffer.c 489

H

handle_IRQ_event
   arch/i386/kernel/irq.c 141
handle_mm_fault
   mm/memory.c 290
handle_pte_fault
   mm/memory.c 292
handle_signal
   arch/i386/kernel/signal.c 335
handle_t
   include/linux/jbd.h 604
hardsect_size
   drivers/block/ll_rw_blk.c 453
hash_page_buffers
   fs/buffer.c 489
hash_pid
   include/linux/sched.h 83
hash_table
   fs/buffer.c 486
hash_table_lock
   fs/buffer.c 486
HeadB
   The shrink_caches Function 565
hh_cache
   include/linux/netdevice.h 613, 617
highend_pfn
   arch/i386/mm/init.c 222
HIGH_MEMORY
   include/asm-i386/e820.h 62
high_memory
   mm/memory.c 256
highmem_start_page
   mm/memory.c 229
HI_SOFTIRQ
   include/linux/interrupt.h 148
htonl
   include/linux/byteorder/generic.h 622
htons
   include/linux/byteorder/generic.h 622
hw_interrupt_type
   include/linux/irq.h 134
hw_irq_controller
   include/linux/irq.h 134
HZ
   include/asm-i386/param.h 196

I

i387_fsave_struct
  include/asm-i386/processor.h 97

i387_fxsave_struct
  include/asm-i386/processor.h 97

i387_soft_struct
  include/asm-i386/processor.h 97

i387_union
  include/asm-i386/processor.h 97

i8259A_irq_type
  arch/i386/kernel/i8259.c 134

I_CLEAR
  include/linux/fs.h 383

I_DIRTY
  include/linux/fs.h 383

I_DIRTY_DATASYNC
  include/linux/fs.h 383

I_DIRTY_PAGES
  include/linux/fs.h 383

I_DIRTY_SYNC
  include/linux/fs.h 383

idt
  arch/i386/kernel/head.S 124

idt_descr
  arch/i386/kernel/head.S 124

idt_table
  arch/i386/kernel/traps.c 124

I_FREEING
  include/linux/fs.h 383

ignored_signal
  kernel/signal.c 329

ignore_int
  arch/i386/kernel/head.S 124

I_LOCK
  include/linux/fs.h 383

IMMEDIATE_BH
  include/linux/interrupt.h 155

inactive_list
  mm/page_alloc.c 561

INADDR_ANY
  include/linux/in.h 622

inb
  include/asm-i386/io.h 429

inb_p
  include/asm-i386/io.h 429

inet_addr_type
  net/ipv4/fib_frontend.c 622

inet_autobind
  net/ipv4/af_inet.c 624

inet_bind
  net/ipv4/af_inet.c 622

inet_create
  net/ipv4/af_inet.c 621

inet_dgram_connect
  net/af_inet.c 624

inet_dgram_ops
  net/ipv4/af_inet.c 625

inet_recvmsg
  net/ipv4/af_inet.c 631

inet_stream_connect
  net/af_inet.c 624

init
  init/main.c 106

init_bh
  kernel/softirq.c 154

INIT_FILES
  include/linux/sched.h 105

init_files
  arch/i386/kernel/init_task.c 105

INIT_FS
  include/linux/fs_struct.h 105

init_fs
  arch/i386/kernel/init_task.c 105

init_IRQ
  arch/i386/kernel/i8259.c 133

INIT_MM
  include/linux/sched.h 105

init_mm
  arch/i386/kernel/init_task.c 105

init_mount_tree
  fs/namespace.c 400

init_MUTEX
  include/asm-i386/semaphore.h 174

init_MUTEX_LOCKED
  include/asm-i386/semaphore.h 174

init_pipe_fs
  fs/pipe.c 637

init_rwsem
  include/asm-i386/rwsem.h 178

INIT_SIGNALS
  include/linux/sched.h 105

init_signals
  arch/i386/kernel/init_task.c 105

init_special_inode
  fs/devices.c 441

init_stack
  include/asm-i386/processor.h 105

INIT_TASK
  include/linux/sched.h 352

init_task
  include/asm-i386/processor.h 105

init_task_union
  arch/i386/kernel/init_task.c 105

init_timer
    include/linux/timer.h   208
init_tss
    arch/i386/kernel/init_task.c   42
init_waitqueue_head
    include/linux/wait.h   85
inl
    include/asm-i386/io.h   429
inl_p
    include/asm-i386/io.h   429
inode
    include/linux/fs.h   381
inode_hashtable
    fs/inode.c   383
inode_in_use
    fs/inode.c   383
inode_operations
    include/linux/fs.h   384
inode_remove_queue
    fs/buffer.c   486
inode_unused
    fs/inode.c   383
insb
    include/asm-i386/io.h   430
__insert_vm_struct
    mm/mmap.c   278
insert_vm_struct
    mm/mmap.c   278
insl
    include/asm-i386/io.h   430
insw
    include/asm-i386/io.h   430
int3
    arch/i386/kernel/entry.S   117
interrupt
    arch/i386/kernel/i8259.c   134
interruptible_sleep_on
    kernel/sched.c   86
interruptible_sleep_on_timeout
    kernel/sched.c   86
invalidate_inode_buffers
    fs/buffers.c   594
invalidate_interrupt
    arch/i386/kernel/i8259.c   144
INVALIDATE_TLB_VECTOR
    include/asm-i386/hw_irq.h   144
invalid_op
    arch/i386/kernel/entry.S   117
invalid_tss
    arch/i386/kernel/entry.S   117
inw
    include/asm-i386/io.h   429

inw_p
    include/asm-i386/io.h   429
ioport_resource
    kernel/resource.c   430
ioremap
    include/asm-i386/io.h   435
ioremap_nocache
    include/asm-i386/io.h   435
iounmap
    arch/i386/mm/ioremap.c   435
ip_build_xmit
    net/ipv4/ip_output.c   626
IPC message header   653
IPC message queue   653
IPC message text   653
IPC message type   653
IPC_CREAT
    include/linux/ipc.h   646
IPC_EXCL
    include/linux/ipc.h   646
ipc_ids
    ipc/util.h   646
IPC_INFO
    include/linux/ipc.h   648
IPCMNI
    include/linux/ipc.h   646
IPC_PRIVATE
    include/linux/ipc.h   646
IPC_RMID
    include/linux/ipc.h   648
IPC_SET
    include/linux/ipc.h   648
IPC_STAT
    include/linux/ipc.h   648
ip_forward
    net/ipv4/ip_forward.c   630
ip_local_delivery
    net/ipv4/ip_input.c   630
ip_output
    net/ipv4/ip_output.c   626
IPPROTO_EGP
    include/linux/in.h   620
IPPROTO_ICMP
    include/linux/in.h   620
IPPROTO_IGMP
    include/linux/in.h   620
IPPROTO_IP
    include/linux/in.h   620
IPPROTO_TCP
    include/linux/in.h   620
ip_rcv
    net/ipv4/ip_input.c   630

ip_route_connect
   include/net/route.h   624
ip_route_input
   net/ipv4/route.c   630
ip_route_output_key
   net/ipv4/route.c   624
ip_route_output_slow
   net/ipv4/route.c   624
iput
   fs/inode.c   392
irqaction
   include/linux/interrupt.h   135
IRQ_AUTODETECT
   include/linux/irq.h   133
irq_cpustat_t
   include/asm-i386/hardirq.h   135
irq_desc
   arch/i386/kernel/irq.c   132
irq_desc_t
   include/linux/irq.h   132
IRQ_DISABLED
   include/linux/irq.h   133
irq_enter
   include/asm-i386/hardirq.h   202
irq_exit
   include/asm-i386/hardirq.h   202
IRQ_INPROGRESS
   include/linux/irq.h   133
IRQ_LEVEL
   include/linux/irq.h   133
IRQ_MASKED
   include/linux/irq.h   133
IRQn_interrupt
   arch/1386/kernel/i8259.c   137
IRQ_PENDING
   include/linux/irq.h   133
IRQ_PER_CPU
   include/linux/irq.h   133
IRQ_REPLAY
   include/linux/irq.h   133
irq_stat
   kernel/softirq.c   135
IRQ_WAITING
   include/linux/irq.h   133
ISICOM_BH
   include/linux/interrupt.h   154
is_orphaned_pgrp
   kernel/exit.c   335
ITIMER_PROF
   include/linux/time.h   216

ITIMER_REAL
   include/linux/time.h   216
ITIMER_VIRTUAL
   include/linux/time.h   216
it_real_fn
   kernel/itimer.c   216

J

jiffies
   kernel/timer.c   199
journal_block_tag_t
   include/linux/jbd.h   603
journal_commit_transaction
   fs/jbd/commit.c   607
journal_dirty_data
   fs/jbd/transaction.c   607
journal_dirty_metadata
   fs/jbd/transaction.c   606
journal_get_write_access
   fs/jbd/transaction.c   606
journal_head
   include/linux/journal-head.h   603
journal_start
   fs/jbd/transaction.c   604
journal_stop
   fs/jbd/transaction.c   604

K

kdev_t
   include/linux/kdev_t.h   438
__KERNEL_CS
   include/asm-i386/segment.h   41
__KERNEL_DS
   include/asm-i386/segment.h   41
kernel_flag
   arch/i386/kernel/smp.c   190
kernel_module
   kernel/module.c   693
kernel_stat
   include/linux/kernel_stat.h   204
kernel_thread
   arch/i386/kernel/process.c   104
kern_ipc_perm
   include/linux/ipc.h   647
kfree
   mm/slab.c   255
kill_pg_info
   kernel/signal.c   343
kill_something_info
   kernel/signal.c   343

kiobuf
    include/linux/iobuf.h   524
kmalloc
    mm/slab.c   255
kmap
    include/asm-i386/highmem.h   229
kmap_high
    mm/highmem.c   229
kmap_init
    arch/i386/mm/init.c   223
kmap_lock
    mm/highmem.c   230
kmap_pte
    arch/i386/mm/init.c   232
kmem_bufctl_t
    mm/slab.c   247
kmem_cache_alloc
    mm/slab.c   251
kmem_cache_alloc_batch
    mm/slab.c   252
kmem_cache_create
    mm/slab.c   244
kmem_cache_destroy
    mm/slab.c   244
kmem_cache_free
    mm/slab.c   253
kmem_cache_grow
    mm/slab.c   246
kmem_cache_init
    mm/slab.c   244
kmem_cache_init_objs
    mm/slab.c   246
kmem_cache_reap
    mm/slab.c   246
kmem_cache_s
    mm/slab.c   242
kmem_cache_shrink
    mm/slab.c   244
kmem_cache_sizes_init
    mm/slab.c   244
kmem_cache_slabmgmt
    mm/slab.c   246
kmem_cache_t
    include/linux/slab.h   242
kmem_freepages
    mm/slab.c   245
kmem_getpages
    mm/slab.c   245
kmem_slab_destroy
    mm/slab.c   246
km_type
    include/asm-i386/kmap_types.h   231

k_sigaction
    include/asm-i386/signal.h   324
ksoftirqd
    kernel/softirq.c   150
ksoftirqd_task
    include/linux/irq_cpustat.h   148
kstat
    kernel/sched.c   204
kswapd
    mm/vmscan.c   572
kswapd_balace
    mm/vmscan.c   573
kswapd_wait
    mm/vmscan.c   572
kunmap
    include/asm-i386/highmem.h   231
kunmap_atomic
    include/asm-i386/highmem.h   232
kunmap_high
    mm/highmem.c   231
kupdate
    fs/buffer.c   494

L

L1_CACHE_BYTES
    include/asm-i386/cache.h   68
LAST_BIND
    include/linux/fs.h   413
LAST_DOT
    include/linux/fs.h   413
LAST_DOTDOT
    include/linux/fs.h   413
LAST_NORM
    include/linux/fs.h   413
LAST_PKMAP
    include/asm-i386/highmem.h   228
last_pkmap_nr
    mm/highmem.c   230
LAST_ROOT
    include/linux/fs.h   413
last_schedule
    kernel/sched.c   355
last_tsc_low
    arch/i386/kernel/time.c   198
LATCH
    include/linux/timex.h   196
link_path_walk
    fs/namei.c   409
linux_binfmt
    include/linux/binfmts.h   675
linux_binprm
    linux/include/linux/binfmts.h   679

list_add
    include/linux/list.h   81
list_add_tail
    include/linux/list.h   81
list_del
    include/linux/list.h   81
list_empty
    include/linux/list.h   81
list_entry
    include/linux/list.h   81
list_for_each
    include/linux/list.h   81
LIST_HEAD
    include/linux/list.h   80
list_head
    include/linux/list.h   80
ll_rw_block
    ll_rw_blk.c   461
load_block_bitmap
    fs/ext2/balloc.c   588
load_elf_interp
    fs/binfmt_elf.c   681
load_inode_bitmap
    fs/ext2/ialloc.c   587
load_script
    fs/binfmt_script.c   675
local_bh_count
    include/linux/irq_cpustat.h   148
local_bh_disable
    include/asm-i386/softirq.h   183
local_bh_enable
    include/asm-i386/softirq.h   183
local_flush_tlb
    include/asm-i386/pgalloc.h   70
local_irq_count
    include/linux/irq_cpustat.h   135
local_irq_restore
    include/asm-i386/system.h   180
local_irq_save
    include/asm-i386/system.h   180
LOCAL_TIMER_VECTOR
    include/asm-i386/hw_irq.h   201
LOCK_EX
    include/asm-i386/fcntl.h   423
lock_kernel
    include/asm-i386/smplock.h   190
LOCK_NB
    include/asm-i386/fcntl.h   423
LockPage
    include/linux/mm.h   219
LOCK_SH
    include/asm-i386/fcntl.h   423

locks_verify_area
    fs/locks.c   419
LOCK_UN
    include/asm-i386/fcntl.h   423
LOOKUP_CONTINUE
    include/linux/fs.h   408
LOOKUP_DIRECTORY
    include/linux/fs.h   408
LOOKUP_FOLLOW
    include/linux/fs.h   408
lookup_mnt
    fs/namespace.c   399
LOOKUP_NOALT
    include/linux/fs.h   408
LOOKUP_PARENT
    include/linux/fs.h   408
LOOKUP_POSITIVE
    include/linux/fs.h   408
lookup_swap_cache
    mm/swap_state.c   548
LOWMEMSIZE()
    arch/i386/kernel/setup.c   62
lru_cache_add
    mm/swap.c   562
__lru_cache_del
    mm/swap.c   562
lru_cache_del
    mm/swap.c   562
lru_list
    fs/buffer.c   485
lru_list_lock
    fs/buffer.c   485

M

machine_check
    arch/i386/kernel/entry.S   118
MACSERIAL_BH
    include/linux/interrupt.h   154
main_table
    net/ipv4/fib_frontend.c   615
MAJOR
    include/linux/kdev_t.h   438
make_pages_present
    mm/memory.c   282
make_private_signals
    fs/exec.c   680
__make_request
    drivers/block/ll_rw_blk.c   462
MAP_ANONYMOUS
    include/asm-i386/mman.h   279, 516
MAP_DENYWRITE
    include/asm-i386/mman.h   279

MAP_EXECUTABLE
  include/asm-i386/mman.h   279
MAP_FIXED
  include/asm-i386/mman.h   279
MAP_GROWSDOWN
  include/asm-i386/mman.h   279
MAP_LOCKED
  include/asm-i386/mman.h   279
map_new_virtual
  mm/highmem.c   230
MAP_NORESERVE
  include/asm-i386/mman.h   279
MAP_PRIVATE
  include/asm-i386/mman.h   279, 516
MAP_SHARED
  include/asm-i386/mman.h   279, 516
map_user_kiobuf
  mm/memory.c   526
mark_bh
  include/linux/interrupt.h   154
mark_buffer_clean
  include/linux/fs.h   485
mark_buffer_dirty
  fs/buffer.c   485
mark_dirty_kiobuf
  mm/memory.c   526
mark_inode_dirty
  include/linux/fs.h   593
mark_page_accessed
  mm/filemap.c   563
mask_and_ack_8259A
  arch/i386/kernel/i8259.c   134
math_state_restore
  arch/i386/kernel/traps.c   98
MAX_MAP_COUNT
  include/linux/sched.h   270
max_queued_signals
  kernel/signal.c   325
max_readahead
  drivers/block/ll_rw_blk.c   507
max_sectors
  drivers/block/ll_rw_blk.c   464
MAX_SWAPFILES
  include/linux/swap.h   531
max_threads
  kernel/fork.c   102
MAX_UNUSED_BUFFERS
  fs/buffer.c   483
mb()
  include/asm-i386/system.h   167

memcpy
  include/asm-i386/string.h   297
memcpy_fromio
  include/asm-i386/io.h   435
memcpy_toio
  include/asm-i386/io.h   435
mem_init
  arch/i386/mm/init.c   225
mem_map
  mm/memory.c   218
memset
  include/asm-i386/string.h   294
memset_io
  include/asm-i386/io.h   435
MINOR
  include/linux/kdev_t.h   438
misc_list
  drivers/char/misc.c   473
MKDEV
  include/linux/kdev_t.h   438
mk_pte
  include/asm-i386/pgtable.h   59
mk_pte_phys
  include/asm-i386/pgtable.h   59
mm_alloc
  kernel/fork.c   267
mmdrop
  include/linux/sched.h   267
mmlist_lock
  kernel/fork.c   266
mmlist_nr
  kernel/fork.c   266
mmput
  kernel/fork.c   267
mm_release
  kernel/fork.c   300
mm_struct
  include/linux/sched.h   265
MOD_AUTOCLEAN
  include/kernel/module.h   701
mod_timer
  kernel/timer.c   208
module
  include/linux/module.h   693
module_exit
  include/linux/init.h   697
module_init
  include/linux/init.h   697
MODULE_LICENSE
  include/linux/module.h   696

module_list
   kernel/module.c   693
mount hashtable
   fs/namespace.c   398
mount_root
   fs/super.c   402
mount_sem
   fs/namespace.c   399
move_first_runqueue
   kernel/sched.c   81
move_last_runqueue
   kernel/sched.c   81
MS_ASYNC
   include/asm-i386/mman.h   522
MS_BIND
   include/linux/fs.h   404
msghdr
   include/linux/socket.h   625
msg_ids
   ipc/msg.c   654
msg_msg
   ipc/msg.c   655
msg_msgseg
   ipc/msg.c   655
msg_queue
   ipc/msg.c   654
msg_receiver
   ipc/msg.c   656
MS_INVALIDATE
   include/asm-i386/mman.h   522
MS_MANDLOCK
   include/linux/fs.h   421
MS_MOVE
   include/linux/fs.h   404
MS_NOATIME
   include/linux/fs.h   404
MS_NODEV
   include/linux/fs.h   403
MS_NODIRATIME
   include/linux/fs.h   404
MS_NOEXEC
   include/linux/fs.h   404
MS_NOSUID
   include/linux/fs.h   403
MS_RDONLY
   include/linux/fs.h   403
MS_REC
   include/linux/fs.h   404
MS_REMOUNT
   include/linux/fs.h   404
MS_SYNC
   include/asm-i386/mman.h   522

MS_SYNCHRONOUS
   include/linux/fs.h   404
MS_VERBOSE
   include/linux/fs.h   404
msync_interval
   mm/filemap.c   522

N

nameidata
   include/linux/fs.h   408
neighbour
   include/net/neighbour.h   617
neigh_resolve_output
   net/core/neighbour.c   626
net_device
   include/linux/netdevice.h   613
net_families
   net/socket.c   620
netif_rx
   net/core/dev.c   629
net_proto_family
   include/linux/net.h   620
net_rx_action
   net/core/dev.c   630
NET_RX_SOFTIRQ
   include/linux/interrupt.h   629
net_tx_action
   net/core/dev.c   627
NET_TX_SOFTIRQ
   include/linux/interrupt.h   627
new_inode
   include/linux/fs.h   592
nopage_sequential_readahead
   mm/filemap.c   521
notify_parent
   kernel/signal.c   334
nr_active_pages
   mm/page_alloc.c   561
nr_buffers_type
   fs/buffer.c   485
NR_CPUS
   include/linux/threads.h   71
__NR_fork
   include/asm-i386/unistd.h   308
nr_free_pages
   mm/page_alloc.c   225
nr_inactive_pages
   mm/page_alloc.c   561
NR_IRQS
   include/asm-i386/irq.h   132
NR_OPEN
   include/linux/fs.h   393

nr_queued_signals
  kernel/signal.c   325
NR_RESERVED
  fs/buffer.c   483
NR_RESERVED_FILES
  include/linux/fs.h   386
nr_running
  kernel/fork.c   81
nr_swapfiles
  mm/swapfile.c   534
nr_swap_pages
  mm/page_alloc.c   535
NR_syscalls
  include/linux/sys.h   305
nr_unused_buffer_heads
  fs/buffer.c   483
__NR_write
  include/asm-i386/unistd.h   317
_NSIG
  include/asm-i386/signal.h   324
ntohl
  include/linux/byteorder/generic.h   622
ntohs
  include/linux/byteorder/generic.h   622
num_physpages
  mm/memory.c   225

O

O   417
O_APPEND
  include/asm-i386/fcntl.h   417
O_CREAT
  include/asm-i386/fcntl.h   417
O_DIRECT
  include/asm-i386/fcntl.h   525
O_DIRECTORY
  include/asm-i386/fcntl.h   417
O_EXCL
  include/asm-i386/fcntl.h   417
O_LARGEFILE
  include/asm-i386/fcntl.h   417
old_mmap
  arch/i386/kernel/sys_i386.c   517
O_NDELAY
  include/asm-i386/fcntl.h   417
O_NOCTTY
  include/asm-i386/fcntl.h   417
O_NOFOLLOW
  include/asm-i386/fcntl.h   417
O_NONBLOCK
  include/asm-i386/fcntl.h   417

open_namei
  fs/namei.c   417
open_softirq
  kernel/softirq.c   148
O_RDONLY
  include/asm-i386/fcntl.h   417
O_RDWR
  include/asm-i386/fcntl.h   417
O_SYNC
  include/asm-i386/fcntl.h   417
O_TRUNC
  include/asm-i386/fcntl.h   417
outb
  include/asm-i386/io.h   429
outb_p
  include/asm-i386/io.h   429
outl
  include/asm-i386/io.h   429
outl_p
  include/asm-i386/io.h   429
out_of_memory
  mm/oom_kill.c   565
outsb
  include/asm-i386/io.h   430
outsl
  include/asm-i386/io.h   430
outsw
  include/asm-i386/io.h   430
outw
  include/asm-i386/io.h   429
outw_p
  include/asm-i386/io.h   429
overflow
  arch/i386/kernel/entry.S   117
O_WRONLY
  include/asm-i386/fcntl.h   416, 417

P

__pa
  include/asm-i386/page.h   65
page
  include/linux/mm.h   218
PageActive
  include/linux/mm.h   219
pagecache_lock
  mm/filemap.c   478
page_cache_read
  mm/filemap.c   507
page_cache_size
  mm/filemap.c   479
PageChecked
  include/linux/mm.h   219

PageClearSlab
  include/linux/mm.h   219
page_cluster
  mm/swap.c   557
PageDecrAfter
  include/linux/mm.h   219
PageDirty
  include/linux/mm.h   219
PageError
  include/linux/mm.h   219
page_fault
  arch/i386/kernel/entry.S   118
page_follow_link
  fs/namei.c   591
page_hash
  include/linux/pagemap.h   479
page_hash_table
  mm/filemap.c   479
PageHighMem
  include/linux/mm.h   219
PageLocked
  include/linux/mm.h   219
pagemap_lru_lock
  mm/filemap.c   561
PAGE_MASK
  include/asm-i386/page.h   56
PAGE_OFFSET
  include/asm-i386/page.h   63
page_readlink
  fs/namei.c   591
PageReferenced
  include/linux/mm.h   219
PageReserved
  include/linux/mm.h   219
PageSetSlab
  include/linux/mm.h   219
PAGE_SHIFT
  include/asm-i386/page.h   56
PAGE_SIZE
  include/asm-i386/page.h   56
PageSlab
  include/linux/mm.h   219
page_symlink_inode_operations
  fs/namei.c   591
pagetable_init()
  arch/i386/mm/init.c   65
PageTestandClearDecrAfter
  include/linux/mm.h   219
PageTestandClearReferenced
  include/linux/mm.h   219

Page_Uptodate
  include/linux/mm.h   219
paging_init
  arch/i386/mm/init.c   65
path_init
  fs/namei.c   407
path_release
  fs/namei.c   409
path_walk
  fs/namei.c   409
pci_read_config_byte
  drivers/pci/pci.c   131
PER_BSD
  include/linux/personality.h   677
PER_IRIX32
  include/linux/personality.h   677
PER_IRIX64
  include/linux/personality.h   677
PER_IRIXN32
  include/linux/personality.h   677
PER_ISCR4
  include/linux/personality.h   677
PER_LINUX
  include/linux/personality.h   677
PER_OSR5
  include/linux/personality.h   677
per-process list of undoable IPC semaphore
        operations   652
PER_RISCOS
  include/linux/personality.h   677
PER_SCOSVR3
  include/linux/personality.h   677
per-semaphore list of undoable IPC
        semaphore operations   652
PER_SOLARIS
  include/linux/personality.h   677
PER_SUNOS
  include/linux/personality.h   677
PER_SVR3
  include/linux/personality.h   677
PER_SVR4
  include/linux/personality.h   677
PER_UW7
  include/linux/personality.h   677
PER_WYSEV386
  include/linux/personality.h   677
PER_XENIX
  include/linux/personality.h   677
PF   609
PF_APPLETALK
  include/linux/socket.h   609

PF_BLUETOOTH
  include/linux/socket.h   609

PF_BRIDGE
  include/linux/socket.h   609

PF_DECnet
  include/linux/socket.h   609

PF_EXITING
  include/kernel/sched.h   107

PF_FORKNOEXEC
  include/linux/sched.h   681

PF_INET
  include/linux/socket.h   609

PF_INET6
  include/linux/socket.h   609

PF_IPX
  include/linux/socket.h   609

PF_LOCAL
  include/linux/socket.h   609

PF_NOIO
  include/linux/sched.h   565

PF_PACKET
  include/linux/socket.h   609

PF_SUPERPRIV
  include/linux/sched.h   102

PF_UNIX
  include/linux/socket.h   609

PF_USEDFPU
  include/linux/sched.h   97

PF_X25
  include/linux/socket.h   609

pg0
  arch/i386/kernel/head.S   64

pg1
  arch/i386/kernel/head.S   64

PG_active
  include/linux/mm.h   219

PG_arch_1
  include/linux/mm.h   219

PG_checked
  include/linux/mm.h   219

__pgd
  include/asm-i386/page.h   57

pgd_alloc
  include/asm-i386/pgalloc.h   60

pg_data_t
  include/linux/mmzone.h   222

pgdat_list
  mm/page_alloc.c   222

pgd_bad
  include/asm-i386/pgtable.h   57

pgd_clear
  include/asm-i386/pgtable.h   57

pgd_free
  include/asm-i386/pgtable.h   61

PGDIR_MASK
  include/asm-i386/pgtable.h   57

PGDIR_SHIFT
  include/asm-i386/pgtable.h   57

PGDIR_SIZE
  include/asm-i386/pgtable.h   57

PG_dirty
  include/linux/mm.h   219

pgd_none
  include/asm-i386/pgtable.h   57

pgd_offset
  include/asm-i386/pgtable.h   59

pgd_offset_k
  include/asm-i386/pgtable.h   59

pgd_present
  include/asm-i386/pgtable.h   57

pgd_quicklist
  include/asm-i386/pgalloc.h   60

pgd_t
  include/asm-i386/page.h   57

pgd_val
  include/asm-i386/page.h   57

PG_error
  include/linux/mm.h   219

PG_highmem
  include/linux/mm.h   219

PG_launder
  include/linux/mm.h   219

PG_locked
  include/linux/mm.h   219

PG_lru
  include/linux/mm.h   219

__pgprot
  include/asm-i386/page.h   57

pgprot_t
  include/asm-i386/page.h   57

pgprot_val
  include/asm-i386/page.h   57

PG_referenced
  include/linux/mm.h   219

PG_reserved
  include/linux/mm.h   219

PG_skip
  include/linux/mm.h   219

PG_slab
  include/linux/mm.h   219

PG_uptodate
  include/linux/mm.h   219

pidhash
  kernel/fork.c   82

pidhash tables   82

pid_hashfn
include/linux/sched.h   82

PIDHASH_SZ
include/linux/sched.h   82

pipefs_read_super
fs/pipe.c   637

pipe_fs_type
fs/pipe.c   637

pipe_inode_info
include/linux/pipe_fs_i.h   636

pipe_mnt
fs/pipe.c   637

pipe_read
fs/pipe.c   638

pipe_read_release
fs/pipe.c   638

pipe_release
fs/pipe.c   638

pipe_write
fs/pipe.c   641

pipe_write_release
fs/pipe.c   638

PKMAP_BASE
include/asm-i386/highmem.h   229

pkmap_count
mm/highmem.c   229

pkmap_map_wait
mm/highmem.c   231

pkmap_page_table
mm/highmem.c   228

__pmd
include/asm-i386/page.h   57

pmd_alloc
include/linux/mm.h   60

pmd_bad
include/asm-i386/pgtable.h   57

pmd_clear
include/asm-i386/pgtable.h   57

pmd_free
include/asm-i386/pgalloc.h   61

PMD_MASK
include/asm-i386/pgtable.h   56

pmd_none
include/asm-i386/pgtable.h   57

pmd_offset
include/asm-i386/pgtable.h   59

pmd_page
include/asm-i386/pgtable.h   59

pmd_present
include/asm-i386/pgtable.h   57

PMD_SHIFT
include/asm-i386/pgtable.h   56

PMD_SIZE
include/asm-i386/pgtable.h   56

pmd_t
include/asm-i386/page.h   57

pmd_val
include/asm-i386/page.h   57

posix_lock_file
fs/locks.c   425

posix_locks_conflict
fs/locks.c   425

posix_locks_deadlock
fs/locks.c   425

prepare_binprm
fs/exec.c   679

printk
kernel/printk.c   124

PRIO_PGRP
include/linux/resource.h   369

PRIO_PROCESS
include/linux/resource.h   368

PRIO_USER
include/linux/resource.h   369

process capabilities
Linux kernel   665

process descriptors
    chained lists   82
    parenthood relationships, representing   83
    pidhash tables   82

processes
    parent, child, and sibling relationships   83

process_timeout
kernel/sched.c   213

protection_map
mm/mmap.c   275

PROT_EXEC
include/asm-i386/mman.h   279

PROT_NONE
include/asm-i386/mman.h   279

proto
include/net/sock.h   612

proto_ops
include/linux/net.h   611

PROT_READ
include/asm-i386/mman.h   279

PROT_WRITE
include/asm-i386/mman.h   279

prune_dcache
fs/dcache.c   570, 571

prune_icache
fs/inode.c   571

prune_one_dentry
  fs/dcache.c   571
PT_DTRACE
  include/linux/sched.h   674
__pte
  include/asm-i386/page.h   57
pte_alloc
  mm/memory.c   60
pte_alloc_one
  include/asm-i386/pgalloc.h   61
pte_clear
  include/asm-i386/pgtable.h   57
pte_dirty
  include/asm-i386/pgtable.h   58
pte_exec
  include/asm-i386/pgtable.h   58
pte_exprotect
  include/asm-i386/pgtable.h   58
pte_free
  include/asm-i386/pgalloc.h   61
pte_mkclean
  include/asm-i386/pgtable.h   58
pte_mkdirty
  include/asm-i386/pgtable.h   58
pte_mkexec
  include/asm-i386/pgtable.h   58
pte_mkold
  include/asm-i386/pgtable.h   59
pte_mkread
  include/asm-i386/pgtable.h   58
pte_mkwrite
  include/asm-i386/pgtable.h   58
pte_mkyoung
  include/asm-i386/pgtable.h   59
pte_modify
  include/asm-i386/pgtable.h   59
pte_none
  include/asm-i386/pgtable.h   57
pte_offset
  include/asm-i386/pgtable.h   60
pte_page
  include/asm-i386/pgtable.h   59
ptep_mkdirty
  include/asm-i386/pgtable.h   59
pte_present
  include/asm-i386/pgtable.h   57
ptep_set_wrprotect
  include/asm-i386/pgtable.h   59
ptep_test_and_clear_dirty
  include/asm-i386/pgtable.h   59
ptep_test_and_clear_young
  include/asm-i386/pgtable.h   59

pte_quicklist
  include/asm-i386/pgalloc.h   60
pte_rdprotect
  include/asm-i386/pgtable.h   58
pte_read
  include/asm-i386/pgtable.h   58
pte_t
  include/asm-i386/page.h   57
pte_val
  include/asm-i386/page.h   57
pte_write
  include/asm-i386/pgtable.h   58
pte_wrprotect
  include/asm-i386/pgtable.h   58
pte_young
  include/asm-i386/pgtable.h   58
PT_PTRACED
  include/linux/sched.h   674
PTRACE_ATTACH
  include/linux/ptrace.h   673
PTRACE_CONT
  include/linux/ptrace.h   673
PTRACE_DETACH
  include/linux/ptrace.h   673
PTRACE_GETFPREGS
  include/asm-i386/ptrace.h   673
PTRACE_GETFPXREGS
  include/asm-i386/ptrace.h   673
PTRACE_GETREGS
  include/asm-i386/ptrace.h   673
PTRACE_KILL
  include/linux/ptrace.h   673
PTRACE_PEEKDATA
  include/linux/ptrace.h   673
PTRACE_PEEKTEXT
  include/linux/ptrace.h   673
PTRACE_PEEKUSR
  include/linux/ptrace.h   673
PTRACE_POKEDATA
  include/linux/ptrace.h   673
PTRACE_POKETEXT
  include/linux/ptrace.h   673
PTRACE_POKEUSR
  include/linux/ptrace.h   673
PTRACE_SETFPREGS
  include/asm-i386/ptrace.h   673
PTRACE_SETFPXREGS
  include/asm-i386/ptrace.h   673
PTRACE_SETOPTIONS
  include/asm-i386/ptrace.h   673
PTRACE_SETREGS
  include/asm-i386/ptrace.h   673

PTRACE_SINGLESTEP
    include/linux/ptrace.h   673
PTRACE_SYSCALL
    include/linux/ptrace.h   673
PTRACE_TRACEME
    include/linux/ptrace.h   673
pt_regs
    include/asm-i386/ptrace.h   138
PTRS_PER_PGD
    include/asm-i386/pgtable.h   57
PTRS_PER_PMD
    include/asm-i386/pgtable.h   57
PTRS_PER_PTE
    include/asm-i386/pgtable.h   57
PT_TRACESYS
    include/linux/sched.h   306, 674
put_unnamed_dev
    fs/super.c   395
put_unused_buffer_head
    fs/buffer.c   484
__put_user
    include/asm-i386/uaccess.h   312
put_user
    include/asm-i386/uaccess.h   312
__put_user_64
    include/asm-i386/uaccess.h   312
__put_user_asm
    include/asm-i386/uaccess.h   312

Q

Qdisc
    include/net/pkt_sched.h   627
qdisc_restart
    net/sched/sch_generic.c   628
qdisc_run
    include/net/pkt_sched.h   627
QM_INFO
    include/linux/module.h   697
QM_MODULES
    include/linux/module.h   697
QM_REFS
    include/linux/module.h   698
QM_SYMBOLS
    include/linux/module.h   697, 698
queue of pending IPC semaphore requests
    652
queue_task
    include/linux/tqueue.h   155

R

rb_entry
    include/linux/rbtree.h   276
rb_erase
    lib/rbtree.c   283
rb_node_t
    include/linux/rbtree.h   273
readb
    include/asm-i386/io.h   435
read_block_bitmap
    fs/ext2/balloc.c   588
read_descriptor_t
    include/linux/fs.h   499
read_inode_bitmap
    fs/ext2/ialloc.c   587
readl
    include/asm-i386/io.h   435
read_lock
    include/asm-i386/spinlock.h   171
__read_lock_failed
    arch/i386/kernel/semaphore.c   171
read_lock_irq
    include/linux/spinlock.h   187
read_lock_irqsave
    include/linux/spinlock.h   187
read_pipe_fops
    fs/pipe.c   638
read_super
    fs/super.c   401
read_swap_cache_async
    mm/swap_state.c   550
read_unlock
    include/asm-i386/spinlock.h   171, 172
read_unlock_irq
    include/linux/spinlock.h   187
read_unlock_irqrestore
    include/linux/spinlock.h   187
readw
    include/asm-i386/io.h   435
recalc_sigpending
    include/linux/sched.h   327
refile_buffer
    fs/buffer.c   485
refill_inactive
    mm/vmscan.c   564
register_binfmt
    fs/exec.c   675
register_blkdev
    fs/block_dev.c   445
register_chrdev
    fs/devices.c   445

register_filesystem
  fs/super.c   396
release_irqlock
  include/asm-i386/hardirq.h   182
release_old_signals
  fs/exec.c   680
release_region
  include/linux/ioport.h   431
release_resource
  kernel/resource.c   431
release_task
  kernel/exit.c   108
remove_bh
  kernel/softirq.c   154
remove_inode_page
  mm/filemap.c   481
REMOVE_LINKS
  include/linux/sched.h   79
remove_page_from_hash_queue
  mm/filemap.c   479
remove_page_from_inode_queue
  mm/filemap.c   479
remove_shared_vm_struct
  mm/mmap.c   519
remove_wait_queue
  kernel/fork.c   85
request
  include/linux/blkdev.h   456
request_irq
  arch/i386/kernel/irq.c   143
request_module
  kernel/kmod.c   700
request_queue_t
  include/linux/blkdev.h   459
request_region
  include/linux/ioport.h   431
request_resource
  kernel/resource.c   431
reschedule_idle
  kernel/sched.c   363
RESCHEDULE_VECTOR
  include/asm-i386/hw_irq.h   144
resource
  include/linux/ioport.h   430
__restore_flags
  include/asm-i386/system.h   180
restore_flags
  include/asm-i386/system.h   182
restore_fpu
  arch/i386/kernel/i387.c   99
restore_sigcontext
  arch/i386/kernel/signal.c   340

ret_from_exception
  arch/i386/kernel/entry.S   156
ret_from_fork
  arch/i386/kernel/entry.S   104, 157
ret_from_intr
  arch/i386/kernel/entry.S   156
ret_from_sys_call
  arch/i386/kernel/entry.S   157
RISCOM8_BH
  include/linux/interrupt.h   154
rlimit
  include/linux/resource.h   89
RLIMIT_AS
  include/asm-i386/resource.h   88
RLIMIT_CORE
  include/asm-i386/resource.h   88
RLIMIT_CPU
  include/asm-i386/resource.h   88
RLIMIT_DATA
  include/asm-i386/resource.h   88
RLIMIT_FSIZE
  include/asm-i386/resource.h   88
RLIMIT_INFINITY
  include/asm-i386/resource.h   89
RLIMIT_LOCKS
  include/asm-i386/resource.h   88
RLIMIT_MEMLOCK
  include/asm-i386/resource.h   88
RLIMIT_NOFILE
  include/asm-i386/resource.h   88
RLIMIT_NPROC
  include/asm-i386/resource.h   89
RLIMIT_RSS
  include/asm-i386/resource.h   89
RLIMIT_STACK
  include/asm-i386/resource.h   89
rmb()
  include/asm-i386/system.h   167
rmqueue
  mm/page_alloc.c   236
rm_sig_from_queue
  kernel/signal.c   329
ROOT_DEV
  fs/super.c   399
root_mountflags
  init/main.c   399
root_vfsmnt
  fs/namespace.c   400
RQ_ACTIVE
  include/linux/blkdev.h   456
RQ_INACTIVE
  include/linux/blkdev.h   456

rtable
    include/net/route.h   616
rt_hash_table
    net/ipv4/route.c   616
rt_sigframe
    arch/i386/kernel/signal.c   339
run_task_queue
    include/linux/tqueue.h   155
run_timer_list
    kernel/timer.c   210
rwlock_init
    include/asm-i386/spinlock.h   171
rwlock_t
    include/asm-i386/spinlock.h   170
rw_semaphore
    include/asm-i386/rwsem.h   178
rwsem_waiter
    lib/rwsem.c   178
rw_swap_page
    mm/page_io.c   549
rw_swap_page_base
    mm/page_io.c   549
rw_swap_page_nolock
    mm/page_io.c   551

S

__s16
    include/asm-i386/types.h   578
__s32
    include/asm-i386/types.h   578
__s8
    include/asm-i386/types.h   578
SA_INTERRUPT
    include/asm-i386/signal.h   135
SA_NOCLDSTOP
    include/asm-i386/signal.h   325
SA_NODEFER
    include/asm-i386/signal.h   325
SA_NOMASK
    include/asm-i386/signal.h   325
SA_ONESHOT
    include/asm-i386/signal.h   325
SA_ONSTACK
    include/asm-i386/signal.h   325
SA_RESETHAND
    include/asm-i386/signal.h   325
SA_RESTART
    include/asm-i386/signal.h   325
SA_SAMPLE_RANDOM
    include/asm-i386/signal.h   135
SA_SHIRQ
    include/asm-i386/signal.h   135

SA_SIGINFO
    include/asm-i386/signal.h   325
SAVE_ALL
    include/asm-i386/hw_irq.h   137
__save_flags
    include/asm-i386/system.h   180
save_flags
    include/asm-i386/system.h   182
save_init_fpu
    arch/i386/kernel/i387.c   98
save_v86_state
    arch/i386/kernel/vm86.c   159
sb_lock
    fs/super.c   379
scan_swap_map
    mm/swapfile.c   543
SCHED_FIFO
    include/linux/sched.h   353
SCHED_OTHER
    include/linux/sched.h   354
SCHED_RR
    include/linux/sched.h   354
schedule
    kernel/sched.c   355
schedule_data
    kernel/sched.c   355
__schedule_tail
    kernel/sched.c   361
schedule_task
    kernel/context.c   156
schedule_timeout
    kernel/sched.c   212
SCHED_YIELD
    include/linux/sched.h   354
scm_cookie
    include/net/scm.h   625
scm_destroy
    include/net/scm.h   625
scm_send
    include/net/scm.h   625
SCSI_BH
    include/linux/interrupt.h   154
search_binary_handler
    fs/exec.c   679
search_exception_table
    arch/i386/mm/extable.c   314
segment_not_present
    arch/i386/kernel/entry.S   117
SEGV_ACCERR
    include/asm-i386/siginfo.h   289
SEGV_MAPERR
    include/asm-i386/siginfo.h   289

sem
  include/linux/sem.h   651

semaphore
  include/asm-i386/semaphore.h   173

semaphore_lock
  arch/i386/kernel/semaphore.c   176

sem_array
  include/linux/sem.h   650

sem_ids
  ipc/sem.c   650

sem_queue
  include/linux/sem.h   652

SEM_UNDO
  include/linux/sem.h   651

sem_undo
  include/linux/sem.h   651

send_IPI_all
  arch/i386/kernel/smp.c   145

send_IPI_allbutself
  arch/i386/kernel/smp.c   145

send_IPI_mask
  arch/i386/kernel/smp.c   145

send_IPI_self
  arch/i386/kernel/smp.c   145

send_sig
  kernel/signal.c   332

send_sig_info
  kernel/signal.c   328

send_signal
  kernel/signal.c   330

SERIAL_BH
  include/linux/interrupt.h   154

set_bit
  include/asm-i386/bitops.h   166

set_current_state
  include/linux/sched.h   76

set_fixmap
  include/asm-i386/fixmap.h   68

set_fixmap_nocache
  include/asm-i386/fixmap.h   68

set_fs
  include/asm-i386/uaccess.h   311

set_intr_gate
  arch/i386/kernel/traps.c   123

SET_LINKS
  include/linux/sched.h   79

SetPageActive
  include/linux/mm.h   219

SetPageChecked
  include/linux/mm.h   219

SetPageDecrAfter
  include/linux/mm.h   219

SetPageDirty
  include/linux/mm.h   219

set_page_dirty
  mm/pagemap.c   554

SetPageError
  include/linux/mm.h   219

SetPageReferenced
  include/linux/mm.h   219

SetPageReserved
  include/linux/mm.h   219

SetPageUptodate
  include/linux/mm.h   219

set_pgd
  include/asm-i386/pgtable.h   59

set_pmd
  include/asm-i386/pgtable.h   59

set_pte
  include/asm-i386/pgtable.h   59

set_rtc_mmss
  arch/i386/kernel/time.c   198

set_system_gate
  arch/i386/kernel/traps.c   123

set_task_state
  include/linux/sched.h   76

set_trap_gate
  arch/i386/kernel/traps.c   123

setup
  arch/i386/boot/setup.S   688

setup_APIC_clocks
  arch/i386/kernel/apic.c   200

setup_APIC_timer
  arch/i386/kernel/apic.c   200

setup_arg_pages
  fs/exec.c   681

setup_frame
  arch/i386/kernel/signal.c   337

setup_idt
  arch/i386/kernel/head.S   124

setup_IO_APIC_irqs
  arch/i386/kernel/io_apic.c   136

setup_irq
  arch/i386/kernel/irq.c   143

setup_local_APIC
  arch/i386/kernel/apic.c   136

setup_memory_region
  arch/i386/kernel/setup.c   62

setup_rt_frame
  arch/i386/kernel/signal.c   339

shmem_inode_info
  include/linux/shmem_fs.h   659

shmem_unuse
  mm/shmem.c   541

shmem_writepage
  mm/shmem.c   659
shmid_kernel
  ipc/shm.c   657
shm_ids
  ipc/shm.c   656
shm_mmap
  ipc/shm.c   658
shm_nopage
  mm/shmem.c   659
shrink_cache
  mm/vmscan.c   567
shrink_caches
  mm/vmscan.c   565
shrink_dcache_memory
  fs/dcache.c   570
shrink_icache_memory
  fs/inode.c   571
shutdown_8259A_irq
  arch/i386/kernel/i8259.c   134
S_IFIFO
  include/linux/stat.h   643
SIGABRT
  include/asm-i386/signal.h   319
sigaction
  include/asm-i386/signal.h   324
sigaddset
  include/linux/signal.h   326
sigaddsetmask
  include/linux/signal.h   326
SIGALRM
  include/asm-i386/signal.h   216, 319
sigandsets
  include/linux/signal.h   327
SIG_BLOCK
  include/asm-i386/signal.h   345
SIGBUS
  include/asm-i386/signal.h   319
SIGCHLD
  include/asm-i386/signal.h   100, 319
SIGCONT
  include/asm-i386/signal.h   319
sigcontext
  include/asm-i386/sigcontext.h   338
sigdelset
  include/linux/signal.h   326
sigdelsetmask
  include/linux/signal.h   326
SIG_DFL
  include/asm-i386/signal.h   324
sigemptyset
  include/linux/signal.h   326

sigfillset
  include/linux/signal.h   326
SIGFPE
  include/asm-i386/signal.h   319
sigframe
  arch/i386/kernel/signal.c   337
SIGHUP
  include/asm-i386/signal.h   319
SIG_IGN
  include/asm-i386/signal.h   324
SIGILL
  include/asm-i386/signal.h   319
siginfo_t
  include/asm-i386/siginfo.h   325
siginitset
  include/linux/signal.h   327
siginitsetinv
  include/linux/signal.h   327
SIGINT
  include/asm-i386/signal.h   319
SIGIO
  include/asm-i386/signal.h   319
SIGIOT
  include/asm-i386/signal.h   319
sigismeber
  include/linux/signal.h   326
SIGKILL
  include/asm-i386/signal.h   319
sigmask
  include/linux/signal.h   327
signal_pending
  include/linux/sched.h   327
signal_struct
  include/linux/sched.h   324
signal_wake_up
  kernel/signal.c   331
signandsets
  include/linux/signal.h   327
sigorsets
  include/linux/signal.h   327
sigpending
  include/linux/signal.h   325
SIGPIPE
  include/asm-i386/signal.h   319
SIGPOLL
  include/asm-i386/signal.h   319
SIGPROF
  include/asm-i386/signal.h   216, 319
SIGPWR
  include/asm-i386/signal.h   319
sigqueue
  include/linux/signal.h   325

SIGQUIT
  include/asm-i386/signal.h   319
SIGSEGV
  include/asm-i386/signal.h   319
SIG_SETMASK
  include/asm-i386/signal.h   346
sigset_t
  include/asm-i386/signal.h   323
SIGSTKFLT   319
  include/asm-i386/signal.h   319
SIGSTOP
  include/asm-i386/signal.h   75, 319
SIGSYS   319
  include/asm-i386/signal.h   319
SIGTERM
  include/asm-i386/signal.h   319
sigtestsetmask
  include/linux/signal.h   327
SIGTRAP
  include/asm-i386/signal.h   319
SIGTSTP
  include/asm-i386/signal.h   75, 319
SIGTTIN
  include/asm-i386/signal.h   75, 319
SIGTTOU
  include/asm-i386/signal.h   75, 319
SIG_UNBLOCK
  include/asm-i386/signal.h   346
SIGUNUSED
  include/asm-i386/signal.h   319
SIGURG
  include/asm-i386/signal.h   319
SIGUSR1
  include/asm-i386/signal.h   319
SIGUSR2
  include/asm-i386/signal.h   319
SIGVTALRM
  include/asm-i386/signal.h   216, 319
SIGWINCH
  include/asm-i386/signal.h   319
SIGXCPU
  include/asm-i386/signal.h   88, 319
SIGXFSZ
  include/asm-i386/signal.h   88, 319
simd_coprocessor_error
  arch/i386/kernel/entry.S   118
size_buffers_type
  fs/buffer.c   485
skb_recv_datagram
  net/core/datagram.c   631
sk_buff
  include/linux/skbuff.h   618

SLAB_HWCACHE_ALIGN
  include/linux/slab.h   248
slab_s
  mm/slab.c   243
slab_t
  mm/slab.c   243
sleep_on
  kernel/sched.c   86
sleep_on_timeout
  kernel/sched.c   86
smp_apic_timer_interrupt
  arch/i386/kernel/apic.c   202
smp_call_function
  arch/i386/kernel/smp.c   144
smp_call_function_interrupt
  arch/i386/kernel/smp.c   145
smp_invalidate_interrupt
  arch/i386/kernel/smp.c   145
smp_local_timer_interrupt
  arch/i386/kernel/apic.c   202
smp_mb()
  include/asm-i386/system.h   167
smp_processor_id
  include/asm-i386/smp.h   94
smp_reschedule_interrupt
  arch/i386/kernel/smp.c   145
smp_rmb()
  include/asm-i386/system.h   167
smp_wmb()
  include/asm-i386/system.h   167
sock
  include/net/sock.h   611
sock_alloc_send_skb
  net/core/sock.c   626
sock_def_readable
  net/core/sock.c   631
SOCK_DGRAM
  include/asm-i386/socket.h   620
socket
  include/linux/net.h   610
sock_queue_rcv_skb
  include/net/sock.h   631
SOCK_RAW
  include/asm-i386/socket.h   620
SOCK_RDM
  include/asm-i386/socket.h   620
sock_read
  net/socket.c   631
sock_recvmsg
  net/socket.c   631
SOCK_SEQPACKET
  include/asm-i386/socket.h   620

SOCK_STREAM
    include/asm-i386/socket.h   620
sock_write
    net/socket.c   625
softirq_action
    include/linux/interrupt.h   148
softirq_pending
    include/linux/irq_cpustat.h   148
softirq_vec
    kernel/softirq.c   148
SPECIALIX_BH
    include/linux/interrupt.h   154
spin_is_locked
    include/asm-i386/spinlock.h   169
spin_lock
    include/asm-i386/spinlock.h   169
spin_lock_init
    include/asm-i386/spinlock.h   169
spin_lock_irq
    include/linux/spinlock.h   187
spin_lock_irqsave
    include/linux/spinlock.h   187
spinlock_t
    include/asm-i386/spinlock.h   168
spin_trylock
    include/asm-i386/spinlock.h   169
spin_unlock
    include/asm-i386/spinlock.h   170
spin_unlock_irq
    include/linux/spinlock.h   187
spin_unlock_irqrestore
    include/linux/spinlock.h   187
spin_unlock_wait
    include/asm-i386/spinlock.h   169
SPURIOUS_APIC_VECTOR
    include/asm-i386/hw_irq.h   145
SS_CONNECTED
    include/linux/net.h   611
SS_CONNECTING
    include/linux/net.h   611
SS_DISCONNECTING
    include/linux/net.h   611
SS_FREE
    include/linux/net.h   611
SS_UNCONNECTED
    include/linux/net.h   611
stack_segment
    arch/i386/kernel/entry.S   117
start_kernel
    init/main.c   691
start_thread
    include/asm-i386/processor.h   682

startup_32
    arch/i386/boot/compressed/head.S   689
    arch/i386/kernel/head.S   690
startup_8259A_irq
    arch/i386/kernel/i8259.c   134
__sti()
    include/asm-i386/system.h   180
sti()
    include/asm-i386/system.h   182
strlen_user
    include/asm-i386/uaccess.h   312
__strncpy_from_user
    arch/i386/lib/usercopy.c   312
strncpy_from_user
    arch/i386/lib/usercopy.c   312
strnlen_user
    arch/i386/lib/usercopy.c   312
stts()
    include/asm-i386/system.h   98
super_block
    include/linux/fs.h   378
super_blocks
    fs/super.c   379
super_operations
    include/linux/fs.h   379
SWAP_CLUSTER_MAX
    include/linux/swap.h   552
swap_duplicate
    mm/swapfile.c   536
SWAPFILE_CLUSTER
    mm/swapfile.c   542
SWAP_FLAG_PREFER
    include/linux/swap.h   537
swap_free
    mm/swapfile.c   544
swap_header
    include/linux/swap.h   532
swap_info
    mm/swapfile.c   534
swap_info_struct
    include/linux/swap.h   533
swapin_readahead
    mm/memory.c   557
swap_list
    mm/swapfile.c   534
swap_list_t
    include/linux/swap.h   534
swaplock
    mm/swapfile.c   535
SWAP_MAP_BAD
    include/linux/swap.h   533

SWAP_MAP_MAX
    include/linux/swap.h   533
swap_mm
    mm/vmscan.c   552
swap_out
    mm/vmscan.c   552
swap_out_mm
    mm/vmscan.c   552
swap_out_pgd
    mm/vmscan.c   553
swap_out_pmd
    mm/vmscan.c   553
swap_out_vma
    mm/vmscan.c   553
swapper_pg_dir
    arch/i386/kernel/head.S   64
swapper_space
    mm/swap_state.c   547
swap_writepage
    mm/swap_state.c   556
__switch_to
    arch/i386/kernel/process.c   94
switch_to
    include/asm-i386/system.h   92
SWP_ENTRY
    include/asm-i386/pgtable.h   535
SWP_OFFSET
    include/asm-i386/pgtable.h   535
SWP_TYPE
    include/asm-i386/pgtable.h   535
SWP_USED
    include/linux/swap.h   533
SWP_WRITEOK
    include/mm/swap.h   533
sync_buffers
    fs/buffer.c   495, 523
synchronize_irq
    arch/i386/kernel/irq.c   183
sync_inodes
    fs/inode.c   495
sync_old_buffers
    fs/buffer.c   494
sync_supers
    fs/super.c   494
sync_unlocked_inodes
    fs/inode.c   494
sys_adjtimex
    kernel/time.c   215
sys_alarm
    kernel/timer.c   216
sys_bdflush
    fs/buffer.c   491

sys_bind
    net/socket.c   622
sys_brk
    mm/mmap.c   301
sys_call_table
    arch/i386/kernel/entry.S   305
syscall_trace
    arch/i386/kernel/ptrace.c   307
sys_capget
    kernel/capability.c   666
sys_capset
    kernel/capability.c   666
sys_close
    fs/open.c   419
sys_create_module
    kernel/module.c   697
sys_delete_module
    kernel/module.c   698
sys_dup
    fs/fcntl.c   393
sys_execve
    arch/i386/kernel/process.c   679
sys_fcntl
    fs/fcntl.c   393
sys_flock
    fs/locks.c   423
sys_fork
    arch/i386/kernel/process.c   101
sys_fsync
    fs/buffer.c   496
sys_getpid
    kernel/timer.c   77
sys_getpriority
    kernel/sys.c   368
sys_getrlimit
    kernel/sys.c   89
sys_gettimeofday
    kernel/time.c   214
sys_init_module
    kernel/module.c   698
sys_ipc
    arch/i386/kernel/sys_i386.c   648
sys_kill
    kernel/signal.c   343
sys_lseek
    fs/read_write.c   378
sys_madvise
    mm/filemap.c   520
sys_mknod
    fs/namei.c   438, 643
sys_mlock
    mm/mlock.c   88

sys_mlockall
   mm/mlock.c   88, 280
sys_mmap2
   arch/i386/kernel/sys_i386.c   517
sys_modify_ldt
   arch/i386/kernel/ldt.c   41
sys_mount
   fs/namespace.c   403
sys_msync
   mm/filemap.c   522
sys_munmap
   mm/mmap.c   518
sys_nice
   kernel/sched.c   368
sys_ni_syscall
   linux/kernel/sys.c   306
sys_open
   fs/open.c   416
sys_personality
   linux/kernel/exec_domain.c   677
sys_pipe
   arch/i386/kernel/sys_i386.c   637
sys_prctl
   kernel/sys.c   667
sys_ptrace
   arch/i386/kernel/ptrace.c   672
sys_query_module
   kernel/module.c   697
sys_read
   fs/read_write.c   419
sys_recvfrom
   net/socket.c   623
sys_recvmsg
   net/socket.c   623
sys_rt_sigaction
   kernel/signal.c   347
sys_rt_sigpending
   kernel/signal.c   347
sys_rt_sigprocmask
   kernel/signal.c   347
sys_rt_sigqueueinfo
   kernel/signal.c   347
sys_rt_sigreturn
   arch/i386/kernel/signal.c   340
sys_rt_sigsuspend
   arch/i386/kernel/signal.c   347
sys_rt_sigtimedwait
   kernel/signal.c   347
sys_sched_getparam
   kernel/sched.c   370
sys_sched_get_priority_max
   kernel/sched.c   371

sys_sched_get_priority_min
   kernel/sched.c   371
sys_sched_getscheduler
   kernel/sched.c   369
sys_sched_rr_get_interval
   kernel/sched.c   371
sys_sched_setparam
   kernel/sched.c   370
sys_sched_setscheduler
   kernel/sched.c   369
sys_sched_yield
   kernel/sched.c   370
sys_sendmsg
   net/socket.c   623
sys_sendto
   net/socket.c   623
sys_sctfsgid
   kernel/sys.c   664
sys_setfsuid
   kernel/sys.c   664
sys_setgid
   kernel/sys.c   664
sys_setitimer
   kernel/itimer.c   216
sys_setpriority
   kernel/sys.c   368
sys_setregid
   kernel/sys.c   664
sys_setresgid
   kernel/sys.c   664
sys_setresuid
   kernel/sys.c   664
sys_setreuid
   kernel/sys.c   664
sys_setrlimit
   kernel/sys.c   89
sys_settimeofday
   kernel/time.c   215
sys_setuid
   kernel/sys.c   664
sys_sigaction
   arch/i386/kernel/signal.c   344
sys_signal
   kernel/signal.c   345
sys_sigpending
   kernel/signal.c   345
sys_sigprocmask
   kernel/signal.c   345
sys_sigreturn
   arch/i386/kernel/signal.c   340
sys_sigsuspend
   arch/i386/kernel/signal.c   346

sys_socket
    net/socket.c   620
sys_swapoff
    mm/swapfile.c   538
sys_swapon
    mm/swapfile.c   536
sys_sync
    fs/buffer.c   495
system_call
    arch/i386/kernel/entry.S   306
sys_umount
    fs/namespace.c   406
sys_uselib
    fs/exec.c   675
sys_vfork
    arch/i386/kernel/process.c   101
sys_write
    fs/read_write.c   419

T

TASK_INTERRUPTIBLE
    include/linux/sched.h   75
tasklet_action
    kernel/softirq.c   153
tasklet_disable
    include/linux/interrupt.h   152
tasklet_disable_nosync
    include/linux/interrupt.h   152
tasklet_enable
    include/linux/interrupt.h   152
tasklet_head
    include/linux/interrupt.h   151
tasklet_hi_action
    kernel/softirq.c   153
tasklet_hi_schedule
    include/linux/interrupt.h   152
tasklet_hi_vec
    kernel/softirq.c   151
tasklet_init
    kernel/softirq.c   152
tasklet_schedule
    include/linux/interrupt.h   152
TASKLET_SOFTIRQ
    include/linux/interrupt.h   148
TASKLET_STATE_RUN
    include/linux/interrupt.h   152
TASKLET_STATE_SCHED
    include/linux/interrupt.h   152
tasklet_struct
    include/linux/interrupt.h   151

tasklet_vec
    kernel/softirq.c   151
task_on_runqueue
    include/linux/sched.h   81
TASK_RUNNING
    include/linux/sched.h   75
TASK_SIZE
    include/asm-i386/processor.h   267
TASK_STOPPED
    include/linux/sched.h   75
task_struct
    include/linux/sched.h   74
TASK_UNINTERRUPTIBLE
    include/linux/sched.h   75
task_union
    include/linux/sched.h   77
TASK_ZOMBIE
    include/linux/sched.h   75
tcp_recvmsg
    net/ipv4/tcp.c   631
tcp_v4_rcv
    net/ipv4/tcp_ipv4.c   630
test_and_change_bit
    include/asm-i386/bitops.h   166
test_and_clear_bit
    include/asm-i386/bitops.h   166
TestandClearPageActive
    include/linux/mm.h   219
test_and_set_bit
    include/asm-i386/bitops.h   166
TestandSetPageActive
    include/linux/mm.h   219
test_bit
    include/asm-i386/bitops.h   166
T_FINISHED
    include/linux/jbd.h   605
thread_struct
    include/asm-i386/processor.h   92
tick
    kernel/timer.c   195
time_after
    include/linux/timer.h   207
time_after_eq
    include/linux/timer.h   207
time_before
    include/linux/timer.h   207
time_before_eq
    include/linux/timer.h   207
time_init
    arch/i386/kernel/time.c   203
timer_bh
    kernel/timer.c   199

timer_interrupt
  arch/i386/kernel/time.c   198
timer_jiffies
  kernel/timer.c   210
timer_list
  include/linux/timer.h   207
timerlist_lock
  kernel/timer.c   209
timer_vec
  kernel/timer.c   210
timer_vec_root
  kernel/timer.c   209
timeval
  include/linux/time.h   203
timex
  include/linux/timex.h   215
TLBSTATE_LAZY
  include/asm-i386/pgalloc.h   71
TLBSTATE_OK
  include/asm-i386/pgalloc.h   71
T_LOCKED
  include/linux/jbd.h   605
total_swap_pages
  mm/swapfile.c   535
tq_context
  kernel/context.c   156
tq_disk
  drivers/block/ll_rw_blk.c   463
tq_immediate
  kernel/timer.c   155
tq_struct
  include/linux/tqueue.h   155
tq_timer
  kernel/timer.c   156
TQUEUE_BH
  include/linux/interrupt.h   156
transaction_t
  include/linux/jbd.h   604
trap_init
  arch/i386/kernel/traps.c   125
T_RUNNING
  include/linux/jbd.h   605
TryLockPage
  include/linux/mm.h   219
try_to_free_buffers
  fs/buffer.c   489
try_to_free_pages
  mm/vmscan.c   564
try_to_release_page
  fs/buffer.c   569

try_to_swap_out
  mm/vmscan.c   553
try_to_sync_unused_inodes
  fs/inode.c   571
try_to_unuse
  mm/swapfile.c   539
tss_struct
  include/asm-i386/processor.h   91
tv1
  kernel/timer.c   209
tv2
  kernel/timer.c   210
tv3
  kernel/timer.c   210
tv4
  kernel/timer.c   210
tv5
  kernel/timer.c   210
tvecs
  kernel/timer.c   209

U

__u16
  include/asm-i386/types.h   578
__u32
  include/asm-i386/types.h   578
__u8
  include/asm-i386/types.h   578
udp_connect
  net/ipv4/udp.c   624
udp_getfrag
  net/ipv4/udp.c   626
udp_getfrag_nosum
  net/ipv4/udp.c   626
udp_prot
  net/ipv4/udp.c   625
udp_queue_rcv_skb
  net/ipv4/udp.c   631
udp_rcv
  net/ipv4/udp.c   630
udp_recvmsg
  net/ipv4/udp.c   631
udp_sendmsg
  net/ipv4/udp.c   625
udp_v4_get_port
  net/ipv4/udp.c   623
udp_v4_lookup
  net/ipv4/udp.c   630
umount_tree
  fs/namespace.c   406
undoable IPC semaphore operation   649

unhash_pid
  include/linux/sched.h   83
unhash_process
  include/linux/sched.h   108
unlazy_fpu
  include/asm-i386/i387.h   98
unlock_kernel
  include/asm-i386/smplock.h   190
unmap_fixup
  mm/mmap.c   284
unmap_kiobuf
  mm/memory.c   526
unmap_underlying_metadata
  fs/buffer.c   512
unnamed_dev_in_use
  fs/super.c   395
unregister_binfmt
  fs/exec.c   675
unregister_blkdev
  fs/block_dev.c   445
unregister_chrdev
  fs/devices.c   445
unregister_filesystem
  fs/super.c   396
unused_list
  fs/buffer.c   483
unused_list_lock
  fs/buffer.c   483
unuse_process
  mm/swapfile.c   541
__up
  arch/i386/kernel/semaphore.c   174
up
  include/asm-i386/semaphore.h   174
update_atime
  fs/inode.c   501
update_one_process
  kernel/timer.c   204
update_process_times
  kernel/timer.c   202, 204
update_times
  kernel/timer.c   203
update_wall_time
  kernel/timer.c   204
update_wall_time_one_tick
  kernel/timer.c   204
up_read
  include/linux/rwsem.h   178
up_write
  include/linux/rwsem.h   178

__USER_CS
  include/asm-i386/segment.h   42
__USER_DS
  include/asm-i386/segment.h   42
user_struct
  include/linux/sched.h   102

V

__va
  include/asm-i386/page.h   65
verify_area
  include/asm-i386/uaccess.h   310
vfree
  mm/vmalloc.c   260
vfs_follow_link
  fs/namei.c   415
vfsmntlist
  fs/namespace.c   398
vfsmount
  include/linux/mount.h   398
vfs_permission
  fs/namei.c   410
virt_to_bus
  include/asm-i386/io.h   436
vma_link
  mm/mmap.c   278
VM_ALLOC
  incliude/linux/vmalloc.h   258
vmalloc
  include/linux/vmalloc.h   258
vmalloc_area_pages
  mm/vmalloc.c   258
VMALLOC_END
  include/asm-i386/pgtable.h   257
VMALLOC_OFFSET
  include/asm-i386/pgtable.h   256
VMALLOC_START
  include/asm-i386/pgtable.h   257
vma_merge
  mm/mmap.c   281
vm_area_struct
  include/linux/mm.h   268
__vma_unlink
  include/linux/mm.h   278
VM_DENYWRITE
  include/linux/mm.h   274
VM_DONTCOPY
  include/linux/mm.h   274
VM_DONTEXPAND
  include/linux/mm.h   274

vm_enough_memory
  mm/mmap.c   281
VM_EXEC
  include/linux/mm.h   273
VM_EXECUTABLE
  include/linux/mm.h   274
vmfree_area_pages
  mm/vmalloc.c   261
VM_GROWSDOWN
  include/linux/mm.h   274
VM_GROWSUP
  include/linux/mm.h   274
VM_IO
  include/linux/mm.h   274
vmlist
  mm/vmalloc.c   257
vmlist_lock
  mm/vmalloc.c   257
VM_LOCKED
  include/linux/mm.h   274
vm_max_readahead
  mm/filemap.c   507
VM_MAYEXEC
  include/linux/mm.h   273
VM_MAYREAD
  include/linux/mm.h   273
VM_MAYSHARE
  include/linux/mm.h   273
VM_MAYWRITE
  include/linux/mm.h   273
vm_min_readahead
  mm/filemap.c   507
vm_operations_struct
  include/linux/mm.h   269
VM_RAND_READ
  include/linux/mm.h   274, 520
VM_READ
  include/linux/mm.h   273
VM_RESERVED
  include/linux/mm.h   274
VM_SEQ_READ
  include/linux/mm.h   274, 521
VM_SHARED
  include/linux/mm.h   273
VM_SHM
  include/linux/mm.h   274
vm_struct
  include/linux/vmalloc.h   257
VM_WRITE
  include/linux/mm.h   273

W

wait_event
  include/linux/sched.h   86
wait_event_interruptible
  include/linux/sched.h   86
wait_for_completion
  kernel/sched.c   179
wait_for_some_buffers
  fs/buffer.c   493
wait_on_buffer
  include/linux/locks.h   469
waitqueue_active
  include/linux/wait.h   85
wait_queue_head_t
  include/linux/wait.h   84
wait_queue_t
  include/linux/wait.h   85
wake_up
  include/linux/sched.h   87
wake_up_all
  include/linux/sched.h   87
wakeup_bdflush
  fs/buffer.c   492
wake_up_interruptible
  include/linux/sched.h   87
wake_up_interruptible_all
  include/linux/sched.h   87
wake_up_interruptible_nr
  include/linux/sched.h   87
wake_up_interruptible_sync
  include/linux/sched.h   87
wake_up_interruptible_sync_nr
  include/linux/sched.h   87
wake_up_nr
  include/linux/sched.h   87
wake_up_process
  kernel/sched.c   81
wake_up_sync
  include/linux/sched.h   87
wake_up_sync_nr
  include/linux/sched.h   87
wall_jiffies
  kernel/timer.c   204
wmb()
  include/asm-i386/system.h   167
writeb
  include/asm-i386/io.h   435
writel
  include/asm-i386/io.h   435
write_lock
  include/asm-i386/spinlock.h   171

__write_lock_failed
arch/i386/kernel/semaphore.c 172
write_lock_irq
include/linux/spinlock.h 187
write_lock_irqsave
include/linux/spinlock.h 187
write_pipe_fops
fs/pipe.c 640
write_some_buffers
fs/buffer.c 493
write_unlock_irq
include/linux/spinlock.h 187
write_unlock_irqrestore
include/linux/spinlock.h 187
writew
include/asm-i386/io.h 435

X

x86_do_profile
include/asm-i386/hw_irq.h 205
xtime
kernel/timer.c 203
xtime_lock
kernel/timer.c 200

Z

zap_low_mappings
arch/i386/mm/init.c 66
zap_page_range
mm/memory.c 284
zap_pmd_range
mm/memory.c 284
zap_pte_range
mm/memory.c 284
ZERO_PAGE
include/asm-i386/pgtable.h 294
ZONE_DMA
include/linux/mmzone.h 220

ZONE_HIGHMEM
include/linux/mmzone.h 220
zonelist_struct
include/linux/mmzone.h 221
zonelist_t
include/linux/mmzone.h 221
zone_names
mm/page_alloc.c 221
ZONE_NORMAL
include/linux/mmzone.h 220
zone_struct
include/linux/mmzone.h 220
zone_t
include/linux/mmzone.h 220

Index

Symbols

. (period) and ..(double period) notation, 13

Numbers

80 x 86 processors, x
    clocks, 194
    exceptions, 115
    I/O architecture, 427–437
    memory, 222
    Task State Segment, 90
802.3 standard, 616

A

aborts, 112
absolute pathnames, 13
Accelerated Graphics Port (AGP), 434
access rights, 15
ACLs (access control lists), 576
active lists, 561
active swap areas, 532
active transactions, 605
address buses, 427
address resolution, 668
Address Resolution Protocol (ARP), 617
address spaces, 10, 264
    creating, 298
    deleting, 300
addresses, 34
address_space objects, 476–478
    page descriptors, 479
adjacent bytes, 449
Advanced Power Management (APM), 43

Advanced Programmable Interrupt
        Controllers (see APICs)
advisory file locks, 420
AGP (Accelerated Graphics Port), 434
alignment factors, 248
anonymous mapping, 294
APICs (Advanced Programmable Interrupt
        Controllers), 113
    CPU local timer, 196
    local, interrupt handlers for, 201
    timers, synchronization, 200
APM (Advanced Power Management), 43
arch directory, 6
ARP (Address Resolution Protocol), 617
arp cache, 617
Assembler OUTput executable format
        (a out), 674
asynchronous buffer heads, 483
asynchronous interrupts, 109
asynchronous notifications, 26
asynchronous read-ahead operations, 506,
        509
atomic operation handles, 603
atomic operations, 23, 164–166
AVL tree, 271

B

base priority, 353
base time quanta, 352
batch processes, 349
bdflush kernel thread, 491–493
big kernel locks (BKLs), 190
big reader read/write spin locks, 172

We'd like to hear your suggestions for improving our indexes. Send email to *index@oreilly.com*.

BIOS, 685
    bootstrap process, 686
    Real Mode addressing, usage of, 686
bitmap, 234
bitmap caches, 586–588
block clustering, 464
block device descriptors, 450
block device drivers, 449–471
    architecture, 455–460
        low-level driver descriptors, 460
        request descriptors, 456
        request queue descriptors, 459
    block I/O operations, 469
    blocks, 453
    buffers, 453
        buffer heads, 453–455
    data structures for, 450
    default file operation methods, 451
    initializing, 451
    kernel, monitoring by, 450
    low-level request handling, 465–468
    page I/O operations, 469–471
    requesting function, 461–465
    sectors, 452
    (see also I/O devices)
block device files, 437
    prepare_write and commit_write
        methods, 513
block device inode, 451
block device request, 456
block fragmentation, 576
block group, 577
block I/O operation, 468
blocked signals, 321
    modifying, 345
blocks, 453
    filetypes, usage by, 582–584
    preallocation, 575
bootstrap, 685
bottom halves, 110, 146, 153–156
    imminent obsolescence of, 146
    TIMER_BH bottom half, 199
BSD sockets, 610
    methods, 611
bss segments, 670
buddy system algorithm, 233–239
    blocks, allocation of, 235
        freeing of, 238
    data structures, 234
    example, 233
    slab allocator and, 245

buffer caches, 474, 481–496
    bdflush kernel thread, 491–493
    buffer head data structures, 482–487
    buffer pages, 487–490
    dirty buffers, flushing to disk, 495
    dirty buffers, writing to disk, 490
    get_blk function, 490
    I/O operations, usage by, 475
    kupdate kernel thread, 493–495
buffer heads, 453
    for cached buffers, 482
    unused buffer heads, 482
buffer pages, 487–490
buffers, 453
bus addresses, 436
bus mouse interface, 432
buses, 427
Busy bit, 91

C

cache controllers, 52
    write-through and write-back, 53
cache descriptors, 242
cache entry tags, 52
cache hits, 52
cache lines, 52
cache misses, 52
cache snooping, 53
caches, 52–54, 241
    allocating slabs to, 245
    slabs, releasing from, 246
    types of, 243
character device drivers, 471–473
character device files, 437
child filesystems, 397
clocks, 194–202
Code Segment Descriptors, 37
code segment registers, 36
Columbus Unix, 645
command-line arguments, 661, 667
commit_write method, 511–513
common file model, 374–377
    object types, 375
completions, 179
concurrency level, 184
context switch, 89
control buses, 428
control registers, 44, 429
Copy On Write (see COW)
core dump, 26
COW (Copy On Write), 295–297

CPL (Current Privilege Level), 36, 120
  segment updating and, 43
CPU local timer, 196
CPU resource limit, 204
CPU-bound processes, 349
cr0 control register, 44
cr3 control register, 45
critical regions, 23, 163
current macro, 78
Current Privilege Level (see CPL)
current working directory, 13
custom I/O interfaces, 431, 432

D

data buses, 427
Data Segment Descriptors, 37
data segment registers, 36
dates, updating by the kernel, 203
deadlocked state, 25
default routers, 614
defective page slots, 533
deferrable functions, 146
  activation of, 147
  disabling, 183
  execution of, 147
  initialization of, 147
  operations performed on, 147
demand paging, 31, 292–295
  limitations, 559
  for memory mapping, 519–521
dentry
  caches, 376
  objects, 376, 389–392
  operations, 391
dependencies, 696
Descriptor Privilege Level (DPL), 38, 120
destination caches, 612
devfs device files, 437, 439
device controllers, 433–436
device drivers, 32, 441–449
  buffering strategies, 443
  IRQ-configuration, 131
  registering, 445
  resource functions, 431
  (see also I/O devices)
device files, 437–441
  examples, 438
  Virtual Filesystem, handling by, 440
device plugging, 463
device unplugging, 464
direct access buffers, 524

direct I/O transfers, 523–527
  direct access buffers, 524
direct mapped caches, 52
Direct Memory Access Controller (see
      DMAC)
directories, 583
dirty buffers, writing to disk, 490
disk caches, 376, 474–496
  buffer caches (see buffer caches)
  page caches (see page caches)
disk controllers, 433
disk interface, 432
disk-based filesystems, 373
  write methods of, 509–511
displacement of a logical address, 34
DMAC (Direct Memory Access
      Controller), 436–437
doubly linked lists, 80
  runqueues, 81
  wait queues, 84
DPL (Descriptor Privilege Level), 38, 120
dynamic address checking, exception
      tables, 313–316
  generating, 314
dynamic caching mode, 585
dynamic distribution of IRQs, 114
dynamic memory, 217
dynamic priority, 353
dynamic timers, 207–213
  example, 212
  handling, 209
  race conditions and, 208

E

e2fsck external program, 576
elevator algorithm, 464
ELF (Executable and Linking Format), 674
emulation, 676
environment variables, 661, 667
epochs, 352
errno variable, 304
ESCAPE instructions, 96
esp registers, 77
Ethernet, 616
exception handling, 125–128
  exception handlers, 126
    down( ) and, 177
    entering and leaving, 127
    nested execution of, 121
exception tables, 313–316
  generating, 314

exceptions, 19, 109, 115–118
  hardware handling of, 119
  process switching, contrasted with, 110
  termination phase, 156–160
  types of, 111
exclusive processes, 85
Executable and Linking Format (ELF), 674
executable files, 661, 662–674
Execute access rights, 15
execution context, 662
execution domain descriptors, 677
exit() library function, 106
Ext FS (Extended Filesystem), 574
Ext2 (Second Extended
       Filesystem), 574–600
  bitmap, 580
  bitmap caches, 586–588
  block groups, 577
  blocks, usage by file types, 582–584
  creating, 588–590
  data blocks, 595–600
    addressing, 595–597
    allocating, 597
    file holes, 597
    releasing, 599
  device files, pipes, and sockets, 584
  directories, 583
  disk data structures, 577–584
  disk space management, 592–600
  features, 575
  group descriptors, 577, 580
  inode tables, 580–582
  inodes, 592–594
    creating, 592–593
    deleting, 594
  memory data structures, 584–588
    filesystem images, 585
    RAM copy, 584
  methods, 590–592
    file operations, 591
    inode operations, 590
    superblock operations, 590
  partition boot sector, 577
  preallocation of blocks, 575
  regular files, 583
  superblocks, 577, 578
  symbolic links, 583
  VFS superblock data, 585
Ext3 filesystem, 600–607
  atomic operation handles, 603
  journaling, 605–607
  journaling block device layer, 602–605

  journaling filesystem, 601
  logging, 602
  metadata, 601
  transactions, 604
Extended Filesystem (Ext FS), 574
extended frames, 339
extended paging, 47
external device, 431
external fragmentation, 233
external object descriptors, 247
external slab descriptors, 243

F

f00f bug, 124
faults, 111
FIB (Forwarding Information Base), 614
FIFOs, 642–644
  creating and opening, 643
  file operations, 644
  pipes, contrasted with, 642
file block numbers, 595
file control blocks, 375
file descriptors, 16, 393
file handles, 381
file hard links, 13
file holes, 597
file locking, 420–426
file modes, 15
file objects, 375, 385–388
file operations, 387, 387–388
file pointers, 16, 386
file soft links, 14
files, 12
  accesses and memory-mapping, 475
  accessing, 17, 497–527
    direct I/O transfers (see direct I/O
      transfers)
    memory mapping (see memory
      mapping)
  addressing of, 17
  closing, 18
  deleting, 18
  device files, 437
  filename length, 12
  fragmentation, 592
  opening, 16
  reading from, 498–509
    page basis of, 498
    read operation descriptors, 499
    read-ahead technique (see read-ahead
      of files)

renaming, 18
undeletion of, 576
writing to, 498, 509–513
    prepare_write and commit_write
        methods, 511–513
    write methods, disk-based
        filesystems, 509–511
filesystem control blocks, 375
filesystem type registration, 395
filesystems, 4, 373
    Ext2 (see Ext2)
    Ext3 (see Ext3 filesystem)
    mounting, 397–406
        generic filesystems, 403–406
        root filesystem, 399–403
    special filesystems, 394
    types, 394–397
    Unix filesystem, 12–18
    unmounting, 406
    (see also Virtual Filesystem)
filetypes, 14
fixed preemption point, 4
fixed-limit caching mode, 585
fix-mapped linear addresses, 67
floating-point unit (FPU), 96
floppy disks, formatting for Linux, 588
flushing dirty buffers, 491
    system calls for, 495
focus processors, 136
Forwarding Information Base (FIB), 614
FPU (floating-point unit), 96
frame buffer, 432
frames, 337, 616
    extended frames, 339
free page frame, 218
full-duplex pipe, 634
fully associative caches, 52
function footprints, 241

G

G granularity flags, 36
GART (Graphics Address Remapping
    Table), 434
GDT (Global Descriptor Table), 36
general caches, 243
general-purpose I/O interfaces, 431, 432
GID (Group ID), 15
Global Descriptor Table (GDT), 36
global interrupt disabling, 180–183
    concurrency and, 185
global kernel locks, 190

GNU/Linux kernel vs. commercial
        distributions, xii
goal, 598
graphic interface, 432
Graphics Address Remapping Table
        (GART), 434
Group ID (GID), 9, 15
group leader, 28

H

half-duplex pipes, 634
hardware cache memory, 52
hardware caches, 52–54
    handling, 68
    lines, 52
hardware clocks, 194–196
hardware context, 90
hardware context switches, 90
hardware error codes, 115
hardware header cache, 617
hash chaining, 82
hash collision, 82
heaps, 300, 670
    managing, 300–302
hidden scheduling, 367
high-level driver, 456
host identifiers, 613
hot spot, 205
hyper-threaded microprocessors, 365

I

idt CPU registers, 118
IDTs (Interrupt Descriptor Tables), 118
    initializing, 122–124
    preliminary initialization, 123
IEEE 802 standards, 616
immutable files, 576
inactive lists, 561
include directory, 6
INET sockets, 611
    methods, 612
info structure, 532
init process, 28, 105
initialized data segments, 670
inode objects, 375, 381–385
inode operations, 384
inode semaphores, 191
inode tables, 580–582
inodes, 14
    caches, 390
    numbers, 375

input registers, 429
insmod program, 696
int instruction, 122
interactive processes, 349
internal device, 431
internal fragmentation, 239
internal object descriptors, 247
internal slab descriptors, 243
Internet, 609
Internet Protocol Suite (IPS) network
    architecture, 609
interpreted scripts, 675
interprocess communications, 26, 632–660
    FIFOs, 642–644
        creating and opening, 643
        file operations, 644
    pipes, 633–641
        creating and destroying, 637
        data structures, 635–637
        limitations of, 642
        read and write channels, 634
        reading from, 638
        writing into, 640
    System V IPC (see System V IPC)
    Unix, mechanisms available in, 632
interprocessor interrupts, 115
Interrupt Controllers, 112
Interrupt Descriptor Tables (see IDTs)
interrupt descriptors, 123
interrupt gates, 118, 123, 134
interrupt handling, 128–145
    interrupt handlers, 20
        for local timers, 201
        nested execution of, 121
        registers, saving, 136
        vs exception handlers, 122
interrupt mode, 448
Interrupt Redirection Tables, 114
Interrupt ReQuests (see IRQs)
interrupt service routines (ISRs), 129, 141
interrupt signals, 20, 109
interrupt vectors, 130
interrupts, 109–115
    actions following, 129
    bottom halves, 110
    disabling, 24, 179–183
    hardware handling of, 119
    IRQs (Interrupt ReQuests) and, 112–115
    laptops and, 110
    multiprocessor systems, handling on, 144
    numerical identification, 112

    process switching, contrasted with, 110
    termination phase, 156–160
    top halves, 110
    types of, 111
    vectors, 112
interval timers, 215
I/O APIC (Advanced Programmable Interrupt
    Controller), 113
    initialization at bootstrap, 136
I/O architecture, 427–437
I/O buses, 428
I/O devices, 427–473
    block device drivers (see block device
        drivers)
    character device drivers, 471–473
    device controllers, 433–436
    device drivers, 441–449
        buffering strategies, 443
        registering, 445
        resources, 430
    device files, 437–441
    DMAC (Direct Memory Access
        Controller), 436–437
    I/O interfaces, 431–433
    I/O operations, monitoring, 447–449
    I/O ports, 428–431
    I/O shared memory, 433
        accessing, 434–436
        address mapping, 434
    kernel, levels of support by, 442
I/O interrupt handlers, 129
I/O interrupt handling, 128–144
I/O-bound processes, 349
IPC (see System V IPC)
    (see also interprocess communications)
IPS (Internet Protocol Suite) network
    architecture, 609
IRQs (Interrupt ReQuests), 112–115
    allocation of IRQ lines, 143–144
    data structures, 132
    I/O APIC and, 114
    line selection, IRQ configurable
        devices, 131
ISA buses, memory mapping, 434
ISRs (interrupt service routines), 129, 141

J

JBD (Journaling Block Device), 602
jiffies, 199
    timer implementation and, 207
journal, 601

journaling, 576, 605–607
Journaling Block Device (JBD), 602
journaling block device layer, 602–605
journaling filesystems, 600

K

kapm, 106
kernel code segment, 41
kernel control paths, 21, 121, 161–163
    interleaving conditions, 162
    Linux, interleaving in, 122
    race conditions and, 163
kernel data segment, 41
kernel master Page Global Directory, 65
Kernel Memory Allocator (KMA), 30
Kernel Mode, 8, 19, 162
    exceptions in, 121
    User Mode, contrasted with, 263
kernel oops, 127, 290
kernel page cache
    self-caching applications and, 523
kernel page tables, 64
kernel requests, issuing of, 161
kernel semaphores, 173–178
    acquiring, 175–177
    releasing, 174
kernel symbol table, 695
kernel threads, 19, 104–106
kernel wrapper routines, 303, 316–317
kernels, 3, 8, 161
    code profilers, 205
    concurrency and global interrupt
        disabling, 185
    concurrency level, 184
    CPU activity, tracking by, 205
    data structures, synchronization of
        access, 184–189
    destination caches, 612
    GNU/Linux vs. commercial
        distributions, xii
    interprocess communications, 26
      (see also interprocess communications)
    interrupt handling, 110
    kernel threads, 3
    Linux compared to Unix, 2
    loading and execution, 685–691
    mappings, high-memory page
        frames, 228–232
    modules, 11
    nonpreemptive, 24

preemptive, 351
    vs. nonpreemptive, 4
priority of, 263
process management, 74
processes, contrasted with, 19
read/write semaphores, handling of, 178
signals, 26
    usage of, 318
source code and instruction order, 166
source code directory tree
    (Linux), 702–706
synchronization, 161–192
    conditions not requiring, 162
    techniques (see synchronization
        primitives)
threads, memory descriptors of, 267
timekeeping, 193–202
Unix kernels, 18–33
    demand paging, 31
    device drivers, 32
    reentrant kernels, 21–24
keyboard interface, 432
KMA (Kernel Memory Allocator), 30
kswapd kernel threads, 531, 571–573
kupdate kernel threads, 493–495

L

L1-caches, 53
L2-caches, 53
lazy TLB mode, 70
ld.so, 669
LDTDs (Local Descriptor Table
    Descriptors), 37
LDTs (Local Descriptor Tables), 36, 42
lease locks, 421
Least Recently Used (LRU) lists (see LRU
    lists)
left children, red-black trees, 271
lightweight processes, 3, 73
    creation in Linux, 100
linear address fields, 56
linear address intervals, 278–285
    allocating, 278–282
    releasing, 282–285
        memory regions, scanning, 282
        Page Tables, updating, 283
linear addresses, 34
    and noncontiguous memory areas, 256
links, 13
Linux, 1
    advantages, 4

Linux (*continued*)
   emulation of other operating
      systems, 676
   filesystems, 4
      Unix filesystem and, 12–18
   hardware dependency, 6
   kernel, 3
   kernel control paths, interleaving, 122
   kernel threading, 3
   lightweight processes, reliance on, 73
   memory barriers, 167
   paging, 54–71
   platforms, 6
   POSIX compliance, 2
   segmentation, 40–44
      segments used, 41
   source code (see source code)
   timekeeping (see timekeeping
      architecture)
   Unix kernel and, 2
   version numbering, 7
Linux kernels (see kernels)
LinuxThreads library, 73
local APICs, 113
   arbitration, 114
   interrupt handlers, 201
Local Descriptor Table Descriptors
   (LDTDs), 37
Local Descriptor Tables (LDTs), 36, 42
local interrupts, disabling, 179
local TLB, 54
locality principle, 52
locking, 167
locks, global kernel, 190
log record, 603
logical addresses, 34
logical block number, 454
login name, 9
login sessions, 28
loopback, 404
low-level driver, 456
low-level driver descriptor, 460
LRU (Least Recently Used) lists, 561
   pages, moving across, 562

M

magic structure, 532
major faults, 291
major numbers, 438
mandatory file locks, 420
maskable interrupts, 111
masked signals, 321

masking of deferrable functions, 147
Master Boot Record (MBR), 686
master kernel Page Global Directory, 64
master memory descriptor, 268
mathematical coprocessors, 96
MBR (Master Boot Record), 686
memory
   initialization of data structures
      for, 222–225
   management, 217–262
      buddy system algorithm, 233–239
      page frames, 217–239
      permanent kernel mappings, 228–231
      swapping (see swapping)
      temporary kernel mappings, 231
memory addresses, 34
memory addressing, 34–71
memory alignment, 248
memory allocation and demand paging, 31
memory arbiters, 35, 164, 436
memory area descriptors, 31
memory area management, 239–262
   cache descriptors, 242
   caches, 243
   interface, slab allocator and buddy system
      algorithm, 245
   multiprocessor systems, 250
   noncontiguous areas (see noncontiguous
      memory area management)
   object descriptors, 247
      aligning objects in memory, 248
   slab allocators, 240–242
   slab coloring, 249
   slab descriptors, 243
   slabs
      allocating to caches, 245
      releasing from caches, 246
memory barriers, 166
memory descriptors, 265–268
   fields, 265
   of kernel threads, 267
   mmap_cache, 276
   read/write semaphores, 191
   red-black trees, 271–273
memory fragmentation, 30
Memory Management Unit (MMU), 29
memory mapping, 23, 513–523
   creating, 516–518
   data structures, 514–516
   demand paging for, 519–521
   destroying, 518
   flushing dirty pages to disk, 521
memory nodes, 221

memory regions, 263, 264, 268–285
  access rights, 273–275
  assignment to processes, 264
  data structures, 270–273
  fields, 268
  flags, 273
  handling, 275–278
    finding a free interval, 277
    finding a region that ovelaps an
      interval, 276
    finding the closest region to an
      address, 275
    inserting a region in the memory
      descriptor list, 278
  linear address intervals, 278–285
  merging, 269
  pages, relation to, 273
  system calls for creation, deletion, 265
memory swapping (see swapping)
memory zones, 219
message queues, 26
metadata, 601
microkernels, 11
microprocessors, hyper-threaded, 365
minor faults, 290
minor numbers, 438
mke2fs utility program, 588
mkswap command, 532
MMU (Memory Management Unit), 29
MMX instructions, 96
modprobe program, 699
modules, 3, 11, 692–701
  advantages, 11
  data structures and, 692
  dependencies, 696
  exception tables, 694
  exporting of symbols, 695
  implementation, 693
  licenses, 696
  linking and unlinking, 696
  linking on demand, 699
  module objects, 693
  module usage counters, 694
  request_module function, 700
mount points, 397
mounted filesystem descriptors, 398
multiprocessing, 10
multiprocessor systems
  caches and, 53
  interrupt disabling and, 24
  interrupt handling on, 144
  memory and, 35

memory area management, 250
nonpreemptive kernels and, 24
processes, scheduling on, 363–365
timekeeping architecture, 199–202
  initialization, 200
multiprogramming, 10
multithreaded applications, 3, 73
multiuser systems, 8

N

named pipes, 642
neighbor caches, 616
Net-4, 608
network addresses, 613
network filesystems, 374
network interface, 432
network interface cards (NICs), 610
network masks, 613
networking, 608–631
  data structures, 609–618
    BSD sockets, 610
    destination caches, 612
    Forwarding Information Base
      (FIB), 614
    INET sockets, 611
    neighbor caches, 616
    NICs (network interface cards), 610
    routing caches, 616
    socket buffers, 617
  frames, 616
  IP (Internet Protocol layer), 613
  network architectures, 609
    Linux, supported by, 609
  network cards, 610, 627–631
    receiving packets from, 629–631
    sending packets to, 627
  network layers, 608, 609
  payload, 617
  programming for networks, 609
  protocols, 609
  sockets
    initialization, 620
  static routing table, 614
  system calls related to, 618–627
    data link layer, 626–627
    network layers, 626
    transport layer, 625
  zones, 615
NGPT (Next Generation Posix Threading
    Package), 73
NMI interrupts, 206
nodes, red-black trees, 271

noncontiguous memory area
management, 256–262
allocating noncontiguous area, 258
descriptors, 257
linear addresses, 256
Page Fault exception handlers and, 297
Page Faults and, 260
releasing memory area, 260
nonexclusive processes, 85
nonmaskable interrupts, 111
nonpreemptive kernels, 24
multiprocessor systems and, 24
nonpreemptive processes, 10
NUMA (Non-Uniform Memory Access), 221
nodes, 221
nodes descriptors, 222
N-way set associative caches, 52

O

object descriptors, 247
object files, 668
objects, 375
caches, allocating in, 251–253
multiprocessors, 252
uniprocessors, 251
caches, releasing from, 253–254
multiprocessors, 254
uniprocessors, 253
general purpose, 254
offsets, of logical addresses, 34
older siblings, 83
old-style device files, 437, 438
operating systems, 8
execution modes, 8
output registers, 429
owners, 477

P

PAEs (Physical Address Extensions), 50
Page Cache Disable (PCD) flag, 53
page caches, 474, 476–481
address_space objects, 476–478
data structures, 478–480
direct I/O transfers, bypassing with, 524
handling functions, 480
I/O operations, usage by, 475
page descriptor fields, 480
page hash tables, 479
page descriptor lists, 478
page descriptors, 479
Page Directories, 45

Page Fault exceptions, 121, 274
Page Fault exception handlers, 285–298
Copy On Write, 295–297
demand paging, 292–295
faulty addresses, 289–292
inside address space,
handling, 290–292
outside address space,
handling, 289–290
noncontiguous memory area accesses,
handling, 297
process flow, 285
Page Faults, noncontiguous memory areas
and, 260
page frame reclaiming, 559–573
algorithm, 560–561
from the dentry cache, 570
functions, 564–570
from the inode cache, 571
kswapd kernel threads, 571–573
Least Recently Used (LRU) lists, 561
pages, moving across, 562
purpose, 559
page frames, 29, 44
avoiding race conditions on, 549
free page frame, 218
high-memory, kernel mapping
of, 228–232
management, 217–239
memory zones, 219
page descriptors, 218
processes, sharing among, 545
request and release of, 225–227
reserved, 61–63
page I/O operation, 468
page slots, 532
defective slots, 533
functions for allocation and release
of, 542–545
Page Tables, 44, 45
handling, 57–61
for kernels
provisional, 64
protection bits, 274
for kernels, 64
for processes, 63
pages, 44
LRU lists, moving across, 562
memory regions, relation to, 273
swapping (see swapping)
paging
demand paging, 292–295
in hardware, 44–54

in Linux, 54–71
  vs. segmentation, 40
paging units, 35
parallel ports, 432
parent filesystems, 397
password, 9
pathname lookup, 407–416
pathnames, 13
payload, 617
PCD (Page Cache Disable) flag, 53
PCI buses, memory mapping, 434
PCMCIA interfaces, 433
pending blocked signals, 345
pending signal queues, 325
pending signals, 321
Pentium processors
  caching, 53
  f00f bug, 124
  three-level paging and, 56
periods in directory notation, 13
permanent kernel mappings, 228–231
  temporary kernal mappings, contrasted
    with, 228
personalities, 677
  Linux, supported by, 677
Physical Address Extensions (PAEs), 50
physical addresses, 35
physical pages, 44
PID (process ID), 76
pipe buffer, 636
pipe size, 636
pipes, 633–641
  creating and destroying, 637
  data structures, 635–637
  FIFOs, contrasted with, 642
  limitations of, 642
  read and write channels, 634
  reading from, 638
  writing into, 640
PIT (Programmable Interval Timer), 195
  interrupt service routine, 198
  multiprocessor systems and, 199
polling mode, 447
ports
  I/O ports, 428–431
POSIX (Portable Operating Systems based on
    Unix), 2
  signals, 26
Power-On Self-Test (POST), 61
preemptive kernels, 351
preemptive processes, 10, 350
prepare_write method, 511–513

primitive semaphores, 649
priority inversion, 367
private memory mapping, 514
Process, 76
process 0, 105
process 1, 105
process capabilities, 665–667
process credentials, 663
process descriptors, 20, 74–89, 353
  hardware context, saving of, 91
  memory, storage in, 77
  process 0, 79
  process descriptor pointers, 76
  process lists, 79
    doubly linked lists, 80
  representation, 77
process group ID, 28
process groups, 28
process ID (PID), 76
process page tables, 63
process switches, 89–99
  hardware context, 90
  interrupt handling, contrasted with, 110
  kernels, performance by, 92–96
process time-outs, 212
processes, 10, 19, 72–108, 661
  address spaces, 22, 263–302
    creating, 298
    deleting, 300
    functions and macros for
      accessing, 312
    linear addresses, 264
  children, 27, 83
  communication between (see interprocess
    communications)
  creating, 99–106
  destroying, 106–108
  execution domains, specification, 677
  files associated with, 392–394
  files, reading from, 497
  implementation, 20
  init, 28
  I/O-bound or CPU-bound, 349
  kernel stack representation, 77
  lightweight processes, 73
    creation in Linux, 100
  management, 27
  memory regions, assignment
    circumstances, 264
  memory requests, 263
  original parents, 83
  page frames, sharing of, 545

processes (*continued*)
    parents, 27, 83
    personality fields, 677
    preemption of, 350
    program execution (see program
        execution)
    quantum duration, 351
    removal, 107
    resource limits, 88
    scheduling, 348–371
        algorithm (see scheduling algorithm)
        base priority, 353
        base time quanta, 352
        data structures, 353–355
        dynamic priority, 353
        epochs, 352
        evaluating priority, 362
        multiprocessor systems, 363–365
        policy, 348–352
        priority, assignment of, 349, 350
        real-time processes, system calls
            related to, 369–371
        schedule function, 355–365
        static priority, 353
        system calls related to, 350, 367–371
    signals, response to, 322
    sleeping processes, 85
    suspending, 346
    swapper, 353
    termination, 107
    time sharing, 348
    types of, 349
    younger siblings, 83
    zombies, 27
process/kernel model, 10
processor-detected exceptions, 111
profile, 205
program counters, 110
program execution, 661–683
    command-line arguments, 667
    environment variables, 667
    exec functions, 678–683
    executable files, 662–674
    executable formats, 674–676
    execution domains, 676
    libraries, 668
    process capabilities, 665–667
    process memory regions, 670
    segments, 670
program interpreters, 669
Programmable Interval Timer (PIT), 195
programmed exceptions, 112

protected mode, 35
protocols, 609
provisional Page Global Directory, 64
pthread (POSIX thread) libraries, 73
PWT (Page Write-Through) cache, 54

Q

quanta, 197, 202, 348
quantum duration, 351

R

race conditions, 23
    dynamic timers and, 208
    prevention, 189–192
    swap caches and, 545
RAM (random access memory)
    dynamic memory and, 217
    swapping (see swapping)
    Unix, usage in, 29
random access memory (see RAM)
Read access rights, 15
read file locks, 421
read operation descriptors, 499
read-ahead algorithm, 504
read-ahead groups, 505
read-ahead of files, 504–509
    asynchronous read-ahead
        operations, 506, 509
    synchronous read-ahead operations, 505,
        507
read-ahead windows, 504
read/write semaphores, 178
read/write spin locks, 170
real mode, 35
Real Mode addresses, 686
Real Time Clock (RTC), 194
real-time processes, 349
    system calls related to, 369–371
real-time signals, 320, 347
red-black trees, 271–273
reentrant functions, 21
reentrant kernels, 21–24
    synchronization, 23
        interrupt disabling, 24
reference counters, 189
registering a device driver, 445
regular files, 583
regular signals, 320
relative pathnames, 13
request descriptors, 456
request queues, 456

Requestor Privilege Level, 38
reserved page frames, 61–63
resource, 430
resource limits, 88
right children, red-black trees, 271
root, 9
root directories, 12, 397
root filesystems, 374, 397
    mounting, 399–403
routers, 613
routing caches, 616
routing data structures, 613
routing zone, 615
runqueues, 81

S

S system flags, 36
schedule function, 355–365
    direct invocation, 356
    lazy invocation, 356
    process switches, 357–362
        actions performed after, 361–362
        actions performed before, 357–361
scheduler, 10
scheduling algorithm, 352–367
    I/O-bound process boosting, effectiveness
        of, 366
    performance of, 365–367
    real-time application support, 367
    scaling, 366
    system load and, 366
scheduling policy, 348
SCSIs (Small Computer System
        Interfaces), 433
    bus, 433
    standard, 433
Second Extended Filesystem (see Ext2)
sectors, 452
Segment Descriptors, 36–39
Segment Selectors, 35
segmentation
    in Linux, 40–44
    vs. paging, 40
segmentation registers, 35
segmentation units, 35, 39
segments, 457
    CPL (Current Privilege Level) and, 43
    Linux, used in, 41
    of logical addresses, 34
self-caching applications, 523

semaphores, 24
    acquiring, 175–177
    kernel semaphores, 173–178
    race conditions, preventing
        with, 191–192
    read/write semaphores, 178
    releasing, 174
    System V IPC, 26
serial ports, 432
Set Group ID (sgid), 15
Set User ID (suid), 15
setuid programs, 663
sgid (Set Group ID), 15
shared libraries, 669
shared linked lists, insertion of elements
        into, 184
shared memory, 26
shared memory mapping, 514
shared page swapping, 546
share-mode mandatory looks, 421
signals, 26, 318–347
    blocked signals, modifying of, 345
    blocking of, 321
    catching, 335–340
        frames, setting up, 336
        signal flags, evaluating, 339
        signal handlers, starting and
            terminating, 339
    changing the action of, 344
    data structures, 322–327
        operations on, 326–327
    default actions, 26
    delivering, 320, 332–334
    descriptors, 324
    exception handlers, 117
    executing default actions for, 334–335
    forcing functions, 332
    generating, 320, 327–332
    ignoring, 334
    Linux 2.4, first 31 in, 319
    masking of, 321
    pending blocked signals, examining, 345
    pending signal queues, 325
    pending signals, 321
    phases of transmission, 320
    process descriptor fields for handling, 323
    processes, response of, 322
    processes, suspending, 346
    purpose, 318
    real-time signals, 320
    real-time signals, system calls for, 347

signals (*continued*)
  regular signals, 320
  sender codes, 326
  sending functions, 328
  SIG prefix, 318
  SIGKILL, 322
  SIGSTOP, 322
  system calls, 320
    for handling of, 343–347
    reexecuting, 340–342
slab allocators, 240–242
  buddy system algorithm, interfacing
    with, 245
slab cache list semaphores, 191
slab caches, 241
slab coloring, 249
slab descriptors, 243
slab object constructors, 240
slab object destructors, 240
slab objects, 240
slabs, 241
  caches, allocating to, 245
  realeasing from caches, 246
sleeping processes, 85
slices, 348
slot indexes, 646
slot usage sequence numbers, 646
slots, 530, 532
Small Computer System Interfaces (see
    SCSIs)
SMP (symmetric multiprocessing), 4, 136
  systems, timekeeping in, 197
socket buffers, 617
socket control messages, 625
sockets, 610
  initialization, 620
softirqs, 146, 147–151
  tasklets, contrasted with, 146
software interrupts, 112, 146
software timers, 206
source code, xi
  GNU/Linux kernel vs. commercial
    distributions, xii
source code and instruction order, 166
source code directory tree, 702–706
special filesystems, 374, 394
specific caches, 243
spin locks, 25, 167–173
  global kernel locks, 190
SSE extensions (Streaming SIMD
    Extensions), 96

stack segment registers, 36
stack segments, 670
static distribution of IRQs, 114
static libraries, 669
static priority, 353
static routing table, 614
static timers, 207
status registers, 429
sticky flag, 15
strategy routine, 456
suid (Set User ID), 15
superblock, 578
superblock objects, 375, 378–381
superblock operations, 379–381
superformat utility program, 588
superuser, 9
supervisor, 9
swap areas, 31, 531–545
  activation, 532
  activation service routine, 536
  deactivation service routine, 538
  descriptors, 533–535
  format, 532
  multiple areas, advantages, 531
  page slots, 532
    allocating and releasing, 542–545
  prioritization, 530
  swap-in and updating function, 539–542
swap caches, 545–548
  helper functions, 548
swapoff program, 538
swapon program, 536
swapped-out page identifiers, 535
  page table value entries, 535
swapper, 79, 105, 353
  timesharing and, 203
swapping, 528–573
  drawbacks, 529
  pages, 529–531
    choosing, 530
    distribution, 530
    functions for, 548–558
    Least Recently Used (LRU)
      algorithms, 531
    page frame reclaiming (see page frame
      reclaiming)
    selection, 531
    swapping in, 556–558
    swapping out, 551–556
    timing of, 531
    transferring, 548–551

of process address space, 529
purpose, 529
share page swapping, 546
swap areas (see swap areas)
symbolic links, 14, 583
symmetric multiprocessing (see SMP)
synchronization primitives, 163–192
  atomic operations, 164–166
  choosing among, considerations, 185
  completions, 179
  kernel data structures, access
        using, 184–189
  memory barriers, 166
  semaphores, 173–178
  spin locks, 167–173
synchronous errors or exceptions, 26
synchronous interrupts, 109
synchronous read-ahead operations, 505,
        507
system administrators, 9
system bootstrap
  I/O APIC initialization, 136
system call dispatch tables, 305
system call numbers, 304
system call service routines, 305
system calls, 19, 303–317
  dynamic address checking, 312
  file-handling, 16
  handler and service routines, 304–316
  initializing, 306
  kernel wrapper routines, 316–317
  networking, related to, 618–627
  parameters, 307–311
        passing, 307–309
        verifying, 309–311
  POSIX APIs and, 303
  process address spaces, accessing, 311
  process scheduling, for, 350, 367–371
  processes, suspending, 346
  real-time processes, related to, 369–371
  reexecuting, 340–342
  signals, 320, 343–347
        changing action of, 344
  system call function, 306
  timing measurements, related
        to, 213–216
  Virtual Filesystem, handled by, 377
system concurrency level, 184
system gates, 123
system load, 366

System Segment, 91
system startup, 685–691
  BIOS, 685
  boot loader, 686
  Linux boot, 687–688
        from floppy disk, 687
        from hard disk, 688
system statistics, updating by kernel, 204
System V IPC (Interprocess
        Communication), 26, 644–660
  IPC identifiers, 645
  IPC keys, 645
  IPC resources, 26, 645–648
  IPC shared memory region, 656
  messages, 653–656
  semaphores, 648–653
  shared memory, 656–660
        data structures, 657
        demand paging, 659
        page swapping, 658
        shm filesystem, 658
  system calls, 648
  (see also interprocess communications)

T

Table Indicator, 38
task gates, 118
task priority registers, 114
task queues, 155
Task State Segment Descriptors (TSSDs), 37,
        91
Task State Segments (TSSs), 42, 90
task switch, 89
tasklet descriptors, 151
tasklets, 146, 151–153
  softirqs, contrasted with, 146
tasks, 72
TCP/IP network architecture, 609
temporary kernel mappings, 231
  permanent kernel mappings, contrasted
        with, 228
text segments, 670
thread groups, 76
threads, 72, 73
three-level paging, 49, 54
  Pentium processors and, 56
ticks, 195
time multiplexing, 348
time quantum, 348
time sharing in the CPU, 202

Time Stamp Counter, 194
timekeeping
    system calls related to, 213–216
    time and date updates, 203
timekeeping architecture, 197–202
    initialization, multiprocessor
           systems, 200
    multiprocessor systems, 199–202
    uniprocessor systems, 198–199
time-outs, 206
timer interrupts, 195
timers, 206
    real-time applications and, 207
time-sharing, 348
timing measurements, 193–216
    via hardware, 194
    types, 193
TLBs (Translation Lookaside Buffers), 54
    handling, 68
top halves, 110
Torvalds, Linus, 1
transactions, 604
Translation Lookaside Buffers (see TLBs)
trap gates, 118, 123
traps, 111
TSC (Time Stamp Counter), 197
two-level paging, 44

U

UID (User ID), 15
umask, 100
uniprocessor systems
    timekeeping architecture, 198–199
unitialized data segments, 670
universal serial buses (USBs), 433
Unix
    process management, 27
    System V interprocess
        communication, 26
Unix filesystem, 12–18
    access rights, 15
    directory structure, 12
    file-handling system calls, 16
    files, 12
        file types, 14
Unix kernels (see under kernels)
Unix operating systems, 1
    Linux and, 2

USBs (universal serial buses), 433
user code segment, 41
user data segment, 42
user group, 9
User ID (UID), 9, 15
User Mode, 8, 19
    exceptions in, 121
    Kernel Mode, contrasted with, 263
    memory, allocation to, 263
    processes, synchronization of (see
        interprocess communications)
    system calls (see system calls)
user threads, 73

V

vectors, 112
VESA Local Buses (VLBs), memory
        mapping, 434
virtual address space, 29
virtual addresses, 34
virtual block devices, 374
Virtual Filesystem (VFS), 372–426
    common file model, 374–377
    data structures, 378–394
        dentry objects, 389–392
        file objects, 385–388
        inode objects, 381–385
        processes, 392–394
        superblock objects, 378–381
    description, 372
    device files, handling of, 440
    Ext2 superblock data, 585
    file locking, 420–426
    filesystems
        types, 394–397
    objects, 375
    pathname lookup, 407–416
    superblock operations, 379–381
    supported filesystems, 373
    system calls, 377
        implementation, 416–420
virtual filesystems, 374
virtual memory, 29

W

wait queue head, 84
wait queues, 84
watchdog system, 206

windows, kernel address space, 231
wrapper routines, 303
    (see also kernel wrapper routines)
Write access rights, 15
write file locks, 421

X

XMM registers, 96

Z

zero page, 294
zombie processes, 27
zone modifier, 227
zones, 220, 615
    size and addressing, 222

About the Authors

Daniel P. Bovet received his Ph.D. in computer science at UCLA in 1968 and is a full professor at the University of Rome, Tor Vergata, Italy. He had to wait over 25 years before being able to teach an operating systems course in a proper manner, due to the lack of source code for modern, well-designed systems. Now, thanks to cheap PCs, as well as Linux, Marco and Dan are able to cover all the facets of an operating system and can hand out tough, satisfying homework to their students. (These young students working at home on their PCs are really spoiled; they never had to fight with punched cards.) In fact, Dan was so fascinated by the accomplishments of Linus Torvalds and his followers that he spent the last few years trying to unravel some of Linux's mysteries. It seemed natural, after all that work, to write a book about what he found.

Marco Cesati received a degree in mathematics in 1992 and a Ph.D. in computer science at the University of Rome, La Sapienza, in 1995. He is now a research assistant in the computer science department of the School of Engineering at the University of Rome, Tor Vergata. In the past, he has served as system administrator and Unix programmer for the university (as a Ph.D. student) and for several institutions (as a consultant). During the last few years, he has been continuously involved in teaching his students how to change the Linux kernel in strange and funny ways.

Colophon

Our look is the result of reader comments, our own experimentation, and feedback from distribution channels. Distinctive covers complement our distinctive approach to technical topics, breathing personality and life into potentially dry subjects.

Mary Brady was the production editor and copyeditor for *Understanding the Linux Kernel*, Second Edition. Ann Schirmer was the proofreader. Sarah Sherman and Claire Cloutier provided quality control. Judy Hoer and Genevieve d'Entremont provided production assistance. John Bickelhaupt wrote the index.

Edie Freedman designed the cover of this book, based on a series design by herself and Hanna Dyer. The cover image of a man with a bubble is a 19th-century engraving from the Dover Pictorial Archive. Emma Colby produced the cover layout with QuarkXPress 4.1 using Adobe's ITC Garamond font.

David Futato designed the interior layout. The chapter opening images are from the Dover Pictorial Archive, *Marvels of the New West: A Vivid Portrayal of the Stupendous Marvels in the Vast Wonderland West of the Missouri River*, by William Thayer (The Henry Bill Publishing Co., 1888), and *The Pioneer History of America: A Popular Account of the Heroes and Adventures*, by Augustus Lynch Mason, A.M. (The Jones Brothers Publishing Company, 1884). This book was converted to FrameMaker 5.5.6 with a format conversion tool created by Erik Ray, Jason McIntosh, Neil Walls, and Mike Sierra that uses Perl and XML technologies. The text font is Linotype Birka; the heading font is Adobe Myriad Condensed; and the code font is LucasFont's TheSans Mono Condensed. The illustrations that appear in the book were produced by Robert Romano and Jessamyn Read using Macromedia FreeHand 9 and Adobe Photoshop 6.